NGO Management

NGO Management

The Earthscan Companion

Edited by

Alan Fowler and Chiku Malunga

publishing for a sustainable future

London • Washington, DC

First published in 2010 by Earthscan

Earthscan Ltd, Dunstan House, 14a St Cross Street, London EC1N 8XA, UK
Earthscan LLC, 1616 P Street, NW, Washington, DC 20036, USA
Earthscan publishes in association with the International Institute for Environment and Development

For more information on Earthscan publications, see www.earthscan.co.uk or write to earth-info@earthscan.co.uk

ISBN: 978-1-84971-119-7 hardback
ISBN: 978-1-84971-120-3 paperback

Typeset by Composition and Design Services
Cover design by Andrew Corbett

A catalogue record for this book is available from the British Library

Library of Congress Cataloging-in-Publication Data

NGO management : the Earthscan companion / edited by Alan Fowler and Chiku Malunga.
    p. cm.
  Includes bibliographical references and index.
  ISBN 978-1-84971-119-7 (hardback) — ISBN 978-1-84971-120-3 (pbk.) 1. Non-governmental organizations—Management. I. Fowler, Alan, 1947- II. Malunga, Chiku Watchman. III. Earthscan.
  HD62.6.N52 2010
  658—dc22   2010027726

At Earthscan we strive to minimize our environmental impacts and carbon footprint through reducing waste, recycling and offsetting our CO_2 emissions, including those created through publication of this book. For more details of our environmental policy, see www.earthscan.co.uk.

Printed and bound in the UK by CPI Antony Rowe, Chippenham.
The paper used is FSC certified.

MIX
Paper from
responsible sources
FSC® C013604

Contents

Part I   Retro-perspective: NGO-ism in a Changing World Order

Part II   From NGOs to Civil Society

Part III   Managing Responsibly

Part IV   Managing Strategically

Part V   Managing Organizational Change

Part VI   Management Applications

List of Figures, Tables and Boxes

Figures

Tables

Boxes

List of Contributors

Anthony Bebbington works at the Brooks World Poverty Institute; and Institute for Development Policy and Management, School of Environment and Development, University of Manchester.

Kees Biekart is a senior lecturer at the Institute of Social Studies of Erasmus University, The Hague.

Harry C. Boyte is founder and co-director of the Center for Democracy and Citizenship at the University of Minnesota's Humphrey Institute.

L. David Brown is a senior research fellow at the Hauser Center for Nonprofit Organizations at Harvard University.

Julius Court was formerly a research associate at the Overseas Development Institute and is a governance adviser with UK Aid, the Department for International Development.

Michael Edwards is a distinguished senior fellow at Demos in New York, and the author of *Small Change: Why Business Won't Save the World*.

Alan Fowler is an adviser on international development and affiliated professor at the Institute of Social Studies of Erasmus University, The Hague.

James L. Garrett is a research fellow at the International Food Policy Research Institute.

Alfonso Gumucio-Dagron works independently as an adviser and is former programme director of Communication for Social Change.

John Gaventa is a senior research fellow at the Institute of Development Studies, University of Sussex.

Georgina M. Gomez is a lecturer at the Institute of Social Studies of Erasmus University, The Hague.

Irene Guijt works independently as an adviser, researcher and facilitator.

John Hailey is an independent adviser, professor and director of the Masters Course on NGO management at the Centre of Charity Effectiveness, University of London.

Sam Hickey works at the Brooks World Poverty Institute; and Institute for Development Policy and Management, School of Environment and Development, University of Manchester.

Bert Helmsing is a professor at the Institute of Social Studies of Erasmus University, The Hague.

Ingeborg Hovland worked at the Overseas Development Institute from 2002–2007. She is now an independent consultant focusing on research communication and evaluation.

Jude Howell was director of the Centre for Civil Society at the London School of Economics.

Alex Jacobs was a founder of MANGO, a capacity building UK NGO, and now works with Keystone Accountability in London.

Jagadananda is a social development practitioner and former leader of the Centre for Youth and Social Development in India.

Rick James is a writer and facilitator working with NGOs on organizational change and capacity building as a consultant with the International NGO Training and Research Centre, Oxford.

David Kelleher is co-director of Gender at Work.

Shannon Kindornay is a research intern at the North–South Institute, Ottawa, Canada.

Chiku Malunga is an independent adviser and founder of CADECO in Malawi.

Emma Mawdsley lectures at Birkbeck College, University of London.

Enrique Mendizabal is a research fellow at the Overseas Development Institute, London.

Henry Mintzberg is Cleghorn professor of management studies at McGill University.

Natascha Mueller-Hirth is a research student at Goldsmith College, London.

Diana Mitlin works at the Brooks World Poverty Institute; and Institute for Development Policy and Management, School of Environment and Development, University of Manchester.

Bill Morton is senior researcher, development cooperation, with the North–South Institute, Ottawa, Canada.

David Osbourne was formerly with the Overseas Development Institute and now works with the Department for International Development, UK.

Gina Porter is senior research fellow in the Department of Anthropology, Durham University, UK.

Brian Pratt is director of the International NGO Training and Research Centre, Oxford, UK.

Aruna Rao is co-director of Gender at Work, Washington, DC.

Paul Ronalds was the chief operating officer of World Vision Australia.

Jan Aart Scholte is a professorial research fellow at the Centre for Globalisation and Regionalisation, Warwick University, UK.

Sue Soal works with the Community Development Resource Association in Cape Town.

James Taylor works with the Community Development Resource Association in Cape Town.

Janet G. Townsend is a research fellow in Geography at the University of Durham.

Robyn Wilford works in the Policy and Evaluation Department of Concern Worldwide in London.

Marilyn Wyatt is a consultant to non-profit boards and the author of the widely used *Handbook of Nonprofit Governance*.

John Young is deputy director of the Overseas Development Institute, London.

List of Sources

Chapter 1: Mike Edwards (2005) 'Have NGOs made a difference? From Manchester to Birmingham with an elephant in the room', *Working Paper Series* 028, Global Poverty Research Group, Manchester University, Manchester

Chapter 2: Diana Mitlin, Sam Hickey and Tony Bebbington (2007) 'Reclaiming development? NGOs and the challenge of alternatives', *Working Paper Series* 043, Global Poverty Research Group, Manchester

Chapter 3: Jude Howell, J. (2006) 'The global war on terror, development and civil society', *Journal of International Development*, vol 18, pp121–135

Chapter 4: John Gaventa, original text for this volume drawn from a longer paper given by the author at a conference of the Development Research Centre on Citizenship, Participation and Accountability (Citizenship DRC) in 2005

Chapter 5: Kees Biekart and Alan Fowler (2009) *Civic Driven Change – Pamphlet*, Institute of Social Studies, The Hague

Chapter 6: Harry Boyte (2008) 'Civic driven change and developmental democracy', in Fowler, A. and Biekart, K. (eds), *Civic Driven Change: Citizen's Imagination in Action*, Institute of Social Studies, The Hague, pp119–138

Chapter 7: Jan Aart Scholte (2007), revised and shortened version of: 'Civil society and the legitimation of global governance', *Journal of Civil Society*, vol 3, no 3, pp305–326

Chapter 8: Jagadananda and Dave Brown (2005) 'Civil society legitimacy and accountability: Issues and challenges', paper prepared for the Program on Civil Society Legitimacy and Accountability of CIVICUS and the Hauser Center, Civicus, Johannesburg

Chapter 9: Alex Jacobs and Robyn Wilford (2008) based on 'Listen first: Practical ways of improving accountability for NGOs', A collaboration by Concern and Mango, December, www.listenfirst.org and draft manuscript submitted to *Development in Practice*

Chapter 10: Marilyn Wyatt (2004) 'Governing for accountability: Principles in practice', an original contribution to this volume adapted from *A Handbook of NGO*

Governance by Marilyn Wyatt with the Central and Eastern European Working Group for Non-profit Governance, European Center for Not-for-Profit Law, Budapest

Chapter 11: Brian Pratt (2010) 'Strategic issues facing NGOs into the foreseeable future', original contribution to this volume

Chapter 12: Chiku Malunga (2009), rewrite of an existing chapter with ideas from extract from *Making Strategic Plans Work: Insights from African Indigenous Wisdom*, Adonis and Abbey, London

Chapter 13: CDRA (2003) 'Phases of Organisational Development', Community Development Resource Association, Cape Town

Chapter 14: Paul Ronalds, original text largely adapted from Chapter 8 of Ronalds, P. (2010) *The Change Imperative: Creating a Next Generation NGO*, Kumarian Press, Bloomfield, CT

Chapter 15: ActionAid (2006) 'Rights-Based Development approaches: combining politics, creativity and organisation', ActionAid, Johannesberg, available at www. actionaid.org/assets/pdf/rights.pdf (last accessed May 2010)

Chapter 16: IDS (2007), Executive Summary and Summary Learning from *Champions of Participation: Engaging Citizens in Local Governance*, Institute of Development Studies, University of Sussex

Chapter 17: Emma Mawdsley, Janet Townsend and Gina Porter (2005) 'Trust, accountability and face-to-face interaction in North–South NGO relations', *Development in Practice*, vol 15, no 1, pp77–82

Chapter 18: Julius Court, Enrique Mendizabal, David Osbourne and John Young (2006) 'Policy Engagement: How Civil Society Can be More Effective', Briefing Paper, Overseas Development Institute, London

Chapter 19: Aruna Rao and David Kelleher (2005) 'Is there life after gender mainstreaming?', Gender and Development vol 13, no 2, pp57–69, Gender at Work, Washington, DC

Chapter 20: Rick James, 'Managing NGOs with Spirit', original contribution to this volume

Chapter 21: Chiku Malunga, 'Civil Society Networks: Of Ants and Elephants', original contribution to this volume

Chapter 22: Natascha Mueller-Hirth (2009) 'South African NGOs and the public sphere: between popular movements and partnerships for development', *Social Dynamics: A journal of African studies*, vol 35, no 2, pp423–435

Chapter 23: James Garrett (2004) 'Bridging gaps: collaboration between research and operational organisations', *Development in Practice*, vol 14, no 5, pp702–709

Chapter 24: Alfonso Gumucio-Dagron, 'NGOs and communication: divorce over the toothpaste', original contribution to this volume

Chapter 25: Shannon Kindornay and Bill Morton (2009) 'Development Effectiveness: towards new understandings', Issues Brief, Development Cooperation Series, September North–South Institute, Ottawa

Chapter 26: James Taylor and Sue Soal (2003) 'Measurement in Developmental Practice: From the Mundane to the Transformational', Community Development Resource Association, Cape Town

Chapter 27: Irene Guijt (2010) 'Reconciling Accountability and Learning', in Ubels, Jan, Acquaye-Baddoo, Naa-Aku and Fowler, Alan, *Capacity Development in Practice*, Earthscan, London

Chapter 28: Ingeborg Hovland (2003), shortened version of 'Knowledge Management and Organisational Learning: An International Development Perspective', Working Paper, no 224, Overseas Development Institute, London

Chapter 29: Alan Fowler (2000) 'Options, Strategies and Trade-Offs in Resource Mobilisation', *The Virtuous Spiral: A Guide to Sustainability for NGOs in International Development*, pp53–79, Earthscan, London

Chapter 30: Georgina Gomez and Bert Helmsing, 'Social entrepreneurship: A convergence of NGOs and the market economy?', original contribution to this volume

Chapter 31: John Hailey and Rick James (2004) 'Trees Die From the Top: International Perspectives on NGO Leadership and Development', *Voluntas*, vol 15, no 4, pp343–354

Chapter 32: Henry Minzberg (2006) 'Developing Leaders? Developing Countries?', *Development in Practice,* vol 16, no 1, pp4–14, Oxfam, Oxford

List of Acronyms and Abbreviations

AASCU   American Association of State Colleges and Universities
ACCESS   Appropriate Cost Effective Centres for Education within the School
             System
AIDS   Acquired Immune Deficiency Syndrome
ALNAP   Action Learning Network for Accountability and Performance
ALPS   Accountability, Learning and Planning System
ANC   African National Congress
ASEAN +3   Association of South East Asian Nations plus China, Japan and
             South Korea
ASEM   Asia Europe Meeting
ATC   Anti-Terrorism Certification
AusAID   Australian Agency for International Development
BOND   British Overseas NGOs in Development
BRAC   Bangladesh Rural Advancement Committee
CBO   Community Based Organization
CDC   Civic-driven Change
CEP   Citizenship Education Programme
CLG   Department for Communities and Local Government
CRDC   Centre for Rural Development Communication
CSO   Civil Society Organization
CSR   Corporate Social Responsibility
CWC   Cultural Wellness Center
DANIDA   Danish International Development Agency
DCF   Development Cooperation Forum
DFID   Department for International Development
DRC   Development Research Centre
EBC   East Brooklyn Churches
EU   European Union
FAO   Food and Agriculture Organization
FBO   Faith-Based Organization
FIM   Montreal International Forum
FSC   Forestry Stewardship Council
FONCAP   Social Capital Fiduciary Fund for Argentina
FXI   Freedom of Expression Institute
G7   Group of Seven
G8   Group of Eight

GCAP	Global Call for Action Against Poverty
GDP	Gross Domestic Product
GEAR	Growth Employment and Redistribution
GM	Genetically Modified
GRI	Global Reporting Initiative
GTZ	Deustche Gesellschaft für Technische Zusammenarbeit
HIV	Human Immuno Deficiency Virus
HLF	High Level Forums
IAF	Industrial Areas Foundation
IASB	International Accounting Standards Board
IBASE	Brazilian Institute of Social and Economic Analysis
ICANN	Internet Corporation for Assigned Names and Numbers
ICCO	Interchurch Coordination Committee for Development Projects
ICT	Information Communication Technology
IDASA	Institute for Democracy in Southern Africa
IDS	Institute for Development Studies
IFAD	International Fund for Agricultural Development
IFPRI	International Food Policy Research Institute
IGOs	International Governmental Organizations
IMF	International Monetary Fund
INGO	International Non-Governmental Organization
INTRAC	International NGO Training and Research Centre
IPU	International Programmes Delivery Unit
ISS	Institute for Social Studies
ITV	Independent Television
IUPUI	Indiana University Purdue University Indianapolis
JAICA	Japanese International Cooperation Agency
JCIF	Japan Centre for International Finance
KM	Knowledge Management
LSE	London School of Economics
LSP	UK Local Strategic Partnerships
M&E	Monitoring and Evaluation
MDG	Millennium Development Goals
MERCOSUR	Southern Common Market
MOSOP	Movement of the Survival of the Ogoni People
NDA	National Development Agency
NGO	Non-Governmental Organization
NGDO	Non-Governmental Development Organization
NSI	North–South Institute
MANGO	Management Accounting for Non Governmental Organisations
OCHA	Office for the Coordination of Humanitarian Affairs
OD	Organization Development
ODA	Overseas Development Assistance
ODI	Overseas Development Institute
OECD	Organisation for Economic Co-operation and Development
OIC	Organization of the Islamic Conference

OSANGO	Organizational Self-assessment for NGOs
OVI	Objectively Verifiable Indicator
PCNC	Philippine Council for NGO Certification
PRIA	Participatory Research in India
RAPID	Research and Policy in Development
RBA	Rights-Based Approaches
RBM	Results Based Management
SAHA	South African History Archive
SANCO	South African National Civics Organization
SEATINI	Southern and Eastern African Trade Information and Negotiations Institute
SIDA	Swedish International Development Agency
SIF	Strategic Initiatives Fund
SPM	Social Performance Management System
SWAPs	Sector Wide Approaches
TAC	Treatment Action Campaign
TD	Trans-Organizational Development
TNCs	Transnational Corporations
UDF	United Democratic Front
UCLG	United Cities and Local Governments
UN	United Nations
UNDP	United Nations Development Programme
UNEP	United Nations Environment Programme
UNICEF	United Nations Children's Fund
UNIFEM	United Nations Development Fund for Women
UNHCR	United Nations High Commission for Refugees
USAID	United States Agency for International Development
W3C	World Wide Web Consortium
WCCD	World Congress on Communication for Development
WESCO	Westside Cooperative Organisation
WTO	World Trade Organization
WWF	World Wildlife Fund
ZOPP	Goal Orientated Project Planning

Introduction: NGOs in a World of Uncertainties

Alan Fowler and Chiku Malunga

Background and Overview

Leading and managing non-governmental organizations involved in international, aided development (NGDOs) is seldom straightforward or easy.[1] The diversity of chapters in this Companion shows, conceptually and practically, why this is often the case. Their topics cover both old and new themes of NGDO interest and concern. For practical reasons, the Companion cannot contain the 'best' or most recent contribution on every theme. But each entry is worthy of the book's purpose: to bring between two covers a comprehensive set of readings for anyone involved with, interested in, or studying NGDOs' leadership, management and development work. Where we saw gaps, an invitation was made to people actively engaged with a missing subject to provide a new contribution. As a result, 8 of the 32 chapters are original pieces from experienced practitioners.

However, this fine-grained approach to the Companion's design runs the risk of not seeing the wood for the trees. In other words, the big forces and factors around and within the evolution of NGDOs and their management might be lost from view. We think that of many internal factors three deserve particular attention. These are issues of NGDO identity, their political economy and achieving effective, accountable development practice. In their own right, and collectively, these factors are adding to the growing internal and external uncertainties NGDO leaders and managers face. All are a source of challenges that are reflected in and cut across topics found in the texts. This introduction therefore reviews these interconnected areas of concern before turning to a guide for navigating the themes and their content.

NGDO Identity

In the past two decades, NGDOs have been 'relocated' so to speak within the concept of civil society. In an attempt to make sense of and adjust to the post-Cold War era, NGDOs have repositioned themselves and have had it done to them by others, particularly by western funding agencies. Following the collapse of the Soviet Union, many official aid agencies wanted to accelerate the 'inevitable' democratization of nation states, of international governance (e.g. Blair, 1998; Scholte, 2005) and of development itself (Clark, 1991). To this end, as an aided part of a civil society, many donor agencies anticipated a critical role for, and hence increased their finance to, NGDOs. The growing outreach of NGDOs from the north into the south and east was expected to pull this 'sector' up by its boot straps so to speak by connecting internationally and building from within (e.g. Eade, 2000; Pratt, 2003). In parallel, official aid would concentrate on promoting an enabling environment for civil society to flourish.

As civic entities, aided NGDOs would become primary actors in developing the number and competencies of civil society organizations (CSOs) across the world towards democratic ends (Ottaway and Carothers, 2000). However, unlike NGO as an antonym, civil society is an unambiguous political category premised on the existence of a modern nation state legitimized by accountability towards its population. Consequently, development was reinterpreted as the attainment of rights and fulfilling responsibilities which required capable citizens (NGLS, 1998). The explicit task of 'NGDOs as civil society' was to help make this happen. However, throughout the 1970s and 1980s, NGDO evolution had concentrated on participatory and people-centred processes in order to make development more sustainable, effective and accountable. A more expressed political function and rights-based agenda reinvigorated old debates about what it meant for NGDOs to be 'alternatives' to official aid thinking, practice. The post-Cold War era re-stimulated contending theories about the meaning and process of development and the economics of poverty and change that bring about social justice with its deep and enduring gender dimensions.

This shift in concept and language of NGDOs towards civil society also added to, rather than helped resolve, existing ambiguity about what it really means to be an NG(D)O. As Terje Tvedt (1998) showed, the definition of an NGDO was far from clear then and has still not become so today.[2] Moreover, Deborah Hilhorst (2003) highlighted ways in which the term 'NGO' had become a discourse – a well-rehearsed set of vocabulary, jargon, assumptions, communication styles and conventional wisdoms – that obscured as much as it defined. In other words, there had emerged a narrative of 'NGO-ism' that was being used for both good and ill. NGO had become a 'non-statement' about an identity that could not be assumed to be trusted or respected across the world. And, because labelling has power (Moncrieffe and Eyben, 2007) being an NGDO placed an escalating demand on leaders and managers to actively deal with an identity, reputation, 'brand' and local credibility which can conjure up potentially competing combinations of charity, social welfare, activism, militant assertion, humanitarianism, self-serving entrepreneurialism and more.

In effect, relocating NGDO identity into a civil society frame of reference had become an additional dimension to be managed: does what you do really mean who you say you are now part of? Is the civic label new, but the content much the same? Does the civil society framework invite expectations that cannot be realized? Is relabelling a potential vulnerability? This latter question became particularly pertinent when, after the Twin Towers attack on 9/11, official development assistance became better aligned with diplomacy and defence in the repertoire of international relations. Such a reinforced connection was accompanied by greater suspicion that non-governmental could be anti-governmental and civil society even more so as a site of potential political opposition to regimes in power. The latter view was often fed by the fact that, historically, while working for political change, members of today's regimes in the south and east had themselves often sought 'refuge' in NGO-ism and in the civic associational life of cultural, sports and chess clubs and (geo)ethnic welfare associations.

The general point is that diverse understandings as well as country-specific interpretations and attitudes of mis(trust) towards what an NGDO is all about have been made more complicated by belonging to civil society. An NGDO's identity – its on-the-ground truth, image promotion, reputation and protection – have risen up the ladder of challenges and uncertainties to be managed, which is linked to issues of resourcing.

The Challenges of NGDO Political Economy

Reliable figures on the totals of NGDO finance are not available.[3] Yet, there is little dispute that, in the past 20 years or so, NGDOs have become increasingly dependent on official aid as a proportion of their total disbursements. From some US$7.3 billion in 2001, informed estimates of total annual budgets of NGDOs in recent years range from US$15–27 billion per annum, with the biggest six accounting for US$7 billion (Ronalds, 2010).[4] Depending on the country concerned, official aid can account for over half of this amount. In addition, there are NGDOs with over 100,000 staff at one extreme and organizations with a handful of volunteers at the other. And, loosely correlated with geo-priorities of official aid, the aggregate and sector-specific importance of NGDOs to development varies significantly between countries (Koch, 2009). Today, the NGDO landscape is both highly asymmetric in terms of distribution of income and size and equally so in terms of an individual organization's reliance on official sources through a widening variety of channels.

The picture of significant economic and institutional growth is not simply attributable to post-conflict financing in Iraq and Afghanistan and elsewhere. As argued above, though very uneven across donor countries, political agendas and liberal, market-driven theories of economic development have generated pro-NGDO policies among providers of overseas development assistance (ODA). But, more significantly, NGDO growth also reflects a deep and enduring moral history of caritas where being financially bigger equates with doing more for those in need. This driver and proxy for NGDO performance is often allied to metrics, board members and a business-like mentality, allied to a quest for self-sustainability. Moreover, such an internal pressure for growth can be interpreted as a strategy to gain leverage and greater impact by gaining a 'policy advocacy' seat at the table of international debate and affairs, where financial size and scale of operations count. This is certainly not to say that small NGDOs do not have international clout. Rather, it suggests that for big international NGDOs money and status are tied, while for small NGDOs money means an ability to advocate, tied to survival. Accordingly, there is a significant management challenge to optimize the political economy of an NGDO's design and relationships as well as choosing its practical work. This demand calls for adjustments that are long-term and structural as well as situation-sensitive and necessarily agile.

An African proverb states that 'when you have your hand in a person's pocket, you must go where they walk'. Over-reliance on ODA, either directly or via southern government contracts, means negotiating terms of engagement but usually from a subordinate position. It means adapting to shifts in the thinking and rearrangement of donors on how they go about aid allocation. With growth and continuity in mind, adapting has meant NGDOs responding to a general trend in ODA to (1) decentralize allocational decisions to within southern countries; while (2) coping with 'harmonization' through budget support; allied to (3) donor moves towards competitive bidding. One result is a complicated strategy of northern NGDOs moving 'downwards' by establishing local entities while simultaneously coalescing upwards.

The ongoing reconfiguration of large international NGDOs into global alliances and federations with locally constituted southern entities as members reflects a response to the downward distribution of donor decision making and opportunities to gain finance from a growing middle class. There are also 'mergers and acquisitions' of smaller northern NGDOs whose viability is under threat.

Substantial management effort is required to bring about these types of organizational change which are needed to both anticipate and stay in tune with global dynamics. To name but a few management challenges of 'coming together': diverse cultures need to be blended without losing their individual value; nationalisms need to be mitigated, particularly where official back-donors are in play; strategies and operating procedures need to be aligned, but without becoming homogenized; financing models, income allocations and overhead cover need to be negotiated; governance and power distributions have to be rebalanced and existing partnerships' need to be revisited and 'rationalized'.

For southern NGOs, the potential gains in such donor trends are a mixed blessing. On the one hand, they should be better placed to access official aid finance, but doing so will increasingly tie them to disbursement by their governments. Issues of compromised autonomy, political sensitivities and dealing with corruption loom larger. In addition, by become locally registered northern NGDOs often emerge as competitors with advantages of international links and alliances to draw on. Northern 'partners' can squeeze out local counterparts. All in all, in-country resource mobilization for southern NGDOs becomes more possible but within a more complicated CSO landscape and trade-offs. Navigating through these types of processes to form effective collaborations that correspond to new funding realities is an ongoing challenge, whose remedies are more in doubt.

To the extent that the past three decades have been generally positive for the economics of NGDO-ism, the forward looking perspective looks less so. Despite the rise of mega-philanthropies on the international development scene (Edwards, 2008), the global financial crisis is taking its toll on both the ODA and the public giving on which NGDOs rely. As in other spheres, the true test of leadership and management are during periods of decline and uncertainty – conditions which are probably more familiar to southern NGDOs than their northern counterparts, inviting a 'reversal' in learning. The demand therefore is to diversify the economics of NGDO-ism away from overwhelming reliance on state subsidy and the gift-economy. The emerging method to do so often reflects the theory and practice of social economy, social enterprise and entrepreneurship (Fowler, 2000a). From a management perspective, this type of movement requires not just an enhanced skill set, but also a shift in organizational behaviour and attitude (Chadha et al, 2003). It opens up the tricky issue of identity management as distinctions between for-profit and non-profit public values and performance measures start to blur. All told, holding on to the tried and trusted political economy of NGDO-ism is unlikely to offer a secure future. Meanwhile, pressures to perform better and to be more accountable do not cease.

The Quest for Effectiveness and Accountability

The new millennium saw a continuation of NGDO efforts to both better understand and improve their effectiveness, but with an added impetus and twist. This concept and its measures of performance were always considered vital for good management as well as critical for satisfying demands for accountability. But this appreciation received a complicated boost when official aid agencies met and announced an initiative to improve their own effectiveness by 'harmonizing' their efforts. Their Paris Declaration (OECD, 2005) set out the rational, methods and goals to be attained to reach the targets set out in the Millennium Development Goals. Recognition of a role for CSOs in this endeavour was conspicuous by its absence. This omission fostered a range of energizing reactions from NGDOs. Ensuing debates signalled divisions between those NGDOs who wanted a place at the table and others who rejected the idea that they should also be 'harmonized' in some way (Eurodad, 2008). In the words of one person heavily involved with the NGDO effectiveness issue:

> I would say that the 'quest' as you term it was prompted initially by the increasing focus on quality and quality assurance by donors. This dialogue and dynamic between NGDOs and their official donors had two prongs ... one was to lead NGDOs to question the notion of quality itself that they were being assessed against, agreeing that quality in aid management was important but it was neither the whole, nor necessarily the most important, issue – hence the need to define for themselves what constituted effective development practice. The second was in their critique of the official aid system and its focus through the Paris Declaration on aid management as a proxy for quality of aid itself.[5]

A focal point for the former NGDO view of harmonization for effectiveness was a meeting in Accra where official aid agencies discussed progress since the Declaration's launch (Booth, 2008; OECD, 2009). Here, NGDOs had a clear presence as well as reaching agreement on processes to systematically debate effectiveness and quality in their own terms, but with engagement with the Paris process in mind.

Unsurprisingly, a lot of this discussion about effectiveness is located within the framework of monitoring and evaluation (M&E). Here, NGDO managers face contention between two schools of thought. One relies on an approach associated with logical frameworks and the idea that, with enough care and thought, development can be achieved as planned. It can be measured using robust numerical techniques. With variations and nuances, this 'plan-able' assumption drives official aid agencies. Adopting this way of thinking and working is a typical requirement of NGDOs to access ODA. An alternative view takes uncertainty as its starting point. Though a desired change in society, on whatever scale and time line, needs to be established, this 'complexity' perspective relies more on continual learning and adjustment to get there. Consequently,

views, effectiveness in development work becomes understood and opera-
quite different ways. Managers are therefore challenged to choose between
er, or to arrive at an organizational blend that satisfies the types of demands
for accountability they face. There are no fixed or proven rules for doing so: another
source of uncertainty.

The effectiveness+accountability issue is set to continue running its course. Moreover, additional reasons to address this area of management concern are coming from
the prospect of cuts in ODA. Unprecedented budget deficits due to the economic crisis
in donor countries are bringing aid allocations under pressure, with unknown results in
both the near and long term. This is but one of the big issues feeding into the assured
future of greater uncertainty that NGDOs will need to cope with. In fact, it could be
argued that the notion of 'professionalism' of NGOs will need to shift from preoccupations with business models and measures. Professionalism will need to reflect a distinct
mix of competencies that *make uncertainty a friend to be embraced with response-ability
rather than an enemy to be defeated.*

Coping with Uncertainties

The African proverb, 'when the beat of the drum changes so must the step of the dance',
advises that when an organization's task environment changes, its management and
leadership must align itself to and seek to influence the context in new ways. Today, the
beat of the drum is changing so fast and in such a seemingly chaotic manner that making
logical adjustments and alignments in the step of the dance is very difficult.

The ongoing changes and complexities in the task environment bring both fundamentally distinct and uncharted combinations of problems requiring new concepts and tools for
managing and leading NGDOs. The 'big' uncertainties mentioned above are compounded,
among many other things, by the HIV and AIDS pandemic, climate change, environmental degradation, increasing frequencies of phenomenal natural and man-made disasters,
the effects of the global financial crisis on poverty and increasing levels of inequalities
between the rich and the poor. The interconnected nature of whatever scenario one envis-
ages requires embracing new ways of managing and leading NGDOs while at the same time
consciously jettisoning those 'old friends' that no longer work.

Navigating through the myriad factors breeding the ever increasing uncertainties
means basing management more on principle-centred approaches that are resilient to
changes in time and space. This is what Stephen Covey refers to as 'leadership by
compass'. He notes:

> correct principles are like a compass: they are always pointing the way. And if we
> know how to read them, we won't get lost, confused or fooled by conflicting voices
> and values ... they provide true north direction when navigating the 'streams' of
> our environments. (Covey, 1992, p19)

Coping with uncertainty therefore means moving away from most of the conventional
approaches towards those that ensure insightful agility despite the storms in the sea of

change (Fowler, 2000b). It also means concentrating more on the organization's desired situation as compared to the plans to get there. It means replacing logical and rigid planning with more flexible and effective organizational learning and knowledge management. It means focusing on learning that ensures increasing relevance, legitimacy and sustainability despite the changes in the task environment and the ensuing unknowns they generate. In short, coping with uncertainties means creating more 'conscious organizations'. In addition to a new perspective on professionalism, reaching this coping capability calls for more self-reflective people, time and processes. Exploring what this type of transformation would entail in ideas and practices is one purpose of this book.

Navigating the Book

There are 10 themes in the Companion. Grouped within them are 32 chapters, each of which can be read on its own. They are intentionally 'uneven'. That is, they span abstract concepts, contending ideas, diverse strategic options and numerous practical solutions that are part and parcel of the life-world of those who lead and manage NGDOs. Inevitably, they will not be of equal interest and accessibility for everyone. Together, they add depth and nuance to the issues of concern sketched and others. Each describes a critical topic in NGDO management. Part 1 begins the volume by assessing and recontextualizing NGDOs in a changing world order that requires greater attention to people as citizens. It does so, initially retrospectively, by (in Chapters 1 and 2) introducing discussion about whether NGDOs have made a difference, what alternatives exist within the NGDO contribution to development and how actually or potentially effective these are. Recognizing that poverty, security and stability have emerged as major justifications for international aid, Chapter 3 contextualizes NGDOs in terms of the impact of the global war on terror and its legacy on NGDOs and civil society more broadly.

Expanding on the issue of identity, the chapters in Part 2 discuss the shift from the concept of NGDOs to that of civil society. Chapter 4 does so through the lens and concept of citizenship, while Chapter 5 concentrates on citizen action. Citizenship implies rights, including that of political choice and a legitimate mandate for those who govern. But the relationship between democracy and development is less clear-cut than is conventionally understood. And democracy itself has many forms that NGDOs need to be aware of. Nationally, this terrain is explored in detail in Chapter 6. An international perspective on NGDOs in terms of legitimizing global governance is set out in Chapter 7.

Part 3 focuses on the governance of NGOs themselves. It covers, in Chapter 8, their legitimacy and accountability as organizations, with special attention in Chapter 9 to the thorny issue of making good on downward accountability. As a specially commissioned contribution, Chapter 10 delves into the realm of NGDO governance from the perspective of the principles and good practices of boards.

Given the uncertainties NGDOs will face, Part 4 discusses how they can reposition themselves to proactively and effectively respond to their changing task environments. The topic is approached from two angles. First, a commissioned contribution in Chapter 11 discusses the major strategic issues facing NGOs today and into the foreseeable future. Chapter 12 looks at the practicalities of ensuring effective strategic responses.

Both require NGDOs to have the ability to change: the theme of Part 5. Here, two complementary approaches are included. Chapter 13 offers an organic view of stages of organizational development and the transitions between them, while a commissioned contribution in Chapter 14 provides an insider's view of the challenges faced when trying to bring about transformation change in large NGDOs.

Containing some 10 chapters, Part 6 is the largest in the volume. This size reflects a conscious choice to concentrate on and group together topics that address practical aspects of NGDO management. Chapters 15 to 24 cover many areas of development practice that managers are assumed to master or oversee with adequate insight. Incorporating some commissioned contributions, these areas include: rights-based approaches, participation, partnership, advocacy, gender mainstreaming, appreciating spirituality and faith, CSO networks, social movements, working with academia and communication.

The theme of effectiveness and producing results is covered in Part 7. Clarifying the confusion about how effectiveness is understood is the task of Chapter 25. And, because power is intimately related to how effectiveness is defined, Chapter 26 takes a careful look at whose measures count. Whatever the measures chosen in order to improve, determining effectiveness means – usually through M&E systems – generating new information and translating this into useable knowledge and learning. Part 8 of the volume gets to grips with these challenges by (in Chapter 27) showing that managers face a false dichotomy between learning and accountability: they can reinforce each other. The ways in which knowledge is understood and used by NGOs is the topic for Chapter 28.

The issue of NGDO resourcing addressed in the first part of the Introduction is tackled at two levels. Chapter 29 provides an overview of resourcing options and their potential implications. Chapter 30, specially commissioned, delves into a specific option increasingly seen on the NGDO landscape: that of social enterprise and entrepreneurship.

It could be argued that leaving the theme of leadership until last is a questionable decision. Many chapters argue that this aspect of NGDOs is often the maker or breaker of success in gaining resilience and coping with unknowns both near and far. So, why not introduce leadership earlier? We decided to place this topic at the end so that previous entries can illustrate the breadth and complexity of what NGDO leadership increasingly means and entails. The complicated relationship between leadership and development set out in Chapter 31 provides a backdrop to what can be done about the development of developmental leadership itself. This challenge is discussed in Chapter 32.

It is obviously our hope that the array of contributions in this volume does what it sets out to do: offer a comprehensive resource that will be a true 'companion' for those interested in and taking on the responsibility of the uncertain world of managing NGDOs into and beyond the next decade of the 21st century.

Notes

1   The management of humanitarian and relief work is intentionally not covered in this volume.
2   The concept of civil society is equally poorly defined (e.g., Hodgkinson and Foley, 2003).

3   The OECD/DAC figures on ODA allocated to NGDOs are reliable in what they seem to say but unreliable in what they actually mean. Many channels – such as contracts by southern governments to NGDOs financed by budget support – are not reported. Finance to NGDOs by mega-philanthropists such as Bill and Melinda Gates, and a plethora of new, small family foundations, are not counted or aggregated. NGDO reporting seldom separates out ODA and non-ODA sources of finance.

4   Obviously, the global war on terror and humanitarian engagement in post-conflict reconstruction in Iraq and Afghanistan, as well as response to natural disasters like the Tsunami of southeast Asia, play a role in these numbers.

5   Personal communication; Conny Lennenburg, Policy and Programme Director, World Vision, Australia.

References

Blair, H. (1998) 'Civil Society and Building Democracy: Lessons from International Donor Experience', in Bernard, A., Helmich, H. and Lehning, P. (eds) *Civil Society and International Development*, pp65–80, Organization of Economic Co-operation and Development, Paris

Booth, D. (2008) 'Aid effectiveness after Accra: How to reform the "Paris Agenda"', *Briefing Paper*, 39, Overseas Development Institute, London

Clark, J. (1991) *Democratizing Development: The Role of Voluntary Organizations*, Earthscan, London

Chadha, P., Jagadananda, and Lal, G. (2003) *Organisational Behaviour: A Framework for Non-Government Development Organisations*, Centre for Youth and Social Development, Bhubaneswar, India

Covey, S. (1992) *Principle Centred Leadership*, Simon & Schuster, London

Eade, D. (ed) (2000) *Development, NGOs and Civil Society*, Oxfam, Oxford

Edwards, M. (2008) *Just Another Emperor? The Myths and Realities of Philanthrocapitalism*, Young Foundation, London, available at www.justanotheremperor.org (last accessed May 2010)

Eurodad (2008) *Turning the Tables – Aid and Accountability Under the Paris Framework; A Civil Society Report*, EURODAD, Brussels

Fowler, A. (2000a) 'NGOs as a Moment in History: Beyond Aid to Social Entrepreneurship or Civic Innovation?', in Fowler, A. (ed) 'NGO Futures: Beyond Aid', *Third World Quarterly Special Issue*, vol 21, no 4, pp637–654, August

Fowler, A. (2000b) *The Virtuous Spiral: A Guide to Sustainability for NGOs in International Development*, Earthscan, London

Hilhorst, D. (2003) *The Real World of NGOs: Discourses, Diversity and Development*, Zed Press, London.

Hodgkinson, V. and Foley, M. (eds) (2003) *The Civil Society Reader*, Tufts, University Press of New England, Hanover

Koch, D.-J. (2009) *Aid from International NGOs: Blind spots on the allocation map*, Routledge, London

Moncrieffe, J. and Eyben, R. (2007) *The Power of Labelling: How people are categorized and why it matters*, Earthscan, London

NGLS (1998) 'Human Rights Approaches to Development', *Roundup*, Non-Governmental Liaison Service, Geneva, November

OECD (2005) *Paris Declaration on Aid Effectiveness: Ownership, Harmonization, Alignment, Results and Mutual Accountability*, European Union, Brussels

OECD (2009) *Better Aid – Aid Effectiveness: A Progress Report on Implementing the Paris Declaration*, Organisation for Economic Cooperation and Development, Paris

Ottaway, M. and Carothers, T. (eds) (2000) *Funding Virtue: Civil Society Aid and Democracy Promotion*, Carnegie Endowment For International Peace, Washington, DC

Pratt, B. (ed) (2003) *Changing Expectations? The Concept and Practice of Civil Society in International Development*, International NGO Training and Research Centre, Oxford.

Ronalds, P. (2010) *The Change Imperative: Creating a Next Generation NGO*, Kumarian Press, Bloomfield, CT

Scholte, J-A. (2005) *Democratizing The Global Economy: The Role of Civil Society*, Centre for the Study of Globalisation and Regionalisation, University of Warwick, Warwick.

Tvedt, T. (1998) *Angels of Mercy or Development Diplomats? NGOs and Foreign Aid*, James Currey, London

Part I

Retro-perspective: NGO-ism in a Changing World Order

Have NGOs 'Made a Difference'? From Manchester to Birmingham with an Elephant in the Room

Michael Edwards

Introduction

In 1991, David Hulme and I found ourselves in a bar at the University of Hull enjoying a post-conference beer. The conversation turned to a mutual interest of ours – the role and impact of non-governmental organizations (NGOs) in development – and after a few more pints we hit on the idea that eventually became the first 'Manchester Conference' on the theme of 'scaling-up', later to be summarized in a book called 'Making a Difference: NGOs and Development in a Changing World' (Edwards and Hulme, 1992). 15 years on, the NGO universe has been substantially transformed, with rates of growth in scale and profile that once would have been unthinkable. Yet still the nagging questions remain. Despite the increasing size and sophistication of the development NGO sector, have NGOs really 'made a difference' in the ways the first Manchester Conference intended, or have the reforms that animated the NGO community during the 1990s now run out of steam?

In this chapter I try to answer these questions in two ways. First, through a retrospective of the Manchester conferences – what they taught us, what influence they had and how NGOs have changed. And second, by picking out a couple of especially important challenges in development terms and assessing whether NGOs 'stood up to be counted', so to speak, and did their best in addressing them. These two approaches suggest somewhat different conclusions, which will bring me to the 'elephant in the room' of my title.

It is obvious that making judgements about a universe as diverse as development NGOs is replete with dangers of over-generalization, and difficulties of attribution, measurement, context and timing. I suspect my remarks may be particularly relevant for international NGOs and to larger intermediary NGOs based in the south. So with these caveats in mind, what does the last decade and a half tell us about the role and impact of NGOs in development?

The Manchester Conferences: A Short Retrospective

As Table 1.1 shows, the theme of the first Manchester Conference in 1992 was 'Scaling-up NGO impact on development'. 'How can NGOs progress from improving local situations on a small scale to influencing the wider systems that create and reinforce poverty?' (Edwards and Hulme, 1992, p7). The conference concluded that were different strategies suited to different circumstances, specifically: (1) working with government; (2) operational expansion; (3) lobbying and advocacy; and (4) networking and 'self-spreading' local initiatives.

All of these strategies have costs and benefits, but the implicit bias of the conference organizers, and most of the participants, lay towards institutional development and advocacy as the most effective and least costly forms of scaling-up, what Alan Fowler later called the 'onion-skin' strategy for NGOs – a solid core of concrete practice (either direct project implementation or support to other organizations and their work), surrounded by successive and inter-related layers of research and evaluation, advocacy and campaigning, and public education. To varying extents, this strategy has become standard practice for development NGOs in the intervening years.

Buried away at the end of 'Making a Difference' was the following statement: 'The degree to which a strategy or mix of strategies compromises the logic by which legitimacy is claimed provides a useful test of whether organizational self-interest is subordinating mission' (Edwards and Hulme, 1992, p213). For reasons that I will come back to later in this chapter, that has turned out to be a prescient conclusion.

Fast forward to the second Manchester Conference in 1994, in a context in which NGOs had begun to 'scale-up' rapidly in an environment in which they were seen as important vehicles to deliver the political and economic objectives of the 'New Policy Agenda' that was being adopted by official donor agencies at the time – deeper democratization through the growth of 'civil society', and more cost-effective delivery of development-related services such as micro-credit and community-driven development. As a result, many NGO budgets were financed increasingly by government aid, raising critical questions about performance, accountability and relations with funding sources: The key question for that conference was as follows: 'will NGOs be co-opted into the 'New Policy Agenda' as the favoured child, or magic bullet for development?' (Edwards and Hulme, 1995, p7). And if so, what would that do to NGO mission and relationships? Will they, as another of the conference books put it, become 'too close to the powerful, and too far from the powerless' (Hulme and Edwards, 1997, p275)?

At the time, our conclusion was that such problems were not inevitable. Whether they arise depends on the *quality* of the relationships that develop between actors, and on how each NGO uses its 'room to manoeuvre' to control the costs of growth and donor-dependence. Therefore, negotiation between stakeholders is vital, requiring innovation in performance-assessment, accountability mechanisms and relations with funding agencies. 'The developmental impact of NGOs', we concluded, 'their capacity to attract support, and their legitimacy as actors in development, will rest much more clearly on their ability to demonstrate that they can perform effectively and are accountable for their actions. It is none too soon for NGOs to put their house in order' (Edwards and Hulme, 1995, pp227–228).

Since 1994 there have been some important innovations in this respect, like the Humanitarian Accountability Project; the rise of self-certification and accreditation

Table 1.1 *The Manchester conferences: A case summary*

Date and location	Theme(s)	Key conclusions	Published outputs
Manchester 1992	*Scaling-up NGO impact on development:*	Different strategies suit different circumstances:	Making a Difference: NGOs and Development in a Changing World
	'How can NGOs progress from improving local situations on a small scale to influencing the wider systems that create and reinforce poverty?'	1) Working with government 2) operational expansion 3) lobbying and advocacy 4) networking and 'self-spreading' local initiatives.	Scaling-Up NGO Impact on Development: Learning from Experience (DIP)
		All have costs and benefits but implicit bias to institutional development and advocacy to control for dangers (the 'onion-skin' strategy):	
		'The degree to which a strategy or mix of strategies compromises the logic by which legitimacy is claimed provides a useful test of whether organizational self-interest is subordinating mission'	
Manchester 1994	*NGO growth raises questions about performance, accountability and relations with funding sources:*	Problems are not inevitable – they depend on the quality of relationships between actors and how 'room to manoeuvre' is exploited.	Beyond the Magic Bullet: NGO Performance And Accountability in the Post-Cold War World (x 2)
	'Will NGOs be co-opted into the New Policy Agenda as the favoured child, or magic bullet for development?'	Therefore, negotiation between stakeholders is vital, requiring innovation in performance assessment, accountability mechanisms, and relations with funders.	NGOs, States and Donors: Too Close for Comfort? (x 2)
	If so, what does that do to NGO mission and relationships – 'too close to the powerful, too far from the powerless?'	'The developmental impact of NGOs, their capacity to attract support, and their legitimacy as actors in development, will rest much more clearly on their ability to demonstrate that they can perform effectively and are accountable for their actions. It is none too soon for NGOs to put their house in order.'	Too Close For Comfort: The Impact of Official Aid on NGOs (WD)
			Policy Arena: New Roles and Challenges for NGOs (JID)

Table 1.1 *The Manchester conferences: A case summary (cont'd)*

Date and location	Theme(s)	Key conclusions	Published outputs
Birmingham 1999	*The changing global context poses questions about NGO roles, relationships, capacities and accountabilities*	This changing context gives rise to 4 challenges for NGOs:	NGOs in a Global Future: Marrying Local Delivery to Worldwide Leverage (PAD)
	'Adapt or die!' Three key changes:	1) mobilizing a genuinely inclusive civil society at all levels of the world system	New Roles and Relevance: Development NGOs and the Challenge of Change
	1) globalization reshapes patterns of poverty, inequality and insecurity	2) holding other organizations accountable for their actions and ensuring they respond to social and environmental needs	NGO Futures: Beyond Aid (TWQ)
	2) 'complex political emergencies' reshape patterns of humanitarian action	3) ensuring that international regimes are implemented effectively and to the benefit of poor countries	Global Citizen Action
	3) the focus of international cooperation is moving from a focus on foreign aid to a focus on rules, standards and supports for those most vulnerable.	4) ensuring that gains at the global level are translated into concrete benefits at the grassroots.	
	Hence, 'NGO Futures Beyond Aid', 'New Roles and Relevance', and 'Global Citizen Action' – transnational organizing among equals for systemic change of north–south transfers and interventions.	NGOs must move from 'development as delivery to development as leverage', or 'marry local development to worldwide leverage'	
		This requires more equal relationships with other civic actors, especially in the south, new capacities (e.g. bridging and mediation) and stronger accountability mechanisms.	

schemes, seals of approval and codes of conduct among child sponsorship agencies and other NGOs; the development of formal compacts between government and the non-profit sector in the UK, Canada and elsewhere; the Global Accountability Project in London; ActionAid's Active Learning Network for Accountability and Performance (ALNAP) system; and simple but powerful things like publicizing the financial accounts of an NGO on public bulletin boards that are being encouraged by MANGO and other organizations (Jordan and van Tuijl, forthcoming).

In retrospect however, NGOs did not heed this call with sufficient attention, and are now suffering from it in a climate in which, unlike 10 years ago, weaknesses in NGO accountability are being used as cover for an attack on political grounds against voices that certain interests wish to silence. Examples of such attacks include the NGO Watch project at the American Enterprise Institute, the Rushford Report in Washington DC and NGO Monitor in Jerusalem. Stronger NGO accountability mechanisms won't do away with politically motivated attacks like these, but they would surely help to expose them for what they are.

In 1999, the Third NGO Conference took place in Birmingham, framed by a rapidly changing global context that posed some deeper questions about NGO roles, relationships, capacities and accountabilities. 'Adapt or die' was the subtext of that meeting, whose organizers highlighted three key sets of changes:

• First, globalization reshapes patterns of poverty, inequality and insecurity, calling for greater global integration of NGO strategies and more 'development work' of different kinds in the north
• Second, 'complex political emergencies' reshape patterns of humanitarian action, implying more difficult choices for NGOs about intervention and the need to reassert their independence from government interests
• Third, a move from foreign aid as the key driver of international cooperation to a focus on rules, standards and support for those who are most vulnerable to the negative effects of global change implies greater NGO involvement in the processes and institutions of global governance, both formal and informal (Edwards et al, 1999, p2).

The thrust of these changes is clearly visible in the titles of the books that emerged from the Birmingham conference – *NGO Futures: Beyond Aid* (Fowler, 2000), *New Roles and Relevance* (Lewis and Wallace, 2000) and *Global Citizen Action* (Edwards and Gaventa, 2001) – holding out the promise of transnational organizing among equals for systemic change as opposed to a secondary role shaped by the continued asymmetries of the foreign aid world.

This changing context, we believed, gave rise to four key challenges resulting from the evolution of a more political role for development NGOs in emerging systems of global governance, debate and decision-making:

1 How to mobilize a genuinely inclusive civil society at all levels of the world system, as opposed to a thin layer of elite NGOs operating internationally
2 How to hold other (more powerful) organizations accountable for their actions and ensure that they respond to social and environmental needs – something that implicitly demanded reforms in NGO accountability too

3   How to ensure that international regimes are implemented effectively and to the benefit of poor people and poor countries (getting to grips with 'democratic deficits' in global institutions and protecting 'policy space' for southern countries to embark on their own development strategies)

4   How to ensure that gains at the global level are translated into concrete benefits at the grassroots (translating abstract commitments made in international conferences into actions that actually enforce rules and regulations on the ground: Edwards et al 1999, p10).

NGOs, we concluded, must move from 'development as delivery to development as leverage', and this would require the development of more equal relationships with other civic actors (especially in the south), new capacities (like bridging and mediation), and stronger downward or horizontal accountability mechanisms.

Since 1999 there have certainly been some examples of innovations like these, like the 'Make Poverty History Campaign' in the UK (which has developed stronger coordination mechanisms among development and non-development NGOs and other organizations in UK civil society), and the development of much more sophisticated advocacy campaigns on aid, debt and trade.

Now, if one believes that there is a credible chain of logic linking these three conferences, their outputs and those of other similar efforts that were ongoing during the same period, with the emergence of a more thoughtful and professional development NGO sector; and going one stage further, linking the emergence of that sector with at least the possibility of a greater aggregate impact on development, then one can begin to answer the question posed by *this* volume in the affirmative, breaking down those answers by country context, type of organization, type of impact, longevity, sector, issue and so on in the ways that other papers try to do.

I think one would have to argue an extreme version of the counterfactual to say otherwise – in other words, to claim that the world would be a better place *without* the rise of development NGOs, however patchy their impact may have been, especially given the huge and complex challenges that face all NGOs in their work today. Perhaps I am not setting the bar very high in making this point, but in critiques of NGOs it is often forgotten. There *has* been a positive change in the distribution of opportunities to participate in development debates and in democracy more broadly, and in the capacities and connections required by NGOs to play their roles effectively, even if global trends in poverty and power relations, inequality, environmental degradation and violence are not all heading in a positive direction.

In other words, some of the preconditions, or foundations, for progress are being laid, brick by brick, organization by organization, community by community, vote by vote. If one believes that democratic theory works, then over time, more transparency, greater accountability, and stronger capacities for monitoring *will* feed through into deeper changes in systems and structures. Civil society may yet fulfill Kofi Annan's prediction as the 'new superpower' – a statement that was largely rhetorical but contained at least a grain of truth. And as context for that conclusion, think back 13 years to the first Manchester Conference when NGOs were still something of a backwater in international affairs. No one could say the same thing today.

Where We Were Wrong, and Why It Is Important

So, so far, so good. There was one major area, however, in which the analysis of previous conferences was seriously awry, and it has some significant consequences for the question of NGO impact in the future. This was the prediction that foreign aid would continue to decline and be replaced by a different, healthier and more effective system of international cooperation in which the drivers of development and change would no longer be based around north–south transfers and foreign intervention.

In fact, as one can see from Figure 1.1, the clear decline in real aid flows that can be observed between 1992 to 1999 – exactly coinciding with the NGO Conferences – turns out to have been an atypical period in recent history. Backed by a growing coalition of celebrities, charities, politicians, journalists and academics, we are firmly back in a period of rising real aid flows, up to around $78 billion in 2004, set to grow still further, and perhaps even reaching the promised land of $150–200 billion a year estimated to be required to meet the United Nations Millennium Development Goals. The critical literature on aid effectiveness, the importance of institutions and the primacy of politics that was developed during the 1990s has largely been marginalized from the current discourse (Edwards, 2004b). From Jeffrey Sachs to Bob Geldof, the new orthodoxy asserts that more money *will* solve Africa's problems, and, if we add in an American twist, make the world safe from terrorism too.

Of course, in 1999 no-one could have predicted some of the key reasons behind this reverse – principally the events of 9/11 and the ensuing 'war on terrorism', or the recent catastrophic Tsunami in Asia – but previous conferences were also guilty of confusing

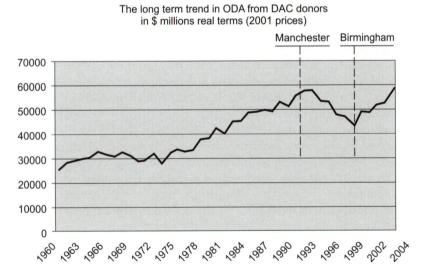

Figure 1.1 *The long term trend in ODA from DAC donors in $ millions real terms (2001 prices)*

Source: German and Ewing (2004)

normative and empirical arguments. Much of the discussion at the Birmingham Conference was driven by what the organizers and participants *wanted* to see happen in the future, not necessarily by a hard-nosed analysis of likely trends and opportunities.

Why is this important for the rest of my argument? The reason is that the perseverance of the traditional aid paradigm, even in its modified version of Millennium Challenge Accounts, Poverty Reduction Strategy Papers, International Finance Facilities and the rest of the current paraphernalia of aid reform, makes any kind of quantum leap in NGO impact much more difficult to achieve because it weakens the incentives for deep innovation by providing a continued 'security blanket' for current practice. Of course, one can read this as a much more positive story, particularly when calls for aid are coupled with serious action on debt relief and trade justice. And I don't mean to imply that investment in developing countries is irrelevant – simply that is difficult to detach the dysfunctional aspects of the traditional aid paradigm from the injection of ever-larger amounts of money by powerful national interests into societies with weak institutions and fragile systems of accountability. To explain what I mean, let me move to the second way in which I've chosen to answer the questions I posed at the beginning of my argument.

The 'Larry Summers Test'

Recently, I attended a dinner at which the keynote speaker was Larry Summers, the ever-controversial President of Harvard University. After his speech was over, one brave member of the audience – a leading Arab academic – asked him point blank whether he thought that America 'has been a force for good in the world'. His answer was unconvincing, but interesting, since he said that it would be impossible to give a sensible answer to that question in any general sense. There are too many 'ifs, buts and maybes', and too many variations of detail, context and circumstance. However, he went on to say, one *can* ask whether America 'did the right thing' at those few moments in history when a certain course of action was unquestionably important – such as intervention in World War I, World War II and the Cold War. And in those cases, the answer was unequivocally 'yes'.

Now, of course one can dispute Summers' conclusion, but I think the way in which he repositioned the question is useful in relation to the topic of development NGOs and their impact. Instead of trying to generalize across the huge diversity of the NGO universe, we can ask ourselves whether NGOs 'did the right thing' on the really big issues of our times.

On the positive side of the balance sheet, I think development NGOs have helped to do the following, albeit with limited practical results thus far:

- Changed the terms of the debate on globalization, leading to the emergence of a new orthodoxy about the need to manage the downside of this process, level the playing field, and expand 'policy space' for developing countries
- Cemented an intellectual commitment to participation and human rights as basic principles of development and development assistance

- Kept the spotlight on the need for reforms in international institutions and global governance on issues such as unfair terms of trade and investment, global warming, Africa, and the kind of warped humanitarian intervention represented by the war in Iraq.

On the other hand, there is a less positive side to this story when one looks beyond the short-term gains that have been made in development discourse to grapple with the underlying goals that NGOs were set up to pursue. In my view development NGOs have not 'stood up to be counted' sufficiently on the following crucial questions.

They have not been very innovative in finding ways to lever deep changes in the systems and structures that perpetuate poverty and the abuse of human rights, despite the recent boom in Corporate Social Responsibility and public-private partnerships. The 'onion', to go back to Alan Fowler's phrase, is still incomplete, made up by layers of fairly conventional development projects and advocacy work.

For example, development NGOs have not changed power relations on anything like the necessary scale in the crucial areas of class, gender and race. They have not faced up to the challenges of internal change – changes in personal attitudes, values and behavior – in any significant way. They have not established strong connections with social movements that are more embedded in the political processes that are essential to sustained change. They have not gotten to grips with the rise of religion as one of the most powerful forces for change in the world today, increasingly expressed in fundamentalism and demanding large-scale action to build bridges between pluralists in different religious traditions.

Equally important, development NGOs have not innovated in any significant sense in the form and nature of their organizational relationships. For example, little concrete attention is paid to downward accountability or the importance of generating diverse, local sources of funds for so-called 'partners' in the south (a weakness that underpins many other problems including legitimacy and political threats to organizations perceived as 'pawns of foreign interests'). They have internalized functions that should have been distributed across other organizations – local fundraising by international NGOs inside developing countries (or 'markets' to use a telling common phrase) provides a good example, and there are others – franchising global brands instead of supporting authentic expressions of indigenous civil society, and crowding out southern participation in knowledge creation and advocacy in order to increase their own voice and profile, as if the only people with anything useful to say about world development were Oxfam and a handful of others.

Of course, there are exceptions to all of these generalizations. I would single out Action Aid for the changes it has made; and on a smaller scale I was struck by the Institute for Agriculture and Trade Policy's decision to transfer spaces on the NGO delegation to the Cancun trade talks from northern NGOs to groups from the south in 2004. But these examples tend to get noticed because they are exceptions that prove the rule. The rules of the international NGO world themselves seem to stay the same. Does anyone believe that development NGOs still aim to 'work themselves out of a job', that old NGO mantra? Maybe it was never true, but there isn't much evidence to suggest that it is taken seriously today. Let's face it – NGOs are a major growth industry, back in the 'comfort zone' and set to continue along that path. There has been little real transfer of roles or capacity in either 'delivery' or 'leverage'. It's almost as though they have taken the entire 'onion' and swallowed it whole!

NGOs may give a nod in the direction of 'levelling the playing field', diversifying NGO representation in the international arena, empowering marginalized voices, building the capacity of actors in the south for independent action, helping them to sustain themselves through indigenous resources, 'handing over the stick', becoming more accountable to beneficiaries and so on, but in practical terms the 'institutional imperatives' of growth and market share still dominate the 'developmental imperatives' of individual, organizational and social transformation (see Table 1.2). And – returning to the quotation I cited from 'Making a Difference' earlier in this paper – this failure places an important, continuing question mark against the legitimacy of development NGOs and their role in the contemporary world.

It is these failings, I believe, that stand in the way of increasing NGO impact in the future, and it is these failings that represent the 'elephant in the room' of my title. We don't want to recognize the beast, but we know it's there. And while it remains in the room – a hulking, largely silent presence – NGOs will never achieve the impact they say they want to achieve, because their leverage over the drivers of long-term change will continue to be weak.

One can read this story under the conventional rubric of institutional inertia, defensiveness and the difficulties of raising money for new and unfamiliar roles. But I think something more fundamental is going on. Underlying this situation is a much broader

Table 1.2 *NGO imperatives*

Developmental imperatives	Institutional imperatives
Bottom line: empowering marginalized groups for independent action	Bottom line: size, income, profile, market share
Downplay the role of intermediary; encourage marginalized groups to speak with their own voice	Accentuate the role of intermediary; speak on behalf of marginalized groups
Democratic governance; less hierarchy; more reciprocity; a focus on stakeholders	More hierarchy; less reciprocity; a focus on donors and recipients
Multiple accountability, honesty, learning from mistakes, transparency, sharing of information	Accountability upwards, secrecy, repeat mistakes, exaggerate successes and disguise failures
Maintain independence and flexibility; take risks	Increasing dependence on government funds; standardization; bureaucracy
Address the causes of poverty; defend values of service and solidarity	Deal with symptoms: internalize orthodoxies even when antithetical to mission
Long term goals drive decision-making; programme criteria lead	Short term interests drive decision-making; marketing criteria lead
Rooted in broader movements for change; alliances with others; look outwards	Isolated from broader movements for change; incorporate others into your own structures; look inwards
Maximize resources at the 'sharp end'; cooperate to reduce overheads and transaction costs	Duplicate delivery mechanisms (e.g. separate field offices); resources consumed increasingly by fixed costs
Maintain focus on continuity, critical mass and distinctive competence	Opportunism – go where the funds are; increasing spread of activities and countries

Source: Edwards (1996)

struggle between two visions of the future – one that I call 'international development,' and the other 'global civil society', for want of a better phrase.

The 'international development' vision is predicated on continued north–south transfers of resources and ideas as its centerpiece, temporarily under the umbrella of US hegemony and its drive to engineer terrorism out of the world, if necessary by refashioning whole societies in the image of liberal, free-market democracy. This vision requires the expansion of traditional NGO roles in humanitarian assistance, the provision of social safety-nets and 'civil society building' (crudely translated as support to advocacy and service-delivery NGOs: Edwards, 2004a). It privileges technical solutions over politics and the volume of resources over their use. The role of the north is to 'help' the less-fortunate and backward south; if possible, to 'save it' from drifting ever-further away from modernity as liberal market democracy (God forbid there is a viable alternative, like Islam); and if that fails, then at least to 'prevent it' from wreaking havoc on northern societies. The 'war on terror', I would argue, reinforces and exacerbates the worst elements of the traditional foreign aid paradigm.

The 'Global Civil Society' vision, and here I'm exaggerating to make a point, takes its cue from cosmopolitan articulations of an international system in which international law trumps national interests, and countries – with increasingly direct involvement by their citizens – negotiate solutions to global problems through democratic principles, the fair sharing of burdens, respect for local context and autonomy, and a recognition of the genuinely interlocking nature of causes and effects in the contemporary world. This vision, to be successful, requires action in all of the areas in which I think development NGOs have been found wanting – levelling the playing field, empowering southern voices, building constituencies for changes in global consumption and production patterns and injecting real accountability into the system, including personal accountability for the choices that NGOs make. The struggle for *global* civil society can't be separated from the struggle for *personal* change, since it is those changes that underpin the difficult decision to hand over control, share power and live a life that is consistent with our principles. In this vision our role is to act as 'critical friends' as I put it on the last page of 'Future Positive,' sharing in 'the loving but forceful encounters *between equals* who journey together towards the land of the true and the beautiful' (Edwards, 2004b, p233).

Recent history can be read as a reversal in what the Birmingham NGO Conference predicted would be a steady, long-term transition from the 'international development' model to 'global civil society'. Led by the United States, we are seeing a retreat from the cosmopolitan vision and a return to culturally-bound fundamentalisms, the hegemony of the nation state and the belief that the world can indeed be remade in the image of the dominant powers through foreign intervention – with Iraq as the paradigm case. That, at root, is why there are so many attacks today on the institutions, or even the idea, of global governance, the rise of non-state involvement and the threats it supposedly carries, the legitimacy of international law and the transnational dimensions of democracy – as opposed to the domestic implantation of versions of democracy in other peoples' countries.

It is no accident that hostility to international NGOs forms a key plank of neo-conservative thinking in America today. 'Post-democratic challenges to American democratic sovereignty should be clearly defined and resisted', writes John Fonte of the

Hudson Institute, one of the key think-tanks of neo-conservatism. 'NGOs that consistently act as if they are strategic opponents of the democratic sovereignty of the American nation should be treated as such. They should not be supported or recognized at international conferences, nor permitted access to government officials' (Fonte, 2004). 'NGOs should be at the top of every Conservative's watch list' says Elaine Chao, President Bush's Secretary of Labor. So, 'you have been warned'. No matter how much additional foreign aid gets pumped through the international system, NGOs are unlikely to get very far unless they recognize that there are much bigger issues at stake. This is nothing less than a battle for the soul of world politics, and NGOs need to decide which side they want to take. I was convinced in Birmingham in 1999, and I'm even more convinced today, that we need to break free from the aid paradigm in order to liberate ourselves to achieve the impact that we want.

Conclusion

To sum up, my case is that the return of foreign aid to favour provides a security blanket for NGOs who might otherwise have been forced to change their ways. There may, of course be more unforeseen events in the near future that, like 9/11, provide an external shock to the system large enough to interrupt current trends and initiate new directions – or, as in this case, return us to old ways of doing business. This might happen to development NGOs, for example, if aid donors ever got serious about cutting intermediaries (national and international) out of the equation, but I don't think this is very likely.

Therefore, I see only incremental increases in impact – shown by the hatched line in Figure 1.2 – unless NGOs can break out of the foreign aid box, as a few pioneers are already doing. As they have recognized, there is a much healthier framework for civic action available to us if we decide to choose it. In my view, the advances made by development NGOs throughout the 1990s – spurred on significantly but not exclusively by the Manchester Conferences – represented a much bigger leap in NGO strategy and

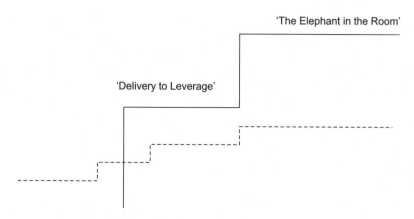

Figure 1.2 *Trajectories of NGO impact*

potential impact, shown by the solid line in Figure 1.2. Dealing effectively with the 'elephant in the room' represents the next such quantum leap.

In conclusion, the question facing development NGOs today is the same question that faced participants in the first NGO Conference in Manchester in 1992, albeit framed in a somewhat different context. That question is less about what NGOs have achieved in the absolute sense, since they can never achieve enough, and more about how they can achieve more, however well they think they are doing. How satisfied are NGOs with their current performance? Do they wait until another 9/11 hits the system and shakes them out of their complacency, or can they 'bite the bullet' and implement their own gradual reforms now?

Perhaps when the development NGO community meets again in Manchester in 10 years time, there will be a different set of answers on the table.

References

Edwards, M. (1996) 'International Development NGOs: Legitimacy, Accountability, Regulation and Roles', in *Meeting the Challenge of Change: the report of the Commission on the Future of the Voluntary Sector*. London: Commission on the Future of the Voluntary Sector

Edwards, M. (2004a) *Civil Society*. Cambridge: Polity Press

Edwards, M. (2004b) *Future Positive: International Cooperation in the 21st Century*. Revised Edition. London: Earthscan

Edwards, M. and Gaventa, J. (eds) (2001) *Global Citizen Action*. Boulder: Lynne Rienner and London: Earthscan

Edwards, M. and Hulme, D. (eds) (1992) *Making a Difference: NGOs and Development in a Changing World*. London: Earthscan

Edwards, M., and Hulme, D. (eds) (1995) *Beyond the Magic Bullet: NGO Performance and Accountability in the Post Cold-War World*. London: Earthscan and West Hartford: Kumarian Press

Edwards, M., Hulme, D. and Wallace, T. (1999) 'NGOs in a Global Future: Marrying Local Delivery to World-wide Leverage', *Public Administration and Development*, 19(2), pp117–136

Fonte, J. (2004) 'Democracy's Trojan Horse', *The National Interest*, Summer, pp117–127

Fowler, A. (ed) (2000) *NGO Futures: Beyond Aid*, Special Issue of *Third World Quarterly*

German, T. and Ewing, D. (eds) (2004) *Reality of Aid 2004: An Independent Review of Poverty Reduction and Development Assistance*. London: Action Aid/ICVA/Eurostep

Hulme, D. and Edwards, M. (eds) (1997) *Too Close for Comfort? NGOs, States and Donors*. Basingstoke: Macmillan and New York: St Martins Press

Jordan, L. and van Tuijl, P. (eds) (forthcoming) *New Frontiers in NGO Accountability*

Lewis, D. and Wallace, T. (eds) (2000) *New Roles and Relevance: Development NGOs and the Challenge of Change*. West Hartford: Kumarian Press

NGOs and Development Alternatives – Revisited

Diana Mitlin, Sam Hickey and Anthony Bebbington

Introduction

In 1987, World Development published 'Development Alternatives: the Challenge of NGOs' (Drabek, 1987). Twenty years later, it has become defensible to claim that 'there is no alternative', that the term NGOs has no analytical or even descriptive value, that development is a form of governmentality rather than a project of emancipation and that it is far more important to ask how the term is used to serve particular interests than to ask what it means. This chapter attempts to restate this reflection on the relationship between NGOs and development alternatives. It begins with a reflection on the concept of 'development', staking out a terrain that gives the term both analytical and normative force. This lays the base for discussing possible meanings of 'alternative' development. Second, it suggests a conceptualization of non-governmental organization and reflects on the meaning of civil society. Third, it places a discussion of NGOs and development in terms of relationships and flows that are as much global as local in their reach, and links processes and actors at different sites across space and time. Fourth, it offers a review of both historical and contemporary experiences of the roles of NGOs in development and the pursuit of something called 'alternatives'.

Thinking about NGOs as alternatives has gone somewhat missing of late. The NGO literature has been voluminous since the 1980s, with these 'new' actors frequently lauded as the institutional 'alternative' to existing development approaches. Critical voices were largely confined to expressing concern that NGOs might be an externally imposed phenomenon, heralding a new wave of imperialism (Tandon, 1991). Much of the literature focused on the importance of NGOs within the emerging 'New Policy Agenda', including 'civil society' and 'democratisation' (Robinson, 1995). The diversification and multiplication of NGO activities and their move to the mainstream came under close critical scrutiny, both from supporters and sceptics. On the one hand were discussions of how to scale-up NGO activities (Edwards and Hulme, 1992), how to run NGOs more successfully and ensure their sustainability as organizations (e.g. Fowler, 1997; Lewis, 2001) and how NGOs might better manage their relationships (Groves and Hinton, 2004). On the other, commentators feared that closeness to the 'mainstream' undermined their 'comparative advantage' as agents of alternative development, citing problems of standardization and upwards accountability (Wallace et al, 1997), NGOs' effectiveness in reaching the poorest (Edwards and Hulme, 1995), and a tendency to employ 'radical' methods of empowerment such as participation as technical means rather than political ends (Lane, 1995). The apparently limited success of NGOs as agents of democratization came under critique (e.g. Fowler, 1993, Stewart, 1997), while the simmering debate over NGOs as an externally driven phenomenon that threatened the development of 'indigenous civil society' re-emerged (e.g. Hashemi, 1995; Mamdani, 1993). Amidst growing calls for 'northern' NGOs to devise new roles and rationales for themselves or risk becoming obsolete (van Rooy, 2000), NGOs were advised to reach beyond the aid system for alternative forms of funding (Aldaba et al, 2000) while also lobbying for a fundamental restructuring of the international aid system itself (Edwards, 1999).

Yet today we are arguably no clearer concerning questions of effectiveness, accountability and successful routes to scaling-up than we were a decade ago, nor are we clearer on what being 'alternative' means at this juncture (Tandon, 2001). And while some NGOs have undergone profound institutional changes (e.g. ActionAid's relocation to South Africa), a sense of complacency concerning these and other key challenges appears to have set in. We therefore ask again whether and how NGOs might re-engage with their founding project of offering genuine 'alternatives'.

This chapter elaborates a framework for discussing the links between development and NGOs, and uses it to review NGO modern history since the 1960s. In light of that review, we suggest possible futures in the relationships between NGOs and alternatives. The paper is both analytical and normative for we are specially interested in particular alternatives – those reworking state-society relationships towards more radical, socially inclusive forms of citizenship (Hickey and Mohan, 2005), and reworking economic relationships such that markets have more potential to become vehicles of social justice.

A Framework for Thinking about Development Alternatives

We address the role of NGOs in development along three dimensions. The first concerns examining development both as an underlying process of social change and as a targeted intervention; the second concerns the tripartite division between state, civil society and market; and the third relates to the relationships between localizing and globalizing tendencies in what NGOs do and are.

D(d)evelopment/A(a)lternative(s)

Cowen and Shenton (1998) distinguish between two meanings of the term 'development' that have been consistently confused: 'development as an immanent and unintentional process as in, for example, the 'development of capitalism' and development as an intentional activity' (Cowen and Shenton, 1998, p50). Hart (2001) amends this slightly to talk of 'little d' and 'big D' d/Development. The former involves the 'geographically uneven, profoundly contradictory' set of processes underlying capitalist developments, while the latter refers to the 'project of intervention in the 'third world' that emerged in a context of decolonization and the cold war' (Hart, 2001, p650). The critical distinction is between notions of intervention and of political economic, structural change when thinking about development, without losing the sense that there are clear relationships between the two (Bebbington, 2003). We can locate NGOs in this simple framework, in the sense that they are – whether as project implementers, knowledge generators or political activists – all involved in intervention, but are also *part of* the societies and political economies in which they operate: they are part of the little *d* development at the same time as they try, through Big *D* Development, to intervene in and modify the nature and/or effects of the broader processes of this little *d* development. NGOs are, then, both endogenous to development (understood in its systemic sense) while often seen as exogenous to it when they undertake their interventions.

The same distinction can also apply to alternatives. Much discussion of alternatives has been in relation to Big D Development – NGOs have been seen as sources of alternative ways of arranging microfinance, project planning, service delivery etc. These are reformist notions of alternatives – different ways of intervening to ensure greater participation, people-centredness etc. However, alternatives can also be conceived in relation to the underlying processes of capitalist (or socialist) development – emphasizing alternative ways of organizing the economy, politics and social relationships in society. When Evo Morales in Bolivia speaks of a commitment to finding non-neoliberal ways of organizing the economy, this is the type of alternative invoked. The distinction, then, is between a partial, reformist, intervention-specific alternative, and a structure changing, radical, systemic alternative to transform society.

Civil society/alternatives

The second element of our framework links these distinctions to a reflection on state, market and civil society. This tripartite division is often used to locate NGOs as civil society actors (Hyden, 1997). This is problematic for two reasons. First, civil society is often seen in normative rather than analytical terms – a source of 'good', distinct from a 'bad' imputed to the state and market. This understates the potential role of the state in fostering progressive change and also downplays the extent to which civil society includes racist organizations, neoliberal research NGOs or other organizations that most of these authors would not consider benign (Hearn, 2001; Lewis, 2002). Second, the fluidity of boundaries among the three spheres – as people move back and forth between NGOs, government and occasionally business – has received less attention though it problematizes the understanding of NGOs as an integral part of civil society. Critically, these discussions of civil society have generally lacked historical depth. NGOs are a relatively recent organizational form which emerged from far more deeply seated social arrangements linked, for instance, to religious institutions, political movements, government and transnational networks of various kinds (Bebbington, 2004). Why they exist, what they do, what they say, who they relate to, can only be properly understood in terms of their relationship to these more constitutive actors in society. This does not mean that NGOs are merely instruments of these actors (though they may be) – it does mean that they are not constitutive and are certainly not the most important actor in civil society.

Civil society – and the place of NGOs within it – must therefore be treated carefully. Ideologically, the notion of civil society has flourished most fruitfully within either the neoliberal school that advocates a reduced role for the state, or a post-marxist/post-structural approach that emphasizes the transformative potential of social movements within civil society. Conceptually, civil society is either treated in terms of associations, or as an arena within which ideas about the ordering of social life are debated. In this paper we work from a broadly Gramscian understanding of civil society as constituting an arena in which hegemonic ideas are established and contested. These contestations, the hegemonies which emerge and the roles of NGOs within this are in turn understood in terms of the relationships and struggles for power among the constitutive actors of society.

These contestations over hegemony can be related to our framing of 'alternatives'. Imagine certain alternatives in the domain of Big D Development, that challenge ideas that are dominant but not foundational – e.g. dominant ideas about how health care or financial service provision should be organized might be contested by actors promoting distinct models of provision. Such alternatives, important though they may be in welfare terms, do not challenge the more basic arrangements in society. Conversely, imagine hegemonic ideas that are far more foundational – e.g. ideas regarding how society and market ought to be governed; or ideas about property rights. These ideas can also be contested with alternatives in the domain of little 'd' development.

Global NGOs

Globalization has (re)shaped NGOs and how they are viewed. NGOs have increasingly become a transnational community, itself overlapping with other transnational networks and institutions (Townsend et al, 2002). These linkages disperse new development discourses, modes of governance and resources throughout the global south; and some southern NGOs have begun to gain their own footholds in the north with outposts in Brussels, Washington and elsewhere. Yet these transnationalizing tendencies have also excluded certain actors for whom engagement in such processes is harder, resulting in the emergence of international civil society elites who dominate the discourses. This raises serious questions as to *whose alternatives* gain greater visibility in these processes.

The transnationalizing of intervention (big D) has also involved increased channel-ling of (national and multilateral) state controlled resources through NGOs – whereby resources become bundled with particular rules and ideas regarding how they must be governed, and contribute to the governing of others. This bundling has made NGOs increasingly subject to the dominant ideas of development finance – especially those related to neoliberalism and security.

Such observations suggest that NGOs are becoming vehicles of neoliberal govern-mentality (e.g. Townsend et al, 2002), disciplining local organizations and populations in much the same way as development programmes have done in the past (Escobar, 1995; Duffield, 2001). Some NGOs *do* manage to resist or negotiate such pressures, and not all transnational NGO networks are characterized by uneven north–south rela-tions – e.g. the experience of Slum Dwellers International (Patel and Mitlin, 2002). Nonetheless, it remains essential to understand NGOs – as well as states, markets and civil societies – in the context of these transnational relations and flows. As noted earlier, NGOs are *part of* while trying to be *apart from* the political economy – and the workings of this political economy are transnational in nature and global in reach. As such, we reiterate the point that, for NGOs to regain a sense of being and offering alternatives, they need to (re)consider themselves in relation to struggles over little 'd' development as a foundational and increasingly globalized form of social change – and not simply in relation to the state or market, or to doing development differently.

NGOs as Development Alternatives: An Abridged History

This section approaches the modern history of NGOs through the lens of our organizing framework, with an overall concern for their place in fashioning alternative forms of development. We divide this abridged history into four main phases, without suggesting any precise dates for each phase.[1]

The *first period* is characterized by the quite long history of a limited number of small agencies seeking to respond – with little external professional support – to the needs of groups of poor people. These largely issue-based organizations combined both philanthropic action and advocacy, e.g. the abolition of slavery and promotion of peace. Mostly northern-based, they were generally embedded in broader movements (e.g. against slavery) and networks that mobilized voluntary contributions, and frequently linked to wider religious institutions and philanthropists. They also interacted with the state around legal reform, as well as with the market which generated most of the resources through foundations. Some were a legacy of colonialism such as volunteer programmes sending experts to 'under-capacitated' countries or organizations that derived from missionary activity. While some organizations recognized the need for structural reform, only rarely was such work alternative in any systemic sense, or in the sense of seeking to change the balance of hegemonic ideas, be these about the organization of society or the provision of services.

Such organizations continued their work during the 1960s and 1970s (broadly our *second phase*). Although they remained relatively small scale, this period marked early stages in NGO growth. Reflecting the geopolitical moment the sector became increasingly critical, understanding the imperative that NGOs elaborate and contribute to alternative arrangements among state, market and civil society (generally on a national scale), and alternatives within, and to, capitalism. Little *d* development was increasingly scrutinized, reflecting the intersection between these NGOs and political struggles around independence and various socialisms. 'Alternative development' itself emerged most strongly in this era (e.g. Nerfin, 1977), albeit by tending to simply invert mainstream forms of 'big D' Development rather than offering alternative forms of 'little d' development.

Such debates happened in both north and south, and led especially in the north to NGOs increasingly populated by people steeped in such debates (Hulme, 1994). 'Alternative' development discourses developed ties to the more formal worlds of development finance and political party funding as evidenced by the growth of co-financing programmes and the *Stiftung* phenomenon (OECD, 1988; Bebbington, 2004). The sector, though small, was increasingly conscious of itself and of the need to build collaborations with other non-governmental actors, particularly across north–south boundaries.

Numerous forces – the imperative of local institutional development, reduction in colonial presence, and the contradictions inherent in the northern NGO model – resulted in a switch from operational to funding roles for northern NGOs and the growth of a southern NGO sector.

During this period growing numbers of NGOs, especially from the political and religious lefts, consciously sought to shift state–market–civil society arrangements through government policy.[2] NGOs developed new strategies and then lobbied for their incorporation into government either directly or indirectly, through fostering social mobilization. Many NGOs negotiated space within and alongside other political and social movements – seeking collaboration among actors who recognized the benefits of their joint existence within the struggle against hegemonic and repressive state structures (e.g. Philippines, South Africa, El Salvador). Such NGOs recognized the need for political change, whilst the political movements recognized the NGO contribution as important means of accessing resources. Often, the relationships between these actors ran far more deeply with NGO staff being simultaneously active in political parties and movements.

These were also the periods when European co-financing resources were (often deliberately) given without many questions, in order to channel resources to oppositional movements via NGOs without any explicit, traceable government knowledge. Other governments and conservative forces – most notably the US – used a similar tactic to support elements of the hegemonic forces and ideas *against* which these NGOs and political movements were struggling. Some of these conservative resources were also channelled through NGOs, and continue to be so today. These competing roles of NGOs, both in strategies of contesting hegemony as well as in strategies aimed at consolidating it, underline the extent to which the non-governmental sector was one of the more important terrains in which civil society was being contested (see MacDonald, 1994) and in which the alternatives at stake were systemic as much as sectoral.

Our *third phase* is defined by the growth in recognition for NGOs and the increasing interest in funding their activities. This NGO 'boom' must be seen in terms of its own relationship to the transforming structures of capitalisms north, south and global – a reminder that NGOs have to be understood in terms of the political economies in which they exist. Two particular shifts in the broader relationships among state, market and civil society are important.

Shifting economics: macro-economic instability and crisis. The 1980s were dominated by structural adjustment programmes and the attendant increase in poverty and reduction in the role of governments. This led to varying demands for NGO intervention – as programme implementers, knowledge generators or as activists. Those interests generally *supportive* of structural adjustment needed NGOs to help deal with its limitations – social emergency and other compensation funds, created to deal with these inadequacies, were increasingly implemented through NGOs. While the negative effects of adjustment were seen as a temporary and internal contradiction, the neoliberal model itself was not in question and certainly this source of support for NGOs did not help them contest it, even if they wished to. Those who *opposed* structural adjustment looked to NGOs to document the scale of suffering caused, and to demonstrate the feasibility of coherent alternatives. Arguably NGOs were far more effective at the first than the second. Expectations of NGOs in this period were unfair and unrealistic – funding was available for collaborative projects but there was no real space to pursue large-scale or system-questioning alternatives. Again the broader context of little d development constrained the possibility that big D interventions – through research, activism, advocacy or experimentation – would achieve very much.

Shifting politics: political democratization. Adjustment was also accompanied by political democratization, partly as the political correlate of neoliberalism, but also as a response to long years of organizing within civil society in which NGOs had played a role. Ironically, democratization brought further complications to NGOs (e.g. Clarke, 1998; Bratton, 1989; Alvarez et al, 1998). Once newly democratic state institutions took up alternatives for which NGOs had pushed, NGOs were left with the uncertainty of what to do next other than help the state make a success of them. Many NGO staff and movement activists moved into government precisely to try and help foster such success. Examples range from NGO leaders gaining seats in national cabinets (e.g. the Philippines) and ministries (e.g. Chile), the women's movement moving into parliament in South Africa and Uganda (Goetz, 2003; Geisler, 2000), and pervasive and important shifts of NGO activists into local government.

If democratization marked a success in delivering a systemic alternative in which NGOs could claim some role, the alternative was incomplete and complex. First, relationships between state and market were largely unaffected, and those between market and civil society appeared to further commodify social relations. Second, the growing closeness of NGOs to the Big D interventions of national and multilateral organizations led to concerns that NGOs had compromised their innovativeness, autonomy, legitimacy and accountability. Many worried that becoming public service contractors (Robinson, 1997) was tying them into mainstream approaches more than ever before – it became increasingly difficult to offer little 'd' development alternatives (Aldaba et al, 2000). Indeed, it has been argued that many local NGOs, particularly in Africa, simply lacked the 'power' to define either their own futures or development paths for poor people (Michael, 2004), alternative or otherwise.

Over the last decade – our *fourth period* – NGOs have hardly become more robust and now face an additional set of threats. We draw attention here to three apparent trends.

Deepening the democratization-neoliberalization agenda. With the creation of the WTO (World Trade Organization), the joint project of liberal democracy and free trade has become increasingly clear and consolidated, making it ever more difficult for NGOs to think or act outside the neoliberal box. There are incentives to engage with hegemonic forms of little d development, as these begin to look more attractive – e.g. the extension of micro-finance services suggests the potential of the market to be inclusive of the poor, and also the poverty reduction strategy papers phenomenon which offers some NGOs unprecedented levels of access to at least part of the policy process. But it also challenges NGOs' capacity and legitimacy as they risk being associated with processes that may in themselves undermine broader democratic norms. Some NGOs have been perhaps too keen to grasp these channels, without thinking through the longer term problems this raises for public accountability.

Hegemony of the poverty agenda. Closely related is the new-found hegemony for 'poverty reduction' in international development, which narrowly focuses on income poverty. Bilateral and multilateral funding to NGOs is increasingly bundled with this poverty reduction agenda. While it is hard to contest the worthiness of such goals, it depoliticizes the range of strategies open to NGOs as they shift attention away from representative social movements to production and credit groups, and seek poverty reduction impacts rather than redistributive effects. It also affects the regions of the world for which NGOs can mobilize funding.

These trends are shifting the political economy of development funding in at least three ways. First, the focus on large scale poverty reduction, coupled with the advance of national government funding in the south, has reinforced a shift back towards the state. This means more money for state programmes and less for NGOs. Second is the increasing tendency to link commercial enterprise and not-for-profits through 'public-private partnerships', which can erode NGOs' potential as agents of systemic social and political change (Fowler, 2004). Third has been a switch to direct funding of NGOs in the south. The requirements of official funding will probably lead to greater concentration in both the northern and southern NGO sector, as smaller south-based NGOs have less capacity to deal with the bureaucracy of this funding type. Meanwhile there is little interest in funding more innovative activities, and certainly not those oriented towards systemic alternatives and challenging hegemonic ideas.

The new security agenda. The third trend marking recent years is the rise of the security agenda (Duffield, 2001; Lister, 2004). NGOs have long operated in the context of global conflicts not only as humanitarian actors but also as active promoters of system change, often in ways related to political and social justice movements. However, the issues have changed significantly with the rise of conflicts framed in terms of Islamic/non Islamic divisions, and leave some NGOs in far more ideologically complex positions. Their existence as western organizations funded by powers viewed as hostile to Islam complicates their relationships with groups and movements with whom they identify. USAID's insistence that its recipients commit to ensuring that no USAID money is associated with potential terror groups, means that NGOs funded by USAID effectively become agents of the US government, responsible for the compliance of their partners with US foreign policy (Fowler, 2004). Even those US NGOs categorically refusing government support must follow tax and legal guidelines to ensure they are not supporting groups antithetical to particular elements of US foreign policy.

Northern NGOs take different positions on this issue. Some refuse to work in countries such as Iraq and Afghanistan, while others have followed what they perceive to be their mission despite opposing the war on terror, or taken the view that their humanitarian aims are compatible with the new imperialism (Lister, 2004, p8). This range of positioning reveals the immense differences among NGOs in how they understand and approach the notion of pursuing 'alternatives'. For those unable or unwilling to extract themselves from the vagaries of big D, today's nexus between security and development means complicity in a wider form of little d that has little discernible link to a project of equity, social justice and political inclusion.

In the very broadest sense these trends present NGOs with new challenges and opportunities. One manifestation of this is the increased weight given to advocacy by some NGOs. This reflects a recognition that in the face of such powerful forces, local level project interventions cannot constitute alternatives of any significance or durability, and that changes to policy and wider norms are required if viable alternatives are to be built. Such NGO advocacy has often been transnational in character, with pressure placed at various points along commodity, policy and other.[3] Although an example of how NGOs read and engage with the globalized character of both big D and little d development, there remains a risk here that the local and the tangible will become lost: as a Ugandan NGO leader warned when ActionAid shifted to a policy focus '… and when we ask villagers what ActionAid does they will tell us "oh, they just talk"'. Furthermore, the move towards advocacy is bound up with another acute challenge for NGOs, that of representation (Jordan and van Tuijl, 2000). Advocacy presumes representation, but how do NGOs assume such representativeness and legitimate the positions taken in advocacy? This dilemma is particularly pressing for northern NGOs, but is also serious for those in the south facing social movements who question the right of NGOs to assume such positions, and occupy such slots in political debate.

On Being Alternative: Reforming Interventions, Transforming Ideas

The business of development alternatives is too large and important a task for NGOs alone; it must necessarily involve other institutional arenas, particularly the state. This is so for both significant reformist alternatives, as well as more radical systemic alternatives. Thus, while one of the most noted examples of reformist 'alternative development' success in recent years – participatory budgeting in Brazil – involved NGOs, most of the key actors have been leftist political parties, civil society activists, social movements and church-related organizations (Cabannes, 2004). The history of radical societal change also demonstrates that either developmental states and/or governments in alignment with broad based social movements have led transformative projects *far* more than have NGOs, think tanks or charities (Tilly, 2004; Leftwich 1995). Through what types of relationships might NGOs therefore reclaim a role in promoting both reformist and radical alternatives?

NGO pathways to reforming 'D'evelopment

The participatory budgeting example illustrates the argument that one NGO route to large scale alternatives is through influencing the interventions of other actors, via direct engagement and by providing alternative models of intervention. The work of BRAC on primary education in Bangladesh constitutes another example of NGOs offering genuine alternatives to the state in terms of public service provision (Nath et al, 1999). The Law of Popular Participation in Bolivia also reflects a policy adoption of NGO-led experiments in participatory development planning (Kohl, 2003). While such examples are relatively scarce, they point to ways in which NGOs have been embedded in larger social processes that ultimately take form in broad-based policy and political change.

Another route to reform is through working within mass movements with the understanding that politics responds to the electoral effects of mobilization. Indeed, there appears to be growing interest in alliances between mass movements and NGOs that can strategically influence candidates, politicians, their professionals and bureaucrats (e.g. Shack/Slum Dwellers International). In these instances, NGOs tend to work with movements to secure their own spaces, rather than to occupy spaces opened by the state – a process *slightly* less prone to clientelism (Appadurai, 2001).

Other alliances engage actors beyond social movements. The basis of many NGOs in class, religious and party political institutions and networks that do *not* derive primarily in the popular sectors further fosters such a tendency. UK NGOs, for instance, have become increasingly aware of their need to reach out to new constituencies who do not necessarily equate NGO activity with the broader and fundamentally political goals of achieving global social justice (Lister, 2004). At a different extreme, in Peru, NGOs that have historically had a very strong position vis-à-vis extractive industries have also begun to open links with both the mining sector with a view to finding a dialogical pathway to reform. Who reforms who in these processes remains far from clear.

NGOs, hegemony and alternative 'D'evelopments

If pushing to reform the 'D'evelopment interventions of other actors is one path towards alternatives, another revolves around strategies to transform the foundational ideas and social relations underlying the contemporary social order. The role that NGOs played in promoting democratization during the 1980s and 1990s as part of broader civil society movements constituted an effort to create a genuine alternative form of politics. Where NGOs engage with social movements and popular organizations demanding the extension of citizenship rights to marginal peoples (in ways that are broadly democratic as opposed to exclusive efforts to secure privileges) they can claim to be engaging with underlying processes of citizenship formation (Appadurai, 2001; Hickey, 2002). Initiatives such as the 'Make Poverty History' campaign likewise reflect a strategy that engages alternatives at the level of foundational ideas rather than projects. Such moves, however, require an acute sense of timing. Arguably the best NGO interventions come from recognizing key moments within underlying development processes and framing interventions in supportive relation to such progressive moves. Getting timing wrong can at best fulfill the prophecy of the Ugandan activist worrying about ActionAid's policy focus, and at worst risk disarticulation, persecution and death of broader movements pushing for more foundational change. All too often it seems unclear whether NGOs (or academics) are capable of recognizing, reading and engaging constructively with underlying processes of development. While the South African NGO activist Allan Kaplan lists 'development knowledge' as the foremost NGO organizational capacity, he also notes that this capacity is rarely well developed (Kaplan, 2001).

Conclusion: New Metaphors for NGOs

How far, and in what ways, NGOs are able to contribute to the reclaiming of development as an alternative project will depend very much on their ability to build relationships with progressive actors operating in the state, in political parties, in social movements and in other domains. An NGO's management of relationships therefore becomes a central development challenge rather than a management challenge (Lewis, 2001). What might some of these relationships be and what do they imply for ways of being an NGO? We close with a reflection on two such modes: 'the NGO as jelly' and 'the NGO as microchip'. Both involve relinquishing to a significant extent the idea of

NGOs being innovative think tanks or pilot projects with brilliant insights capable of articulating alternatives that are so convincing that politicians lay down the red carpet and capitalism abandons the profit motive. Both involve groups that accept they are in a long-term battle over hegemonic ideas against very powerful forces that will reorganize to ensure continued elite control of resources.

The NGO as jelly. In this model the NGO accepts it has little power except that which is generated by being a convener. The NGO builds alliances with more powerful groups, social movements, political parties, rich donors, etc. and they seek to respond to opportunities that emerge within these relationships. They put emphasis on a process that draws in pro-poor individuals and groups, and they are essentially responsive to that process. They have to be a jelly because they are dealing with powerful entities who don't hesitate to contest the process; and they are realistic enough to recognize that they have little power within the development process so by necessity they fit into gaps. The NGO gets pushed and pulled but its gelatinous nature helps it hold something together – its role is above all else to convene. This gelatinous nature draws on what the context offers; for southern NGOs, it often involves links (family, education, religious) between social elites that cross market, state and civil society divides. For both north and south, it may draw on international connections (with associations of informational and finan- cial resources). Their cross-sectoral relationships may help to encourage social move- ments and sometimes the corporate sector and the state to share ideas and begin a negotiation process. In such a model, NGOs make a significant contribution in terms of supporting a governance model that is more inclusive than traditional approaches to state consultation processes. The emphasis on process can, though, be difficult, and in some cases reducing their own visibility can be detrimental as it can give space to other actors who *do* wish to claim profile.

The NGO as microchip. The second model is one in which NGOs seek to be more proactive around content. They are still concerned with process but the NGO is less willing to relinquish leadership to others than in the jelly model. Their relative lack of power means that they still have to be subtle and persuasive, slipping their ideas into discourses as they are reworked. They may seek to convince a more powerful actor, such as a state minister or agency professional, of the merit in their approaches. Some of these NGOs find that their convening legitimacy depends on their playing a microchip role: it is their intellectual contribution that enables them to bring actors together with some legitimacy. NGOs can add real insight to local grassroots and political strategies by broadening horizons and helping people learn and see things differently. At other times, their capacity to overview other experiences means that they define the boundaries within which alternatives can be discussed. It is for this reason that research-based NGOs in particular are able to take on a convening role.

Both types of NGO are small (or may be a component of a bigger NGO), both essentially intermediate. Sometimes they need to implement – in the same sense that the best advocacy work done by NGOs often draws on their operational experience – but they are not essentially doers (although they may work with other NGOs who are). The more successful alternative models avoid getting drawn into operational roles because these increase administrative burdens for NGOs that divert them from thinking strategically. They therefore employ limited numbers of high-quality versatile people and invest in their skills and capacities. In each case being an NGO worker becomes a vocation rather than a job, and the goal is that the networks built will be enduring. These networks accompany political changes and exploit opportunities with wisdom rather than opportunism.

We have sought to suggest that NGOs can still contribute significantly to development alternatives, and that this requires a direct and critical engagement with development as a long-term process of social change, driven primarily by particular and increasingly globalized forms of capitalism, (re)shaped by states at different stages of formation, endlessly contested within civil society and with specific outcomes in terms of citizenship and social justice for people and societies. In the end the key issue remains the extent to which the political economy of NGOs will persuade them of the need to reclaim a role for themselves as agents of transformative approaches to development. To the extent that NGOs maintain a significant slice of the overall cake of development finance, they may be a long way from feeling the pinch.

Notes

1   This omits the deeper history to which Lewis refers. In addition, we do not specifically discuss the type of relief-oriented NGO that has historically emerged throughout each of our four stages, in direct relation to specific emergencies, as with the Sahelian drought of the 1970s, Hurricane Mitch or the earthquakes in Gujarat.

2   As just two examples from the urban sector, consider the Orangi Pilot Project (OPP) and the Centro Operacional de Vivienda y Poblamiento AC (COPEVI). OPP works in Karachi (Pakistan) and seeks to improve levels of infrastructure and services in low-income settlements. Over time their strategy has changed, but during the 1980s they very deliberately set out to demonstrate alternatives to the state. COPEVI is a Mexican NGO whose ideas for improving low-income urban settlements were later taken up in the government programme FONHAPO (Connolly, 2004).

3   See for instance advocacy strategies around mining by Oxfam America.

References

Aldaba, F., Antezana, P., Valderrama, M. and Fowler, A. (2000) 'NGO strategies beyond aid: Perspectives from Central and South America and the Philippines', *Third World Quarterly* Vol 21, No 4, pp669–683

Alvarez, S., Dagnino, E. and Escobar, A. (eds) (1998) *Culture of politics/politics of cultures. Re-visioning Latin American social movements*, Boulder: Westview

Appadurai, A. (2001) 'Deep democracy: Urban governmentability and the horizon of politics', *Environment and Urbanization*, Vol 13, No 2, pp23–44

Bebbington, A. J. (2003) 'Global Networks and Local Developments: Agendas for Development Geography', *Tijdschrift voor Economische en Sociale Geografie*, Vol 94, No 3, pp297–309

Bebbington, A. J. (2004) 'NGOs and uneven development: Geographies of development intervention', *Progress in Human Geography*, Vol 28, No 6, pp725–745

Bratton, M. (1989) 'The Politics of Government: NGO relations in Africa', *World Development*, Vol 17, No 4, pp569–587

Cabannes, Y. (2004) 'Participatory budgeting: A significant contribution to participatory democracy', *Environment and Urbanization*, Vol 16, No 1, pp27–46

Clarke, G. (1998) *The Politics of NGOs in South East Asia: Participation and Protest in the Philippines*, London: Routledge

Connolly, P. (2004) 'The Mexican National Popular Housing Fund', in Mitlin, D. and Satterthwaite, D. (eds) *Empowering Squatter Citizen*, Earthscan, London, pp82–111.

Cowen, M. and Shenton, R. (1998) 'Agrarian doctrines of development: Part 1', *Journal of Peasant Studies*, Vol 25, pp49–76

Drabek, A.G. (1987) 'Development Alternatives: The challenge of NGOs', *World Development* Vol 15 (supplement), Autumn

Duffield, M. (2001) *Global Governance and the New Wars: The Merger of Development and Security*, London: Zed Books (3rd Edition 2005)

Edwards, M. (1999) *Future Positive: International Co-operation in the 21st Century*, London: Earthscan

Edwards, M. and Hulme, D. (eds) (1992) *Making a Difference? NGOs and Development in a Changing World*, London: Earthscan/Save the Children

Edwards, M. and Hulme, D. (eds) (1995) *NGOs: Performance and Accountability: Beyond the Magic Bullet*, London: Earthscan (reprinted 1996)

Escobar, A. (1995) *Encountering Development: The making and unmaking of the Third World*, Princeton: Princeton University Press

Fowler, A. (1993) 'Non-governmental Organisations as Agents of Democratization: An African perspective', *Journal of International Development*, Vol 5, No 3, pp325–339

Fowler, A. (1997) *Striking a balance: A guide to enhancing the effectiveness of non-governmental organisations in international development*, London: Earthscan

Fowler, A. (2004) 'Aid Architecture and counter-terrorism: Perspectives on NGO futures', INTRAC OPS 45, Oxford: INTRAC

Geisler, G. (2000) '"Parliament is another terrain of struggle": Women, men and politics in South Africa', *Journal of Modern African Studies*, Vol 38, No 4, pp605–630

Goetz, A.-M. (2003) 'The problem with patronage: Constraints on women's political effectiveness in Uganda', in Goetz, A.-M. and Hassim, S. (eds) *No shortcuts to power: African women in politics and policy-making*, London: Zed, pp110–139

Groves, L. and Hinton, R. (2004) *Inclusive Aid: Changing Power and Relationships in International Development*, London: Earthscan

Hart, G. (2001) 'Development critiques in the 1990s: *culs de sac* and promising paths', *Progress in Human Geography*, Vol 25, pp649–658

Hashemi, S. (1995) 'NGO Accountability in Bangladesh: Beneficiaries, donors and the State', in Edwards and Hulme (1995) pp103–110

Hearn, J. (2001) 'The Uses and Abuses of Civil Society in Africa', *Review of African Political Economy*, No 87, pp43–53

Hickey, S. (2002) 'Transnational NGDOS and participatory forms of rights-based development: Converging with the local politics of citizenship in Cameroon', *Journal of International Development*, Vol 4, No 6, pp841–857

Hickey, S. and Mohan, G. (2005) 'Relocating participation within a radical politics of development: From practice to theory', *Development and Change*, Vol36, No2, pp237–262.

Hulme, D. (1994) 'Social development research and the third sector: NGOS as users and subjects of social inquiry', in Booth, D. (ed) *Rethinking Social Development: theory, research and practice*, Harlow: Longman, pp251–275

Hyden, G. (1997) 'Civil Society, Social Capital, and Development: Dissection of a complex discourse', *Studies in Comparative International Development*, Vol 32, pp3–30

Jordan, L. and van Tuijl, P. (2000) 'Political responsibility in transnational NGO advocacy', *World Development*, Vol 28, No 12, pp2051–2065

Kaplan, A. (2001) 'Capacity Building: Shifting the paradigms in practice', in Eade, D. (ed) *Debating Development*, Oxford: OXFAM

Kohl, B. (2003) 'Non Governmental Organizations and Decentralization in Bolivia', *Environment and Planning C: Governance and Planning*, Vol 21, No 2, pp317–331

Lane, J. (1995) 'Non-governmental organizations and participatory development: The concept in theory versus the concept in practice', in Nelson, N. and Wright, S. (eds), *Power and Participatory Development: Theory and Practice*, Intermediate Technology Publications, London, pp181–191.

Leftwich, A. (1995) 'Bringing politics back in: Towards a model of the developmental state', *The Journal of Development Studies*, Vol 31, No 3

Lewis, D. (2001) *The Management of Nongovernmental Organizations*, London: Routledge

Lewis, D. (2002) 'Civil society in African contexts: Reflections on the "usefulness" of a concept', *Development and Change*, Vol 33, No 4, pp569–586

Lister, S. (2004) *The future of international NGOs: New challenges in a changing world order*, Paper presented at the British Overseas NGOs for Development (BOND) Futures Programme, London (28 April).

MacDonald, L. (1994) 'Globalizing civil society: Interpreting NGOs in Central America', *Millenium: Journal of International Studies*, Vol 23, No 2, pp267–285

Mamdani, M. (1993) 'Social Movements and Democracy in Africa', in P. Wignaraja (ed) *New Social Movements in the South: Empowering the People*, UK: Zed Books, pp101–118

Michael, S. (2004) *Undermining Development: The absence of power among local NGOs in Africa*, Oxford: James Currey

Nath, S.R., Sylva, K. and Grimes, J. (1999) 'Raising Basic Education Levels in Rural Bangladesh: The impact of a non-formal education programme', *International Review of Education*, Vol 45, No 1, pp5–26.

Nerfin, M. (1977) (ed) *Another Development: Approaches and strategies*, Uppsala: Dag Hammarskjöld Foundation

OECD (1988) *Voluntary Aid for Development: The role of non-governmental organizations*, Paris: Organization for Economic Cooperation and Development

Patel, S. and Mitlin, D. (2002) 'Sharing Experiences and Changing Lives', *Community Development Journal*, Vol 37, No 2, pp125–136

Robinson, M. (1995) 'Strengthening civil society in Africa: The role of foreign political aid', *IDS Bulletin*, Vol 26, No 2, pp70–80

Robinson, M. (1997) 'Privatising the voluntary sector: NGOs as public service contractors?', in Hulme, D. and Edwards, M. (1997) *Too Close for Comfort? NGOs, States and Donors*, Basingstoke: Macmillan and New York: St Martins Press, pp59–78

Stewart, S. (1997) 'Happy Ever After in the Marketplace: Non-government Organisations and Uncivil Society', *Review of African Political Economy*, No71, pp11–34

Tandon, R. (1991) 'Foreign NGOs, Uses and Abuses: An African perspective', *IFDA Dossier*, Vol 81, pp67–78

Tandon, R. (2001) 'Riding high or nosediving: Development NGOs in the new millenium', in Eade, D. and Ligteringen, E. (eds) *Debating Development*, Oxford: OXFAM, pp44–59

Tilly, C. (2004) *Contention and democracy in Europe: 1650–2000*, Cambridge: Cambridge University Press

Townsend, J., Porter, G. and Mawdesley, E. (2002) 'The role of the transnational community of development non-governmental organizations: Governance or poverty reduction?', *Journal of International Development*, Vol 14, pp829–839

van Rooy, A. (2000) 'Good news! You may be out of a job: Reflections on the past and future 50 years for Northern NGOs', *Development in Practice*, Vol 10, Nos 3–4, pp300–317

Wallace, T., Crowther, S. and Shepherd, A. (1997) *Standardising Development: Influences on UK NGOs' Policies and Procedures*, Oxford: World View Publishing

3

The Global War on Terror, Development and Civil Society

Jude Howell

Introduction

Following George W. Bush's declaration of a 'global war on terror' in the aftermath of the 11 September attacks, politicians across the world have introduced a swathe of counter-terrorist measures and legislation. Not only have the purposes of such measures been riddled with ambiguity, but their actual and potential effects on civil liberties and citizen rights have drawn considerable concern. In the field of development the global war on terror has highlighted the strategic relevance of foreign aid to both national interests and global security at a time when its ideological rationale in the post-Cold War era had almost disappeared. Aware of the perceived threat to global security and global markets, a melee of actors including leaders of low income countries, US and European politicians, UN leaders and many developmental NGOs have for diverse reasons lobbied for an increase in aid. However, the introduction of repressive measures coupled with the increasingly explicit subordination of foreign aid to military, foreign policy and economic interests has altered the context in which foreign aid is framed and implemented. This in turn not only affects the way certain civil society actors are perceived and included in development processes, but also unsettles the hitherto benign understanding of civil society that has permeated donor documentation and policy since the late 1980s.

In this chapter, we examine the consequences and implications of the 'global war against terror' for civil society and development practice. We begin by outlining the effects of the 'global war on terror' on the ideological justification of aid, the interconnections between development, foreign policy and security and the direction, nature and reporting of aid flows. We then consider the effects on civil society, highlighting the constriction of spaces, the casting of suspicion over relations between northern and southern development agencies, and the compromising of humanitarian principles of neutrality and impartiality. We go on to consider the implications of some of these immediate consequences for civil society organizations in preserving separate public identities from the state and military, in engaging around sensitive issues concerning social justice, redistribution and ethnic oppression, and in enhancing their legitimacy and accountability.[1] Civil society is a historically and contemporarily contested concept.[2] Having fallen from usage during most of the 20th century, it has enjoyed a renaissance from the mid-1980s onwards as East European dissidents drew upon the language of civil society to express their dissatisfaction with an authoritarian state and their aspirations for a better life. Since then the term has been appropriated by a diversity of actors across the world for different ideological purposes and political ends. In this chapter we use the term civil society to refer to the arena of purposive collective action around shared interests and values. Civil society commonly embraces a diversity of actors, spaces and institutional forms, varying in their degree of formality, autonomy and power. Its institutional forms are theoretically distinct from those of the state, family and market, though in practice the boundaries are complex, blurred and negotiated.

The Global War on Terror, Aid and Development

The launch of a 'global war on terror' by the USA against an amorphous and elusive enemy has ushered in a new politics of aid that in turn has repercussions for both non-governmental humanitarian and development agencies and for other civil society organizations across the world. The term 'global war on terror', coined by George W. Bush in the aftermath of the 11 September attacks, crystallizes a complexity of meanings and functions, which render it highly malleable and potent for leaders of diverse political hues. Here we understand the term 'global war on terror' to embrace the following: first, a mobilizing discourse, used by global and national leaders in pursuit of military and political objectives; second, the expression of a polarizing vision of the world, which pits modernity against backwardness, civilization against barbarism and freedom against oppression; third, a militaristic content, reflected both in the choice of language such as 'war' and 'terror' and in its shorthand justification for pre-emptive military intervention; fourth, a global political reordering, creating new alliances and divisions among states, constructing new foes and friends; and finally, a new set of institutional and policy arrangements, expressed most vividly in the closer interweaving of development and security.

Foreign aid has always been part of donor states' soft approach to pursuing foreign policy, military and commercial objectives (Cassen, 1994; German and Randel, 1995; Belgrad and Nachmias, 1997; Reusse, 2002). In the Cold War era, aid policy was embedded in a global political framework of ideological and geo-political superpower rivalry. With the end of the Cold War the apparent supremacy of liberal democracy and free markets freed aid policy somewhat from the constraints of ideologically-informed global political rivalries. Donor agencies and Western governments began explicitly to place issues of governance onto the development agenda, making human rights, democracy, the rule of law and accountability conditions for aid. In the humanitarian field the emphasis shifted from humanitarian intervention in the new wars towards conflict resolution and post-war reconstruction, which involved strengthening the rule of law, building representative institutions and improving state capacity (Duffield, 2002). This approach reflected not only the consolidation of governance as a key goal of development policy, but also an emerging view of the south as a source of international crime, terrorism and conflict that contributed to global instability. At this point the practical implications of conceptualizing the south as a source of instability were most visible in conflict and post-conflict countries.

Northern donors looked to civil society as a key ingredient in promoting 'good governance', stressing its key role in ensuring transparency, accountability and participation. Civil society appeared as the natural counterpart to privatized markets and liberal democracies, and for some politicians, a useful way of reducing aid budgets and public expenditure (Howell and Pearce, 2002). Rights-based approaches to development, voice and participation became leitmotivs of development practice and writing. In this spirit bilateral and multilateral agencies throughout the 1990s began to establish civil society units and develop programmes of support to strengthen civil society in the south.

The events of 11 September 2001 ushered in a new phase in aid policy and practice, the seeds of which were already being sown in the 1990s. For, as John Davis (2005, p8) notes, the war on terror was not just about Afghanistan and Iraq or other rogue states, but 'an expansive campaign that covers the globe'.[3] By creating a climate of fear, withdrawing certain basic liberties and embarking on unilateral military interventions, the global war on terror has redefined the environment within which international aid is framed, constructed and implemented. Though the 'good governance agenda' and the discourses of civil society, participation and rights-based development remain key ingredients in donor policies, the overall environment within which aid policy and practice is played out has changed. In particular global security issues and the national geopolitical and economic interests of the USA and other Western governments have become increasingly prominent, consolidating a process that was already underway in the 1990s. Characteristic of this new phase in aid policy and practice is a shift in the ideological justification of aid, a closer alignment of aid with foreign policy and security issues and concomitant new institutional arrangements.

By pasting together the themes of poverty, alienation, global insecurity and terror, Western politicians have forged a new justification for aid that is premised on the defence of a global economic system that is weighted towards the interests of rich countries. Experiences of alienation, poverty, deprivation and racism are given as the pervasive underlying causes of extreme acts such as suicide-bombing,[4] thereby eschewing the political rationales underlying these acts of violence (Hage, 2003). In an interview for an ITV documentary in November 2004, UK Chancellor of the Exchequer, Gordon Brown, for example, spoke of poverty as 'a breeding ground for discontent'.[5] Similarly George Bush, in his remarks to the Inter-American Development Bank in March 2002, linked the 'hopelessness and despair' emanating out of poverty and oppression to the emergence of terrorism, particularly in failed states such as Afghanistan (Bush, 2002). Similar sentiments were voiced by other national leaders during the UN Monterrey conference in March 2002.[6] With aid as a potential soft tool for maintaining global economic stability whilst also counterbalancing the belligerent thrust of foreign policy, politicians such as Gordon Brown and Tony Blair have canvassed leaders of wealthy countries at key events such as the Monterrey conference in 2002, the G7 meeting and the G8 summit in 2005 for an increase in aid budgets and a commitment to meet the UN target of 0.7 per cent of GDP (Grass Domestic Product) devoted to aid.

This thematic pastiche of leading Western politicians has seeped quickly into the discourses and programmes of development agencies. Though the ideological justification of aid as a panacea for both poverty and global instability was already finding expression in the policy statements of international development agencies from the mid-1990s onwards,[7] its full expression blossomed after 2001. In his report to the UN

General Assembly in March 2005 the Secretary-General of the UN, Kofi Annan, underlined the links between development and security[8] and called upon member states to commit to implementing a new security consensus that recognized the interdependency of development, security and human rights. Bilateral development agencies, such as DANIDA and JAICA and multilaterals such as the EU began to link explicitly their development agendas to security and foreign policy objectives. In its 2004–2008 programme, for example, the Danish government nominates security and the fight against terrorism as its second key challenge in fulfilling its overall objective of reducing poverty (Royal Danish Ministry of Foreign Affairs, 2003). The Australian government depicts terrorism in its 2003 report on counter-terrorism and aid as a key challenge to the aid programme's objective of 'advancing the national interest by reducing poverty and promoting sustainable development' (Australian Government/AusAID, 2003). A year later, it increased its support for two programmes that seek to enhance the capacity of partner countries to manage terrorist threats and to promote environments conducive to growth and poverty reduction, so as to limit the risk of terrorist networks emerging (Parliamentary Library, 2004). In the US, President Bush has proposed long-term development support for education in countries with large Muslim populations so as to divert potential students away from madrassas, thereby linking developmental and security objectives firmly together (Tujan et al, 2004, p62).[9]

The approximation of development, policy and security interests is in turn reflected in the direction and nature of aid flows, in institutional arrangements to facilitate these linkages and in the reporting of aid statistics. Though Western governments have made rhetorical commitments to increase aid,[10] the concern with security issues and especially the foreign policy interests of the USA has seen a large increase in aid to Afghanistan and Iraq. Substantial commitments of military aid have been made to strategically important countries. OECD aid to Afghanistan increased tenfold between 1999 and 2003, from US$143 million to US$1,533 million, with Afghanistan outstripping India as the largest recipient of ODA in South and Central Asia (OECD, 2005). In the case of the UK, Iraq became the top recipient of bilateral aid with £209 million in 2003/2004, usurping India. This has been achieved in part through a diversion of existing aid budgets away from middle-income countries in Latin America. Between 2002 and 2004, Pakistan and Afghanistan received the highest allocations of USAID in Asia, reflecting their strategic and military importance to the USA (USAID, 2005). Much of the increase in foreign aid that Bush promised after 11 September has gone towards military aid (Lobe, 2002). In particular the USA has increased significantly its development assistance and military aid to countries with large Muslim populations such as Pakistan, Philippines and Indonesia (Tujan et al, 2004, p56).

The increasing convergence of development, foreign policy and security agendas emanating out of the global war on terror has also led to changes in the institutional arrangements of aid policy. At the domestic level this is reflected in the increased interaction between government agencies concerned with defence, development and crime. In the UK, the Ministry of Defence, Department for International Development (DFID) and the Foreign and Commonwealth Office have regularly held cross-ministerial meetings to coordinate their policies in relation to Afghanistan and Iraq, and have established a pan-Whitehall post-conflict reconstruction unit to deal with the UK response to conflicts. This has brought the making of UK development policy much closer in line with foreign policy and security interests and contrasts with the early years of New Labour when the then Secretary of State for Development, Clare Short, achieved a more independent role for DFID. In the EU the Solana proposal marks a similar move towards military and civil joint operation. At the global level the UN has established integrated missions, which comprise a politically appointed special representative to the Secretary General, the UN military, UN operational agencies and the OCHA, thereby bringing together military and humanitarian concerns and institutions under political leadership.

The tighter overlap between military and development activities has also complicated the reporting of aid statistics. Distinguishing the activities that should be categorized as military assistance as opposed to official development, assistance has become increasingly complex since the UN began peace-keeping operations in the 1990s.[11] Key areas of controversy in the Organisation for Economic Cooperation and Development (OECD) relate to the training of security forces in human rights and principles and the proposal of a blanket ban on using overseas development assistance (ODA) for any military activity, even where it is in practice non-military. Similarly proposals to include the financing of peace-keeping missions from the European Development Fund for African, Caribbean and Pacific countries, which would require revising aid eligibility criteria, have also raised concerns about the intermeshing of development, foreign policy and security objectives (Tujan et al, 2004, p59).

In brief, these ideological, strategic and institutional changes in aid policy suggest a departure from the more sanguine era of the 1990s, when aid policy was momentarily freed from the constraints of Cold War objectives. Though the new wars of the 1990s had laid the seeds for a convergence of security interests with development, the launch of the global war on terror in 2001 generalized this trend beyond the narrow confines of post-conflict states to all aid-recipient countries. In this changed context the goals of 'good governance' and related ideas of civil society, human rights, participation and the rule of law that came to prominence in the 1990s take on a new meaning. In the 1990s they reflected the ideological victory of liberal democracy and free markets over communism and an agenda that positioned the domestic state as a key element in the pervasiveness of poverty. At the turn of the millennium they become subsumed under a much broader strategic canopy that is concerned with maintaining global stability and preserving Western economic power. In this context civil society has become a more suspect arena, one that may potentially harbour enemies of Western interests and values as well as allies in the dual fight against poverty and terror. In the next section we look more closely at the effects of the changed context of the global war on terror on civil society.

Impact on Civil Society

The spate of counter-terrorist legislation and measures that has been enacted since 2001 has evoked considerable concern among human rights and civil liberty lawyers and activists across the world eager to defend basic civil liberties such as the right to freedom of expression and the right to a fair trial (Gearty, 2003; Greenwood, 2005; Sassen, 2002; Sparks, 2003).[12] However, its effects on civil society, the vibrancy of which hinges upon certain basic rights, has received far less attention. In this section we show how the global war on terror has led to the constriction of civil society space, a clampdown on NGOs with a concomitant smothering of Muslim organizations, the unsettling of an overzealous embrace of civil society by donor agencies and the undermining of the principles of neutrality, impartiality and independence among humanitarian agencies.

The effects of the global war on terror on civil society-donor relations cannot be understood without situating these relations within the broader historical context of state-civil society relations in donor and recipient countries. There are two emerging tendencies here that frame the environment in which development agencies operate. These are the appropriation of the language of terror by governments to repress perceived political opponents and the veil of suspicion that governments cast over all civil society actors as potential terrorist fronts.

After 2001 many governments have skilfully deployed the language of terrorism to undermine and oppress their perceived enemies. Even where previously governments may have used the language of extremism and terrorism to label opponents, in the post-11 September context such terms have a heightened resonance and justificatory power. The Uzbekistan government, for example, has been accused of torturing and imprisoning Muslim civilians on the grounds of religious extremism and terrorism (Walsh, 2005). In April 2005 the Chinese government signed a memorandum of understanding with other members of the Shanghai Cooperation Organisation[13] and the Commonwealth of independent States to cooperate inter alia on counterterrorism, the key target here being so-called East Kurdistan' terrorist forces.[14] In this way secessionist struggles as in Xinjiang province and Tibet are castigated as 'terrorist activities', and their demands and justifications effectively discredited and depoliticized. Similarly in Zimbabwe, Robert Mugabe has accused his legitimate opponents of being terrorists, whilst in Kenya members of the Muslim community have complained about harassment by security forces (Dagne, 2005, p101). India has managed to gain apparent acceptance by the international community of its labelling of military incursions from Pakistan into India as 'cross-border terrorism', a concession no doubt for willingness to cooperate with the USA in its war on terror (Ollapally, 2005, p156).

Apart from targeting specific political opponents, some governments have also begun to scrutinize the activities of charitable organizations, foundations and non-profit organizations. In the USA, Britain and Saudi Arabia (MacAskill, 2004) charitable agencies, and in particular Muslim groups, have been investigated for operating as 'terrorist fronts' and some have even been closed down (Benthal and Bellion-Jourdan, 2003; Bell, 2004).[15] In June 2004, Saudi Arabia disbanded its largest overseas charity, the Al-Haramain Islamic Foundation, and established a commission to manage all Saudi charitable activities overseas in an effort to prevent charitable funds from being diverted to Al-Qaeda or other terrorist groups. In the UK the NGO Interpal was listed by the USA as a Specially Designated Global Terrorist organization in August 2003. Following an investigation by the Charity Commission, no evidence was found to support these claims and the charity has been allowed to continue its activities in the UK. In the USA it is noteworthy that only Muslim charitable organizations figure in the list of Specially Designated Global Terrorists of the Treasury Department, even though other non-Muslim charities provide assistance in conflict-ridden areas across the world. The specific targeting of Muslim organizations not only creates an unhealthy construction of Islam as enjoying a special affinity with terrorism, a view that defies all history of terrorism, but also identifies Muslim population as a 'dangerous other' that unless observed and disciplined risks behaving in uncivil and violent ways. Apart from the alienating effects of such a discourse, it also undermines the basic rights of Muslims to associate and organize, as such action immediately draws suspicion.

From the late 1980s onwards, as described earlier, donor agencies embraced enthusiastically the idea of civil society, establishing special civil society strengthening programmes, channelling more funds to NGOs and engaging civil society actors in policy processes. The events of 2001 have unsettled, however, the benign view that donors held of civil society as the bearer of democracy, participation and social justice. Compelled in part by their governments, donor agencies and foundations have begun to examine more critically their grantees and partner organizations. Since 2001 the USA authorities have scrutinized foundations and non-profit organizations for signs of extremist language, terrorist activities and any connections with terrorist organizations. US funding has been withdrawn from several NGOs operating in Palestine because they could not adequately demonstrate that they had no links with terrorism (Naidoo, 2004). The Ford Foundation came under particular scrutiny because of its alleged funding of Hamas, a listed terrorist organization in the Middle East, and has since instituted more stringent security checking mechanisms on its grantees.[16] The USAID now requires its grantees to sign an Anti-Terrorist Certification (ATC), stating that no project participants have been involved or are involved in terrorist or religious extremist activities.[17]

Whilst Western governments have cast a suspicious eye on civil society organizations for fear of links with terrorism, in China, Russia and Uzbekistan leaders have used this broader climate of scrutiny for other purposes. Concerned about the role of foreign NGOs and their links with domestic NGOs in the democratic colour revolutions in Ukraine, Georgia and Kyrgyzstan, leaders of China, Russia and Uzbekistan have seized the opportunity to justify a parallel crackdown on NGOs using the veil of countering terrorism. In Uzbekistan, President Karimov has woven together the language of extremism and terror not only to discredit his political opponents but also to restrict the activities of international NGOs and local NGOs funded by external donors.[18] Western attempts to export democracy through civil society-building initiatives are portrayed as a threat to sovereignty and the maintenance of the Karimov regime and juxtaposed with Islamic fundamentalism.[19] In this vein the Uzbek government has clamped down on the transfer of funds from donors to local NGOs, justifying this as a way to cut off funding to terrorist groups.[20] In Kazakhstan legislators close to President Nazarbaev introduced draft legislation to restrict NGO activity, justifying this in terms of 'strengthening national security' (Corwin, 2005).[21] Similarly in Russia, President Vladimir Putin gave a speech in July 2005 in which he denounced foreign funding of Russian NGOs that engaged in political activity. By leaving the term 'political activity' vague, Putin has created uncertainty among local NGOs as to what kind of advocacy work or criticism is acceptable. In the wake of the 'colour revolutions', the Chinese government began in late spring 2005 to investigate foreign NGOs in China and domestic NGOs receiving grants from external sources. Conferences on topics perceived as sensitive such as labour issues that involve external sponsorship have been postponed.[22]

At the operational level the fusion of security, foreign policy and development objectives has blurred the boundaries between civilian, military and governmental actors. Indeed since the late 1980s, lines between government and NGOs have become increasingly obscured as bilateral and multilateral agencies have channelled more of their funds through NGOs and drawn NGOs into policy consultation through joint committees and platforms for dialogue. In the humanitarian field, too, closer engagement between military and civilian institutions was already being established during the new wars of the 1990s. By 2001 relations of cooperation, dialogue and negotiation between NGOs, UN, bilateral donors and the military and private companies were increasingly common in humanitarian work, albeit often uncomfortable.

These interlocking webs of activity between military, civilian and governmental actors have intensified since 2001 and caused alarm among aid officials and NGOs such as Oxfam, Save the Children Fund and BOND (British Overseas NGOs in Development). For example in a recent report to the House of Commons (2002–2003, pp28–29) questions were raised about the blurring of lines between civilian and military operations in Afghanistan that were likely to be exacerbated with the establishment of joint regional teams involving both military and civilian personnel. Particularly worrying for NGOs such as Save the Children Fund, Oxfam, BOND and Care International has been the growing involvement of the military in relief and development work since 2001. In the cases of both Afghanistan and Iraq, US military forces have strategically matched their militaristic interventions with campaigns and actions to win over the local population. Any loosely structured organization such as Al-Qaeda has to rely to some extent on local support for its survival, earned variously through claims to truth and morality, symbolic acts of destruction and feats of acclaimed martyrdom. Hence the opponent, too, has not only to engage in physical conflict but also in an ideologically charged battle of ideas. Military personnel have appropriated the language of development, civil society and rights to dilute their militarism and to gain support locally. This strategy of 'hearts and minds' has taken various forms such as handing out sweets to children on the streets, distributing leaflets portraying the enemy in a negative way, building schools, hospitals and wells and delivering food aid.[23]

All this has created difficulties on the ground for humanitarian and development workers, who are often perceived to be allied to the external military forces. This has not only highlighted issues of safety but also of the difficulties of maintaining humanitarian principles of neutrality, independence and impartiality, particularly for US NGOs, which are more dependent on bilateral funding than their European counterparts. NGO workers in Iraq and Afghanistan have sometimes become targets for kidnapping or ambush. The well-publicized case of the director of CARE International in Iraq, who was kidnapped and eventually murdered in 2005, underlines the growing perception of humanitarian and development NGOs as 'Western' rather than as impartial or neutral actors.

Humanitarian and development workers have always had to struggle to maintain their declared neutrality and impartiality, not least because these ideas are hotly contested. The failure of the International Red Cross, for example, to reveal its knowledge of the existence of labour camps in Nazi Germany illustrates well the moral dilemmas of remaining 'above politics' and practising self-censorship (Rieff, 2002, p76).[24] With the global war against terror this has become further complicated as the enemy does not take the form of a conventional army and the rules of engagement are not shaped by conventional treaties. Though in the 1990s voluntary guidelines were developed, such as the Code of Conduct designed by the International Red Cross and Red Crescent Movement, to establish principles of neutrality for relief agencies, these have proven an insufficient defence in a context where military and civilian work is becoming increasingly confused.

Challenges for Civil Society

The manipulation of the discourse of the war on terror to undermine political opponents and to cast suspicion over the activities of civil society organizations, especially Muslim groups, points to a disturbing development in state-society relations. Furthermore, the questioning of Western donor support to civil society organizations in the south and the thickening of relations between civilian, governmental and military forces pose a range of immediate and longer-term challenges to civil society organizations, and specifically to developmental NGOs across the world.

An immediate challenge for foundations and grant-making organizations is how to handle the processes of monitoring award-holders, whilst also maintaining relations of trust. For small foundations or other international grant-makers the administrative costs of complying with the US ATC and the 2002 Anti-Terrorist Financing Guidelines and similar measures in other countries are formidable (Baron, 2004). Furthermore, these kinds of requirements alter the relationship between donor agencies and grantees, particularly in countries where information required on organizations has to be obtained from police, intelligence or security agencies (Baron, 2004, p12). To the extent that donor agencies are required to monitor and report on their grantees, it undermines relations of trust, renders the notion of partnership increasingly vacuous and exposes the deeper imbalances of power that have always underpinned relations between grant-makers and recipients. Moreover there already is some evidence in the USA that the counter-terrorist measures have led to a drop in giving to international projects (Odendahl, 2005).

Another immediate challenge for humanitarian and development agencies working in conflict and post-reconstruction contexts is how to maintain a commitment to neutrality and impartiality as their operations become confused with and subordinated to broader military objectives. Reasserting a commitment to a Code of Conduct is unlikely to be a sufficient response. In the longer term it will require humanitarian and development agencies to analyse more closely their own role, whether intentional or unintended, in the foreign policy agenda of their own countries and to devote greater effort to understanding the complex politics of the countries in which they have chosen to operate. Part of this process will involve development and humanitarian NGOs defining more carefully and defending more vigorously their identities, and in particular, whether they wish to portray themselves as 'nation-less' international agencies which stand above territorial divisions or as national agencies operating in an international field. Though the former option may do little in practice to counter the perception that US or European developmental and humanitarian NGOs represent national interests, it will nevertheless be an important step in NGOs asserting greater control over the construction of their own identities.

For developmental NGOs, social movements and other civil society actors another key challenge concerns how to continue to organize, advocate and campaign around marginalized interests, particularly where certain social groups are being associated with terrorism. This is rendered even more complex as organizations labelled by some as terrorists, such as Hamas in Palestine, appropriate the language of development and civil society, and act as key providers of social welfare. In the USA counter-terrorist measures have already begun to impinge on non-profit advocacy groups that challenge the Bush administration (Odendahl, 2005). Given the complex interweaving of meanings and language around terrorism, Islam, refugees and asylum-seeking, any kind of claim-making actions, social movements and organizations advocating around issues of justice, religious freedom, immediately become suspect.

It is not easy to assess the effects of this subtle interlinking of meanings on civil society in any particular context as they concern more the intangible creation of climates of opinion, the shifting of attitudes and the semantic construction and manipulation of 'others' and 'enemies' than the visible effects of massive repression. However, it is likely that as development agencies seek to engage with civil society actors, either for the purposes of programme implementation or to strengthen civil society, the cast of actors involved in these processes becomes more tightly controlled and subject to suspicion. The concern here is that groups and organizations that seek to articulate the interests of marginalized people are left out as they are seen as too risky or too unfamiliar. Donors then become not only more conservative in their judgements but also the spaces for participation and inclusion that were being prised open in the 1980s and 1990s became increasingly constricted.

These processes should put advocates of particular causes on the alert, and especially where these relate to refugees, asylum-seekers, Palestine, religion and secessionist demands, for this negotiation of meanings embodies the contestation of power both with the state and within civil society. On the other hand in countries that have become part of the US coalition of allies, the US government is likely to cast a blind eye to any abuses of human rights or constriction of space for civil society actors, much as happened during the Cold War era. In these circumstances civil society organizations need to continue, as during the Cold War era, to expose human rights abuses, to highlight the hypocrisies in the foreign policy objectives of dominant Western powers and to challenge social injustices. In doing so they need to look afresh at strategy. When governments portray essentially political problems as cultural, social or economic, this reduces the discursive resources available to groups seeking just political outcomes (Megoran, 2005, p93).[25] This then raises the question of how best to frame demands and shape actions so as not only to avoid being accused of being a terrorist organization, associate or sympathizer but also to ensure that certain issues are not cast as illegitimate and beyond discussion.

A final issue relates to the perceived legitimacy and accountability of NGOs. With the increasing engagement of non-governmental actors in global processes such as parallel UN summits, there has been growing concern over the sources of legitimacy and systems of accountability of NGOs, particularly among elected parliamentarians. The suggestion that charities, NGOs and foundations have served as conduits for money laundering by terrorist organizations, especially in the USA, has intensified the pressure on NGOs to improve their transparency of operations and procedures. For example, in

2004 the American Enterprise Institute for Public Policy and the Federalist Society for Law and Public Policy Studies, two highly influential think-tanks serving the Bush administration, launched a website, NGO Watch, to address issues of accountability, and in particular a concern that NGOs were overstepping their mandates (Carter and Carter, 2004). Muslim charities in the US have already taken steps to demonstrate greater accountability and transparency such as publishing annual reports and conducting audits (Al-Marayati, 2004). However, in a climate of suspicion and fear, it is vital that all civil society organizations pay greater attention to issues of accountability and transparency ahead of governments.

Conclusion

It is only five years since the launch of the Global War on Terror.[26] In this short period governments across the world have introduced repressive legislation and measures aimed ostensibly at limiting the opportunities for organizations labelled as terrorist to take action but also often opportunistically to clamp down on perceived political opposition. Foreign aid policy has become more tightly intermeshed with the security and military objectives of national governments, consolidating a trend that was emerging in the 1990s. In conflict and post-conflict situations the boundaries between military and civil operations have become increasingly blurred, rendering the work of humanitarian and development actors ever more complicated and ambiguous. Furthermore, the requirement by USAID and some US foundations that grantees sign statements that they do not support terrorism has cast a shadow over the once euphoric embrace by aid agencies of civil society actors. In the 1990s donor agencies viewed civil society as an important ingredient in the process of democratization and poverty reduction, indeed the sociological mirror image of the market. Since 2001 donor agencies have been forced to take a more circumspect approach to civil society, recognizing its benign and less savoury elements.

These are but some of the immediate effects of the global war on terror on civil society, and effects that proponents of civic engagement should remain alert to. In the longer term civil society actors will need to engage more strategically and astutely in the defence and expansion of spaces to organize and deliberate. In particular such a defence must be mounted not only in the interests of dominant groups but also of those on the margins of society.

Notes

1   I am grateful for the very useful comments on this paper provided by an anonymous reviewer and David Lewis.

2   For an overview of the historical roots of the term see Keane (1988), Cohen and Arato (1995) and for discussions of the cultural appropriateness of a term that owes its origins to Western political thought see Comaroff and Comaroff (1999), Kaviraj and Khilnani (2001), Hann and Dunn (1996), and Glasius et al (2004).

3   See also Tujan et al (2004, p53).

4   Placing the emphasis on deprivation and poverty detracts, however, from the fact that some of the 11 September hijackers and leaders such as Osama Bin Laden come from relatively privileged backgrounds. More sophisticated analyses distinguish between those who are highly educated from middle-class families, often with backgrounds in engineering or information technology, and those who are less educated, alienated from society and from deprived backgrounds.

See also UK Prime Minister Tony Blair's speech to Congress on 17 July 2003, where he juxtaposes poverty, lack of freedom and terrorism: 'The threat comes because, in another part of the globe, there is shadow and darkness where not all the world is free ... where a third of our planet lives in poverty ... and where a fanatical strain of religious extremism has arisen ... and because in the combination of these afflictions, a new and deadly virus has emerged. That virus is terrorism ...' (Blair, 2003).

5   For example, the Peruvian President Alejandro Toledo, stated that 'to speak of development is to speak also of a strong and determined fight against terrorism'. The President of the UN General Assembly, Han Seung-Soo, describe the world's poorest countries as 'the breeding ground for violence and despair' (BBC World News, 2002).

6   See for example the World Bank, The State in a Changing World: World Development Report, 1997, OECD, 1998 and DAC, 1997.

7   See section IB, paragraph 16, 'Not only are development, security and human rights all imperative: they also reinforce each other ...While poverty and denial of human rights may not be said to "cause" civil war, terrorism or organised crime, they all greatly increase the risk of instability and violence ...' and paragraph 17 '... we will not enjoy development without security, we will not enjoy security without development ...' UN General Assembly (2005).

8   Similarly, following the London bombings in July 2005, the British government put pressure on Pakistan to tighten its control over madrassas, which were portrayed as sources of extremist ideology, and to reform the curricula. By the end of July General Pervez Musharraf had ordered all 1400 foreign students studying in the country's madrassas to leave.

9   For example in the run up to the UN conference on Financing for Development in Monterrey, Mexico, in March 2002, the USA promised US$10 billion in aid over three years followed by a permanent increase of US$5 billion a year after that.

10   I am grateful to Judith Randel for explaining some of the technical difficulties around these issues.

11   Examples of such measures include in the US the Presidential Executive Order 13224 issued in September 2001, the US Patriotic Act passed by Congress in October 2001, the Anti-Terrorist Financing Guidelines issued by the US Treasury Department in November 2002 and in the UK the 2000 Terrorism Act, the Anti-Terrorism, Crime and Security Act of 2001.

12   These are Kyrgzstan, Kazakhstan, Uzbekistan, China and Russia.

13   See Xinhua News Agency, 'Shanghai body, CIS sign accords on terrorism, cooperation', Beijing, 12 April 2005.

14   By April 2002 the UK had frozen the assets of more than 100 organizations and 200 individuals suspected of terrorist financing, complying thereby with the new FATF 8 Special Recommendations on terrorist financing (Brown, 2002).

15   Grantees are required to countersign a letter of agreement that includes a clause requiring them to agree that their organization will not promote or engage in violence, terrorism or bigotry or make sub-grants to any organizations that engage in such activities.

16   On 31 December 2002 USAID issued Acquisition and Assistance Policy Directive 02–19, also known as the Anti-Terrorism Certification (ACT). This requires all USAID grantees to certify that they do not support terrorism. Following concerns raised by NGOs about the

    language used in the certification, the ACT was reviewed by the government and revised versions were issued in March and September 2004.

17 For example, in December 2003 the Ministry of Justice required all international NGOs to re-register with them by March (instead of with the Ministry of Foreign Affairs). This led to tighter monitoring of international NGOs and to the closure of the Open Society Institute, funded by George Soros. The activities of Internews, an NGO working with independent media and supported by USAID, were suspended for six months. I am grateful to Daniel Stevenson for drawing my attention to and providing me with detailed information about the situation in Uzbekistan.

18 For example, official Uzbekistan media have linked the Andijon protests of May 2005 with Islamic fundamentalists, sponsored by outside agencies seeking regime change as happened in Georgia, Ukraine and Kyrgyzstan. Moreover they have described the Uzbek refugees who fled to Kyrgyzstan as 'escaped extremists' (Kimmage, 2005).

19 In February 2004 resolution number 56 entitled 'On measures on increasing efficiency of the accountability pertaining to financial means, grants and humanitarian aid received from international and foreign governmental and non-governmental organizations' was adopted. This required NGOs receiving funds from donors to use accounts in two state controlled banks. This has made it difficult for NGOs to access money and most donors have seen their money returned to them. Given the dependency of local NGOs on donor funding, this clearly has a constricting effect on their activities. Again I am grateful to Daniel Stevenson for sharing this information with me.

20 The original proposal required NGOs to provide local executive organs with detailed information about any financial transaction with a foreign donor. The version eventually passed required them only to alert local authorities about the direction of the financial flow (Corwin, 2005).

21 Personal communication, August 2005.

22 Illustrative of the confusion between civil and military work is the use in the first phase of the Afghanistan response of military planes to drop food parcels that were the same colour as those used to drop cluster bombs.

23 This moral dilemma surfaced again during the Biafra War in 1967. Bernard Kouchner, a French doctor working for the ICRC in Biafra, challenged the principle of self-censorship fostered by the ICRC when he spoke out publicly about the atrocities he had witnessed. He went on to found the medical relief organization, Médecins Sans Frontières, which, with its commitment to the moral obligation to speak out, charted a new course in humanitarian action (Rieff, 2002, pp82–87).

24 In a skilfully crafted satire of conflict prevention and civil society-building in Central Asia, Megoran (2005, p93) demonstrates how the discursive labelling of political issues as cultural and social shapes and limits the possibilities for seeking just political settlements.

25 This article was published in 2006. For a more recent analysis of the legacy of the Global War on terror and NGOs, see Fowler and Sen 2010.

References

Al-Marayati, L. (2004) American Muslim Charities: Easy Targets in the War on Terror. Paper presented at the Pace University School of Law Symposium 'Anti-Terrorist Financing Guidelines: The Impact on International Philanthropy', on 3 December

Australian Government/AusAID (2003) Counter-Terrorism and Australian Aid. August 2003

Baron, B. F. (2004) 'Deterring donors: anti-terrorist financing rules and American Philanthropy', *The International Journal of Not-For-Profit Law* 6(2): pp1–32

BBC World News (2002) Poverty 'fuelling terrorism'. 22nd March. Downloaded from http://news.bbc.co.uk/1/hi/world/1886617.stm on 6 September 2005

Belgrad, E. and Nachmias, N. (1997) *The Politics of International Humanitarian Aid Operations*, Praeger: Westport, Connecticut

Bell, S. (2004) *Cold Terror: How Canada Nurtures and Exports Terrorism around the World*, John Wiley and Sons. Etobicoke: Ontario

Benthall, J. and Bellion-Jourdan, J. (2003) *The Charitable Crescent: Politics of Aid in the Muslim World*, I.B. Tauris: London

Blair, T. (2003) Prime Minister's Speech to Congress. Office of the Prime Minister. 17 July, downloaded from www.ppionline.org/ppi_ci.cfm on 6 September 2005

Bush, G. W. (2002) Remarks to the Inter-American Development Bank, March 14th, released by the White House, Office of the Press Secretary, downloaded from www.state.gov/e/eb/rls/rm on 6 September 2005

Brown, G. (2002) Statement by Gordon Brown. International Monetary and Financial Committee Fifth Meeting, Washington, D.C. 20 April. Downloaded from www.imf.org/external/spring/2002/imfc/stm/eng/gbr.htm on 5 September 2005

Carter, T. S. and Carter, S. S. (2004) Worldwide implications of America's emerging policies concerning NGOs, non-profits and charities. Anti-Terrorism and Charity Law Alert 5. 30 November

Cassen, R. (1994) Does Aid Work? Report to Intergovernmental Task Force. Clarendon Press: Oxford

Cohen, J. L. and Arato, A. (1995) *Civil Society and Political Theory*, The MIT Press: Massachusetts

Comaroff, J. L. and Comaroff, J. (eds) (1999) *Civil Society and the Political Imagination in Africa. Critical Perspectives*, The University of Chicago Press: Chicago and London

Corwin, J. (2005) Will Putin follow in Nazarbaev's footsteps on NGOs? Radio Free Europe/Radio Liberty Newsline 9(144) Part I, 2 August 27

DAC (1997) DAC Guidelines on Conflict, Peace and Development Cooperation. Development Assistance Committee, OECD.

Dagne, T. (2005) 'Africa and the war on terrorism', in *The Global War on Terrorism. Assessing the American Response*, Davis J. (ed) Nova Science Publishers, Inc: New York; pp95–112

Davis, J. (2005) 'Introduction', in *The Global War on Terrorism. Assessing the American Response*, Nova Science Publishers, Inc.: New York

Davis, J. (ed) Nova Science Publishers, Inc.: New York; ppvi–xiii

Duffield, M. (2002) *Global Governance and the New Wars: the Merging of Development and Security*, Zed Books: New York.

Fowler, A. and Sen, K. (2010) 'Embedding the War on Terror: State and Civil Society Relations', *Development and Change*, Vol. 41, No. 1, pp1–47

Gearty, C. (2003) 'Reflections on civil liberties in an age of counter-terrorism', *Osgoode Hall Law Journal*, 31: pp185–210

German, T. and Randel, J. (1995) The Reality of Aid 95. An Independent Review of International Aid. Earthscan

Glasius, M., Lewis, D. and Seckinelgin, H. (eds) (2004) *Exploring Civil Society. Political and Cultural Contexts*, Routledge: London and New York

Greenwood, C. (2005) 'International law and the "War on Terrorism"', in *The Global War on Terrorism. Assessing the American Response*, Davis J (ed) Nova Science Publishers, Inc.: New York; pp45–59

Hage, G. (2003) 'Comes a time we are all enthusiasm: understanding Palestinian suicide bombers in times of exighophobia', *Public Culture*, 15(1): pp65–89

Hann, C. and Dunn, E. (eds) (1996) *Civil Society. Challenging Western Models*, Routledge: London and New York

Howell, J. and Pearce, J. (2002) *Civil Society and Development. A Critical Interrogation*, Lynne Rienner Publishers: Boulder, Colorado

House of Commons International Development Committee 2002–2003. Afghanistan: The Transition from Humanitarian Relief to Reconstruction and Development. First Report of Session 2002–2003, HC 84

Kaviraj, S. and Khilnani, S. (eds) (2001) *Civil Society. History and Possibilities*, Cambridge University Press: Cambridge

Keane, J. (ed) (1988) *Civil Society and the State. New European Perspectives*, University of Westminster: London

Kimmage, D. (2005) Uzbekistan's President Battens Down the Hatches. Radio Free Europe/ Radio Liberty Newsline 9, no. 143, part I, August

Lobe, J. (2002) Billions for Defense, Pennies for Development. Inter Press Service, 2 March. Downloaded from www.globalpolicy.org/socecon/ffd/2002/0302billions on 6 September 2005

MacAskill, E. (2004) Saudis crack down on Islamic charities, The Guardian, 3 June 2004; p16

Megoran, N. (2005) 'Preventing conflict by building civil society: post-development theory and a Central Asian-UK policy success story', Central Asian Survey March 24(1): pp83–96

Naidoo, K. (2004) 'Coming clean: Civil society organisations at a time of global uncertainty', *The International Journal of Not-For-Profit Law*, 6(3): pp1–3

Odendahl, T. (2005) 'Foundations and their Role in Anti-Terrorism Enforcement: Findings from a Recent Study and Implications for the Future', Speech given at The Foundation Center, Washington, D.C., 9 June

OECD (1998) 'Conflict, peace and development cooperation on the threshold of the 21st century', Development Cooperation Guideline Series, Organisation for Economic Cooperation and Development: Paris

OECD (2005) OECD Receipts and Selected Indicators for Developing Countries, Table 25 downloaded from www.oecd.org, 6 September 2005

Ollapally, D. (2005) 'America's war on terrorism in South Asia. Political and military dilemmas', in *The Global War on Terrorism. Assessing the American Response*, Davis J. (ed) Nova Science Publishers, Inc.: New York; pp145–158

Parliamentary Library (2004) 'The Changing focus of Australia's aid program: budget 2004– 2005' Research Note. Department of Library services. No. 59, 31st May

Reusse, E. (2002) *The Ills of Aid. An Analysis of Third World Development Policies*, University of Chicago Press: Chicago

Rieff, D. (2002) *A Bed For the Night. Humanitarianism in Crisis*, Simon and Schuster: New York

Sassen, S. (2002) 'Governance hotspots: challenges we must confront in the post-September World', *Theory, Culture and Society*, 19(4): pp233–244

Sparks, C. (2003) 'Liberalism, terrorism and the politics of fear', *Politics*, 23(3): pp200– 206

Royal Danish Ministry of Foreign Affairs (2003) A World of Difference. The Government's Vision for New Priorities in Danish Development Assistance 2004–2008. June

Tujan, A., Gaughran, A. and Mollett, H. (2004) 'Development and the "global war on terror"', *Race and Class*, 46(1): pp53–74

UN General Assembly (2005) 'In larger freedom: towards development, security and human rights for all', Report of the Secretary-General. A/59/2005, March

USAID (2005) FY 2002–2005 USAID Country Allocation Summaries. Downloaded from www. USAID.org on 6 September 2005

Walsh, N. (2005) 'Uzbekistan kicks US out of military base', The Guardian. 1 August 2005; p10

World Bank (1997) 'The State in a Changing World', *The World Development Report*, Washington DC, World Bank

Part II

From NGOs to Civil Society

4

'Seeing Like a Citizen': Re-claiming Citizenship in a Neoliberal World[1]

John Gaventa

Introduction

In this chapter, I will argue that neoliberalism and globalization are radically reshaping the terrain of citizenship in a way that particularly challenges our understandings of how citizenship is constructed and the sites in which it is claimed. I suggest that dominant approaches to citizenship as shaped in the neoliberal model are producing 'thin' versions of the concept, in which citizens are treated as residuals to other categories, be they the market, the state, 'democracy', or even 'civil society'.

Reversing the telescope – looking at citizenship through the perspective of citizens as actors in the development process – gives us a very different view. Rather than understanding citizens as products shaped by other forces – e.g. as consumers, users, voters or beneficiaries – we gain an image of citizens who are actively engaging to claim their rights and to assert their voice, but not necessarily in the ways or spaces ascribed to them by the dominant institutions. Rather than seeing citizenship along a single dimension of relations to the state or market, we see a more multidimensional view – one that grows from action and identities in multiple spheres, not only in relationship to the state or the market alone.

Such an approach has important consequences for how we understand civil society and the specific role of NGOs as civil society actors. The idea that civil society 'speaks for' citizens and protects their interests in relationship to states and markets has long held sway in development discourse and practice. A 'citizen-centred' approach challenges such a view, arguing that civil society is only one of the arenas through which citizens express their identities and claim their rights, and that civil society organizations do not necessarily represent 'the citizens'. This approach argues that NGOs should go beyond a view of citizens as their 'beneficiaries' to one which recognizes citizens as rights-bearing actors who engage constantly with states, markets and civil society itself. Their role becomes less one of speaking *for* citizens and more one of working *with* citizens to deepen state-society relationships, and to support the construction of new understandings of citizenship and the deepening of rights themselves.

The Changing Terrain of Citizenship in a Neoliberal World

Though to do so risks great oversimplification, I will briefly argue that a citizen-centred approach can be seen in contrast to four other approaches, each of which are under-girded by broad tenets of neoliberalism: a) a neoliberal market-based approach; b) a narrow state reform approach; c) a 'thin' democracy approach and d) a 'thin' civil society approach which focuses largely on NGOs as deliverers of services, and as professional mediators between the state, market and citizen in the development process. Each of these approaches focuses on getting particular institutional forms of development right, with the assumption that if this is done, stylized views of citizenship will follow. In each, 'citizens' are treated as a residual category, who act and respond as a by-product of other forces of development, framing citizens as consumers, users and choosers, voters, or beneficiaries, not as rights-bearing actors in and of themselves (Cornwall and Gaventa, 2000).

The market approach to citizenship

A neoliberal market approach argues for transforming the category of citizen in relationship to the state by focusing on citizens as consumers in the global market. As Dagnino observes in the book on *Inclusive Citizenship:*

> neo-liberal discourses establish an alluring connection between citizenship and market. To be a citizen comes to mean individual integration into the market as consumer and producer. This seems to be the basic principle implicit in a vast number of projects to enable people to 'acquire citizenship', that is to say, learning how to initiate micro-enterprises, how to be become qualified for the few jobs still on offer, and so on. In a context where the state progressively withdraws from its role as guarantor of rights, the market is offered as a surrogate arena of citizenship. (Dagnino, 2005, p159)

Similarly, Munck argues neoliberalism seeks to convert the citizen into a consumer, in which 'the complex and empowering vision of citizenship in its classic democratic presentation was reduced, in the era of neoliberalism, to the power of the credit card and the pleasures of the shopping mall' (Munck, 2005, pp65–66). Through such an approach, citizens theoretically exercise power through market choice – yet, clearly, such a route is limited if we are concerned with poor people who, by definition, lack market or consumptive power.

Throughout the Citizenship DRC's (Development Research Centre) work, we have seen examples of the ways in which the rise of market forces have altered and changed the citizenship terrain, thus challenging many assumptions about traditional patterns of authority and ways in which rights are protected. In Bangladesh, Kabeer describes how neoliberalism has led NGOs to a focus on 'market participation as the route to empowerment', and contrasts a more rights-based approach taken by the NGO Nijera Kori (Kabeer, 2003, p2). Work by Robins (2005b) shows how approaches by the NHS in the

UK which treat persons with HIV-AIDS as consumer citizens actually served to de-politicize notions of citizenship and to 'kill activism'. In Mexico, the work by Pare and Robles (2006, p81) demonstrates how 'the neoliberal development model's privileging of market forces has accelerated environmental destruction and the erosion of traditional institutions' and in so doing has altered the balances of power between citizens and the state.

The state approach

Neoliberal approaches also carry with them projects to reform the state, seen as redesigning institutions and streamlining bureaucracies in order to increase their efficiency and effectiveness. Alongside this approach, a narrow, technocratic approach to governance emphasizes rules and procedures, downplaying the importance of power and politics, and weakening the focus on the state as a protector of the rights of citizens. In this view, citizens are often called upon to play a conflicting role both as providers of services, and also as 'users' and clients of the state, who through the expression of their voices can help to make it more accountable and transparent.

The cases studies from the Citizenship DRC illustrate time and again how as the state is being reconfigured, it is also weakened as the arbiter of rights or even as the deliverer of basic services, thus challenging liberal, state-based assumptions about where and how rights and citizenship can be realized. For instance, in work examining the right to water in South Africa, Lyla Mehta (2006) examines the conflicts between market-based frameworks in which citizens are expected to gain rights as consumers through implied contracts with private water utilities rather than through rights-based frameworks, where rights are mediated by the state. Other work also challenges the idea civil society participation by itself can serve as an effective means to hold the state accountable. Simply creating new spaces for institutionalized participation with the state does not necessarily alter power relations, and may in fact reinforce the status quo (Cornwall and Coelho, 2007). Newell and Wheeler challenge 'technocratic framings of accountability, arguing that they 'generate a kind of naivety that reform processes can generate pro-poor change without challenging power inequities' (Newell and Wheeler, 2006, p22).

The 'thin democracy' approach

Neoliberal forms of the state also carry with them notions about democracy and how it is to be constructed. Rather than seeing democracy in its 'thicker' and 'deeper forms' in which citizens mobilize and struggle to express their voice and claim their interests (Fung and Wright, 2003; Gaventa, 2006), 'the new democracy is thin and anaemic, it is restricted and delegative at best' (Munck, 2005, p66). Democracy in this view focuses not on struggles of citizens, but on a uniform set of institutional designed approaches to elections, representation and the rule of law (Carothers, 1999). In such a weaker view, citizens are seen largely as voters, who express their consent from time to time, but leave governance to the elected rulers and informed elites.

Even where states are 'democratic', they may not play the role expected by liberal theory as the protector of rights. As Naila Kabeer (2005, p181) writes on Bangladesh, though the Constitution and state policy are all committed to upholding and supporting a broad array of human and social rights, 'the reality however bears little relation to these constitutional provisions. It is characterized instead by corruption and clientelism. The state does not merely fail to protect the rights of citizens, it actively contributes to their violation'. In Brazil, Wheeler shows how the failure of the state to deliver to poor *favelas* strips citizens of their self-respect. 'Dignity is everything for a citizen,' she quotes one woman, 'and we have no dignity. We are treated like cattle in the clinics, on the buses and in the shops. Only in rich neighbourhoods are people treated with dignity' (Wheeler, 2005, p109). Other work in Nigeria and India shows the power of social exclusion drawing from ethnic identity or caste to create and reinforce citizenship as a form of 'exclusion' rather than its more 'inclusive forms' (Abah and Okwori, 2005; Pant, 2005).

The narrow civil society approach

While each of the above approaches reduces citizens to consumers, users or voters, some theories argue that it is through a robust civil society that a deeper notion of citizenship can be realized. Civil society becomes both the vehicle and the arena through which citizens mobilize and organize for their rights. However, a number of other writers argue that civil society also risks being captured by the same neoliberal forces which it is meant to confront. As Dagnino (2005, p158) points out:

> In recent years … this concept [*participación ciudadana* or citizen participation] has been appropriated and reinterpreted by the state as part of its strategy for the implementation of neo-liberal structural adjustment. There is thus a perverse confluence between, on the one hand, participation as part of a project constructed around the extension of citizenship and the deepening of democracy, and on the other hand, participation associated with the project of a reconfiguration of the state that requires the shrinking of its social responsibilities and its progressive exemption from the role of guarantor of rights. The perversity of this confluence reflects the fact that, although pointing in opposite and even antagonistic directions, both projects require an *active, proactive civil society.*

In the neoliberal discourses we have seen a depoliticized view of citizen participation emerge in which civic engagement is seen as the involvement of the civil society sector, through more professionalized organizations and associations such as NGOs, who enter new consultative spaces to speak for the citizens themselves. Such an approach, Thelda Skocpol (2003, p11) warns, leads to the emergence of 'diminished democracy', in which public involvement has lost its link to political life. Similarly, Crenson and Ginsberg (2002, pxx) warn of the 'downsizing of democracy', in which collective citizen action has given way to narrow interest groups, and in which citizens are treated like customers, who communicate to elites through opinion polls and electronic market research processes. The arena of civil society becomes the arena of professionalized organizations and activists who also, in the name of effectiveness, assume the right to speak for citizens who are reduced to the role of 'beneficiaries' of the NGOs rather than active citizens in their own right.

Reversing the Telescope: Seeing Like a Citizen

While perhaps portrayed in a stereotyped way, each of the above approaches constructs and uses the concept of citizenship as a residual to other approaches. For the market approach, the assumption is that if one can get the market right, the benefits will follow for the citizen as consumer. If one can get the institutions of the state right, then citizens can also play a role in holding it accountable and delivering its services. If democracy can be designed and spread effectively, then citizens can play a role as voters and watch-dogs of those in power. If NGOs and civil society sector can grow and become more professional, they can help communicate the messages for its beneficiaries to market, state and elected leaders.

Alternatively, the 'seeing like a citizen' approach taken by the Citizenship DRC reverses the telescope on the other dominant approaches. Rather than focusing on insti-tutional designs as a starting point, it starts with the perceptions of citizens themselves and asks how they interact and view the institutions from which they are expected to benefit. In doing so, the actor-oriented view taken by the DRC suggests a picture of citizenship, participation and accountability that goes beyond citizenship as a residual, or as a product of legal status or institutional design alone.[2]

Such an approach to citizenship builds upon and reinforces a number of traditions and debates which attempt to stand counter to the dominant approach. Picking up themes and debates from emergent 'rights-based' approaches to development, it focuses on issues of inclusion, participation through organized collective action and the devel-opment of democratic institutions which have obligations to protect and promote rights. Building on debates about the multiple forms of citizenship, especially from Latin America, citizenship is seen as an important arena of contestation, which is fully attained not only through the exercise of political and civic rights, but also through social rights, which in turn may be gained through participatory processes and struggles (Dagnino, 2005; Avritzer, 2002). In such a view, citizen participation itself may be seen as a social right, which enables the capacity to claim other rights (Gaventa, 2002).

Such an actor-based approach also re-politicizes our understandings of participa-tion, moving it from that of 'beneficiaries' of the development process to one of rights-bearing citizens. Interacting with debates in the literature on deepening democ-racy, this approach focuses on the process through which citizens exercise ever-deep-ening power over decisions which affect their lives, and in which democracy is extended 'from a democracy of voters to a democracy of citizens' (UNDP, 2004). As David Beetham argues:

> the core idea of democracy is that of popular rule or popular control over collec-tive decision-making. Its *starting point is with the citizen rather with the institu-tions of government*. Its defining principles are that all citizens are entitled to a say in public affairs, both through the associations of civil society and through partic-ipation in government; and that this entitlement should be available in terms of equality of all. Control by citizens over their collective affairs, and equality between citizens in the exercise of that control, are the key democratic principles. (1999, p3, emphasis added)

In this view, 'thicker' and more participatory forms of citizenship move beyond passive engagement as voters, beneficiaries or consumers. Citizens are seen as the 'makers and shapers' of policies not only the 'users and choosers' of development or as the 'clients' of other actors (Cornwall and Gaventa, 2001).

Citizenship as a Process of Construction

By taking such a view, research across each of the working groups of the DRC offers a dramatically different view from those of the dominant approaches to how citizenship is constructed.

First, while acknowledging the colonial and often exclusionary origins of the concept of citizenship, case studies from the DRC give a view of citizenship-in-practice which is far more robust than that portrayed and constructed in its more neoliberal forms. Citizens are engaging on key issues that affect their lives, and in ways that challenge traditional notions of passivity or disengagement. Case studies from contexts as diverse as Nigeria, South Africa, Brazil, Mexico, India and Bangladesh signal common impulses at the grassroots for values of justice, recognition, self-determination and horizontal solidarity, which offer potential for building more vibrant forms of citizenship, and for realization of fundamental rights (Kabeer, 2005).

However, while citizens are acting to claim their rights and assert their voice, it is not always done in relationship to the state. Rather, the DRC's work argues for understanding citizenship in a more multidimensional way, in which citizens may express their voice and demands not only in the political realm, but also in relationship to other social, ethnic and religious identities and in other social, economic, household, global, or local spheres.

Case studies, for instance, show the articulation of citizenship in struggles for the right to have a recognized identity by migrant populations in both India (Pant, 2005) and the United States (Ansley, 2005); for a sense of place and sense of belonging in Kenya (Nyamu-Musembi, 2006) and Brazil (Wheeler, 2005); in the workplace struggles 'for dignity and daily bread' (Mahmud and Kabeer, 2006) and in terms of biological citizenship, or control over one's own health (Robins, 2005a). The work also points to the fact that citizenship is expressed not only in vertical relations to the state, but in horizontal, social relations as well; and that in everyday practice, citizenship is not a singular identity, but an ensemble of identities, affiliations and forms of action. Just as participatory approaches to understanding of poverty over the last decade have led to a more multidimensional understanding of what poverty entails, so too do the empirical investigations of rights and citizenship call for more robust understandings of these concepts, and argue for dimensions of citizenship which go beyond the nation state-based understanding alone.

Much of the empirical work from the DRC thus supports recent trends in citizenship studies which suggest that citizenship must be understood in social as well as in political spheres, and expressed in non-state as well as state arenas. In this sense, like the concept of democracy, citizenship may have 'thick' and 'thin' versions:

> So-called 'thick' citizenship' which gives people real power over their lives is desirable, but 'thin' citizenship (in terms of formal legal and political entitlements) is better than no citizenship at all. The right to self-rule is important and central to citizenship: but it becomes absurd and paradoxical when placed in the context of the state. This is why the case for an inclusive citizenship makes it essential that we look beyond the state ... (Hoffman, 2004, p13)

In the 'thick' view of citizenship, a sense of citizenship is deeply related to a sense of personhood and identity. As Kabeer (2003, p1) writes, 'how people define themselves, and are defined by others, is relevant to citizenship as practice because of its implications for their capacity to act as citizens'. Yet, as she goes on to write 'while individual agency may be a central aspect of claiming rights and observing duties, history tells us it has been the collective struggles of those who have been denied citizenship status that have driven processes of transformation towards more inclusive definitions and practices' (Kabeer, 2003). Such struggles for inclusive citizenship often begin with demands for recognition and dignity and around concrete issues and immediate needs in the social and community sphere, not in the first instance with struggles for greater political voice in state-based processes. Such engagement is not always by invitation, nor inspired by liberal or even neoliberal concepts of what a citizen ought to do or be. Rather, it springs from impulses for social justice, for desires for recognition and dignity, and from the need to confront concrete social needs and issues that affect everyday life (Kabeer, 2005).

While such action for social inclusion may begin outside the state sphere, there are political consequences: it is through engagement for recognition on local issues that broader awareness, skills and networks are acquired, and through which social citizenship is converted to political engagement. Through acting and mobilizing on key issues and identities, citizens learn and acquire new identities as political actors; they become conscious of their rights, and their right to have rights. They build the alliances and solidarities which allow them to exercise power.

For instance, in South Africa Robins (2005b, p5) writes about how the 'extremity of "near death" experiences of full-blown AIDS, and the profound stigma and "social death" associated with the later stages of the disease ... can produce the conditions for AIDS survivors' commitment to "new Life", social activism and "responsibilized" citizenship'. In sharp contrast to the biomedical interventions which treat HIV/AIDS patients as clients to be protected through anonymity, the activist discourses associated with the movement known as Treatment Action Campaign served to revitalize 'isolated and stigmatized AIDS sufferers' as social activists, aware of their rights and responsibilities as citizens.

Similarly, in Bangladesh, Shireen Huq (2005, p168) writes that in relationship to the work of Naripokko, 'our experience of discrimination as women led us to demand fair treatment and respect for our dignity as human beings, and only thereafter to claim our rights and entitlements as *citizens*'. In this sense, political citizenship is constructed *through* engagement, not the other way around. That is, one does not create citizens who then act; rather action creates the sense and practice of citizenship itself. From this perspective citizenship is constructed from below, not given from above. It is claimed, not bestowed.

Implications for NGOs and Development Practices

Such an approach has implications for broader debates that are relevant to development policy, as well as to how NGOs may act to achieve their goals.

First, such an approach means going beyond the state-society binary which has often affected approaches to development. On the one hand, the reconfiguring of the state and changing patterns of authority are themselves pointing to the importance of non-state actors to do what the state once did. For NGOs, this may mean that they play the role of service providers, rather than playing the role of helping citizens claim rights and accountability from the state. In this approach, there is a risk that NGOs simply replicate patterns of dependency: where once citizens may have been clients or subjects of the state, rather than actors and claimants on it, they now become passive beneficiaries of NGOs instead. The relations of power between provider and recipient do not change.

But on the other hand, we have also seen that the social sphere itself is an important arena in which citizenship is expressed and constructed. It is often here, through action on immediate issues in daily life, where citizens build their political skills, identities and self-awareness as actors. In turn, as a sense of citizenship is constructed outside of the state, it can contribute to the emergence of citizens who engage with the state and who claim rights and accountabilities from the state.

This recognition of the ways in which states and societies interact has important consequences for how NGOs who seek to take a rights-based approach go about their work. First, even where they are working on community-based issues or on service delivery projects which do not directly engage with the state, they can approach these as potential learning grounds in which a sense of citizenship and rights are developed and strengthened. Over time, *how* they work with citizens in enabling a sense of rights and agency in these spaces can be as important as *what* they actually do.

Secondly, even as NGOs and civil society organizations help strengthen spaces for the construction and expression of citizenship outside of the state, they can also engage with the state to help protect these spaces and to build a sense of responsiveness to the citizen voices which do emerge. In this sense, the Citizenship DRC has argued that building effective relationships between states and citizens, means 'working on both sides of the equation' (Gaventa, 2004, p27). The in-depth work by Coelho on the health councils in Brazil provides demonstrable empirical evidence on this point. In testing the significance of a) committed public managers, b) civil society activism or c) an appropriate institutional design in building more inclusive health care services, her work confirms the importance of all three acting together (Coelho, 2007).

The case studies in the DRC call also for recognition of the multiple ways in which power and identity serve to mediate between the legal frameworks and institutional procedures which are designed to support the rights of citizens and what actually happens in everyday life. Yet simultaneously, the claims for rights also can serve to challenge and change power. It is through the mobilization and demands of citizenship that rights are made real, new legal rights are created and meanings of citizenship are expanded.

Citizenship in this sense is contextual but also historical – it is created and realized over time, in different ways in different places and points in time. To suggest that citizenship is gained through practice, and that a fundamental right of participation is the right to create rights, in turn makes both rights and citizenship emergent concepts. If that is the case, to support the realization of rights and citizenship is not only to support the capacities of states and citizens to realize *existing* rights, but also to enable and support the process by which new formulations emerge. Historically, if one had simply applied an agenda of upholding *existing* rather than supporting the struggles for *emergent* rights, then the rights-based agenda would simply have strengthened the status quo (in the case of the US, for instance, a democracy of white, male property owners). Forces from below pressing new rights – such as inclusion of women and minorities in democratic processes – would have been ignored.

Understanding this emergent character of citizenship also has important implications for development practice, as well as for the role of NGOs. First, it suggests that the success of new democratic experiments and assertions of citizenship can only be measured in decades, not in the course of a few years. Struggles for inclusive forms of citizenship do not fit neatly with approaches to development that measure success through indicators of efficiency and performance, delivered within project or budget cycles. Neither will support for the deepening of rights and citizenship from below mesh easily with new aid approaches which focus on budget support, aid harmonization and national ownership – almost by definition emergent demands against exclusion are not likely to be key budget priorities, nationally owned nor harmonious.

Rather, the work of the Citizenship DRC points to the need for approaches that affirm the central role which demands for recognition and rights play in constructing more robust forms of citizenship and more inclusive states over time. Civil society organizations which are deeply rooted in the societies in which they are a part have the potential to contribute to creating stronger citizens, and in turn to strengthen the relationship between citizens and state institutions. To do so, however, means that NGOs must engage *with* citizens, starting with their own identities and local struggles, not simply speak *for* them, or reduce them to beneficiaries in the development process.

Notes

1 This title is a play on the title of the very important book by James C. Scott, 'Seeing Like a State' (New Haven: Yale University Press 1998). However, beyond the title, the approach here and that taken by Scott are very different.
2 In one of the early working papers which helped to define the Citizenship DRC's work, Celestine Nyamu-Musembi (2002, p1) described this actor-based approach as one in which rights and citizenship are 'shaped through actual struggles informed by people's own understanding of what they are justly entitled to'.

References

Abah, S. O. and Okwori, Z. J., in Kabeer, N. (ed) (2005) *A nation in search of citizens: Problems of citizenship in the Nigerian context*, London: Zed Books, 71–84

Ansley, F., in Kabeer, N. (ed) (2005) *Constructing citizenship without a license: The struggle of undocumented immigrants in the USA for livelihoods and recognition*, London: Zed Books, 199–218

Avritzer, L. (2002) *Democracy and the Public Space in Latin America*, Princeton: Princeton University Press

Beetham, D. (1999) *Democracy and Human Rights*, London: Polity Press

Carothers, T. (1999) *Aiding Democracy Abroad: The Learning Curve*, Washington DC: Carnegie Endowment for International Peace

Coelho, V. S. (2007) 'Brazilian Health Councils', in Cornwall and Schattan, (eds) 2007, *Spaces for Change? Participation, inclusion, and voice*, London: Zed Books, 33–54

Cornwall, A. and Gaventa, J. (2000) 'From Users and Choosers to Makers and Shapers: Repositioning Participation in Social Policy', *IDS Bulletin* 31 (4): 50–62, Brighton: Institute of Development Studies

Cornwall, A. and Coelho V. S. (eds) (2007) *Spaces for Change? Participation, inclusion, and voice*, London: Zed Books

Crenson, M. and Ginsberg, B. (2002) *Downsizing Democracy: How America Sidelined its Citizens and Privatized its Public*, Baltimore: John Hopkins University Press

Dagnino, E., in Kabeer, N. (ed) (2005) 'We all have rights, but ... ' Contesting concepts of citizenship in Brazil, London: Zed Books, 149–163

Fung, A. and Wright, E. O. (2003) *Deepening Democracy: Institutional Innovations in Empowered Participatory Governance*, London: Verso

Gaventa, J. (2002) 'Exploring Citizenship, Participation and Accountability, in Making Rights Real: Exploring Citizenship, Participation and Accountability', *IDS Bulletin* 33 (2): 1–11, Brighton: Institute of Development Studies

Gaventa, J. (2004) 'Towards Participatory Governance: Assessing the Transformative Possibilities', in Hickey, S. and Mohan, G. (eds), *From Tyranny to Transformation*, London: Zed Books

Gaventa, J. (2006) 'Triumph, Deficit or Contestation: Deepening the Deepening Democracy Debate', *IDS Working Paper*, No. 264

Hoffman, J. (2004) *Citizenship beyond the state*, London: Sage Publications

Huq, S., in Kabeer, N. (ed) (2005) *Bodies as sites of struggle: Naripokkho and the movement for women's rights in Bangladesh*, London: Zed Books, 164–180

Kabeer, N. (2003) 'Making rights work for the poor: Nijera Kori and the construction of "collective capabilities" in rural Bangladesh', *IDS Working Paper*, No. 200

Kabeer, N. (ed) (2005) *Inclusive Citizenship: Meanings and Expressions*, London: Zed Books

Kabeer, N., in Kabeer, N. (ed) (2005) *Editorial introduction: 'Meanings and expressions of citizenship: perspectives from the north and south'*, London: Zed Books, 1–30

Mahmud, S. and Kabeer, N. in Newell and Wheeler (eds) (2006) *Compliance versus accountability: Struggles for dignity and daily bread in the Bangladesh garment industry*, London: Zed Books, 223–244

Mehta, L. in Newell and Wheeler (eds) (2006) *Do human rights make a difference to poor and vulnerable people? Accountability for the right to water in South Africa*, London: Zed Books, 63–78

Munck, R. (2005) 'Neoliberalism and Politics and the Politics of Neoliberalism', in Saad-Filho, A. and Johnston, D., *Neoliberalism: A critical reader*, London: Pluto Press, 60–69

Newell, P. and Wheeler, J., in Newell and Wheeler (eds) (2006) *Rights, Resources and the Politics of Accountability*, London: Zed Books

Nyamu-Musembi, C. (2002) 'Towards an Actor-Oriented Perspective on Human Rights', *IDS Working Paper*, No. 169

Nyamu-Musembi, C., in Newell and Wheeler (eds) (2006) *From Protest to Proactive Action: Building Institutional Accountability Through Struggles for the Right to Housing*, London: Zed Books, 122–143

Pant, M., in Kabeer, N. (ed) (2005) *The quest for inclusion: Nomadic communities and citizenship questions in Rajasthan*, London: Zed Books, Chapter 5

Pafe, L. and Robles, C., in Newell and Wheeler (eds) (2006) *Managing watersheds and the right to water: Indigenous communities in search of accountability and inclusion in Southern Veracruz*, London: Zed Books, 79–100

Robins, S. (2005a) 'Rights passages from "near death" to new life': AIDS activism and treatment testimonies in South Africa', *IDS Working Paper*, No. 251

Robins, S. (2005b) 'From "medical miracles" to normal (ised) medicine: Aids treatment, activism and Citizenship in the UK and South Africa', *IDS Working Paper*, No. 252

Scott, J. C. (1998) *Seeing Like a State: how certain schemes to improve the human condition have failed*, New Haven, Yale University Press

Skocpol, T. (2003) *Diminished Democracy: From Membership to Management in American Civic Life*, Norman: University of Oklahoma Press

UNDP (2004) 'The Challenge: From a Democracy of Voters to a Democracy of Citizens', in *Democracy in Latin America: Towards a Citizens' Democracy*, UNDP, 35–48

Wheeler, J., in Kabeer, N. (ed) (2005) *Rights without citizenship? Participation, family and community in Rio de Janeiro*, London: Zed Books, 99–113

5

Civic-driven Change: A Concise Guide to the Basics

Kees Biekart and Alan Fowler

The world is not working well. For more and more people, life is unfair and insecure. In fact, for years now the global future has looked less rather than more politically certain, financially stable and ecologically viable. This chapter introduces novel ideas about citizen efforts that can turn this alarming reality around. In doing so, it adds to debates about how the impasse of ineffective aided-development policies and practices can be broken.

It is clear that neither governments nor markets can bring solutions to the range of problems faced by societies everywhere. Yet, too often, as citizens, people do not take up or are not allowed to play essential roles in creating answers to critical social and political ills and issues, such as countering poverty, discrimination, injustice, inequity, conflict, corruption and environmental unsustainability. It is time, therefore, for citizens to reclaim their rightful place as agents of development, guiding how society evolves to what ends and on what terms.

The following pages start a new phase of a long-term process. Its goal is to bring to centre stage approaches to social problem solving that are driven by citizens, i.e., civic-driven change (CDC). The first phase involved an international core group of practitioners and critical analysts, supported by an independent review process. During 2008, they worked on the question: what would a citizen-centred story of change in society look like? Initial results of this effort have been published as essays on the ISS website as well as in a book and as policy papers (see Annex 1). All were presented and discussed at a seminar in The Hague, in October 2008, attended by about 180 people. This second phase is directed at communicating results more widely. The task is to spread both knowledge of and stimulate discussion about civic action and drivers as a distinct approach to social change within and beyond the aided-development community.

This concise guide to CDC serves two key communication purposes. One is to cut through the detail to explain major characteristics of CDC as conceived by the core group. Second is to place CDC within the evidence, ideas and arguments generated by the critical commentary available so far as responses to a lead article in *The Broker Issue 10*, 'Reinventing citizen action'. These objectives will involve comparisons between CDC and current mainstream development thinking.

Characteristics of Civic-driven Change

The CDC framework can perhaps best be explained in terms of (1) location in existing debates, (2) a basic precondition and (3) five defining characteristics. In terms of location, this narrative of CDC draws together and positions itself within contentious discussions. These are enduring and unresolved debates about context-specific substance and 'optimal' relationships between:

- effective states and empowered citizens;
- public and private spheres of life;
- pro- and anti-social values;
- voters and political parties and processes.

CDC offers a compelling lens which connects these debates in a novel way. It helps unpack and focus on deep causes of poverty and injustice which societies and agencies of aided-development continue to grapple with.

The precondition is a situation where people enjoy basic civic rights and freedoms. Where these are denied, full exercise of citizenship becomes the real issue to be addressed, often by expanding the 'imaginative space of democracy' (Boyte, 2008a). In more open contexts, the advent of modern sovereignty casts citizenship as a fundamental, legitimizing relationship between a state and its population.

What citizenship means is written in a state's constitution. But, in practice, being a citizen has a wide range of (in)significance for people's identity and self-understanding. Nevertheless, all constitutions regulate the extent of people's freedoms towards each other and towards the state. In these relationships, CDC is premised on a quality of citizenship which is 'civic'. That is, citizens behaving in ways which respect differences between people, allied to a concern for the whole of society and its natural environment.

CDC operates in terms of rights and obligations. These can function both *towards* and *within* institutions. For example, people have rights in relation to criminal charges – they are innocent until proven guilty. But they also have obligations towards fellow workers or employers: such as not to sexually harass or racially abuse.

A CDC view of society also questions any statement about a 'natural' boundary between what is public and what is private. Such ideas are often projected through political dialogue into the public mind and people's world view. In other words, CDC confronts divisions between what is a 'shared' issue and what is not. For example, if private banks are 'too big to fail' because the economy and society would 'collapse' along with them, who, then, should they belong to? Similarly, it questions the principle that, through corporate taxation, the public takes on responsibility for 'externalized' environmental damage they cause. CDC is at the forefront of the public/private debate, where the idea of a 'global commons' reinforces attention to interdependence on one planet.

A CDC approach does not simply accept historically evolved rules of the game within society as prescribed or as having no alternative. Rules and social formations can be unravelled and rewoven as part of a change agenda. This process happened with the civic-driven reconfiguring of society in post-Soviet east and central Europe. Mass, self-organized and self-propelled assertiveness of China's farmers to change the Communist Party's policy on land ownership is a recent example of civic agency. The efforts (and risks) carried by the Chinese middle class and intellectuals to establish and sign up to Charter 08 for greater political freedoms are another. Some might even argue that the recent election of Barack Obama signals a civic-driven reconstitution of the politics of race in America because it was founded on a tradition of community self-organizing, 'public work' and culturally appropriate practices for collective action (Boyte, 2008b).

Language

Understanding CDC requires a particular language associated with a set of key concepts. The terms and meanings shown in the box are particularly important.

CDC does not rely on the 'three Ps' that are central to the theory and practice of mainstream aided change. These are Projects, Participation and Partnership. These terms serve and reinforce an institutionalized way of understanding socio-political processes, typically with government in the lead and in control. Over time, this terminology has come to both anticipate and label a 'harmony' model of change. That is, all types of change in society can be negotiated, creating win-win situations for all parties. In turn, this view assumes and requires the 'civility' of everyone involved. Apparently, economic exploitation, corruption, state immunity and abuse of official positions are never in play.

In distinction, the CDC framing rests more on assertive self-organization. People negotiate countless forms of collaboration. Asymmetries in power and grappling with associated contention are common place. This process is itself valued as an organic form of socio-political capacitation, or civic self- empowerment.

Box 5.1 *CDC language*

Development is bringing about change in the 'political project' pursued by a society.

(Deep) democracy is a condition where the polity effectively exert a shared influence over those with public authority and holds them to account.

Agency is the application of a person's energy towards realizing an imagined future.

Civic behaviour is pro-social and premised on exercising the rights and obligations of citizenship that contribute to public benefit.

Civic agency is the self-willed action of people to create the society they individually imagine and collectively want. It involves empowerment in crafting and navigating political space.

Collaboration is, with power in the foreground, about negotiating and forming relationships that further civic agency.

Civic self-organization is a capacity-enhancing ability to produce public value, often though public works.

The Basic Elements of Civic-driven Change

The broad characteristics of civic-driven change arise from many social and political elements. They can be grouped in many ways. Context is important because it will usually determine which way of bringing them together makes most sense. The grouping below is meant to be illustrative with no specific situation or history in mind. Though somewhat stereotypical, mainstream development thinking is described in order to focus comparative attention on CDC perspectives.

Socio-political relationships

Mainstream aided development thinking typically takes (western-style) citizenship for granted. There is an implicit modelling along the lines of what donors want to be the case, but without explicit attention to the political philosophy on which rights and obligations are based. For example, what is the balance – if any – between loyalty to the nation and freedom to criticize authority? The centrality of the state as development actor is also simply assumed. Not to do so would invite problems about sovereignty.

A CDC approach:

- starts with the centrality of citizenship as a political relationship between a state and its population: full legitimacy of the former requires informed active engagement by the latter;
- pays careful attention to the power and interests hidden within the language and discourse employed by whom;
- recognizes that societies are continually evolving as 'political projects' – that is, they are driven by the beliefs, interests, desires and aspirations, world views and representations of what society should be which guide political action. People's imagination matters.

Trust in people's experience and knowledge

Mainstream aided development relies on (external) technical experts for virtually everything it engages with. The ritual of donor mission after mission is a well-known syndrome. Associated is a prescriptive formulaic 'three sector' institutional framing and explanation of social structure, roles and responsibilities. The premise of 'participation' is that professional views are best. People can take part in change processes defined by others. Citizen's experience and knowledge is not necessarily ignored, but it is scripted into a predefined progression to be financed.

A CDC approach:

- gives primacy to civic agency – people's action in shaping society – which happens in all walks of life;
- challenges institutional prescriptiveness and civic irresponsibility of any sector or actor;
- opens up to multiple types of knowledge and sites of knowledge-making. Priority is not accorded to external specialists or 'disembodied' science. This does not mean

that people are always 'wise' or right in their understandings, but that they need to organize and find this out for themselves in order to 'self-capacitate'.

Contention in values, measures and processes: Where do outsider 'developers' belong?

With varying degrees of sensitivity to what exists, mainstream development brings a baggage of norms, values and metrics tied to resources and local abilities to use them well. This combination can cause serious dilemmas when the process of change required cannot be 'harmonious'. For example, civic resistance is required to remove corrupt 'winners' and diverters of aid finance. Similarly, measures made meaningful for mainstream aid have, eventually, to translate into money and return on investment. Other measures do not carry as much weight, even if they do so locally. Finally, the system of aid relationships rests on a structural asymmetry in terms of risks of change. Outsiders are seldom held to account locally and can withdraw when change gets rough. Insiders have to cope as best they can with what remains of good intentions gone wrong.

A CDC approach:

- works with the fact that change in society is normative and is as often conflictual as it is collaborative. Attaining democracy often means facing the dilemma that civic ends sometimes call for uncivic means, such as civil disobedience;
- is sensitive to who carries risk, with caution about the role of outsiders in bringing about change to, for, or with others: value-imposition and 'expertized' disempowerment are too frequent outcomes.

Beyond party-political systems

Ostensibly, mainstream aid respects the principle of non-interference in the internal affairs of a country. Adherence to this principle is most sensitive when party politics is involved. Zimbabwe today is a case in point. But mainstream aided development ignores the deeper issue of the extent to which party politics is the most appropriate instrument to ensure popular control over those in authority. There are many signs that this mechanism is past its sell-by date as a means to distribute power and enforce accountability for its use.

A CDC approach:

- pins down context-specific historical processes of power accumulation that have marginalized the polity, typically recasting citizenship in terms of clients to be served by privatizing rights, public space and fulfilment of government obligations;
- responds to the failure of party-based politics exhibited in voter apathy, tied to electoral manipulation and widespread mistrust in today's political systems and leaders. Democracy as currently practiced is being eroded from within and will not self-reform. Local citizen action is a critical starting point for reform to happen;
- knows that media and communication matter. Information – its substance and source – is a vital factor in shaping civic agency. Understanding origin, control and 'spin' are fundamental.

CDC has a different perspective on equity

As an almost an axiomatic philosophy, mainstream development relies on *equity of economic opportunity* as the engine of social change. Empowerment is typically viewed in terms of expanding people's choice through economic gains to get above a poverty line set in financial terms. Other benefits flow from this gain. Examples are increasing capabilities to access goods and services and to engage in market transaction from a stronger position.

A CDC approach:

- CDC differs in this basic premise. Development – aided or otherwise – is not defined by economic measures, but as a political project pursued by all parts of a society;
- its axiom is that what is needed to reduce poverty and marginalization is *equity of political agency* – that is a condition where all citizens have the capabilities needed to co-determine the life and society they want in its many dimensions and possibilities, including the leadership and economic model a country chooses;
- this principle reframes the metrics of (un)aided development processes and intended outcomes.

Lurking behind this summary are many familiar and less familiar stories and theories about how societies work and alter over time. This leads to an obvious first reaction: what's new? And, what is missing? One way of addressing this type of response is to reflect on the comments posted on *The Broker* and the summary overview (Verkoren, 2008). This publication provides a valuable open forum for debate which has been actively taken up in commentaries that continue to grow.

By its nature and timing, *The Broker* piece (Bieckman, 2008) was a compressed and early summary of both the process and substance of the group's collective reflection. And, of course, there are many other stories and angles. For example, the economics of CDC is not covered: a gap that needs to be addressed. And, inevitably, the article 'Deepening Democracy' could not capture the whole body of ideas, experiences and real life cases that made up the CDC story. One outcome is interpretations of what CDC is about that may not correspond with what is presented. Another is the impression of CDC as an abstraction. In other words, it is not grounded in reflections on practical experience – which it is. However, comments which reflect such outcomes are important. They communicate critical ideas and feedback that merit a thoughtful response, not to defend CDC, but to help clarify and test its value for further reflection and action.

The Novelty of CDC

'What is really new about CDC?' This reaction reappears in debates following the presentation of the CDC essays. In one way, the question is justified. But when uncommon avenues and ideas are being explored, it represents only one logic among many.

Responding to this question also requires caution. Why? Because there seems to be a pressing need within NGO circles to always come up with something 'new'. As if 'new' always implies an improvement and a step forward. Perhaps this stance results from the push for constant innovation in aid policies as signs of progress and learning because the evidence does not tell its own unequivocal, compelling story.

Rather than 'new' we argue that CDC offers a different – potentially inspiring – perspective on recurrent issues that aid agencies are grappling with. This perspective is not necessarily 'new' in terms of innovating a particular practice or strategy. Instead, CDC can offer a refreshing angle into examining persistent issues or enduring 'thorns in agencies' flesh'. From recent discussions we suggest seven areas where CDC offers interestingly 'different' perspectives.

Shifting the focus from 'civil society' to 'civic action'

For many years, civil society has been used as a concept in aid discourse to differentiate between governmental and non-governmental channels of aid delivery and to locate the sphere in which partner organizations and networks operate. However, increasingly there has been a tendency to embrace 'civil society' not only as 'the good guys' but also as an actor for change in and of itself, a stance that causes much confusion. To begin with, civil society cannot be perceived as a single actor or mono-purposeful entity. In most definitions, civil society is characterized by a variety of societal actors representing different – and often opposing – world views and interests. An extreme example of these opposing interests is the occurrence of anti-democratic or 'uncivil' actors in civil society, such as neo-Nazis, criminal cartels and intolerant, anti-social groupings. CDC puts the 'civic' element central in its analysis. It makes explicit the need to recognize and counter change that could be characterized as 'uncivic'. Given the conventional approach to civic society as an ostensibly benign location providing socially valuable functions, this can be regarded as a significant clarification.

CDC rearticulates the centrality of citizens and citizenship

A second area where CDC offers a renewed perspective is the centrality of citizens as key actors in change processes. Citizens are entitled to a range of political and civil rights with associated (moral) obligations that are central to the understanding of citizenship. This assertion adds considerably to their 'contained' roles of being mere voters, inhabitants of a geographical space, or consumers of products and services. CDC re-emphasizes the importance of citizenship and puts citizens back in as the primary members of the polity. Of course, citizens are different from 'civic actors'. The latter is a wider concept including organizations, movements and networks that manifest 'civic agency'. But citizens also have 'civic agency' and are certainly part of the family of 'civic actors'. This perspective challenges positions in debates where the individual role of citizens is often subordinated to the interests of social institutions, (umbrella) organizations and their representatives.

CDC is a tiered, cross-boundary viewpoint on society and change

A third area where a civic-driven framework can help to inform new perspectives on change is the important observation that civic action is not limited to – nor oriented at – civil society alone. Some commentators argue that CDC is 'overloading the arena of civil society with too much responsibility'. The CDC essays actually argue the opposite. Civic action – as well as uncivil action – takes place in all possible arenas of social life: in civil society as well as in politics, in markets as well as in the realm of the household. After all, public servants have civic agency, so do employees, consumers, parents and children, voters and citizens. Planned or otherwise, people's actions operate simultaneously, habitually and strategically in all these spheres. As commentators note, the co-creation of public life is something that often goes beyond 'public action' and emerges from the private sphere of the family, in terms of world view, education, gender roles and more personal aspects of socialization.

From the standpoint of citizenship and CDC, the classical sectoral approach in which society is split up into three sectoral 'balloons' or institutional domains, further divided by public and private spheres, is too simple. This framework is an increasingly distorting approximation of reality. The nature of citizenship pervades all spheres of society. Social innovation and social entrepreneurship continue to blur institutional boundaries. And there are growing tiers and density of connections – where 'globalized' means 'many localities joined up'. These and other processes that shift human relations and the power differences within them call for a fundamental revision to the schemas used to comprehend (interdependent) social change. CDC is one lens for doing so.

CDC does not take 'aided change' as a starting point

This position seems to be a controversial feature of the CDC approach in terms of its argument that social change will not essentially depend on the initiatives of (non-governmental) aid agencies. It is civic actors who decide about structural and enduring changes in their society. At best, aid agencies with good intentions and practices that – at a minimum 'do no harm' – can play at most a facilitating role. This 'proportionality and humility' point is not original. The new element is that this 'thinking project' has been initiated by some key Dutch aid agencies who accept that their – or their partner organizations' – future existence is no longer the point of departure for strategizing. This major milestone makes a new and fresh approach possible to what we have called 'aided change', which too often turns out to be a less sustainable type of social change.

CDC primarily focuses on the process of social change, rather than only on the social actors themselves

This is a complex point, which can be easily misunderstood. CDC puts citizens central into processes of social change. One result is to emphasise important tools such as empowerment, self-organization, popular education and cultural organizing. However, mainstream aided change over the years has increasingly emphasized an 'implementation logic'. This stance focuses mainly on the particularities of change-driving actors (capacity building, accountability, sustainability, etc). The implication has been a shift away from what is actually being achieved. In many contexts, the corresponding invest-ment in the creation of NGO bureaucracies hinders social change rather than triggering it. That is why a CDC approach tends to focus more on the outcomes of empowering processes (social change) rather than mainly on the roles and capacities of its key actors. The CDC framework certainly requires more elaboration in order to cope with partic-ular contexts and value-systems. But the essential shift of effort is to explore more systematically the eventual results of transformative change that benefit the previously excluded and marginalized.

CDC has the potential to link local to global change

Another criticism has been that the CDC framework starts from the assumption that local change will automatically generate change at the global level. At least, it has not been specified how the two are linked. From a CDC perspective transformative change always implies changes taking place in complementary – but seldom synchronized – ways at multiple socio-political scales and tiers. But since CDC takes a perspective of citizen-led change, this obviously is a bottom-up process that is articulated and linked at higher levels. This may be classed as 'romantic'. Which is, indeed, a positive way of looking at it. But, everything 'global' has some form of local manifestation. A CDC approach stresses the fact that local processes of social change will have to engage with each other in order to achieve larger transformations. This point is illustrated as much by Obama's presidential campaign in the 21st century, as it is by the campaigns to abolish slavery and struggles for women's right to vote in the 19th and 20th centuries.

CDC actually does not pretend to be 'new'

The criticism that the CDC approach is 'too academic' and that the authors lack relation-ships with day-to-day reality is simply unfounded. The CDC perspective was elaborated on the basis of reflection on practical engagement and real life cases. But, indeed, many more experiences or 'CDC narratives' will have to be analysed in order to really work towards an academic 'theory' of CDC. What is on paper so far are a range of pointers and ideas worked out in, and emerging from, individual essays. There is no pretension to be a new paradigm of social change. However, it can be argued that a new element signalled by the various comments is a valued recognition of a necessary effort to explore the dynamics of social change that do not initially stem from within an 'aid-driven box'.

Overall, we are pleased that an intended debate is coming on stream and look forward to further initiatives and exchanges in the spirit of critical innovation. A few concluding observations may help stimulate thinking about ways ahead.

CDC Follow-up Activities

The CDC initiative is not alone. As the published materials note, other institutions are tackling similar issues from complementary angles and different scales of enquiry. It may therefore be the moment to bring together these various activities and their lessons in a knowledge-exchange.

The CDC initiative is a work in progress. We think that the following elements would merit more detailed work in the period ahead.

- Tracing the threads of CDC to previous development theories and placing it and them in the 21st century
- Examining more and more experiences through a CDC lens to test both its ideas and substance. Does CDC improve our understanding of how social change occurs and to whose benefit? And, is it practice-relevant?
- Undertaking a thorough look at what a CDC approach implies in terms of existing strategies, policies and practices of public aid agencies. To help in grounding – perhaps different work contexts could be used – from autocratic governance and conflict situations through to stable settings where civic agency is alive and well
- Understanding the system-wide and organizational processes involved in 'interrogating' novel ideas like CDC. How and why do aid-based institutions respond in the way they do when an innovation appears on the landscape? The value of such an effort would be to help leaders of organizational change learn from the experience of others. Given future world scenarios that are likely to require a capability for agility and continuous adaptability, CDC might be a useful 'guinea pig'.

An overarching guide to these types of initiatives is to promote ways in which 1001 CDC stories can be told and shared, including those that are uncivic. We hope that the characteristics of a CDC lens generate new knowledge from reflections on existing practices and cases; that stories are told which cross and connect institutional boundaries. And which increase stories which provide access to and learning about unaided actions by citizens in all walks of life that are dedicated to solving the social, ecological and other problems that are making the world unjust, insecure and unwell.

References

Bieckmann, F. (2008) 'Special Report: Deepening democracy', *The Broker*, No. 7, August.

Boyte, H. (2008a) 'Civic Driven Change and Developmental Democracy', in Fowler, A. and Biekart, K. (eds) *Civic Driven Change: Citizen's Imagination in Action*, pp119–138, Institute of Social Studies, The Hague.

Boyte, H. (2008b) 'Civic Driven Change: Organizing Civic Action', *ISS-CDC Policy Brief*, No. 3, Institute of Social Studies, The Hague.

Fowler, A. and Biekart, K. (2008a) 'Introducing Civic Driven Change', *ISS-CDC Policy Brief*, No. 1, Institute of Social Studies, The Hague.

Fowler, A. and Biekart, K. (2008b) 'Civic Driven Change and Aided Development', *ISS-CDC Policy Brief*, No. 2, Institute of Social Studies, The Hague.

Fowler, A. and Biekart, K. (eds) (2008) *Civic Driven Change: Citizen's Imagination in Action*, Institute of Social Studies, The Hague.

Konijn, P. and van der Ham, A. (2008) 'Civic Driven Change – A New Impetus to the Debate', *ISS-CDC Policy Brief*, No. 5, Institute of Social Studies, The Hague.

Mathie, A. and Cunningham, G. (2008) *From Clients to Citizens: Communities Changing the Course of Their Own Development*, Intermediate Technology, Rugby.

Rai, S. (2008b) 'Civic Driven Change: Facing Risk', *ISS-CDC Policy Brief*, No. 4, Institute of Social Studies, The Hague.

Verkoren, W. (2008) 'Debating Civic Driven Change: People's Power', *The Broker*, No. 10, December.

Useful websites (all last accessed July 2010)

www.iss.nl/cdc
www.ids.ac.uk/citizenshipdrc/
http://democracy.carnegieuktrust.org.uk/civil_society
www.thebrokeronline.eu
www.oxfam.org/en/policy/from_poverty_to_power

Annex 1 Contents of Civic-driven Change: Citizen's Imagination in Action

The following essays can be downloaded at: www.iss.nl/cdc (last accessed July 2010)

1 Civic-driven Change: Citizen's Imagination in Action
  Alan Fowler & Kees Biekart
2 Civic-driven Change and Political Projects
  Evelina Dagnino
3 Civic-driven Change: Spirituality, Religion and Faith
  Philomena Mwaura
4 Six Degrees and Butterflies: Communication, Citizenship and Change
  Alfonso Gumucio-Dagron
5 Civic-driven Change: Of the Law and the Role of Outsiders
  Nilda Bullain
6 Civic Driven Change: Opportunities and Costs
  Shirin Rai
7 Civic Driven Change and Developmental Democracy
  Harry Boyte
8 Civic Driven Change for Deepening Democracy
  Rajesh Tandon
9 Global Civic-driven Democratization as Political Agency
  Teivo Teivainen
10 Civic Driven Change: Implications for Aided Development
  Alan Fowler & Kees Biekart

6

Civic-driven Change and Developmental Democracy[1]

Harry C. Boyte

Too often transformation has come to be seen as a way of compensating previously disadvantaged people rather than creating opportunities for all citizens to contribute their talents, experience and skills to the process of developing our country. Development can't be done 'to' people. People have to become the agents of their own development.

Mamphela Ramphele, 2008

Summary: The Public Work and Workers of Developmental Democracy

Mamphela Ramphele, a former leader of the Black Consciousness Movement, recently a vice president of the World Bank, calls for what can be termed civic-driven change in her new book *Laying Ghosts to Rest: Dilemmas of the Transformation in South Africa*. The book is rich with insights about what it will take to develop capacities of all South Africans to work together. While recognizing the importance of leadership and democratic institutions, it is mainly an argument for bottom-up development that taps the energy and develops the capacities of ordinary people to be 'agents of their own development'. When I worked as a field secretary for his organization in the 1960s, I often heard such views from Martin Luther King, describing 'the unlettered men and women' as 'the real heroes' of the freedom movement.

Though the implications of this perspective for understanding democracy and citizenship need to be drawn out, I am convinced that Ramphele's stress on people becoming the agents of their own development implies a radical shift of meanings from 'representative democracy' and 'participatory democracy' to 'developmental democracy'. This entails a shift from the citizen as a rights-bearing individual whose highest act is voting and demanding government be held accountable, or a citizen who deliberates and participates in civil society, to the citizen as the co-creator of a democratic society and government as catalyst and enabler of civic action.

Representative democracy, which emphasizes rights-based citizenship and free and fair elections, is an enormous achievement. Such democracy has been deepened through the struggle for 'the right to rights', in the excellent phrase that co-writer Evelyn Dagnino borrows from Hannah Arendt as well as through international standards and codes of rights which Nilda Bullain describes. But with its focus on fair distribution of resources – 'who gets what' in the language of mainstream political science – representative democracy and the language of rights alone fuels a consumer culture in which the collaborative 'we' disappears and an omnivorous 'me' takes center stage. Participatory democracy has arisen in recent decades in response, with a stress on rebuilding community, providing venues for citizen voice and regenerating concern for the common good. Jonathan Sacks, chief rabbi of Britain's United Hebrew Congregations, gives wise expression to this view in *The Politics of Hope*. Sacks contrasts the hopeless circumstances of many poor today with his family's background, economically impoverished but rich in cultural and relational resources. He calls for renewal of community. 'Every age has its characteristic preoccupations', he writes. Since the Enlightenment, intellectuals have been concerned to create space for individuals 'to be themselves' against the weight of constricting tradition or totalitarian systems. '[Today] it would be fairer to say that we stand in the opposite situation. In today's liberal democracies, it is not that we are too much together but that we are too much alone and seek to learn again how to connect with others.'[2] Ramphele echoes such views in the South African context, calling for a 'neo-republican' conception of citizenship that involves sacrificing self-interests for the common good.[3]

In contrast, public work, work by the public, in public, for the public, harnesses self-interests to public ends. Representative democracy focuses on structures. Participatory democracy focuses on processes. Developmental democracy focuses on the work of growing capacities for self-directed collective action across differences for problem solving and the creation of individual and common goods. It depends on citizen health

Table 6.1 *Models of democracy*

	Representative democracy	Participatory democracy	Developmental democracy
Who is the citizen?	Voter, consumer, rights bearing individual	Community member	Co-creator – solving problems, co-creating public goods
What are the main tasks?	Fairly distributing rights and services	Strengthening social capital, communicating	Developing civic agency
What is the method?	Mobilizing	Deliberating	Organizing
What is government's role?	Delivering the goods	Promoting community and participation	Catalyst, resource, convener
Tag line	'For the people'	'Of the people'	'By the people'
Who is the government worker?	Service provider	Facilitator	Civic partner, organizer, catalyst
How are self interests understood?	In consumer terms	Put aside for the common good	Integrated and expanded with civic purposes through work
What is power?	Power over	Power with	Power to

workers, teachers, clergy, homemakers, cab drivers, trade unionists, business owners, civil servants and others who recognize the civic potentials of their fellow citizens and are themselves liberated by work with larger meaning and the increase in civic energies such work generates. It conceives of democracy as a society, promoting action across 'state', 'civil society' and 'markets'. It points towards institutional and cultural change.

Understanding citizenship as public work illuminates collaborative work traditions in every society. It draws from religious and social thought including Catholic social teachings, feminism, Jewish philosophy and Marxism. For all their differences these traditions have asserted the dignity and social meaning of work. This lens also highlights how much the public dimensions of work are eroding in a world of invisible home-making, undocumented workers, human trafficking, child labour and dependency-creating expert systems which define people as deficient and needy. To turn this around requires 'organizing' civic action with a strong focus on popular education to develop skills and habits of civic agency. These ideas are expressed in a chart comparing three models of democracy, which build on each other and also produce hybrid forms.

The Re-emergence of Agency

Civic-driven change points to a shift to a bottom up development paradigm in which people are agents of their own development, contrasted with top down development in which people are 'helped' or 'saved' by others, often with the best of progressive and redistributive intentions. The idea is elaborated in the collection of essays, *Culture and Public Action*, by scholars of development, drawing on UN Development Programme and World Bank experiences. As the editors, Vijayendra Rao and Michael Walton put it:

> Although there are disagreements stemming from different paradigms ... there is broad agreement that [we need] a shift from equality of opportunity to 'equality of agency'... creating an enabling environment to provide the poor with the tools, and the voice, to navigate their way out of poverty.[4]

Agency can be defined as the navigational capacities to negotiate and transform the world around us, which is understood to be fluid and open. As Mustafa Emirbayer and Ann Mishe have observed in their detailed treatment, 'What Is Agency?', through most of the 20th century attention to agency 'has been overshadowed by an emphasis upon clear and explicit rules of conduct, concepts that permit relatively little scope for the exercise of situationally based judgment'.

Though it goes against the trends of modern institutions, agency can be understood as a basic 'driver' of human behaviour. Richard M. Ryan and Edward L. Deci, writing in the *American Psychologist*, summarized a considerable body of research that showed while social-contextual conditions dramatically facilitate or forestall the natural tenden-cies towards self-motivation, such self-direction is a basic tendency across cultures. 'Whether people stand behind a behavior out of their interests and values or do it for reasons external to the self, is a matter of significance in every culture and represents a basic dimension by which people make sense of their own and others' behavior.'[5]

Civic agency adds a collective action dimension. It is the capacity not only to direct one's life and shape one's environment but also to collaborate with others across differences to address common challenges and to make a common world. Circumscribed in the 20th century, civic agency was kept alive in community organizing and popular education movements in the Third World, as well as in parts of Europe and the US.

In the early years of the new century civic agency is re-emerging in many settings, the results of the spread of popular education methods and organizing and also new structural changes like the global telecommunications revolution. For instance, it has surfaced in the US presidential election in the campaign of Barack Obama, who has translated the civic agency themes that he learned as a community organizer in Chicago into larger political terms. 'I'm asking you not only to believe in my ability to make change; I'm asking you to believe in yours', reads his website. The concept is expressed in campaign slogans such as 'yes we can', and 'we are the ones we've been waiting for', drawn from a song of the freedom movement of the 1960s. The organizing mindset which promotes agency has found expression in parts of the campaign organization. As Tim Dickinson, a reporter for *Rolling Stone* magazine, put it in a review of the field operation, '[The] goal is not to put supporters to work but to enable them to put themselves to work, without having to depend on the campaign for constant guidance. "We decided that we didn't want to train volunteers", said [campaign field director Temo] Figueros. "We wanted to train *organizers* – folks who can fend for themselves."' In the Obama campaign local participants have far more freedom to innovate and organize than is usual in election efforts, in which messages and action scripts are typically handed down from on high. Obama has also started to articulate what a focus on civic agency might mean in policy terms. Thus, his speech on 23 May 2008 in Miami challenged the Bush foreign policy doctrine towards the Americas. Obama said that 'It is not enough to come to the defense of freedom with epic and intermittent efforts when it is threatened at moments that appear critical. Every moment is critical for the defense of freedom'. He sketched a vision for a new paradigm with resemblance to Ramphele's. 'After decades pressing for top-down reform, we need an agenda that advances democracy, security, and opportunity from the bottom up.'

An organizing perspective also helps to illuminate 'what's gone wrong' in civic life.

Technocratic Creep

Intellectuals from different traditions have described how humans develop and express agency through 'work', understood as the activity of transforming the world around us and ourselves in the process. They have also detailed obstacles. Karl Marx denounced modern factory life in which 'the individual characteristics of workers are obliterated' and machines themselves 'appear as a world for themselves quite independent of and divorced from the individuals'. The modern women's movement helped to bring out of the shadows the hidden labors, injustices and generative qualities of women's work.

In a similar vein, in his major statement *On Human Labor*, which impacted workers from Poland to Latin America, the late Pope John Paul II argued that work most importantly is 'subjective'; that is, work's most important outcome is not 'objective' products but rather how well work serves human development. John Paul described this development as three dimensional: how much work develops human capacities; how much work helps people forge social solidarity with others; and how much work provides opportunities for people to add through co-creative effort to the common store of their societies and humanity as a whole. John Paul also detailed many obstacles to such development.

Recent studies such as Robert Putnam's *Bowling Alone* have shown the erosion of many forms of civic life in the US. And critics have proposed a variety of explanations, from the influence of television to the rise of consumer culture and growing inequalities. All have merit. But a work-centred civic agency view adds other dimensions. It shows how technocracy, control by outside experts, has eroded people's civic development as professionals have lost respect for local knowledge and people's capacities.

Technocracy is widespread in a 'service economy'. To use the analysis of the Asset Based Community Development Institute (where Michelle Obama has long been a faculty member), the dominant service economy trains professionals to look at people and poor communities in terms of their deficiencies, not their capacities. This generates a culture of rescue. As a result, institutions that once were civic meeting grounds became providers of services. Even such deeply rooted popular institutions as religious congregations have suffered from this pattern. As community organizers often quip, ministers are taught to see everyone as 'walking wounded' in need of pastoral care. The South African public intellectual Xolela Mangcu, writing out of the Black Consciousness Movement tradition, calls all this 'technocratic creep'.

In the US, technocratic creep has been at work for many decades and higher education bears a significant share of the responsibility. Higher education educates professionals to be mobile individualists, detached from the communities in which they work and the cultures from which they come, who see people in terms of their deficiencies. The historian Thomas Bender calls this shift over the last 50 years in the US the change from 'civic professionalism' to 'disciplinary professionalism'. Technocracy also dominates in African, Latin American or Asian universities with global aspirations.

Technocratic creep has refashioned professional education to be narrowly disciplinary. For instance, in seminaries and divinity schools, according to Mary Fulkerson, a professor at Duke Divinity School who studies theological education in the US and Europe, the 'practice courses' typically pertain to matters internal to the life of the congregation, such as preaching, counselling and church organization. Teaching skills and habits needed to engage with places where congregations are located is slighted. Philamena Mwaura tells me that the pattern is similar across Africa

Similarly, the pattern that Joe Nathan, director of the Center for School Change at the Humphrey Institute, observes about US teacher education applies to South Africa. Teacher education curricula typically include little or nothing on learning to work collaboratively with parents and other stakeholders, who have often far different backgrounds and interests. When such learning is absent, graduates come to understand themselves as detached experts providing service *for* people, not as citizens working *with* fellow citizens on public problems.

In a recent issue of *Change* magazine, Parker Palmer described the weak sense of civic agency and the posture of 'value free' practice that result from student experiences in US higher education. 'The hidden curriculum of our culture portrays institutions as powers *other* than us, over which we have marginal control at best.' Palmer continues:

We turn our graduates loose on the world as people who *know* but do not *recognize* that our justice system often fails the poor ... that practical politics is more about manipulating public opinion than discerning the will of the people ... that science and technology are not neutral.[6]

The power dynamics of technocracy are disguised by the fact that dominating experts are full of egalitarian and inclusive intentions to 'help'. A 1989 lecture at the University of Illinois by Donna Shalala, then chancellor of the University of Wisconsin, soon to be Secretary of Health and Human Services in the Clinton administration, illustrated this. Shalala made an impassioned plea for public service and social justice, for struggles against racism and sexism, for environmentalism and peace. She called for public universities to engage the world. Her good intentions were palpable – and tied explicitly to technocracy. For her, 'the ideal [is] a disinterested technocratic elite' fired by the moral mission of 'society's best and brightest in service to its most needy'. The imperative was 'delivering the miracles of social science' to fix society's problems 'just as doctors cured juvenile rickets in the past'.

However suffused with good intentions, the rescue approach is the opposite of an agency approach – for both professionals and non-professionals. Most people have little to do except to give thanks (or to complain if they don't like the cure), while professionals are burdened with the total responsibility. Technocratic professionalism undermines the confidence of people without credentials, degrees and university training, while devaluing their talents and capacities. It shapes a citizenry who are needy clients, in Rajesh Tandon's terms, not co-producers. Technocracy calcifies settings which once served as sources of civic learning, turning not only schools, but also congregations, unions, non-profits and government agencies into service delivery operations. This dynamic renders civic life as off-hours activities in 'civil society' like 'volunteering' or 'community service', seen as oases of civic ideals and decency in a degraded world.

As civic muscle weakened, progressive politics became 'mass politics' that emphasizes redistributive justice, rights and a consumer view of the citizen. Mass politics is based on what Steve Fraser in *Rise and Fall of the New Deal Order* called the concept of 'a new man – existentially mobile, more oriented to consumption than production, familiar with the impersonal rights and responsibilities of industrial due process'. This politics 'was inconceivable apart from a political elite in command of the state, committed to a programme of enlarged government spending, financial reform, and redistributive taxation, presiding over a reconstituted coalition in the realm of mass politics'.[7]

Mass politics crystallized in the mobilizing approaches to citizen action and elections that emerged in the 1970s in the US. Mobilizing includes the door to door canvass (going house to house to raise money and get petition signatures for an issue), direct mail fundraising and, recently, internet and other electronic mobilizations. All are based on a formula: find an enemy to demonize, stir up emotion with inflammatory language, create a 'script' that defines the issue as good versus evil and shuts down critical thought. Mobilizing, implicitly or explicitly, conveys the idea that elites will save the victims. Mobilizing approaches more subtly shape professional practices and identities in many ways. This is because higher education generally prepares students to be mobile individualists, detached from the communities in which they work and the cultures from which they come. Who see people in terms of their deficiencies, not capacities and who learn few skills of collaborative work in which experts are 'on tap not on top'. Professionals characteristically learn to 'mobilize'. They seek to activate groups around goals and objectives they have determined in advance.

Such approaches fail to address complex problems that require work across lines of difference, public judgement, and imaginative collective action. These problems especially plague the Third World, from organized crime syndicates to sectarian violence and global warming, from trafficking in women to pandemics and poverty. Mobilizing approaches leave governance and economic systems unchanged – or, even worse, they foster cultures of guilt and rescue among professionals. They do not develop agency.

A great challenge of our time is to develop a civic agency politics as an alternative to technocratic politics, a politics in which people are not empowered *by* leaders but rather empower themselves, developing skills and habits of collaborative action, changing institutions and systems to make them more supportive of civic agency.

Stories of such politics are beginning to appear in many settings. These stories illustrate how professionals' self-interests are not inevitably narrow or static. Contrary to the arguments of some critics, professionals have multiple interests, not simply increasing their 'market share' of social life. Organizing liberates both professionals and amateurs.

Organizing, Popular Education and Liberation through Public Work

> The world is deluged with panaceas, formulas, proposed laws, machineries, ways out, and myriads of solutions. It is significant and tragic that almost every one of these proposed plans and alleged solutions deals with the structure of society, but none concerns the substance – the people. This, despite the eternal truth of the democratic faith that the solution always lies with the people.[8]

In his 1946 book *Reveille for Radicals,* Saul Alinsky, sometimes called the father of modern community organizing, was passionately restating the basic organizing and popular education tradition and its animating faith. Alinsky's ideas were rooted in the great organizing and civic efforts of the Great Depression and the Second World War, especially those activists and public intellectuals who liked 'popular front' organizing but didn't like Soviet-style Marxism. Though his experiences were in the US, they were also part of the global 'people's fronts' that gave birth to national liberation and independence movements across the Third World, like the Freedom Charter movement in South Africa.

Organizing is tied to popular education, democratic learning methods with an emphasis on civic agency. In the US, popular education in the 1930s included labour schools, study circles and folk schools like the Highlander Folk School in Tennessee, a popular education centre founded by Myles Horton who had travelled through Scandinavia to study the schools. Highlander trained many civil rights leaders including Rosa Parks and Martin Luther King. Rajesh Tandon reports that he also spent time at Highlander before founding PRIA. Highlander initiated the Citizenship Education Program (CEP), taken over by SCLC in 1961 that I worked for as a young man.

In Scandinavia, folk schools generated cultures rich in adaptive and innovative resources, norms and behaviours with implications for civic-driven change. Marie Ström of Idasa in her study of folk schools, popular libraries and study circles in Sweden has shown how they played a powerful role in the transformation of the nation from a very poor society into a society of abundance. Folk schools, originating in the 19th century, were closely associated with communities in which they were located, and communities had a strong sense of ownership in the schools. Today 147 folk schools are owned by a wide variety of groups, including municipalities and organizations like the Red Cross.

They have a particular focus on educating marginalized and vulnerable groups such as new immigrants, ex-offenders, unemployed, disabled people, older people with little schooling and youth who have dropped out of state schools. 'Far from offering a second-rate education, they tend to serve as a kind of avant-garde. Innovations in methodology and curriculum from the folk schools have often been adopted over time by the formal educational system.' Folk schools form the grounding for associated study circles, self-directed learning groups that operate on an enormous scale in Sweden (one-quarter of the adult population participate each year). In both folk schools and study circles people 'develop high levels of accountability both in terms of taking responsibility for realizing their personal learning objectives and participating in a broader learning community'. Popular education emphasis 'developing citizen competence and building a culture of democracy' and translates to encouragement of learners 'to develop a public orientation to their learning, nurturing a sense of public purpose whatever the topic of study may be and building commitment and confidence to shape a public world'. Popular education takes participants 'beyond the role of consumers and spectators' to unlock creative energies, deepen members' sense of who they are, develop intellectual life, and foster skills of dealing with diversity'.[9]

One can see all these elements today in the Abahlali movement and the 'University of Abahlali', a remarkable organizing and self-directed popular education movement in South Africa created by tens of thousands of shack dwellers in 34 townships in Kwa Zulu Natal. Fighting for land and housing, an end to forced removals and access to education, water, electricity, sanitation, health care and refuse removal, the Abahlali movement has also been at the forefront of fighting xenophobic violence. Sympathetic professionals and intellectuals play a variety of roles, but 'on tap, not on top', in the organizing phrase. In its mode of organizing, Abahlali has impacted civic life, gender relations and governance, as well as creating a cosmopolitan culture that asserts the humanity of immigrants.[10] It has also developed the concept of 'living politics' contrasted with 'party politics'. 'Abahlali has been an intellectually serious project from the beginning', reads the website. 'Our struggle is thought in action', says S'bu Zikode, one of Abahlali's leaders. 'We define ourselves and our struggle.'

In the last generation, community organizing with popular education has developed in networks like the Industrial Areas Foundation, PICO, the Gamaliel Foundation, and DART in the US. These have counterparts in developing nations in groups like PRIA, Church Based Community Organization, the grassroots training efforts of Idasa in South Africa and other African countries and HakiElimu in Tanzania. Organizing groups focus on developing people's public skills and capacities.

Organizing and popular education have normative dimensions, infused with values such as inclusion, equality, cooperation, work, dignity and freedom. But they begin 'where people are at', not where organizers think they should be. Organizing and popular education develop concepts, methods and learning environments ('free spaces') in which people shape for themselves a more inclusive understanding of themselves and 'the people' as they develop confidence, skills and public life. Organizing is always grounded in the cultural life of communities.

In organizing, people learn the skills of engaging others' self-interests, understood not as selfishness but rather as each person's unique stories, passions and relationships rooted in everyday life. People learn to map power in different situations. They become attentive to the dangers that Shirin Rai describes, which come from an idealized sense of possibility. Organizing stresses the necessity of holding in tension 'the world as it is' and 'the world as it should be' and living on the border between the two poles, the pre-figurative Ghandian challenge of 'being the change you want to see in the world' observed by Teivo Teivainen.

In organizing, people learn to understand human complexity and human potential, the immensely rich stories and motivations of others of different income, religious, cultural or partisan backgrounds. They refrain from quick ideological or categorical judgements, and learn to negotiate diverse institutional interests. They do not put aside anger and disagreement. Citizen politics often surfaces conflicts that were previously submerged. But they learn to contain quarrels and discipline anger, to avoid violence and to produce public outcomes of general benefit. People learning organizing skills and habits become adept at creating what are called 'public relationships' across differences for the sake of public action, even with those they once saw as enemies. They learn to think in long term and strategic ways. They pay close attention to local cultures and networks. Finally, at its broadest, organizing changes institutions and also cultures, returning them to earlier insights.

Through diverse partnerships, the Center for Democracy and Citizenship has found it useful to conceptualize organizing and popular education as 'public work'. Public work is sustained effort by a mix of ordinary people who develop capacities to work across differences to create things of lasting civic value. Public work is work 'in public', visible, open to inspection, whose significance is widely recognized. It is cooperative effort of 'a public', a group whose interests, backgrounds, views and resources may be quite different. Public work is at the heart of organizing, both requiring and developing civic agency. It also revives older concepts of 'citizen professionals' who see themselves as on tap, not on top. Citizen professionals take pride in their knowledge and craft, but they shift from the deficiency mindset that erodes civic muscle to an appreciation of the abundant potentials of ordinary people.[11]

The following two stories illustrate public work and the civic agency it develops. They also point towards a systems approach attentive to the potential role(s) of culture shaping institutions such as the media and higher education in developing citizen professionals.

Nehemiah Homes[12]

The Nehemiah Homes organizing effort was undertaken by East Brooklyn Churches, an affiliate of the Industrial Areas Foundation, or IAF. The IAF is a network of large-scale citizen organizations made up of poor, lower and middle class groups. IAF is much like Obama's former network, the Gamaliel Foundation.

IAF organizing went through two stages of development after the death of its founder, Saul Alinsky, in 1972. Organizers and local leaders sought to ground the organizing process more deeply in community institutions and value traditions, preeminently those of local religious congregations of mainstream Catholic, Protestant, Jewish and more recently Muslim orientation. Such a development gave rise to 'value based organizing'. Value-based organizing weds the struggle for agency to communal values and communal fabric. It was accompanied by a shift in the theory of leadership from positional leaders to 'relational leaders', enlisting groups of community sustainers, most often women, who maintain the networks and relationships of community life, who are almost never central in mobilizing politics. In my observations, the public confidence and skills which women gain through organizing and public work often significantly lessens 'private' injustices, such as domestic violence.

As these groups experienced growing successes and began to think about larger rationale, they added a second dimension to their self-awareness, coming to understand themselves as 'schools for public life'. Schools of public life are settings where people learn civic skills which are much more multidimensional than voting or protest and where people develop new intellectual life. They experience what Doran Schrantz, a leading organizer in the Gamaliel Foundation, calls 'public growth'.

East Brooklyn Churches (EBC) is a citizen organization based largely among African American churches in impoverished neighborhoods of Brooklyn, New York. The group began modestly in 1978 with a small group of Catholic and Protestant clergy and laity to discuss the formidable array of community issues they faced. They followed the organizing dictum to start with small 'winnable' issues around which poor and powerless people can experience confidence-building success and develop clear-eyed assessment of risks (the approach that Shirin Rai urges). EBC members forced clean-ups of rotten meat in local food stores, pressured the city to install hundreds of street signs, forced renovation of local parks and worked together to clean up vacant lots. Slowly they forged a sense of solidarity and potency. 'We are not a grassroots organization', thundered the Rev. Johnny Ray Youngblood, a key leader in the organization, at one rally. 'Grass roots are shallow roots. Grass roots are fragile roots. *Our* roots are deep roots. Our roots have fought for existence in the shattered glass of East New York.'

In the early 1980s, EBC took on a project to build thousands of houses affordable for working class and low income people, a scale that dwarfed not only their own prior activities but any other low income housing development initiative in the country. The EBC turned to housing out of the conviction that only widespread home ownership could create the kind of 'roots' essential for renewed community pride and freedom from fear. Teaming up with a well-known newspaper columnist and former developer, I.D. Robbins, they adopted his controversial argument that for half the cost of high-density, high rise apartments, it would be possible to build large numbers of single family homes, owned by low income families that could create stable neighbourhood anchors.

EBC named their undertaking the 'Nehemiah Plan', recalling the Old Testament prophet sent back to Jerusalem by the King of Persia in 420 BC to lead in the rebuilding of the city after the Babylonian captivity. Nehemiah was a skillful politician as well as apparently a great orator. He gained permission from the king of Persia in 446 BC to return to Jerusalem in order to lead the Jews in rebuilding the city walls. 'You see the trouble we are in; Jerusalem is in ruins, its gates have been burned down', he told the assembled crowd. Nehemiah did not present himself as a Moses-like rescuer. Rather, he called people to work and helped develop their capacities for such work. 'Come, let us rebuild the walls of Jerusalem and suffer this indignity no longer.' The people responded. 'Let us start! Let us build.' The Bible recounts that 'with willing hands they set about the good work' (Nehemiah 2, verses 17–18).

During the Babylonian captivity, enemies of the Jews had multiplied. Jews persevered in the face of ridicule and posted guards against plots. More subtly, rebuilding the walls required civic restoration. A culture of greed and instant gratification had produced fragmentation and a decline in morale in the community. Nehemiah held together a motley crew – 40 different groups are named – including merchants, priests, governors, nobles, members of the perfume and goldsmiths' guilds and women. At one point he organized a great assembly to call to account nobles making excessive profit from the poor. As the Jewish people rebuilt their walls, they renewed their purpose and identity.

The cultural aspects of the Nehemiah story held important lessons for the East Brooklyn Churches group. 'The story connected our work to something real, not something bogus', explained Mike Gecan, EBC organizer. 'It got it out of the "housing" field and the idea that you have to have a bureaucracy with 35 consultants to do anything. It made it a "nonprogram", something more than housing.' As the EBC leader Celina Jamieson put it, 'We are more than a Nehemiah Plan. We are about the central development of dignity and self-respect.' Like the biblical story, 'Nehemiah' symbolized the regeneration of community and civic life and a sense of shared control over the future.

Although the group had financial commitments from an impressive array of backers, the project's success depended on city funding for a loan pool. Early in 1982, they had waited for weeks for word from the New York mayor Edward Koch about whether he would support their plans. He refused to meet with them, citing a negative experience with a sister organization in the Queens area of New York. Leaders held a press conference to publicize his indecision. That evening, the local CBS television affiliate broadcast clips of the desolate area, while an announcer read from the Book of Nehemiah: 'You see the trouble we are in, how Jerusalem lies in ruins with its gates burned. Come, let us build the wall of Jerusalem, that we may no longer suffer disgrace.' Viewers were outraged and audience reaction was immense. The following day, Mayor Koch declared himself the new Nehemiah and pledged his support for the effort. He gave Nehemiah speeches for several months thereafter. Thousands of Poles and Italians and other ethnics from Catholic parishes in Queens joined an interfaith religious celebration at the groundbreaking of the first Nehemiah homes. Nearly 4000 were built, and it became the spark for national low-income housing legislation.

The story suggests lessons of successful civic initiative: public work politics that is visible, large in import, involves a variety of people, generates a different model of civic leadership and uses government tools but is not dependent upon government services, can change people's sense of themselves and produce also new 'citizen professionals'.

A story with some parallels has taken shape in recent years in the neighborhoods surrounding Indiana University Purdue University Indianapolis (IUPUI).

He believes that while global consciousness and connections are important – fostered by an international public university – public work also depends on a vital sense of place. 'Public work is local work through the institutions of communities – clubs,

> ## Box 6.1 *Overcoming a legacy of bitterness: IUPUI and WESCO*[13]
>
> William Plater was Executive Vice Chancellor of the IUPUI from 1987, four years after he arrived there, until 2006 when he left that post to work full time on international community development for the university. He has become a key leader in the higher education movement to 're-engage' with the life of communities and their populations in respectful, reciprocal, sustained fashion, carrying with him the values and practices he learned as a student activist in the civil rights movement of the 1960s. Plater has become a champion of what he describes as the public work method for public engagement of universities, elaborating the concept in the process. In his view public work is voluntary, non-coerced action for the public good. It generates a variety of civic outcomes and enlists a myriad of civic talents. He argues that 'When all citizens are included in the possibility of acting together for the common good, the things they do and the assets they create are always greater than what government alone can do.' He sees public work as a means to realize values of inclusion, equality and productive contribution. 'Public work recognizes the individual citizen – and not only her elected representative – as a relevant, valued, and even powerful co-creator of the democratic process. This is the generative power of inclusiveness because it engages everyone who would participate, and because ideas, projects, actions and works produced do not depend on government or on enfranchisement through voting status. Youth, immigrants, religious minorities and – in some places still – women can contribute equally with voting citizens, even when they are officially excluded from political processes.'

schools, non-profit organizations, businesses and corporations, religious organizations, sports and voluntary groups of all kinds, even when it reaches to other places in other nations.' Finally, Plater believes civic agency – 'the capacity of ordinary people to act on their own behalf without relying on experts or deferring to the mystique of the technical or the professional' – builds capacity to do public work. 'Civic agency is the means to achieve public work, and it has skills, methods and capacities that can be taught and learned.'

Translating values he learned as an activist in the civil rights movement to higher education turned out to be a process over years filled with conflict and learning.

In the 1960s and 1970s, IUPUI expanded rapidly. The school now has more than 30,000 students and includes one of the two largest medical schools in the United States. As it expanded, hundreds of families were displaced from the surrounding neighbourhoods, which once formed a vital center of small businesses, jazz clubs and street life. Most of those displaced were African American, low income whites and Mexican Americans. In their view the university, working with local government, had manipulated building and traffic regulations, political boundaries, school placements and other levers to move them out, across the White River. In the Westside neighbourhoods across the river bitterness and resentment was widespread. When Plater met community residents in the mid-1980s at the performance of a student-created play, *The Bridge*, about what had happened, he heard story after story of anger. 'Families got up and told stories about how they had been moved about, about the sense of loss they felt and the fragmentation that had occurred.' Anger and despair was passed on to children and grandchildren.

In the late 1980s, a group of neighbourhood residents and organizations decided to reverse the downward spiral. They created a community organization, the Westside Cooperative Organization (WESCO). They took advantage of a variety of resources created by the city of Indianapolis, a leader in the local government movement for collaborative civic work. It is worth noting the motivation of the local government in Indianapolis, driven by self-interests of local officials who want to get productive work done. As Matt Leighninger, who has worked closely with the National League of Cities and hundreds of local communities in the new movement for 'shared governance' observes, 'Practitioners in planning, education, law enforcement, human relations, environmental protection, housing, economic development and public health are realizing that they need more support if they are going to succeed.'[14]

Organizing gave people new hope and power. 'We began to realize that we as a community had value in ourselves', said Olgen Williams, president of the group. 'We could make changes. We empowered ourselves and things began to look a little better.' WESCO was able to create a non-profit economic development corporation, to address crime and to look at improving schools. This created a background to work with IUPUI in a new way. 'We asked them to come to have a conversation with us about how we could work together to create a better community and a stronger urban university', said Williams. On the university side, Plater voiced strong verbal support and backed it up with university commitment of resources. University cooperation with the community was based on three principles, according to Plater:

- The first principle was a candid statement that the university wanted to join the neighbourhoods out of self-interest because the proximity of a poor community with a high crime rate was adversely affecting its ability to attract students from the suburbs and other regions. This principle of mutual benefit was articulated on both sides; parties had things they wanted to get out of working with each other.

- The second principle was based on reciprocity and the idea that the community had something of equal value to contribute along with the university's expertise, resources and access to power in local and state governments ... The greatest asset was the emergence of talented, natural leaders who found their voice and the respect of their neighbours in the process of talking about what to do. In 'speaking truth to power', their civic agency established them as co-equals with government officials and experts.

- The third principle was sustainability and a commitment of the neighbours to each other to persist even when enthusiasm waned and specific initiatives failed. This required a commitment from the university that its involvement was not defined by the length of a semester term when students were assigned class projects in the neighbourhood or the duration of a research grant when faculty wanted to study someone or something. The only way to prove the principle was through time, but the commitment of the university took the form of providing a full-time staff member whose role was to attend meetings, to listen and to participate as a member of the community – not as a faculty member with expertise or a student doing a project or an administrator with some hidden agenda for renting space or creating a medical waste recycling center.

Many community projects have emerged from the process, including the opening of the first public schools in many years, a new library, a health clinic, a bank, a grocery store and other businesses. Community residents have developed a plan to turn a formal mental hospital into a park and zone for economic development. There has been a significant increase in school retention and college attendance among young people. But the most important changes may be attitudinal. Plater says that the years of public work collaborating with the community in a variety of ways has significantly impacted attitudes and approaches of staff, faculty, students and whole professional programs. '[Community engagement] is now a matter of pride at IUPUI', he observes. Significant changes have taken place on the community side as well. 'The people are comfortable on the community side that the university is not going to come over across the river and take this whole community over', argues Williams. 'There is room for us to co-exist. We have trust and communication now, whereas before they ignored us. We are also more educated and knowledgeable about how to do business with the powers that be.'

Transformative Leadership

I agree with Rakesh Rajani's assessment that in a turbulent world of growing dangers, 'Small is no longer beautiful.' The stories of Nehemiah and the WESCO-IUPUI partnership hold lessons about how to promote large system change.

Mamphela Ramphele describes the challenges. She calls for 'credible, visionary leadership that expands the boundaries of possibilities for all citizens'.[15] She also details enormous obstacles in the way. In Africa, many liberation leaders 'delinked' themselves from poor people in the fight for freedom, either in exile or through alienation from families and communities. Against the background of North Atlantic condescension and the vast humiliations of colonial rule, 'Making it [became] associated with leaving the village, the township, even the language of one's community.' Too often Third World leaders look to Western models. Such detachment is reinforced by patterns of learning and identity formation in many school systems and higher education.

To use an ecological analogy, just as environmental work involves restorations of wetlands and other habitats, the long range task of civic renewal requires a systems point of view. Systems thinking looks at forces of change as a dynamic, interconnected whole; it emphasizes the influences of the parts on each other and the way they function together, generating an overall direction to a given system. A systems approach contrasts with the event-oriented perspective that dominates in most policy fields. This linear perspective examines a particular problem or event in sequential terms without taking into account the larger patterns out of which events emerge. In a case often used by systems theorists, if six drops of reagent are needed to achieve crystallization in an experiment, an event-oriented causal analysis would conclude that the first five drops were ineffective and the last drop caused the change. In this view, the way in which the accumulating drops work together to create the change is ignored. In contrast, a systems view is about finding the right vantage with which to understand the dynamic properties of a whole system.[16]

From a systems perspective, the long-range tasks of civic renewal must not only address the symptoms of civic decline, but also must go upstream to the roots of the problem, changing major institutions of culture formation and developing new generations of citizen professionals who respect people's capacities for self-organization and self-empowerment and learn skills of collaborative public work. Both Nehemiah and the

IUPUI story show how public work can transform identities and practices so that leaders come to see people in terms of their talents, not their deficiencies, and themselves as 'on tap not on top'. It is useful to conclude with a group focused on this process.

The Cultural Wellness Center

In Minneapolis, Minnesota, the Powderhorn Phillips Cultural Wellness Center (CWC) explicitly challenges the dominant values of acquisitive individualism by promoting and revitalizing 'indigenous' values as a source of strength, health, and wellbeing and it prepares community leaders who share this view. The Cultural Wellness Center is located in a bank building on the border of the Powderhorn and Phillips neighbourhoods. This is the most culturally diverse area in Minnesota, with the largest combined concentration of African Americans, Native Americans, Asians and Latinos. The neighborhoods also include many people from European American backgrounds.

It began in the mid-1990s, when Atum Azzahir, a leader in the culturally grounded 'Way to Grow' initiative teamed up with Mike Christianson, director of the giant Medica Health Plans. They explored the idea of focusing on one place, South Minneapolis, through the prism of her core philosophy, and Medica provided financial resources.

'Rather than focusing on what was wrong with Black people – that they have high infant mortality rates, and other public health problems – I wanted to explore the other side: Why it is that some children live and flourish in the exact same conditions?' she says. 'What are the sources of resilience? What is it that gave us as African American people the capacity sometimes to transcend oppressive conditions?'

The principles behind CWC's philosophy, what they call the People's Theory of Sickness, include the idea that people are responsible for their own recovery and healing, that community provides the container and the resources for living a healthy life and that connection to culture and a sound identity transform the historical trauma of racism. Azzahir and Janice Barbee, who came to her own commitment to cultural restoration after seeing her family, of Welsh descent, buffeted by the medical system, spent two years holding conversations with different cultural communities. They discovered that other cultural groups – Hmong, Latinos, Native Americans and European Americans as well – had similar issues. 'I know of the collective aloneness of the African American because I am a member of this group', said Azzahir, 'but to hear the Dakota, Lakota, Nakota and Ojibwe people, Mexican and Hmong American people speak of their deep sense of disconnectedness and aloneness has amazed me. I thought these groups had culture, language and a home base, even if they didn't control it. I became more and more driven to be a part of and give direction to an effort to alleviate this condition for these great peoples of ancient heritage.'

The CWC prepares transformative leadership. For instance, its Invisible College explicitly addresses the meaning of education for people of all ages by conveying a different view of 'educator' and 'education'. This involves an extensive series of class offerings, including cultural competence courses for health professionals. It also consciously challenges the overly expert centered education dominant today. Thus, a class on old ways of parenting begins with parents asking what kind of values and practices they want to teach their children, how they want them to grow up and what their traditions have to say about preparing children to contribute to community life. This, in Azzahir's account, helps families – many of whom feel marginalized by public school educators – reclaim their heritage as a source of wisdom and power.[17]

Strategic mapping of possibilities for leadership development in the US has drawn our attention to networks such as the regionally based schools of the American Association of State Colleges and Universities (AASCU), an association with an explicit commitment to becoming reconnected with local communities and developing the civic agency of students. The Center for Democracy and Citizenship and AASCU have launched a Civic Agency Project to strengthen education of students to be 'stewards of place', professionals attentive to the assets of communities and the talents of others.

Conclusion

For all the differences between North Atlantic societies and the Global South, there are also many parallels when it comes to building civic agency, developing facilitative environments and creating new visions of democratic society. New initiatives by donors that support development of civic agency, schools for public life and transformative civic leadership among poor populations can help address the greatest challenges for the 21st century: how to tap and vastly expand the civic talents and energies of whole societies to address multiplying problems that no expert systems or government agencies can begin to 'fix' by themselves; how to reverse patterns of civic decay and regenerate civic muscle. Support for initiatives that change cultures of poverty and despair into places of agency, abundance and hope can help provide inspiration and guidance for us all.

Notes

1   Many thanks to Paul Graham, Marie Ström, Gerald Taylor, Xolela Mangcu, Alan Fowler, Kees Biekart, Allert van den Ham, Fons van der Velden, Sharin Rai, Evelina Dagnino, Rakesh Rajani, Philamena Mwaura, William Plater and Paul van Hoof for feedback on this chapter and public work concepts in relation to development. Graham suggests developmental democracy as also 'constructive democracy'.

2   Jonathan Sacks, 2000, *The Politics of Hope,* Vintage, London.

3   Mamphela Ramphele, 2008, *Laying Ghosts to Rest: Dilemmas of the Transition in South Africa,* p147, Tafelberg, Cape Town.

4   Vijayendra Rao and Michael Walton (eds) 2006, *Culture and Public Action,* pp. 26, 259, Stanford University Press/World Bank.

5   Richard M. Ryan and Edward L. Deci, 2000, 'Self-Determination Theory and the Facilitation of Intrinsic Motivation, Social Development and Well-Being', *American Psychologist,* Vol. 55:1, p69.

6   Parker Palmer, 2007, 'A New Professional: The Aims of Education Revisited', *Change* November–December, p4, www.carnegiefoundation.org/change/ (last accessed June 2010).

7   Steven Fraser and Gary Gerstle, (Eds), 1989, *The Rise and Fall of the New Deal Order: 1930– 1980,* p70, Princeton University Press, Princeton.

8   Saul Alinsky, 1946, *Revielle for Radicals,* Vintage Press, New York.

9   Marie-Louise Ström (ed), 2008, Living and Learning Democracy: Nonformal Adult Education in Sweden and South Africa, Institute for Democracy in South Africa, Cape Town.
10 See www.abahlali.org (last accessed June 2010).
11 *The Citizen Solution* describes examples of citizen professionals from whom we have learned, such as William (Bill Doherty), a family therapist whose shift from 'service delivery' to 'community organizing' has generated striking movements among families. Albert Dzur describes a fledging citizen or democratic professional movement in his book *Democratic Professionalism*, and this is a major theme in Michael Edwards' work as well. Public work practices can be found in the cultural histories of many other societies. There are many African parallels to public work in the US. In Sesotho, the term *letsema* means cooperative village work on common projects and in isiZulu, *ilimo* is a close equivalent. In Xhosa, *dibanisani* means 'let's work together for a better future', while in Afrikaans, *saamspan* means 'let's get to work'. In Swahili the phrase *kidole kimoja hakivunji chawa* – literally, one finger cannot kill the lice – is used to convey the importance of cooperative work on a project.
12 Adapted from Harry C. Boyte, 1989, *Common Wealth: A Return to Citizen Politics,* Free Press, New York.
13 The following account is taken from 'Habits of Living: Building an Inclusive Society through Public Work, Civic Agency, Voluntary Action, and Academic Diplomacy', a speech delivered by William M. Plater at the 2nd UCLG ASPAC Congress on July 15, 2008, in Pattaya, Thailand; and also US Department of Housing and Urban Development, The Power of Partnership: 1994–2004, www.oup.org/files/pubs/copc10.pdf, pp98–101 (last accessed June 2010).
14 Matt Leighninger, 2006, *The Next Form of Democracy: How Expert Rule Is Giving Way to Shared Governance*, Vanderbilt University Press Nashville.
15 Ramphele, 2007, pp295, 301.
16 Here, as Teivo Teivainen observes, factors of scale, boundaries of inclusion and the negotiating the politics of 'open space' become critical for the progress of civic agency towards a new type of politics and democracy.
17 Adapted from The Citizen Solution.

Bibliography

Thomas Bender, 1993, *Intellect and Public Life: Essays on the Social History of Academic Intellectuals in the United States*, John Hopkins University Press, Baltimore, MD

Harry C. Boyte, 2008, *The Citizen Solution: How You Can Make A Difference*, Minnesota Historical Society Press, St Paul

Harry C. Boyte, 2008 'Against the Current: Developing the Civic Agency of Students,' *Change: The Magazine of Higher Learning*, May/June, available at www.carnegiefoundation.org/change/ (last accessed June 2010)

Albert Dzur, 2008, *Democratic Professionalism: Citizen Participation and the Reconstruction of Professional Ethics, Identity, and Practice*, Pennsylvania State University Press, University Park

Michael Edwards, 2004, *Civil Society*, Polity Press, London

Nan Kari and Nan Skelton, (Eds), 2007, *Voices of Hope: The Story of the Jane Addams School for Democracy*, Kettering Foundation, Dayton OH

Peter Levine, 2007, *The Future of Democracy: Developing the Next Generation of American Citizens*, Tufts University Press, Boston

Xolela Mangcu, 2008, *To the Brink*, University of KwaZulu Natal, Durban

7

Civil Society and the Legitimation of Global Governance

Jan Aart Scholte

Introduction

Contemporary history would attest to the importance of effective global governance for the good of any society. And it is widely supposed – by activists, officials and researchers alike – that, by engaging with civil society, the shortcomings of global regulatory institutions can be redressed. In particular, the participation of civil society would enhance the legitimacy of those agencies. It is believed that civil society involvement could inject values and voice that bolster the moral and democratic authority of global governance. In addition, civil society associations could – through the provision of vital information, insights and methods – enhance the technical performance of global governance agencies. Furthermore, civil society initiatives could promote the formalization of those global governance activities that have previously operated with little or no legal frameworks. Civil society associations could moreover support charismatic leaders for global governance, albeit hopefully executive heads who also follow a moral, democratic, competent and legal course.

Yet does the record fulfil these hopes and expectations? How far have the activities of civil society in practice advanced the legitimacy of global regulation to date? What do the experiences of several decades of intensified civil society engagement with global governance institutions suggest regarding ways to enhance these legitimation effects in the future?

This chapter argues that – although there are of course considerable variations across different global governance institutions and different civil society initiatives – the general picture has been one of but partially realized potentials of legitimacy promotion. Like the tip of the proverbial iceberg, civil society activities concerning global regulation have so far made visible only a fraction of the total mass of possibilities. Hence prescriptions for the future centre on 'more' and 'better'.

To develop this argument the discussion below reviews the expansion of civil society engagement of global regulatory arrangements and the positive contributions (actual as well as prospective) of these activities for the legitimation of those regimes. It then elaborates on shortcomings in current civil society relations with global governance agencies that limit positive legitimation effects, and offers suggestions to practitioners in civil society and official circles to improve matters.

Global Governance and Its Legitimacy Gaps

Conventional political thought has usually equated 'global governance' with 'intergovernmental organizations'. However, other kinds of global regulatory apparatuses have also appeared over recent decades, in part because the growth of traditional multilateral institutions has not kept pace with the needs of rapid globalization. As a result one might today distinguish half a dozen institutional types of global governance arrangements. The most familiar form of planet-spanning regulatory body is indeed the formal intergovernmental agency, the old-style 'international organization'. This category includes well-known entities like United Nations (UN) institutions, as well as less publicized bodies like la Francophonie and the Organisation of the Islamic Conference (OIC). In addition, recent decades have witnessed major growth of planetary-scale regulation through transgovernmental networks and accompanying global administrative law (Raustiala, 2002; Slaughter, 2004; Kingsbury and Krisch, 2006). In these cases senior officials from multiple states jointly pursue governance of common concerns with informal collaboration through memoranda of understanding, conferences and day-to-day communication. Examples include the Competition Policy Network, the Group of Eight (G8) and the Nuclear Suppliers Group.

Less extensive to date, but potentially more important for the future, is global governance through interregional arrangements. In these cases, regulation of global issues is pursued among several macro-regional bodies, for example, between the EU and MERCOSUR (the Southern Common Market) or between the EU and ASEAN+3 (the Association of Southeast Asian Nations plus China, Japan and South Korea). Still further global regulatory networks have a translocal character, linking provincial and municipal governments across the planet in initiatives like United Cities and Local Governments (UCLG). Meanwhile, other expansion of global governance has transpired in recent decades through private regulatory mechanisms run by business consortia and/or civil society associations. Examples of private global governance include the Forestry Stewardship Council (FSC, to promote ecologically sustainable logging), the Global Reporting Initiative (GRI, to advance corporate social responsibility) and the International Accounting Standards Board (IASB, to elaborate and harmonize modes of financial reporting). A final category of growing global governance in contemporary history involves hybrid arrangements that combine public and private elements. Examples include the Internet Corporation for Assigned Names and Numbers (ICANN, started in 1998), the Global Compact (launched in 2000) and the Global Fund to Fight AIDS, Tuberculosis and Malaria (established in 2002).

Appreciated in this multifaceted way, considerably more global governance has developed over recent decades than is suggested by looking at intergovernmental multilateralism alone. Accounts of global governance particularly tend to underestimate, or overlook altogether, the substantial contemporary significance of transgovernmental networks and private global regulation. In addition, interregionalism, translocalism and public–private hybrids are important in certain areas and may become major forms of global regulation in the years to come.

Yet for all of this institutional innovation and expansion, global governance today still falls far short of needs. Much more and much better transplanetary regulation is needed to ensure that globalization impacts positively on core attributes of a good society such as cultural vibrancy, democracy, distributive justice, ecological integrity, material well-being, morality and peace.

A governance framework can derive legitimacy from several sources, especially the five qualities of morality, legality, technical competence, democracy and charismatic leadership. With respect to morality, fair trade schemes with their explicit orientation to distributive justice generally enjoy greater legitimacy with global publics than the WTO. With respect to legality, grounding in international law tends to give the UN greater legitimacy than the informal G8. With respect to technical performance, the achievements of the United Nations Children's Fund (UNICEF) in promoting education and health of young persons bring that agency substantial public endorsement, whereas the legitimacy of the IMF (International Monetary Fund) has suffered from various failings of the macroeconomic adjustment policies that it has promoted. With respect to democracy, comprehensive direct stakeholder participation and control arguably secures the FSC more legitimacy than the United Nations Environment Programme (UNEP). With respect to charisma, James Wolfensohn by his person arguably bolstered public support for the World Bank at a time of considerable challenge, while the success of the World Wide Web Consortium (W3C) in global regulation of the internet owes largely to the inspiration of Tim Berners-Lee.

The dynamics of legitimation are of course more complex than an artificially neat analytical distinction of five sources may suggest. However, there can be little dispute that the overall current balance sheet for the legitimacy of global governance stands deeply in the red. Moral foundations, legal grounding, material delivery, democratic practice and charismatic leadership are sooner weak than strong in transplanetary regulation today. Again, this problem is critical: without greater legitimacy, global governance will not obtain the greater resources and powers that are needed to make the required major regulatory advances.

The Legitimizing Potentials of Global Civil Society

Arguably civil society involvement in global governance can do much to address these legitimacy deficits. Civil society activities are pervasive in contemporary global governance (Florini, 2000; Edwards and Gaventa, 2001; GCS, 2001–9; Clark, 2003; Batliwala and Brown, 2006). Parallel NGO Forums alongside UN-sponsored global issue conferences are one highly visible manifestation of this engagement. In addition, civil society is also involved in transgovernmental processes like the G8 and interregional processes like the Asia-Europe Meeting (ASEM). In some cases of private global governance like the FSC and fair trade schemes, it is civil society associations themselves that formulate and administer the rules. Among the public–private hybrids, civil society associations have sat on the boards of ICANN and the Global Fund.

Diversity of civil society in global governance efforts

The civil society associations that engage global governance institutions take many forms. Some are non-governmental organizations (NGOs), that is, issue-based non-profit agencies with a formal organization, legal personality and professional staff. Many (albeit far from all) citizen initiatives on consumer problems, democracy promotion, development cooperation, environmental degradation, health, human rights, humanitarian relief, market regulation, the status of women and youth questions are largely pursued through NGOs. Other civil society activities vis-à-vis global governance occur through social movements involving large, often informally organized, and sometimes even underground mobilizations of non-professional activists. Examples include many citizen actions on animal rights, caste discrimination, indigenous peoples, land tenure, peace, racial solidarity, religious belief and working conditions. Thus the civil society that is relevant to global governance extends far wider than the transnational NGOs who cluster around Geneva, New York and Washington.

Civil society initiatives in respect of global governance also vary widely in other respects. In terms of size, for example, tens of thousands may gather around a G8 summit, while other actions involve only handfuls of people. In terms of duration, the Anti-Slavery Society has several centuries behind it, while other NGOs are 'come-and-gos'. In terms of geographical scope, the campaign to ban land mines spanned all inhabited continents, while civil society actions on the use of debt relief monies can be highly localized. In terms of cultural context, many global civil society activities are steeped in western modernity, while others involve the assertion of indigenous life-worlds or religious revivalism. In terms of resource levels, Amnesty International and Greenpeace can draw on large funds and the most sophisticated technology, while the peasants of *Vía Campesina* often lack even their own land. In terms of constituencies, civil society interventions in global governance may advocate for anyone from multinational companies to the mentally ill. In terms of broad strategies, global civil society houses everything from the neoliberalism of the Cato Institute to the Trotskyism of the Fourth International. In terms of tactics, some parts of civil society will don establishment attire for face-to-face meetings in the offices of global governance agencies, while other citizen activists steadfastly refuse any direct contact with global authorities.

Legitimization in practice

All of this diverse civil society activity can in principle significantly advance the legitimation of global governance on the several grounds discussed earlier. For example, with regard to legitimation on the basis of moral stature, many civil society associations have donned the mantle of 'conscience of the world' in respect of global governance institutions (Willetts, 1996). In this vein citizen group initiatives have prodded transplanetary regulatory agencies to promote righteous ends like decolonization, human rights, poverty eradication, fair trade, anti-corruption, peace and ecological sustainability. Pressures from civil society have figured centrally in the development of countless global governance policies with a pronounced moral dimension, including sanctions against the former apartheid regime in South Africa, measures to advance gender equality, promotion of the Millennium Development Goals, the rescheduling and eventual cancellation of many poor-country debts, the Kimberley Process against so-called 'blood diamonds', initiatives to protect biological diversity and so on.

Conversely, civil society interventions have at other times undermined the legitimacy of global governance by highlighting purported moral flaws, for instance, with charges that policies of the WTO deepened social injustice. True, civil society also houses 'uncivil' groups of fundamentalists, militarists, racists and ultra-nationalists; so its interventions in global governance do not always and inherently carry positive moral effect.

Civil society energies have also in different contexts helped to generate legitimation (and de-legitimation) of global governance in relation to legality. Advocacy by citizen groups has figured centrally in the formulation and ratification of countless treaties and resolutions with global legal force. Already in the 1940s, civil society inputs were instrumental in promoting the San Francisco Charter that set up the UN. Half a century later, civil society actors figured prominently (especially through the World Economic Forum) in launching the Uruguay Round that delivered the WTO in 1994. Likewise, the entry into force of the Convention to Prohibit Anti-Personnel Mines in 1999 and the creation of the International Criminal Court in 2002 resulted in good part from civil society campaigns. Conversely, civil society associations have questioned the legitimacy of some global governance by highlighting weak legal groundings, for example, in relation to trans-governmental processes like the G8 and certain private global governance mechanisms like instruments for corporate social responsibility (CSR). Similarly, several million street demonstrators in February 2003 undermined the legitimacy of a forthcoming invasion of Iraq that lacked full and specific legal sanction under the United Nations.

From a third angle, civil society associations have often contributed to the legitimation of transplanetary regulation by abetting the successful delivery of material objectives. Competent inputs from civil society can enhance policy development and operational work in global governance. Civil society groups can inject valuable information, insights, methods and advice into policy processes. On other occasions civil society interventions prompt adjustments to policy, for example, by bringing the latest news fresh from the field or by providing alternative views from quarters that official circles do not readily access. Challenges from civil society quarters to established policy can provoke a global governance agency to sharpen its thinking and improve its instruments. Engagement with civil society can also provide global regulatory institutions with an important gauge of the political viability or otherwise of a given project or programme. In certain situations civil society actors moreover themselves perform global regulation. For example, they may hold formal positions in transplanetary governance mechanisms, e.g. as parties to the FSC and as supervisors of fair trade schemes. In addition, some global governance bodies subcontract parts of their operations to civil society agencies, particularly in situations where the citizen groups can perform the services in question more effectively than official bureaucracies. Needless to say, where civil society inputs undermine material delivery – e.g. with faulty information or flawed performance – they sooner contribute to a de-legitimation of global governance.

Still another way that civil society activities can raise the legitimacy (or conversely emphasise the illegitimacy) of transplanetary regimes relates to democracy. From this fourth angle global governance can be legitimate when – along with, or in some cases instead of, morality, legality, material delivery and charismatic leadership – it rests on participation by and accountability to the affected public(s). Civil society can promote 'rule by the people' in global governance in at least seven complementary ways (Scholte, 2003). For one thing, civil society associations can contribute significantly to public education about global governance, thereby empowering citizens to involve themselves meaningfully in these regulatory processes.

Civil society interventions can stimulate public debate about current and possible future courses of global governance, thereby fuelling the active critical deliberations that lie at the heart of a vibrant democracy. Second, civil society groups can connect citizens directly to global governance authorities, through consultation exercises and the like. Third, civil society pressures can induce global governance authorities to be more open, visible and transparent about their operations, so that citizens are able to intervene more effectively in policy processes. Fourth, civil society organizations can serve a watchdog role that extracts greater public accountability from global regulatory agencies for their actions and omissions. Fifth, civil society actions can counter the various arbitrary social hierarchies (*inter alia* on lines of age, class, culture, gender, geography and race) that prevent citizens from having adequate and equal opportunities to shape global governance. Sixth, civil society initiatives can provide recognition and voice for political identities (for example, of indigenous peoples, religious revivalists and sexual minorities) that tend generally to be undemocratically marginalized and silenced in global politics. Of course, civil society can and does also fail to realize these democratizing possibilities vis-à-vis global governance. In some cases civil society groups even exacerbate failings of global democracy through shortfalls of accountable practices in their own quarters. So civil society's democratic impacts on global governance are potential rather than automatic, but many positive effects of this kind have been had, and many more could be obtained.

Finally, civil society activities can advance legitimacy in global governance by promoting charismatic leadership of these regulatory institutions. As noted earlier, transplanetary regulation has, in contrast to contemporary national government, not usually sought or secured much legitimacy on the basis of the popular appeal of its executives. Usually these organizations have been headed by relatively faceless technocrats, and civil society groups have for the most part not challenged this tendency. That said, civil society associations themselves have inserted into global politics some charismatic personalities who have helped to draw media and popular attention to pressing issues of transplanetary regulation. Examples include José Bové, the Dalai Lama, Wangari Maathai and Comandante Marcos.

Across all five main dimensions, then, civil society can do much to bolster – or where warranted to undermine – the legitimacy of global governance. True, civil society activities are not the only source of such legitimation; nor are civil society groups always sufficiently legitimate in their own right. Nevertheless, civil society houses some of the most powerful forces available today for the badly needed greater legitimation of global governance. Hence the final part of this discussion turns to steps that could bring a fuller realization of the possibilities.

Global regulatory agencies have broadly (if sometimes rather belatedly and reluctantly) recognized the legitimizing potentials of relations with civil society. As a result, most global governance institutions have over recent decades pursued notable initiatives to engage citizen associations. In several cases civil society groups have actually held seats on global policymaking bodies like ICANN committees and the UN Commission on Sustainable Development. In various other cases global institutions have convened civil society advisory committees. Almost all global governance agencies have institutionalized some kind of mechanisms for civil society consultation. Even the UN Security Council has since the late 1990s permitted occasional informal briefings by civil society organizations under the so-called 'Arria formula' (GPF, 2007). A number of global regulatory agencies have appointed specially designated civil society liaison officers. Several including the IMF, the United Nations Development Programme (UNDP) and the World Bank have also prepared written staff guides for relations with civil society actors. A few multilaterals have furthermore introduced staff training courses on the subject. Most of these steps to 'open up' to civil society were barely conceivable thirty years ago.

Critics may enquire sceptically what kind of legitimation results from such civil society engagement with global governance. Do these relationships veritably enhance the moral, legal, technical, democratic and/or charismatic qualities of transplanetary regulation? Or do the overtures from official quarters to civil society amount to a hegemonic disciplining and cooptation of dissent, whereby a surface legitimation disguises and suppresses a deeper illegitimacy?

Answers to these questions can go either way, depending partly on concrete evidence relating to specific contexts and partly on the theoretical and political predispositions of the questioner. However, commentators of all persuasions would affirm (albeit in different ways) a need for better civil society legitimation of global rules.

Positioning Civil Society for More Global Governance Influence

What could be done to improve the legitimation dynamics of civil society relations with global governance institutions? What steps are advisable both to increase the interchanges and to generate a positive rather than a hegemonic legitimation of global regulation? In a word, what is wanted in the period ahead is more, more inclusive, more competent, more coordinated and more accountable civil society engagement at the heart of policy processes of the full range of global governance processes.

More relations

Greater and better legitimation of global governance could be obtained through sheer increases in civil society engagement of the regimes in question. Important though the relations to date have been, the scale could be substantially larger. On the one hand, more civil society associations could direct more of their work towards questions of global governance. At present the circle of serious engagers remains relatively small.

It is also important that civil society efforts on global governance better cover the full range of relevant institutions. Current civil society attentions are disproportionately concentrated on the older generation of intergovernmental agencies and remain comparatively neglectful of newer arrangements like transgovernmental networks and private governance instruments that generally suffer greater legitimacy deficits. Anne-Marie Slaughter (2004, pp220–1; 240) has argued that civil society engagement offers one of the best ways to enhance justice in respect of transgovernmental regulation. Yet to date few citizen associations have taken up this challenge, apart from sporadic attention to the G8. Likewise, key private global governance arrangements in areas like communications and finance have so far usually stayed off the civil society campaign map, again limiting important prospective (de)legitimation effects.

Indeed, civil society associations should arguably construct future advocacy more in terms of issues than in regard to specific institutions. A global problem tends to be regulated through a diffuse, trans-scalar, multi-actor complex, rather than in a centralized fashion through a single agency. Thus, for example, civil society initiatives would better engage the polycentric network that governs global trade rather than direct efforts at the WTO alone. The notable impacts of civil society campaigns on debt relief and women's rights have resulted partly from a strategy of engaging the overall relevant governance framework instead of just one or the other institutional node.

Yet wherever in global governance civil society associations engage, greater positive legitimation effects could result if these citizen inputs were integrated more into the whole policy process, starting from initial agenda setting and continuing all the way through to retrospective evaluation. In many cases, global regulatory agencies have mainly limited civil society involvement to later stages of policy formulation, after the principal decisions have been taken. Official circles then expect 'consultation' of civil society to give a veneer of public endorsement to policy that has in effect already been decided.

More inclusive relations

A key step in improving the quality of relations is to develop more inclusive interchanges that encompass the whole of society, in particular marginalized and subordinated people. To date the 'civil society' that engages global regulatory institutions has on the whole disproportionately involved limited and structurally privileged sectors of humanity. Past exchanges have especially favoured a global elite of culturally western, university-educated, English-speaking professionals. In the process many other citizen voices have been sidelined. As a result, patterns of civil society relations with global governance have generally reproduced the arbitrary inequalities of society at large. To this extent diversity and dissent are suppressed (however subtly and in many cases also unintentionally).

To counter these exclusionary tendencies there is need for more proactive efforts at wider involvement than witnessed so far. A *laissez-faire* approach to civil society engagement of global governance invariably leads, as in any 'free market', to an overwhelming dominance of the strong. A positive development of the past decade has seen the growth of a rhetoric of inclusion in global politics, particularly in respect of 'the south', 'the grassroots' and 'gender mainstreaming'. However, in practice the prevailing pattern remains for better resourced and more forceful north-based professional advocates (more often than not men) to speak in global governance quarters instead of (and sometimes purportedly for) south-based and otherwise marginalized constituencies. Much more sustained deliberate actions are needed to advance equality of opportunity to enter civil society relations with global governance.

Meanwhile NGOs themselves could in general also pursue greater efforts to develop better understandings of and communications with social movements on global governance issues. Some NGOs have nurtured substantial links of this kind, including organizations like the Brazilian Institute of Social and Economic Analysis (IBASE), Focus on the Global South and NGOs supporting the Movement for the Survival of the Ogoni

People (MOSOP). Since 2001 the World Social Forum has also provided a constructive meeting ground for NGOs and social movements. However, most NGO interlocutors with global regulatory agencies rarely trade elite corridors for squatter camps.

One way to counter this NGO inbreeding with official power is to encourage more rotation of the civil society actors who enter into dialogue with global governance agencies. True, as is elaborated under the next heading, an enhanced legitimation dynamic also wants the greater competence that is born of experience, which implies a certain continuity of personalities. However, as in any other vocation, too much continuity of personnel in civil society relations with global governance can lessen capacities to deliver new information, critical analysis, alternative worldviews and out-of-the-box advice. Civil society careerists ensconced in Brussels and New York can sometimes jealously guard their privileged access to global policy processes. In the worst cases a tired civil society establishment may counterproductively obstruct the entry of energetic newcomers who could reinvigorate moral sensibilities, convey the latest technical advances and inject wider democratic voice. Civil society offers veritable legitimation at the global governance table not by co-optatively warming up the seats, but by counter-hegemonically heating up the proceedings.

More competent relations

Relations between civil society associations and global governance institutions need to be marked by ample mutual comprehension if the interchanges are fully to realize their potentials to advance legitimation. Both sides include parties who have impressive information and insight about the other, but overall the current picture is often marked by considerable ignorance. Thus a major requirement for greater legitimacy of global governance through relations with civil society is improved competence on the part of activists and officials alike to deal with one another.

Improved competence on engagement of global governance often requires that campaigners stay the course on specific issues and institutions. Some civil society organizations have through long-term sustained efforts developed a deep engagement regarding certain agencies and areas of global regulation. Illustrative examples include the Southern and Eastern African Trade Information and Negotiations Institute (SEATINI) and the Japan Center for International Finance (JCIF). However, many civil society initiatives fail to acquire sufficient depth on any policy area, following the caprice of headlines and sponsors to flit from one global governance problem to the next. In this way civil society herds have moved from debt to trade, from trade to war, from war to CSR and so on.

Much as global governance officials require training in respect of civil society, citizen activists for their part also generally need more capacity enhancement in respect of transplanetary regulation. The current emergence of university courses on global public policy can help to deepen future civil society competence, particularly in NGOs. In addition, however, greater activist education through 'popular universities' of the kind found in Brazil and Scandinavia is needed to raise capacities in social movements that campaign on global governance issues.

Along with upgraded conceptual insight, civil society campaigners on global governance issues often also need a sharper strategic orientation. Even many veteran activists have not systematically and explicitly thought through the underlying values and overarching visions that motivate their engagement. The World Social Forum initiative has been helpful in highlighting issues of overall strategy. Several texts on globalization and its governance (e.g. Klein, 2000; Bello, 2002; Stiglitz, 2002) have served a manifesto-like purpose for some civil society practitioners. However, most citizen activists have not carefully and precisely identified what they find lacking in currently prevailing policy paradigms, let alone how more specifically they would reconstruct those strategic frameworks. In short, civil society efforts to promote more legitimate global governance are hampered to the extent that the advocates lack a clear conception of what, beyond the issue immediately at hand, they are advocating.

Increased civil society competence can also be pursued in respect of campaign tactics. True, the effectiveness of citizen group initiatives on global governance is often highly constrained by limited resources. The best devised action plans are naught without sufficient people, equipment and money to execute them. Thus more – and more reliable – resourcing of civil society engagement of transplanetary governance is an obvious priority for the future. A chronic lack of means has led too many able campaigners to abandon their efforts in despair.

That said, improved tactics can also make limited resources go further. One key step in this direction is discussed at greater length below: namely, better coordination of civil society initiatives regarding global regulation. In addition, civil society groups working on global governance could generally do more to exploit the possibilities of mobilizing constituents through the internet and other mass media. More cleverly still, citizen advocates can pursue emancipatory causes in ways that harness hegemonic forces and their superior resources. For example, the civil society campaign for access to essential medicines has prompted global capitalists to question and qualify the existing regime of intellectual property rights. Similarly, poorly resourced movements of Dalit women, indigenous peoples and other subordinated groups have been able to turn a largely hegemonic discourse of global human rights to their advantage.

As these examples show, civil society associations can draw on rich past experiences to further their campaigns for more legitimate global governance. What is generally lacking, however, are effective mechanisms for the sharing of, and mutual learning from, this accumulated competence. Arguably civil society associations could make much more and better use of publications like the *Global Civil Society Yearbook* (GCS, 2001–9), studies on civil society engagement of global governance agencies commissioned by the Montreal International Forum (FIM, 2007), reports prepared through the North–South Institute (NSI, 2007) and a number of edited collections and monographs (Willetts, 1996; Florini, 2000; Edwards and Gaventa, 2001; Scholte and Schnabel, 2002; Clark, 2003; Martens, 2005). Likewise, the fruitful collaborations nurtured over the past decade between campaigners and researchers on global governance would help-fully be much expanded and deepened (Brown, 2001).

Alongside academic research, more could also be done for capacity development through civil society conferences and workshops where activists engaged with questions of global governance can productively exchange experiences across issues, institutions and campaigns. However, these costly gatherings are perforce rare and involve only limited numbers of advocates. Complementary efforts might therefore be dedicated to developing a permanent resource centre for civil society initiatives on global governance. Such an institute could provide activists with services such as: assembling records of previous campaigns on global governance questions; mapping networks of regulation and power in relation to different global issues; translating important civil society and global governance documents into relevant languages; and acting as an incubator for new ideas and programmes on collective citizen engagement of global governance agencies.

More coordinated relations

As well as enhancing campaigner competence, a global civil society resource centre could also help to address a more general need for improved coordination in civil society activities vis-à-vis global governance. Many past citizen initiatives on issues of global regulation have seen their limited resources dissipated through fragmentation, duplication of efforts, and internecine competition.

Several initiatives have developed, especially over the past decade, to assemble civil society voices vis-à-vis global governance. For example, the Conference of Non-Governmental Organizations in Consultative Relationship with the United Nations (CONGO, dating from 1948) and Social Watch (launched in 1995) have provided venues for civil society associations to congregate in relation to the UN system. The Montreal International Forum (started in 1998), the Bridge Initiative (begun in 2001) and the World Forum of Civil Society Networks-UBUNTU (formed in 2001) have sought to facilitate civil society coordination in respect of a wider range of multilateral institutions. The World Economic Forum (1971), CIVICUS-Worldwide Alliance for Citizen Participation (1993), the State of the World Forum (1995) and the World Social Forum (2001) have also constructed broad tents for civil society, albeit without seeking specifically to engage global governance agencies.

Welcome though these efforts to foster more coordinated civil society engagement of global governance have been, they have generally suffered from some of the other shortcomings highlighted in the present analysis. Thus, for example, the initiatives have tended to limit their scope of 'global governance' to the most visible intergovernmental organizations, while overlooking transgovernmental networks and private global regulation as well as incipient interregionalism and translocalism. Moreover, with the exception of CONGO in relation to the UN, existing mechanisms to coordinate civil society activities on global governance have usually focused on the macro-level of major conferences and general policy frameworks, giving less attention to day-to-day processes of policy formulation and implementation. Furthermore, aside from the World Social Forum these initiatives have generally limited coverage of 'global civil society' to NGOs, and the more globally connected NGOs at that, thereby excluding large swathes of global citizen action in social movements and more locally based associations. In addition, apart from the World Economic Forum, most of these projects have worked with small and fragile resource bases. Nor – anticipating the next discussion point below – have these mechanisms for civil society coordination incorporated systematic processes to secure their accountability, either towards the participating civil society groups or towards constituencies in wider society.

More accountable engagement

Finally, the potentials for civil society legitimation of global regulation can be furthered with increased accountability on the part of the citizen groups to their various constituencies. Constructive accountability dynamics can promote increased civil society relations with global governance agencies, since the authorities and the general public would then have more confidence in the bona fides of these citizen associations. At the same time, when pursued in a positive fashion, greater attention to accountability can prompt civil society groups to become more inclusive, competent and coordinated in their relations with transplanetary regimes.

Civil society activities largely advance the legitimacy of global governance by making those regimes more accountable. With accountability, holders of power (in this case transplanetary regulatory authorities) are made to answer for the ways that they use or fail to use that power, particularly when their actions and omissions result in harms. Civil society monitoring of the moral, legal, technical and democratic credentials of global governance bodies has been one important way to promote the legitimacy of those regimes, particularly in the absence of strong formal oversight by parliaments and courts. In a watchdog function citizen groups endorse transplanetary regulatory agencies when these rulers perform well and call them to task when they fall short.

Yet civil society watchdogs of global governance must also be accountable themselves. After all, the actions and omissions of civil society groups vis-à-vis transplanetary regulation can also do damage, including by the frequent shortfalls of inclusion, competence and coordination described above. In particularly bad cases, civil society organizations in global politics lack a clear public constituency, rarely if ever consult their supposed beneficiaries, fail to report on their activities, escape rigorous financial controls and offer aggrieved parties no channels for complaint and redress.

To correct such flaws in their own operations civil society associations require devices to ensure their own accountability – and through it their own legitimacy in exercising influence on global governance. The need for secure accountability on the part of actors in global civil society has been increasingly recognized of late, also by those actors themselves (Edwards, 2000; Chapman and Wameyo, 2001; Scholte, 2003, pp87–94; Blagescu and Lloyd, 2006; Jordan and van Tuijll, 2006; Ebrahim and Weisband, 2007, Part III). Less clear, however, is precisely for what these civil society groups should be accountable, to whom and by what means.

To be sure, certain important measures are already in place to foster the accountability of civil society associations in their engagement of global governance processes. For example, formal civil society organizations are usually registered under relevant national statutes and thereby become accountable to state authorities. In such cases the executive or the judiciary can curtail or disband civil society bodies that break the law. In addition, certain global governance agencies operate accreditation schemes to vet civil society associations that seek a formal consultative status. Meanwhile those civil society groups that have memberships and/or a board of governors are accountable to these supporters and may lose their backing in response to poor performance. Many civil society initiatives are also accountable (via project reports and financial statements) to donors that fund their work, with the sanction of losing vital monies in cases of immoral, illegal, incompetent or undemocratic conduct. Organizational accountability further exists to staff inasmuch as employees may blow whistles on misconduct or resign. Critical assessments of a given civil society association published in the mass media, academic research and consultancy reports can also promote its accountability to the general public. Moreover, civil society organizations working in the area of global governance have promoted mutual accountability within their sector through the development of self-regulatory codes of conduct and other quality assurance schemes. A notable recent initiative in this regard is the INGO Accountability Charter inaugurated in 2006 (INGO, 2007).

Yet arrangements to enhance the accountability of civil society activities in respect of global governance could be improved in three key respects. First, the credibility of the mechanisms just described depends in good part on the accountability in turn of the various monitors of civil society activities. Otherwise these controllers (be they governments, donors, mass media, academics or consultants) can abuse their power and use arguments about 'accountability' as a tool to suppress civil society. Every agent of accountability also needs in its turn to be sufficiently answerable for its own actions on this subject. Thus constructive, effective and just oversight is better obtained when the various social actors involved are enmeshed in complex networks of multilateral mutual accountability. To this end substantial future efforts could be devoted to furthering not only the answerability of civil society bodies to officials, funders, journalists, researchers and consultants, but also vice versa.

A second major problem in existing accountability arrangements regarding civil society engagement of transplanetary governance is that they are heavily biased towards the powerful. Citizen group initiatives in global politics are mainly monitored by actors from elite quarters: donors, corporate media, academics, etc. In contrast, civil society work on global governance rarely includes systematic accountability to subordinated circles, even though it is often claimed that poor people and various minorities are major beneficiaries of civil society interventions in global regulation. Such asymmetric accountability reflects and reinforces the dynamics of marginalization. When civil society associations are mainly made answerable to elites, accountability easily becomes part of hegemony rather than – as is often presumed – a way to resist it (Weisband and Ebrahim, 2007). Thus the future wants far more attention paid to ways that subordinated circles can obtain accountability from the powerful in civil society work on global governance issues.

A third significant improvement in measures to obtain accountability in civil society campaigns on global governance could be had with reorientation from negative and blunt policing to positive and imaginative learning. Current oversight of global civil society associations is heavily geared towards bureaucratic surveillance and punishment in relation to targets imposed by funders and other outside parties. Although controls against malfeasance are doubtless necessary, accountability exercises can and should also be a supportive process for reflective learning, with positive and creative initiatives to rethink visions, goals and the ways that they are pursued. Without such learning civil society organizations fail to correct their shortcomings and underachieve. Thus on the whole future practices of accountability in civil society work concerning global governance need relatively less technocratic surveillance and relatively more organizational learning.

Conclusion

As the foregoing third part of this analysis has indicated, many challenges confront the enlargement and improvement of civil society engagement of global governance. To acquire greater consequence in the legitimation of global governance these relationships need substantial advances in terms of expanded proportions, enhanced inclusiveness, upgraded competence, raised coordination and improved accountability. Achieving these ends will take major efforts patiently sustained on multiple fronts over multiple years. These efforts will be worthwhile for the ample fruits that they can bear. Though civil society interventions are not the only way to raise moral standards, legal bases, material delivery, democracy and charismatic leadership in transplanetary regulation, civil society actors offer some of the most substantial and immediately available possibilities in this regard.

References

Batliwala, S. and Brown, L.D. (eds) (2006) *Transnational Civil Society: An Introduction*, Bloomfield, CT: Kumarian Press

Bello, W. (2002) *De-Globalization: Ideas for a New World Economy*, London: Zed

Blagescu, M. and Lloyd, R. (2006) *2006 Global Accountability Report: Holding Power to Account*, London: One World Trust

Brown, L.D. (ed) (2001) *Practice-Research Engagement and Civil Society in a Globalizing World*, Cambridge, MA: Hauser Center for Nonprofit Organizations, Harvard University

Chapman, J. and Wameyo, A. (2001) *Monitoring and Evaluating Advocacy: A Scoping Study*, London: ActionAid

Clark, J.D. (ed) (2003) *Globalizing Civic Engagement: Civil Society and Transnational Action*, London: Earthscan

Ebrahim, A. and Weisband, E. (eds) (2007) *Global Accountabilities*, Cambridge: Cambridge University Press

Edwards, M. (2000) *NGO Rights and Responsibilities: A New Deal for Global Governance*. London: Foreign Policy Centre

Edwards, M. and Gaventa, J. (eds) (2001) *Global Citizen Action*, Boulder, CO: Rienner

FIM (2007) Website of the Montreal International Forum, available at www.fimcivilsociety.org (last accessed March 2007)

Florini, A.M. (ed) (2000) *The Third Force: The Rise of Transnational Civil Society*, Tokyo/Washington, DC: Japan Center for International Exchange and Carnegie Endowment for International Peace

GCS (2001–9) *Global Civil Society Yearbook*, Oxford: Oxford University Press (annual)

GPF (2007) 'Arria and Other Special Meetings between NGOs and Security Council Members', website of the Global Policy Forum, www.globalpolicy.org/security/mtgsetc/brieindx.htm, accessed on 24 February 2010

INGO (2007) website of the INGO Accountability Charter, available at www.ingoaccountabilitycharter.org/ (last accessed February 2007)

Jordan, L. and van Tuijll, P. (eds) (2006) *NGO Accountability: Politics, Principles, and Innovations*, London: Earthscan

Kingsbury, B.W. and Krisch, N. (eds) (2006) 'Symposium on Global Governance and Global Administrative Law in the International Legal Order', *European Journal of International Law*, vol. 17, pp1–278

Klein, N. (2000) *No Logo*, London: Flamingo

Martens, K. (2005) *NGOs and the United Nations: Institutionalization, Professionalization and Adaptation*, Basingstoke: Palgrave Macmillan

NSI (2007) Website of the North–South Institute, www.nsi-ins.ca (last accessed March 2007)

Raustiala, K. (2002) 'The Architecture of International Cooperation: Transgovernmental Networks and the Future of International Law', *Virginia Journal of International Law*, vol. 43, no. 1 (Fall), pp1–92

Scholte, J.A. (2002) *Civil Society Voices and the International Monetary Fund*, Ottawa: North–South Institute

Scholte, J.A. (2003) *Democratizing the Global Economy: The Role of Civil Society*, Coventry: Centre for the Study of Globalisation and Regionalisation, available at www.csgr.org (last accessed June 2010)

Scholte, J.A. with A. Schnabel (eds) (2002) *Civil Society and Global Finance*, London: Routledge

Slaughter, A.-M. (2004) *A New World Order*, Princeton: Princeton University Press

Stiglitz, J. (2002) *Globalization and Its Discontents*. New York: Norton

Weisband, E. and Ebrahim, A. (2007) 'Forging Global Accountabilities', in Ebrahim and Weisband (eds), *Global Accountabilities*, Cambridge: Cambridge University Press, pp1–38

Willetts, P. (ed) (1996) '*Conscience of the World': The Influence of Non-Governmental Organizations on the UN System*, Washington, DC: Brookings Institution

Part III

Managing Responsibly

8

Civil Society Legitima
Accountability: Issues and

Jagadananda and L. David Brown

Introduction

One of the most complex challenges facing Civil Society Organizations (CSOs) today is the question of their legitimacy as social and political actors and their accountability to key stakeholders. Challenges to the legitimacy and accountability of CSOs have emerged as they have begun to play increasingly important roles in development and governance processes at local, national and international levels.

This chapter attempts to unravel the evolving complexities of civil society legitimacy and accountability and to analyse existing systems and practices for responding to legitimacy and accountability challenges. It provides the base for a series of dialogues and consultations about these issues with CSOs and their stakeholders in the future. It suggests steps for developing systems to enhance the legitimacy and accountability of civil society organizations and multi-organization domains.

Why Legitimacy and Accountability?

Why are CSO legitimacy and accountability such contentious issues now? There are a number of reasons for the emergence of the issues.

First, questions about civil society legitimacy and accountability have come to reflect deeper concerns about the legitimacy and accountability of institutions. Concerns about corruption in government agencies and unacceptable practices by business organizations often assume greater urgency than concerns about civil society. Illegal activities at Enron in the US or Bofors in India raise questions about both business and government accountability, and undermine the legitimacy of the sectors. The impacts of such events can spread throughout the society, affecting public perceptions of many other institutions as well. Thus, in part, the growing concern about legitimacy and accountability reflects a more general 'crisis of governance'.

Second, commitments to social values and visions are at the heart of civil society's ability to mobilize people and resources, and their reputation as legitimate and accountable

ose missions is vital to their effectiveness as social actors and their ability
taff and allies to their causes. Gandhi and the Indian Independence Move-
Martin Luther King Jr and the Civil Rights Movement, and Solidarity and the
Liberation Movement all depended on their credibility as legitimate embodi-
ents of widely held social values. If questions about legitimacy and accountability
remain unanswered, they can corrode the identity and operational capacities of organizations that depend on leader, staff and volunteer values and voluntary commitments.

Third, some legitimacy and accountability questions grow out of the problematic
behaviour on the part of some civil society organizations. Publicity about the accusa-
tions of board self-dealing at the Nature Conservancy or the mistaken analysis made
by Greenpeace of the proposed Brent Spar oilrig disposal in the North Sea raise questions about the extent to which CSOs live up to their professed values and whether
mechanisms exist to enforce minimum standards of practice. CSOs, like agencies
operating in other sectors, are not uniformly altruistic nor are their actions always
consistent with their values. Some challenges to their legitimacy grow out of their own
mistakes or malfeasance.[1]

A fourth set of challenges is posed by agencies that have been targets of civil society
advocacy activities. When CSOs exert political and social pressure on behalf of marginalized constituencies, for example, they may inspire counterattacks by powerful interests. Civil society advocacy has brought challenges to corporations, governments and
global governance institutions. Government agencies charged with corruption, corporations pressed to change bad business practices and intergovernmental institutions challenged to alter projects or policies may be motivated to cast aspersions on the legitimacy
or the accountability of their challengers.[2] Of course, it is important that CSOs explain
their legitimacy and their accountability to key stakeholders, but it should not be
forgotten that demands for such explanations may be inspired by motives other than a
desire for transparency.

Fifth, CSOs often have diverse stakeholders that make competing accountability
claims. Unlike a corporation or a democratic regime, CSOs are not primarily accountable to a single set of stakeholders. Businesses are ultimately accountable to their owners
and shareholders, and democratic regimes are accountable to voters. Civil society organizations, in contrast, are accountable to donors for their resources, to clients for delivery
of goods and services, to allies for performance of joint activities, to staff and members
for meeting their expectations and to government regulators for following relevant regulations. Dealing with many different accountability claims may be extremely difficult,
and where stakeholders have different or contradictory interests, being fully accountable
to all of them is impossible. So legitimacy and accountability may constitute a challenging problem for CSOs because of the very nature of the sector.[3]

All these demands on CSOs have been further complicated by their expanding roles
in the sphere of social development and change. For some the shift amounts to a 'global
associational revolution' that may be as important as the emergence of nation states as
critical institutions in governance.[4] Civil society actors have often been seen as 'gap
fillers', providing services not available from the market or the state. However, in recent
years they have increasingly taken on capacity building and policy advocacy roles that
make them participants in multi-sectoral governance processes.[5] While much civil
society work has historically been focused on local problems, CSOs now increasingly

work at national and transnational levels as well.[6] Their emerging roles in large-scale initiatives may call for new approaches to legitimacy and accountability.

CSO Legitimacy and Accountability: A Framework

As a recent report on UN and civil society points out, global civil society networks and social movements increasingly inform citizens about policy choices and influence policy debates on international issues. They open up a global public space for debating issues and informing global public opinion. The UN report suggests 'Civil Society is as much a part of today's global governance as governments'.[7] The Secretary General of the UN, the President of the World Bank and a number of national political figures have agreed that civil society should be a key player in strengthening democracy and promoting social development. The Human Development Report 2002 identifies 'expanding the space for non-state actors to influence policies and hold powerful actors accountable' as a key element in deepening democracy.[8] But this potential can be fulfilled only if civil society actors respond quickly and clearly to questions about their legitimacy and accountability.

Legitimacy

The concept of legitimacy refers to perceptions by key stakeholders that the existence, activities and impacts of CSOs are justifiable and appropriate in terms of central social values and institutions. For example, Edwards has defined legitimacy as 'the right to be and do something in society – a sense that an organization is lawful, admissible, and justified in its chosen course of action'.[9] Legitimacy is lost or gained in the eyes of stakeholders, and different stakeholders may differ considerably in their standards and perceptions of the legitimacy of a particular CSO.

CSOs may be concerned about their legitimacy as institutions that seek to play credible and accepted roles in society. Institutional legitimacy can be grounded in regulatory, normative or cognitive bases.[10] CSOs may gain regulatory legitimacy by conforming to rules and regulations, such as meeting state standards and procedures for organizational registration and reporting. They can build normative legitimacy by exemplifying values and moral obligations, such as cultural expectations for protecting children, supporting the poor or delivering safe goods and services. CSOs may also gain cognitive legitimacy by aligning their activities with shared meanings and definitions that define – often tacitly – 'the way things are'. Many civil society organizations recruit eminent trustees and follow the reporting and organization forms of well-regarded agencies to enhance their own credibility. From this perspective, CSOs might emphasize quite different bases for their institutional legitimacy, depending on the extent to which their fields of operation have well-defined rules and regulations, shared values and moral perspectives, or widely held-meanings and explanations for how the world works.

CSOs may also seek to define their legitimacy with respect to particular issues. For example, CSOs that seek to influence the actions of other actors, such as government agencies or private firms, need to establish their credentials as appropriate and accepted voices on the issues in question. Four bases for legitimacy may be identified.[11] These bases are related, but not identical, to the bases for institutional legitimacy.

- Legal Legitimacy: Legitimacy can grow from compliance with legal and regulatory requirements, such as meeting state registration requirements or delivering goods and services that meet professional standards. Sometimes CSOs gain legitimacy from their support of regulatory standards that constrain the activities of their advocacy targets, such as World Bank policies that Bank staff fail to follow in projects.
- Political Legitimacy: Some civil society actors claim issue legitimacy on political grounds, such as democratic representativeness, participation, transparency, and accountability to their constituents affected by the issue. Democratic legitimacy depends on decision-making processes that allow those represented to understand issues, participate in decisions, influence results, and hold organization leaders accountable.
- Moral Legitimacy: CSOs can ground their claims to legitimacy through their action on behalf of widely held moral values and norms. Bringing food to the victims of a famine or campaigning to stop mutilation of children by land mines are activities grounded in widely held values. Such moral legitimacy is often important to CSOs, whose missions spring from values and visions of a better world.
- Technical or Performance Legitimacy: A fourth basis for legitimacy is expertise, knowledge, information or competence relevant to the issues in question. When a coalition of international relief and development agencies lobbies the UN on actions to cope with complex emergencies, their claims are grounded in years of experience of providing relief and development support in similar circumstances. When an alliance of senior environmental scientists takes a position on climate change, they rely on scientific expertise as a basis for legitimacy.

Institutional legitimacy is a long-term attribute of a CSO, typically gained over years of activity with, and observation by, many stakeholders. Issue legitimacy refers to credibility in respect to a particular issue. General institutional legitimacy is not a guarantee that a CSO will be seen to have legitimacy on a particular issue: a grassroots CSO known for representing the interests of its members will not necessarily have legitimacy on the best way to deliver rural health care. But issue and institutional legitimacy do interact: stakeholders may well give institutionally legitimate CSOs the benefit of the doubt about accountability on particular issues, and clear accountability over time can build institutional legitimacy.

Accountability

The concept of accountability refers to a responsibility to answer for performance expectations. It may be seen as an identity issue in the sense of feeling responsible to one's ideals and commitments. It may also be seen as a relational issue in the sense of being answerable to and held responsible by other actors.[12] While the issue of CSO identity and its expression in ongoing loyalty to its mission is important, our focus here will be on accountability associated with CSO relations to the stakeholders that affect or are affected by their activities. CSOs are accountable in relationship terms when they are answerable to key

Table 8.1 *Models of accountability relationships*

	Representative	Principal/agent	Mutual
Status of parties	Constituents most important	Principal most important	All parties important
Influence relationship	Representative acts for constituent	Agent is subordinate to principal	Mutual respect, trust and influence
Desired outcomes	Defined in general by constituents; specifics by representative	Defined primarily by principal; agent gets compensation	Defined by shared values and problem definitions
Transparency	Representative open to constituents	Agent is open to principal	Parties are open to each other
Source of incentives and sanctions	Political support; media publicity; regulator oversight	Legal and economic; courts enforce contracts	Social and moral; peer networks enforce

stakeholders for their performance promises.[13] Relational accountability is usually defined in terms of accountability for performance to some stakeholder implemented through a process for assessing, reporting and sanctioning that performance.

Table 8.1 summarizes differences among the underlying models of accountability relationships. CSOs may use a variety of models of accountability in their relations with different stakeholders. Relations with donors often depend on principal agent negotiations and contracts; relations with members may be driven by representative roles of elected leaders; and relations with allies may depend on mutual accountability grounded in long histories of cooperation. Relations constructed as one model may evolve over time into another, as when a long-term relationship between a donor and a CSO evolves from a principal-agent contract for specific outcomes to a more mutually accountable compact to accomplish shared social objectives. When parties understand their relationship in terms of different underlying models, serious problems can arise. Many northern and southern CSOs, for example, have used the language of mutual accountability in constructing their 'partnership,' and when northern CSOs – sometimes under pressure from their own donors – invoke principal-agent concepts to administer the partnership, their southern colleagues may feel misled or even betrayed.[14]

The interaction of legitimacy and accountability

Legitimacy and accountability are related. CSO legitimacy can be enhanced by clear lines of accountability to appropriate stakeholders, and accountability can be clarified and improved through attention to the organization's bases for legitimacy.

CSO missions and strategies offer clues about bases of legitimacy and stakeholders who might hold them accountable. CSO strategies define approaches to accomplishing their missions: many CSOs focus on relief and providing services; others emphasize local organization and capacity building; still others engage in policy advocacy and exercising influence on government and corporate agencies; and an increasing number use combinations of these and other strategies.

Criteria for legitimacy and accountability vary across strategies. Service delivery CSOs may be required to demonstrate the quality and reach of their services to establish their legitimacy, and make themselves accountable to donors and service regulators to establish that they are effective in carrying out their missions. Capacity building CSOs may work closely with clients to define needs and develop programmes that enable effective local action, and so emphasize accountability to clients whose capacities cannot be enhanced without their active cooperation. Advocacy CSOs may need to build legitimacy with both the constituents they represent and the targets they seek to influence. Accountability to constituents is central to preserving their legitimacy as a voice for otherwise unheard populations; legitimacy with targets may grow out of technical, normative or legal standards as well as the CSOs' relationship to constituents. In the multi-stakeholder world of CSOs, it is not always clear how to deal with complex and sometimes conflicting demands that can affect agency legitimacy.

CSOs that do not explicitly grapple with the issues of legitimacy and accountability often end up paying more attention to stakeholders with loud voices and substantial power – such as donors and government agencies – and paying less attention to stakeholders with less clout, such as clients or agency staff.[15] In later sections we turn explicitly to the possibilities of building systems for constructing and maintaining legitimacy and managing accountabilities to many stakeholders. Such accountability systems include definitions of performance, identification of key stakeholders, approaches and standards for assessing performance, mechanisms for communicating those assessments and vehicles for enabling stakeholders to create performance consequences for the CSO.

Figure 8.1 summarizes this discussion. The 'strategic triangle' of value creation, legitimacy and support and operational capacity on the left reflects the critical questions that CSO leaders must answer in creating organizational strategy. It is important for CSO leaders to recognize not only what value the CSO will create (such as services delivered, capacities built, or policies influenced), but also to think through how the

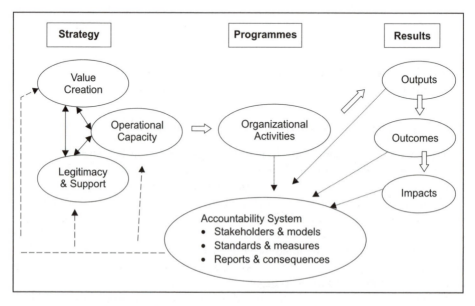

Figure 8.1 *Strategy, accountability and legitimacy*

CSO can gain and preserve resource support and legitimacy for its work and how it will develop and maintain the operational capability to carry out its strategy.[16] The CSO's activities then produce direct outputs (such as health services, capacity-building workshops or policy analyses), outcomes in the form of changed behavior by targets (such as better nutrition by mothers, more self-help by villagers, changed policies by legislators) and longer-term social impacts (such as healthier babies, improved conditions in villages and improved government services), as indicated by the large arrows.

Accountability systems can assess information about activities, outputs, outcomes and impacts, report it back to relevant stakeholders and enable selected stakeholders to hold the CSO accountable for its performance. Thus the dashed arrows from the accountability system to legitimacy and support, operational capability and value creation reflect the use of performance information to press for enhanced legitimacy, improved organizational capacity and performance management and organizational learning to improve value creation. Enhanced accountability can increase institutional and issue legitimacy over time. This legitimacy may also reduce pressures for accountability, at least in the short run.

Sources of standards

How do standards for accountability and legitimacy become established? One possible way is to develop definitions of legitimacy and accountability standards on the basis of general principles. If principles could be constructed to span the differences across sectors and countries, they could be the basis for defining legitimacy and accountability for a wide range of organizations and settings.

One ambitious study in this tradition, the Global Accountabilities Project, is briefly described in Box 8.1. The Project has developed a framework of standards of accountability that can be applied to transnational organizations across the government, business and civil society sectors. Box 8.1 presents an initial set of eight accountability standards and some findings from comparing civil society, business and governmental organizations on the basis of member control and access to information.

This study demonstrates some of the challenges posed by attempts to find common standards across sectors. The study's definition of 'members', for instance, illustrates the problem: 'members' were defined as country governments for the intergovernmental organizations (IGOs), as shareholders for transnational corporations (TNCs) and as national offices for international NGOs (INGOs). INGOs were somewhat less likely than other organizations to systematically bias decision-making in favour of a few powerful members – but this definition glosses over the multiple stakeholder problems of NGOs. The diversity of definitions of 'member' suggests that differences across sectors are such that principles general enough to span them may offer only limited assistance in dealing with particular sectoral problems.

A second source of legitimacy and accountability standards is the articulation of societal ideals that are established by laws or widely held social norms and expectations. CSOs are expected to obey basic laws and norms of the societies in which they are embedded, and governments may set more specific expectations to regulate their formation, resources and activities. When a government legislates standards they become legal expectations for civil society. Social norms and 'customs having the force of law' also

---

Box 8.1 *The global accountabilities project: General principles?*

The GAP created a framework of internal and external accountability dimensions, and then used some of those dimensions to assess the accountability of a sample of international NGOs (INGOs), transnational corporations (TNCs), and intergovernmental organizations (IGOs).

The internal stakeholder accountability dimensions included:

1   Member control over the organization's actions
2   Appointment of senior staff procedures
3   Compliance mechanisms for enforcing decisions on members (only IGOs)
4   Evaluation processes to assess and report performance.

The external stakeholder accountability dimensions included:

1   External stakeholder consultation that involves them in decision-making
2   Complaints mechanisms that enable stakeholders to register and pursue issues
3   Corporate social responsibility to report social and environmental impacts
4   Access to information that is available to the public online.

The project assessed 18 agencies on the first and eighth dimensions. In general it appeared that international NGOs (with some exceptions) tended to score higher than other organizations on member control, and to score lower on making information available online.

Source: Kovach, H., C. Neligan & S. Burall (2003) *Power without Accountability?* London, One World Trust, Global Accountability Project.

---

amount to standards based on societal ideals. When very high salaries for chief executives of some charitable organizations in the US became public knowledge, many of their branches and donors disassociated themselves in view of their violation of norms relating to 'reasonable compensation'. Rigorous state regulation of civil society organizations is relatively infrequent, however. In part this lack of attention reflects civil society's relative obscurity in many countries; in part, it may also reflect interest in preserving the flexibility and ease of entry that are critical to the operation of civil society as a source of social energy and innovation.

Box 8.2 briefly describes the evolution of the Philippine Council for NGO Certification (PCNC) as an example of an effort to negotiate and enforce domain standards for development and environment NGOs in cooperation with government agencies, so the resulting societal standards meet the concerns of both sectors.

The PCNC experience demonstrates that codes of conduct and peer review can reduce the likelihood that the sector will be dominated by fraudulent NGOs created to gain access to money and tax breaks, though the certification process has also involved substantial commitments of volunteer time and energy. Such initiatives can catalyse sector-wide debate on the key elements of a code of conduct, and help to construct understanding and commitment to minimum standards. The involvement of the state in supporting those standards begins to invest them with the status of societal ideals.

Where societal ideals remain ill-defined, communities of CSOs may agree on negotiated domain standards on the basis of their specialized experience. Arriving at agreement within the sector may be a basis for building wider agreement with many other stakeholders on good practices in the longer term. Such domain standards can be negotiated to set accountability expectations in many multi-organizational contexts, from

---

Box 8.2 *Societal standards: The Philippine Council for NGO Certification*

PCNC emerged as the product of a negotiation between the Department of Finance and networks of civil society organizations. In the mid-1990s the Department proposed to abolish tax deductions for contributions to NGOs because lack of oversight was leading to rampant abuse and corruption. The NGOs, on the other hand, believed that the change would affect their resources quite negatively.

Six networks of Philippine NGOs agreed to develop a code of conduct and to carry out the peer reviews needed to certify NGOs as being in compliance with the code, and the Government agreed to maintain tax deduction for certified NGOs. The evaluation process was expected to be funded by fees from evaluated NGOs as well as member contributions and initial support from foundations.

By 2005 more than 350 NGOs had been certified through the peer review process that involves hundreds of volunteer evaluators from member NGOs. Roughly 10% of the applicants were initially denied certification, though many of them were certified in subsequent assessments. Those certified have been granted tax deductions for contributions received.

Source: R. A. Chamberlain, Regulating Civil Society: The Philippine Council for NGO Certification, Manila: PCNC. Also see PCNC website at www.pcnc.com.ph

---

communities of organizations in the same sector to alliances for campaigns across local, national and regional differences, to coalitions to solve problems that bring together business, government, civil society and other actors.[17]

Initiatives to build domain standards out of the experience of CSOs and then to certify those complying with these standards is becoming increasingly common for NGOs in many countries, from Pakistan and India to Australia and the United States. Box 8.3 briefly describes the Credibility Alliance in India, which reflects a widespread discussion among CSOs about sector standards.

Creating sector standards can provide opportunities for constructive debate about CSO practices and problems. It may also, as in the Credibility Alliance, provide avenues to increased financial support from many sources. But building detailed standards is not always easy. It is often relatively easy to come to agreement on general principles, but creating detailed standards and mechanisms for sanctioning violations of those standards may be very difficult. We will return to the issue of building domain accountability systems in more detail in a later section of this chapter.

When domain standards have not yet been established and societal ideals leave open many possibilities, agencies may have to create their own accountability standards and priorities that support achievement of their missions through organizational strategic choice. Organizations may have considerable leeway in defining how accountable they will be to various stakeholders, particularly when their stakeholders vary in interests and power. Ambiguity about societal and domain standards allows space for CSO leaders to make strategic decisions about accountabilities to different stakeholders. Those choices have consequences, of course; leaders cannot choose to ignore stakeholders without legal, moral or prudential risks. But CSOs often make less use of space for choice than they might if they gave systematic attention to their options. In the absence of strategic choice, some stakeholders are likely to receive much more attention than others. Thus it is common for donors and government regulators to have their accountability claims

---

Box 8.3 *Negotiating sector standards: The Credibility Alliance in India*

The Credibility Alliance is a consortium of organizations that is working to establish a set of norms for the voluntary sector grounded in a sector-wide consensus. They shared an initial set of norms with 15,000 CSOs and found strong support for articulating the norms and creating a body to develop and propagate them.

At a series of regional conferences organized by regional networks in 2001 and 2002, and a national meeting in 2002, hundreds of participants reinforced the support for norms and their propagation. The draft norms emphasized disclosure and objectivity on two major issues, identity and governance:

Identity norms include, for example:

*   The organization is registered as a Trust/Society/Section 25 company.
*   Registration documents are available upon request.

Governance norms include, for example:

*   The organization has a governing board.
*   All remuneration or reimbursements to Board members are to be disclosed.

These norms have now been adopted by the GIVE Foundation as the standards for including CSOs in their portal for private donations. It is expected that these standards will also be useful to government and international donors seeking to support CSOs in the future.

Source: Gupta, S., & N., V. K. (2004) The Credibility Alliance and Indian Non-profits, *Accountability Forum* (2, Summer), 58–69.

---

honored, while the claims of less powerful constituencies like poor and marginalized beneficiaries receive less attention.[18]

Organizational strategic choice and domain negotiated standards offer arenas in which civil society actors can shape the terms of their accountability and legitimacy. The next two sections focus on innovations in building accountability systems at the organization and interorganizational domain levels. A general set of approaches to the challenge has been formulated, which have been illustrated with innovations from around the world that show how civil society and other actors are responding to legitimacy and accountability problems.

Constructing Organizational Legitimacy and Accountability

The strategic choice perspective focuses on direct action by CSOs to strengthen their legitimacy and accountability in ways that increase their capacities to accomplish their missions. CSOs can build on their missions and strategies to construct accountability systems that reinforce performance and mission accomplishment. These systems may make use of a range of accountability mechanisms, such as governing boards consisting of outsiders who oversee organizational policy and finances; adherence to standards for disclosure and public reporting; independent assessments or audits of finances and programme impacts; and consultation with stakeholders in assessing programmes and activities.

Building accountability systems involves using such elements to accomplish four tasks: (1) identifying and prioritizing organizational stakeholders, (2) setting standards and performance measures, (3) assessing and communicating performance results, and (4) creating performance consequences by which stakeholders can hold the CSO accountable. We consider each of these elements below and illustrate them with examples drawn from current initiatives around the world. This section aims to provide an overview of possibilities available to particular organizations, before turning in the next section to the possibilities available to multi-organization domains.

Identifying and prioritizing organizational stakeholders

Who are the key stakeholders for CSOs? Answers to this question vary considerably across CSOs, depending on their missions and strategies, the contextual forces they face and the capacities they can bring to bear. As suggested earlier, the stakeholders that are critical to disaster relief or service provision may be quite different from those central to local capacity building or to policy advocacy or to other strategies. Since CSOs have many diverse stakeholders – donors, members, regulators, clients, allies, staffs, targets – trying to be fully accountable to all of them may be a recipe for paralysis or constant firefighting that can undermine work on strategic goals. So, prioritizing accountabilities critical to mission accomplishment can be vital to effectiveness.

The strategic triangle in Figure 8.1 offers a simple way to identify and map stakeholders who have important accountability claims on the organization. This mapping focuses on analysing which stakeholders affect or are affected by the organization in three areas: (1) the creation of value envisioned by its mission and strategy, (2) the creation and maintenance of its legitimacy and support, and (3) the development of its operational capability to carry out the strategy. Figure 8.2 illustrates how the strategic triangle can be used to identify stakeholders for the case of an international NGO that builds the capacities of marginalized communities, southern NGOs and local government agencies.

When the relevant stakeholders have been identified, CSO leaders can assess the strategic importance of being accountable to them. At least three questions relating to that assessment have been raised. First, is the CSO accountable on legal grounds? Some stakeholders can use law and the courts to hold the CSO accountable, such as suing it to compel compliance with contractual obligations to provide donors with audited accounts. Second, is the CSO accountable morally to the stakeholder? Some stakeholders can call for accountability on grounds of values and norms held by the society and/or by the CSO, such as client demands that it live up to its mission to help rather than exploit the poor. And third, is the CSO accountable on prudential or practical grounds? Some stakeholders can exact high costs for accountability failures, as in regulators withdrawing government certification or donors refusing to re-fund programmes.

Stakeholders may have strong claims on all three questions, or strong claims relating to some but not others, or relatively weak claims relating to all three. Donors often have strong claims on legal and prudential grounds, while clients may have strong moral claims but little prudential clout or legal standing. One approach has been to assess stakeholders on all three questions and then combine those assessments for an overall

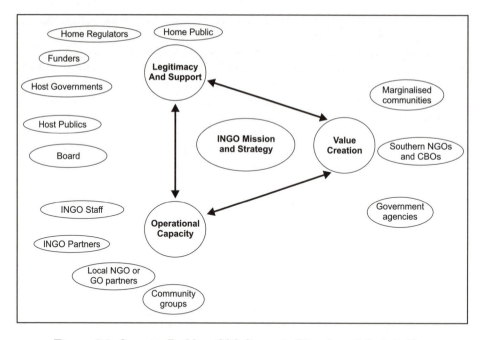

Figure 8.2 *Capacity Building CSO Strategic Triangle and Stakeholders*

Source: Brown, L. D., M. H. Moore, & J. P. Honan (2004). Building Strategic Accountability Systems for International NGOs. *AccountAbility Forum* 1 (2), pp31–43

priority rating.[19] Deciding which stakeholders are relevant and then establishing which ones take priority is essential to constructing accountability systems that support mission and strategy achievement. Many CSOs recognize the temptation to pay more attention to stakeholders with strong prudential and legal claims, such as donors or government regulators, and pay less attention to value-based claims, such as those of clients, even when those values are at the core of CSO missions. Recognizing and discussing those tensions is a prerequisite to constructing accountability systems better designed to achieve CSO missions.

Setting standards and measuring performance

Accountability systems depend on agreements about performance and how it can be measured. Measuring performance is particularly challenging when a CSO seeks to accomplish long-term social impacts, since it is extremely difficult to measure such impacts or the contributions of various actors to them. The framework overview in Figure 8.1 suggests that CSO immediate outputs activities, client outcomes and longer-term impacts are all important elements of assessing CSO performance – but they are increasingly difficult to assess as they become more causally distant from CSO activities.

The challenges of assessing social and environmental impacts have received increasing attention in the last 10 years. While many initiatives have examined ways to assess immediate outputs of programmes, others have paid attention to their outcomes in terms of

---

Box 8.4 *Building practitioner-led social performance systems*

The problem of accountability is closely intertwined with the crisis NGOs face in the growing gap between the reality and the rhetoric of reaching the very poor, creating people-centered development, delivering high-quality services and producing sustainable change in the lives of people and their communities. The practitioner-led Social Performance Management system (SPM) is designed to equip microfinance institutions to measure social as well as financial performance and to build new forms of accountability. The Imp-Act network, drawing on the resources of the Universities of Bath, Sheffield and Sussex in the UK, is working to develop processes and tools for assessing social performance around the following questions:

- What are the social performance objectives of the organization, and how does it seek to achieve them?
- How does the organization monitor, whom does it reach and whom does it exclude, how and why?
- How does the organization monitor and understand the effects/impacts of its work on the people/their communities?
- How does the organization use social performance information to improve its services?
- How does the organization improve the system through which it answers these questions?

As an internal quality control system, SPM is designed to consciously refine the tools and the processes to enhance the quality and ownership of the organization and track its own engagement in terms of its own mission and performance targets.

Source: www.imp-act.org

---

changed behaviour on the part of programme targets.[20] The work of organizations like the New Economics Foundation, AccountAbility and ACCESS (Appropriate Cost Effective Centres for Education within the School System) have all contributed to expanding awareness of measures and standards for assessing social and environmental impacts.

Box 8.4 describes an initiative to grapple with some of the problems of assessing social as well as financial performance for microfinance institutions that seek to have social impacts as well as make capital available to microenterprises.

It is not uncommon for donors to negotiate for results, measures and evaluation plans for the programmes that they fund. But donor interests are not always identical to those of other stakeholders, and so the results of their evaluations may not serve the interests of clients or allies or staff. Indeed, some CSOs collect information required by donors but create quite different systems to support their own learning. The challenges of creating performance measurement systems that serve multiple stakeholders have inspired a number of innovations, such as the OSANGO assessment system briefly described in Box 8.5. Note that this approach emphasizes working with stakeholders, and particularly clients and beneficiaries, to define problems, to identify indicators and measures of impact, and to assess and interpret results. The system is designed to foster joint learning about programme outcomes and impacts, stressing enhanced independence and capacity of programme clients and beneficiaries as well as that of the CSO.

Creating a performance measurement system that makes sense to the CSO is an important step, but it does not guarantee that the resulting measurements will constitute adequate evidence for key stakeholders. The OSANGO system emphasizes working with other stakeholders to develop goals and objectives, generate information

---

Box 8.5 *Organizational self-analysis for NGOs (OSANGO)*

This self-managed assessment system was created by Indian NGO support organizations to enable NGOs to assess their performance with respect to their missions, values and operating principles. If offers a framework for analysing organizational structures and processes and can provide computerized feedback that compares the organization to others.

OSANGO emphasizes NGO accountabilities to stakeholders and particularly to beneficiaries by encouraging agencies to:

- be aware of statutory obligations and other legal requirements;
- develop goals and objectives in cooperation with stakeholders;
- engage in dialogue with beneficiaries to solve local problems;
- seek feedback on programme impacts from beneficiaries and other stakeholders;
- measure performance in cooperation with other stakeholders.

Source: Jagadananda (2004). 'The Need for Self Assessment-Reflection: Organizational Self-Analysis for NGOs (OSANGO) in South Asia'. *AccountAbility Forum* (2, Summer): 98–106.
For additional information on OSANGO: http://www.cysd.org/osango.htm

---

about impacts and interpret the results. Often the value of information for accountability purposes will turn on the extent to which the CSO has negotiated agreement on performance measurement with key stakeholders early in the process. Early negotiations can help the CSO and its stakeholders to define desirable performance in the same general terms.

Assessing and communicating performance

The results of CSO performance can be assessed in many ways. Some organizations invest time and resources in self-evaluations, deploying staff to collect and analyse information about programme performance and how much their activities have the intended impacts. Others commission external evaluations (or have evaluations imposed on them) to gain the advantage of technically sophisticated and organizationally independent feedback. Communications include disclosure statements, annual reports or publication of internal and external evaluations. The critical issue here is making information available in forms that are comprehensible and useful to various stakeholders. Stakeholder diversity means, of course, that some will find communications more difficult to decipher than others.

A particularly interesting innovation in the area of assessing and communicating performance is the ACCESS initiative, described in Box 8.6. This initiative builds on the assumption that better performance and reporting standards could expand the resources available for social programmes.

If ACCESS achieves its goals, it will influence both the substance of result reporting on social and environmental CSO programmes and the context in which those results are communicated. It will help create shared standards for assessing the capabilities of CSOs, enhance the capabilities of CSOs and their abilities to learn from their work and enable potential social investors to identify, assess and support effective programmes. Its founders hope that these changes will enable funding for social results on a much larger scale than is now possible.

Box 8.6 *The ACCESS initiative: Shared standards of performance*

Access Reporting has been organized to build a widely accepted reporting standard for social and environmental results that can be used to improve CSO performance, strengthen account-abilities and consequently expand social investment. To do this it fosters multi-stakeholder dialogues on the need for accountability and transparency and it fosters action research to build a reporting standards framework in a number of pilot projects with partners around the world.

The reporting framework focuses on the competencies of CSOs that are predictive of future performance. Features of the standard include:

- ratcheted reporting, so that more mature CSOs meet higher standards;
- open, inclusive and participatory processes to enable mutual learning;
- capacity development emphasis rather than picking winners;
- capability based analysis focused on likely future performance;
- graduated external verification, from self to peer to external assessments;
- flexibility in prioritizing rating aspects, so potential donors can assess CSOs according to their particular concerns.

Source: Bonbright, D. (2004). 'NGO Accountability and Performance: Introducing ACCESS'. *AccountAbility Forum* (2, Summer): 4–13. See also www.accountability.org.uk

---

Another important initiative in assessing and reporting CSO impacts has been the rise of social auditing. Much of the initial work in this area has focused on private sector initiatives, but it is highly relevant to CSO work as well. Box 8.7 summarizes

---

Box 8.7 *Social auditing*

Social audits assess the social impact and ethical behaviour of an organization in relation to its aims and those of its stakeholders. Social audits in principle are:

- Inclusive. The social accountability process must reflect the views of all stakeholders, not only those with the most influence.
- Comparative. The performance of the organization must be comparable over time or with standards drawn from experience of other organizations, regulations or norms.
- Comprehensive. No area of the organization's activities can be deliberately or systemati-cally excluded from the assessment.
- Regular. An organization's performance cannot be assessed in at any one point. Issues vary over time, as do composition and expectations of key stakeholder groups.
- Embedded. It is essential that the organizations develop clear policies and procedures to support social auditing are regularized and recognized by the organization.
- Communicated. Disclosure of findings is an active means of communication with key stakeholders and the wider public. Merely publishing a document is not 'good practice' if it is difficult to obtain, costly or unintelligible to key stakeholders.
- Externally Verified. The role of an independent verifier is an important means for strength-ening accountability and legitimacy both of the process and of the organization.
- Linked to Continuous Improvement. An organization must be committed to improving its performance in relation to the assessment process and to be audited against commitment in subsequent cycles.

Source: Sue Davidson & Peter Raynard, *Ahead of the Field: Pilot Agencies and the People in Aid Code, 1997–2000*, London: People in Aid, 2001

some of the main elements of social auditing as an approach to assessing and communicating results.

As the pilot action research projects of ACCESS and the applications of social auditing to CSO activities develop, the challenges of assessing and communicating results of CSO activities may become much less formidable. Building performance measurement systems and communicating their results to important stakeholders are critical steps to enhancing organizational accountability. But they are not enough in themselves.

Creating performance consequences

Since the interests and capacities of CSO stakeholders vary a great deal, making information available to all of them in the same format does not ensure that they can hold the CSO accountable. While government officials and donor agency staff may be quite happy with audited accounts or external evaluation reports, grassroots constituents may neither have the languages (e.g. English) nor the skills (e.g. accounting) to interpret the reports, nor the resources to compel attention to their concerns if they voice them. 'Creating performance consequences' assumes some degree of voice and influence from the relevant stakeholders, and some balance of power among the actors that ensures that the CSO listens to those who are most important to accomplishing its mission.

This problem is often recognized by CSOs – but less often solved. Box 8.8 describes an initiative by an international NGO concerned with the difficulties of managing information from local assessments while promoting enhanced local accountability.

Since development is often understood as 'empowering' grassroots constituents, creating the context for mutual assessment and joint learning with them is an attractive goal – but not one that is easily accomplished. Accountability to clients and beneficiaries is an empty term if they do not have the power to demand attention to their concerns, but that power does not happen by accident. The ALPS experience suggests that mutual learning and accountability has to be explicitly woven into programmes and implemented with considerable commitment if it is to be effective.

Box 8.8 *Accountability, Learning and Planning System (ALPS)*

This system was created by ActionAid to help focus programme reporting and evaluation on important outcomes and to bring together clients, partners and staff to learn from experience.

The ALPS process emphasizes appraisal, strategy formation, programme review and annual reflections in cooperation with community groups and partners, with a special emphasis on downward accountability. It includes elements to ensure:

- participation by primary stakeholders in various phases of work;
- transparency, sharing and reporting across stakeholders;
- recognizing different forms of literacy, communication and reporting;
- emphasis on learning with stakeholders about achievements and failures;
- downward accountability to poor people.

For additional information about ALPS: www.actionaid.org.uk/800/alps.html

Organizational learning, performance management and legitimacy

The information generated by accountability systems has a number of uses. It offers opportunities to organizations operating in complex and changing contexts for organizational learning from information about programme outputs, outcomes and impacts. This information can help the CSO learn what works at the operational level as well as how well its theories of social change in fact predict and explain the results it produces. In Figure 8.1 the dashed arrow from the accountability system to the value creation aspect of the CSO strategy reflects the organization's ability to adapt by making use of organizational learning.

Within the organization, information from the accountability system can be used for performance management purposes, clarifying roles and responsibilities and defining performance expectations to focus organizational energies where they will have the greatest impact. The dashed arrow in Figure 8.1 from the accountability system to operational capability indicates the possibility of using new information to foster more effective performance.

Finally, the existence of clear standards and information about performance can be used to strengthen internal and external legitimacy of the CSO, as indicated by the dashed arrow from the accountability system to legitimacy and support. The more clearly the organization can state its core mission and then produce data that indicate performance in the service of that mission, the more credible the case for legitimacy. Critics may challenge the relevance or value of the mission – but at a minimum the CSO can demonstrate that its actions are consistent with its words–that it 'walks its own talk' in behaving consistently with its values.

In short, constructing accountability systems at the organizational level offers CSO leaders opportunities to assess the importance of various stakeholders and design systems that align internal and external accountabilities to press for mission accomplishment. Defining organizational accountabilities makes it possible for key stakeholders to support accomplishment of critical objectives. There is no complete freedom to decide which accountabilities will be primary – accountability choices have consequences, particularly when powerful stakeholders get less than what they want. But there is enough latitude for many CSO leaders, given chances to negotiate with donors and other stakeholders, to build accountability systems that support and reinforce key strategic commitments.

Building domain legitimacy and accountability

Civil society legitimacy and accountability systems can also be constructed at the domain level, so that communities of organizations agree about appropriate standards, practices and relations with key stakeholders. While building organizational accountability systems focuses on the strategies and activities of individual organizations, constructing domain accountability systems lays emphasis on interorganizational negotiations to define standards for community members and identify accountabilities to key domain stakeholder. Often domain expectations about legitimacy and accountability are developed out of the experiences of their members, so agreement on standards and practices emerges from past practice. Domain standards, practices and expectations may become embedded in wider social norms and legal standards and so evolve into societal ideals of legitimacy and accountability. Domain standards that emerge from negotiations with governments can easily become embedded in the regulations and statutes associated with societal definitions of legitimacy and accountability.

Building domain legitimacy and accountability systems is more complicated than building organizational accountability systems, in part because of the many independent organizations involved and the need to create new organizational arrangements to implement collective action. But it is also clear that the importance of the issues of legitimacy and accountability is catalysing a wide range of initiatives to grapple with these issues across many regions and countries.

Continuing Dilemmas

There are many initiatives under way to strengthen the legitimacy and accountability of civil society organizations and domains. We expect that those initiatives will be broadened and strengthened over the next five years, as more and more civil society leaders recognize the critical importance of building the legitimacy of the sector and clarifying the values, goals and stakeholders to which it will be accountable. We also expect that some challenges will not succumb easily – if ever – to simple solutions. Some dilemmas will continue to be sources of tension and inspiration for further innovation.

We expect, for example, that there will be a continuing need to balance the power differences among organizational and domain stakeholders. As long as civil society organizations are working across the boundaries that separate the rich and the poor, the powerful and the disenfranchised, the global north and south, they will continue to face diverse demands for accountability – some explicit and others unspoken. To the extent that civil society agencies seek legitimacy with and accountability to less powerful stakeholders, they will need to create mechanisms and processes to balance the demands of unequally powerful stakeholders. The tug and pull of different constituencies is inherent in the nature of civil society and its multiple allegiances, but responding to upward, downward and lateral accountabilities can leave little time and energy for pursuing core civil society priorities if leaders are not thoughtful about balancing those demands.

To the extent that civil society organizations and domains foster action on complex social problems, an ongoing dilemma involves measuring social performance when its causes are ambiguous and multiply-determined. We have suggested that performance measurement is a critical element in building organizational and domain accountability systems, since legitimacy and accountability is so intimately bound up with delivering on performance promises. Organizational, domain and societal learning needed to deal more effectively with complex social problems is at the heart of many civil society initiatives, and learning depends pivotally on information about the outputs, outcomes and impacts of social interventions. For most complex problems unambiguous proof of impact will never be available, but civil society actors are gradually learning to make plausible and convincing cases for the relevance of their work, and so buttress their claims for legitimacy and accountability to interested stakeholders.

The call for clarifying strategies, performance measurement and accountability to key stakeholders as bases for legitimacy and improved practice has found responsive ears within civil society as well as in other sectors. But clear standards and tightly-enforced accountability can undermine many of the characteristics we value in civil society: independence, diversity, flexibility, innovativeness and willingness to take on unpopular causes. The challenge will be in balancing high standards with space for continued innovation, diversity and responsiveness. Had civil society actors remained accountable to the 'best practice' of requiring collateral for small loans, no microcredit movement would have provided working capital to millions of micro-entrepreneurs. In many cases 'one size will not fit all' and preserving room for innovation and invention will be central to solving local problems. In other cases failure to identify and follow key standards will undermine the effectiveness and impact of civil society initiatives.

A related dilemma is the challenge of using organizational learning to catalyse domain and societal development. Civil society organizations can sometimes define their accountabilities on the basis of strategic choices and so mobilize stakeholders to support their initiatives. As areas of work evolve, however, the emergence of many organizations grappling with similar problems can create a range of practices and the identification of some that are better than others. The development of a community of organizations with experience in some form of service, or an issue or a multi-stakeholder problem may set the stage for negotiating domain standards or even societal ideals. Thus the rise of standards for development NGOs in Pakistan, the Philippines and Australia that are explicitly backed by government authority is moving from domain standards enforced by NGOs to societal standards laid down in government regulations. Civil society organizations may have to trade the autonomy of setting standards by strategic choice for the wider impact of setting standards by domain negotiation or societal norm-setting. The loss of organizational autonomy may be offset by the expanded impacts of best practices widely deployed – or perhaps not.

Conclusion

We began with the idea that legitimacy and accountability have become central issues for civil society. It has emerged in response to several factors – global questions about the 'crisis of governance' in many sectors, the centrality of legitimacy and accountability to valued-based civil society organizations, highly visible problems with some civil society actors, attacks from powerful targets of civil society advocacy, conflicting demands from multiple civil society stakeholders, the increasing importance of civil society roles in social problem-solving and so on. The stakes of improved answers to legitimacy and accountability questions are high: civil society actors have public legitimacy in many countries and growing capacities to play central roles in governance and social problem solving. But their legitimacy is central to that capacity. If wider publics become convinced that civil society actors – like governments, businesses and many other social institutions – are not legitimate and value-driven social actors, their efficacy in arenas dominated by more wealthy and powerful actors will sharply decline.

This chapter has suggested a framework for understanding civil society legitimacy and accountability, and used that framework to suggest ways to strengthen organizational legitimacy and accountability by strategic choice and interorganizational domain legitimacy through negotiated standards. We have drawn on a wide range of innovative initiatives focused on enhancing the legitimacy and accountability of civil society organizations and domains.

We believe that it is imperative for civil society organizations and domains to continue to respond to questions about their legitimacy and accountability if they are to live up to their potential for constructive influence on governance and problem-solving. Recent experience suggests that civil society actors can successfully challenge abuses by national governments, private firms, intergovernmental organizations and transnational corporations. Indeed, that success is in part responsible for escalating challenges to civil society's legitimacy and accountability. Such challenges may limit abuses or catalyse preventive policies for the future. But successful civil society response to questions about legitimacy and accountability can also form the basis for more collaborative initiatives, in which the social goals and values of civil society actors are joined with the resources and power of governments and businesses to accomplish local, national and global results which the participants can not accomplish by themselves. Challenges to civil society legitimacy and accountability amount to recognition of their potential in the drama of globalization and sustainable development; effective and persuasive responses to those challenges can be the basis for new models of governance and problem-solving so desperately needed in a rapidly changing world.

Notes

1   See Naidoo, K. (2004). The End of Blind Faith? Civil Society and the Challenge of Accountability, Legitimacy and Transparency. *AccountAbility Forum* (2, Summer): 14–25; and Clark, J. (2003). *Worlds Apart: Civil Society and the Battle for Ethical Globalization.* Bloomfield, CT, Kumarian Press, pp102; and Gibelman, M. & Gelman, S. R. (2004). A Loss of Credibility: Patterns of Wrongdoing among Nongovernmental Organizations. *Voluntas, 15*(4), pp355–381.

2   See Fox, J. and L. D. Brown (1998). *The Struggle for Accountability: NGOs, Social Movements, and the World Bank.* Cambridge, MA, MIT Press; and Jordan, L. and P. v. Tuijl (2000). 'Political Responsibility in Transnational NGO Advocacy'. *World Development* 28(12): pp2051–2065.

3   See Edwards, M. (2000). *NGO Rights and Responsibilities: A New Deal for Global Governance.* London: The Foreign Policy Centre; Brown, L. D. & Moore, M. H. (2001). Accountability, Strategy and International Nongovernmental Organizations. *Nonprofit and Voluntary Sector Quarterly, 30*(3), pp569–587; and Ebrahim, A. (2003). Accountability in Practice: Mechanisms for NGOs. *World Development, 31*(3), pp813–829.

4   See Clark, J. (2003A) op. cit.; and Salamon, L. M. (1994). 'The Rise of the Nonprofit Sector'. *Foreign Affairs* 73: pp109–116.

5   For discussion of the transnational roles of CSOs, see Clark, J., Ed. (2003F). *Globalizing Civic Engagement: Civil Society and Transnational Action.* London, Earthscan; Florini, A. (2000). *The Third Force: The Rise of Transnational Civil Society.* Tokyo, Japan Center for International Exchange; and Khagram, S. and K. Sikkink, Eds. (2001). *Restructuring World Politics.* Minneapolis, University of Minnesota Press.

6 For discussion of the transnational roles of CSOs, see Clark, J., Ed. (2003F). *Globalizing Civic Engagement: Civil Society and Transnational Action*. London, Earthscan; Florini, A. (2000). *The Third Force: The Rise of Transnational Civil Society*. Tokyo, Japan Center for International Exchange; and Khagram, S. and K. Sikkink, Eds. (2001). *Restructuring World Politics*. Minneapolis, University of Minnesota Press.

7 Panel of Eminent Persons on United Nations-Civil Society Relations (2004). *We the peoples: civil society, the United Nations, and Global Governance*. United Nations Civil Society Relations Report. United National General Assembly; June 11, 2004; 58th Session, Agenda Item 59.

8 United Nations Development Programme (2002). *Human Development Report 2002: Deepening Democracy in a Fragmented World*. New York, Oxford University Press.

9 Edwards, 2000, op. cit. pp20.

10 For a discussion of the institutional aspects of legitimacy, see Scott, W. R. (1995). *Institutions and Organizations*. Thousand Oaks, CA: Sage, pp45.

11 Brown, L. D. and Others (2001). Civil Society Legitimacy: A Discussion Guide. In L.D. Brown (ed), *Practice-Research Engagement and Civil Society in a Globalizing World*. Washington, DC, CIVICUS: World Alliance for Citizen Participation: pp31–48.

12 See Ebrahim, (2003) op. cit.; Fry, R. (1995). 'Accountability in Organizational Life: Problem or Opportunity for Nonprofits?' *Nonprofit Management and Leadership* 6(2): pp181–195; and Edwards, M. & Hulme, D. (Eds.). (1992). *Making a Difference*. London: Earthscan.

13 Brown, L. D. & Moore, M. H. (2001), op. cit.

14 See Ashman, D. (2001). 'Strengthening North–South Partnerships for Sustainable Development'. *Nonprofit and Voluntary Sector Quarterly* 30(1): pp74–98.

15 See Ebrahim (2003), op. cit; and Edwards & Hulme, (1992) op. cit.

16 Moore, M. (2000). Managing for Value: Organizational Strategy in For-profit, Nonprofit, and Governmental Organizations. *Nonprofit and Voluntary Sector Quarterly*, *29*(1, Supplement,), pp183–204; and Brown & Moore, 2001, op. cit.

17 For discussion of domain accountability systems see Brown, L. D. (2006). Building Civil Society Legitimacy and Accountability. *Philanthropy and Social Change in the Americas*. C. Sanborn, R. Villar and F. Portocarrero. Cambridge, Harvard University Press. For descriptions of what may be involved see Royo, A. (1998). Against the People's Will: The Mount Apo Story. In J. A. Fox and L. D. Brown (Eds.). *The Struggle for Accountability: NGOs, Social Movements and the World Bank*. Cambridge, MA, MIT Press; and Weber, E. (2003). *Bringing Society Back In: Grassroots Ecosystem Management, Accountability and Sustainable Communities*. Cambridge, MA, MIT Press.

18 Ebrahim (2003), op. cit.

19 Brown, Moore and Honan (2004), op. cit.

20 For work on assessment of development outcomes, see for example Earl, S., Carden, F. & Smutylo, T. (2001). *Outcome Mapping: Building Learning and Reflection into Development Programs*. Ottawa: International Development and Research Centre; and Estrella, M. & Others (2000). *Learning from Change: Issues and Experiences in Participatory Monitoring and Evaluation*. London: Intermediate Technology Publications.

Listen First: A Pilot System for Managing Downward Accountability in NGOs

Alex Jacobs and Robyn Wilford

Introduction

This chapter presents the results of a pilot project by Concern and Mango (two international NGOs) to develop a set of practical approaches, called 'Listen First', which provide a systematic way of managing 'downward accountability'. The project took place from 2006 to 2008, involving field trials in six countries and work with over 530 staff and advisors.

Some exciting breakthroughs were made, which echo similar advances elsewhere in NGO practice, such as creating a flexible performance framework to define what downward accountability means in practice and generating quantified feedback from local communities on their perceptions of an NGO's work. While already of value, further research and testing of the skeleton and its associated processes could provide of a management system that explicitly fosters, measures and rewards downward accountability. This chapter locates the project within the academic literature and current practice on NGO accountability. It provides a brief description of Listen First and how it was applied in Concern's programme in Angola in 2008. It ends with lessons learnt and further information is available at www.listenfirst.org.

NGO Accountability

In 1995, Edwards and Hulme framed the debate on NGO accountability. They analysed major dynamics and concluded that the need for NGOs to improve their performance assessment was 'central to their continued existence as independent organizations with a mission to pursue' (Edwards and Hulme, 1995, p224). Since then, further academic research has described and explored these issues and many practical initiatives have been undertaken by donors and NGOs to respond to their challenge. However, it is reasonable to conclude that NGOs have not yet satisfactorily resolved these issues (HAP, 2009; Ebrahim and Weisband, 2007; Wallace 2007).

The literature does not recognize a single, widely accepted definition of 'accountability'. For example, see the different definitions used by Edwards and Hulme 1995,

Bendell 2006, HAP 2009, Lloyd et al 2008, Kilby 2006. But some common elements can be identified. They recognize accountability as an attribute of a relationship between two or more actors, which involves three central elements: negotiating commitments, reporting performance and restitution.

These elements allow one actor to influence another's actions. So accountability is closely related to the distribution and enactment of power. In itself, this has the same potential to entrench oppressive power relations as it does to rebalance them in favour of the less powerful.

As a result, accountability mechanisms have an important influence on on-going relationships between organizations. In order to be effective, NGOs need to maintain the trust and support of different stakeholders, including the intended beneficiaries of their work (be they individuals or organizations) and donors. In the context of complex social interventions, this is often initiated by a joint dialogue about the nature of the issues faced and appropriate responses. This dialogue may typically be shaped by accountability mechanisms (for instance, designing potential interventions with local partners and negotiating contracts with donors). Both sets of stakeholders may reasonably expect to hold an NGO to account for these commitments.

As a result, NGOs have to manage a complex set of relationships, particularly in the light of power dynamics and the flow of funds. The challenge becomes how an NGO can align the commitments it makes and the dialogue it pursues with different stakeholders: some who have little power over it, but are immediately affected by its work, and some who have substantial power over it, but are distant from the field of action. This is all made significantly harder when NGOs and intermediary organizations become large organizations, with their own internal systems, politics and bureaucracy.

The literature tackles these issues by distinguishing between 'upward accountability' and 'downward accountability' (Bendell, 2006). 'Upward accountability' is associated with relationships that face 'up' existing power relationships, where a more powerful actor (such as a donor) uses accountability mechanisms to influence the actions of a less powerful actor (such as an implementing NGO). 'Downward accountability' is associated with relationships that face 'down', flowing against existing power relationships, where a less powerful actor (such as an intended beneficiary) uses accountability mechanisms to influence the actions of a more powerful actor (such as an implementing NGO). These issues are of real practical importance, as they relate to control over funds and the design and implementation of NGOs' activities.

Whereas powerful actors can require accountability from less powerful actors, less powerful actors cannot so easily require it of the powerful. Instead, powerful actors often have to choose to establish and submit themselves to mechanisms of 'downward accountability', which involves releasing some of their power. This may strengthen their legitimacy (in the eyes of the less powerful), but it may also contradict their short term interests and create significant discomfort among managers, around the loss of control. The tensions faced by managers around these choices were a consistent theme in the Listen First pilot, described below.

Downward accountability is closely related to the concept of empowerment, a central component of a great deal of development practice (see for example Freire, 1996, or Chambers, 1997). Both involve people with limited power engaging more effectively with those with more, to increase their influence on decisions which affect their lives.

From the perspective of poor communities, this may be just as important in their inter-actions with an NGO as it is in their interactions with other service providers and authorities, such as government. So, systems to manage downward accountability may provide an important link between the means and the ends of development. NGOs have the opportunity, and arguably the obligation, to model good practice.

As mentioned above, these concepts find concrete form in the management systems used by NGOs and donors. This creates the general questions: do the domi-nant management systems currently used by NGOs and donors achieve an appro-priate level of both upward and downward accountability in the majority of situations? If not, how can they be improved?

Current research shows that the mechanisms used for upward accountability system-atically undermine and distort downward accountability. Wallace presents detailed research on the use of results-based management tools (including logical framework analysis, known as 'logframes') that are currently widespread in the NGO sector (Wallace, 2007). She describes a fracture between the tools used for upwards accounta-bility to donors – project plans, indicators and impact assessment – and the reality of field work actually undertaken.

This contributes to a substantial literature describing the inadequacies of results-based management tools for NGO work (for instance see Chambers, 1997; Earle, 2004; Groves and Hinton, 2004; Kaplan, 2000). Ebrahim (2003a) has described in detail how these management tools divert field managers' attention away from the changing reali-ties of people's lives and towards pre-designed activities. They encourage NGO staff to take the view that social change is linear and predictable and that NGOs have an inflated influence in creating social change. Donors often require staff to deliver the specific activities described in their initial plans. This makes staff less inclined to listen to the changing and contested views of different interests in beneficiary communities, and less able to adapt their work accordingly. In other words, the accountability mechanisms used by donors have a substantial impact on the priorities and practice of field staff.

In addition, researchers including Chambers, Ebrahim and Wallace have described in detail how current widely used accountability systems deliver unreliable reports of performance and achievements up the aid chain. This is a serious effect, undermining the quality of reporting achieved as well as the quality of work. Literature from the anthropology of development provides fine grained descriptions of the gaps between rhetoric and reality (for instance see Mosse, 2004; Hilhorst, 2003).

The debate on downward accountability is rooted in a different discourse, including in particular the literature on participation. The term downward accountability is often used loosely to describe the extent to which an NGO is transparent about its actions, and listens and responds to those lower down the aid chain (Keystone, 2006). Participa-tion is also notoriously loosely used as a term, covering a similar range of activities which vary from expecting local people to participate in pre-designed projects through to sensitive processes of locally-led analysis and design (Brock and Pettit, 2007). There is a significant overlap between the two sets of concepts, which both describe the nature of the interactions between an NGO and the people it aims to assist.

Ellerman draws on substantial philosopher-activists to make the case that develop-ment work is only effective when its activities are owned by local people themselves and build on their priorities (Ellerman, 2005). Many others have written on the same subject. This work implies that the relationship between an NGO and its beneficiaries is the foundation of effective NGO interventions. A report by British Overseas NGOs in Development (BOND), based on research across 60 NGOs, concluded that 'the quality of an NGO's [field]work is primarily determined by the quality of its relationships with its intended beneficiaries' (Keystone, 2006, pv). The same principles have been crystallized into a set of standards for humanitarian work by the Humanitarian Accountability Partnership (HAP, 2007).

A central element of the problem is that results-based management systems tend to create rather inflexible bureaucracy. While it has been argued that they *can* be used in a sensitive and adaptable way (for instance Wield, 2000), Wallace describes how in practice they are not: 'staff engaging in these procedures while trying to work with local realities all said that the tools do not work once implementation starts. There were no exceptions; this was a really striking finding' (Wallace, 2007, p165). These findings are consistent with other research, such as by Earle, 2004; Bakewell and Garbutt, 2005.

Many NGOs subscribe to the values of 'empowerment' and 'participation' and recognize that participation is critical for successful field work. However, curiously, most NGOs do not manage 'participation' or 'downward accountability' in a systematic way. The terms themselves are used to mean different things by different people (Brock and Pettit, 2007), which further confuses their management within organizations. One author has commented that the extent of downward accountability is a matter for the discretion of individual managers, relying on their 'grace and favour' (Kilby, 2006, p952). This was the entry point for Listen First: the project investigated systems for managing downward accountability on a systematic basis, across a variety of different interventions, rather than methods, for strengthening downward accountability in specific circumstances.

Much of the literature concludes that NGOs need new approaches to managing and reporting their performance that provide a reliable description of actual performance (for donors and senior managers) and which also encourage field staff to develop effective, respectful relationships with their intended beneficiaries. In other words, NGOs need systems that align the incentives created by upward accountability with good practice in downward accountability (for instance, Edwards and Hulme, 1995, p 224; Fowler, 1997, p57; Kilby, 2006, p960; Wallace, 2007, p177; Ebrahim and Weisband, 2007, p220).

During the Listen First project, a literature review was conducted to identify published case studies of NGOs' mechanisms for downward accountability. Over 500 documents were reviewed from a wide variety of sources. But very few reliable case studies were identified with enough detail to understand how processes had functioned at the local level. This was a striking finding in itself, suggesting a substantial lack of published material to support efforts in this area.

A number of pioneering innovations are emerging in the literature and practice. While some exciting approaches are emerging, these are still largely at an experimental stage: further innovation and research is needed before they can be applied more widely.

ActionAid took a major step with their radical, values-based Accountability Learning and Planning System (known as ALPS), launched in 2000. This attempted to place downward accountability at the heart of organizational systems (ActionAid, 2006). However, a 2007 review found that the quality of implementation remained variable. Arguably, this is because ALPS has not been managed to a consistent standard within ActionAid

International: individual managers have applied it at their own discretion. While some adapted the principles carefully to local contexts, others have not applied them to a significant extent and are not even familiar with them. They have not been supported adequately and held accountable for their performance in this area (ActionAid, 2007).

The Humanitarian Accountability Partnership's 2007 Standard for Humanitarian Accountability and Quality Management is a milestone in creating working definitions of downward accountability and locating them within quality management policies for NGOs (HAP, 2007). Their 30 members are generating a host of innovations (HAP, 2009; Jordan and Van Tuijl, 2006). The HAP standard creates a framework of organizational level policies; managers have to develop ways of meeting these commitments at the local level and demonstrate compliance with them. This locates HAP at the opposite end of a spectrum of organizational oversight from ALPS. It appears that the NGO sector is still struggling to develop organizational systems for managing diverse cross-cultural teams, which balance the demands of central oversight and consistency with those of decentralization and the need to inspire greater commitment to specific values in staff.

Chambers has recently described a methodological revolution, using participatory methods to generate quantified measurements of qualitative factors (such as empowerment) (Chambers, 2007). A particularly powerful example from Bangladesh shows how this can resolve the tensions for an organization to be accountable to different stakeholders. In this case, local groups rated their progress using a standard model, with three different levels of performance across four areas. The groups found this useful to review their work and inspiring for future action; senior decision-makers used the quantified summaries to manage the performance of field staff and report to donors (Jupp and Ali, 2008).

Other researchers have also experimented with similar approaches to measurement. Kilby (2006) developed a model to quantify and measure empowerment. Keystone is piloting methods for generating comparative feedback from recipients of funds and assistance, with a view to balancing local learning and management reporting. They are part of an emerging field, including the Center for Effective Philanthropy and Dara International's Humanitarian Response Index (Jacobs, 2009).

The Listen First project was developing along similar lines at a similar time, perhaps reflecting a wider convergence in the sector around the problems faced and potential solutions.

Listen First

Listen First is an emerging system for managing downward accountability in NGOs. It involves a central framework and three key processes, developed through a series of innovations and field trials. It is still a work in progress.

The framework defines what downward accountability means in practical terms. In itself, it is a substantial output from the pilot project. It sets out four levels of flexible performance standards across each of four areas. The framework can be presented on one side of A4 paper, albeit using a small font. The four areas are: providing information publicly, involving people in making decisions (participation), listening and staff attitudes and behaviours. The four performance levels are labelled: sapling, maturing, flowering and fruit-bearing. These were also easily translated into ratings: one, two, three and four.

For each performance level in each area, the framework sets out a series of example behaviours for field staff. The behaviours are all couched in positive, progressive terms, with the aim of encouraging staff to build on their existing efforts and inspiring them to do more, where appropriate. This establishes a set of expectations about what downward accountability means, and what different levels of performance would entail.

The framework aims to balance the flexibility needed for sensitive, context-specific interventions with the consistency needed for a management system. Field staff can adapt the specific behaviours, constituting different performance levels, in line with local circumstances. It also allows the same processes to be followed, and comparisons made, across different interventions. It plays a central role in structuring the three processes, below. During the research project, the framework was translated into a number of languages, including Portuguese and Khmer. It is directly compatible with the central four benchmarks in HAP's 2007 Standard (HAP, 2007). During the project, Concern joined HAP and preparing for their baseline exercise became a significant priority. Senior managers emphasized the need for this compatibility.

The structure of the framework was developed in discussion with pro bono advice from staff of the professional services firm PricewaterhouseCoopers and experienced NGO practitioners. The content for the first draft was drawn from Mango's Accountability Checklist (Mango, 2005). Subsequent drafts were developed by the research team in response to field testing with staff and local communities in Cambodia, Ethiopia and Angola.

The three key processes are:

- self-assessment workshops for staff to reflect on current levels of downward accountability, and identify potential improvements;
- community research, into local people's perceptions of the level of downward accountability actually achieved and how useful they find an NGO's work (disaggregated by gender);
- management reports, summarizing the levels of downward accountability actually achieved.

This approach was developed in response to some significant challenges in managing downward accountability identified during the course of the research. Downward accountability mechanisms had to be carefully adapted to the local context; standard solutions were not effective. There were significant tensions between downward accountability and other management priorities. By its nature, downward accountability requires significant personal courage and humility in order to listen actively to others, release power and challenge personal assumptions. So, achieving downward accountability in practice relied to a great extent on staff attitudes. It was not effective to instruct staff to change their attitudes. Instead, the research team worked with staff to reflect on the importance and implications of downward accountability in their work. These issues are described further below.

Field Trial: Angola

In February 2008 the research team worked with Concern's country programme in Angola, one of the six pilot countries. This section describes the methods used and research findings. The field trial built on experience from the preceding five pilot countries, allowing the team to pilot a full set of tools. It provides a practical example of the three Listen First processes in action and the type of findings they generated. Similar findings were generated in the other field trials and lessons from these are included in the section on 'lessons and implications'.

Background

With changes in Angola's political situation, Concern Angola was moving their programme from short-term emergency work (and direct implementation) to longer term development work (and working with local partners). They had started exploring approaches to improving their accountability to local communities and were interested in being part of the Listen First pilot project, specifically focusing on a major livelihoods programme. The livelihoods programme was working with 100,000 vulnerable people in two provinces in rural Angola. It had a budget of 9.2 million Euros and was scheduled to run from 2006 to 2010, with a second phase planned from 2010 to 2015.

Methods

The methods were discussed and refined with the team in Angola. They included the three elements of Listen First processes.

Self-assessment workshops for field staff: Two workshops were carried out with Concern and partner staff, one in Huambo and one in Kwito. They were one and a half days long, carried out in English with translation to and from Portuguese. They had three sections:

- staff reflected on being in a disempowered relationship and identified the key elements of a more effective relationship;
- staff identified the constraints and opportunities for improving how they worked with communities, across each of the elements of the Listen First framework;
- staff used the full framework to assess their current performance and identify plans for improvement.

Community research: 12 focus groups, six female and six mixed, of approximately 10 people each, and 12 key informant interviews were carried out across six villages. The villages were randomly selected from all those Concern works with, with three from 'hard to reach' and three from 'easy to reach' categories. The community research was guided by an ethical statement. It used a peer review process whereby field staff from one location conducted research in another project location. This was a practical compromise, bringing a measure of independence to the research process, reducing costs and keeping learning within the staff team.

A set of research questions was designed linked to the four elements of the Listen First framework, with two additional questions to explore peoples' perceptions of the value of Concern's work. The six research questions were:

1   How easy is it for you to find out the following key information about Concern: who is the main person assigned to your village; how to contact Concern; what Concern's objectives are here; who Concern is trying to help; what Concern's budget is for its work here, and how funds are being spent?
2   How much have you contributed to making important decisions on project activities?
3   How much does Concern listen to your ideas and comments?
4   How comfortable do you feel discussing your personal issues with Concern's staff?
5   How useful has Concern's work been for you personally?
6   How wisely has money been spent on this project?

Researchers were trained on participatory exercises to introduce, discuss, rate and record people's perceptions. Cartoons were commissioned to illustrate four different performance levels for questions one to four. Each question was closed by asking participants to rate performance by allocating 20 beans across four different levels: low, medium, high, very high. These could be compared to the four performance levels in the Listen First framework.

Reports for managers: The quantitative and qualitative findings were written up by one of the programme managers, and discussed with country management and head office management.

Findings

Self-assessment workshops: Staff were observed engaging enthusiastically in the self-assessment workshops. One manager said they created 'space for us to debate and discuss how we can further improve our approach in increasing participation … transparency, etc'. There were lively conversations about what Concern was fundamentally trying to achieve and communities' capacities to do things for themselves.

When field staff and their managers were split into separate groups, field staff were observed challenging their manager's self-assessment scores, based on their own experience working directly with communities. For instance, in one workshop managers scored the level of participation at two, but field staff scored it lower at one. After discussion, the field staff changed this to two. In both workshops, staff settled on a self-assessment level of two out of four for all of the four areas of the Listen First framework.

Community research: The focus groups and interviews produced a rich mix of qualitative and quantitative feedback. The detailed feedback varied by location. However, some similarities and trends were identified. For example, about half of the focus groups knew the face of the relevant Concern field staff and some could mention the name of the individual assigned to their village. Eighty per cent of the focus groups said that they participated in a number of project related activities including for example: project identification, changes to activity plans and selecting group leaders for the project activities. However, their level of participation was being 'informed' about what was happening, the first level of the framework. As one focus group respondent said 'We don't contribute in decision, they come and had already make plan for us on what we will be going to receive'.

In relation to 'listening' the focus groups and interviews found that people felt they had the opportunity and confidence to speak to Concern staff. However, feedback raised questions about the depth of this engagement. Two typical quotes were:

It easy to contact Concern to send our ideas and comments through staff assigned in the field, but not all ideas/comments has been responded and in many cases … no responses are given back to us.' (Focus group respondent)

It is too difficult to encourage people to talk [at meetings], we always hear someone from the community who are vocal enough or village chief speaking sometimes on our behalf.' (Women's focus group respondent)

The quantitative findings from the bean ranking exercises were summarized in tables and charts. This made it easy to compare perceptions between villages and to compare staff self-assessments with villagers' rankings. It also allowed performance to be aggregated.

The individual focus group scores provided data which field staff could use, in addition to the qualitative findings. For example the women in one village were the only focus group to place beans on level one, the lowest level, for how well they felt listened to. As a group, they placed three beans on level one and the remaining seventeen on level two. This allowed for more nuanced descriptions and further discussion.

Reporting and management: The programme managers had been closely involved in the pilot and were very supportive of the results. One of the programme managers commented that his team found it a useful exercise, saying that 'lots of information was provided by the respondent[s] which gave us to rethink and staff start reflecting of what we are doing. We have discussed initially the reports with the staff and partners and agree to many of the issues presented …'. He continued to comment that the community research 'provided a signal to the community and respondents that we are willing to listen and improve our work and relationship with them'. He also said that his team 'definitely might repeat this research sometime, to make sure if there are any changes over time'.

However, the programme managers also faced many other priorities and, six months after the field research, one programme manager said they had not yet fully considered the final report and drawn up strategies to improve their accountability. Other priorities included a pressure to focus on 'fast track projects', achieve targets and spend budgets.

The acting Country Director said he found the process useful, as the exercise had 'given management a way to control the performance and behaviour of our staff in the field which in the past was lacking'. This was very encouraging, albeit the emphasis on control could have been explored further. However, in practice this was not possible as he left the organization shortly afterwards. He also had many other priorities on his plate. In his monthly report to head office, covering the research period, he reported eight other major issues he was dealing with alongside the on-going work of managing the programme, including: mainstreaming HIV/AIDS work, contributing to government initiatives, and engaging with other external stakeholders such as the UN. All managers involved in the project said that staff turnover in Concern Angola, particularly at management level, had been a big challenge. During the last 13 years there had been

11 Country Directors. The Regional Director agreed that accountability to communities needed to be improved. She said the pilot exercise could provide a baseline upon which to monitor improvement. She also had many other priorities contending for her attention. The research team had a one hour meeting to go through their entire report.

Lessons and Implications

Lessons

Throughout the research, field staff appeared to find the Listen First processes useful and relevant to their everyday work. They were observed engaging enthusiastically in the workshops and provided many practical examples of the importance of downward accountability for their work. A number of key lessons emerged from the pilots, including the following.

The way the ideas and tools were introduced was important for generating engagement, reflection and learning among staff and managers. The research team quickly learnt that implementing head office initiatives, like this one, require careful handling. To work well, non-threatening spaces for reflection had to be created. Power dynamics always risked distorting this process. For example, in an early pilot using the Mango Checklist, field staff were primarily concerned with scoring themselves as highly as possible, as they felt their scores might affect the level of funds available to them. This feedback prompted a review of the approach taken by the research team, in particular how to work with the principle of supporting people's own efforts and critical reflection. Before the detailed pilots, head office management tended to prefer the certainty of the checklist as a basis for managing accountability.

The same principles were equally important when field staff took steps to improve downward accountability. When standardized or externally designed mechanisms for downward accountability were applied without careful consideration they often did not work. There were always local complexities. For instance, some of Concern's partners in Cambodia put up notice boards and complaints boxes. But local people did not use the boxes, for reasons to do with local political history, cultural norms and out of date information on the notice boards.

During the first pilot in Pakistan it was not possible for men to speak to women alone in the pilot villages, emphasizing the importance of having female and male members as part of the research team. Gender issues were therefore made more explicit in the framework and research project. Women-only focus groups were run, to hear their views of Concern's work. This direct feedback from women could potentially be expanded, to provide a way of assessing the impact that interventions have on women, as distinct from and in comparison to men.

The self-assessment workshops provided staff with an opportunity to consider the effects of existing relationships and power dynamics within the community on these initiatives and their work. For example, during one workshop in Cambodia staff considered the efficacy of holding public meetings as a way of hearing from intended beneficiaries. Staff concluded that even if the poorest in the village were present at the meeting they were not comfortable saying anything. Staff suggested this could make local people feel less confident, rather than helping tackle discrimination and inequality. During the workshop, staff developed alternative approaches to hear from local people such as visiting them at home. Facilitation skills proved crucial for implementing the Listen First processes and improving downward accountability.

The research team faced significant language challenges in the first pilot in Pakistan pilot. Many of the poorest people in villages spoke a local dialect, not the national language, Urdu. But some staff members did not speak the dialect. During one of the focus groups, the wealthier members of the community translated between staff members and the poorest in the community, which risked distorting the process and entrenching oppressive power dynamics. The same issue occurred in Cambodia, Angola and Ethiopia.

Translating key concepts could create substantial misunderstandings. Sometimes there was no direct translation for the word 'accountability', and translators instead chose from a number of options, including words that meant 'policing' or 'checking up'. The pilots seemed to work better when the word accountability, or its translation, was not mentioned, and instead the work was described as being about developing good relationships with local communities.

With careful facilitation, the same processes of reflection were carried out with partner NGOs. This approach was sometimes in opposition to less flexible, 'donor-recipient' approaches to handling relationships with partners. Staff were more comfort-able considering partners' downward accountability than their own. It emerged from the research that the relationships between Concern and its partners were not generally characterized by the Listen First principles. For example, the head of a long standing partner organization in Cambodia, asked politely but directly if Concern would also improve its accountability to his organization. In the following year the partner had taken steps to improve their own downward accountability, but Concern had not changed how they worked with that partner.

Managers had many other priorities, such as getting project plans and budgets approved, completing activities laid out in project logframes and spending budgets within fixed time scales. Downward accountability was sometimes in active opposition to these. When field staff were asked about the main constraints to making progress in this area, staff in two different pilots said: 'Leadership ... how senior managers are serious enough to promote this participation and not becoming activity oriented' and there was 'no motivation from line manager'. Managers had little incentive to prioritize downward accountability, and were not held to account for performance in this area.

The use of quantified summaries of performance and a standardized framework caused sharp differences of opinion. Some saw the summaries as important for reporting performance in a short, comparable way across projects. They argued this was necessary for senior managers, so they could manage the levels of downward accountability actu-ally achieved. Other people were concerned that quantified findings would be taken out of context by managers and this would create incentives to inflate scores which would undermine reflection and learning at field level. There was a danger that the system would be reduced to unhelpful bureaucracy. Some also questioned whether the four criteria were too simplistic for use across a wide variety of organizations and communi-ties. However, some staff involved in the research reported that they liked the quantified findings as it helped them understand how well they were performing.

Implications

The findings may have significant implications for managing downward accountability in international NGOs like Concern. The key factors in improving downward accountability were: (a) the quality of local leadership, management and support available to field staff and (b) the attitudes of front line staff to the importance of downward accountability, releasing power to local people and partners, and helping local people build their self-confidence. These factors could shape a management agenda, for instance around encouraging country-level managers to consider what downward accountability means for them, how they can promote it and its implications for their relationships with staff.

An NGO may also have to review the relationships between head office and field programmes, and field programmes and partners, to ensure managers have the space and flexibility to implement downward accountability. To support this, managers may have to be consistently held to account for the level of downward accountability they actually achieve. Without this incentive, it is hard to see how improvements will be possible in practice. A system like Listen First could potentially form the basis of an organizational system to achieve this.

The pilot project also concluded that some general policies could be applied across more interventions, in most circumstances, to create an enabling environment, encouraging staff to develop effective downward accountability practices. They resonate closely with the HAP Standard and include areas such as: an open information policy; informing partners and local people about contact details, project plans and their rights (in relation to the NGO); focusing staff attention on building dialogue and trust with partners and local people; holding regular review meetings with all stakeholders every six or 12 months; and collecting systematic feedback from partners and local people.

Further research

The Listen First approach needs further research in a number of areas, including:

- understanding representation within communities: who is speaking on whose behalf, with what legitimacy, and making this more explicit within an analysis of downward accountability;
- performance reporting may be improved by using finer grained scales (e.g. 1–10) rather than 1–4, particularly for community research;
- different participatory methods may improve community research and staff self-assessment. It may be useful to look at trends, either reported retrospectively or monitored over time;
- understanding whether stronger relationships generate more critical feedback from communities (or partners), because people feel more free to be honest. Weaker relationships may be more distorted by power dynamics, as people only feel able to make positive comments about decision-makers;
- understanding the relationship between reporting quantified summaries of performance and the quality of reflection and learning processes at field level; and the implications of repeating Listen First processes with the same individuals over time.

Conclusion

The academic literature concludes that there is an urgent need for NGOs to develop better ways of managing and reporting their performance, which are aligned with the fundamental principles of good development practice. Some exciting new possibilities are emerging; the sector as a whole is at the stage of developing innovative approaches.

Listen First was trialled as one such innovation. Through field research over six countries, a central framework and three management processes were developed. They were used to generate critical self-reflection by field staff, feedback from local communities and summary quantified data for managers – all three of which emerged as necessary components for managing downward accountability on a systematic basis.

As a result, Listen First could be a step towards developing a consistent way of managing and reporting performance for NGOs. It appears to be part of a new wave of approaches and methods. A number of areas need further research, in particular testing the impact this form of measurement has on relationships over time and refining specific methods further. However these issues appear manageable, particularly in the light of the potential gains available from improving accountability.

This research, and related initiatives, suggest that there are significant opportunities for NGOs to take hold of the debate around accountability and ensure that their internal systems are built on the core principle of consistently achieving empowerment and downward accountability in their own practice.

References

ActionAid (2006) *Accountability Learning and Planning System*, ActionAid

ActionAid (2007) *ALPS Review*, ActionAid

Bakewell, O. and Garbutt, A. (2005) *The Use and Abuse of the Logical Framework Approach*, SIDA

Bendell, J. (2006) *Debating NGO Accountability*, New York and Geneva: UN-NGLS

Brock, K. and Pettit, J. (eds) (2007) *Springs of Participation*, Rugby: Practical Action Publishing

Chambers, R. (1997) *Whose Reality Counts*, ITDG

Chambers, R. (2007) *Who Counts? The Quiet Revolution of Participation and Numbers*, IS Working Paper 296, Brighton: IDS

Earle, L. (2004) *Creativity and Constraint*, Oxford: INTRAC

Ebrahim, A. (2003a), *NGOs and Organizational Change*, Cambridge: Cambridge University Press

Ebrahim, A. (2003b) 'Accountability in Practice: Mechanisms for NGOs', *World Development*, Vol. 31(5) 813–829

Ebrahim, A. and Weisband, E. (2007) *Global Accountabilities*, Cambridge: Cambridge University Press

Edwards, M. and Hulme, D. (eds) (1995), *NGO Performance & Accountability*, London: Earthscan

Ellerman, D. (2005) *Helping People Help Themselves*, Michigan: University of Michigan

Fowler, A. (1997) *Striking a Balance*, Earthscan

Freire, P. (1996) *Pedagogy of the Oppressed (revised edition)*, London: Penguin

Groves, L. and Hinton, R. (2004) *Inclusive Aid*, London: Earthscan

HAP (2007) *HAP 2007 Standard in Humanitarian Accountability and Quality Management*, Geneva: HAP

HAP (2009) *The 2008 Humanitarian Accountability Report*, Geneva: HAP

Hilhorst, D. (2003) *The Real World of NGOs*, London: Zed Books

Jacobs, A. (2009) *Constituency Voice*, unpublished presentation, London: Keystone

Jupp, D. with Ali, S. I. (2008) *Measuring Empowerment? Ask Them*, unpublished article available at http://quality.bond.org.uk/index.php?title=Measuring_Empowerment (last accessed August 2009)

Jordan, L. and van Tuijl, P. (eds) (2006) *NGO Accountability*, London: Earthscan

Kaplan, A. (2000) 'Understanding Development as a Living Process', in Lewis, D. and Wallace, T. (eds) *New Roles and Relevance*, Kumarian Press

Keystone (2006) *A BOND Approach to Quality in NGOs*, London: BOND

Kilby, P. (2006) 'Accountability for Empowerment', *World Development*, Vol. 34 (6): 951–963

Lloyd, R., Warren, S. and Hammer, M. (2008) *2008 Global Accountability Report*, London: One World Trust

Mango (2005) *Accountability to Beneficiaries: A Practical Checklist*, Oxford: Mango

Mosse, D. (2004) 'Is Good Policy Unimplementable?', *Development and Change* 35(4): 639–671

Wallace, T. (2007) *The Aid Chain*, Rugby: Practical Action

Wield, D. (2000) 'Tools for Project Development within a Public Action Framework' in Eade, D. (ed) *Development and Management*, Oxford: Oxfam

Governing for Accountability: Principles in Practice

Marilyn Wyatt

Introduction

The maturation of NGOs around the world has led, inevitably, to a keen interest in their governance. This interest is inevitable for several reasons. First, more mature organizations are generally larger and more complex. With growth comes increased pressure from donors, beneficiaries, media and other external stakeholders for more information, better programmes and more meaningful guarantees against malfeasance and mismanagement. Second, post-Enron efforts to strengthen corporate governance worldwide have had a spill over effect on NGOs. Though this trend may originate in new regulations aimed at businesses, it is reinforced by the NGO sector's increasingly intimate relationship with the private sector in terms of funding and shared management practices and personnel. Finally, internal tensions in maturing NGOs themselves lead to a new appreciation for functioning boards. Chief executives who have single-handedly led smaller NGOs find that in growing organizations they are no longer able to exercise all leadership roles simultaneously. An engaged and competent board can provide the leadership capacity any larger organization needs to operate efficiently while meeting the expectations of a proliferating number of stakeholders.

In short, good governance comes to the forefront when an NGO begins to think seriously about itself as an accountable organization. Externally, good governance ensures accountability as an adherence to applicable laws and standards, an open dialogue with stakeholders and the regular provision of accurate information and high-quality programmes. Internally, good governance ensures accountability as the clear flow of authority, rational procedures, sustainable operations and avoidance of conflict of interest. As a function of accountability, then, good governance is no less important to NGOs than to the private and public sectors. Indeed, an NGO's approach to governance expresses the degree of its commitment to responsible and democratic leadership – values that are essential to civil society overall.

But while the principles underlying NGO governance are relatively straightforward, in practice governance can be quite the reverse. NGOs have been slow to put their governance house in order precisely because, as freely constituted organizations, they are loath to introduce systems and structures seen as intrinsically bureaucratic. Moreover, the governance of organizations can be a messy and vague affair. Governance takes places in the innermost sanctum of an organization, where personalities predominate and prefabricated approaches may be inadequate for individual needs. As a result, uncertainty over the 'whats' and 'hows' of governance is rife among NGOs. In turn, this condition encourages a host of other dysfunctionalities: power struggles between boards and executives or sometimes even staff, a lack of shared organizational purpose between the board and staff or the misapplication of effort and resources, to name just a few.

This brief overview of the basic governance practices assumes that, far from being a prefabricated approach, they are a flexible tool that **can** be adapted to individual organizations, enabling good governance, not as unwanted bureaucracy, but as responsible, accountable leadership.

What Is Governance?

The English word *governance* derives from the Latin word meaning 'to steer, guide, or direct'.[1] The term generally refers to the way in which power is assumed, conveyed and exercised within a society or an organization. According to western political theorists, good governance is a sharing of decision-making authority that prevents power and resources from accumulating in the hands of a single individual or group. Good governance is rooted in a system of checks and balances between the different branches of government and a process of regular consultation between those who govern and those who are governed. This approach ensures that authorities serve the common good and are held accountable to the public trust invested in them.

In non-profit organizations, governance works in much the same way. Good governance exists when an NGO has an internal system of checks and balances that restrains the control of any one person or group and ensures the public interest is served. This emphasis on the public interest is crucial, since NGOs derive tax relief and other benefits from their pledge to serve the larger community rather than put profits in the pockets of owners.

Models for NGO governance generally derive from the corporate sector, where governance is understood as involving the relationships among owners, management, the board and other stakeholders.[2] NGO governance similarly defines the relationships among stakeholders both inside and outside the organization to ensure the fulfilment of its reason for being – which, in the absence of owners seeking profits, is its non-profit mission. As in companies, the authority to govern is invested in 'boards' which are bodies charged with the stewardship of the organization.[3] Boards are basically responsible for organizations' legal compliance, organizational performance as well as their longer-term direction and sustainability. Whereas among corporations there are two major traditions of boards – a unitary board largely or entirely independent of management and a dual structure with a management board composed of executives and a supervisory board composed of external controllers – non-profit governance models generally assume the existence of one board only.[4] In form, function and personnel, this board is understood as operating independently of management and as exercising authority over it, as shown in Figure 10.1.

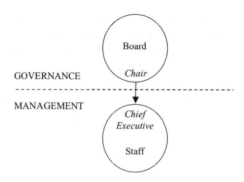

Figure 10.1 *Basic governance model*

Governance and Organizational Setting

In most legal systems, a governing board is required to incorporate or register a non-profit organization. Though their duties may vary, the board is named in the founding documents – that is, the statutes, charter or act of incorporation – as invested with legal responsibility for the organization. This explicit designation of the board as the governing body is important, for it clarifies where decision-making authority originates in the organization. Even in countries where the legal code does not require a board, NGOs are wise to include such a body in their organizational make-up, since an explicit governance structure is the first and most important step towards establishing a stable framework for accountability.

The founding documents are usually brief and may not specify the board's role beyond the time of founding. For this reason, they are ideally supplemented by a set of internal rules, or by-laws. A well-crafted set of by-laws helps ensure consistent leadership by the board and lays the groundwork for it to govern collectively, that is, with each board member engaged equally according to agreed roles and responsibilities. The by-laws usually outline the duties of the board, the roles and responsibilities of individual board members and the board's relationship to other organizational entities, especially the chief executive. The by-laws also contain rules for the board's operation, including:

- the minimum number of board members;
- membership rules (including eligibility criteria, the method of appointment or election, and grounds for expulsion);
- terms of office (that is, the length of terms and limits on the number of terms);
- the minimum number of board meetings per year;
- the manner of convening meetings and setting agendas;
- decision-making procedures (including the number needed for quorum and procedures for voting and recording decisions);
- conflict-of-interest provisions;
- the board's self-assessment procedures (the board and individual board member assessment).

Another document aiding organizational stability and accountability is an organizational chart. The organigram should show, among other things, the flow of authority from the board through the chief executive to employees and volunteer staff. A good exercise to help strengthen governance is for board members and chief executives to draw their organizational chart, inserting a dotted line to separate governance and management functions. If this proves difficult or if significant variations emerge, the chances are that the organizational structure needs clarifying or even overhauling, so that checks and balances are in place and there is a common understanding of the distinct roles of board and the staff.

Board composition

Perhaps no area of organizational governance has received more attention in recent years than board composition. Founding documents, by-laws and organograms may set forth a solid framework for governance, but in the end an organization is only as good as the people who lead it. Even with the most sophisticated structures and systems, the quality of individuals serving on the board can, in the words of author Jim Collins, make the difference between an organization that is merely good and one that is great.[5] Hampering the effectiveness of many NGO boards is a membership drawn exclusively from the sector itself. Such boards may have deep understanding of the programmes but are all too often limited in their outlook and outreach or riddled by conflicts of interest. Other NGOs have recruited celebrities to their boards in the hope that such names will lend their organizations visibility, glamour and legitimacy. But they often find themselves saddled with board members who feel that lending their names is enough and resist contributing more actively to the board's work. Recruiting people just because of their names often makes it difficult for such people to commit as they are too busy for the organization. Such people are usually in 'big demand'. Still other NGO boards consist of hand-picked friends or family members of the founder or executive director, who are unwilling or unable to operate as a counterweight to that person's influence. Around the world, NGOs have been slow to break out of these sterile patterns of board composition to recruit members who can govern fairly, with integrity, foresight and flair.

Creating a board that is both respectful of the framework for governance and flexible and innovative in its approach demands deliberate attention to the recruitment of its members. A balanced, capable board necessarily includes people from varied professional and personal backgrounds who are genuinely committed to the NGO's mission. They must also be prepared to work together as a team, overcoming differences and personal agendas. Finding dedicated and diverse board members is a major challenge in settings where volunteerism is unfamiliar or the NGO sector is still building credibility. Some organizations have turned to professional associations, chambers of commerce and retiree groups as sources of candidates; others have even tried advertising with good results. Whatever the approach, the main aim should be to build a board that has sufficient diversity to understand a complex environment, sufficient expertise to lead with competence and sufficient patience, prudence and humour to work together and deal productively on the tasks, tensions and untidiness that come with governance work.

Regarding size, experience shows that boards generally work best with five to 12 members, though this range is by no means absolute. At the smaller end, the board is more coherent as a team, whereas a larger number of members enables more effective committee work. Often boards grow in size as an organization develops and the board's tasks become more diverse. This trend is fine as long as a concerted effort is made to keep all members engaged and new positions are not created just to offset non-contributing board members.

Board roles and responsibilities

The main duties of NGO boards are often described in terms of lists, and there is little disagreement among experts that boards are responsible for such activities as 'protecting the organization's mission', 'ensuring adequate resources', 'hiring and firing the chief executive' and 'opening doors to new contacts'. While such lists encompass the broad range of board duties, they often lack an overall conceptual framework. Therefore it may be more productive to consider governance as a combination of function and focus (see Table 10.1). The board *focuses* on four primary, overarching concerns that are essential

Table 10.1 *The governance matrix*

	Policy (What do we stand for?)	Oversight (How are we doing?)	Guidance (Where are we going?)
Mission	• Mission and mission statement • Programmatic priorities • Approaches to planning and evaluation	• Mission-programme alignment • Monitoring of programme effectiveness	• Organizational vision • Recalibration of mission • Strategic planning • Goal setting (both near- and long-term)
Values	• Legal framework • Professional standards • Code of conduct • Conflict of interest policy	• Compliance with applicable laws • Projection of organizational values • Implementation of code of conduct, conflict-of-interest policy	• Enhancing culture of accountability and transparency • Setting example through board's own behaviour
Resources	• Definition of relationship with chief executive • Parameters for acquiring, using and preserving all resources • Internal controls	• Supervision of chief executive • Monitoring of disposition of resources • Financial oversight and audits	• Identification of longer-term resource needs • Resource development/fundraising • Risk management
Outreach	• Standards for transparency and accountability • Other parameters for relationships with donors, government and other stakeholders	• Timely and accurate reporting • Openness to feedback from stakeholder groups • Compliance with other accountability expectations	• Scanning for environmental trends • Promotion of organization in the community • Forging of new links with donors, beneficiaries, partners and other stakeholders

to the organization's core identity: mission, values, resources and relationships with the larger community. In so doing, the board engages in three major *functions:* setting policy; overseeing organizational performance and providing guidance in terms of strategic direction, and long-term sustainability.

In the governance matrix, a policy is understood to be a statement of principle or procedure meant to guide individual actions and regulate internal activity. Setting *policy* means generally determining the way an organization behaves (and does not behave). Exercising *oversight* means monitoring the execution and outcomes of programmes and activities, especially with an eye towards stated policies and goals. The board's supervisory responsibilities are largely exercised over one employee, the chief executive, to whom it delegates responsibilities for other activities. Providing *guidance* means determining a vision for the NGO and ensuring that planning is adequate to realize that vision through the acquisition of human, material and financial resources. The board's own behaviour has an important exemplary function insofar as it sets a standard for the entire organization, especially in the area of ethics and policy adherence.

The governance matrix suggests the most important areas in which the board should engage its attention, but many permutations are possible. Above all, boards should approach governance as a matter of inquiry. The board governs by asking questions, especially of the chief executive: questions that test assumptions, clarify procedures, identify goals and query outcomes, all in an effort to hold the NGO accountable for fulfilling its mission in a responsible, sustainable way. The three questions shown in the governance matrix are basic but they too have endless variations. A board that wants to assess its governance performance can ask whether it is effectively posing these and related questions and receiving acceptable responses in return.

Board members govern collectively, but they have individual duties as well. In the common law tradition, board members are expected to fulfil the duties of loyalty and care.[6] These duties hold for NGO board members too. In practice they mean attending meetings regularly, contributing actively to board deliberations, demanding accurate information and avoiding conflicts of interest that can lead a board member to put personal, professional or organizational gain above organizational interests. Many organizations find that a written agreement or job description for board members, including a conflict of interest policy, helps them better understand and realize their role.

To execute their duties efficiently, boards often delegate responsibilities to individual members. Nearly all boards appoint a chair who coordinates the work of the board and serves as the main liaison with the chief executive. In addition, a financial expert who serves on the board might be appointed to coordinate an audit or oversee preparation of financial reports, while a lawyer on the board may be given broad authority to oversee the NGO's legal affairs. Such delegation of specific responsibilities should be minuted in writing and must not be automatically assumed according to the professional qualifications of individual board members. By the same token, it is not enough for board members to limit their board service to specialized professional services. The first and most important duty of every board member is to contribute to the collective deliberations of the board as a whole.

Relationships between the board and management

NGO stakeholders usually regard the separation of management and governance as one of the most crucial measures of accountability. This separation involves the division of both duties and personnel. The usual rule of thumb is that management runs the organization from day to day, while the board is concerned with the big picture, especially where the organization is headed and how. Of course this does not mean that the staff has nothing to do with strategy, or that board members never contribute on the day-to-day level. What it does mean is that there is a fine but important line between these two areas that is jealously guarded by both sides.

Separation of authority: A tricky border line

One way to maintain the distinction between governance and management is to ensure the same people do not perform both jobs. This expectation may seem counterintuitive, since the staff usually know more about the NGO than board members and thus may seem in a better position to provide strategic direction or evaluate performance and needs. However, conflicts of interest arise when staff members serve on the board and, in a governance role, approve their own budgets, set their own pay, assess their own programmes and otherwise try to monitor and oversee their own activities. Their judgment is not impartial, and there is no way that a board composed of staff or of people intimately connected to staff can objectively ensure that the organization is well managed. In short: a board that is not separate from management operates in a perpetual state of conflict of interest and may, even with the best of intentions, interfere with the realization of a sustainable, accountable, mission-focused organization.

For this reason, staff members are discouraged from serving as voting members of the board. An exception is sometimes made for the chief executive, who provides the board with a useful bridge between policy or strategy and implementation. However, apart from the obvious conflict of interest, having a chief executive as a voting member of the board can strain that person's relationships with other board members, blur the distinction between governance and executive roles and cause external stakeholders to view the NGO as less accountable than it should be. The compromise many NGOs find acceptable is to include the chief executive on the board as a non-voting member, who withdraws from any discussion about a topic of direct interest, such as salary and performance assessment. If, for whatever reason, the chief executive does serve on the board as a voting member, it is important that he or she does not act as the board chair, as this would represent a concentration of power in the hands of one individual that could severely undermine accountability throughout the entire organization.

Delegation of authority: A difficult judgement call

One of the most important ways in which the board leads the organization is by hiring, and delegating authority to, the chief executive. The board does not give up all of its power; important duties the board retains for itself usually include conducting audits and deciding the disposition of large sums. The tasks delegated to the chief executive are generally of an operational nature: for example, staff supervision, programme implementation, the daily management of financial accounts and most stakeholder relations. Even as it delegates duties, the board remains the principal decision-making authority, and the chief executive remains answerable to the board for his or her actions. This supervisory relationship should be spelled out in the founding documents and by-laws as well as including a job description. Written expectations help to smooth cooperation, ease tensions or misunderstandings and keep the board from relinquishing too much responsibility or, at the other extreme, micro-managing the staff.

Although the lines of authority may be vertical, on a practical level the relationship between the board and the chief executive work should be a close and cooperative one. There is usually a considerable grey area separating board and staff roles, which needs an open and cordial relationship to sort out and resolve. A productive partnership between the board and the chief executive demands hard work, patience, mutual respect and honesty. Each side plays a supporting role for the other, offering advice and encouragement as well as constructive feedback. The key to success is good communication: the chief executive owes the board accurate, thorough and timely information about the NGO and its environment, and he or she must be frank about the guidance needed – and not needed – from the board. The board, for its part, should be clear and direct in its instructions, guidance and feedback. The board should not only monitor, but also mentor, the person it has hired to run the organization. Good board members probe, prod and praise in a way that leaves the chief executive with no doubts about what is expected and with feelings of motivation to do his or her best.

Effective Board Processes

There are three main areas demanding close attention if the board is to operate effectively as a governing body: (1) meeting preparation, conduct and follow-up; (2) committee structure and operations; and (3) board training and evaluation.

Making meetings work

As a collective body, boards are normally obliged to conduct their business in legally convened meetings rather than through email, phone conversations or other ad hoc channels. The organization of meetings – a primary responsibility of the chair – should be regular and well developed. Board meeting preparation is cyclical in nature, as shown in Figure 10.2.

The founding documents or by-laws usually specify a required number of board meetings per year. While there is no perfect number, one meeting annually is rarely enough for the board to discharge its full range of duties. Some boards find they can do their job in two or three long meetings yearly, while others prefer to meet monthly. Whatever the choice, board members need to be informed of the dates well in advance and have sufficient time to prepare for the meetings. Most NGOs find that attendance is better if a schedule of meetings is agreed at the start of the year.

For the sake of efficiency, meetings should be run with a carefully prepared, strictly enforced agenda. Key to this effort is a disciplined chair who knows how to guide discussion, encouraging participation while keeping to the main purpose in view. The chair

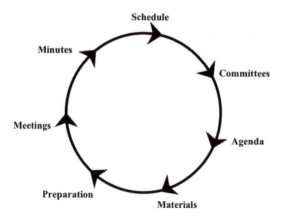

Figure 10.2 *The board meeting cycle*

normally prepares the agenda in cooperation with the chief executive. Other board members, especially committee chairs, should be given a chance to contribute to the agenda. Once set, the agenda becomes the blueprint for the meeting, and any deviation from it should be limited and well founded.

Background materials developed by committees and the staff in support of items on the agenda should be distributed at least a few days in advance. As part of their duty of care, all board members are expected to prepare for the meeting, mainly by being familiar with the agenda, understanding the issues and reading background materials in advance.

Some boards meet behind closed doors to protect confidentiality while others prefer open meetings to enhance transparency. Either approach is justified as long as it is conducive to the main business of the board. The board's approach to decision-making is usually dictated by tradition, organizational culture, efficiency and personal taste. Some boards aim for consensus while others vote in accordance with parliamentary procedure. Again, either approach is justified as long as it promotes sound judgment and teamwork on the board. For decisions to be binding, a quorum as specified in the founding documents or by-laws must be present.

A record of board meetings is a form of institutional memory and a basic instrument of accountability. The board should appoint a board secretary to keep a record of all meeting proceedings, including their time and place, attendance (including the presence of a quorum), the agenda, decisions taken and business deferred till a future meeting.

Members attending the meeting approve the minutes in draft before they are distributed in final form. Policy decisions by the board can be gathered together in a separate policy manual, to be made available throughout the organization. The secretary, working with the board chair, is responsible for ensuring that the policy manual is updated as needed.

In the case of emergencies, boards may need to conduct business outside of legally-convened meetings. To enhance accountability the by-laws should stipulate the procedures to follow on such occasions, such as contacting board members, conducting business by phone or email and ratifying any decisions at the next board meeting. Some boards appoint an executive committee to act on its behalf between board meetings.

Even with such extraordinary powers, the executive committee remains accountable to the full board and never governs in the board's place.

Board committees: Roles and added-value

Boards that have taken on the full range of governance duties find their work is easiest to accomplish through committees. Indeed, an effective committee structure is a hallmark of a highly developed, fully functioning board. Committees take on the tasks that in the smaller and newer NGOs may be performed by staff, such as the definition of issues to be addressed by the board, the preparation of materials for board meetings and the training and recruitment of new board members. In this sense, the formation of committees represents a shift of responsibility for its own work from the staff to the board itself.

Committees are delegated with authority to explore issues and propose decisions for consideration by the full board. They do not perform the work of the board itself. The reasons for this are that committees meet outside of legally convened board meetings and generally do not include a required quorum of board members. To maintain their focus and accountability, committees should operate with a written mandate or scope of work approved by the full board. The most common board committees are finance (overseeing the NGO's financial performance and account management) and governance (responsible for overseeing the work of the board itself). Development, planning and programme committees are also popular.

Committees work best when they follow a cycle similar to that of board meetings. Committee meetings should be scheduled at least one week before board meetings, so that there is ample time to prepare background materials for meetings of the full board. An agenda and background materials are distributed in advance and minutes are kept of proceedings. The minutes are most useful if they are geared to the needs of the full board for information or recommendations rather than simply regurgitating committee proceedings.

The majority of committee members should be from the board, though it is useful also to bring in outside members who have the necessary professional skills or are good candidates for eventual selection to the board. Staff members may also serve on board committees as non-voting members. Like the board as a whole, committees should set goals and evaluate their performance yearly.

Tending to the board's performance: Training and evaluation

Periodic attention to the performance of the board is now mandatory in most top corporations, and NGOs are following suit. Training usually includes team-building exercises and a discussion of the duties of the board and of individual board members, such as active participation and avoidance of conflict of interest. Orientations are frequently combined with the board's annual self-evaluation and setting of goals. Many boards find it works best to bring in an outside facilitator if possible. In any case, it is not desirable for the chief executive to conduct board trainings since it implies that the board lacks independence.

Annual self-evaluations help the board sharpen its vision and more clearly define its goals. They are also a good way to address dysfunctional behaviour on the board, such as poor attendance, tensions among members or simply a lack of team feeling. Board evaluations (self-assessments) are ideally performed yearly in a process that can be simple: time set aside at a meeting for a discussion of the board's strengths and weakness, or complex: a weekend retreat, complete with an outside facilitator. Most boards approach self-evaluations by asking board members to fill out a questionnaire individually and then compare the results. The questionnaire should ask how well the board performs its job as described in the founding document or another source, whether goals have been fulfilled and, more generally, whether the board adds value and works effectively on behalf of the NGO. The process, whether simple or complex, should result in candid assessment and honest discussion. Since the process of evaluation is only as valuable as the resolutions that come out of it, it should conclude with concrete plans for following up. Many boards find that an annual evaluation (self-assessment) is usefully paired with the setting of board goals for the subsequent year, which can then be used as benchmarks for the next evaluation (assessment).

Conclusions

NGO boards have long struggled with a lack of clarity about their purpose and a lack of pressure to perform. Chronic governance weaknesses are now being addressed in a gathering trend to establish standards, codes of conduct and other self-regulatory initiatives for NGOs worldwide.[8] Designed to unite and strengthen the NGO sector or a particular sub-sector in a common framework of accountability, these initiatives nearly always emphasize deep engagement and competent oversight by the board. Despite divergent national traditions and legal frameworks, boards are no longer acceptable as passive, non-contributing appendages to their organizations. Instead, aspirations to a higher level of professionalism are finally pushing NGO boards to live up to their responsibility to serve as stewards and protectors of the public trust.

Another trend contributing to new attention to NGO boards is the development of infrastructures for federated organizations. The large sums of money flowing through large humanitarian assistance, and social service organizations in particular, have prompted a search for rigorous, consistent standards. Striking the right balance between local autonomy and centralized control in federated organizations leads necessarily to a focus on boards. As they straddle the lines separating inside from outside in organizations, local, country and regional boards can provide robust guarantees for accountability in all its forms – from responsiveness to beneficiaries, international donors, home offices and manifold other stakeholders, to efficient, mission-directed operations.

Both of these trends are long overdue and certainly welcome. Good governance should be a central pillar of the NGO sector, and capable boards are central to that effort. One can only hope that current interest in NGO boards continues to grow even keener. If it does, civil society as a whole will prosper.

Notes

1   Much of this chapter is adapted from *A Handbook of NGO Governance* by Marilyn Wyatt with the Central and Eastern European Working Group for Non-profit Governance (Budapest: European Center for Not-for-Profit Law, 2004), available at www.ecnl.org.hu/index. php?part=13publications&pubid=18&PHPSESSID=bf7e858e6734eed46d8e4ba52780 e0fa (last accessed June 2010). The Handbook is now available in many translations; see the ECNL website (www.ecnl.org) for more information.

2   See *OECD Principles of Corporate Governance* (Paris: Organisation for Economic Co-operation and Development, 2004), p11, available at www.oecd.org/dataoecd/32/18/31557724. pdf (last accessed June 2010). This document is the basis of many national-level corporate governance codes.

3   Non-profit governing bodies can go by a variety of names: 'board', 'leadership council' and 'advisory committee' are among them. In this chapter, the word *board* is used generically to encompass them all.

4   In countries where NGOs have dual boards, the model of governance proposed here applies to the independent supervisory board. In the case of a non-profit association, the board is understood as being distinct from the membership or general assembly, which remains the highest governing body while delegating most of its duties to the board.

5   Collins, Jim (2001) *Good to Great: Why Some Companies Make the Leap ... and Others Don't.* New York: HarperBusiness.

6   See *OECD Principles of Corporate Governance*, p59.

7   A good discussion of this topic is offered by Karl Mathiasen in *Board Passages: Three Key Stages in a Non-profit Board's Life Cycle* (Washington: National Center for Non-profit Boards, 1990).

8   See, for example, *Study on Recent Public and Self-Regulatory Initiatives Improving Transparency and Accountability of Non-Profit Organisations in the European Union* (commissioned by the European Commission Directorate-General of Freedom, Justice and Security and submitted by the European Centre for Not-for-Profit Law, 2004), available at www.ecnl.org.hu/index. php?part=14news&nwid=259&PHPSESSID=9c6866902ae7d79c9dc6cd18e4f29ca2,   as well as One World Trust's database on self-regulatory initiatives available at www. oneworldtrust.org/csoproject (both last accessed June 2010).

Part IV

Managing Strategically

11

Strategic Issues Facing NGOs into the Foreseeable Future

Brian Pratt

Introduction

Working on issues of relief and development creates an almost infinite number of challenges for any organization. Given the impossibility of listing the vast array of economic, social, scientific and political challenges development entails, as a sort of opinion piece, this chapter focuses on the strategic issues organizations are likely to face in the foreseeable future. This choice does not seek to deny or underestimate the daily problems found in political repression, inadequate health care provision, effects of environmental shifts, insecurity and so on. Rather, a strategic approach is adopted because missing from many contemporary debates is a reflection on whether global factors – such as climate change and the transfer of a geopolitical axis from the Atlantic to somewhere between Mumbai and Shanghai – will impact on the world of international development as we know it. In my view, it is already apparent that macro factors of climate change, geo-economic and geo-political reordering are having wider-spread impacts: food security, conflict and deteriorating quality of (global) governance being but three examples. It does not, therefore, follow that new challenges will necessarily be met by the existing architecture of aid, where new entrants with large budgets such as the global funds, new mega-philanthropy and non-OECD donors are already disputing accepted ways of 'doing development'.

Within this broad area of debate, my focus is the potential effects on and possible responses of international development entities, particularly non-governmental organizations (NGOs), as inadequacies in the current aid architecture become exposed. From my vantage point, the themes of primary concern can be loosely grouped under the headings of:

- structure and identity;
- commercialization;
- governance and management;
- roles;
- transition from an aided to an unaided development sector.

Running through these themes are other potentially major issues, which are also discussed. Examples are loss of independence and values, and possibly loss of civic vision and energy, replaced by the emergence of more organically-based social movements and other civil society groups. Indeed, at several points in this chapter a conclusion is reached that many NGOs simply fail to align and be clear about their operational and organizational strategies. This shortcoming works against ensuring that who they are will enable them to effectively deliver what they want to do! The resulting gap between words and deeds is a sort of debilitating schizophrenia that invites public mistrust. An interesting question, therefore, is whether or not reform in an inadequate aid architecture presents NGOs with opportunities to 'rediscover' and regenerate themselves?

Strategic Issues Facing NGOs into the Foreseeable Future

An overarching issue for NGOs is one of conceptual location. While charity, humanitarianism or solidarity are voiced as inspirations, NGOs in development have been based on a simple principle of transferring resources from developed to developing countries. Despite being refined and amended, transfer underpins the whole NGO development model. At different times and with different agencies, the resources being transferred have ranged from goods (blankets, food, wheelchairs), technical expertise (volunteers, specialists), information (books, IT), capacity building expertise and, of course, money. The simplest structure has connected the source of funds directly through to the intended recipient with no further intermediation. Despite many arguments to the contrary[1] this function still underpins the model for most NGOs. For most if not all, it has represented their core business.[2] Therefore regardless of values, ideologies and management fads, there is a certain imperative behind the structures adopted which permit and facilitate cross-border transfers of resources. This model has enabled possibly millions of poor people to receive an array of assistance from basic needs such as food, water to help with productive enterprises, education, infrastructure and support for empowerment.

However, this perspective and function may be on the wane. As the absolute or proportional transfer of concessionary resources and grants is reduced, or possibly even comes to an end as some countries reach middle income status, southern governments can assume responsibilities for many services. A result may be the emergence of very different types of non-governmental organizations. Proponents of the concept of a global civil society would argue that joint or common concerns create a very different set of organizations on the international stage. Some will pursue wide political interests while others will reflect cooperation and alliances between people with very specific shared concerns, for example sufferers from a specific disease or disability. Others will try to advance more traditional interests such as unions representing members from common trades or professions. Domestically, in post-aid countries we would expect to see a greater diversity of civil society groups representing specific local interests, and the demise of the generalist 'development' NGO running large projects in, for example, agriculture or 'community development'. This general shift in the concept of an NGO and NGO-ism as a narrative may also play out in other ways, starting with structure.

Structure and identity

Structurally we will probably see more NGOs in both developing and developed countries transfer from being a part of civil society (I am loathe to use the value word here as values may survive but the structure and function may not) to being not-for-profit semi-commercial contractors, primarily to the state. In many agencies, this move is causing management problems. The transfer is not always smooth. Some staff object, boards are often caught unaware and the demands of contract management are often different from grant management.[3]

A second structural issue must be the growth of the transnational NGOs and the emergence of *global brands*. NGO development and relief work is increasingly commoditized and, as noted above, negotiated into contracts. The commercial response is to develop global branding. Internationally recognizable brands appropriate to the world of BBC and CNN dominate images gathered from around the globe. As communication and fundraising become increasingly more competitive – no longer just an Anglo Saxon NGO phenomena as it was in the past – it is easier to buy into such a brand in order to ensure that you can legitimately claim presence across the globe. This strategy is especially prevalent in the case of humanitarian emergencies. A rush for global presence and recognition has spawned international alliances, some with brand-seeking names: Oxfam International, Save the Children federation, Care, World Vision, Plan International. Meanwhile others are trying to create new brands: ACT and Alliance 2015 are but two examples.

Many global alliances start with a common assumption of size being equal to strength. One rationale for global 'confederating' is that international coverage goes beyond access to in-country funding and the need to beat off the competition in order to better focus on joint advocacy. Although she was rather dismissive of NGOs as a historical blip linked to the aid business, Mary Kaldor (2003) probably summarizes the federating approach to what she called global civil society being able to assemble pressure internationally around common themes.

A further assumption behind global reconfiguring is that it solves demands for simpler aid, epitomized in the ideas of harmonization and alignment to be found in the Paris declaration. The practical idea is that a federated form will reduce duplication (one NGO donor rather than six); simpler procedures, such as a single reporting format; and reduced transaction costs, seen in having fewer offices in a developing country.

There will be challenging times ahead for staff and boards to continue to refine and justify this trend. Is it purely structural, as a means of reducing transaction costs and duplication, or global marketing, or coordinated civil society advocacy action? Or will it threaten the very diversity of civil society and ape multinational companies driving small cafes to the wall to replace them with franchises of golden arches or the NGO logo-based equivalent?

Decentralization is a third structural issue. For many years, international (INGOs) have run field offices in developing countries. Initially such set ups were led by expatriates, usually from and directly responsible to decision-makers in a sponsoring country. From this base, many changes in management structure and culture have taken place. A usual start is for small expatriate-run offices being localized by recruiting local management and staff, followed by various forms of decentralization. Some of this movement was justified on the grounds of: (a) being less expensive, which often turned out to be erroneous; (b) getting closer to the action for better decision-making; (c) involving local people more; (d) ensuring a higher in-country or in-region (like in the case of ICCO and HIVOS setting up regional offices) profile; and (e) last but not least, raising funds locally, replicating in order to 'capture' resources stemming from decentralization of official donors to in-country decision-making. In management terms this has led to several major dilemmas. Firstly, how to retain central control and accountability? A main response has been to tighten financial controls, audits, authorizing procedures, reporting and monitoring. The degree of success in this approach is dubious, given reportedly increased internal corruption in many of the larger organizations.[4] Secondly, a raft of issues arise from becoming an international employer. This move brings challenges to standardized employment conditions, adapting to local labour law, surrendering flexibility (e.g. the ability to move out of a country at short notice is no longer possible) in favour of stability, and an in-country presence which can no longer be viewed as temporary whilst the visiting NGO 'worked its way out of a job'. The notion of a permanent INGO presence, however constructed in terms of international governance, is a significant shift in the rules of the game.

The degrees of actual devolution of decision-making power and accountability vary, but confront the contemporary NGO manager with a reinvigoration of old problems as well as new ones. Not least is the enduring issue of withdrawal from 'partnership' commitments once funding comes to an end. More and more, donors remove countries from their lists of priorities and other countries achieve middle income status. It would seem that success, in terms of increased average per capita income, was not something many NGOs planned for![5] One reaction to this contradiction is for some agencies to assume an indefinite presence in a specific country. For many others exit strategies are still an urban myth, shattered only when funding shortages suddenly makes action inescapable and hence we see agencies leaving quickly with little attention to how, or whether, some form of phased withdrawal would be more appropriate.[6]

It is very likely that as some INGOs will continue to decentralize, some will try to retain control in the centre and others will try to move accountability out to their local offices. Other INGOs will re-centralize and cut out what they now regard as superfluous layers of regional and country-level management and functions. Several major groups are already reducing large numbers of local staff in their regional offices. Managers are often untested, and unused to making staff redundant and closing or reducing offices. The down-side costs of earlier decentralization were not foreseen as redundancy costs and staff resistance come to play. In reaction, shrinkage can be stemmed or avoided if incomes are diversified, for example by becoming more commercial.

Commercialization of NGOs

The past decade has been particularly characterized by a heightened market-oriented approach to aid thinking and allocation. This move has sharpened a structural headache of NGOs shifting from grant finance to contract funding. This commercialization of NGOs and its implicit alienation from 'civil society' will probably continue. In doing so, it creates different management problems for those who follow the distinct paths of civil society actor or (social) service contractors. The latter option creates a particular type of 'corporatized' NGO, the 'not-for-profit service providers'. David Korten (1990) was perhaps the first to identify this outcome when he used the term 'public service providers'. Their origins are still in the original concept of the 'voluntary' organization which utilized various forms of 'charitable' or 'not-for-profit' legislation designed to allow organizations to engage in a series of activities without the burden of paying tax on their often donated income. Now a common hybrid exists of not-for-profit companies, providing services on a contractual basis as part of the privatization of social welfare, but still claiming the tax advantages on the basis of their providing a 'public good'. This arrangement – already common in the UK and the US – is being propagated globally as a part of the free market approach to social welfare and protection. Rather than large state run service institutions, not-for-profits provide public services on contract. Such agreements have become increasingly constraining in what is permitted, and expected from the contractor. Flexibility is ever reduced. Correspondingly, the mooted autonomy or independence of the not-for-profit contractor becomes truly a myth. Organizations (INGOs) which 20 years ago would have survived on freely donated cash from the public, or reasonably untied grants from state and other donors, now find themselves hurdled into the contract culture. It is surprising how detailed these contracts can be.[7] This system is changing INGOs into management platforms for the implementation of contracts, moving them further away from being part of civil society and closer to being a part of the market place.

This model is also being passed on to local NGOs in developing countries. Indeed it is conscious policy of some donors that the future for NGOs in developing and transitional states will be through the institutionalization of local contracts from local government to local NGOs (or not-for-profit service providers in our terms). Thus some major funding bodies have already started the process of moving civil society funding to recipient country governments. New, in-country, funding mechanisms are being set up with the intention that, over time, they can be reproduced locally, primarily through the tax base. In the interim NGOs are supported through official aid, sometimes channelled as part of budget or sector wide support. This move makes an implicit assumption that NGOs are primarily about service delivery and hence their 'institutional sustainability' will lie in large tax-based contracts. Experience from emerging economies would seem to indicate that indeed some work will be funded by local government. However, other forms of NGO activity are suffering. For example, impressive independent research centres and think tanks in Latin America are losing ground rapidly. Likewise, social movements and indigenous groups find it harder to identify independent support for alternative sources of funding. There is also an issue of how civil society organizations can play a watchdog role against a government that is funding them. One of the many implications of commercialization is to be found in NGO governance.

Governance and management: A confusion of approaches

The issues raised so far lead to a worrying concern regarding governance. Few agencies have thought through the implications of moving to a transnational structure with 'localized' country programmes. There is a clear governance tension in the old centralized model based in the initiating donor countries, between the 'parent' organization and the partners or subsidiaries in the recipient countries. A few agencies have decided that, indeed, their first loyalty is the governance structure at the home base in the parent agency's country. This includes most of the Nordic agencies for whom local membership is a precondition to qualify for government funding. Conversely, others are working towards some form of confederation of independent national bodies (WWF, World Vision). Some NGOs seem to swing back and forth between these models.

Of greater concern is where these uncertainties and lack of sound strategy lead to governance being weakened towards the donor end, yet not strengthening it at the recipient end of the aid chain. The counter reaction to this concern has been a not-altogether successful attempt to tighten 'accountancy' rather than accountability. Such moves have been based on the unproven assumption that tight accounting procedures can compensate for ill-defined governance. Whilst others continue to argue that genuine partnership can only come when the old model – of donor-recipient, described at the beginning of this chapter – finally gives way to a confederation of equals each with their own governing structure and tied together with a democratic system of governance for their international character and mission.

Challenges of governance are intimidating enough without the extra problems of unclear management models and challenges to overall organizational legitimacy.[8] Two predominant models seem to be emerging. The first is donor-based accountability through traditional not-for-profit boards. The other attempts to set up international boards (sometimes of a family of donors, others including representatives of developing countries). A risk is of an ill-informed board trying to engage with a large professional staff spread across the globe engaged in a range of work in different contexts. Internationalizing is likely to exacerbate and not improve this distance between the board and their organization. Further challenges are the linkages of accountability (mainly to donors), the failure to be accountable to clients and the tenuous accountability to the governance structures, except through minimal and formal accounting and auditing. Indeed strict accountability in terms of 'accountancy' practices is often seen as sufficient evidence of good governance, when this is clearly not the case, the two often being confused.

The perennial lack of a 'bottom line' undermines the ability of managers and board members alike to agree on indicators of success and performance. The lowest common denominator therefore tends to lead to an emphasis on reporting against activities, with too little review of strategy and impact. The confusion between management and governance will continue to be a key issue in the future, undoubtedly inspiring a range of options and solutions, while the failure to fully investigate alternatives could further undermine the legitimacy of many organizations.

If a manager's role, along with other stakeholders of course, is to assess constantly whether their organization is 'fit for purpose' this will inevitably lead into further discussions about the role of their organization. We have already referred to changing roles through reference to the increased dominance of contracts for services among some NGOs, and for others the implications of changing concepts of partnership as well as appropriate engagement in 'advocacy'. Increasingly many NGOs will be obliged to revisit the question of their own role and whether indeed they are fit for purpose. This will lead them into revisiting missions and strategy, as well as their own structures and relationships.

The challenge will be to review these not only from an internal perspective but also against a changing global context. The past decades of growth have allowed internal decisions to be postponed, or, in some cases, managers were able to use growth as a sufficient indicator of success to avoid other more profound questions. Now it is becoming clear that growth and turnover are not sufficient to justify an organization's work. What they do in response is not going to be uniform. Some will look to more evaluations of impact. Others will review external stakeholders' perception of their organization, or explore other means of external justification or validation. With relevance becoming an increasingly important issue, such reviews will certainly need to happen.

Difficult issues will have to be confronted. Not least of all whether ensuring fitness for purpose means actually doing less better, and not assuming that more is always good. For example, if more means losing strategic focus, and independence, would downsizing be a better option? A failure to make such strategic decisions can only lead to unplanned downsizing or change later. Better surely to plan and move by design rather than be forced by events.

Roles

In terms of role options the larger NGOs will have a range of options open to them. Some will revert to being supporters to civil society through capacity-building and other services. Others will become the commercial market-centred end of the not-for-profit sector. Yet others will rebuild contacts with different civil society groups internationally around specific common interests. Examples might include the global call for action against poverty, climate change advocacy or more specific concerns over genetically modified (GM) crops, access to retroviral drugs etc.

There is a sign that too few donors and INGOs are sufficiently concerned to make all-important, but often modest, support available to groups dealing with issues which politically cannot easily access local resources. Thus independent lobbying groups, think tanks, research bodies, minority representation, legal and human rights challenges may be as vital in a middle income as in a poor country, but these are likely to be the last areas to pick up local funding. However, it is also true that northern-based donors do not always find it easy to raise funds for such work either and as their free unrestricted funds are under pressure they will find it more difficult to support such entities and activities.

In certain parts of the world, predicted to be a smaller part, some NGOs will still find the ability and demand upon them to act as an alternative to the state through provision of key services to many poor people – mission hospitals and schools emergency water, refugee camps etc. In such circumstances the classic transfer of resources will still have some logic.

As more countries move into middle income status and find themselves no longer eligible for external funding, one of the biggest challenges for locally-based NGOs will be the transfer from being a part of what some call the aided civil society to the unaided. We have noted that some NGOs will move towards government contracts for service provision or even the administration of microcredit which is increasingly seen as a way of protecting organizational sustainability. An array of organizations will disappear along with the available funds, some leaving little mark behind whilst others will be sorely missed. Other NGOs will have to rediscover their constituencies and to see what is possible with less funding and more voluntary inputs. This shift from external funding to domestic resource mobilization demands serious work on reviewing strategies, but also missions and vision. It may also mean dismantling staffing and organizational structures and reinvigorating voluntarism.

One of the issues plaguing NGOs is that they were born out of innovation but as a sector they have become conservative. They feel the need for a structure and staffing which can last indefinitely or at least for several years. A recent INTRAC workshop concluded that it is the nature of the sector that structures and approach should change regularly to meet changing needs and external factors.[9] Flexibility and courage will, however, still be needed to tackle the overtly political constraints and discrimination suffered by many women and excluded groups. Given the intractable nature of some persistent forms of inequality, it is likely that the resource transfer model will be less important than a long-term commitment to confronting such injustices, and it is possible this is where smaller international, often niche organizations will have an advantage because of their low level of financial and infrastructural exposure.[10]

Overlying many of these other challenges of both the external environment as well as internal structures and mission, let alone developmental challenges, there is some consensus that NGO management has not always been well served by NGO managers. There are differences among boards who appoint chief executives, between those who see NGO directors as *managers of existing strategies* and those selected in order to *lead and inspire with new ideas*, representing their members or constituents, leaving daily management to support staff. Whilst some have regarded the appointment of business and public sector senior staff as a positive move towards professionalizing management, others see this as part of the decline of the sector along with the loss of the higher moral ground, intellectual leadership, independence and innovation. Boards are presumably choosing between these criteria. And ideally the choice is based on a sound reading of the organization's current condition and accurate perspectives on its needs to fit an uncertain future.[11] In the absence of leadership many boards assume this mantle themselves, with mixed results. It is tempting to take a generational approach to this and bemoan the loss of leadership in the sector. Or is it a sign of its coming of age and institutionalization?

Towards a Conclusion?

One friend I have worked with for many years from a Dutch NGO rightly reminded me that civil society itself is very strong. New movements are emerging across the globe. What is in doubt is the future of many of the NGOs, or at least the model we have become accustomed to over the past generation or so. Indeed, in many middle income countries people have more time to do voluntary work. They have the education and competencies to manage local campaigns and pull together people with common interests.[12] The future will probably see a further burgeoning of civil society but not necessarily the professional (i.e. with paid staff) NGO except where governments have indeed adopted a policy of privatizing certain public services.

Therefore we can foresee a situation where many organizations will either change, evolve or possibly die. There is a challenge in knowing how to manage these difficult processes. However, there are also likely to be difficult decisions which, in reality, may be made by default rather than as a result of conscious processes. Decisions about whether to revert to supporting civil society (nationally or globally)[13] or to seek a future as commercial not-for-profits providing services on contract to the state. Civil society as represented by citizen-run groups or associations will indeed continue to expand in overt and more subtle ways that reflect openness or the repression of autocratic governments that seek to reduce the space for civil society along with other freedoms.

Overall, good management may be portrayed not by who is bigger than whom and whose growth rate outstrips those of their neighbours, but who can be flexible and agile in front of a changing world with differentiated and more nuanced needs.

Notes

1   People may talk of being partners, of promoting ideas, and although people prefer to think of themselves as development workers rather than donors or aid administrators, this doesn't detract from this basic core business.

2   Recent moves towards trying to put advocacy centre stage implicitly challenges this resource transfer model. But there is an inevitable tension in many NGOs which preach advocacy yet their funding comes primarily for resource transfer. This tension will increase.

3   It is only a matter of time before commercial companies mount legal challenges to the tax free status of not-for-profits. Indeed there have been some legal tests cases, including in developing countries, already. They include issues of unfair competition by microcredit institutions operating as NGOs, when in fact they are commercial finance institutions relying on profit from transactions to pay their costs.

4   Confidential interviews and discussions with major INGOs over the past year.

5   Clearly average per capita incomes levels are not or should not be the only indicator of a country's progress, and high levels of inequality can quickly leave many areas and populations way below international poverty lines despite high average incomes.

6   Teobaldo Pinzas talks of 'a stampede rather than thought out retirement' as INGOs left Peru. T. Pinzas (2009) 'The end of an era', *INTRAC*, No 43, September.

7   I visited a refugee camp in Rwanda where the birthing room was clearly too small and barely fitted the length of the birthing couch. But the size of the room had been specified by the UNHCR (United Nations High Commission for Refugees) contract.

8   Unclear to the extent of unplanned hybrids, e.g. some offices with advisory committees, others with random southern representatives on international boards, overlapping boards (country members, international confederations/alliances), some country offices with local boards, others with none, etc.

9   Intrac workshop: New Directions in International NGO structures, 10 November 2009, available at www.intrac.org (last accessed June 2010).

10 See, for example, the work of those supporting isolated indigenous groups compared to the large environmental agencies, where the former continue to fight for indigenous rights and the latter feel they have to play safe due to large scale operations and investments.

11 It should be added that there is a similar debate in the private sector.

12 Recently Intrac ran a programme with both communities in northern and southern Cyprus. It was notable that most people we worked with were volunteers running various groups on the island hence all of our training and other activities tended to be held in the evenings.

13 In India I met NGO directors who have already moved from running large-scale community development programmes to directing much smaller operations offering capacity building

and other support to local civil society (in the form of community groups, peasant federations and the like). This move was consciously made in light of the changing demands and realities of certain sections of the rural poor and was seen as a sign of long term success of earlier work.

References

Kaldor, M. (2003) *Global civil society: An Answer to War*, Polity Press, London

Korten, D. (1990) *Getting to the 21st Century: Voluntary Action and the Global Agenda*, Kumerian Press, West Hartford, CT

12

Strategic Planning: The Cultivation of Organizational Beauty

Chiku Malunga

A beautiful girl does not need to be a great dancer
(African proverb)

Introduction

Aided civil society organizations find themselves in complex task environments described in Part II of this volume. This chapter discusses how, through strategic planning and implementation, civil society organization (CSOs) can position on a changing landscape by making themselves beautiful. It does so by revisiting the meaning of strategic planning, reviewing the constraints CSOs face in doing so and describing how they could be overcome in practice.

For our purposes, strategic planning is interpreted as how a CSO organizes itself to respond to the changes in its task environment and, more importantly, how to influence the political, economic, socio-cultural and technological factors involved in its favour. Organizing in defence and expansion of spaces in the interests of those at the margins of society, which is the *raison d'être* for aided civil society, is only possible through effective strategic planning.

This chapter is based on the author's experience in facilitating strategic planning processes among southern and northern CSOs and on his research work on their strategic planning processes and practices. A central argument is that, to be effective, strategic planning must be viewed as a process and practice of 'cultivating organizational beauty'. In rapidly changing and increasingly complex operational contexts strategic planning today is a conscious and collective continuous cultivation of attractiveness. In other words, strategic planning moves from being merely formulation and implementation of strategic plan documents to ensuring that the organization is consciously and collectively in an agile and strategic state all the time. This is a condition where an organization is strategically 'fit'. The challenge of strategic planning is to make an organization fit by making it beautiful.

Organizational Beauty

In traditional African communities marriage was and is still a very strong institution. Most girls looked forward to getting married someday. The ability to attract suitors or a good husband therefore is a major concern among many girls and their parents. Obviously girls who are naturally beautiful do not have a lot of pressure as it is easier for them to attract men using their natural attributes. Those who are less fortunate with socially valued endowments are encouraged to develop compensatory skills and behaviours. One skill frequently emphasized is the ability to sing and dance. Men would therefore be attracted to a woman because she was very beautiful or maybe because she was a great dancer or she had a valued skill or behaviour. The same was also true for men though to a lesser degree. Less fortunate men could also develop such skills as being great dancers, great hunters, great singers or great story tellers. This resulted in proverbs such as 'if you are not a butterfly in beauty be an elephant in size' and 'a beautiful girl does not need to be a great dancer'.

The proverb 'a beautiful girl does not need to be a great dancer' talks about the essence and purpose of strategy or how organizations can gain advantage more effectively. An objective of strategic planning is to gain advantage over competitors in a sustainable manner. Civil society voice is in competition with many other voices. If there was no competition strategic planning would not be necessary. The proverb shows that organizations can compete using 'beauty' or 'great dancing'. And competition is about getting the required attention or being noticed by the people critical to the success of the organization. For instance the purpose of business is to compete for and create a satisfied customer (Drucker, 1974, p56). Businesses therefore need the attention of the customer. The purpose of government or political parties is ultimately to win the next elections (Drucker, 1990: 34). Governments therefore need the attention of the voter. The purpose of CSOs is to bring about good change or transformation in people's lives (Chambers, 2005, p184). CSOs therefore need the attention of the people they serve and the donors financing their work. They also need the attention of the other stakeholders critical to their success. All organizations are 'asking for eyes' or for attention because, beauty becomes useless if there is no one to admire it. The proverb 'the beautiful girl does not need to be a great dancer' metaphorically shows that there are two ways to attract and get the needed attention or recognition. These are *great dancing* and *cultivating beauty* or *being a great dancer* or *a beautiful girl*. Great dancing implies getting the attention we need through pushing or aggressively forcing one's way.

Cultivating beauty implies getting the needed attention through pulling or being a magnet rather than pushing. It means using leverage or the least effort and people coming to us out of their own accord without any feeling of coercion. The proverb encourages organizations to become *beautiful girls* rather than *great dancers*. It encourages organizations to invest more in cultivating beauty rather than aggressively pushing for attention. If we take two non-profit organizations for example, a beautiful organization is one that donors are attracted to because of its evident impact on the lives of the people it serves. Its results speak for themselves as *good merchandise advertises itself*. An organization like Nelson Mandela's AIDS Foundation is an example of a 'beautiful' organization as it has Mr. Mandela's charisma and magnetism. A beautiful organization may not need to push donors for funding as they are already convinced. A great dancer on the other hand is the non-profit organization that has not taken time to invest in its capacity to demonstrate impact on the lives of the people it serves and therefore be attractive to donors. This organization will need to do a lot of work in fundraising and convincing donors to support its work. Cultivating organizational beauty in this case is investing in the capacity to demonstrate impact.

It is important to clarify at this point that 'beauty' strategies need not exclude 'great dancing' strategies. In real life the two are complementary and need to go together. Successful politicians for example craft 'beautiful messages' to be attractive and then aggressively campaign to get the messages across in order to win elections. The point of the message in the proverb and this chapter is that in strategic planning processes organizations generally emphasize more on what they must do (great dancing) as compared to what they must be (beauty). When organizations have done their home work – investing in capacity to be beautiful – their need for aggressive dancing will be less and it will mostly be downhill rather than uphill. Though great dancing may appear to produce required results in the short term, these results are not sustainable because in the long run, organizations cannot give what they do not have and what they have is in their being. Cultivating organizational beauty enables an organization to invoke the law of attraction or to become a magnet of success in a sustainable way. An ability to attract through beauty corresponds to a strategic fit – creating a landscape of admirers.

Strategic Fit

This section expounds the concept of organizational beauty as it relates to strategic planning by describing its components which are organizational relevance, legitimacy and sustainability (Atack, 1999, p860). Strategic planning therefore involves asking and answering the three key questions: how can we remain or improve our relevance? How can we maintain or enhance our legitimacy? How can we sustain our organization, its work and benefits to the people we serve?

A beautiful organization therefore is one that is relevant, legitimate and sustainable. These three concepts define the organization and its relationship with its task environment or how the organization positions itself in the task environment.

Relevance is based on the competences of the organization being in alignment with the needs and demands of its task environment. When this happens, the task environment will 'own' the organization thereby legitimizing it and the task environment will also provide the resources the organization needs making it sustainable. Relevance goes beyond implementing a needed project or delivering a needed service. It means the results of the projects or the services transforming people's lives. Relevance also means implementing unique projects or at least implementing the projects in a unique, creative and innovative manner as a way of reducing competition.

Legitimacy means being accepted by the people we serve and other stakeholders in a deep enough way to gain their commitment and ownership of the efforts. It means connecting with the people in the values, emotional or affective domain. Key questions for legitimacy include: who is the CSO accountable to? How representative is it of the people it serves? How deeply do the people feel attached to it? And whether the people

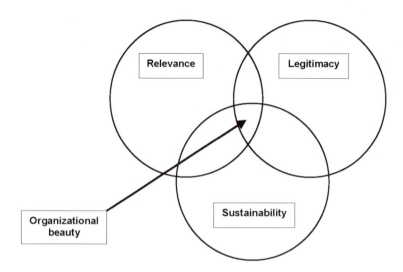

Figure 12.1 *Locating organizational beauty*

feel the organization is reflecting their own values. Taken further, legitimacy is the basis for the CSO's involvement in facilitating civic-driven change – the concept of people acting as citizens to change the society they live in, not necessarily as needy beneficiaries, participants, public clients or economic producers and consumers, but as agents of their own future (Fowler and Bierkart, 2008). Facilitating processes that enable the people to be agents of their own future is also the true meaning of relevance.

Sustainability refers to the continued existence of the organization, its projects and its project benefits for as long as these are needed by the people the organization exists for. At the organizational level, sustainability goes beyond having adequate financial and material resources. It means the ability to attract and retain high quality and competent personnel. It also means the ability to handle succession from one leader(ship) to another. Project benefit sustainability refers to the continued flow of benefits from a project after the project has closed down. It means having well thought through and effective exit strategies.

Where the three concepts of relevance, legitimacy and sustainability intersect is called the strategic fit (Hatch, 1997, pp102–103). The ultimate beauty of an organization is the attainment of its strategic fit. Strategy therefore must be concerned with actively identifying and managing the fit in order to achieve and sustain competitive advantage. The proverb 'no matter how far you are from your house, you will keep going until you get home' illustrates this point well. The organization's home is its strategic fit. It is not easy to achieve strategic fit and once achieved it is never permanent. But since it is the organization's home or desired destination it is worth the continuous effort required. Strategic fit is the ideal position that the organization strives to attain. This is the position of beauty and grace for the organization. At this position it becomes possible to say 'good merchandise sells itself' as the organization becomes a magnet attracting all it needs for its progress and success. But this is easier said than done.

Factors Constraining Cultivation of Organizational Beauty

In most strategic planning efforts there is a conspicuous lack of 'process consciousness' because strategic planning is mostly limited to the formulation stage. Limited or no conscious attention is paid to the preparation, implementation and monitoring and evaluation stages. Strategic planning is taken as an event, often being equated to the document which is the output of a strategic planning workshop.

Specific factors tend to help or hinder sound strategic planning. At the preparation stage they include: the need to have an agreed and shared purpose for undertaking strategic planning among all the key players; ensuring adequate awareness and understanding of what is intended to help clarify expectations; ensuring ownership especially by the staff and board; not having a task force to manage the process; and not conducting organizational assessments to identify issues to guide the tasks involved. Preparation is also hindered by failing to negotiate and agree on the roles and responsibilities to be played by the different levels (the organizational, intermediate/country/field and operational/intervention levels) in the strategic planning process. This creates confusion as to what to expect from each level and how to balance the 'top-down and down-top' negotiations needed to ensure a successful process. CSOs generally pay less attention to the preparation stage: this undermines the whole process as preparation forms the foundation stage for the whole process.

The formulation stage involves developing the organization's ideal picture – the future situation the organization aspires to. It also involves an analysis of the organization's uniqueness – to enable the organization to identify factors that can help it stand apart from others; crafting the vision, mission and values statements. It also involves identifying issues to address (on its relevance, sustainability and legitimacy or in the organizations work, capacity needs and collaboration or networking needs); goals to accomplish on each identified issue; and the strategies to pursue in accomplishing the goals. Strategies are the 'prioritized, broad, alternative, preferred conceptual how of achieving the goals'. Strategies are turned into activities through chosen programmes and projects, the conscious day to day implementation of which is the nurturing of organizational beauty. A strategy document is supposed to be a 'loose' roadmap in cultivating the organization's attractiveness.

The strategic plan also includes a performance-monitoring framework for the monitoring and evaluation of the projects and the strategic plan as a whole. It also includes a budget, for the whole period of the strategic plan, on all activities, for example, under the three main areas of relevance, legitimacy and sustainability, including administrative costs.

Factors constraining organizational beauty at the formulation stage include inadequate 'strategic' capacity of the participants and the need for competent facilitators. Inadequate strategic capacity is demonstrated by a general lack of 'outward and future orientation'. Most CSOs are still stuck in an 'inward and present or past orientation'. Effective formulation is also constrained by 'inadequate will to change' resulting from fear of loss of position by staff and fear of loss of donor funding if the priorities identified go against the organization's current donor priorities.

Constraining factors at the implementation stage include inadequate knowledge and organizational capacity to implement the strategic plans and the influence of donors on the organization's priorities. Implementation is also constrained by staff who may feel that their participation in the process was false because decisions were already made at the top and they were required just to rubber stamp. The disruption in human relationships caused by the loss of jobs for some colleagues (as is usually the case in many strategic planning processes) may negatively affect the morale and commitment of some of the remaining staff. Failure to focus and concentrate on a few key projects, capacity issues and collaboration or networking issues is another key constraint to effective implementation. Aided civil society organizations usually take on too many activities as a survival technique (to maximize chances of funding). This usually results in the amount of work planned outstripping a capacity to implement especially in terms of time, 'energy' and money.

Lastly, at the monitoring and evaluation stage, obstacles include overemphasizing accountability to donors at the expense of learning, and a culture of busyness undermining reflection and learning. In addition, there is a common inability to differentiate between the monitoring and evaluation of strategic plans from monitoring and evaluation of projects and activities.

Effective Strategic Planning

By introducing the *levels of complexity model*, this section provides a further and more comprehensive analysis of the constraints aided CSOs face in their strategic planning processes. It also discusses the key challenges the different players face in attempting to address these challenges. It then concludes by presenting some suggestions on how to address the identified challenges.

Applying the levels of complexity model

The *levels of complexity model* is an analytical tool that helps organizations locate the problems they face at different organizational levels. A level indicates the gravity or seriousness of the problem, the amount of energy or effort needed to address it and the types of interventions that can be used as possible remedies. By placing strategic factors at the appropriate levels, a CSO can identify the strengths it needs to build on, problems to tackle, blockages to clear and the weak areas to strengthen. Table 12.1 below shows the levels from simple to those more complex.

The analysis above shows factors influencing the effectiveness of a strategic planning process from simple to the most complex. It also shows that most of the factors involved are at the lower levels of material and financial resources and skills and competences.

While it is important to address these lower factors, if the factors at the higher levels have not been addressed (even if they are unrelated) interventions at the lower levels will have little or no value. This is because the higher factors form both the framework and the foundation that ensures effective and sustainable use of the lower level interventions. To ensure effective strategic planning therefore it is important to address all the levels simultaneously.

Secondly, the highest level and therefore the most complex is the task environment. In their external environment, CSOs usually have little if any control over donors'

Table 12.1 *Factors affecting the effectiveness of the strategic planning process*

Level of complexity	Factor affecting the strategic planning process
1 Financial and material resources	Limited time given to preparation No time for monitoring and evaluation Not enough time for transition from current to new strategic plans No money given to projects that are not donors' priorities Less money given to capacity building efforts
2 Skills and competences	Lack of collective understanding of the strategic planning process Inadequate assessment to gauge organizational priorities to address in strategic planning No task force to manage and lead the strategic planning process Low competence of facilitators or consultants Inability of participants to engage at strategic level – low outward and future orientation Inadequate knowledge among CSO leaders to implement, monitor and evaluate strategic plans CSOs not aware of national and international frameworks guiding donor funding priorities
3 Policies, systems and procedures	Short term, project based funding from donors No monitoring and evaluation systems for the strategic plans Organizational structure, policies, systems and procedures not consciously reviewed, adapted or aligned to the new strategic plan
4 Relationships	Unequal power relationships between donors and CSOs Lack of clarity of the roles and responsibilities of the different personnel levels in the organization Facilitators or consultants employed on one off basis and not on partnership basis
5 Vision and mission	More emphasis on strategic plans being viewed as an accountability and marketing tool rather than being viewed as a governance, management and learning tool Insufficient outward and future orientation
6 Values	Limited ownership of the strategic planning process by the CSOs CSO leaders wanting strategic plans only as fundraising tools Culture of 'busyness' constraining organizational learning
7 Task environment	Diminishing levels of donor (financial) support Donors funding only their priorities Donors not keen on funding 'CSOs self-sustainability efforts'

purposes and priorities in their funding practices. Building their internal organizational capacity, however, would still give them room for manoeuvre, either through gaining negotiating power with the donors or identifying alternative sources of funding. Edwards (1996, p1) observed that, 'the environment is crucial but not determinant; therefore, organizational choices always provide some room for manoeuvre'.

While the task environment is largely outside the circle of control of the civil society organizations, they can best invest their energies working on those levels that they have some control over. This is the essence of strategizing. Aided CSOs can find alternative sources of 'unrestricted funds'. They can also create monitoring and evaluation systems for the strategic plans. Through these efforts, they can become more empowered to negotiate more developmental relationships with donors. These moves may also help them to develop enough 'shock absorbers', enabling them to ignore non-developmental donors while they are looking for funders who are genuinely interested in their development. When the CSO leaders consciously invest within their circle of influence, it begins to expand and they gain more and more control over their task environment. The more they do this the more they will be able to engage donors at a collegial level rather than as in a child–adult relationship.

Lastly, the way to deal with the challenges in level 1 or the material and financial resources is to provide the needed resources. Simply signing a cheque or making time available can solve most of the problems at this level. Problems in level 2 or skills and competences can be solved by provision of information, knowledge and training. Provision of financial and material resources, information, knowledge and training are the most straightforward and common forms of intervention. One reason for the primary attention they receive is that challenges at these levels are the most visible and most felt (James, 2002, pp126–127).

Problems at the higher levels are often less visible, less tangible, less felt and least addressed. These problems cannot be resolved by training or provision of resources. The most effective approach to tackling these challenges is through process interventions. Process interventions are based on reflection and learning in the organization. Reflection and learning help the organization to surface and confront its contradictions. The starting point is the ideal picture – the organization's collectively hoped for and agreed desired destination some years into the future. The organization creates regular space and time to reflect on how its policies, systems and procedures, its relationships, structures, role as and responsibilities, leadership styles and its vision and mission and values are helping or hindering it from reaching its destination as stipulated in the ideal picture. Answers from this reflection guide the modifications or changes the organization needs to make so that it is aligned to its ideal picture.

It is worth remembering that process interventions to address the higher level challenges require more energy and consciousness in the organization. This is why most aided CSOs avoid it and rush to the familiarity of training and resource provision. However, without the foundation of process interventions, training and resource provision cannot bring about lasting change in the organization that will eventually ensure effective strategic planning processes and organizational effectiveness.

Players in strategic planning

All players in a strategic planning process face challenges, be they the board, management, donors, consultants or the communities.

Common challenges faced by the board include low commitment, inadequate capacity and failure to provide strategic leadership. For the management the factors include inadequate knowledge and capacity to effectively implement the strategic plans or to move from an operational to a strategic orientation.

For donors, challenge factors include stringent, inflexible conditions attached to their money, project rather than organizational-based funding, short-termism and failure to establish genuine partnerships with the organizations they support. Consultants usually fail to establish partnership relationships with the CSOs they serve. They typically limit the scope of strategic planning by excluding it from a wider OD framework, promoting a 'service rather than developmental or civic agency' approach to their work. Communities usually fail to participate at a 'strategic level' in the strategic planning process and fail to hold the organizations accountable for the performance of the strategic plans.

There is still low awareness of the roles and responsibilities of the players in the strategic planning process. There is need for more knowledge, capacity and commitment among all the players.

Strategies to Cultivate Organizational Beauty

Strategy is the 'grand, conceptual how' to reach the organization's goals in the areas of relevance, legitimacy and sustainability. The intersection of the organization's relevance, legitimacy and sustainability is its beauty or attractiveness. Strategic planning therefore is the organization's conscious effort to cultivate its beauty or attractiveness. This section discusses how aided CSOs can address the above constraints in order to improve their strategic planning processes thereby enhancing their beauty or attractiveness.

The way to cultivate organizational beauty is to *kindle a fire* in the organization. Traditionally, in African societies, the elders would occasionally sit around the fire in the evenings to discuss issues of concern to the community in order to maintain stability and unity. If the fire is not kindled for this purpose, literally or symbolically, the proverb 'it is easy to defeat the people who do not kindle their own fire', warns that the community will be defeated in the time of trial. 'Lighting a fire' in the organization means creating space and time to discuss how the organization is managing its strategy and draw lessons for improvement of practice. If organizations do not light this fire they will easily be defeated by threats in the task environment and weaknesses within the organization. They will not be able to seize opportunities in the task environment and make best use of their strengths.

A way to cultivate organizational beauty is to have a strong strategic team that regularly lights a fire in the organization as a basis for effective practice. Lighting a fire involves establishing a learning and knowledge management system in the organization. A detailed discussion of learning and knowledge management is made in another chapter but I will present two tools that organizations can use to regularly light a fire with the aim of improving strategic behaviour. These are the after action review checklist and environment scan checklist.

After action review

After action review is a simple tool that enables continuous assessment of organizational performance looking at successes and failures, ensuring that learning takes place to support continuous improvement. It works by bringing together a team to discuss tasks, events, activities or projects in an open and honest manner. A systematic approach of this tool is crucial in driving organizational change. It is the key aspect for organizational learning and motivation. The essence is to bring together the relevant group to think

Table 12.2 *An after action review*

Question	Purpose
What was supposed to happen? What actually happened? Why were there discrepancies?	These questions establish a common understanding of the work item under review. Differences from plans should especially be explored.
What worked well? Why? What did not work well? Why?	These questions generate reflection about success and failures during the course of the project, activity, event or task. The question why generates understanding of the root causes of these successes and failures.
What would you do differently next time?	This question is intended to help identify specific actionable recommendations. They must be crisp and clear and achievable and future oriented.

about a project, activity, event or task (under the headings of: relevance, legitimacy and sustainability) and pose the questions shown in Table 12.2.

The after action review needs to be administered regularly to detect changes within the organization that may require strategic shifts as a response. It is important to document what comes out of the reviews because documented rather than memorized knowledge is more important as 'the palest ink is much stronger than the strongest memory'. Organizational learning is the changing of organizational behaviour which occurs through a collective learning process. This is why it is important to involve as many people as possible in the process as 'knowledge is like a baobab tree, no one person can embrace it alone'. An organization can only learn if its individual members are learning and there are systems to capture the learning. Without individual learning there can be no organizational learning. Consciously learning from its practice makes an organization to continuously improve its practice because 'a person is taller than any mountain they have climbed'.

Environmental scanning tool

The second tool is the task environment scan tool presented below. The aim of the environment scanning is to regularly detect changes in the environment that may present opportunities or threats to the organization and the organization needs to proactively respond to because 'when the beat of the drum changes so must the step of the dance'.

This is administered through answering a set of questions:

• What changes have taken place in the organization's task environment in the last year (or the agreed period of time) that have implications on our organization's work or what trends or patterns are unfolding in the task environment that have implications on our organization's work?
(Hint: Look at the external environment in the terms of: politics, economy, socio-cultural factors, technology and donor funding practices.)
Limit your observations to the country but also draw from the region, continent and global trends that have relevance to the country.
• Based on these observations, what do you predict for the next year? What opportunities and threats do you see for the organization?

- What priority issues therefore must our organization address in the coming year to continue moving towards its ideal picture or achieving its strategic fit?

Strategic awareness and reflection

It is important to improve the understanding of key players that 'strategy' involves a never-ending process of connecting organization and context rather than a one-off event. This could be done as a special session with the organization at the beginning of the process. It could also be done by taking a learning approach throughout the whole process as discussed above. Another way would be organizing joint inter-organizational reflective sessions where leaders from different organizations would come to reflect and share experiences on their strategic planning processes.

Preparation for the strategic planning process would be improved by ensuring that there is an agreed and shared purpose for going through the strategic planning process among all the key players. This could be achieved through the awareness session discussed above and some political 'buy in activities' by the organization's leaders. Such sessions and activities would also help to establish ownership. Having a special task force or a strategic planning team with specific responsibilities for the whole process is a key success factor. Conducting an organizational assessment to determine the issues to address in the strategic planning process is critical. To be more effective, consultations for the assessment must be guided by a board approved framework which includes factors shown in Box 12.1:

Box 12.1 *Factors in strategic awareness*

Relevance

- A (re)statement of organizational identity: beliefs, values and mission.

- A statement of organization – wide thematic priorities for development – for example, environment or income generation or human rights.

Legitimacy

- A (re)statement of key principles to be applied throughout the organization – for example, on relations with government, participation, gender, organizational and individual account-ability.

- A (re) statement of the cause and change analysis which justifies the overall approach to development work and provides the basis for the interpretation of events.

- An indication of any desired changes in relationships that significantly affect the organiza-tion's position in society – for example, working more (or less) with civic actors, such as trade unions. Informal sector organizations, or with private business, governments and official aid agencies.

- Sustainability.

- A statement of intentions with respect to qualitative and quantitative growth.

- A statement on how the organization intends to finance itself and its work given the 'predicted' funding environment over the period of the planned strategic plan.

Adapted from Fowler, 2002, p81

Formulation of strategic plans would be improved by ensuring the participants have adequate competences and 'strategic thinking ability'. Enough time must be provided. When the organization does good work in the preparation stage, they free a lot of time for the formulation stage. There must be sufficient diversity among the participants to make sure the interests of all the organization's stakeholders are taken into account.

Implementation of strategic plans would be enhanced by ensuring that the organizations have adequate knowledge and capacity to meet the often 'higher demands' implied by the strategic plan. They also need to develop capacity to move beyond 'unhealthy donor dependence' in order to maintain autonomy to pursue their priorities. This means developing capabilities to negotiate with donors as partners and/or to access alternative and unrestricted sources of funding.

Monitoring and evaluation of the strategic plans would be enhanced if the accountability and marketing purpose of the monitoring and evaluation does not override the learning, governance and management purpose. The organizations would also need to introspect themselves and challenge themselves to embrace a 'culture of accountability in performance'. This means they need to develop effective monitoring and evaluation and performance appraisal systems. Lastly, there is a need to build specific skills especially among the boards in monitoring and evaluation of strategic plans as a related but distinct discipline from monitoring and evaluation of project activities.

Conclusion

The recommendations given above illustrate how to cultivate organizational beauty. There are two principle options available to CSOs: to become 'more beautiful girls' or 'great dancers'. What shall we choose? We see great dancers everywhere. We see them in politics, in business, in religion and in the media. They are not relevant, they do not have genuine legitimacy, their promises and benefits are not sustainable. Beautiful girls are in short supply or maybe *the beautiful ones are not yet born?* I believe they are but organizational beauty must be cultivated through more effective strategic planning processes. With genuine beauty what you see is what you get – relevance, legitimacy and sustainability. We need more beautiful CSOs not fewer!

References

Atack, I. (1999) Four Criteria of Development NGO Legitimacy. *World Development* (25): 855–865

Chambers, R. (2005) *Ideas for Development*. London: Earthscan

Drucker, P. (1974) *The Practice of Management*. Oxford: Butterworth-Heinemann

Drucker, P. (1990) *Managing the Non-Profit Organization*. London: Butterworth-Heinemann

Edwards, M. (1996) *NGO Performance – What Breeds Success?* Kathmandu: Save the Children (UK)

Fowler, A. (2002) Organizing Non-Profits for Development, in *The Earthscan Reader on NGO Management* (Edwards, M. and Fowler, A. eds), London: Earthscan

Fowler, A. and Biekart, K. (2008) *Introducing Civic Driven Change*, ISS – CDC Policy Brief Number 1

Hatch, M. (1997) *Organizational Theory: Modern Symbolic and Postmodern Perspectives*. New York: Oxford University Press

James, R. (2002) *People and Change: Exploring Capacity Building in NGOs*, Oxford: INTRAC

Part V

Managing Organizational Change

13

The Phases of Organization Development

James Taylor

The Nature of Initiatives and Organizations

Underlying the following discussion of initiatives are three basic assumptions, all quite obvious yet all important. The first is that all initiatives and organizations are human creations, no matter how old and well established. They are created by people with an idea in response to a perceived need and they are continuously being modified by people's ideas and actions. A school, a cafe, a company, may well carry something of the personality of the founders, but it is changed by the ideas and aspirations of those who now share responsibility. So we live and move in a world created by nature and in a large and increasingly complex institutional world created by people.

The second assumption is that this institutional world of shops, restaurants, NGOs, schools and even government agencies is one in which each initiative, like a human being, goes through characteristic phases of development. Organizations are not mechanical; they are living systems with phases of crisis, adaptation, growth and development. This means that organic metaphors such as seed, stalk, bud and flower, or childhood, adulthood and old age, are more relevant to the life cycle of organizations than mechanical metaphors such as input, output, clockwork or a smooth running engine. It also implies the third assumption, namely that one of the central tasks of initiative takers is keeping the organization alive and developing as a healthy living organism.

In working in NGOs, I am frequently surprised by how little awareness initiative takers have about their whole organization and its stage of development and how relieved they are when they realize that, while unique, it shares characteristic phases of crisis and development with other organizations.

The following description paints a general picture of the phases of an initiative development over time, as an aid for individuals to more consciously shape and develop their organizations. The picture presented in no way seeks to deny the uniqueness of individual initiatives, but rather to describe the characteristic challenges and opportunities which exist in the life cycle of most organizations.

ɔneer phase – improvising in response to needs

at from the view point of an organization's life phases, one can say it starts with ːtion period when one or more individuals are walking around with an idea – an which is slowly ripening. This gestation period may be shorter or longer – often it ːeply connected with that individual's life and destiny. Henry Ford he wanted ⸱ be an engineer when he was 12. He also knew he wanted to found his own automo-ɔile company when he was in his late twenties. But it took him until 40 to finally create the Ford Motor Company.

Following the gestation period is a moment of birth – when the school first opens its doors, the company delivers its first product or NGO receives its first grant. This is a very important moment in the biography of all initiatives and it should be celebrated like a birthday. Usually this is done, often unconsciously, through a party, a festive meal or even just saving the first dollar or pound earned by the new co-op. However, if this can be done consciously, as a foundation or a birth ceremony, inviting friends, customers, and helpers, it will help to get the new baby off to a good start.

If the initiative flourishes, it enters a period which is analogous to childhood: vibrant, exciting, full of surprises and of growth. Co-workers are involved in many activities, routine is limited and the direction of the initiative is clear. It is a time full of ups and downs – a mood similar to the early 20s in an individual's life.

A couple who initiated a futon manufacturing and retail business only a few years ago gave a picture that describes many early initiatives which got off to a successful start: endless activity in deciding on staff, setting wage levels, ordering supplies, supervising production, keeping the books, getting bank loans, planning future activities and occasionally stopping to catch a breath. They also mentioned two qualities essential to any starting enterprise: concern for the quality of their futon (cotton) bedding, and doing their utmost to assure customer satisfaction. The same qualities apply to a new school, a literacy project or any endeavour. Its reputation rests on the satisfaction of its clients, customers or parents. If it provides a quality service or product, it will generally thrive.

Being concerned with quality and client satisfaction means that a new initiative, a pioneer organization, has to act like a large sense organ, continuously monitoring the satisfaction of those it serves, while at the same time sensing how the initiative is functioning internally. If a literacy project spends more time developing programmes than helping people read and write, or if a school is unable to maintain discipline, interest and support from pupils and parents will begin to decline.

Sometimes people wonder whether it is better to start an initiative alone or together with others. In reality this is never an abstract question; a couple will decide to open a furniture store, one individual to start a college or two partners to begin a consulting service NGO. In the past a single individual – a pioneer – tended to start a new venture and others then joined him or her, attracted by the personality and vision of the individual. They then need to be certain that they have a common vision and are equally committed with their time and energy. Absent and half-hearted initiative takers are not readily accepted by those who are in it full time. Also the group should not be too large and should be capable of working together. If these conditions are met, then a group of individuals – because of their combined talents and wider set of destiny connections – definitely has a greater potential than a single pioneer.

As the pioneer organization grows, one can observe a number of characteristic qualities in organizations as diverse as schools, co-operatives and community clinics:

- It is generally of small to medium size, although I have worked with a community college with a teaching staff of 600, still in its pioneer phase
- It has a shallow, flexible structure with a limited hierarchy. Key decision-makers are often involved in the full scope of organizational activities
- It is person-oriented, rather than function oriented. If you ask a pioneer about his or her organization, you are usually told that Tom does publicity, Mary, craft therapy, Steve, counselling and so on
- Leadership is personal and direct with people generally knowing who makes what decisions. However, throughout the initiative's growth there is the need to clarify the role of the central carrying group vis-à-vis detailed work groups and supporters. This is especially important and problematic in initiatives largely dependent on volunteer help
- Decision-making is intuitive. Things are decided more by hunch or by feel than through a long process of rational analysis. This style of arriving at decisions usually means that the pioneer organization is able to respond rapidly to changes in the environment
- The pioneer organization has a family atmosphere about it. Everyone contributes as they are able and most of the staff have a strong sense of loyalty to the founding group, and to the initiative
- Motivation and commitment in a pioneer organization are high
- The goals of the organization are implicit – carried in the minds and personalities of the carrying group.

This phase of an organization's life is exciting, somewhat insecure and very creative. It is really about developing something out of an idea, a hope, and seeing it grow into an institution with services or products, a physical space and staff. Another way of describing this is to say that one is bringing a child into the world – a child with its unique personality – full of vitality and potential.

As the initiative grows, a number of problems begin to appear. This may be 2, 5, 10 or even 25 years after its beginning. One issue is size: not everyone knows everyone anymore. New people join the organization in substantial numbers and do not share the joys and struggles of the early days, having no relation to the institution's past or the people who made it what it is. Another issue is that new structures of decision-making are needed to cope with increased size and complexity. Leadership often becomes unclear and motivation decreases. A sense of uncertainty, of crisis, exists. In many smaller NGO initiatives this crisis of the pioneer phase includes some of the following phenomena.

Loss of confidence in leadership. Increasing criticism, usually by newer people, about the 'autocratic' and 'non-democratic manner' in which decisions are made. Newer people have little relationship to the starting situation and the sacrifices that the original group made in getting things going. In some case, these issues are also generational with a new generation of people both wanting to have more influence and wanting to work in new ways.

Lack of clarity about goals and directions. At an earlier time these were embodied in the carrying group. Then, there was a personal relationship, and if there was a question everybody knew who to go to. I remember attending a faculty meeting in an educational institution and watching all heads turn towards one person when a question of significance arose. In the absence of close personal relationships, the need for clearly understood goals and policies arises. What was implicit and personal needs to become explicit and objective.

The need for a definition of responsibilities and decision-making authority. When things are smaller and informal one decision-making centre is adequate. But if you have a kindergarten, a lower school and a high school, or upper school, who has what responsibilities? In a college, what is the relationship between the teaching faculty and the administration, or between the departments or divisions? In a furniture cooperative, how will purchasing, accounting, merchandising and hiring be divided in an orderly fashion? Such questions become burdensome and indeed become the source of conflicts.

In both large and small organizations the crisis of the pioneer phase is perplexing and painful. The need for change is recognized but its direction and how to achieve it often remains obscure. It is in such circumstances that a developmental picture can help, not as a prescription but as a rough road map so that at least the nature of the next landscape is discernible.

The differentiation phase: The challenge of diversity with consciousness

The challenge of the phase of differentiation is how one can move from the personal, intuitive, improvising mode of a smaller pioneer organization to a more objective, clear and functional way of meeting a growing organization's objectives. In my experience, there is a trade-off between consciousness and form in meeting this challenge. The more conscious people are of goals and policies – the direction and guiding principles of an organization – the less there is need for rigid forms and control mechanisms. However in the absence of shared goals and policies, hierarchical principles, procedural handbooks and rigid reporting relationships seem to become imperatives.

Cultural institutions such as schools, development organizations, primary health care centres and the like often resist pressures for greater functional clarity by attempting to muddle through. This tendency is quite pronounced in faculty-run schools, partly because most teachers have limited administrative and organizational experience. The trend in most businesses is the other way – replacing people by systems and so rationalizing operations that individuals feel like a cog in the proverbial machine. The tendency to muddle through, to cling to a vague longing for the old unity, generates chaos and the struggle for power between individuals. The opposite emphasis reduces individuals to numbers and robs them of their creativity.

The central question for all organizations in this phase of development is to bring about functional differentiation without sacrificing human creativity and commitment. Achieving this balance, and entering a healthy differentiation process, involves paying attention to four critical organizational needs.

The first is to renewing the identity and purpose of the initiative by developing a vision of the future and a clear mission statement. This means a renewed dialogue with the spirit, developing a vision – a struggle for the original and now newly willed central aims of the organization. The process of developing a vision of the future is akin to an individual asking him or herself what is really central to their life. It should involve many people in different parts of the organization so that a commonly shared sense of direction emerges. A colleague I know took over a year to develop an image of the future while including faculty, administrators and support staff in the process. While lengthy, it was time well spent as it generated a new hope and commitment. In many organizations suggesting such a process raises fears. Will teachers and administrators, or leaders, not want totally different things? I have never experienced this to be the case. Generally, people see the same organizational reality and share a common picture of the values they want to pursue in the future. In this process of renewing the culture, the identity of the institution, it is essential to also call to mind the initiative's biography, the rich texture of its history, personalities, failures and successes.

Second, in conjunction with renewing the organization's sense of purpose, comes the need to create a new understanding of the different functions of leadership. What are the differences between goals and policies, and where and how does evaluation and review take place? Such differences are seldom understood and yet such a differentiation in awareness, in consciousness, needs to be present to provide a healthy basis for differentiation in form and function. While there are different ways of describing the main leadership functions in organizations, they often include the following aspects:

- goal setting;
- policy formulation;
- establishing plan and procedure;
- integrating functions;
- organizing and executing work activities;
- innovating and renewing;
- evaluating and reviewing.

Goal-setting consists of setting long and medium term goals for the initiative. It is a central responsibility of those guiding the organization, although ideally as many people as possible should be involved.

Policies are different from goals. They provide a framework, a set of guidelines, according to which individuals can make decisions and act. Examples are policies on hiring or promotion, purchasing, remuneration and the like. If a hiring committee at an Educare Centre has an agreed upon policy that an Educare trained teacher with at least half a year's experience are essential qualifications, then they have something to go on.

Establishing plans and procedures for particular work activities can be done if goals and policies are shared. The scholarship committee of a school can develop its plans and procedures knowing what policy there is on financial aid and what restrictions exist in terms of the projected budget (a statement of financial goals). A small manufacturing company can plan production of annual goals if a marketing plan exists. In short, the delegation of responsibility becomes possible to sub-units, committees, or even to individuals, within a broad goal and policy framework. Developing such a framework is, of course, helped when the organization has already reviewed its sense of purpose.

The first three functions of leadership have been mentioned. They tend to be the responsibilities of all or most of the leadership in smaller service or professional organizations. The fifth function, from the list above – that of organizing and executing work activities, while belonging to the whole organization, the focus is on the individual rather than the leader. In a school it is the teachers or in a cafe the cook and the waitresses who need to organize and carry out the myriad of daily activities.

Likewise, innovation and renewal are everyone's responsibility, although for the organization as a whole it tends to lie with those individuals or groups having a central leadership role.

Evaluation and review is usually understood as financial review and quality control in product organizations. Other types of institutions seldom pay much attention to it, yet it is absolutely central to an initiative's learning and development. In schools or service agencies, in shops, farms or medical facilities, it should be like an extended New Year reflection. How has this past year gone? What successes or failures have we had? Why did things go wrong in this class or with this particular product? What can we improve upon next year? What new activities can we engage in? Questions of this type are vital, and the more members of an organization grapple with these issues the more a responsible work community is created.

A third organizational need in the differentiation stage is that of functional specialization and structural clarity. In self-administered schools there is a need to differentiate the upper or high school from the lower grades and from the preschool. Administration, records, accounting, fund-raising and publicity activities need to be consciously picked up and calls for committees to be established as everything can no longer be decided and implemented by one decision-making group. The phase of differentiation can also be called an administrative phase, in which what was done semi-consciously to make things run in the early years now needs conscious attention.

An important principle during this phase of development is that of giving clear mandates and responsibilities to sub-groups or committees of an initiative. This means that each committee needs to have clear terms of reference regarding their tenure and areas of responsibility.

The fourth function, that of integration, is like five, six and seven: everyone's concern, yet it tends to fall heavily on those having a leadership function. They must relate more general specific tasks to goals and principles.

Bringing about awareness of the leadership functions in an organization is by itself not enough – they must be exercised. Where and by whom are long and medium term goals set? How are they communicated and responded to by other parts of the organization? I have worked with some clients where goals were set but it was largely a paper exercise for outside consumption, and people within the initiative knew little about it. Policy formulation is equally important. Where and by whom are policies to be defined? Plans and procedures are established and carried out in many parts of an organization, as are the other functions, yet what is important is that people are aware of what functions of leadership are being exercised by whom and how the results are communicated to the rest of the institution. Generally as many people as possible should be involved in developing policy. In this way a sense of ownership is created.

If we step back from this functional description and ask what really lies behind the differentiation process in organizations, then we can say that the soul of the organization is being developed. This inevitably involves multiplicity and differentiation just as in the individual the development of soul in the 20s and 30s manifests through becoming aware of the complexity of thoughts, emotions and intentions. This process of differentiation is difficult for many initiatives because it involves some task specialization. But if overall goals and policies are shared by people in the initiative, then a conscious division of tasks can take place so that the whole benefits.

The fourth critical organizational need of the differentiation process in any organization is the need for a change in leadership and decision-making styles. In most new initiatives leadership is personal and decisions are made by hunch, by intuition. As the organization grows and becomes differentiated leadership has to become more functional – related to areas of expertise and responsibility – and decision-making becomes more rational and analytical. Both of these style characteristics will develop over time, but the transition is often difficult as individuals used to the more free-willing and informal style of the pioneer phase resent the more rational and sometimes more 'bureaucratic' approach appropriate to the differentiation phase.

As with the 30-year-old, a differentiated organization runs the risk of too much rationality. The need for social contact, for a nurturing of human relationships is very important. Can the staff of a well-established school continue with the vitality of shared research work and create regular opportunities for meeting, for sharing meals, for knowing each other? Can a group of architects or workers in a shop create possibilities for the 'soul' of the initiative to live? Differentiation needs to be balanced by conscious attention to building the human team to have fun, as well as work.

Many organizations reach this phase in their life cycle often unconsciously and with great struggle. Yet it is clear that this phase too has its limitations, its period of crisis, as anyone who has worked in a large corporation or a big state institution knows. This crisis is most visible in those institutions where differentiation has been carried through by mechanistic structures, systems and procedures without considering their impact on human capacities or motivation. In these types of institutions a marked loss of vitality, decreased motivation, high levels of absenteeism and continued communication difficulties are evident.

While symptoms of this crisis are clearest in large bureaucracies and many companies in traditional manufacturing sectors, they also appear in smaller NGOs which have been in the differentiation phase for some time. The weight of the past, endless committee meetings, a lack of purpose, gossip, conflict and limited innovation are symptoms which become evident in well established development agencies, schools and smaller cooperative production companies. Being well established and in most cases quite secure, it is as if they too were experiencing a kind of mid-life crisis, searching for new meanings and a new way of working. The interest in cooperative and associative models among NGOs suggests that there is a conscious and widespread search underway in all societies for possible answers to the crisis of differentiation.

The integration phase: Initiation

In their best-selling book, *In Search of Excellence*, Peters and Waterman point to a number of basic qualities which have made some mature large companies successful. These include:

- clear-cut goals and a culture of commitment and excellence;
- treating people as people and valuing their contribution;

- a decentralized and flat structure;
- an awareness of the central work processes in organizations and greater support for these processes rather than to administrative procedures and control.

Our work in many different organizations suggest that a mature institution facing a crisis of the 'administrative' or differentiation phase needs to consciously enter a new cycle in its development, opting for a new set of values, a different orientation towards work activity and simpler, decentralized structures. We believe this is as true for manufacturing companies as it is for service institutions, schools and NGOs which have reached maturity. Practically, this means that a mature institution needs to formulate a new set of simple, yet meaningful goals related to the essential products or services provided to clients. These goals need to be an integral part of the organization's past – its biography – to be authentic and to have the capacity of motivating both clients and co-workers or employees. What are a school's central educational goals and its educational philosophy, and how do they relate to the needs of both parents and students? What is a group of literacy teachers really seeking to offer a client? Is a co-op actually offering a set of quality products? It does not do to say quality or service to customers is number one if they have never been so and there is no intention of making it a reality. Implied in this effort to reformulate goals or purposes is the recognition that people need to be able to find meaning in their work and in their lives. An organizational culture that responds to this need in an honest way gains the commitment of its people and a sense of direction and purpose for itself.

In the differentiation phase the basic aims of a school, a community clinic or a company tended to get lost over time as technical, administrative and financial concerns became paramount. The focus of attention had quite properly shifted inward to make sure things were functioning rationally. But the price of this inward focus is a loss of connection to clients and a dimming of the vision which made the initiative what it is.

The integration phase: Towards full and conscious maturity

As in the beginning of the differentiation phase, an entry into full and conscious maturity, into the integration phase of the organization's life cycle, requires renewed attention to the initiative's central tasks and goals. This can be done through a detailed study of the organization's biography, a conscious celebration of its uniqueness and a restatement of its central goals.

Implied in this reformulation of goals is waking up to the 'sleeping partners' of the initiative, the customers and clients. The principle of association, of dialogue, needs to be adopted so that the initiative really knows the needs and preferences of those it seeks to serve. A school needs an active parent council and student council so that teachers, parents, students and the community can have a frank discussion of needs and possibilities. A clinic or therapeutic centre requires a patient group, and a farm or food store a consumer circle. Only by taking such steps can the mature initiative avoid the one-sidedness of deciding by itself what an outside group needs, and keep its goals, products and services in touch with changing people and changing culture.

A second important aspect of the integration phase is the further development of the values and criteria which are central in the organization's decision-making process.

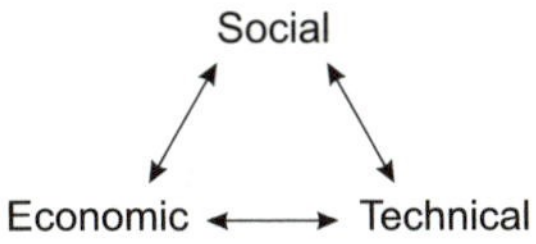

Social

Economic ←——→ Technical

Figure 13.1 *Organizational systems*

In the pioneer phase, customer satisfaction and survival was paramount, while the base of the initiative was being built. In the next phase of development, administrative and technical criteria played an ever greater role, so that the implementation of new information systems or production systems to increase efficiency were often more important than their impact on people. In the integration phase, technical, financial and social or human criteria need to be conscious balanced. If one looks at an initiative as containing these three sub-systems, then a decision in one area has implications for the others.

A new technical system will affect social relationships and financial outcomes. A new product line requires investment, training, shifts in work patterns and new equipment. Consequently, any important decision needs to consider the consequences in these three areas and to include those measures or activities which will assure an integrated approach. Most importantly, the human impact of change needs to be considered and human needs taken more consciously into account in the integration phase.

A third area is related to this latter point – namely a conscious understanding of the human as the essential ingredient in any successful initiative. Most organizations going through the differentiation phase divide the work process in such a way that some people are involved in planning and delegating (leaders), others are involved in doing (field workers) and still others in controlling and checking (administration). This is, of course, most visible in large product organizations making cars, refrigerators or tubular steel. However, it is also a tendency in development agencies, doctor's offices, hospitals and other initiatives where senior leaders plan work, less senior people do it and others check and control.

This simple division of labour is important, yet it has the consequence of using the capacities of people in a one-sided way. Who has not laughed or cried at the architect who designed an office that is uninhabitable or a house that cannot be built because the designer did not understand the building materials? Equally, we have all experienced a person doing a specific job and following instructions but not being able to carry it out properly because he did not really understand how it related to a customer's need. In the first case, the architect is using the ability to think in order to design; in the second a person is using their will to do. Human beings, however, have three capacities: to think and plan, to will and do, and to feel and be responsible. The modern division of labour and the related high levels of specialization foster a one-sided development of individuals. This tendency is particularly pronounced in the differentiation phase of an initiative.

In the integration phase the three capacities again need to be more consciously taken into account in building semi-autonomous work or project teams which, over time, acquire the quality of planning, executing and controlling their own work within general guidelines. The creation of such groups or teams within general guidelines require delegation, open sharing of goals and other information and often time and training. But without steps in this direction, people will use their ingenuity to circumvent time or quality systems, their feelings to 'challenge' the organization and their will to enter politics or play sport.

A culture of excellence, of commitment, means creating not only an organization with worthwhile goals, but also one in which people have the opportunity to use their innate faculties for the benefit of the whole. Recognizing the full potential of human creativity also involves a commitment to professional development activities, flexibility in work hours and scheduling, and the fostering of individual initiative.

Self-administered initiatives in the cultural or service spheres may feel that this does not apply to them. But here too differentiation inevitably leads to the hiring of administrators, bookkeepers, secretaries, maintenance people, cooks and others. Teachers also should have an insight into the bookkeeping and the supply ordering system. Having the same people doing the same jobs for many years fosters one-sidedness. The question then emerges, how can people be helped to both broaden their insights and balance the use of their capacities?

When an organization has moved towards integration, its ability to respond to its environment is enhanced, its internal functioning is more streamlined and people can have a renewed sense of ownership and pride in their work. One could say it has achieved full maturity and a collective wisdom which also allows it to help other initiatives and to serve the wider needs of its community. In summary, the qualities of the integration phase include:

- renewing central aims and the organization's values and culture to provide meaning;
- working proactively to attain this shared vision instead of reacting to every request or problem that arises;
- creating the organization for an association – a conscious dialogue with customers, clients, suppliers and the community in which the initiative is active;
- a leadership and decision-making style which takes human needs into account, explicitly balancing financial, technical and social criteria;
- an enhanced understanding of human beings and the creation of work processes and structures which take this new understanding of human capacities into account;
- creating a process organization in which structures reflect the requirements of central work processes rather than administrative control mechanisms. Paying attention to and enhancing the rhythmic quality of the initiative's life;
- building teams and smaller, decentralized and flatter organizational forms;
- process, horizontal thinking, rather than vertical and hierarchical thinking.

These qualities do not add up to an organizational blueprint. Rather, they suggest a type of awareness, a way of looking at and understanding organizations and people from a less analytical, but deeper, more whole and conscious perspective. This perspective and the resulting direction are being explored by many initiatives today, for we all face the question of what new organizational forms are appropriate for the growing individualized consciousness we have in our societies.

A conscious ending

If the pioneer stage can be likened to childhood, the differentiation phase to early and middle adulthood, and the integration phase to full maturity and old age, what can be said about the death of an initiative? A convenient response is to say that they die when they fail and are no longer needed. However, I feel that many institutions have not only become old, but also sclerotic, disposing of vast resources but no longer really serving human needs. It has been suggested that the life cycle of institutions should approximate that of individuals if they are to serve the needs of the times. What a revolutionary idea! What would happen to cultural, social and economic creativity if institutions over 70 or 80 years old turned over their resources to new groups wishing to respond to similar needs in new ways? What a peaceful ongoing creative revolution society would experience. To do this would require institutions to contemplate a conscious death process in order to allow a new resurrection. It is an intriguing thought, if not a present reality.

The Image of Development

What has been presented is a sketch of developmental patterns in organizations. Frequently I am asked, can't a stage be missed? The answer is no if organizations have a true life cycle moving from simple to more complex, from one central organizing principle to another. This means that true development is a discontinuous, irreversible process in time, moving from a stage of growth through differentiation to a higher stage of integration and passing through states of crisis which offer the impetus for development. This pattern is, I believe, true for all living forms, for the human being and for organizations.

However, it is possible for initiatives to move more or less rapidly through these phases. A school that starts with six grades and a kindergarten will face questions of differentiation sooner than one which starts with one grade, adding a new grade each year. A company which has three employees the first year and 17 the second will also face developmental issues more rapidly than one which grows more slowly. Furthermore, it is quite common for large organizations to have different segments, albeit at different stages of development. A new product division may be in the pioneer stage, the mother company may be going through the crisis of differentiation, while one older division may already have started working with the principles of integration. The described image of an initiative's development over time is incomplete. Like all ideal-type descriptions it cannot do justice to the rich texture of organizational life, nor to the uniqueness of each initiative. Its purpose is rather to describe a landscape of possibilities, indicating paths to be pursued and pitfalls to be avoided so that we may become more conscious and responsible co-creators on earth.

14

The Change Challenge: Achieving Transformational Organizational Change in International NGOs

Paul Ronalds

Introduction

In the two decades since the fall of the Berlin Wall, the world has changed dramatically. Globalization, a process of increasing economic, social and political connectedness, has facilitated the spread of democracy, helped to lift millions out of poverty and enabled the almost instantaneous global transfer of information. It has also brought unprecedented challenges. The global economic crisis precipitated by the collapse of Lehman brothers in September 2008, the impact of climate change and the threat of terrorist networks like al Qa'ida are just some of the issues that our current global governance arrangements struggle to cope with. At the same time, we may well be seeing a historic transfer of power from west to east, illustrated by the growth in power of China and India and the increasing importance of the G20.

Globalization is producing a similar combination of benefits and challenges for the world's largest international non-government organizations (INGOs). On the one hand, globalization has contributed to the unprecedented growth in their size and influence. For example, in the 10 years from 1999 to 2008 the combined revenue of the six largest INGOs has grown from around US$2.5 billion to more than US$7 billion (Ronalds, 2010, Table 1.1). Even more significant has been the increase in their influence. The largest INGOs are now routinely involved in formal norm creation and standard setting, are key sources of information and comment for the media and their extensive public communication activities help to shape and influence public opinion. They are also involved in the functioning of many international inter-government organizations (IGOs) and exercise direct influence on the economies and governments of many developing countries through their long term development work, humanitarian activities and by promoting political development.

On the other hand, the political, economic and social changes wrought by globalization create significant strategic challenges. With their growing size and influence, questions about INGO's legitimacy are increasingly raised and there are growing calls for them to better demonstrate their effectiveness and accountability. Politically, they must adjust to an international context that is far more multilayered, complex and fluid than anything they have experienced in their relatively short histories. They must also adapt to a plethora of new aid and development actors. The success of campaigns like Make Poverty History have not only increased total official development assistance (ODA) by OECD countries to around US$120 billion in 2008, it has also led to an incredible explosion in the number and variety of actors now engaged in tackling global poverty.

On top of this, reduced food security, rising oil prices, climate change, rapid urbanization and a more politicized operating environment present significant new development challenges for INGOs. Climate change in particular is likely to have a highly disruptive impact on their operations and finances. For example, World Vision has already seen the proportion of its global budget expended on aid (relief work) rather than development increase from 15 per cent in 1998 to 35 per cent in 2008. As climate change contributes to the increasing frequency and severity of natural disasters in coming decades this is likely to rise even further.

To navigate these challenges, INGOs must attract and retain increasingly skilled staff in a job market where they are at a competitive disadvantage due to the relatively low salaries they offer. As a result, some commentators are forecasting an enormous INGO 'leadership deficit' in the years ahead, leading to a 'talent war' with the business and government sectors (Tierney, 2006). INGOs can also expect new technologies to create significant strategic disruptions. Many new technologies, such as the mobile phone and the internet, are network technologies whose benefits increase as more people use them. With global internet penetration still at only around 23 per cent, this suggests that many of the transformative effects of this technology are still ahead of us.

To remain relevant and effective in this environment, INGOs will need to become experts at organizational change. Organizational change can be divided into three main forms. The first type, 'strategic adjustments', are the day to day tactical changes or modifications to an organization's activities that assist them to more effectively achieve their strategic goals. Such change is very important for making incremental improvements to development and relief programmes, advocacy campaigns or operating systems and processes and, over time, such strategic adjustments can result in significant progress. The second type of organizational change is that which results from regular strategic reviews that identify new strategic goals for a future period of time, normally between three and five years. This type of process can be described as 'strategic reorientation' (Lawler and Worley, 2006, pp9–10). While entailing a greater degree of change than 'strategic adjustments', a new strategic plan still normally builds off the base of the previous one: increasing revenue or beneficiary targets, identifying new advocacy campaigns or opening new field or fundraising offices. As such, it is rare that strategic reorientations lead to revolutionary change. Both strategic adjustments and strategic reorientation can be distinguished from the third form of organizational change – transformational organizational change – that radically changes the governance, operating model or effectiveness of the organization.

Most INGOs continuously engage in strategic adjustments and regularly undertake strategic reorientation, but neither are likely to be sufficient to meet the demands of the dramatic changes in INGOs' strategic context. Yet, examples of large INGOs successfully implementing transformational organizational change are becoming increasingly rare. Even the change undertaken by ActionAid, one large aid and development INGO that has been recognized for its organizational change in the past few years, while ambitious, is still yet to be cemented and may be insufficient to meet the demands of its changed strategic context.[1] As a result, this chapter will argue that despite their reputation for innovation and responsiveness, growing bureaucracy, the long term failure to invest in professional development and their diffuse governance structures means that many large INGOs are unable to implement the required level of organizational change. This chapter will conclude by proposing some critical elements for successfully achieving transformational organizational change in INGOs.

The Change Challenge

Radical change is difficult for any organization. As Lawler and Worley (2006, pxv) state in *Built to Change*, 'most change efforts in established organizations fail to meet expectations because the internal barriers to change are so strong'. They conclude, pessimistically, that most attempts at revolutionary organizational change are doomed to failure from the start. Lawler and Worley's conclusion echo John Kotter's findings in *Leading Change* a decade earlier that only 30 per cent of change programmes succeed and is consistent with a 2008 McKinsey survey of 3199 executives around the world that found only one transformation in three succeeds (Aiken and Keller, 2009). However, as difficult as organizational change has been historically, globalization is probably making the situation even worse. Four factors in a globalizing world are particularly in play.

Adapting to speed and contagion

It took centuries for information about the smelting of ore to cross a single continent and bring about the Iron Age. In the age of sailing ships, it took years for knowledge to be shared. However, in the modern age innovations in communication technology make it possible for information to cross the globe almost instantaneously. One consequence of this change is that the time available to organizations to determine how they will adapt to a changing environment and implement that change has shrunk dramatically. Thus, globalization's compression of time and space has made organizational change even more difficult. The reduced time that organizations have to respond to massive disruptive change is well illustrated by the recent global economic crisis. Each update on the global financial crisis swept across the globe in seconds and within less than three months from the collapse of the investment firm Lehman Brothers, on 14 September 2008, the 'contagion' had spread across Europe and Asia resulting in the economy of one country after another falling into recession. While one needs to be careful making comparisons, the speed at which the Asian Economic Crisis spread just 10 years earlier appears relatively leisurely in comparison (it took more than 12 months to eventually engulf Russia and Brazil and to lead to the collapse of the US Hedge Fund, Long-Term Capital Management).

Pressures to harmonize and centralize

Over recent years, INGOs have faced growing pressure for increased alignment and conformity from a number of sources (both internal and external) which have arguably reduced their ability to change and adapt. For example, pressure from donors, especially governments, to be more accountable and to harmonize programming with other development actors has encouraged aid and development INGOs to seek alignment, stability and equilibrium to improve management control and coordination.

Similarly, improved coordination and increased centralization within INGO 'families' such as World Vision, Plan International and Save the Children has reduced the freedom of individual members to change and adapt to their particular context. While the nature and extent of the 'internationalization' of INGO families can vary significantly, it requires individual INGOs to cede some decision-making authority or agree to act collectively on some issues, usually under a common brand. For example, regional investment decisions are made centrally in World Vision and the growth rates of individual countries are agreed collectively at annual regional strategy forums. At Plan, each individual affiliate undertakes all development programmes in developing countries through Plan International. Since all Plan projects are collectively funded, Plan has had to develop a common approach to development across all affiliates. At World Vision and ActionAid, internationalization has also led to affiliates in developing countries taking a much greater role in the global governance of the organization. For example, World Vision's international board comprises representatives appointed from the local boards of both developed and developing countries.

While internationalization can have a number of benefits, global strategies, increased bureaucracy and additional stakeholders can also reduce flexibility, constrain innovation and slow decision-making. For the most part, it appears that the internationalization undertaken by the largest INGOs has been too shallow to capture many of the expected benefits but has led to more complex and diffuse international power structures that make organizational wide change very hard to achieve.

Culture as constraint to transformation

The large INGOs have developed an organizational culture that is not supportive of change and adaptation. As Nielson et al (2006, pp109–110) argue, organizational culture of itself 'inhibits the reform that necessitates the fundamental disruption of staff members' "mental models"'. As new employees begin to learn the characteristics of an organization's culture, their strategies and choices become constrained, at first strategically and then, over time, habitually by those characteristics. However, in large INGOs, the inherent change inertia created by organizational culture is increased by a range of specific cultural factors that further inhibit organizational change. These include: concerns over professionalization and corporatization; a strong bias for internal appointments in senior human resource recruitment which has meant they have not accessed the external skills they need to help improve organizational practice or adopt new practices; unhealthy conflict management approaches (for example, a tendency to be 'passive aggressive' and suppress conflict in favour of superficial agreement); and a lack of institutional rewards for innovative thinking or planning beyond immediate problems.[2]

In addition, as the amount of funding they receive from governments has grown they have been required to adopt additional processes and procedures that have further increased organizational bureaucracy. And, as Nielson et al (2006, p113) argue, a bureaucratic culture, 'once entrenched, can be highly stable and robust'. This bureaucratic culture has then been reinforced by management's response to the exponential growth in revenue large INGOs have enjoyed over recent decades. Since rapid growth can lead to managers feeling like they are losing control of the organization, they respond by putting in place control and accountability systems that further reduce flexibility and strangle innovation (Walker, 2008). This has been compounded by the usual barriers to organizational change: apprehension of the new, uncertainty, inconvenience, threats to individual's status and competency anxieties that all remain strong in INGOs. The result is an organizational culture that not only promotes inertia to change but sometimes appears to strongly resist it. A conducive organizational culture is the key to organizational change yet the culture of large INGOs has become increasingly unsupportive of such change and changing a large INGO's existing culture can be very difficult indeed.

Learning disabilities and feedback shortcomings

Failure to become learning organizations has further reduced large INGOs' ability to change, since learning is a key attribute that allows organizations to adapt to an uncertain future or, as Senge (1990, p13) says, 'through learning we re-perceive the world and our relationship to it'. INGOs' failure to invest in information technology also means that they have not developed the processes and systems that may help to offset the drag of an increasingly bureaucratic culture.

Making the situation worse, INGOs have generally lacked a sufficiently compelling motivation to overcome the internal barriers to change. While for-profit organizations have the discipline of markets and democratic governments the ballot box, the largest INGOs do not face any similar external accountability mechanism. This is due to the limited ability of donors to assess underlying performance, beneficiaries having little effective choice and INGOs' paying insufficient attention to issues of 'downward accountability'. Anheier (2000, p13) argues that management of INGOs needs to be far more pro-active than that in corporations because 'performance signals from markets and electorates are incomplete, if not totally missing'.

The result is that despite widespread understanding about many of the problems facing INGOs, they continue to recur. For example, the Tsunami Evaluation Coalition's evaluation of the first two years of the Tsunami response concluded that, despite the quality measures that the sector has developed over recent years, the 'lack of quality enforcement mechanisms means that the same problems keep reappearing in emergency responses' (Cosgrove, 2007). While they identified the potential for donor feedback to play a role as an external enforcement mechanism, since public knowledge is often limited and media coverage lacks detailed analysis, they were not seen as sufficient. The Tsunami Evaluation Coalition therefore recommended a 'regulatory system … to oblige agencies to put the affected population at the centre of measures of agency effectiveness, and to provide detailed and accurate information to the donor public and taxpayers on the outcomes of assistance, including the affected populations' views of that assistance' (Cosgrove, 2007).

The recent investigation of Plan International's child sponsorship practices suggests that this problem is more widespread than just agencies' emergency responses. For example, the report suggested that 'few if any of the critical findings reported here are new to Plan staff' (Pettit and Shutt, 2008, p3). The lack of an external accountability mechanism also explains why there are so few mergers among INGOs. There is simply insufficient motivation, despite the fall in income experienced due to the global financial crisis, to overcome the egos, jealousies, territoriality and pettiness that are usually encountered by those promoting such activity.

Even INGOs' built environment tends to conspire against change. INGOs often house themselves in pokey, poorly laid out buildings. While this may superficially appear to be good stewardship it is likely to reduce performance in the long run. As a result, INGOs need to adopt a much more evidence based approach to their investment in property. For example, Becker (2007) argues that 'in organizations faced with substantial change, high degrees of uncertainty and a need for agility, innovation and rapid problem solving, it is critical that the physical environment is one that facilitates multi-disciplinary collaboration and speedy, free-flowing information sharing.' He identifies five aspects that are important: the amount of variation in work settings; spatial transparency (can staff see one another?); the degree of functional inconvenience (does the space promote chance encounters?); the human scale of spaces; and the number of neutral zones.

In some ways, the leaders of large INGOs have successfully created organizations 'built to last' rather than organizations 'built to change'. This is illustrated by the fact that the make-up of the six largest INGOs have not changed during the last decade. In contrast, over a similar period, there has been a dramatic change in the make-up of the world's largest corporations. While such stagnation always threatens an organization's relevance and effectiveness, in the rapidly changing and chaotic environment that INGOs now face it is likely to be fatal. Accordingly, the next section will focus on ways that leaders of large INGOs can achieve radical organizational change.

Achieving Transformational Change in INGOs

While change is difficult in any large organization and particularly hard in large INGOs, it is nonetheless possible. However, large INGOs not only have to face up to the critical need for radical organizational change but also seek to learn from the experience of change in other organizations. Case studies from business, government and non-government organizations point to a number of preconditions for any successful organizational change in large organizations and therefore provide very useful guidance for the larger INGOs.

The compelling case

Firstly, the lack of a sufficiently compelling motivation for change must be overcome. While a plunging stock price or loss of market share often provides the motivation in for-profit organizations, and the bureaucrats of democratic governments have the pressure of implementing the new policies of each incoming government, such external motivations are largely absent when it comes to INGOs. As a result, it must come from other sources. Reform at the World Bank, at the end of the 1990s, was driven by the significant and sustained public criticism the Bank received from former staff such as Joseph Stiglitz, advocacy networks such as *Jubilee* and *50 Years is Enough* and the media, which combined to create a strong motivation for change (although there are mixed views on the overall success of this reform: see Nielson et al, 2006).

In large INGOs, it is possible that loss of significant donor funding, resignation of large numbers of staff, sustained operational stress or organization-wide recognition of a dramatically changed external environment may individually or collectively contribute to strong motivators for change. However, given large INGOs' demonstrated resistance to change, these factors are probably insufficient by themselves. Most leaders of the largest INGOs are well aware of the threat posed by the changed strategic context, experience the pressure for improved performance from major donors and are struggling to recruit the necessary 'talent'. As Michael Edwards argues the 'constant strategic reviews that you see now among international NGOs are a sign that they recognize the necessity of change, but most lack the intellectual clarity and courage to see what needs to be done, and to do it' (Lewis, 1998). In this context, the board of Plan International are to be commended for their decision not only to commission a detailed review of their child sponsorship practices but to commit, ahead of time, to making it available on their website whatever the outcome (see Pettit and Shutt, 2008). Commissioning such an independent report has the potential to create a broad and compelling case for transformational organizational change and its publication contributes to creating an external compliance mechanism that will help to maintain reform momentum as the inevitable organizational barriers to change exert themselves.

Failing such an internally-generated compelling case for change, one can envisage how a difficult worldwide economic environment such as that generated by the global economic crisis, combined with significant adverse media, finally creates sufficient motivation for necessary organizational change. While such a situation would be unfortunate and create additional transitional pain, it is preferable to the alternative of irrelevance. However, even where strong, multiple sources of motivation are present, they will not, by themselves, be sufficient to enable significant organizational change.

Change managers also need to ensure that the motivation for change is shared not only among an organization's senior management but with employees, board members and external stakeholders. In fact, some organizational change specialists argue that external stakeholders are the most critical audience to convince if the change is to be successful. This can be extremely difficult and time consuming since different stakeholders are often motivated to change by different drivers. In the case of INGOs, it is further compounded by the sheer number and variety of stakeholders and their diverse interests. The benefits of change to poor communities, to donors and other supporters, to volunteers and to employees all need to be carefully communicated.

Internal change agents and champions

The second precondition for successful transformational organizational change is the presence of internal change agents who are able to articulate a coherent change agenda that is aligned with organizational values. This is especially the case in large INGOs where the personal values of staff are central to their professional motivations. If a new leader cannot identify such change agents among existing staff, then a key priority must be the recruitment of new staff who share the desired new world view and other attributes. In this regard, a major structural reorganization can be useful. Not only does it allow a new leader to recruit the desired change agents, it can also serve to disrupt the underlying organizational culture and in its place create new structures of authority and incentives that help to realign staff expectations and behaviour to the desired forms.

Once change agents are identified or recruited, it is important that they strategically engage the existing organizational culture towards their own ends. Nielson et al (2006, p110) argue that this can be achieved by these reformers or 'norm entrepreneurs', as they describe them, 'couching change goals in ways that do not appear "counter-hegemonic" but which are instead culturally compatible'. In other words, these change agents must articulate the new 'ideas and goals and fit new incentives to existing norms in ways that do not require current staff to wholly discard their pre-existing worldviews or behavioural habits' (Nielson et al, 2006, p110). In this way, organizational culture can be used to support broader organizational change rather than inhibit it.

Incentives as attractors

Thirdly, as the new organizational culture is being embedded, it is critical that organizational leaders and change agents are constantly aware of the signals that their decisions send about the way that new behaviour will be rewarded. Not surprisingly, an organization's 'people systems' have a significant influence over organizational behaviour and outcomes (Taylor, 2005).[3] This is one of the reasons why promotion decisions during a period of organizational change become so important. They signal to the organization that old organizational behaviours are no longer accepted and new behaviour 'rewarded'. Promote members of the 'old guard' and employees will interpret the change process as a facade and become cynical.

Similarly, if a change agenda is not funded, employees will rightly suspect that management is not committed to it. As a recent article in the *Harvard Business Review* argued, 'a theory of change that can't be funded isn't real' (Bradach et al, 2008, p94). Since resources are always scarce while good initiatives are usually plentiful, this requires INGO leaders to make hard prioritization decisions. If leaders avoid making these decisions it is almost certain that the organizational reform will fail. On the other hand, if an organization's leadership demonstrates that it is willing to make such decisions, it reinforces to the organization's staff that they are committed to the change agenda and that aligning with it will be rewarded, in this case, in the form of increased resources.

For example, as part of World Vision Australia's 2009 budgeting process, a multi-million dollar 'strategic initiatives fund' (SIF) was set up. This fund not only created a pool of resources for meeting new development challenges, for process re-engineering and for the development of new fundraising products, it also helped management signal its strong commitment to the organizational change agenda. In fact, the difficult economic conditions prevailing at the time meant reducing 'business as usual' activities in order to create the SIF sent an even more significant signal than would otherwise have been the case, underlining the transformative opportunity provided by a crisis. The message sent by the creation of the SIF was complemented by a strong commitment to invest in professional development, despite the economic conditions. There was an associated re-allocation of resources to address new development challenges such as climate change, urbanization and growing energy and food insecurity, coupled to a strong emphasis on developing new fundraising products that would provide sustainable funding to the organization's new development priorities.

The information imperative

Fourthly, it is critical that cultural change and new reward and incentive structures are supported by objective information. Such information will promote better decision-making, assist in building organizational wide consensus for the desired change and help to more readily identify aligned and non-aligned behaviour. As Sorgenfrei and Wrigley (2005, p12) argue, '[O]rganizations, like individuals, observe and interpret reality according to previous experiences which may then be fitted into received/accepted ways of viewing the world'. To overcome this inherent bias against change will require a much greater focus by INGO leadership on their organization's analytical and adaptive capacity.

While individuals within the large INGOs may have analytical and adaptive capacities, these capacities must become institutionalized for an organization to be able to effectively respond to change and adapt to the unpredictable.[4] Likewise, an investigation of reform at the World Bank demonstrated that organizational reform is more likely to succeed where the 'desired behaviours and organizational outcomes are measurable ... and thus information is more symmetric and deviant behaviour is easily identifiable' (Nielson et al, 2006, p110). This finding reinforces the need for large INGOs to invest in human resource and information technology systems that are able to support such measurement.

Leadership matters

The fifth factor is leadership. Not only must senior leaders be genuinely supportive of the change agenda, they must repeatedly communicate the vision and the rationale for change. They must also work towards creating a more supportive cultural environment, one that encourages experimentation, seeks to learn about new practices and technologies, monitors the environment, assesses performance and is genuinely committed to continuously improving performance. However, this cultural change and its intended effects must be achieved without increasing the gap between the INGO and beneficiaries in communities. Furthermore, leaders of the largest aid and development INGOs have to abandon the myth that their organizations are effective simply because they are large or growing. As Crutchfield and Grant (2008) argue, NGO size does not necessarily correlate to impact. In the past, ongoing income growth has sometimes been used to undermine motivations for change. Organizational growth must be motivated by its relationship to increased impact rather than increased organizational or executive status.

High quality human resources

Finally, the quality of an INGO's human capital is critical. In fact, the quality of INGO leaders and the professionalism of staff may be the single most critical element to these organizations effectively responding to the increasingly complex and unpredictable challenges they face. While organizational strategy is important, it always lags behind the strategic context in fast changing environments and cannot, by definition, accommodate the unpredictable. If large international NGOs are going to successfully meet the strategic challenges of the 21st century they will need to focus far more on developing higher quality human resources and significantly upgrade their human resource systems.

Can International Restructuring Make a Transformational Difference?

It was argued above that the internationalization undertaken by the largest INGOs has been too shallow to capture many of the expected benefits from improved coordination and scale, yet has led to more complex and diffuse international power structures that make meaningful organization-wide even change harder to achieve. This raises the question about how further changes to the global structures of the large INGOs would impact on their capacity for organizational change. This question is particularly relevant given that a number of large INGOs are either undertaking or contemplating governance changes that would deepen their internationalization. For example, since the 'Our Future' organizational change process commenced in 2004 in World Vision, changes to the organization's by-laws and operations have led to significantly increased international coordination and centralization. In 2009, Save the Children decided to radically change its global operating model by creating a single international programme delivery unit (IPU) similar to Plan's model. Even Oxfam is seeking to increase international cooperation by appointing a 'lead' agency from among its affiliates in most developing countries, similar to the CARE operating model.

Where power is highly decentralized, as is the case with Médecins Sans Frontières, individual entities retain a high level of autonomy and therefore the ability to be more entrepreneurial and innovative. On the other hand, an organization with highly dispersed decision-making and a large number of entities runs the very real risk of being unable to obtain agreement to significant organization-wide change, reducing the potential for scale and other benefits. In a globalized world, different marketing strategies and brand identities among affiliates sharing a common name can also create significant brand risk and confusion among donors and other stakeholders. This situation is exacerbated where there is a strong culture of consensus-based decision-making or where some members have an actual or effective veto. The problems of achieving change within the European Union and reform of the United Nations are both examples of these limitations.

The federation model adopted by World Vision and ActionAid seeks to balance this tension. In theory, they allow individual entities sufficient autonomy to respond to changes in their strategic context while also retaining sufficient decision-making power at the centre to allow them to implement organization-wide change. The devolved governance structures adopted by federations also encourage a network culture that is likely to be a key element of success in the 21st century. However, in practice this balancing act is extremely hard to perform. Federations can also be exhausting to govern. The result is that these organizations have historically moved between periods of centralization and decentralization without putting in place the necessary preconditions to make a federated model successful.

There is also pressure on large INGOs to 'broaden' their internationalization by giving southern-based affiliates and partners a greater role in the organization's management and governance. For example, over recent years ActionAid has intentionally sought to improve the involvement of southern-based affiliates in its global governance and relocated its international head office to Johannesburg. Similarly, Plan changed its governance in 2006 to increase southern representation on its international board, part of a 'commitment by the organization to participative governance'. At least three of Plan's international board members must now be from the south. Such a 'broadening' of an INGO's internationalization should increase their legitimacy, improve 'downward' accountability and facilitate more informed decision-making. It may also make them more attractive to international donors. However, more complex and diverse governance structures can also slow down decision-making, increase the effort required to manage internal stakeholders, reduce the time organizational leaders have to engage externally and increase bureaucracy. Such factors can all lead to a more representative global organization being less able to respond to a rapidly changing strategic environment.

A critical issue, therefore, for those INGOs seeking to either deepen or broaden their internationalization is how to enjoy the benefits of this process without undermining their capacity for organizational change. While more research is clearly required into this issue, interestingly, solving this dilemma may rely on similar factors to those required to achieve transformational organizational change. For example, if a compelling case for improved southern participation has been successfully communicated to internal and external stakeholders, organizational resistance to the change is likely to be reduced, helping to ameliorate the drag on decision-making from increased participation. And if this case was supported by strong, objective information, internal and external critics could not dismiss the change as easily. If there is genuine support from INGO leaders for improved southern participation and the organization's people systems are aligned with it, the underlying cultural change may proceed more smoothly. If there has been appropriate investment in building the facilitation skills and cultural awareness of senior managers, directors and trustees, the benefits to organizational decision-making from improved southern participation are more likely to be realized. This is also an area where improved use of new communication technologies could help to realise the benefits of broader internationalization while minimizing organizational costs.

Conclusion

Over the past 10 years, large INGOs have encountered fundamental change at three levels. First, global politics has become much more multilayered, complex and fluid. Second, the aid and development industry has become more fragmented, there has been a dramatic rise in non-aid financial flows to developing countries and we have seen the emergence of some powerful new actors. Third, at the organizational level, large INGOs have experienced enormous growth in their financial resources and influence. This has placed considerable strain on their management, people and processes. It has also dramatically increased stakeholder expectations. As a result, the greatest challenge facing large INGOs in our rapidly changing world is to change and adapt faster than their strategic context. However, achieving significant organizational change in any type of large organization is difficult and most attempts fail. In addition, large INGOs face a number of additional, inter-related, challenges. Nonetheless, significant organizational change in INGOs is possible. The most critical factors for achieving success are:

- a compelling motivation for change that creates a high degree of shared worldview and a mutual commitment to change across the organization and among stakeholders;
- the presence of internal change agents who are able to present their change objectives in a manner that is compatible with the organization's current culture and thereby leverage it to achieve change;
- a compensation and reward structure that reinforces the desired behaviours;
- accurate and objective information that supports the case for change and institutionalized analytical capability;
- genuinely committed leadership who continually reinforce the vision and the rationale for change;
- high quality human resources.

The changed international context and the new expectations that it has created provide a clear and urgent rationale for change. Only those INGOs that can create an organizational culture and intentionally pursue strategies that allow them to change at least as fast as their external environment can survive in the long run. It will be those organizations that adapt the best and where change becomes 'business as usual' that will be most successful. This is the key challenge for the 21stcentury INGO.

Notes

1   Interview with Richard Miller, ActionAid UK, 19 November 2008.
2   See also Fowler (1997: p204) for a long list of organizational, human and relational sources of resistance to change in development NGOs.
3   'People Systems' include the processes for the selection of employees, the promotion of employees, talent management, individual goal setting, evaluation, remuneration and dismissal (Taylor, 2005: pp218–223).
4   Sorgenfrei and Wrigley (2005: pp40–42) suggest a number of ways to encourage this institutionalization process.

References

Aiken, C. and Keller, S. (2009) 'The Irrational Side of Change Management', *The McKinsey Quarterly*, April
Anheier, H. (2000) 'Managing Non-profit Organisations: Towards a new approach', *Civil Society Working Paper, No. 1*, Centre for Civil Society, London School of Economics, London
Becker, F. (2007) 'Organizational Ecology and Knowledge Networks', *California Management Review* 49 (2): pp42–61

Bradach, J., Tierney, T. and Stone, N. (2008) 'Delivering on the Promise of Nonprofits', *Harvard Business Review*, December: pp88–97

Cosgrove, J. (2007) 'Synthesis Report: Expanded Summary', Joint Evaluation of the international Response to the Indian Ocean Tsunami, Tsunami Evaluation Coalition, London

Crutchfield, L. and Grant, H. (2008) *Forces For Good. The Six Practices of High-Impact Nonprofits*, Jossey-Bass, San Francisco

Fowler, A. (1997) *Striking a Balance. A Guide to Enhancing the Effectiveness of Non-Governmental Organisations in International Development*, Earthscan, London

Kotter, J. (1996) *Leading Change*, Harvard Business Press, Boston

Lawler, E. and Worley, C. (2006) *Built to Change: How to Achieve Sustained Organisational Effectiveness*, Jossey-Bass, San Francisco

Lewis, D. (1998) 'Interview with Michael Edwards on the Future of NGOs', *Nonprofit Management and Leadership* 9 (1): pp89–93

Nielson, D., Tierney, M. and Weaver, C. (2006) 'Bridging the rationalist-constructivist divide: re-engineering the culture of the World Bank', *Journal of International Relations and Development* 9 (2): pp107–139

Pettit, J. and Shutt, C. (2008) *The Development Impact of Child Sponsorship*, Institute of Development Studies, Brighton

Ronalds, P. (2010) *The Change Imperative: Creating a Next Generation NGO*, Kumarian Press, Bloomfield, CT

Senge, P. (1990) *The Fifth Discipline: the Art and Practice of the Learning Organisation*, Doubleday, New York

Silverman, L. and Taliento, L. (2005) *What You Don't Know About Managing Nonprofits – And Why It Matters*, McKinsey & Company, New York

Sorgenfrei, M. and Wrigley, R. (2005) 'Building Analytical and Adaptive Capacities for Organisational Effectiveness', *Praxis Paper No. 7*, International NGO Training Research Centre, Oxford.

Taylor, C. (2005) *Walking the Talk: Building a Culture for Success*, Random House, London

Tierney, T. (2006) *The Nonprofit Sector's Leadership Deficit*, The Bridgespan Group, Boston, MA

Walker, P. (2008) 'Complexity and Context as the Determinants of the Future', *Opinion Paper*, Feinstein International Centre, Medford, MA

Part VI

Management Applications

15

Rights-based Development Approaches: Combining Politics, Creativity and Organization

ActionAid

The use of rights language in development work has increased in recent years and, as with many concepts, there are disagreements about definitions and approaches to rights and rights-based development. For us, people-centred advocacy and rights-based approaches share the same world view and reflect the African poet, Ben Okri's hopeful vision of humanity's capacity 'to create, to overcome, to endure, to transform, (and) to love' (see Box 15.1). However, we make the distinction that people-centred advocacy looks at social change through a lens of who the actors are, while rights-based approaches look through a lens of how the desired change is viewed.

Our Understanding of Rights-based Approaches

Many social movements and NGOs have recognized the importance of integrating rights work into development work, not as a separate approach but as an essential part of a holistic process. Traditional development programmes have tended to focus almost exclusively on meeting basic needs. Yet in trying to address them, people have gradually framed needs such as food, jobs, health and respect as human rights and worked collectively to

---

Box 15.1 *Ben Okri's vision*

We are greater than our despair.
The negative aspects of humanity
Are not the most real and authentic;
The most authentic thing about us
Is our capacity to create, to overcome,
To endure, to transform, to love,
And to be greater than our suffering.

From *Mental Fight*, Ben Okri, Nigeria/UK[1]

ensure their incorporation into laws and policies and to change attitudes that affect their fulfilment. Thus rights-based approaches to development build on people's desire for inclusion and dignity and the satisfaction of their basic needs.

The struggle for rights

Rights, however, are not bestowed from on high. They are part of a never-ending human struggle to improve people's lives, drawing on both visions of a better future and a desire to prevent reoccurrence of past atrocities. As such rights have been articulated, defined and legalized by the collective efforts and struggles of many people over many years, and will continue to evolve (or be lost) as time goes on. One key success of these struggles is the wide recognition that the actual concept of rights applies to all people, in all places, at all times. Yet, as with any right, this concept in itself needs protecting and strengthening as it is challenged by ideologies such as patriarchy, racism and fascism.

This component of rights – the collective human struggle to win and protect rights – is a vital element of rights-based approaches to development. Rights are not cold legalistic formulae to be arbitrated by well-meaning, well-educated and sophisticated experts on behalf of the majority. Rather they are a manifestation of what the human spirit aspires to and can achieve through collective and positive struggle. As such they can only be made real by the involvement and empowerment of the community at large, particularly those whose rights are most violated. With people's involvement, the exploitative power relationships that deny rights can be challenged and eventually overturned.

Ethics and inclusiveness

A second aspect of rights-based development incorporates a vision of ethics and inclusiveness. Value-based, it is grounded in the belief that poor and marginalized people everywhere have certain rights and responsibilities purely by being members of the human race. Many of these economic, social, cultural and political rights have been enshrined in UN conventions and procedures which encapsulate universal aspirations for freedom and fairness and provide a set of guiding principles. Other rights are not enshrined in law but are moral entitlements based on values of human dignity and equity. These rights are indivisible, i.e. there is no hierarchy of rights. As put by Cheria et al 'respect for the dignity of an individual cannot be ensured without that person enjoying all her rights'.[2] Some of these principles include:

- people having the right to a voice in the decisions shaping the quality of their lives;
- basic economic and social resources and protections – from health care to freedom from violence in the home – not being special privileges but basic rights.[3]

Integrating different aspects

Rights-based approaches to development fulfil their promise when they integrate the political, organizing, practical and creative aspects of work on poverty and injustice. The political aspect focuses on making legal frameworks more just and supportive of the poor and excluded and advancing their rights. The organizing side builds people's organizations, leadership and synergy for the collective struggle. The practical and creative side supports capacity building and innovations in development alternatives that give meaning to rights and lay the basis for challenging oppressive practices and paradigms – such as the creation of more effective irrigation or credit systems, health delivery approaches or decision-making and negotiation processes. This new synergy can promote strong social movements, political awareness, solidarity and concrete alternatives to the current development models that prevent people from meeting their needs and fulfilling their rights. Integrating these dimensions of change brings potential for increased impact.

In summary

As we understand them, rights-based approaches to development focus on strengthening people's dignity, solidarity, participation and creativity as well as their organizations and leadership. They work to improve the legal and political context in which people live and to support their economic and social initiatives so that their rights can have meaning. Values of justice, equity, equality, dignity, respect, solidarity and inclusion are at the centre of a rights-based approach as shown in Figure 15.1.

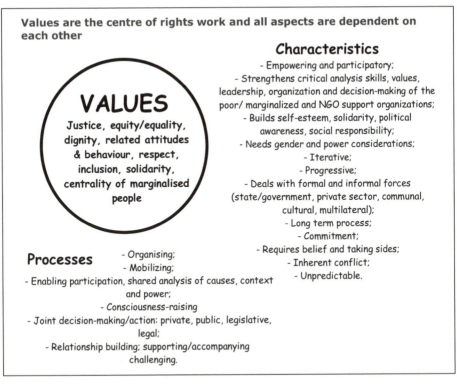

Figure 15.1 *Values, characteristics and processes*

Source: Adapted from ActionAid in Practice, ActionAid International, November 2003, Addis Ababa, Ethiopia

Box 15.2 *Rights are political*

The notion of rights as universal standards of human dignity belies their inherently political and conflictual nature. Rights do not come in neat packages, but rather are part of dynamic, some-times messy, processes of resistance and change that work to engage and transform relations of power. Despite the existence of the international human rights system, the terrain of rights remains an ever-changing, political arena where some groups' rights compete and conflict with others.

Source: VeneKlasen et al, 2004[3]

Box 15.3 *The diversity of advocacy approaches*

The rapid growth of advocacy training in the last decade has generated a wide variety of defini-tions, approaches and strategies. Diverse advocacy approaches are not just different ways of reaching a similar end. They embody different values, political views and goals, and thus seek different ends. The distinctions have important implications for excluded groups such as women, indigenous communities and ethnic minorities. Advocacy initiatives concerned with empowerment, citizenship, and participation appear different from those that only focus on policy reform.

Source: VeneKlasen, Lisa, with Miller, 2002[4]

Box 15.4 *Main features of rights-based approaches from a people-centred perspective*

In summary we consider the main features of rights-based approaches for NGOs to be:

- Identifying and clearly taking sides with poor and marginalized people who confront injus-tice in their daily lives

- Attempting to address not only the effects of poverty, marginalization and injustice, but also their causes

- Facilitating and supporting poor and marginalized people's own empowerment, leader-ship, organization and action to restore and advance their rights and promote social justice

- Affirming that individuals and civil society have both the right and the responsibility to define, defend and advance people's rights; the state has similar obligations and, most importantly, the fundamental responsibility to ensure justice and the application of those rights fairly across society

- Recognizing that making rights and development real in people's lives requires changes in deeply engrained attitudes and behaviours at all levels of society

- Understanding the inextricable links between rights, development and power, and the resulting need for integrated strategies that address the policy and political aspects of making rights and development meaningful as well as the organizational and creative side which involves leadership development and testing and promoting concrete development alternatives.

Source: Developed from ActionAid Asia, Operationalising a Rights Approach to Development, 2000

Good Governance

If we are to challenge the way power operates in our societies, we should have an alternative vision of how we would like power to operate in a more inclusive and just manner. Our understanding of rights gives us a basis for defining a vision of good governance as open and participatory paying particular attention to promoting the voice of excluded members of society. However, supporting the most marginalized is very difficult in the current 'one-size fits all' neoliberal development model that basically sees the role of government as facilitating the flourishing of markets. Rather than sharing and balancing power and advancing human rights for all, this approach tends to concentrate power and wealth. Because of the dominance of this approach to governance it is important that people work with their own organizations and governments to create alternative economic, political and social models that can support and advance their rights and confront this narrow ideological perspective.

Implications of Rights-based Approaches

The implications of a development NGO truly adopting rights-based approaches are massive. Despite the current popularity of rights rhetoric in the development field, these implications have not been fully appreciated. First, a rights based approach is inherently a political approach – one that takes into consideration power, struggle and a vision of a better society as key factors in development. It opposes a depoliticized interpretation of development which portrays problems 'as purely technical matters that can be resolved outside the political arena' without conflict when in fact, they are rooted in differences

NGOs often find the development of rights-based approaches difficult and sometimes reframe what they have done for years into rights-based language without any real changes in strategy. Incorporating rights and development is a continual challenge.

Figure 15.2 *The good old days*

of power, income and assets.[5] Rights cannot be truly realized without changes in the structure and relationship of power in all their forms – changes in who makes decisions, whose voice is heard, what topics are seen as legitimate, people's sense of relative self-worth and in the confidence of people to speak out.

This means that power analysis and developing an understanding of how change can happen in a particular context and can be sustained over time becomes much more central in our work.

Interconnectedness of rights, participation and empowerment

Many people see rights and participation as separate concepts and programme approaches. We view them as connected, with empowerment being vital to their success. Whereas advocacy or campaigning has become a common intervention in rights-based approaches, questions arise about who carries these strategies out, on what issues and using what approaches.

Many advocacy approaches do little to change power structures or dynamics; instead they promote a singular focus on policy reform which often results in advocates being consumed by lobbying and joining elite groups of decision-makers thus losing touch with their constituency and grassroots base. This not only makes change much less likely to be sustained but does nothing to transform power structures, leaving the marginalized as politically excluded as before and sometimes alienated from their own leadership.

Role of Development NGOs in Rights-based Approaches

The above understanding of rights-based approaches implies that the primary roles of development NGOs and donors shift from being implementers and drivers of development to being allies and fellow partners with people's organizations and social movements in a collective struggle for change. This implies a much more complex mix of roles that involves sharing and negotiating power in new ways, challenging assumptions and taking clear, often risky, political stands in favour of the poor and marginalized. Inferences about the nature of these roles and relationships can be drawn from John Samuel's definition of people-centred advocacy (see Box 15.5).

One issue that needs careful thought is that of people's own agency – their ability and willingness to act and work with others to improve society. Central to our vision of development and good governance is the inclusion of all people in collectively building the society they would wish to see. This means that neither development nor good governance are possible without the inclusion of the most marginalized – thus people's own agency in bringing about social change is both a means and an end. However, it is not morally defensible or feasible to put the full burden of making society more just solely on the shoulders of those who are most disadvantaged. We all, as individuals and organizations, have a moral obligation to fight injustice and discrimination.

Finding the balance between promoting the leadership and voice of the marginalized and speaking on their behalf can be a challenge. In certain circumstances, it may be

---

Box 15.5 *People-centred advocacy*

To be effective and efficient, people-centred advocacy needs to:

- Empower those who have less conventional economic, social or political power, using grassroots organizing and mobilization as a means of awareness and assertion of the rights and social responsibilities of citizens

- Resist unequal power relations (like patriarchy) at every level: from personal to public, and from family to governance. The challenge for public advocacy groups is to accomplish this using our meagre financial, institutional and human resources to effectively influence government or corporate power structures. Public advocacy can draw on five major sources that cost nothing:

  1 the power of people or citizens;
  2 the power of direct grassroots experience or linkages;
  3 the power of information and knowledge;
  4 the power of constitutional guarantees;
  5 the power of moral convictions

- Bridge micro-level activism and macro-level policy initiatives. Public advocacy initiatives that are practiced only at the macro-level run the risk that a set of urban elites, equipped with information and skills will take over the voice of the marginalized. Public advocacy groups must make sure they are continually sensitive to the grassroots situation and organically bridge the gap between citizens and policy change.

Grassroots organizing and mobilization lends credibility, legitimacy and crucial bargaining power to public advocacy. In the Indian context, grassroots support and constituency are the most important factors that determine the credibility of the lobbyist – not his or her professional background or expertise. Activists with an adequate level of expertise and mass support have proven to be better lobbyists than professional experts. Grassroots mobilization and advocacy must work together if we are to achieve real progress at the macro-level.

Source: John Samuel, People-Centred Advocacy, National Centre for Advocacy Studies, 1997, Pune cited in VeneKlasen, 2002, *A New Weave of Power, People & Politics: The Action Guide for Advocacy and Citizen Participation*

Box 15.6 *Popular experiences*

'Before we used to think that we are only Dalits and when we fought for basic human rights, we did so as Dalits. But now when we are involved in advocacy campaigns for rights, we first believe in ourselves and that there is no such thing as Dalits and non-Dalits. We fight for basic human rights as individual members of the same community ie the same humanity.'

'Before our involvement in the action research we used to speak on behalf of the oppressed and the victims, but now we have come to realise that our role is not to speak for them but to help them speak for themselves.'

Source: Shrestha, 2004

---

difficult or dangerous for the marginalized to speak for themselves, such as in the case of political prisoners who are suffering or facing possible torture, or their families who are being threatened. The reality of power dynamics means that sometimes NGOs and donors need to intervene directly to try to defend and guarantee the rights of the most

---

Box 15.7 *Rights and development from a village perspective*

In 1994, The Community Self Reliance Centre, a Nepali NGO, carried out a Participatory Rural Appraisal in two rural areas. The appraisal showed that a large proportion of inhabitants of both areas were tenants cultivating other people's land and that the insecurity of their tenure was a cause of poverty for a large number of families in the district. They found that the area's land-lords collected large portions of the harvest as rent and could change the amount at will. Landlords could also transfer permission to cultivate from one tenant to another, forcing tenants to farm with only a short-term perspective, resulting in low productivity from the land and increasing poverty for the farmers.

A further baseline study carried out in the same year, found that of almost 1500 households in the two villages, 45 per cent were tenant farmers cultivating others' land and that more than 95 per cent of these were not obtaining receipts for the rent they paid. Without a receipt the farmers had no proof of cultivation and therefore no claim to rights over the land. This baseline study confirmed that insecure tenancy on agricultural land was a fundamental cause of poverty in the area.

In response to these findings, CSRC held meetings with the villagers to discuss and plan a development programme to assist them. Initially CSRC offered to support the development of an irrigation system with the aim of increasing the land's productivity. The farmers did not respond enthusiastically as they thought the benefits of this effort would go largely to the land-lords. This helped highlight that the farmers' insecurity of tenure was at the root of many of their problems and needed to be addressed. At the farmers' request, CSRC staff were flexible enough to change their initial ideas and instead began to plan a programme to assist the local farmers to address the tenancy rights issues they faced. This led to a campaign on tenancy rights which spread to other villages and by December 2003, over 3000 tenant farmers had received the security of tenure rights to their land, meaning that they could no longer be arbitrarily removed, of which almost 1000 received full land ownership titles.

Having achieved security of tenure, farmers are now showing considerable initiative in improving the productivity of their own land. As one farmer said:

> I had never dreamt of getting my own piece of land. I feel a sense of dignity now that I have gained ownership. I got six ropanis of land after two years' of struggling for my land tenancy right. I used it as collateral at the local agricultural development bank and got a Rs. 18,500 loan to buy a buffalo and now I have begun selling six litres of milk every day at the local milk collection centre and earn Rs. 3200 a month. I want to pay the debt in one year's time. The buffalo will then be mine and I will get more benefit from the milk sales. I am meeting the household expenses with some amount of income. For me, ownership of land has encouraged me to increase the productivity of the land and grow more grains to meet the needs of my family.

---

impoverished and excluded sectors of society. Whatever the case, NGOs need to find the most inclusive way of making decisions about strategies and roles. It may be that different strategies are implemented simultaneously in public and private spaces. Where it is difficult for the poor and marginalized to take a lead advocacy role NGOs may speak in public, while at the same time supporting efforts of conscientization, empowerment, organization and leadership building in the spaces that are available. In all cases NGOs need to be cautious that their actions do not undermine local organizations or place people unduly at risk. Strategies that might incur harm need to be negotiated with and decided upon by those most affected and in potential danger.

Notes

1 Okri, B. (1997) *Mental Fight*, Weidenfeld & Nicolson.
2 Cheria, A. and Sriprapha Petcharamesree, E. (2004) *A Human Rights Approach to Development*, Books for Change, Bangalore, India.
3 VeneKlasen, L., Miller, V., Clark, C. and Reilly, M. (2004) *Rights-based approaches and beyond: Challenges of linking rights and participation*, Institute of Development Studies, Brighton.
4 VeneKlasen, L. with Miller, V. (2002) *A New Weave of Power, People & Politics: The Action Guide for Advocacy and Citizen Participation*, World Neighbors.
5 Harriss cited in Dochas (2003) 'Application of Rights Based Approaches – Experiences and Challenges', Report on Dochas Seminar on Rights Based Approaches to Development, 12 February 2003.

16

Participation[1]

Institute of Development Studies

What happens when you bring together 'champions of participation' from countries in every continent to explore the problems and the potential for strengthening citizen participation in local government? What do their experiences, drawn from such different contexts, have in common? What are the lessons and how can sharing this experience inform and shape policy and practice in the UK and elsewhere?

Champions of Participation

The Champions of Participation event in May 2007 brought together 44 people (24 from the UK and 20 from 14 other countries involved in local government) to discuss these questions.[2] They comprised elected officials, including mayors from the Philippines and Brazil; city councillors from New Orleans and UK authorities; local government officials and other service providers; community activists; workers from local and national NGOs; academics and representatives of central government in the UK and in India.

The aim was to look at the challenges local governments face in responding to growing demands for citizen engagement and more participatory forms of governance. This report summarizes the discussions and debates held over a five-day period which included a two-day workshop, two days of visiting sites in the UK of particular interest and one day of policy dialogue with UK policy-makers in the Department for Communities and Local Government (CLG) and the Department for International Development (DFID).

It is impossible to do justice to the broad range of experience that was brought together by the participants in this workshop. Broadly speaking the experiences and innovative approaches included:

- participatory approaches to budgeting which provide more transparent methods for allocating public resources, involving citizens, elected representatives and local government officials, such as in Porto Alegre in Brazil, Malaga in Spain and Bradford, Newcastle and Salford in the UK;
- processes of participatory planning, which range from public involvement in the construction of small community-based projects, to larger neighbourhood action plans, to strategic area planning and the rebuilding of an entire city as in the case of

New Orleans following Hurricane Katrina, or in human rights participatory planning in post-war Bosnia and Herzegovina;

- new forms of partnerships between citizens, the government and other stakeholders, as in the UK Local Strategic Partnerships (LSP) and at neighbourhood level through local agreements, or in places like Brazil and the Philippines where citizens and officials sit as 'co-governors' on key decision-making bodies;
- new forms of public scrutiny to hold elected representatives and government officials to account, ranging from local scrutiny groups in Shropshire, citizen-led organizations holding independent public forums with politicians in East London and citizen monitoring of public tenders in Chile;
- new methods of consultation and inclusion, such as community study circles in Wisconsin, US, and community radio and mobile phone feedback in Nigeria;
- opportunities for citizen participation in service delivery, such as housing, employment and community safety service through neighbourhood renewal and tenant management programmes in the UK, delivery of healthcare in Brazil and education in the Philippines.

To hear what is happening outside of the UK context in India, Bosnia, Norway, etc. has helped me think outside the box. In other countries power is often more equally shared between national and local/regional government. This can create both a healthy tension and places for discussion – which is good for participation.

> Vince Howe, Neighbourhood Renewal Officer, Newcastle City Council, UK

Letting people know they can make a difference is key to making participation work. Showing that they can affect change really makes a difference to participation.

> Angela Smith MP, Department for Communities and Local Government, UK

Participating in the budget is not the only way for citizens to participate, but I think without it, it would be impossible for citizens to feel empowered ... I will leave with a strong care and respect for the participatory process which enables the individual to build solidarity and enables communities to strengthen and deepen democracy.

> Olivio Dutra, former Mayor of Porto Alegre, Brazil, the birthplace of participatory budgeting

Summary Learning

Participation and empowerment

- Community involvement is at the heart of sustainable change and is central to the task of revitalizing democracy, improving service delivery, tackling poverty and building strong, resourceful communities. It is not an optional extra, but is essential if we are to achieve meaningful and sustainable outcomes for people and society.
- Citizens should have a right, not just an invitation, to participate which is enshrined in some form of enabling legislation, rather than simply being invited to respond to

the government. They should be encouraged and have the right to become active participants in their own development and self-governance.

- Citizens should be 'makers and shapers' of policy and practice rather than merely 'users and choosers' of public services. They should also be encouraged to speak and act as part of a community, as well as exercise the freedom to make their voices heard as individuals.
- Empowerment should be seen as an outcome in its own right, instigating a fundamental change in the way a community sees itself and relates to others. More work is needed to identify measures that enable us to monitor and assess this kind of change in order to reinforce its importance and value.

Citizens and communities

- The stakes for participation can be very high, especially in former authoritarian regimes where speaking out could mean a person risking their freedom or their life. Even in the UK, participation demands a lot, especially of community leaders and other volunteers. It depends on 'champions' who need to be supported, whether they operate inside the government or within local communities.
- Community participation can take a variety of forms, such as through involvement in self-help projects, working in partnership and the development of independent civil society organizations. It is helpful to recognize that community leaders are expected to play different roles and meet different expectations in each context.
- Partnerships make tough demands on community representatives where the rules of engagement mean that they can feel marginalized and lack the resources they need to operate as equal partners. They are expected to become 'expert citizens', reflecting community views to partners and taking partnership decisions back to their communities.
- Civil society needs to engage 'politically' beyond the government and make their views heard and seek solutions through advocacy, protest and direct action, in relation not only to the government but also to large employers, trade unions and global corporate institutions. In a healthy democracy, the government should support the right of communities to organize, set their own agenda and take action on the issues that most affect them, and non-government funding bodies should support this activity in order to protect the independence of such organizations.
- Resources should be targeted to reduce inequality and focus on the poorest neighbourhoods and most marginalized communities where the fight against poverty and the need to build strong, vibrant and cohesive communities is most urgent.

Central and local government

- The role of local government is changing and has become a key agent of social change. It is expected to work closely with citizens in delivering a complex agenda which includes tackling poverty, delivering area regeneration, stimulating economic development and supporting community empowerment.
- Participation should be part of mainstream local government practice and integral to the way it works, not something done occasionally in an ad hoc and partial way.

But there are resource implications as those involved will need new skills. New management styles are also needed to reflect a more participatory approach to public leadership that is more open, enquiring and responsive – less 'top-down' and more accountable.

- Changing political culture and entrenched views is difficult. It involves challenging entrenched and negative attitudes, whether they are held by people in the government who exercise power or by local communities who have very little. It involves building new relationships between citizens, elected politicians and service providers, based on mutual respect, a more equal balance of power and greater local accountability.

- Local politicians need to 'go deeper' into their communities and reconnect with the people they represent. This will demand new skills to broker different views and potentially conflicting demands, and to build alliances with local communities. It will also mean respecting other community champions and, rather than feeling threatened, recognizing their role as legitimate leaders and spokespeople.

- Participation takes time and resources to really understand the issues; to create new spaces for engagement; to demonstrate political will and the leadership necessary to drive the process; to be prepared to act so that participation leads to results that make a difference; and to support and sustain participation over the long term.

- There needs to be something real on the table so people can see that their input will make a difference, that they will be listened to and that those with power will include them in making decisions. This often means involvement in budgets and spending decisions. Without a sense of real benefits, there is a high chance of 'consultation overload and fatigue'.

- Central government needs to provide appropriate leadership by setting out a clear policy for participation and establishing systems for public scrutiny and evaluation – possibly including minimum standards. But it should also step back and allow local government and local communities to work out how best to implement policy at the local level, while maintaining close scrutiny to ensure progress is made. In the UK this will involve removing centrally-driven requirements that work against participation, such as those linked to targets, timescales and frequently changing policy priorities.

Notes

1   This chapter is the Executive Summary and Summary Learning from *Champions of Participation: Engaging Citizens in Local Governance*, Institute of Development Studies, University of Sussex, 2007.

2   The countries were: China, the Philippines, India, Nigeria, Kenya, South Africa, Brazil, Chile, Bosnia, Spain, Hungary, Bulgaria, Norway, US, plus 20 participants from the UK.

17

Trust, Accountability and Face-to-face Interaction in North–South NGO Relations

Emma Mawdsley, Janet G. Townsend and Gina Porter

Introduction

In this brief chapter we set out a qualified argument for greater personal interaction between northern and southern NGOs as a formal mechanism of partnership. We argue that increasing the number and quality of face-to-face visits can, in some circumstances and with appropriate safeguards, help enhance the effectiveness of both northern and southern NGOs by fostering more open dialogue between partners; improving upward and downward accountability; and by making monitoring and accountability more rigorous and meaningful. At the heart of this argument is faith in individual professional judgement. At present, while everyone working in or around the development NGO sector is well aware of the primacy of personal relations (Lister, 1999; Hailey, 2001; Hailey and Smillie, 2001; Shameem Siddiqi, 2001), formal development discourses and institutions tend to be anxious, silent or even hostile on the subject. This opposition to the personal arises partly from understandable concerns about corruption and partly because of the more contentious issue of 'professionalization'. Following the wider turn to the culture(s) and agenda(s) of 'new public management', donor demands for greater transparency, monitoring and accountability have often taken the form of a micro-managing obsession with audits, targets and performance indicators. Just as in the UK's public sector, these can result in distorted efforts, immense paperwork, the demoraliza-tion of the workforce and significant extra costs (Allsop, 2003). The chapter is based on two research projects and a longer research and personal engagement with NGOs in Ghana, India and Mexico.

Professionalization, Trust and 'New Public Management'

Over the last 15 years or so, the development NGO sector has been transformed. Notwithstanding their global diversity, the southern 'NGOs' of the 1960s and 1970s often emerged from earlier social movements which had been founded in opposition to the state. They tended to be high in motivation and low in formal organization. Some were supported by ideological and/or humanitarian organizations in the north, which provided funding and occasionally technical assistance. Often these relationships were highly personal in nature and finances and procedures tended to be more informally regulated than at present. One of our respondents in Dehra Dun, India (interview, September 1999), talked about a 'past age', when he would meet someone from a northern development organization at a party, sketch out an idea and, over a breakfast meeting, be given the nod for funding to carry it out. During the 1980s and 1990s, the growth of donor interest in the 'third sector' led to an explosion in funding. One outcome has been the emergence of a new generation of southern NGOs, most of which employ middle-class, educated and urban-based men and women in their offices, while the scope of NGOs has widened from relief and disaster response to service delivery, and most recently to advocacy and policy analysis.

As the NGO sector has expanded in terms of funding and functions, there has been a growing concern with the dual issues of professionalization (organizational development and capacity building) and accountability (financial probity and transparency). In part, this can be attributed to the 'good governance' agenda – NGOs are now widely taken to be key constituents of 'civil society' (as well as vehicles of its wider development) and therefore as targets of intervention and reform. A new 'support industry' has arisen around capacity building and training to improve the organizational development of southern NGOs. Some argue that this has robbed NGOs of their autonomy, as they have lost their radical origins and been co-opted into serving the neoliberal project (Tvedt, 2001; Wallace, 2004). For others, this professionalization has allowed NGOs to work more effectively, and to act as 'authorized critical voices' that have the ability to stir governments and global institutions to more positive change (Tandon, 2003). Setting this debate to one side, we are concerned here with the form that 'professionalization' has taken. From a UK background, we can observe parallels with recent public-sector reforms in Britain (Desai and Imrie, 1998). Core features of 'new public management' include the surveillance and management of the professions and public sector through the establishment of quantifiable indicators and targets, associated with an explosive demand for documentation. Onora O'Neill is highly critical of the impact that this has had in the UK, arguing that:

> The idea of audit has been exported from its original financial context to cover ever more detailed scrutiny of non-financial processes and systems. Performance indicators are used to measure adequate and inadequate performance with supposed precision ... The new accountability is widely experienced not just as changing but I think as distorting the proper aims of professional practice and indeed as damaging professional pride and integrity. Professionals and public servants understandably end up responding to requirements and targets and not only to those whom they are supposed to serve. (O'Neill, 2002)

We find many parallels between O'Neill's analysis of the current 'culture of suspicion' in the UK and the new management regime being imposed upon both northern and southern NGOs. As we have argued elsewhere (Mawdsley et al, 2002), although many southern NGOs are supportive of the goal of improving effectiveness and accountability, they are critical of the manner in which these objectives are being pursued. Some of the main problems concern the distorting impact of chasing targets and key indicators; the time burden imposed by reporting demands; and the exclusionary effect on smaller NGOs that are unable to master the new technical requirements (e.g. logframes) or language (e.g. English, French, Spanish) needed to produce the necessary glossy applications and reports. As northern NGOs have increasingly withdrawn from direct implementation to a more financial and technical supporting role for their southern partners, and in conjunction with the policy of 'indigenization', these reports have become increasingly central to monitoring and accountability.

The NGO sector is handling large flows of public and private money, and we support the need to monitor their effectiveness in achieving development goals. However, we believe that there are creative ways of managing this that may be more rigorous than the current over-reliance on reports and documentation and yet which would also have benefits for southern NGO effectiveness, diversity of approach and the personal and professional well-being of NGO personnel in the north and the south (see also Brehm, 2003).

Being There: The Value of Visits, Observation and Interaction

The practical measures we identified with our respondents included:

- the substitution of a significant proportion of standard documentation (reports etc.) by visits between southern and northern partners and donors;
- visits from northern personnel to the south should focus on the clients (a term we prefer to 'beneficiaries') and on fieldworkers, as well as on NGO leaders;
- this strategy depends on a continuity of personnel (individuals and/or teams) on both sides. Relations have to be built up over time, as do knowledge and experience of specific sites, the real issues facing the poor in those areas and the changes that are being made on the ground.

What are the benefits of this approach? We suggest that, to some extent, some or all of the following might be achieved:

1   It would reduce some of the tremendous time burden imposed by office-based tasks, about which both northern and southern NGO workers complained vociferously. The last few years have witnessed an extraordinary proliferation of documentation, in part facilitated by information and communications technology (ICT) developments. Many respondents told us that they often feel that they don't have enough time for their core work, let alone for critical reflection and discussion

2   For many in both the north and south, reduced documentation and more field visits would help improve personal job satisfaction and motivation. Many of our respondents felt that they were no longer development professionals but rather

paper pushers and managers, and they regretted the fact that they had less time to spend in the field and/or to engage in discussion and learning

3   A greater focus on in-country visits would help northern NGO workers to learn more about their southern NGO partners and their clients. Visits would help sensitize them to local/regional specificities and to the realities of lives, livelihoods, needs and limitations in that area. Through greater interaction on the ground, they would be in a better position to discuss and understand the issues confronting their partner NGOs and their clients. This would, ideally, help to improve dialogue and enable southern partners to have more of a voice in setting the agenda. Ideally, therefore, it would help address the tendency towards universal prescriptions and solutions from expensive jet-setting consultants

4   Talking more to the clients of NGOs would contribute to 'downward accountability' – something that is the subject of much discussion at present (INTRAC, 2004)

5   Southern NGOs, especially smaller ones, would have more opportunity to learn about their northern partners – their mission, goals and styles of working – and have greater opportunity for feedback and dialogue. This might stimulate closer and more respectful 'partnership'. Face-to-face interactions facilitate a depth of relation that is almost impossible to initiate and difficult to sustain through e-mails, letters and faxes. This may be particularly true in many parts of the south where a high priority is often placed on oral and interpersonal communication

6   More visits could contribute to a more rigorous monitoring system – if they were to the grassroots, and if they were repeat visits from the same person/team. First, it would help eliminate the minority of outright corrupt NGOs, whose reports and claims have absolutely no basis in reality. For genuine NGOs, direct and repeat visits are one way of developing more accurate and vigorous monitoring processes over the longer term. In part, this is because visits would help monitor what counts: change on the ground. The current insistence on quantifiable targets and outputs is of limited value and in some cases even harmful to more effective change. There are two main problems. First, they can distort NGO efforts towards what can be counted (number of groups formed, amount of money loaned, amount returned, etc.). The effort to meet targets can overtake the original mission – microfinance return rates are improved when one does not lend to the poorest of the poor (or, as in the UK, hospital waiting lists shorten if one concentrates on the speedy but not especially important operations). Second, less tangible indicators may be equally important, but neglected. Sometimes the most meaningful changes – self-respect, the exercise of greater choice and so on – are the most difficult to massage into figures. For example, Kameshwari Jandhyala, a senior woman in Mahila Samakhya (MS) whom we interviewed in 1999 in New Delhi, told us of a low-caste, poor woman who after five years of participation in an MS group had actually gone into the courtyard of the male, high-caste village leader's house to confront him about something. This was an extraordinary change, a real result, but as Kameshwari said, how could you put that down as a 'target'?

There is, of course, value in measuring what can be counted – how many children inoculated, how many standpipes built and so on. But these need to be set within their context, and recognized as partial and proxy indicators of 'development'. Targets and indicators have their place, but they need to be balanced with other evidence, and contextualized within more complex social, economic and political realities. Again, this requires that donors have a greater depth of knowledge of specific situations, and an ability to trust in one's own and others' informed, qualitative, professional judgements.

What are the potential problems of this approach?

- There are significant time and money implications for northern and southern NGOs, although, as we have suggested above, the former should be offset against a reduction in time spent on paperwork. This implies a policy choice over priorities for funding, and a weighing up of costs and benefits
- Visits are not foolproof ways of examining an NGO's organizational structure, procedures and culture, or the impact it is making on its clients. Language issues will probably intervene between northern visitors and NGO fieldworkers and clients, biasing them towards the interpretations of leaders. Visits can be manipulated to showcase the best achievements of the NGO, and hide failures and problems. However, these problems confront all monitoring systems – we suggest that making direct, repeat visits to the NGO and the grassroots, in conjunction with other forms of monitoring and reporting, is likely to be more rigorous than most
- Southern NGOs may feel that such visits, as well as being expensive and time consuming, are intrusive. Trust can be eroded, as well as improved, through greater personal interaction
- There are obvious dangers in an over-reliance on personal interactions. Some people are better at getting on than others, and this may start to affect judgement and create unhelpful inclusions and exclusions. Good personal relations and trust may start to degenerate into complacency and even corruption. For these reasons, we believe that the proposals outlined here need to be subject to checks and balances, and complemented (rather than drowned) by reports, audits and so on
- Those NGOs that are willing to experiment would have to convince their funders of the potential efficiency and effectiveness of greater personal interaction as a means of monitoring and ensuring accountability.

Conclusions

Our critique of the dominant methods of monitoring and accountability within the NGO community chimes closely with O'Neill's analysis of the 'crisis of public trust' in the UK. Like her, we suggest that an over-reliance on documentation, targets and indicators, as well as the devaluation of professional working practices and relations, have deeply problematic outcomes. We do not advocate a return to the more informal and irregular funding and partner relations of 20 years ago – the sector has changed and so has the world around it. Neither do we suggest that we have set out a universal nor coherent 'solution' to the many challenges of contemporary management, monitoring and accountability in a highly diverse sector. However, we do feel that there are potential benefits for northern and southern NGOs, and for their clients, in thoughtfully encouraging more personal interaction and contact and moving away from an over-reliance on documentation and quantitative indicators. In this, we concur with Sarah Lister's observation, that:

> The dominance of personal relations within the organisational relationships calls into question much of the theory currently being developed for NGOs in terms of capacity building, institutional strengthening, scaling-up and diffusion of innovation, which all rely on organisational processes as the basis for change. This study suggests that a more actor-oriented approach may be appropriate for the development of NGO theory. (Lister, 1999, p15)

References

Allsop, I. (2003) 'Preparing for a hike?', Charity Finance December 2003:16–27

Brehm, V. (2003) 'Fostering autonomy or creating dependence? A case study of Norwegian Church Aid's partnerships in Brazil', unpublished paper, Oxford: INTRAC

Desai, V. and Imrie, R. (1998) 'The new managerialism in local governance: North–South dimensions', Third World Quarterly 19(4):635–650

Hailey, J. (2001) 'Beyond the formulaic: process and practice in South Asian NGOs', in B. Cooke and U. Kothari (eds) Participation: The New Tyranny?, London: Zed Books

Hailey, J. and Smillie, I. (2001) Managing for Change, London: Earthscan

INTRAC (2004) Creativity and Constraint: Grassroots Monitoring and the International Aid Arena, Oxford: INTRAC

Lister, S. (1999) 'Power in Partnership? An Analysis of an NGO's Relationships with its Partners', CVO International Working Paper 5, London: CVO, London School of Economics

Mawdsley, E.E., Townsend, J.G., Porter, G. and Oakley, P. (2002) Knowledge, Power and Development Agendas: NGOs North and South, Oxford: INTRAC

O'Neill, O. (2002) A Question of Trust: The BBC Reith Lectures 2002, Cambridge: CUP, available at www.bbc.co.uk/radio4/reith2002/lectures.shtml

Shameem Siddiqi, M. (2001) 'Who Will Bear the Torch? Charismatic Leadership and Second-line Leaders in Development NGOs', CCS International Working Paper 9, London: CCS, London School of Economics

Tandon, R. (2003) 'The civil society – governance interface: an Indian perspective', in R. Tandon and R. Mohanty (eds) Does Civil Society Matter? Governance in Contemporary India, London and New Delhi: Sage

Tvedt, T. (2001) Angels of Mercy or Development Diplomats: NGOs & Foreign Aid, 2nd edition, London: James Currey; Philadelphia, PA: Africa World Press

Wallace, T. (2004) 'NGO dilemmas: Trojan horses for global neoliberalism?', in L. Panitch and C. Leys (eds) The New Imperial Challenge: Socialist Register 2004, New York, NY: Monthly Review Press

18

Briefing Paper: Policy Engagement for Poverty Reduction – How Civil Society Can Be More Effective

Julius Court, Enrique Mendizabal, David Osbourne and John Young[1]

Acting alone, CSOs' impact is limited in scope, scale and sustainability. Civil society organizations (CSOs) are enormously important players in international development. They provide development services and humanitarian relief, innovate in service delivery, build local capacity and advocate with and for the poor.

Acting alone, however, their impact on policy is limited in scope, scale and sustainability. CSOs need to engage in policy processes more effectively.

Despite more open and accessible policy contexts, CSOs are having a limited impact on public policy and practice in developing countries and ultimately on the lives of poor people. All too often, CSOs appear to act on their own, leading to questions about their legitimacy and accountability. Their policy positions are also increasingly questioned: researchers challenge their evidence base and policymakers question the feasibility of their recommendations.

Key points:

- CSOs could have greater impact by engaging in policy processes more effectively
- Better use of evidence by CSOs would increase their policy influence and pro-poor impact
- Regardless of context, there are ways CSOs can maximize policy impact.

This briefing paper focuses on why and how CSOs can engage more effectively in policy processes in international development. Section 1 sets the scene and highlights the opportunities and challenges facing CSOs policy work. Section 2 focuses on why evidence matters for CSOs' work in international development. Section 3 provides a framework that matches the engagement mechanisms and evidence needs to the critical stages of policy processes. Section 4 summarizes strategic and practical advice regarding how CSOs can ensure their policy engagement is more effective, influential and sustained.

> **Box 18.1** *CSOs and development: Some estimates*
>
> - Non-governmental development organizations have estimated annual revenues of US$12 billion
> - It is said that NGOs reach 20 per cent of the world's poor
> - CSOs in Ghana, Zimbabwe and Kenya provide 40 per cent of all healthcare and education
> - There are an estimated 22,000 development NGOs in Bangladesh alone
> - Recent evidence-based health reforms in rural Tanzania contributed to over 40 per cent reductions in infant mortality between 2000 and 2003.

Changing Context: Opportunities and Constraints

The last 15 years have seen significant changes in the contexts affecting the relationship between CSOs and policy-makers. This period has been characterized by globalization, democratization, reductions in conflict and advances in information and communication technologies (ICTs). In general, there is potential for progressive partnerships involving the public and private sectors and CSOs in more and more developing countries.

The number of CSOs is growing. Many CSOs have become aware that policy engagement can lead to greater pro-poor impacts than contestation. We see more and more examples of CSOs engaging in informed advocacy as an important route to social change and a means of holding governments to account. Sometimes this is leading to impressive outcomes.

Why then are CSOs having a surprisingly limited influence on policy and practice in developing countries? The evidence suggests that adverse political contexts are partly responsible. Often, however, the main obstacles are internal to CSOs.

Figure 18.1 highlights the main obstacles to CSO engagement in policy processes (from a survey of CSOs). The most common barriers were internal to CSOs, with respondents listing insufficient capacity and funding (62 per cent and 57 per cent respectively) as significant constraints. Others cited the closed nature of the policy process as an impediment to their participation, with 47 per cent of respondents noting policy-makers do not see CSO evidence as credible.

CSOs, Evidence and Policy

Recent ODI (Overseas Development Institute) work shows that: (i) better outcomes stem from better policy and practice; (ii) better policy and practice occur when rigorous, systematic evidence is used; (iii) CSOs that use evidence better will have greater policy influence and greater pro-poor impact. Figure 18.2 outlines our framework.

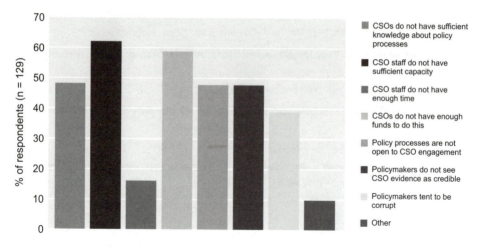

Figure 18.1 *Main obstacles to CSO engagement in policy processes*

Better use of evidence by CSOs can increase the policy influence and pro-poor impact of their work in three ways. First, it can help improve the impact of CSOs' service delivery work. Second, better use of evidence can increase the legitimacy and effectiveness of their policy engagement efforts, helping CSOs to gain a place and have influence at the policy table. Finally, it can help ensure that policy recommendations really do help the poor.

CSOs engage with policy processes engage in many different ways. They can:

* *identify* the political constraints and opportunities and develop a strategy for engagement;
* *inspire* support for an issue or action; raise new ideas or question old ones; create new ways of framing an issue or 'policy narrative';
* *inform* the views of others; share expertise and experience; put forward new approaches;
* *improve*, add, correct or change policy issues; hold policymakers accountable; evaluate and improve their own activities, particularly regarding service provision.

Box 18.2 *Key terms*

* CSOs refer to any organization that works in the arena between the household, the private sector and the state, to negotiate matters of public concern. CSOs includes NGOs, community groups, research institutes, think tanks, advocacy groups, trade unions, academic institutions, parts of the media, professional associations and faith-based institutions

* We take the view that policy and practice should be informed by research-based evidence. But we adopt a general, though widely accepted, definition of research as 'any systematic effort to increase the stock of knowledge'

* We use the term 'policy' to denote a purposive course of action followed by an actor or set of actors

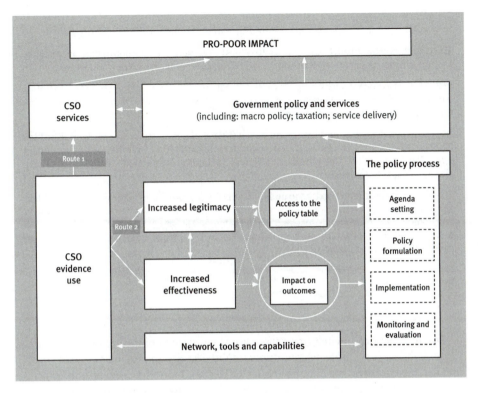

Figure 18.2 *CSOs, evidence, policy and pro-poor impact*

And research-based evidence can be influential in each of the four main stages of policy processes: agenda setting, policy formulation, implementation, monitoring and evaluation.

At the agenda setting stage, evidence can help put issues on the agenda and ensure they are recognized as significant problems which require a policy-maker's response. CSO inputs can be even more influential if they also provide options and realistic solutions. Better use of evidence can influence public opinion, cultural norms and political contestation and indirectly affect policy processes.

At the policy formulation stage, evidence can be an important way to establish the credibility of CSOs. Here, evidence can be used to enhance or establish a positive reputation. CSOs can adapt the way they use evidence to maintain credibility with local communities and with policy-makers, combining their tacit and explicit knowledge of a policy issue. A key issue is to outline the theory of change – how the proposed policy measure will result in pro-poor services. CSOs may also present evidence of their political position, as much as their competence, in order to be included within policy discussions.

At the implementation stage, evidence helps CSOs translate technical skills, expert knowledge and practical experiences, so as to inform others better. CSOs have often been successful innovators in service delivery that informs broader government implementation. The key to influencing implementation of policy is often to have solutions that are realistic and generalizable across different contexts.

Box 18.3 *Evidence and policy influence: Coalition 2000 in Bulgaria*

The Coalition 2000 initiative was launched in 1998 to counteract corruption in Bulgarian society through a process of cooperation among NGOs, governmental institutions and citizens.

In 2003, the Corruption Monitoring System of Coalition 2000 identified the education sector as a corruption-prone area. University professors and school teachers were consistently rated by the general public in the top five most corrupt professions in Bulgaria.

Based on this evidence, and to support governmental efforts to tackle the problem, Coalition 2000 developed and tested a set of instruments for teaching on corruption for use in secondary and tertiary education. This included designing textbooks, online study materials, manuals, and teaching programmes.

These experiences demonstrated to public institutions the benefits of introducing the topic into civic education curricula. They also underscored the usefulness of creating new anticorruption programmes and ready-made teaching materials for the Ministry of Education and Science. As a result, anticorruption classes were introduced in the official curricula of the Bulgarian secondary schools in the fall of 2004.

Source: Dimitrova, N. P. (2005) Introduction of Anticorruption Education in the Bulgarian Secondary Schools, London:ODI

Finally, evidence can be further used to influence the monitoring and evaluation of policy. It helps to identify whether policies are actually improving the lives of their intended beneficiaries. For example, many CSOs have pioneered participatory processes that transform the views of ordinary people into indicators and measures, garnering the interest of the media or other external groups. This can make help improve policy positions and make policy processes more accountable.

CSOs could have greater influence if they were more strategic about:

- whether to engage in policy processes;
- which part of the policy process actually matters for the lives of poor people;
- which component of the process a CSO is trying to engage with;
- what mechanism and evidence tends to matter at each stage.

Approaches for Effective Policy Engagement

There are a number of obstacles, both external and internal, which restrict CSO policy engagement. Adverse political contexts or problematic policy processes constrain or prevent CSO work. However, the main obstacles are often internal to CSOs. Below we highlight some of the ways to overcome the main obstacles facing CSOs. More detail on each is in the full report.

While our focus has been on what CSOs can do, there are also ways in which progressive policy-makers and donors could help. Progressive policymakers could help by: working to ensure political freedoms are in place; making policy processes more transparent; providing access to information and providing space for CSO contributions on

Table 18.1 *Approaches for effective policy engagement*

Key obstacles to CSOs	Potential solutions for effective policy engagement
External	
Adverse political contexts constrain CSO policy work	• Campaigns – to improve policy positions and governance contexts • 'Boomerangs' – working via external partners to change national policy. • Pilot projects – to develop and test operational solutions to inform and improve policy implementation.
Internal	
Limited understanding of specific policy processes, institutions and actors	Conduct rigorous context assessments. These enable a better understanding of how policy processes work, the politics affecting them and the opportunities for policy influence. We outline key issues and some simple approaches to mapping political contexts.
Weak strategies for policy engagement	Identify critical policy stages – agenda setting, formulation and/or implementation – and the engagement mechanisms that are most appropriate for each stage. We provide a framework that matches the different approaches and evidence requirements to each stage in the policy process.
Inadequate use of evidence	Ensure that evidence is relevant, objective, generalizable and practical. This helps improve CSO legitimacy and credibility with policymakers. We outline sources of research advice and mechanisms for how CSOs can access better evidence.
Weak communication approaches in policy influence work	Engage in two-way communication and use existing tools for planning, packaging, targeting and monitoring communication efforts. Doing so will help CSOs make their interventions more accessible, digestible and timely for policy discussions. We provide examples and sources of further information.
Working in an isolated manner	Apply network approaches. Networks can help CSOs: bypass obstacles to consensus; assemble coalitions for change; marshal and amplify evidence; and mobilize resources. We outline the key roles of networks (from filters to convenors) and the 10 keys to network success.
Limited capacity for policy influence	Engage in systemic capacity building. CSOs need a wide range of technical capacities to maximize their chances of policy influence. We outline some key areas where CSOs could build their own capacity or access it from partners.

specific policy issues. Donors could help by providing: incentives and pressure for governments to ensure political rights and a space for CSO engagement in policy, diversifying their support to the CSO sector (beyond NGOs) and ensuring funding for informed CSO policy engagement.

Conclusions

In some countries, adverse political contexts continue to be the main barrier to informed policy engagement. CSOs can try to improve the situation and influence policy but their options are limited. In many contexts, the extent of CSOs impact on policy is in their own hands. By getting the fundamentals right – assessing context, engaging policy-makers, getting rigorous evidence, working with partners, communicating well – CSOs can overcome key internal obstacles. The result will be more effective, influential and sustained policy engagement for poverty reduction.

Sources and Further Information

This chapter draws on the report: Court, J., Mendizabal, E., Osborne, D., and Young, J., 2006, *Policy Engagement: How Can Civil Society be More Effective* London: ODI.

The report is based on literature reviews; a survey with responses from 130 CSOs; a range of case studies, thematic studies and practical action research projects; and a series of 22 learning workshops involving over 800 people in Africa, Asia and Latin America.

The full report, other research and policy influence toolkits can be seen at: www.odi.org.uk/rapid/. To get involved, email: rapid@odi.org.uk.

Join The RAPID Network

We hope this chapter provides insights and stimulates others to work in this area. An emerging network, coordinated initially by ODI, will focus on:

- generating greater awareness of the importance of evidence use by CSOs;
- providing more 'how to' information to CSOs interested in informed policy influence;
- working with others to build systematic capacity in this area;
- undertaking new research on informed CSO policy engagement;
- supporting policy engagement on issues where CSOs can have an impact.

Notes

1   Overseas Development Institute: ODI is the UK's leading independent think-tank on international development and humanitarian issues (email publications@odi.org.uk). Briefing Papers present objective information on important development issues. Readers are encouraged to quote or reproduce material from them for their own publications, but as copyright holder, ODI requests due acknowledgement and a copy of the publication. This and other ODI Briefing Papers are available from www.odi.org.uk (last accessed July 2010). © Overseas Development Institute, 2006, ISSN 0140-8682.

19

Is There Life after Gender Mainstreaming?

Aruna Rao and David Kelleher

Impressive Gains and Staggering Failures

In the last decade, efforts to make the mainstream work for women have resulted in impressive gains as well as staggering failures. In the wake of Beijing Plus 10, one review after another documents the strategic partnerships forged over the last decade between the women's movement and policy reformers in putting equity and women's rights at the heart of development debates (UNRISD, 2005; Millennium Project Gender Task Force Report, 2005). Women's leaders have made striking gains in getting elected to local and national governance bodies and entering public institutions, girls' access to primary education has improved sharply and women are entering the labour force in increasing numbers.

Under the banner of gender mainstreaming in institutional practice, there are numerous examples of positive outcomes for women's lives beyond policy measures. They include bringing women to the peace table during the Burundi peace process; strengthening or establishing organizations, networks to promote gender equality in mainstream agencies; mainstreaming gender issues into law reform processes in Botswana including national policy regarding HIV/AIDS; gaining greater visibility for women's work as a result of engendering the census in Nepal, India and Pakistan; protecting widows and orphans from dispossession on the death of the male 'owner' by supporting a primary justice mediation process Malawi; and in Rwanda, where women were systematically raped and murdered during the civil war, women now have gained 49 per cent of the seats in parliament and formed local women's councils elected solely by women.

The problem is that these examples are not the norm. Practices that successfully promote women's empowerment and gender equality are not institutionalized into the day-to-day routines of state and international development agencies.

More important are the myriad, insidious ways in which the mainstream resists women's perspectives and women's rights. Economic orthodoxy promoting unmanaged, export-led growth through competitive market capitalism, free trade and fiscal austerity including the drastic reduction of government social spending, has hurt poor women the most. Governance reforms have not forced states to address their accountability failures when it comes to women's access to resources and services and institutional reform for the most part still means fiscal and administrative reforms rather than making systems work better for the poor, including women.

In South Africa, where Gender at Work has organized numerous consultations over the past two years, the unease generated by the gap between promise and reality is palpable. Feminist activists speak of the fundamental difficulty in shifting the paradigm of patriarchy within which they operate and the resultant high fallout and burnout. They tell you that they have only managed to chip away at how power is exercised – there is no major shift here. They point to the enormous contradictions they see with good gender equity policies and high number of women in positions of power and at the same time some of the highest levels of violence against women in the world. In India, where Gender at Work is also active, social justice activists point to the rise in the power of the state and right wing politics and a concomitant decrease in commitment to human rights principles.

At the level of formal institutions whether they are trade unions, NGOs, women's organizations, community based organizations, state bureaucracies or corporate structures, not much has changed either. Organizational structures tend to reinforce power being vested in a few and for the most part men are unwilling to part with privileges of power. On the other hand when power is shared, responsibility is not exercised by more than a few. Moreover, the management discourse dominates institutional life. The strength of traditional management theory and organizational development thinking and practice is to focus on efficiency and results. Its weakness, particularly as applied to social change organizations in many southern contexts, is that it does not explicitly deal with power dynamics, cultural change, strategic objectives derived from a nuanced analysis of relational and material hierarchies and outcomes aimed to change all of those dysfunctionalities.

In the world of feminist activism, the time seems ripe now for review and reflection – taking stock, asking why change isn't happening, what works, what doesn't work. This rethink is happening at a time of unprecedented militarization globally and an equally unprecedented mobilization of citizens against war and the negative effects of globalization, as well as *for* social justice. Calls for a restructuring of the global governance infrastructure such as the Global Call for Action Against Poverty (GCAP) led by citizen action groups are focusing attention on accountability of global institutions, new terms of trade and development. But by and large, these global movements and their grounding notions of citizenship and accountability are gender blind.

Moreover, while 'citizens' are mobilizing, the infrastructure and resources for supporting women's activism, women's movements and challenging gender power relations in the home, communities, organizations, markets and the state are being dismantled. The architecture to support women's empowerment and gender equality is being eroded at international and national levels, and new aid modalities such a budgetary supports and SWAPs (Sector Wide Approaches) may make it even more possible to fudge on gender equality goals. Gender concerns are falling through the cracks. Institutional change, capacity building, political partnerships and women's organizing are being marginalized in what is increasingly a bean-counting approach to development deliverables.

Gender Mainstreaming: Wedged between a Rock and a Hard Place?

Gender mainstreaming is grounded in feminist theoretical frameworks and its appeal to 'femocrats' and to gender activists was its promise of transformation. But gender mainstreaming has been caught between a rock and a hard place. At a macro level, it is operating in a policy environment increasingly hostile towards justice and equity which is further feminizing poverty. At the meso institutional level, there is still active resistance to the value of women's rights and gender equality goals, or where allies exist their hands are tied by policy priorities as well as poor infrastructure and decreased funding levels. Gender mainstreaming has become a grab bag of diverse strategies and activities all ostensibly concerned with moving forward a gender equality agenda but often not working in ways we would have hoped. Finally, at a micro level, first generation development objectives enshrined in the MDGs (Millennium Development Goals) are trumping support for women's organizations and women's organizing – the vanguard of the political fight.

The need for political strategizing at multiple levels and deeper, institutional change has made the inadequacy of previous strategies apparent. Old solutions are inadequate but it is unclear what the new solutions are. Most acknowledge the need for new approaches that address the gender biased implications of macroeconomic policies on employment, wages, food security and welfare services that work with power to structure opportunities for women, that hold systems accountable and that allow for learning on the part of women and men. Those approaches are being formulated. They range from calls for a new social contract (Sen, 2004), innovative managed market approaches (Elson, 2005), transformation of institutions and organizations (Goetz and Hassim, 2003; Rao and Kelleher, 2004; Millennium Project Gender Task Force Report, 2005) and a re-energized and re-politicized women's movement. All these approaches for gender equality must have a political component because gender relations exist within a force field of power relations and power is used to maintain existing privilege. Here we will elaborate on the dimensions of institutional change.

What Are We Trying to Change?

Our understanding of how to work towards gender equality has evolved to the realization that we need to change inequitable social systems and institutions. Generally, people now speak of 'institutional change' as the requirement for getting to the root causes of gender inequality. This means changing the rules of the game, meaning the stated and unstated rules that determine who gets what, who does what and who decides (Goetz, 1997; North, 1990; Rao and Kelleher, 2002). These rules can be formal such as constitutions, laws, policies and school curricula, or informal such as cultural arrangements and norms such as who is responsible for household chores, who goes to the market, who decides on the education of children or who is expected to speak at a village council meeting. It also means changing organizations which, in their programmes, policies, structures and ways of working discriminate against women or other marginalized groups.

Different organizations have focused on either one or the other of the four areas highlighted below. Some organizations for example work on legal and policy change, while others focus on changing material conditions. In order to change gender inequality in fundamental ways change must occur both at the personal level and at the social. It must occur in formal and in informal relations. This gives us the four clusters which impact on each other:

- women's and men's individual consciousness (knowledge, skill, political conscious-ness, commitment);
- women's objective condition (rights and resources, access to health services and safety, opportunities for voice);
- informal norms such as inequitable ideologies and cultural and religious practices;
- formal institutions such as laws and policies.

Often we assume that change in one will lead to change in the others, for example women who have started and maintained micro businesses report being more self-confident. But we also know for example that it is possible to have material resources but no influence; it is possible to be 'economically empowered' but not free from violence. Since sustainable change requires institutional change, that is, the clusters of informal norms and formal institutions at the bottom of Figure 19.1, the question is how does institutional change happen and most importantly, what is the role of development organizations in that change process? The organizations that will be supporting those interventions also exist in the same force field and will require certain capacities not only to want to intervene in a significant way, but to be able to intervene to work with these forces. Typically, it will require an on-going change process to build and maintain these capabilities.

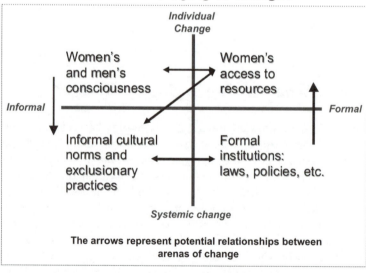

Figure 19.1 *What are we trying to change?*

This diagram may be helpful in the following ways: first, it shows in an abbreviated way, the whole universe of changes that might be contemplated to enhance gender equality and can serve as an outline to document the particular situation in these clusters in a particular context. Second, it allows change agents to make strategic choices as to where and how to intervene and finally, it points to the fact that changes in resources, capacity and knowledge are necessary but not sufficient for sustainable change. Ultimately, changes of formal and particularly informal institutions are required.

What Are Some of the Key Challenges We See?

As we reflect on lessons from organizational experience and those of our own, we see four key challenges:

1 Challenges of institutional change on the ground: programme and project evaluations point to the difficulty of moving from rhetoric to reality or from individual change and learning to social change. They describe the problem of sociocultural acceptance of ideas of gender equality, the lack of capacity of implementing partners and the difficulties of attitudinal and behavioral changes at the individual and institutional level

2 Challenges of clarity: a number of analysts have recently pointed out how a lack of clarity endangers implementation of gender mainstreaming strategies (Hannan, 2002; Subrahmanian, 2005). However the most pernicious misunderstanding is the separation of gender mainstreaming from women's empowerment work and the withdrawal of resources from projects focused on women's empowerment in the name of mainstreaming. Much work needs to be done with both men and women but we cannot reduce commitment to programming that focuses on women because that is where crucial gains towards gender equality are being made

3 Challenges of organizational change: the lack of senior management support, lack of accountability, lack of knowledge and skill of senior staff on gender issues, marginalized, under-qualified and under-resourced theme groups and specialists – these are all problems in organizations mandated to mainstream gender concerns in development

4 Challenges of measurement: at the first level, there are on-going difficulties of obtaining sex-disaggregated data. At the second level, there is a lack of tracking mechanisms that can notice relative contributions to different goals in a particular project. For example in a sanitation project – how much of the project budget can be said to be responding to the needs of women? This would require a social impact analysis at the design stage of the project and a sophisticated tracking mechanism. More deep, however is the problem of measuring the intangibles that are at the root of social change of any sort – the change in consciousness of women and men, the change in community norms or the change in attitudes.

Beyond Mainstreaming to Institutional Transformation

Transformation of gender relations involves access and control over material and symbolic resources. It also requires changes in deep-seated values and relationships that are held in place by power and privilege. Transformation is fundamentally a political and personal process. Amartya Sen says that institutions limit or enhance poor people's right to freedom, freedom of choice and action. Without a critical understanding of how institutions need to change to allow different social groups to secure their entitlements and access opportunities for socioeconomic mobility, development goals cannot be achieved. From the perspective of poor people, institutions are in crisis and a strategy of change must 'start with the poor people's realities; invest in organizational capacity of the poor; (iii) change social norms; and (iv) support development entrepreneurs' (Narayan, 1999).

Feminist thinking about empowerment directly engages with resources, power, ideology and institutions (Batliwala, 1996) implying a symbiotic relationship between power and ideology which gains expression and perpetuation through structures of all kinds – judicial, economic, social and political. Empowerment in this framework therefore means a transformation in power relations. Specifically, it means: control over resources (physical, human, intellectual, intangible); control over ideology (beliefs, values, attitudes); and changes in the institutions and structures that support unequal power relations.

Notions of citizenship, like institutions, are inextricably bound up with relations of power. 'Like power relations, citizenship rights are not fixed, but are objects of struggle to be defended, reinterpreted and extended' (Meer, 2004). The negotiation is around societal positions that discriminate against women and gender roles including the public/private divide that acts to contain women and their agency primarily within the private sphere and while opening men's agency to the public sphere. It is also around unequal power formed on the basis of class, caste, ethnicity and other key markers of identity. But not only that, it is also a challenge to ideas that frame how we see the world and how we act.

Similarly, claiming rights is a political process and it is played out as struggles between interests, power and knowledge of differently positioned actors. A rights-based approach basically argues that all people are entitled to universal human rights and development should be oriented to meeting those rights. Ferguson says that a rights perspective politicizes needs. While a needs-based approach identifies the resource requirements of particular groups, a rights-based approach provides the means of strengthening people's claims to those resources. According to Jones and Gaventa (2002), the challenge of the rights-based approach is 'in maintaining equal emphasis on the need to build both citizens' capabilities to articulate rights *and* the capabilities of political-economic institutions to respond and be held to account'. For individuals and groups, making demands for accountability requires a sense that they have a right to do so (claiming that political space) and mechanisms through which their demands can be made and responded to. And on the other side, accountability according to the UNDP Human Development Report 2000 is judged by whether appropriate policies have been implemented and progress achieved.

Figure 19.2 *Social and public accountability*

Transformation: The Role of Development Agencies

We think that such transformatory goals exist uneasily within large development organizations as they are likely to be overcome by technical considerations more amenable to administrative practice. The key questions are: given the uneasy relationship between transformation and large organizations how can we strengthen the capacity of state and development bureaucracies to deliver on their operational mandates and how can we shift organizational practice as necessary to better focus on equity and exclusion.

In order to strengthen practice in the project of transformation, we need to disaggregate the range of diverse strategies and activities that are dumped in the gender mainstreaming bag – such as policy reform, advocacy, capacity building, analytical frameworks, programme development, monitoring systems – and analyze their gains and their failures (Subrahmanian, 2005). This also should help in strategic thinking about what these institutions are well placed to do. Concurrently measurement systems need to be developed that can capture the full range of gender equality outcomes – tangible and intangible.

Our change strategies should envision institutional change. This doesn't mean reducing programmes such as education or increased resources for women's entrepreneurship. It means seeing these not as ends but means towards equality and realizing that political activity and more is required to translate education or improved health care into equality. One important idea is that of working on both demand and supply of the institutional change equation. By the supply side, we mean shifting opportunity structures in institutional environments towards equality of women's agency, changing incentives and capacity in global, state and community agencies to respond to women including delivering on services and on rights. On the demand side, we mean strengthening women's awareness of their own agency, voice and mobilization, and their influence over institutions, and their ability to hold them to account

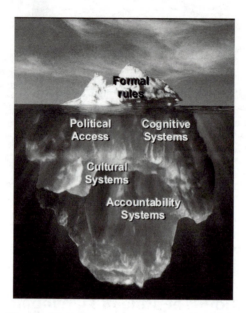

Figure 19.3 *Deep organizational structures*

Organizational Deep Structures

Organizational change needs to go far beyond policy adoption and large scale processing of staff through gender training workshops. It is clear that like any other complex skill, the evolution of knowledge and values (particularly for men) is a long process requiring practice. Gender theme groups and specialists need to be better resourced but more importantly need to be part of decision-making. Even when senior managers agree that gender is important, gender equality still has to displace other important competing values in decision-making. Only by ensuring a strong gender voice in decision-making will gender concerns be represented in the day-to-day discussion of competing needs and values that are at the heart of development work. Numerous analysts have emphasized the importance of strong leadership, accountability structures, including performance appraisal and better monitoring, and while we would agree that these are needed, 30 years of research and practice in the private sector is saying that these 'command and control' strategies are not enough for significant organizational change.

In our own work, we have described the 'deep structure' of organizations that, like the unconscious of individuals, is largely unexamined but constrains some behaviour and makes others more likely (Rao et al, 1999). The deep structure is that collection of taken-for-granted values; ways of thinking and working that underlies decision-making and action. Power hides the fact that organizations are gendered at very deep levels. More specifically, women are prevented from challenging institutions by four inter-related factors:

1   Political access: there are neither systems nor powerful actors who can bring women's perspectives and interests to the table

2 Accountability systems: organizational resources are steered towards quantitative targets that are often only distantly related to institutional change for gender equality

3 Cultural systems: the work-family divide perpetuated by most organizations prevents women from being full participants in those organizations as women continue to bear the responsibility for child and elderly care

4 Cognitive structures: work itself is seen mostly within existing, gender-biased norms and understandings.

It should not come as a surprise to learn that much of the deep structure of most organizations is profoundly gender biased and acts as a brake on work for gender equality. For example, one aspect of the deep structure is the separation between work and family. As Joan Acker pointed out, a key assumption in large organizations is that work is completely separate from the rest of life and the organization has first claim on the worker. From this follows the idea of the 'ideal worker' dedicated to the organization, unhampered by familial demands, and … male (Acker, 1990). Another aspect of the deep structure is the image of heroic individualism. As organizations were originally peopled by men they are not surprisingly, designed and maintained in ways that express men's identity. Heroic individualism can lead to a focus on winning and noticeable achievement in the place of the largely processual and sometimes long-term business of understanding gender relations in a particular context and acting for equality. Also, given stereotypic gender roles, heroes tend to be men, further contributing to the idea of male as ideal worker and women as other.

Generating Power to Change Organizations

We believe that there is a web of five spheres in which power can be generated to move an organization towards doing good gender equality work. These five spheres are:

1 political;
2 bureaucratic politics;
3 organizational culture;
4 organizational process;
5 programmatic interventions.

The political sphere begins with assumption that because they live within gendered societies, few organizations will devote the time, energy and resources to effective gender equality work unless pressured to do so. So the questions here are whether or not there is a women's constituency that is exerting sufficient pressure for gender to be on the radar of the organization as an issue requiring attention. In some cases donors or boards of directors have been the source of some pressure but local political pressure has more potential for holding organizations accountable. The key skills required here are organizing and advocacy. The pressure generated by this sphere may have many results – they are dependent on work in the other spheres.

Organizational politics refers to the day-to-day bargaining that goes on between bureaucratic leaders as they struggle to make their particular views a reality. This sphere is all about access of gender advocates to power, bargaining ability and skill in the use of power. Power is built from position, coalitions, clarity of analysis and purpose and assets such as who has access to whom and who is able to provide valued goods (information, technical expertise, material resources) to whom. The strong voice of an outside constituency is a tremendous asset but far from all that is needed for a bureaucratic player. The outcome of bureaucratic 'victories' may be stronger policy or increased resources or even an evolution of organizational culture.

Institutional culture is that collection of values, history and ways of doing things that form the unstated rules of the game in an organization. Most importantly, culture defines what is valued as being truly important in the organization (often at odds with official mission statements). This sphere is important because of its capacity to make things happen as well as to block them. Another way to describe culture is as organizational ideology – 'Ideology is a complex structure of beliefs, values, attitudes, and ways of perceiving and analyzing social reality – virtually, ways of thinking and perceiving' (Batliwala, 1996).

Culture then can be a powerful ally in making work on gender equality a valued part of the organization's work – the normal, the reasonable, 'just good development'. Similarly, culture can exclude, make the organization difficult for women, force a focus on 'harder' more 'real' outcomes such as infrastructure projects. Cultures are changed generally by the influence of leaders and by the understanding of others that the new directions are valuable.

Organizational process is the vehicle that turns the intangibles of bureaucratic politics, organizational culture and political pressure into organizational action – programme, policies, and services. The first question is whether there are sufficient resources, sufficient skilled and knowledgeable people to lead the process of learning and change. However, ultimately, it must be asked if knowledge is sufficiently spread through the organization, that it is part of the organizational skill set along with other aspects of development. If resources and expertise are the grease of organizational process than approval mechanisms that require gender analyses are the drivers. For example, some development agencies require a gender analysis and strategy as a component of all projects. Finally, because achieving gender equality has never been accomplished in any society organizational learning needs to seen as a key capacity. This leads us to work on the ground.

Programmatic interventions constitute the last (and first) sphere of power. It is here that the work of the other spheres is validated. It is also here that the organization delivers value or not. In the area of gender equality, what is of value is still contested – what used to be thought of as good practice is now challenged as insufficient. What this means is that this sphere must be energized by applied research and the development of new methodologies that can make a difference and capture the attention and support of other parts of the organization as well as its partners.

The following diagram shows some of the relationships between these spheres of power.

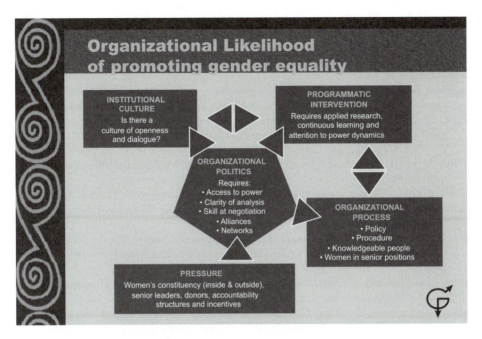

Figure 19.4 *Five spheres of power to change organizations*

Building Knowledge for Transformation and a 'Politics of Solidarity'

Even when the focus is at this level, however, we have deep reservations regarding organizational change strategies as being useful in making large organizations more interested in working towards gender equality. These strategies are helpful when there is strong and continued pressure to change felt by managers but in many cases in large multilateral organizations the pressure for work on gender is intermittent and muted. The difficulty with governmental systems is similar – seldom is there significant pressure to take gender equality seriously and many government officials are isolated from the pressure in any case. Our track record to date is telling us we need to better understand how to intervene for organizational change that can support gender equality. In particular, we need to better understand the work of gender advocates within these institutional settings and support their work. This has primarily to do with understanding how these institutions work, how to help them develop strategies appropriate to their contexts and how to create alliances that work in constrained environments.

Finally, in these times of political and economic conservatism, gender advocates within development organizations and feminists working in all kinds of spaces need to come together to build what some have called 'a politics of solidarity'. This is needed both to infuse our work with vision and energy but also to strategically assess how to advance this transformatory agenda when different political and institutional arenas are not working in synergy with our understanding of social change.

References

Acker, J. (1990) 'Hierarchies, jobs and bodies: a theory of gendered organisations', Gender and Society, 5: 390–407

Batliwala, S. (1996) 'Defining Women's Empowerment: A Conceptual Framework', in Education for Women's Empowerment, New Delhi: Asia South Pacific Bureau of Adult Education

Elson, D. (2005) 'Section 1: Macroeconomics, well being and gender equality', presentation at a panel organised by UNRISD at The Ford Foundation, New York in March 2004, to launch the UNRISD publication Gender Equality: Striving for Justice in an Unequal World, 2005

Goetz, A. (1992) 'Gender and Administration', IDS Bulletin, 23, Brighton: Institute of Development Studies

Goetz, A. (1997) Getting Institutions Right for Women in Development, London: Zed Books

Goetz, A. and Hassim, S. (2003) No Shortcuts to Power: African Women in Politics and Policy Making, London: Zed Books

Hannan, C. (2003) 'Gender Mainstreaming: Some Experience from the United Nations', paper presented at a conference on Gender Mainstreaming – A Way Towards Equality, Berne, 20 June 2003

Jones, E. and Gaventa, J. (2002) 'Concepts of Citizenship: A Review', IDS Development Bibliography 19, Brighton: Institute of Development Studies

Meer, S. with Sever, C. (2004) Gender and Citizenship: Overview Report, Bridge Pack on Gender and Citizenship, Brighton: Institute of Development Studies

Millennium Project Gender Task Force on Education and Gender Equality (2005) 'Taking Action: Achieving Gender Equality and Empowering Women', www.unmillenniumproject. org

Narayan, D. (1999) Can Anyone Hear Us? Washington D.C.: The World Bank North, D. (1990) Institutions, Institutional Change, and Economic Performance, Cambridge: Cambridge University Press

North, D. (1990) Institutions, Institutional Change, and Economic Performance, Cambridge: Cambridge University Press

Rao, A. and Kelleher, D. (2002) Unravelling Institutionalized Gender Inequality, AWID Occasional Paper No. 8, Toronto: AWID

Rao, A., Stuart, R. and Kelleher, D. (1999) Gender at Work: Organizational Change for Equality, Connecticut: Kumarian Press

Sen, G. (2004) 'Remaking Social Contracts: Beyond the Crisis in International Development', Irene Tinker Lecture Series, International Center for Research on Woman, Washington DC, 16 November 2004

20

Managing NGOs with Spirit

Rick James

Spiritual and religious values inspired the birth of many civil society organizations (CSOs) across the world. While this may be obvious for faith-based organizations (FBOs), many secular agencies, including the Red Cross, Oxfam, Amnesty International, Greenpeace, Save the Children Fund, were founded by people with strong religious beliefs (Benthall, 2008). Such spiritual values continue to play a major role today. Yet despite this history, spirituality has been largely ignored in NGO management. Management is treated as an entirely secular process, even by many FBOs.

Human behaviour is more complex than rational logic alone. It is affected by a multitude of factors including culture, emotions and beliefs. Neglecting the spiritual therefore misses out an important factor in human behaviour. Many mainstream business management writers and practitioners now realize this. In the last decade, there has been an 'explosion of interest in spirituality as a new dimension of management' (Howard, 2002, p230). Spirituality in management may be even more relevant for the NGO sector which is so steeped, inspired and still motivated by spiritual values. Effective NGO management therefore engages with spiritual values and beliefs. But it does so in an inclusive, sensitive and humble way.

The subject of spirituality is a personal, sensitive and flammable subject. It can easily be abused. Some attempts to bring spiritual perspectives into management have been reckless, exclusive and damaging. But the importance of the subject makes it imperative to develop our understanding and ability to discuss the spiritual more explicitly. Spirituality, after all, is clearly not the monopoly of any one religion and is informed by a wide variety of beliefs. Although the spiritual is very personal, it does not necessarily follow that it must also remain private. In any discussion of spirituality and management differences of opinion and interpretation are guaranteed, but these very differences may uncover new understandings to make NGO management more effective.

This chapter explores the interrelationship between spirituality and NGO management. It starts by looking at some of the definitional challenges, before identifying common elements in a number of definitions. It then highlights the many dangers of bringing spirituality into development and management. The chapter goes on to outline how attitudes, both in development and in management, are becoming more positive to integrating spirituality into management. It then identifies what spirituality in organizations looks like, before highlighting implications for NGO management. The chapter concludes that if spirituality can be integrated into NGO management in an inclusive, sensitive and respectful way, this can make a major contribution to NGO performance and impact.

What Do Different People Mean by Spirituality?

Part of the sensitivities and disagreements over spirituality in organizations arise from the wide variety of definitions of spirit and spirituality. One of the foremost authors on spirituality in organizations, Harrison Owen admits: 'Although I have written much on the subject of Spirit, I have never been able to define it.' (N.D). People naturally interpret spirituality from a personal frame of reference and belief system, but still need to communicate using common language. Wisely and Lynn highlight the limitations of language when they say, 'the spirit cannot be said it can only be shown' (in Conger, 1994, p104). Just as it is difficult to see the wind, we know it is there because we can see its effects, so with the spirit. We know it when we see it.

In trying to define spirituality it is easier to start by stating what it is not. Spirituality is not the same as religion. Ver Beek puts it clearly:

> Spirituality is a relationship with the supernatural or spiritual realm that provides meaning and a basis for personal and communal reflection, decision and action, while religion is an institutionalised set of beliefs and practices regarding the spiritual realm. (2000, p32)

Some common themes emerge from the variety of definitions of spirituality in management (McCormick, 1994; Wong, 2003; Korac-Kakabadse et al, 2002; Dehler and Welsh, 1994; Harris, 2000). They include:

- an animating life force;
- an inner, intangible experience;
- an awareness of connectedness or relationship with something more;
- it concerns the meaning in life.

The main area of difference in definitions is whether people are simply talking of the inner human spirit or whether they are also talking about a sacred and, to a degree, external spirit. Many are comfortable with the term spirit to refer to an inner human spirit. This inner spirit includes things like intuition, emotions and love. We frequently use the words 'team spirit', 'community spirit' or say someone is in 'high or low spirits' and we know what is meant.

Other people believe more contentiously that as well as this human spirit there is something more – an unseen, transcendental, external power – a divine spirit. In Greek, Latin and Hebrew, spirit originally meant 'breath' or 'wind' and inspire literally means 'to in-breathe'. People of many different faiths believe that there is something sacred at the core of existence that breathes in life. As John Adair observes: 'In all traditions, there is a deeper tradition, that all inspiration flows from God, named or nameless, just as the sun is the ultimate source of energy in nature.' (2002, p318)

Why the Spiritual Is Largely Ignored in NGO Management

Few NGOs consciously integrate the spiritual into their management processes. One reason for this is the on-going ambivalence towards religion in their development programmes in communities. Religion has had an intense but chequered relationship with development. As well as providing the motivation for much development work over the years, religion has also been:

- divisive – a rallying point for division and conflict;
- regressive – maintaining (if not indeed promoting) historical injustices such as slavery, colonialism, apartheid, and on-going caste and gender inequalities;
- irrelevant – development being an autonomous technical discipline, about which 'otherworldly' religion has nothing valuable to say;
- insensitive – exported in culturally highly inappropriate ways;
- proselytizing – seeking to convert others to their faith in a coercive way.

The NGO sector understandably wants to distance itself from these negative contributions of religion to development. In management too, spirituality can be all too easily abused. There are examples of NGO leaders who have used spirituality in management to attempt to manipulate their staff to think or behave in a particular way. Even when it is done well, spiritual issues are highly personal. In many countries, discussion of spirituality at work is taboo. It is a flammable subject, which easily causes offence.

Bringing the spiritual dimension into management also requires time. Many NGO managers are simply too busy to stop and create the necessary spaces for the spiritual. It also requires courage – courage to look inside ourselves at our own beliefs about life. But as Sogyal Rinpoche observes: 'We are so addicted to looking outside ourselves that we have lost access to our inner being almost completely. We are terrified to look inwards' (in Edwards and Fowler, 2002, p151).

Changing Attitudes to Spirituality

Such negative attitudes to spirituality in NGO management, however, are coming under pressure from two sides. In the development world, donors and policy-makers are increasingly interested in the role and potential of faith and religion. In the mainstream business world, there is far greater attention to spirituality in management. We consider each of these in turn.

Increasing attention to faith in development

Donor attitudes to faith in development are changing. For decades religion has been subject to 'long-term and systematic neglect' by donors (Lunn, 2009, p937). Yet the last few years have seen a reassessment of the role of faith in development. Some of the 20th century certainties are being challenged. Instead of the predicted decline in religion, in most parts of the developing world it is increasing. Many are realizing that the past secular materialistic approaches are failing to deliver the hoped for change. Faith is once again under the spotlight. There is increasing evidence that faith communities make a significant contribution to development (see for example World Bank 'Voices of Poor' study (Narayan, 2000), ARHAP studies, current work at Berkley Center at Georgetown University and the 'Religions and Development' research at University of Birmingham).

Faith organizations offer the potential to 'add value' to development in a number of ways. They can:

- provide efficient development services;
- reach the poorest at the grassroots;
- have a long-term, sustainable presence;
- be legitimate and valued by the poorest;
- provide an alternative to a secular theory of development;
- elicit motivated and voluntary service;
- encourage civil society advocacy.

While these are generally accepted potential advantages of faith organizations, there are three more contentious 'spiritual' advantages from faith itself (that people of faith may point to but others may discount or react against):

- spiritual teaching;
- hope, meaning and purpose;
- divine power.

Donors recognize the need to engage with faith, given the important role it plays in shaping worldviews and behaviours of the vast majority of people in the world. Currently donors are moving from 'estrangement to engagement' with faith (Clarke and Jennings, 2008). The tipping point came with 9/11. It showed in a violent way the power of religion to motivate extreme action. Prior to 2001 Jim Wolfensohn, then President of the World Bank, was unable to interest the Bank's board in engaging with religions. After 9/11 the board reversed their decision. Faith was clearly a powerful motivating force, for good or evil. The previous strategy of ignoring faith as irrelevant in aid was defunct.

Since then the World Bank even set up a 'Directorate on Faith' (now called the Development Dialogue on Values and Ethics). According to Katherine Marshall, its first director, the World Bank now recognizes: 'we cannot fight poverty without tending to people's spiritual dimension and its many manifestations in religious institutions, leaders and movements' (Marshall quoted by Barron, 2007). Official aid departments in North America and Europe are now actively trying to understand and engage with the faith dimension to development. Bi-lateral donors also exhibit new interest in engaging with faith in development. In the UK, there is a 'growing interest among DFID departments for a more systematic understanding of the role that faiths play in achieving the Millennium Development Goals' (DFID, 2005, p14). Consequently DFID launched five-year, £3.5 million research programme on Religion and Development in 2005. The 2009 White Paper promises to double funding to faith based groups (DFID, 2009).

Other European government aid departments are also seeking to develop their under-standing in this area. The Dutch government created a Policy Platform on faith and recently surprised some church-related agencies they fund by asking them to articulate: 'What is the added-value of your faith to your work?' In 2004 SIDA convened a workshop to explore the 'Role of Religion in Development'. The USA has gone the furthest, though perhaps more for electoral considerations. Under President Bush US foreign aid dollars going to faith based groups almost doubled from 10.5 per cent of aid in 2001 to 19.9 per cent in 2005. Under the Obama administration, this is likely to continue.

As peoples' spiritualities are increasingly recognized as important with development work in communities, this raises questions as to the role of people's spirituality within the management of development organizations themselves.

Increasing attention to spiritual in business management

The academic world of management is also changing in its attitude to spirituality. Howard asserts that 'the present spiritual trend is probably the most significant trend in management since the 1950s' (2002, p230). There are numerous conferences, arti-cles, books, influential websites and courses springing up on the subject. The American Academy of Management – 'arguably the most mainstream and venerable professional association' (Dean et al, 2003, p378) – has recently formed a special interest group on Management, Spirituality and Religion. Harvard Business School now hosts an annual Conference on Leadership, Values and Spirituality and there are now at least 12 other conferences each year in the US alone on spirituality and organizations (Harris, 2000). In the UK, Cranfield School of Management has an MBA elective on 'Spirituality and Organisational Transformation'. Major academic journals such as the Journal of Organisational Change Management had two special issues on spirituality in 1999 and another in 2003. The Journal of Management Psychology also had a focus issue on spirituality in 2002. The interest prompted the launch of a new journal, 'Management, Spirituality and Religion' in 2004.

There has been a convergence of thinking and practice in the three fields of organi-zational change, organizational behaviour and leadership. According to Lee Robbins of the Academy of Management: 'Leadership, particularly transformational leadership, depends heavily on spiritual perspectives, values and assumptions of leaders and on how these perspectives connect them to potential followers.' (Academy of Management, 2003) This resonates with the words of Mahatma Gandhi: 'Such power as I possess for working in the political field is derived entirely from my experiments in the spiritual field.' (Academy of Management, 2003, p6)

The interest in spirituality is not confined to the rarefied atmospheres of academia. Organizational consultants and popular writers such as John Adair, Peter Senge, Tom Peters, Peter Vaill, Steven Covey, Charles Handy, Peter Drucker and Harrison Owen are increasingly explicit about the spiritual dimension to organizational life. John Adair, one of the foremost authors on leadership, concludes, 'the vital difference, the X factor, which enables you to transcend limits, is called inspiration ... There is guidance and help avail-able in strategic leadership from God, or as if from a god if you would prefer it' (2002, p266). Steven Covey states: 'I believe that there are parts to human nature that cannot be reached either by legislation or education, but require the power of God to deal with' (1989, p319). Or as Owen points out: 'Real or lasting change is rarely, if ever, affected by memo and command. Such change occurs when the spirit changes' (Owen, 1985).

These spiritual perspectives on organizations have also permeated the real world of hard-nosed management practice. Wagner-Marsh and Conley observe that 'a great number of highly diverse firms are moving ahead with attempts to instil a spiritual approach to their corporate cultures' (1999, p292). They highlight Fortune 100 firms such as TDIndustries, Xerox, Exxon and the Bank of Montreal which 'all have a spiritual dimension to leadership and management development programmes' (1999, p294). Hewlett Packard, Semco, Ben and Jerry's and Toyota are also identified by Marcic as implementing a spiritual approach to management. Other large firms such as Boeing have Christian, Jewish and Muslim prayer groups while others have what they call 'Higher Power Lunches'. Research in the US by Biberman and Whitty revealed that an 'increasing number of managers are turning to various types of meditation and spiritual disciplines to cope with their turbulent work environments' (1997, p132). This finding is echoed by Howard's UK research which found that 'in the midst of high-flying business careers, participants talk explicitly about prayer and reflection upon wisdom literature as the foundation of their ability to have discernment' (2002, p237). Paul Wong concludes: 'The movement to bring spirit and soul to business is no passing fad; it continues to grow and shows no signs of abating. Clearly something significant is stirring the corporate world.' (2003, p1)

What Are the Key Elements of the Spiritual in Organizations?

Although definitions of the spiritual vary, there is a general consensus among writers on what this looks like when applied to organizations and also to leadership. Some of the major elements common to most are an emphasis on:

- vision and values;
- service and love for others;
- empowering others;
- courage to overcome fears;
- changing from within;
- the role of a transcendental spirit or divine power.

We consider each of these elements in turn.

Vision and values

The management world is increasingly emphasizing the importance of organizations being visionary and value-led. These are a key element of a spiritually-based organization. Influential longitudinal research by Collins and Porras in 1997 on 18 visionary companies that had been leaders in their industries for 50 years showed that their success was due to focusing on *non-economic* values and an empowering culture. They actually outperformed their competitors by as much as 16:1 (Korac-Kakabadse et al, 2002, p165). As people are increasingly searching for meaning from their workplace amidst a cacophony of activities, so values becomes more of a driving factor (Katherine Tyler Scott in Conger et al, 1994). Harrison claims: 'Strategic planning is a search for meaning rather than a search for advantage.' (1995, p177)

This is consistent with the growing interest in leadership as a value-transmitting activity and a creator of meaning. According to Lebow and Simon, 'the primary human motivator comes from values. Values do not have to be sold to people, because all of us already have a set of fundamental values deeply embedded' (1997, p48). People have a yearning to be inspired with a vision. Bennis and Nanus advise that 'by focussing atten-tion on a vision the leader operates on the emotional and spiritual resources of the organisation, on its values and commitment' (Conger et al, 1994 referring to 'Leaders', 1985, p92). The most effective organizations are seen to be those that have shared values that harness emotional energies of people. Peter Senge says that real learning organiza-tions, 'talk of being part of something larger than themselves' (Wisely and Lynn in Conger et al, 1994, p122). In a similar vein John Adair states that 'the greatest leaders have been sustained by a belief that they were in some ways instruments of destiny, that they tapped hidden resources of power, that they truly lived as they tried to live in harmony with some greater, more universal purpose or intention in the world' (2002, p306).

Service and love for others

The emphasis on service to others has underpinned many of the quality management change programmes in the last two decades. As organizations are increasingly perceived to be interconnected with stakeholders, so there has been greater attention paid to the needs of the customers and more recently to the needs of the wider community through corporate social responsibility programmes. Within the leadership field, there has been considerable emphasis on the concept of the leader as the servant of others – servant leadership (Greenleaf, 1998; Blanchard, 1999; Adair, 2001).

Some describe this focus on meeting the needs of others or wanting the best for others as 'love'. Marcic relates: 'In my search to understand what has been happening in organisations, I began to see that dysfunctional managers are not the causal factor as I had previously thought, but symptoms of some deeper problem. The root cause is lack of love.' (Marcic, 1997, p14). She goes on to say that 'Spiritual power comes from one's being and is the capacity to influence others, not by controlling them as in political power, but through love. Those who have it do not feel arrogant or self-satisfied, but rather gain a greater humility realising that the true source of power comes from a higher power, not from themselves' (1997, p49). This mirrors James Autry's assertion that 'Management is in fact a sacred trust in which the well-being of other people is put into your care during most of their waking hours' (Marcic, 1997, p95).

Empowering others

Closely linked with the notion of service is the concept of empowering others. As organ-izations are perceived to be more about relationships and interconnections, so there is an emphasis within 'spiritually-based organizations' on empowering others – making people free to take decisions, to develop their potential and work creatively with others. David Dotlich put it powerfully when he said 'Show me a leader who is decisive, fiercely independent, dominant and in control and I'll show you someone who doesn't have a clue about how to lead in today's organisations' (Dotlich and Noel, 1998, pxi). Or as John Buchan pointed out: 'The task of leadership is not to put greatness into humanity, but to elicit it, for the greatness is already there' (quoted by Adair, 2002, p256).

Courage to overcome fears

The desire to control is usually rooted in fear. 'Fear is one of the greatest diseases of mankind and it is rampant in organisations and group decision-making processes' (Marcic, 1997, p110). In the turbulence of today's world, such efforts at control are proving counter-productive, so spiritually-based firms emphasize the importance of courage in overcoming fears. Parker Palmer observes that 'All the great spiritual traditions at their core say one single thing: be not afraid'. His advice to leaders is 'Do not be your fears. Lead from an inner place of trust and hope thus creating a world that is more trusting and hopeful' (in Conger et al, 1994, p40).

Changing from within

Spiritually-based organizations and leaders believe that we are part of an interconnected whole. If we want to change that whole, we must change ourselves. Margaret Wheatley points out: 'The source of change and growth for an organisation or an individual is to develop increased awareness of who it is, now. If we take time to reflect together on who we are and who we could choose to become, we will be led into the territory where change originates.' (Wheatley and Kellner-Rogers, 1998, p100).

For an individual or an organization to be open to such change, they need to be very self-aware, without being self-centred. Key writers (such as Kakabadse and Kakabadse, 1999; Quinn, 2000; Adair, 2002) emphasize that effective leaders are highly self-aware as 'Leaders with self-awareness are more likely to move quickly and confidently and in different directions, without needing to be consistently right and in control' (Dotlich and Noel, 1999, p187). Leaders and organizations need to look at their glasses rather than just through them. As Larry Bossidy, Jack Welch's deputy at GM said: 'I can only change this company as quickly as I can change myself' (MSR Newslettter, 2003, p6).

Such honesty with self is part of humility. According to Covey, humility is the mother of all virtues (1994, p3) and by implication pride is the mother of all problems. In fact it was pride that was identified by executives at a NASDAC conference, as the major cause of leadership failure. Pride is so damaging because it leads to impatience, an unwillingness to build consensus, inability to receive criticism and unwillingness to endure periods of trial and uncertainty (Delbecq, 1999, p348). Roman generals had an understanding of the destructive potential of pride, for when they were being carried on chariots in triumphal processions, they had a slave constantly whispering in their ear, 'Remember you are only human' (Carr, 1998, p28).

So Is Anything New in This?

The first five of these 'spiritual' elements are generally accepted as current good organizational practice even by those who profess no spiritual belief (except perhaps in the power of the human spirit). Some question whether the current emphasis on a spiritual dimension in organizations adds anything new to accepted good practice in management. Others answer saying that this good practice today is actually based on centuries-old spiritual principles and that underlying spiritual laws are the foundation for good practice (Milliman et al in Academy of Management, 2003; Marcic, 1997). Still others go further to assert that the involvement of a divine power certainly can add a different dimension to normal management practice.

The role of a transcendental spirit

The crux is the question of whether or not there is an outside spiritual force that complements, and indeed even empowers the work of the human spirit. This would make improvement more than simply self-help. MODEM investigated this with 30 UK managers. Using in-depth semi-structured interviews and focus group discussions they examined spiritual energy at work and concluded that participants described a sense of empowerment by a 'contagious energy' that was 'exceptional and often unexpected' (Pettifer, 2002, pp5, 19). This enabled them to achieve far more than they had anticipated would be possible. This force was left mostly undefined by participants – as a mysterious and elusive phenomenon – but can be 'best described as spiritual' (Pettifer, 2002, p3). While the source of energy may be hidden, the research concluded that a spiritual force 'can be relied on and is available to anyone if they are open to it'.

Another research project designed to explore what actually happens in the moment of transformation, interviewed in depth three major organizational theorists and practitioners, Peter Senge, Bill Torbert and Ellen Wingard. It found that:

> in all cases the transformations they helped to generate were sparked, not through rational efforts at all: the actual 'cause' of transformation, according to the data, was expressed by these practitioner/theorists in terms of 'grace', 'magic' and a 'miracle'. By definition these are phenomena that cannot be scientifically or logically explained, supernatural events going beyond theory and rational action ... The cause of transformation may indeed be spirit, yet the result may indeed be an increase in effectiveness and productivity within the system (Neal et al, 1999, p180).

Such research will never be able to prove something that ultimately is a matter of faith, but many practitioners active in such fields believe that it is needed and exists. Because 'as much as 75 per cent of planned, humanistic change efforts fail' (Cameron, 1997, quoted by Quinn, 2000, p198), this has led people to look for more innovative and deeper solutions to organizational change issues. Roger Harrison points out: 'the tools and approaches that have got us where we are today are not the ones we can use to advance to another level. The real answers to our dilemmas lie in the dark, beyond the circle of illumination given by our current concepts and methods' (1995, p167).

Harrison Owen, who developed the concept and practice of Open Space technology, entitled one article 'Open Space and Spirit Shows Up'. He says in the text that from his 15 years experience with open space, 'The most significant occurrence could not be seen with the eyes of flesh. Spirit showed up. Call it inspiration, inspired performance – call it what you like, but in some indefinable way the group becomes electric' (Owen, undated).

Implications for NGO Management

So what are the implications for NGO management? It may be that for a sector like that of NGOs, which is so steeped, inspired and still motivated by spiritual values, bringing the spiritual into management is even more relevant than for the business world. It is clear that organizational and staff behaviour in NGOs is too complex for simplistic solutions. NGO management needs to go beyond the rational and engage with emotions, motivations, values and even beliefs.

The different spiritual elements of organization highlighted in the previous section have implications for NGO management. How these should be applied will obviously depend on the particular context. The following example of one aspect of NGO management – capacity building – illustrates this. A recent study of the management of NGO capacity building (James and Hailey, 2007) concluded that NGOs actually know what is good practice yet consistently fail to implement what they know. They are held back by underlying problems that go deeper than mere rational knowledge. Indeed in this example of capacity building the challenges experienced resemble common spiritual problems, known by some as the 'seven deadly sins' (Box 20.1).

The extent to which these deadly sins are common to all religions is a moot point. Some argue that they are not even common to Christianity as a whole, only to traditional Catholicism. But many would see a resonance with other beliefs systems. While the words used are different, in Islam, Hinduism and Buddhism there is general acknowledgement of the dangers of greed (usury); lust (adultery, rape); sloth (not fulfilling duties) and pride. As a Hindu, Mahatma Ghandi considered the seven most perilous traits to be: wealth without work; pleasure without conscience; science without humanity; knowledge without character; politics without principle; commerce without morality; worship without sacrifice. There are obvious overlaps with the notions of gluttony; lust; pride; greed and sloth

Addressing such spiritual problems requires spiritual solutions. Managing NGO capacity building effectively means putting into practice the antithesis of these deadly sins – namely the spiritual virtues of humility, compassion, patience, commitment, generosity, self-control and honesty. Such virtues may be even more important to work with than values.

Values are now common parlance in management, but virtues have been largely ignored until recently. Yet virtue is obviously not a new concept. Aristotle described virtue as 'the state which makes a man good and which makes him do his work well (quoted by Caza, 2002, p10). Virtues are not the same as values because they bring in notions of moral absolutes; of right and wrong. While values looks at peoples' underlying

---

Box 20.1 *Seven deadly sins of INGO in managing capacity building*

Pride *– seeing ourselves as better than others –*
Pride is the original of seven deadly sins and the source from which others arise. Pride underpins INGO thinking that 'we know better' or 'we can do it ourselves'.

Greed *– the acquisition of wealth or a longing to possess something –*
INGOs preoccupied with their growth often take on work that could and should be done by local partners. They prioritize visible results for donors before impact on the poor.

Lust *– seeing others as means to our gratification or an impure love for others –*
Some INGOs lust after control, power and status. They are primarily interested in what others can provide for them. They use other 'partners' as means to their ends.

Gluttony *– thoughtless excess, over-consumption or habitual greed –*
Some INGOs are guilty of gluttony, through their over-consumption of limited local human resources; in 4X4 vehicles overwhelming communities; in inflating salary levels and fees ...

Envy *– a desire to have something possessed by another –*
Envy may be at the root of INGO failure to collaborate with other stakeholders. INGOs can view others as competitors. As a result, they fail to work together and learn from each other.

Wrath *– intolerance, impatience, discrimination or extreme anger –*
Wrath undermines development when it leads to impatience. When artificial project deadlines prove unrealistic, this can lead to frustration and even anger.

Sloth *– reluctance to work or make an effort, laziness, fail to use/develop talents –*
Most INGOs are very busy, but can be lazy in prioritizing. They may not actively seek to develop and implement learning. Some lack the determination to see it through.

---

assumptions and expectations (which can be good or bad), virtues ask about what is right and what brings life. Talking about good and bad have become politically incorrect or at least gone out of fashion in our relativist and post-modern world.

But this neglect of virtues in management appears to be changing. An increasing number of organizational writers and theorists are investigating the apparently positive relationship between organizational virtues and performance (Caza, 2002; Cameron et al, 2003; Moore and Beadle, 2006; Manz et al, 2008). They are exploring the relationship between being able to practice excellence in a particular field and the institutional virtues needed to protect and extend that. They focus on institutional character, which depends on the relationship between the individual staff, the institution itself and the external environment. They argue that institutional virtues are needed to resist 'the corrupting influences and constraints in the external environment' (ibid).

Conclusion

The traditional separation between spirituality and NGO management is breaking down. Not only are donors and policy-makers engaging more with notions of religion and faith in development, but increasingly spiritual perspectives pervade mainstream management writing and thinking. Spirituality is no longer seen as the domain of the uneducated or of a lunatic fringe.

NGO management needs to keep pace with these changes (if not actually lead them). It needs to maintain and develop spiritual values into management. There are obvious dangers in doing this. Spirituality can be introduced in an intolerant, arrogant and aggressive way. It can be used to manipulate and coerce. But if done well, it can positively influence important determinants of human and organizational behaviour.

To integrate the spiritual in management needs courage, integrity, humility and wisdom. It needs NGO managers to have the courage to get in touch with their own spirits and motivations. They need the integrity to live out the virtues they encourage in others. Above all, NGO managers need humility and wisdom to bring spirituality into their work in an inclusive, sensitive and respectful way. It is not about forcing beliefs on others. It is about creating and managing spaces for people to get in touch with their own sense of purpose and animating life force. Doing this well, managing NGOs with spirit, can make a major contribution to NGO performance and impact.

References

Academy of Management (2003) *Spirituality and Religion Newsletter*, Winter, MSR SIG

Adair, J. (2002) *Effective Strategic Leadership*, Macmillan, London

Autry, J. A. (1992) *Love and Profit: The Art of Caring Leadership*, Avon Books, New York

Barron, M. (2007) 'The Role of Pastoral Care in Development – is it really development?, *IMU Report*, March – May

Bennis, W.G. and Nanus, B. (1985) *Leaders*, Harper and Row, New York

Benthall, J. (2008) *Returning to Religion: Why a secular age is haunted by faith*, Macmillan, London

Biberman, J. and Whitty, M. (1997) A post-modern spiritual future for work, *Journal of Organizational Change Management*, Vol. 10, No. 2, pp130–138, MCB University Press

Blanchard, K. (1999) *Leadership by the Book*, Harper Collins, London

Cacioppe, R. (2000) Creating spirit at work: re-envisioning organization development and leadership – part II, *Leadership and Organization Development Journal*, Vol. 21, No. 2, pp110–119, MCB University Press

Cameron, K., Dutton, J. and Quinn, R. (eds) (2003) *Positive Organizational Scholarship: Foundations of a New Discipline*, Berrett-Koehler Publishers

Carr, S., McAuliffe, E. and MacLachlan, M. (1998) *Psychology of Aid*, Routledge, London

Caza, A. (2002) Organisational and leadership virtues and the role of forgiveness, *Journal of leadership and Organisational Studies*, available at www.allbusiness.com/human-resources/employee-development-leadership/345316-1.html (last accessed July 2010)

Clarke, G. and Jennings, M. (2008) *Development, Civil Society and Faith Based Organisations: Bridging the Sacred and the Secular*, Palgrave Macmillan, Basingstoke

Collins, J. and Porras, J.I. (1997) *Built to Last: Successful Habits of Visionary Companies*, Harper Business, New York

Conger, J. (1994) *Spirit at Work: discovering the spirituality in Leadership*, Jossey-Bass, San Francisco

Covey, S. (1989) *The 7 Habits of Highly Effective People: Powerful Lessons in Personal Change*, Simon and Schuster, New York

Covey, S. (1992) *Principle Centred Leadership*, New York: Simon and Schuster

Daft, R. and Lengel, R. (1998) *Fusion Leadership: Unlocking the Subtle Forces that Change People and Organisations*, Berrett Koehler, San Francisco

Dean, K., Fornaciari, C. and McGee, J. (2003) 'Research in spirituality, religion and work: walking the line between relevance and legitimacy', *Journal of Organizational Change Management*, Vol. 12, No. 4, pp378–395, MCB University Press

Dehler, G. and Welsh, M. (1994) 'Spirituality and Organizational Transformation: Implications for the New Management Paradigm', *Journal of Managerial Psychology* Vol. 9, No. 6, pp17–26, MCB University Press

Delbecq, A. (1999) 'Christian spirituality and contemporary business leadership', *Journal of Organizational Change Management*, Vol. 12, No. 4, pp345–349, MCB

DFID (2005) 'Faith in Development', available at https://repository.berkleycenter.georgetown.edu/RD-20051207-Benn-FaithinDevelopment.pdf

DFID (2009) 'Building Our Common Future' white Paper. Downloadable from www.dfid.gov.uk/documents/whitepaper/building-our-common-future-print.pdf

Dotlich, D. and Noel, J. (1998) *Action Learning*, San Francisco: Jossey-Bass

Edwards, M. and Fowler, A. (eds) (2002) *The Earthscan Reader on NGO Management*, Earthscan, London

Edwards, M. and Sen, G. (2001) 'NGOs Social Change and the Transformation of Human Relationships: A 21st Century Civic Agenda' in Edwards, M. and Fowler, A. (eds) (2002) *The Earthscan Reader on NGO Management*, Earthscan, London

Frankl, V. (1946) *Man's Search for Meaning*, Washington Square Press, Boston

Greenleaf, R. (1998) *The Power of Servant Leadership*, Berrett Koehler, San Francisco

Harris, H. (2000) 'The spiritual dimensions of courage in management', unpublished paper presented to the Philosophy Graduate Student Conference, Marquette University, Milwaukee, WI

Harrison, R. (ed) (1995) *A Consultant's Journey: A Dance of Work and Spirit*, Jossey-Bass, San Francisco

Howard, S. (2002) 'A spiritual perspective on learning in the workplace', *Journal of Managerial Psychology*, Vol. 17, No. 3, pp230–242, MCB University Press

Howard, S. and Welbourn, D. (2004) *The Spirit at Work Phenomenon*, Azure, London

James, R. (2004) *Creating Space for Grace: God's Power in Organisational Change*, SMC, Stockholm, available at www.missioncouncil.se/download/18.25948b3d117af90ec978000388/04_02_space_for_grace.pdf

James, R. (2009) 'What is distinctive about FBOs', INTRAC Praxis Paper 22, available at www.intrac.org/data/files/resources/482/Praxis-Paper-22-What-is-Distinctive-About-FBOs.pdf

James, R. and Hailey, J. (2007) *Capacity building for NGOs: Making it work*, INTRAC

Jaworski, J. (1998) *Synchronicity: the Inner path of Leadership*, Berrett Koehler, San Francisco

Kakabadse, A. and Kakabadse, N. (1999) *Essence of Leadership*, International Thompson Business Press, London

Kaplan, A. (2002) *Development Practitioners and Social Process: Artists of the Invisible*, Pluto Press, London

King, S. and Nicol, D. (1999) 'Organisational enhancement through recognition of individual spirituality', *Journal of Organizational Change Management*, Vol. 12, No. 3, pp234–242, MCB University Press

Korac-Kakabadse, N., Kouzmin, A. and Kakabadse A. (2002) 'Spirituality and Leadership Praxis', *Journal of Managerial Psychology*, Vol. 17, No. 3, pp165–182, MCB University Press

Lebow, R. and Simon, W. (1997) *Lasting Change*, Wiley, New York

Lichtenstein, B. (1997) 'Grace, Magic and Miracles: A "chaotic logic" of organizational transformation', *Journal of Organizational Change Management* Vol. 10, No. 5, pp393–411, MCB University Press

Lunn, J. (2009) 'The Role of Religion, Spirituality and Faith in Development: A critical theory approach', *Third World Quarterly*, July, Vol. 30, No. 5, pp937–951

McCormick, D. (1994) 'Spirituality and Management', *Journal of Managerial Psychology*, Vol. 9, No. 6, pp5–8, MCB University Press

Manz, C., Cameron, K., Manz, K. and Manz, R. (2008) *The Virtuous Organization: Insights from some of the World's Leading Management Thinkers,* World Scientific Publishing

Marcic, D. (1997) *Managing with the Wisdom of Love: Uncovering Virtue and People in Organisations*, Jossey-Bass, San Francisco

Moore, G. and Beadle, R. (2006) 'In search of organizational virtue in Business: Agents, practices, institutions and environments', *Organization Studies*, No. 27, pp369–390

Narayan, D. (2000) *Voices of the Poor: Can Anyone Hear Us?*, Washington OUP, World Bank

Neal, J., Lichtenstein, B. and Banner, D. (1999) 'Spiritual perspectives on individual, organisational and societal transformation', in *Journal of Organizational Change Management*, Vol. 12, No. 3, pp175–185, MCB University Press, Bradford

Owen, H. (undated) Open Space and Spirit Shows Up, downloaded from internet: www.openspaceworld.com/spirit_shows.htm (10.10.10)

Owen, H. (1985) 'Leadership by Indirection', published in *Transforming Leadership*, Miles River Press

Owen, H. (1999) *The Spirit of Leadership: Liberating the Leader in Each of Us*, Berrett Koehler, San Francisco

Owen, H. (2000) *The Power of Spirit: How Organizations Transform*, Berrett Koehler, San Francisco

Pettifer, B. (ed.) (2002) Management and Spiritual Energy, Report on the Hope of the Managers, MODEM

Quinn, R. (2000), *Change the World: How Ordinary People can Accomplish Extraordinary Results*, Jossey-Bass, San Francisco

Vaill, P. (1998) *Spirited leading and Learning: Process Wisdom for a New Age*, Jossey-Bass, San Francisco

Ver Beek, K. (2000) 'Spirituality: a development taboo', *Development in Practice,* Vol. 10, No. 1, February, Oxfam, Oxford

Wagner-Marsh, F. and Conley, J. (1999) 'The fourth wave: the spiritually-based firm', *Journal of Organizational Change Management*, Vol. 12, No. 4, pp292–301, MCB University Press

Wheatley, M. and Kellner-Rogers, M. (1998) *Bringing Life to Organisational Change*, Barkana Institute

Wong, P. (2003) Spirituality and Meaning at Work, downloaded from internet: www.meaning.ca/articles/presidents_column (10.10.03)

World Faith's Development Dialogue (2002) Key Issues for Development, Occasional Paper 1, Oxford

Zohar, D. and Marshall, I. (2000) *Spiritual Intelligence: the ultimate intelligence*, Bloomsbury, London

21

Civil Society Networks: Of Ants and Elephants

Chiku Malunga

Introduction

Ants united can carry a dead elephant to their cave.

Ants could be among the smallest visible animals. An elephant is the largest mammal that walks on land. The metaphor of ants carrying an elephant is intriguing because of its vividness and apparent contradiction or contrast. In the metaphor, ants are able to carry the dead elephant to their cave because of a number of factors. The ants have a common goal. They are all going to the same cave. Each ant makes an effort. The collective effort miraculously and magically lifts the mighty elephant and moves it to the cave. There is also common interest. The elephant will be turned into a major feast once in the cave and all the ants will take part in the feast. The effort is therefore for the benefit of all. Through collaborative effort and the synergy created the ants achieve the impossible. They carry a dead elephant to their cave. This is the rationale for networks and networking.

The principle of 'ants united can carry a dead elephant to their cave' has inspired the rise of networks and partnerships as a preferred form of organization among non-profit and civil society organizations. Networks are already changing what we have known about governance, management and sustainability of individual organizations. If one works for an HIV and AIDS organization for example, the board can no longer have the final say on strategy, it has to follow what national, regional or global coalitions are saying. Individual organizations have to engage in trans-national networks because this is crucial to bringing about social change, organizational development and personal development. Networks and partnerships therefore are rising in prominence, and discussing organizational effectiveness cannot be complete without discussing networks, partnerships and other forms of collaboration. For instance, 'Networks are the most important organizational form of our time' (Miller, 2005, p215); 'The formal network has become the modern organizational form' (Church, 2003); 'Networks have become the donors' and sponsors' choice with the aim of maximizing reach and impact of organizations' (Ashman, 2005).

The main difference between networks and partnerships is the number of organizational members: networks include multiple organizations while partnerships include only a few. A further distinction is made between networks and coalitions (Cohen et al, 2001, p90). Networks are perceived to exist for information sharing, ideas and support. A common interest may be the only membership requirement, a network's structure is often informal – members invest little and are free to benefit, contribute or quit whenever they wish. Coalitions on the other hand exist for joint action. To reach a specific goal, members invest significant resources, share decision-making power and coordinate their strategies, messages and action plans. In addition to a common interest, coalition members must share high levels of trust. A coalition's structure tends to be more formal, and skilled leadership is needed to guide the members through differences so that the coalition can function.

In this chapter coalitions are seen to be 'a more matured and effective stage of networks' and therefore the word 'network' will be used to mean both networks and coalitions. The main purpose for the partnerships and networks is collaboration. Collaboration means working with individuals and groups who share a common focus or interest (Cohen et al, 2001, p90).

In an increasingly interrelated and rapidly changing world, organizational challenges or issues and opportunities come in 'elephant size' that no single organization or 'organizational ant' can carry alone. In an increasingly globalized world, challenges or issues are no longer confined to national or continental borders making networks and networking at all levels – local, national, regional, continental – the most relevant form of organization for dealing with the issues. In the past we used to say: *think globally, act locally*, now we say: *think locally and act globally through networks.* This is why individual organizations have to engage in trans-national networks because this is crucial to bringing about social change, organizational development and personal development.

Benefits of Networks and Partnerships

The key benefit of networks and partnerships is found in the word 'synergy' (or $2 + 2 = 17$) which simply means together the partners and members can achieve more than they could by working individually. In other words, together *they can carry their elephant-size challenges and opportunities to their cave*, a thing they can't do working individually. It is very simple: friendships that do not add value are not worth initiating or keeping. Friendships must be assets and not liabilities. As a result of the synergy from collaboration, the members are expected to achieve a number of things.

One is more effective delivery because of expanded skills, ideas and resources. By providing mutual support and services based on joint assessment of needs, networks are expected to contribute directly to upgrading the quality of activities, outputs, outcomes and impact of the member organizations. This releases more time for other work for members by using the skills and capabilities of other members. They contribute towards enhanced skills and capabilities of the network members by working with others who have skills and abilities the organization lacks. This connects the network members to a larger like-minded community and helps combat isolation. Networks are also expected to facilitate a collective learning process among their members. This may also enable members to learn from others' experiences of what works well and what does not.

Box 21.1 *Deciding whether your organization should join a network or partnership*

- Is the issue the network is addressing of priority to our organization? Will joining the network help further our organization's agenda?

- Do we have the organizational capacity to commit resources to the network? Or will joining the network drain our organization's leadership or other resources?

- How will joining the network affect our relationship with our constituents and members? How do we stay accountable to them?

- Can we achieve our goal if we don't work with others? Do we have the resources and support we need? If we don't join a network, is there another way to achieve our goals?

- Who else will be involved? Do we have – or want to have – a relationship with any of the potential network members? Do we share similar values? If not, are we willing and able to work through our differences so that the network can function? Do the other members demonstrate the same commitment to 'agree to disagree?'

- What trade-offs, will we be making if we join the network? If we don't join?

Source: Adapted from Cohen et al, 2001, p91.

In addition networks are expected to contribute to 'lifting up' civil society organizations' activities and directing them towards national and international audiences for wider impact. Networks are expected to result in greater efficiencies through resource sharing and coordination, improved quality of services through more rapid development and dissemination of activities. New donor and sponsor contacts as networks may accord opportunities to source new funds for an idea rather than drawing from the same donors who have always been there. Lastly, there is increased recognition from peers, donors, sponsors, government departments and communities that the organization works with. Networks enable organizations to pilot and demonstrate new models. This can enhance reputations.

Network functions

Networks perform four major functions. These are:

1   Learning through joint reflection. This is what sets networks apart from other types of human organizations. The learning helps to raise the quality of member organizations' work. The learning is aimed at helping members improve their performance. Networks are successful if they improve member organizations' performance. If they do not, the networks cannot be sustainable

2   Providing services like training, communication, documentation and information services. Network secretariats are able to provide these services in a more cost-effective manner than individual member organizations could

3   Advocacy – on behalf of the member organizations. The collective voice thus created is much more powerful than individual small voices speaking separately and in isolation – as it is said *when one person complains it is gossip when two or more speak it is a voice*

Box 21.2 *Networking at an individual level*

Individual networking capacity can be increased in a number of ways, including:

- writing articles;

- making speeches;

- collecting business cards, filing them and occasionally linking up with the owners of the business cards on issues of mutual interest;

- giving out business cards to potential 'partners';

- creating a newsletter in a timely and consistent manner and getting feedback;

- blogging on the internet, e.g blogging on speeches or pictures that can be captured by the media or shared in a network.

---

4 Network management – facilitating the networking process itself. This includes caring for network communication, infrastructure and operating procedures, maintaining network resources, activities and outputs, coordination with other organizations and networks. A list or directory of members is among the first results of most networks.

Network secretariats are kept as lean as possible and many functions are distributed among member organizations.

The above are the main activities that networks are involved in. This should not be confused with individual networking activities. Individual networking is mostly for individual benefit and examples of the main activities are presented below.

Managing Networks and Partnerships

However, many of the above desired benefits are more theoretical than practical. This section therefore discusses the key challenges that networks usually face. According to Ashman (2005, p1), in practice, the performance of networks and partnerships often falls short of expectations, at times with such negative consequences that some donors and civil society organizations have begun to abandon the idea of networks and partnerships altogether. Much of the original infatuation with networks is waning. Why are 'organizational ants' failing to carry their 'dead elephants' to their caves? The model on stages of development by Livegoed (1969; 1973) helps shed light on this.

The key point to make from the above model is that networks and partnerships are more successful among organizations at the interdependent phase of development, when they can contribute to and not just consume and take away from the network or partnership relationship. Many of the challenges that networks and partnerships face can be explained by the differences in stages of development among members and partners. The more developed members feel they are 'selling more than they are buying'. When they feel that they are 'working more than they are netting' they eventually get discouraged. Conversely, those 'buying more than selling' get discouraged once the

---

Box 21.3 *Stages of organizational development*

Development organizations go through three distinct stages of development. These are the dependent, independent and the interdependent phases. At the dependent phase the organization is newly formed and led by one or more charismatic leaders. The organization is run almost as a family unit, personally and informally. Decision-making is very informal and intuitive with the leader personally involved in every aspect of the organization. Internal systems are very rudimentary and there are high levels of informality, energy, motivation and commitment. This is an insecure but very creative and dynamic phase.

But this pioneer or dependent phase eventually becomes overripe and a crisis leads to further development. As the organization grows, the need for structure and procedures gradually eclipses informality. Staff are no longer content simply to follow – they have themselves been developing all the time. At this time the organization enters the independent phase: formation of specialized sub-systems, of formal structures and procedures. The crisis of this phase enters when standardization leads to feelings of isolation and alienation.

At this point integration is necessary and organizations reach an interdependent phase. This involves becoming a more conscious organization which is no longer driven by structures and procedures but by purpose, a sense of meaning and direction. Leadership is developed throughout the organization. The most important feature of this phase is that the organization becomes conscious.

---

benefits they used to get from the networks decrease or cease. The performance of networks and partnerships therefore is determined by the stages of development and therefore capacity of the members – often the weakest members slow down progress of networks or partnerships. In this scenario the network or partnership becomes counter-productive as synergy cannot be achieved. For genuine partnerships and networks, such relationships are not worth going into.

Because of the differences in stages of development and capacity, challenges in networks and partnerships appear in four main areas: identity, leadership, strategy and funding. (James and Malunga, 2006; SANSAD, 2007).

Identity

Because the members are at different stages of development and capacity, their needs and therefore what they are seeking or hoping to get from the relationship varies. This leads to a multiplicity of visions. Unconsciously the partnership and the networks are made to focus on many issues, and this undermines its impact in the process. The lack of a unified and shared vision confuses the identity of networks and the expectations that beneficiaries may have of the network or partnership.

Often when networks establish secretariats, register and secure project funding from donors and sponsors, the secretariats may find themselves working increasingly independently from their members. Because of lack of capacity among the members, network secretariats may be forced to start implementing projects mainly due to pressure from donors to meet deadlines. When this is practiced regularly, the secretariat may 'forget' its coordination role and start competing with its members. Many network secretariats have become organizations in their own right, killing the network as a result.

In addition, members often do not implement network activities because of problems in their own organizations. CSO staff are usually not paid or appraised on time spent on network activities. The more time they give to the network the more their own organization and their own work suffers. For this reason network activities may be treated as a luxury and are pushed to the background (Freeth, 2005 p23).

Many CSO networks lack clear membership criteria – especially regarding minimum capacity requirements that enable members to contribute towards the effectiveness of the network. This leads to many members joining mostly in the hope of getting some benefits rather than making some contribution – more netting than working.

Related to the above, many networks do not have effective codes of conduct to enforce compliance to agreed norms. Where codes of conduct are there they are not adhered to and there are no systems to reward compliance or punish non-compliance.

Leadership

In many CSO networks there are no clear terms of reference for the board, the secretariat and members. If the terms of reference are there, they are not clearly communicated and therefore not internalized. Networks often lack clear job descriptions for the board, the secretariat and the members, hence none of them is clear on their roles and responsibilities. A related point is representation: often the stronger network members or partners are perceived to monopolize positions and control of the network. Yet when members from weak organizations are given the same positions they may not deliver at the same level due to limitations in capacity. To be effective however, members and partners must feel that they can influence major decisions of the network or partnership. They need to have confidence that each of the others will effectively carry out their roles and fulfil their responsibilities.

In relating with members, secretariats often lack a democratic and consultative mindset. There are usually challenges with communication and logistics arrangements. Secretariats are supposed to be a support system to coordinate the members and their activities, but they are often perceived as a separate and independent organization. This is aggravated by lack of interest among the network secretariats to make leadership development for members a priority. Over time members begin to feel inferior to the secretariat and the normal situation of the secretariat being a servant of the members is reversed. This leads to members abdicating responsibility to the secretariat, which in turn leads to overloading the secretariat and sometimes diverting the coordination role of the secretariat to the implementation role as described above.

Most network boards are weak and do not discharge their governance role effectively. Nor do they effectively contribute towards financial oversight, financial sustainability, performance monitoring and general strategic direction. Most networks lack the capacity to build collective leadership and develop future leaders for the sustainability of the network. This is a key area where the board could play an important role.

Commitment by the leaders of member organizations is critical for the success of networks and partnerships. Sometimes leaders from member organizations will only send junior staff to attend to network issues, thus not giving the networks the attention they deserve. When leaders demonstrate that they are personally committed to the network, this motivates staff to participate more actively in that network.

Strategy

Because of the differences in stages of development and capacity, networks' strategic plans tend to display a number of weaknesses. They often fail to help members to have a public 'voice' or publicize themselves. Strategic plans sometimes do not spell out clear roles and responsibilities for board, secretariat and the members, or clear membership criteria. Other critical issues often missing from networks' strategic plans include: the need to have clear, regular, meaningful interaction between secretariat and members; how to enable secretariats to coordinate collective action by members, for example by breaking large networks into smaller strategic sub-groups for more efficient and effective management, or by building internal capacity of secretariats and members for sustainability and impact; and how to enhance cooperation with the government and build relationships with donors. Most importantly, the strategic plans fail to help networks demonstrate their relevance to and legitimacy from the member organizations and intended beneficiaries.

Funding

Many CSO networks are not self-financing: they depend on donors and sponsors. Failure to enforce payment of membership fees and relying only on donors to finance the network undermines ownership of the network by its members. When writing their organizational funding proposals, member organizations often forget to include a budget line for subscription to the networks they belong to which is why members can find it difficult to pay their network membership fees.

Networks often lack capacity for results-based programming to demonstrate impact to stakeholders and donors to ensure their continued support and confidence. A network that is demonstrating clear results will rarely lack financial supporters. The low performance of many networks has led to caution and even scepticism among donors and sponsors.

Some donors are expressing concerns that network weaknesses are forcing them to find alternative ways of funding as the 'synergy assumption' of working with networks is becoming questionable. Of course some of the network funding has been for donor selfish reasons of administrative simplicity and efficiency as donors may find they can achieve the same in advocacy and capacity building by focusing on one network secretariat as compared to 20 individual organizations (James and Malunga, 2006 p10).

While it is certainly administratively simpler to fund one organization instead of 20, in a real sense this diverts support from network members to network secretariats. As a result, the work of individual members remains under funded and therefore members cannot support their networks adequately.

Being mostly donor dependent, most aided-CSO networks' lives are responding to funders' priorities. Ideally networks are supposed to close when their work is over. But many close when donors shift their preferences. And some continue to exist long after their purpose has been achieved simply because donor money is still available.

The challenges discussed above have two main implications for network and partnership effectiveness. First, networks need to develop clear and strict membership criteria to make sure that each member adds value to the network. Second, networks and partnerships need to invest more in capacity building of their members so that collective capacity can result in real interdependence which is the prerequisite for network and partnership performance and success.

Improving CSO Network Effectiveness

A network's effectiveness refers to the ability to improve member organizational performance and achieve crosscutting goals through networking (PACT, 2008, p37). Well-capacitated networks that are capable of *carrying their dead elephants to their caves* would need to ensure that they have critical network and partnership success factors. These would enable the creation of a truly interdependent and effective network or partnership. Improving the effectiveness of networks and partnerships therefore starts with an assessment of the key network organizational elements. These are:

Clear vision/mission and goals: the individual organizations are asked separately what they would want to see changed in society as a result of the work of the network or partnership. The responses are compared for similarities and differences. These show the congruence or divergence in the vision, mission and goals among the members. It also shows differences in emphasis and expectations from the network. This aspect also includes assessing whether the network members have an agreed and shared 'ideal picture' of the network in the future. The ideal picture describes the 'future desired network' five or more years into the future. The picture acts as a magnet pulling the network to its desired future because *what the eyes have seen the heart cannot forget.*

Setting out a clear destination of where it wants to go enables the network not only to learn from its past but also from its future. It acts as a benchmark against which the network measures its progress and success.

Strategic plan: this enables an understanding on whether the network can realistically achieve relevance, legitimacy and sustainability. Very importantly it enables understanding on whether the members can consciously connect or link their own strategic plans to the network strategic plan. Often network strategic plans remain secretariat strategic plans with no connection whatsoever with the members' strategic plans. The assessment also needs to determine whether the network strategic plan clearly defines the results sought by the network in terms of efficiency, effectiveness, impact, legacy and transformation. Ashman, (2003, p2) advises that a network's strategic plan must enable the network achieve a strategic fit. A strategic fit has four main elements:

1 Network goals address needs and issues perceived to be significant by all participants, members, donors and beneficiaries
2 Methodology employed is based on a proven successful model for addressing social needs that is shared by the members and major stakeholders. It is however important also to note that while we can learn from the successes of other networks, networks are not fully replicable – an existing and successful network is one piece of a jigsaw puzzle, a piece that has found its place within a wider framework of reshaping society. The network would not have emerged as it did without the contextual factors that shaped it (SANSAD, 2007, p170)

3   The network represents meaningful value-added to member organizations' portfo-
     lios. It enables partners to achieve benefits they could not achieve alone
4   The functional roles of the members in the network are complementary.

Agreed ground rules: help determine whether the network has an agreed code of conduct, if this code of conduct is being adhered to and whether members are actually rewarded or punished for adherence or non-adherence.

Clear decision-making procedures and the way communication is handled: this refers to the actual roles and responsibilities played by the board, secretariat and members, assessed against what these groups are supposed to be doing. It also refers to clarity on what decisions need to be made, at what level and by whom. Communication is the life blood of networks. Often however information tends to be clogged. There is either too much information leading to information overload, or too little leading to gossip, suspicion and conflict.

Appropriateness of the network's organizational structure: networks at different stages of development require different organizational forms. New and young networks need a strong hub or secretariat to which all the members are connected. The centre or hub plays the entire coordination role. As the network grows, the centre becomes overloaded and needs to decentralize. Network members dealing in similar themes can group and form 'sub-networks' within the main network. The main hub begins to play a support role to smaller decentralized hubs. At this stage the network operates as a matrix. As it continues to develop and grow the sub-networks decentralize to even smaller sub-networks and the hubs disappear, creating a web like structure for the network. The 'spider web' denotes the type of relationships among the members at this stage.

The assessment aims to identify the stage of development of the network and therefore what form of organizational structure would be more appropriate. Most networks suffer from over-structuring. When over-structured they cannot be sustainable as efficiency is hampered by bureaucracy. When under-structured, they cannot deliver effectively.

Whether benefits for membership outweigh the costs of membership: the network can only be sustainable if the benefits for membership outweigh the costs. According to Ashman (2001) networks and partnerships are defined as effective when they satisfy partners and members. In other words, for the members, *the juice must be worth the squeeze*.

Whether the network has a financial plan and how adequately the plan is financed: this includes both resources for running the secretariat, supporting board activities and activities to be carried out by members. When the secretariat or members have more money than the other, there will be a relationship of dependence making an 'adult to adult' relationship impossible. This undermines the spirit of partnership and networking. This is also related to the network's relationships with donors. To be effective, networks require 'good quality funding' that can facilitate the growth of local rather than imposed agendas and autonomy. With 'good quality funding', donors' formal agreements, monitoring and reporting procedures are flexible, promote mutual accountability, avoid burdensome reporting and promote an 'adult to adult' relationship between networks and their donors.

After the consultation, key capacity gaps in the network are identified and appropriate interventions agreed on to address the prioritized issues. The aim of the intervention is to build the capacity of individual members to help them move towards the

---

Box 21.4 *Critical network success factors*

- A considerable number of people must share the view that networking will add a specific value to their work

- The importance of communication and participatory methods: if the network is to be supported by a wide group of non-profit organizations they must be allowed to participate intensively in the formulation of the objectives, approach and organization

- The development of a shared conceptual framework that will facilitate exchange of ideas, experiences and knowledge: this helps to make sense out of the idea of setting up a network, checking the need for it and defining its potential for supporting its members in doing their work better. This involves developing a 'theory of joint intervention' that makes sense to everyone who will participate

- Tangible activities the members or prospective members of the network are already performing in their respective areas: the immediate needs arising from the fieldwork of each of the institutions are the basis and reasons for being a network. Network activities must provide support to the actual work of the organizations involved

- Minimum resources required for the establishment and maintenance of vital communication facilities, create opportunities for interaction and stimulate participation.

Source: Engel, 1993.

---

interdependent phase which is the prerequisite for effective networks and partners. A further aim is to bring consciousness of the critical success factors of networks and partnerships mentioned above and build these capacities within the network or partnership as a whole.

Network Development

The process for facilitating the development of networks and partnerships is called trans-organizational development (TD) (French and Bell, 1995). Many networks evolve unconsciously but effectiveness can be enhanced if networks are deliberately and consciously established, developed and nurtured. TD involves getting more than one organization, or getting a number of stakeholders, to 'work together collaboratively towards a common goal or objectives'. TD is useful in establishing and managing networks, business alliances or consortia formed with the aim of creating synergy among the organizations involved. The proverb *no matter how powerful a person, they cannot make rain fall on their farm only* illustrates the essence of TD well. It is based on the principle that no matter how strong it is, no organization can be self-sufficient in the sense of not needing the support of other organizations to achieve its goals. 'Synergy' is the key word in TD. The TD process involves four main phases:

1   Identifying potential members: the main activities of the TD practitioner are to help people with the idea of forming the 'network' to form a steering committee and establish the preliminary membership criteria. He or she may also facilitate the induction of new members into the network

2   Bringing together the member organizations: the TD practitioner facilitates a work-shop or a session for representatives of the member organizations to agree on the necessity of forming the network. This session enables the members to clarify their expectations and fears. Much more importantly, the TD practitioner must help the members to agree on working values for the 'network'. Many networks fail because of unshared expectations and values among the members

3   Establishing the network: after agreeing on the purpose and generating enough energy and enthusiasm, the TD practitioner helps the members to create and agree ground rules, roles and responsibilities, decision-making processes, communication mechanisms, appropriate structure and ways to secure the required financial and material resources. Most importantly, the TD practitioner helps the members to agree on how the network will be coordinated

4   A key role that a TD practitioner plays is to facilitate periodic reflection sessions on how the 'network' is doing. The TD practitioner helps the members to identify their successes and challenges and what they are learning from these and, more impor-tantly, how they can use the lessons to improve the performance of the network.

The TD practitioner may require much more 'energy' as much of his or her work will be to facilitate 'power-sharing and political interventions' especially at the beginning of the process. Being seen to be neutral and not taking sides is key to success in such interventions.

Conclusion

Networks are complex organizational systems because they assume that the participating members and partners are at the interdependent stage of development, which in practice is very difficult to attain. Truly interdependent organizations are a rare phenomenon in real life. The real management challenge for networks therefore is to invest more in the capacity building of their members so that the collective capacity will enable conscious interdependence and then allow the *united organizational ants to carry the dead elephant to their cave.* This will enable the secretariats to play an increasingly facilitative and coor-dinating role rather than growing bigger than the members and eventually becoming independent organizations that begin to compete with, and eventually replace, the members. The interdependent spirit is a cooperative spirit in contrast to the competitive spirit of the independent phase. To achieve this interdependence and therefore effective-ness, CSO networks must allow space for evolution, accommodating difference, converging and dispersing, for engaging in dialogue and collective decision-making among the members (SANSAD, 2007, p170).

References

Ashman, D. (2001) *Building Alliances with Civil Society*, IFCB
Ashman, D. (2005) *Supporting Civil Society Networks in Institutional Development Programs*, Washington: AED Center for Civil Society and Governance

Church, M. (2003) *Participation, Relationships and Dynamic Change: New Thinking on Evaluating the Work of International Workshops*, DPU UCL, Working Paper 121: London

Cohen, D., Vega, R. and Watson, G. (2001) *Advocacy for Social Justice: A Global Action and Reflection Guide*, Kumarian Press: Bloomfield, USA

Engel, P.G.H. (1993) *Daring to share: networking among non-government organisations,* in 'Linking with Farmers, networking for low-external-input and sustainable agriculture', ILEIA Readings in Sustainable Agriculture

Freeth, R. (2005) 'Networks: Amorphous, Ambivalent and Powerful', *Mulberry Series*, Durban: Olive Publications

French, W. and Bell, C. (1995) *Organization: Behavioral Science Interventions for Organization Improvement* (5th edition), New Jersey: Prentice Hall Inc

James, R. and Malunga, C. (2006) 'Organizational Challenges Facing Civil Society Networks in Malawi', *KM4D Journal*, 2 (2): pp48–63

Livegoed, B. (1969) *Managing the Developing Organization*, Oxford: Blackwell

Livegoed, B. (1973) *The Developing Organization*, London: Tavistock

Miller, P. (2005) 'The Rise of Network Campaigning', in McCarthy, H., Miller, P. and Skidmorw, P. (eds) *Network Logic: who governs in an interconnected world?* available at http://www.demos.co.uk/files/networklogic.pdf

PACT (2008) *Building Effective Networks,* Unpublished Research Paper

SANSAD (2007) *Networking: Towards a Better Tomorrow*, New Delhi: South Asian Network for Social and Agricultural Development

22

South African NGOs and the Public Sphere: Between Popular Movements and Partnerships for Development

Natascha Mueller-Hirth

Introduction

There are a number of South African non-governmental organizations (NGOs) whose objectives include enhancing public debate and participation and building civil society capacity. Generally donor-funded, the activities of such NGOs are understood as deepening democracy and supporting a healthy civil society. This chapter seeks to assess claims about the role of NGOs in the public sphere: does their work open up the sphere of debate and critique or are their endeavours by definition elitist, excluding the experiences and socio-economic realities of the majority population? A number of interrelated processes are charted by which certain actors are included and others excluded in conceptions of civil society in South Africa. This, it is argued, may in fact impact negatively on the existence of spaces of public deliberation and on the shape of post-apartheid democracy. The chapter thus seeks to contribute to a critical reading of formalized South African NGOs and their relationships with other components of civil society. In the first part, I examine how particular donor understandings of civil society, chiefly its conflation with professionalized NGOs, contribute to a limited definition of civil society in post-apartheid South Africa. In the second part, reconceptualizations of public-sphere theory are employed in order to direct attention to popular movements and their potential to open up spaces for a critique that NGOs may structurally be unable to engage in. In examining the relationships of formalized NGOs to social movements, I argue that processes of NGO-ization as well as NGOs' own 'reformism' of civil society may contribute to a narrowing of spaces for public debate.

The organizations sampled for this research are what I refer to as intermediary NGOs. Unlike pure service-delivery NGOs, the work of such formalized organizations seeks to promote and extend democracy through capacity building, research, advocacy, monitoring and organizational development. Given their heterogeneity, it is not possible to give adequate space to the political and organizational differences between the NGOs considered here; this chapter focuses on the processes by which NGOs may come to represent civil society in South Africa.[1]

Civil society, Donors and Post-apartheid Democracy: What Role(s) for NGOs?

Theoretical perspectives on civil society and public sphere

South African political scientist Adam Habib characterizes civil society as 'the organized expression of various interests and values operating in the triangular space between the family, state and the market' (Habib et al, 2003, p228).[2] The term has plural and often contradictory meanings for different civil society actors: many of those interviewed rejected it outright as a donor discourse, some saw it as an ambivalent category with limited use and others employed the term strategically. Yet, the notion of civil society is perpetually evoked in the language of donors and international institutions. Its revival in the 1980s, when it was picked up by the development mainstream, resulted in a huge extension of civil society support programmes; by the end of the decade, a new orthodoxy had evolved which discredited the state as at best inefficient. Civil society was hailed as a benign area through which to improve the democratic performance of governments in the developing world, with NGOs identified as primary agents of this vision.

Turning first to mainstream approaches of civil society, it is perhaps Putnam's (1993, 1995) interpretation that has been most influential on institutional civil society discourse in the last two decades. Putnam's approach builds on Alexis de Tocqueville's work on early American democracy in the first half of the 19th century. Here, civil society is understood as the sum of voluntary organizations. The strength and stability of liberal democracy depends on a vibrant sphere of such associational participation as a means of ensuring equality and protecting the individual from conformity to the will of enfranchised masses (Howell and Pearce, 2001). This approach to civil society is embedded in liberal democracy, placing great emphasis on political stability and the safeguarding of individual interests. Despite the fact that Putnam's work was specifically concerned with democratization processes in Italy and associational life in the United States, the revived notion of civil society was adopted as global development consensus. Assumptions that it can be transposed to any given political, economic or cultural context were justified by an appeal to the universality of (neo)liberal democracy. By the mid-1990s, the term had become a fixture in debates on South Africa's democratic future as well. This was not least due to the influx of international development funding and knowledge into the country in the period between 1990 and 1994, during which global policy discourses such as 'good governance' and 'civil society' were adopted and circulated by national NGOs (Pieterse, 1997).

Other theoretical approaches can be traced back to a Gramscian conception of state and civil society, the latter a site where hegemony and counter-hegemony are played out. Such a framework allows accounting both for NGOs as articulated with the consent and legitimating functions of the state and for potentially more progressive movements seeking to carve out counter-hegemonic spaces. Habermas (1987) argues that the 'colonization of the lifeworld', for example, through commercialization and commodification of media or education, reduces the public sphere by bureaucratizing and commodifying social life and replacing open dialogue by bureaucratic procedures and economic transactions. However, this process also gives rise to new social movements which can then construct relatively autonomous spaces for public debate about the legitimacy of the political and economic system: 'Civil society is composed of those more or less spontaneously emergent associations, organizations and movements that, attuned to how societal problems resonate in the private life spheres, distil and transmit such reactions in amplified forms to the public sphere' (Habermas, 1996, cited in Chambers et al, 2002, p96). In Habermas's account, social movements are thus identified as the principal actors for resistance and emancipation, responsible for generating and extending the public sphere in democratic systems. From this perspective, civil society provides a site for the 'production and circulation of discourses that can in principle be critical of the state' and of the goals and values of governance (Fraser and Elliott, 2003, p84). His arguments further reveal how economic rationalities come to dominate other rationalities in the public sphere – a point which I believe can be applied to the commercialization of NGOs discussed below and challenges an orthodox understanding of NGOs as necessarily strengthening democracy.

Some claim that the heyday of civil society discourse is 'passé' (Edwards, 2004), but this is certainly not backed up by an analysis of recent donor requirements and institutional policy texts, nor was it reflected in the interviews for this study. The link between civil society and democracy is frequently framed in terms of active citizenship, participation and debate – language immediately reminiscent of public-sphere theories. Donor-funded civil society projects in South Africa sometimes address the subject of the public sphere directly, arguing for instance that 'civil society must be able to participate in and influence public debate', thus advancing the democratization process (Böll Foundation, 2007). The funding guidelines of other donors similarly assume linkages between democratic civil societies and increased participation in public affairs.[3] Accordingly, many formalized intermediary NGOs are involved in related activities: organizations as diverse as the Wolpe Trust, the Centre for Public Participation, Media Monitoring Africa and Agenda held grants for projects seeking to facilitate public dialogue and foster political participation in 2007. Other organizations that focus directly or indirectly on building capacity for dialogue and critique include the Institute for Democracy in South Africa (IDASA), the Freedom of Expression Institute (FXI), the Edge Institute and the South African History Archive (SAHA), to name but a few.[4]

The construction of civil society in liberal theory as a binary opposite to the state, as encountered above, oversimplifies the complex relationships and frequent collaboration between state and civil society actors. Habib et al (2003) distinguish three different sets of civil society organizations (CSOs) which display distinct modes of engagement with the South African state: formalized NGOs, social movements and survivalist community-based organizations (the latter of which have little, if any, interaction with the state). These distinctions are not rigid; social movements such as the Treatment Action Campaign (TAC) have taken on characteristics of formalized NGOs, a process I discuss later in this chapter, whereas NGOs such as the FXI see their role as supporting popular movements.[5]

Nonetheless, the formal NGO sector in particular interlinks with the state in a number of ways, for instance through partnerships, through subcontracting or through personal histories and political affiliations. It is therefore more apt to speak of a spectrum of relations that are fluid and contingent on individuals in CSOs as well as in the state's agencies. In order to further elucidate this argument, a brief history of CSOs in South Africa, charting the increasing conflation of civil society with NGOs, is discussed next.

From civics to NGOs: State-civil society relations in South Africa

Under apartheid, service organizations were working explicitly against the state, providing a shadow welfare system to the majority of the population neglected by the state's separate development policy. Foreign governments and international donor agencies channelled funds through these organizations to fight apartheid. Besides the objectives of a non-racial democracy, however, the values of the various parts of the anti-apartheid movement were not always clearly defined and differed on essential issues such as the form of democracy and the economic system to be adopted after the end of apartheid. Tensions were largely suspended with the formation of the United Democratic Front (UDF). This provided an umbrella organization for hundreds of civics mobilizing against National Party rule, but clear ideological and organizational divides remained among the different components of South African civil society.

The transition and immediate post-1994 period was mainly characterized by a harmonization of development objectives and cooperation between civil society and the newly democratic state. This was the result of a consensual model of nation building in the 'new South Africa' that attributed a service delivery role to CSOs. The shift, in 1996, away from a framework seemingly emphasizing reconstruction towards the neoliberal Growth, Employment and Redistribution plan (GEAR) moreover favoured 'institutionalized corporatist relationships involving all social forces in the project of "nation building" through political/ideological "consensus"' (McKinley, unpublished). The adoption of GEAR also marked the increasing exclusion of civil society from consultation in policy processes. Structural and legislative changes included the establishment of the South African National Civics Organization (SANCO), the National Development Agency (NDA) and legislation such as the Non-Profit Act. Many organizations folded as a consequence of funding modalities changing towards bilateral relations with the ANC (African National Congress) government and much of the expertise of the sector being absorbed into the new state bureaucracy. Other NGOs survived the funding crisis, but found that they needed to reposition themselves either as service-delivery organizations or to carry out contracting work for government bodies. As a result of these processes, the sector was weakened in terms of capacity, reduced in numbers and increasingly dependent in terms of activities, and had restructured itself partly in line with government policies and priorities. This transformation and formalization mirrored the global development priorities of institutionalism and inclusion as encapsulated in the Post-Washington Consensus.[6] Civil society effectively became equated with NGOs that had successfully professionalized.

These changes gave rise to what we may call new-generation NGOs. Having innovative funding models and a variety of resource mobilization strategies, such NGOs are organizationally configured towards strong partnerships with the public and the corporate sector. The partnership mode can be contrasted with NGOs that remain structured around a more classical donor-beneficiary model. Clearly, all NGOs are currently forced to seek new income-generating strategies and develop self-financing strategies. Also, adherence to monitoring and evaluation standards leads donor-based NGOs to corporatize to some extent. The South African NGO sector is highly differentiated: 'new' NGOs by no means encapsulate the entire NGO sector nor do I argue that partnerships have the same impact on all organizations. That said, the model that new-generation NGOs are employing has important effects on the whole NGO sector in that it renders partnerships as a necessity in the eyes of donors and establishes a blueprint for a stream-lined NGO. Many of the case NGOs have narrowed their programmatic focus, expanded their activities into the Southern African region and subcontracted to government in recent years. Around the time of the second democratic election in 1999, South Africa also began to witness an eruption of mass protests and mobilizations expressing dissent over the government's failures in service delivery.

Broadening participation or extending partnerships?

Intertwining national and global processes of professionalization and homogenization have produced as ideal-typical CSO a formal and streamlined NGO with cross-sectoral linkages. In this study, the organizations that emerged as most successful in accessing donor funding in the spheres of civil-society strengthening and public participation were NGOs based in the three urban centres; they had professionalized and all had considerable quantitative-analytical skills. Being able to adhere to the stringent reporting requirements demanded by donors already implies a high level of financial, manage-ment and language expertise. The point to emphasize in relation to donor demands of monitoring and evaluation is their organizational-structural effects. Project evaluation and performance reviews overemphasize quantitatively measurable outcomes, therefore they are changing the ratio between financial/administrative and project staff, impacting on organizational culture and producing specific types of expertise. Monitoring and evaluation practices thus require certain organizational conditions which not only favour but indeed produce highly professionalized types of NGOs.

In addition to favouring such types of organizations, donors delineate specific roles for CSOs, such as 'partnering with government to improve the quantity and quality of basic services' or 'engaging in policy formulations' (Charles Stewart Mott Foundation, 2007). The emphasis placed on partnering is central to a contemporary understanding of development that sees partnerships between civil society and the state as a means to deliver inclusively and efficiently. At the same time, the fact that many donors support the South African government via bilateral aid means that they shy away from supporting NGOs that work with social movements which may be seen as critical of government. The constantly shifting alliances in partnerships have severe implications for NGO accountabilities to their supposed constituencies. However, a simple argument of inter-national donors putting into place the existing development regime does not capture the complexities of the South African non-profit sector for which the state is in fact the biggest donor. Civil society-enhancing programmes continue to be constructed by external actors, but they overlap, and occasionally conflict, with other (for instance, state-led or community-based) versions of development. Many NGOs have themselves incorporated donors' interpretations of their roles.

The often internally divided relationships of NGOs with the state are further complicated not only by their involvement in partnerships, but also by their subcon-tracting for government as part of a drive for sustainability. A number of NGO staff characterized their location as necessitating a constant tightrope walk. IDASA was said to have a 'schizophrenic capacity to work in different ways with different people'.[7] On the one hand, civil society should be a site for the production of discourses that can be critical of the state, especially in the context of high levels of poverty and inequality. Given that NGOs are tasked with building capacity for and extending civil society, they are assigned a critical role that goes beyond holding the state accountable. This is why a celebration of civil society's plurality must be carefully formulated: NGOs working with other parts of civil society have a responsibility to strengthen these formations in their own abilities to advance dialogue and critique. On the other hand, collaboration with national government or provincial ministries on particular policies can impede their ability to exercise this twofold critical role. Service-related NGOs by definition are in more collegiate relationships with the government than many of the NGOs considered here that are working in the fields of human rights, advocacy or monitoring. Nevertheless, even for this set, assisting government and hence 'contributing to change seriously' can be an important aspect of their work.[8] The dualism of supporting government in implementation while remaining in a critical watchdog role that holds government accountable is difficult to accomplish, especially given the state's apparent definition, for much of the post-apartheid period, of appropriate state-civil society relations as collegiate and uncritical, and its branding of non-adherence as unpatriotic. This dilemma is particularly evident where NGOs' perspective on popular movements is concerned, the latter of which have been subject to state marginalization and repression for challenging government policies and its failures in service delivery. NGOs' engagement with the state clearly affects their positioning towards other components of civil society.

The link between expanding the public sphere and democratic growth is regularly evoked, but – as those involved in initiatives designed to stimulate public dialogue readily acknowledge – remains under-researched.[9] Precisely because of this lack of evidence, it is important to question whether NGOs are the appropriate agents to engage those excluded from political processes and to encourage criticism of the narrowing of spaces for debate. After all, NGOs have for many years been criticized for frequently not reaching the marginalized, having little legitimacy with communities and having a specific base. Donor objectives of supporting a diverse civil society seem largely rhetorical where it is almost exclusively formal NGOs that qualify for funding intent on broadening public participation and strengthening civil society. The structural location of formal NGOs may result in donors supporting very particular interests and reproducing existing elites. Donors' focus on NGOs could then be seen as limiting civil society and democratic participation, running the danger of 'thwart[ing] the formation and effectiveness of interest groups that could push for state accountability' (Howell and Pearce, 2001, p185). With civil society itself being constructed, discursively and materially, according to often narrow donor criteria, its extension through capacity building projects can arguably result in more of the same civil society, as opposed to contributing to greater participation.

NGOs and Social Movements

From the public sphere to counterpublics

The fact that most funded NGOs may structurally not be in a position to forge critical debate necessitates the question of which other civil society formations are able to open up such spaces. In particular, it is popular movements and their repression by the state that bring the relationships of NGOs towards non-elitist forms of participation and protest into sharp focus. South Africa now has the greatest number of protest actions in the world: 10,000 per year, according to some (Bond, 2007). The persistence of high levels of poverty, unemployment and inequality, resulting from the restructuring of the economy and the adoption of a cost-recovery model in service provision, has given rise to the upsurge of movements out of such protests. What are sometimes referred to as new social movements encompass a whole array of issues and constituencies that vary considerably in scale, organizational form, capacity and strategies.[10] While movements tend to be vociferous in their critique of the state, their positioning can be divergent, ranging from confrontation to partial engagement on specific issues. The differences between NGOs and movements are not in all instances clear-cut either, as was stated earlier: TAC, for example, bridges the space between NGO and movement, employing a range of tactics to hold the state accountable. Nonetheless, community movements are usually excluded from donors' definition of civil society and the public sphere. Donor-funded NGOs similarly struggle with defining their identity in relation to movements, as the next section of the article explores: while situating themselves in alliance with movements, their relationship is also characterized by attempts to contain or shape movements.

To direct attention to social movements as potentially offering spaces for debate and critique requires briefly revisiting Habermas's work on the public sphere. While his analysis can provide a tool to understand the commercialization of NGOs, more problematic for the present context is his assumption that social movements have shifted their attention from capital/labour struggles to grievances connected to the colonization of the lifeworld by state and economy. This is difficult to uphold in the context of South African community mobilizations against the neoliberal reordering of the economy.[11] Habermas's thinking on the public sphere also falls short in this context because it assumes that a multiplicity of alternative public spheres indicates fragmentation and democratic decline. Fraser and Elliott (2003), for instance, have shown that, in stratified societies, existing structural inequalities are exacerbated if there is only one single public sphere: members of subordinated groups have no spaces for deliberation among themselves, resulting in a danger of absorption into a comprehensive public sphere. Their concern certainly resonates with the stigmatizing of public protests as seemingly constituting a betrayal of the national democratic revolution and of national democratic citizenship. The discourse of nation building as it is circulated by political elites is in fact central to this understanding of the public sphere as necessarily consensual and homogenous. Mangcu (2008) argues that nationalism, instead of being a tool in the struggle against repression, has become an instrument of rule. Based on the same logic is the inclusive vision of development and social change that is encapsulated in the contemporary emphasis on multisectoral partnerships.

Conversely, Fraser's concept of counterpublics captures the 'plurality of competing publics', providing spaces for subordinated groups to 'invent and circulate counterdiscourses to formulate oppositional interpretations of their identities, interests and needs' (Fraser and Elliott, 2003, p91). Her notion challenges the oft-criticized assumption that members of the Habermasian public sphere are able to debate as equals, notwithstanding their economic or social status. In the context of post-apartheid South Africa, with its formally inclusive public sphere but historical structural relations of dominance and inequality, greater attention to discursive interactions and the rules governing inclusion and exclusion in public spaces is necessary. Support of formalized NGOs' work for the purpose of widening democratic participation has to be carefully reassessed taking into account these concerns. Moreover, the ongoing attempts by certain sectors of government and other centres of power to contain critical voices present in the convened public sphere point to the essential role for counterpublics in South Africa. As sites enabling public deliberation, critique and active citizenship, social and community movements have the potential to act as counterpublic spheres.[12] Turning now to NGO relations to movements, several positions are highlighted: while some cast movements as providing much-needed critical voices, there is also a tendency to draw these alternative spaces into a consensual civil society.

Relationships of NGOs to movements

A small set of NGOs, such as the FXI or Khanya College, has in recent years played a supportive role to movements by providing legal resources, training and publicity, or by building capacity.[13] The repression of protest by the state has defined such NGOs' positioning.[14] While NGOs may see themselves as supportive of the activities of social movements, the extent to which they are able to support them materially is dependent on their own funding modalities: 'quite a few NGOs ... have shunned working with social movements because they don't want to be tainted with the aura of radicalism', as Jane Duncan, Executive Director of the FXI, put it.[15]

The majority of NGO staff felt that the appropriate relationship between their NGOs and movements should be one of 'solidarity' and 'mutual respect', yet the NGOs were not actively supporting movements. Similar to the first set of organizations, such NGOs understood the contribution of social movements to democracy as positive: social activism and protest are signs of the maturity of post-apartheid democracy. NGO accounts often drew on an idea of civil society as plural, depicting populist movements as the vanguard that demonstrates to NGOs their failure in challenging the status quo: '[Social movements] have become that critical voice to say that's the role you should have been playing. They just went and they did it. They just marched.'[16] Again, decisions not to support social movements despite pronouncements of solidarity may be motivated by concerns about their own funding.

A perhaps surprisingly large number of NGO staff, consciously or unconsciously, distanced themselves from social movements. For instance, the contribution of social movements to democratic practice was praised in the abstract, but the strategies and tactics they employ were critiqued by the director of Agenda:

> You know, I have always worked at a grass roots level. So for me social movements are critical. And I think we as civil society organizations, as NGOs that might give you a different flavour from a social movement, I think there is a need for civil society organisations to put their weight and put their resources and thoughtfully move social movements to a place where it is much more credible.[17]

Commonalities with movements by virtue of shared values or politics were often evoked, for example, by drawing on the reified 'we' of civil society. However, marching or 'burning the tyres outside' loomed large in NGO narratives of community activism. This is appropriate in that one characteristic of post-apartheid movements is their high degree of popular participation. Yet, they cannot be reduced to it. In fact, many social movements have used a variety of strategies and have developed a 'maturity around when to use the courts, when to use struggle-on-the-streets tactics, when to use publicity, and when to use all three together', argues Jane Duncan.[18]

Another way in which NGO staff distanced themselves from social movements was by pitting 'constructive engagement' with the state against 'marching on the street'. Institutionalized politics, the media and the courts were in some interviews portrayed as the legitimate and proper channels through which policy can be impacted on in the democratic era. Conversely, mass mobilization was portrayed as outdated, with the effect of it seemingly being no longer acceptable to use what was constructed as backward apartheid-era struggle tactics. This discursive opposition throws up interesting parallels to development discourses on modernity, progress and liberal democracy. It also resonates strongly with a dominant understanding of civil society as an arena for formal organizations suited to a liberal model of organizing society. Besides establishing which means are appropriate to register protest, NGO accounts of social movement activity thus also work to define what a modern CSO should be. Others argued that while protest was justified given the lack of service delivery, social movements were simply not effective enough: 'If you are going to engage with the major policy issues and try to shift the way your society operates, you are going to have to have organized forms of civil society. The best model would appear to be, at this stage, some kind of sensitive NGO'.[19] NGO constructions of social movements resonate with the above-encountered donor understanding of civil society in that they envisage an organization that mediates between communities and the state. The liberal tenet requires more and more civil society, but not the kind of civil society that social movements embody. The kind of organization supposedly best suited to post-apartheid liberal democracy is an effective, efficient and formal NGO, staffed with 'well-mannered activists who play by the rules, settle conflicts peacefully, and do not break any windows', to cite one commentator (Carothers, 1999, cited in Howell and Pearce, 2001, p42).

The following extract from an interview with the director of an NGO that focuses on strengthening democracy through citizen participation and civil society promotion points further towards some of the politics underlying NGO relationships with movements:

> And we've offered them: if you want to use our training manuals here; if you want capacity building, having a workshop and sandwiches and stuff, we can provide that. And we have materials and manuals that you want to use, that's fine ... But one of them came to me and said they'd smashed their car. And they came to us;

you know what, can we get a car? I said no I can't do that ... that is where we differ;
I have to be completely accountable for how I spend the money of the organisation.
It does not work like that. I said you also have to learn how these things operate.[20]

Holding the purse strings in a potential relationship does not just indicate a resource
inequality that may or may not play itself out similarly to a classical donor-beneficiary
relationship; the provision of training itself establishes particular practices and provides
access to communities and their immediate organizations.[21] As I implied above, the
capacity building role that many NGOs are sponsored to fulfil in civil society is itself
problematic. Organizational development, one of the fields of activity for intermediary
NGOs, may itself contribute to the restructuring of their civil society partners in line
with a particular version of civil society.

Whether supportive or critical of their work, wanting to 'move social movements to
a more credible place' or the teleology characterizing the above account of a meeting
with members of Abahlali base, Mjondolo betrays a sense of NGOs wanting to change
social movements' practices in line with their own version of civil society. Such
'reformism' is a central issue in NGOs' relations to social movements. This argument
underlines how civil society practice is also defined by NGOs wanting to shape social
movements in their own image, and highlights the potential for an NGO-ization of
movements. In accessing funding or other resources, CSOs have to engage with a variety
of bureaucratic questions arising from the need for accountability. The quantitative-
analytical skills required for reporting, monitoring and evaluation practices are one
example. Moreover, once an NGO has entered into funding and monitoring regimes, it
becomes increasingly difficult to work with less formalized organizations since these are
not structurally equipped to prove results-based management or adhere to complicated
reporting systems. As the director of an NGO that provides education and research for
the labour and social movements put it: 'we only work with the ones who do have a
photocopying machine, who can account for all the money and so on'.[22] As a result,
CSOs may become – in terms of activities and organizational structure – more like
NGOs. In important ways, the professionalization and formalization of the NGO sector
that were charted earlier translate to civil society more broadly.

There is a parallel as well between NGO-ization and the processes of homogenization that are the outcome of NGO partnerships with the public and private sectors. The
expertise that NGO-ization produces is organizational, financial and managerial; the
channels through which it is circulated are organizational practices and procedures that
are connected to the responsibilization of CSOs. While NGO attempts at reforming
movements may be purely discursive, they serve to define what civil society should be,
thus marginalizing certain forms of CSOs and contributing to a narrow definition of
civil society. NGO-ization and NGO reformism have the potential of institutionalizing
community struggles over the meaning of development and democracy, thereby
containing and civilizing them. However, it is necessary to bear in mind that the institutionalization of movements is an incomplete project; there are constantly challenges
to NGOs' discourses and practices within civil society (see Li, 2007).[23]

Conclusion

This article has examined the idea that post-apartheid democracy can be deepened and civil society strengthened by NGO activities in the sphere of public debate and participation. I do not wish to imply that such activities are futile. On the contrary, the case NGOs are all committed to opening spaces for participation and critique. I have sought, however, to emphasize that the overwhelming focus of donors on NGOs as the only legitimate representative of civil society may in fact narrow spaces for critique by excluding CSOs that do not fit their criteria. A gap between donor rhetoric and funding practices was identified where a plural civil society is regarded as central to democratic development, but in practice it is mainly formal and urban NGOs that are supported to carry out public sphere-enhancing activities. This funding preference may well contribute to a homogenous and institutionalized public sphere, thus reinforcing societal elites and marginalizing the majority population. NGOs increasingly acting as a development partner for government and the corporate sector further cast doubt on their ability to open up spaces for critical public debate and engagement as their involvement in multi-sectoral partnerships impacts on their positioning towards wider civil society.

While some NGO accounts celebrate the pluralism of civil society, I have asked whether the capacity building activities of NGOs may not ultimately construct less professionalized components of civil society as something to be reformed and drawn into a circle of consensus. The danger here lies not only in a marginalization of other CSOs, but also in the homogenization of civil society through processes of NGO-ization. This certainly raises concerns over the institutionalization of community struggles and the containment of counterpublic spheres. I have only tentatively indicated what the democratic deficit resulting from narrowly conceived notions of civil society and processes of NGO-ization may be. Nonetheless, the exclusion of less formal types of organizations runs a danger of excluding actors that could push for state accountability, where NGOs may be structurally unable to do so. Attention must be paid to the processes of governmentality by which NGOs themselves come to define and transfer what civil society should be and in how far they limit or contain the existence of counterpublic spheres.

Notes

1 This chapter draws on data gathered from interviews with directors or senior staff of NGOs. Consent was given by all participants to be named and for their institutional affiliation to be given. Clearly, though, these do not necessarily represent the often divided opinions within their organizations on key questions of location and identity.

2 There is considerable discussion about what is included and excluded in civil society, and particularly whether the economy should be included in the definition of civil society. See Edwards (2004) and Elliott (2003) for overviews of the debate.

3 See, for example, the Mott Foundation, Ford Foundation and the UK Department for International Development (DFID), as well as a number of northern NGOs that act as grantmakers in South Africa.

4   There are also academic institutions whose public lectures and research programmes seek to foster debate and bridge the gap between communities and academia but which do not fit the description of NGO as I employ it here. Many of the case NGOs are also involved in capacity building initiatives with local or community-based organizations as a way of extending civil society and strengthening democracy.

5   As I indicated in the introduction, the NGOs sampled for this research are what I have chosen to call intermediary organizations, rather than straightforward service-delivery NGOs providing welfare to the population.

6   The term Post-Washington Consensus describes the shift in economic thinking and development policy, in the last decade, towards recognizing the centrality of institutions and social factors in the efficient functioning of markets.

7   Interview with R. Calland, Director, Governance Programme, IDASA, 23 April 2007.

8   Interview with A. Motala, Executive Director, CSVR, 4 May 2007.

9   Interview with T. Bailey, National Coordinator, Harold Wolpe Memorial Trust, 25 April 2007.

10 See, for example, the edited volume by Ballard et al (2006), which contains chapters on the Landless People's Movement, the Concerned Citizens Forum, the TAC, the Anti-Privatisation Forum and other movements.

11 For reasons of space, it is not possible to discuss the critiques of Habermas's original account, such as his exclusion of women and workers. Rather, this section is concerned with reconceptualizations of his account as they may apply to the politics of civil society sponsoring in South Africa.

12 While it is not implied that every protest action is indicative of public debate or the existence of emancipatory public spaces, social movements continue to formulate alternative policies and approaches to development, democracy, the state, etc.

13 There are other donor-funded organizations that are aligned with or supportive of social movements, such as the University of KwaZulu Natal's Centre for Civil Society, SAHA, International Labour Research and Information Group or the Alternative Information Development Centre. Some of these reject the characterization as an NGO, others are academic research centres and therefore not included in this analysis. Conversely, some international NGOs also support relatively more formalized movements such as the Anti-Privatisation Forum (APF) or the TAC. This article is not concerned with NGO-social movement relations, although a shift in terms of how such organizations conceive of popular movements has taken place in recent years (personal conversation with D. McKinley, Anti-Privatisation Forum, 11 July 2007).

14 Following the mobilizations around the World Conference against Racism and the World Summit on Sustainable Development in 2001 and 2002, respectively, the government started to ban gatherings and repress movements – sparking new struggles and increasing support for existing movements. These events represented the first very public rejection of the ANC and its economic policies and also signified collective national action of previously highly localized community struggles (Desai, 2002). They are noteworthy also because they marked a defining point in terms of repositioning the relationships between some of the movements and NGOs, with a small set of progressive NGOs and donors now beginning to support these movements (interview with J. Duncan, 30 March 2007).

15 Interview with J. Duncan, Director, FXI, 30 March 2007.

16 Interview with anonymous NGO director, 25 June 2007.

17 Interview with M. Oyedan, Director, Agenda, 27 June 2007.

18 Interview with J. Duncan, 30 March 2007.

19 Interview with W. Bird, Director, Media Monitoring Africa, 13 June 2007.

20 Interview with anonymous NGO director, 25 June 2007.

21 However, it is important to note that rather than seeking funding or collaborations with NGOs, those movements that come from an autonomist tradition would reject funding from NGOs or other donors or NGOs outright.

22 Interview with L. Gentle, Director, ILRIG, 24 April 2007.

23 An analysis of social movements' understanding of NGOs would clearly yield quite different results which go beyond the scope of this article. Far from seeking relationships with NGOs, some movements come from a strong autonomist tradition and would reject funding from donors or NGOs outright (such as the Western Cape Eviction Campaign). Other movements, such as the APF, receive some funding from NGOs, work with them on a number of clearly specified projects, but similarly do not see a natural connection or political alliance with them – their relationship is at best a 'tactical temporary alliance' (personal conversation with D. McKinley, 11 July 2007). Many contemporary movements in South Africa have theorized their ideas of development and democracy in opposition to NGOs (including left NGOs). Richard Pithouse, for instance, writes about Abahlali that it has been driven by a commitment to intellectual autonomy from its beginnings, further noting that '[r]ival state and NGO vanguards have responded to the emergence of a politics of the poor with strikingly similar paranoia and authoritarianism' (2008, p86; also see Gibson, 2008). Conversely, some NGO leaders are acutely aware of the danger of institutionalizing the struggles of emerging movements or of speaking for them.

References

Ballard, R., Habib, A. and Valodia, I. (eds) (2006) *Voices of protest. Social movements in post-apartheid South Africa*, University of KwaZulu-Natal Press, Scottsville

Böll, Foundation (2007) *Democracy and human rights in Africa*, available from www.boell.de/worldwide/africa/africa-4834.html [Accessed 2 December 2007]

Bond, P. (2007) Volatile capitalism and global poverty. *SANPAD Poverty Challenge Conference* Durban, South Africa

Chambers, S., Chambers, S. and Kymlicka, W. (eds) (2002) 'A critical theory of civil society', *Alternative conceptions of civil society*, Princeton University Press, Oxford

Charles Stewart Mott Foundation (2007) *About Mott: civil society*, available from www.mott.org/about/programs/civilsociety/southafrica.aspx [Accessed 2 December 2007]

Desai, A. (2002) *We are the poors. Community struggles in post-apartheid South Africa*, Monthly Review Press, New York

Edwards, M. (2004) *Civil society*, Polity, Cambridge

Edwards, G., Roberts, J.M. and Crossley, N. (eds) (2004) Habermas and social movements: what's 'new'?. *After Habermas: new perspectives on the public sphere*, Blackwell, Oxford

Elliott, C.M. (ed) (2003) *Civil society and democracy. A reader*, Oxford University Press, Oxford

Fraser, N. and Elliott, C.M. (eds) (2003) Rethinking the public sphere: a contribution to the critique of actually existing democracy. *Civil society and democracy. A reader*, Oxford University Press, Oxford

Gibson, N.C. (2008) 'Introduction: a new politics of the poor emerges from South Africa's shantytowns', *Journal of Asian and African Studies*, 43:(1), pp5–17

Habermas, J. (1987) *The theory of communicative action. Vol. 2. Lifeworld and system: a critique of functionalist reason*, Polity, Cambridge

Habermas, J. (1996) *Between facts and norms: contributions to a discourse theory of law and democracy*, MIT Press, Cambridge, MA

Habib, A., Daniel, J. and Southall, R. (eds) (2003) 'State-civil society relations in post-apartheid South Africa', *State of the nation. South Africa 2003–2004*, Human Sciences Research Council, Cape Town

Howell, J. and Pearce, J. (2001) *Civil society and development. A critical exploration*, Lynne Rienner, London

Li, T.M. (2007) *The will to improve. Governmentality, development and the practice of politics*, Duke University Press, London

Mangcu, X. (2008) *To the brink: the state of democracy in South Africa*, University of KwaZulu-Natal Press, Scottsville

McKinley, D. (unpublished) *Wither civil society in South Africa?*

Pieterse, E. (1997) 'South African NGOs and the trials of transition', *Development in Practice*, 7:(2), pp157–166

Pithouse, R. (2008) 'A politics of the poor: shack dwellers' struggles in Durban', *Journal of Asian and African Studies*, 43:(1), pp63–94

Putnam, R. (1993) *Making democracy work: civic traditions in modern Italy*, Princeton University Press

Putnam, R. (1995) 'Bowling alone: America's declining social capital', *Journal of Democracy*, 6:(1), pp65–78

23

Bridging Gaps: Collaboration between Research and Operational Organizations

James L. Garrett

The Potential of Collaboration

Information is essential to improving organizational effectiveness. The potential for benefits from collaboration between a research organization and an operational NGO seems large. The NGO can tap into the latest knowledge and learn how to improve its own survey and analytical methods. This can in turn strengthen its show of impact and innovation to donors. By working with NGOs, researchers can get a better sense of critical policy and programme questions and shape their work to demand, thereby increasing the probability that others will actively make use of their findings.

This Practical Note builds on the insights of Laura Roper's 2002 article on 'Achieving successful academic – practitioner research collaborations' by reviewing one example of such collaboration, a partnership between CARE and the International Food Policy Research Institute (IFPRI). Since 1997, CARE and IFPRI have collaborated on increasing knowledge about urban livelihoods that will be of use to programme development. The two have worked in a number of countries, including livelihood assessments in Tanzania, issue-based research in Bangladesh, technical assistance in Mozambique and programme assessment in Peru and Ethiopia. Examining their collaborative efforts, this paper provides a concrete illustration of how to build bridges and profit from synergies between two such organizations while highlighting potential bumps to expect along the way and what to do about them.

The Gap

Despite the apparent benefits, explicit collaborations between research and operational organizations are not common. Institutional perceptions throw up barriers to working together. The roots of the problem may be primarily differences in organizational culture and intellectual approach (Roper, 2002). NGOs may see research organizations as too theoretical, too slow, too expensive and ignorant of the 'Real World'. On the other hand, some researchers believe that NGOs are too ideological, too activist, too 'quick and dirty' and generally ignorant of what it takes to generate reliable information.

These perceptions are too stark to reflect reality, but there are differences between the two types of organization. Many of these differences revolve around useful parallels. In broad strokes, research organizations produce information. Operational organizations use it. Research institutions analyse policies, evaluate programmes, think in general terms and usually target higher-level audiences, such as policy-makers, donors and academics. Operational organizations work under (and may attempt to change) policies, implement programmes, act more concretely and target their programmes to individuals and households. These parallels can provide important commonalities around which actions can fit and shared interests emerge.

The most outstanding commonality is information: as users, NGO staff want information that is practical, provides concrete, specific answers and gives clear direction for action. They seek information that adds value to what they already know. NGO staff often have years of experience. What does a researcher know that they don't about project design, implementation, monitoring and evaluation of programmes?

As information suppliers, researchers must be able to relate their often general knowledge to a specific context. Any additional research must focus on the specific situation. The research community, though, pulls researchers in the opposite direction, asking them to draw general conclusions from their work.

Collaborators should build on these different perceptions, not attempt to remake the other in their own image. Ultimately, NGOs have a comparative advantage in terms of knowledge about the design, implementation and operation of programmes in the field. Research organizations have a comparative advantage in methods to produce, analyse, publish and disseminate information produced by rigorous processes. Researchers can often raise key questions about programme operation, while implementing organizations often focus almost exclusively on specific management and reporting issues. For instance, when CARE staff in Bangladesh identified questions for research, they highlighted personnel and reporting requirements, not 'higher-level' issues of potential design changes to improve impact.

Bridging the Gap

Understanding these needs and differences is key to bridging gaps. Roper (2002) identifies several models of cooperation, whereby the researchers serve as consultants or trainers, document organizational practice, develop the theoretical literature or pursue a more collaborative process of learning. These models are not exclusive and the type of engagement differs depending on the type of NGO (and research or consulting firm) involved. The internal dynamics of each institution will also shape the nature of the collaboration.

Regardless of the model, some principles to bridge the gap include:

- identification of common ground, institutional advantages and synergies;
- identification of a mutually understood knowledge gap;
- identification of usable activities and outputs to fill that gap;

- identification of entry points for research via current institutional mechanisms;
- dissemination of information.

How did the IFPRI-CARE partnership reflect these principles?

Common ground and synergies

The two organizations had a mutual interest in urban poverty and hunger. CARE-USA headquarters had highlighted urban livelihood insecurity as an area to emphasise in future programming. A few country offices had urban programmes, such as Peru and Zambia. Others, like Bangladesh, were planning work in urban areas. Their interests meshed with IFPRI's, which had just begun a multi-country research programme on urban livelihood, food and nutrition security.

The organizations also shared institutional missions: to be leaders in how to help the poor and vulnerable in developing countries. CARE and IFPRI both had a commitment to innovation and excellence, with IFPRI aiming to produce cutting-edge policy analysis and CARE seeking to develop effective programming in a creative way. Interests and goals overlapped.

Finding the part of the organization that shares a research perspective on knowledge is important. Cash-strapped country offices are not likely to support research that generates 'general knowledge' (rather than information relevant to a specific project), unless it is for a new programme area. In addition, country funds are often only for operational purposes. An NGO's head office, however, is usually more interested in gleaning lessons applicable across countries and may be able to assist.

Cross-project synergies can open up possibilities for funding and knowledge generation. For studies of community-driven development in Madagascar and Zambia, for instance, IFPRI leveraged funds from a World Bank project looking at the same topic while CARE headquarters, regional offices and country missions added their own funds to the pool. Synergies also arise as the research organization brings to bear knowledge generated by other projects. For example, recently completed research from other IFPRI studies on public works in South Africa shed light on CARE's experiences with food-for-work (FFW) programmes in Ethiopia and Peru.

Knowledge gaps

Head office advisers were aware that country offices had limited experience with city-based programmes or had not yet documented their urban experiences. IFPRI had recently completed a comprehensive literature review on urban issues. IFPRI and CARE could then match knowledge needs with knowledge availability and identify gaps to be addressed.

Usable activities and outputs

Different types of collaboration may be appropriate at different times. An initial engagement might simply build trust through categorization of the organization's current knowledge. Later work could proceed to more rigorous research (Roper, 2002). Researchers and CARE staff together identified specific activities or outputs that would be useful in the short, medium and long term. These included technical assistance and guidelines for rapid assessments as well as specific studies on various aspects of urban livelihoods.

Products generally fell into the following categories:

- conceptual frameworks, to use for understanding potential areas of intervention and designing programming activities;
- general knowledge to provide context, lessons and insights;
- methods for data collection and analysis in monitoring and evaluation;
- best practices, identifying what works and what doesn't in programme design and implementation;
- capacity building to conduct, direct and use research.

Entry points

Operational organizations often follow a specific project cycle in carrying out programming: consultation, assessment, formulation and design, implementation, operation, monitoring and evaluation. This cycle can provide strategic points of entry for the research, with research supporting each stage as needed. For instance, in Mozambique and Tanzania IFPRI joined CARE teams in the diagnostic phase to plan and carry out rapid livelihood security assessments. In Bangladesh, IFPRI worked with CARE staff to strengthen monitoring and evaluation methodologies and train them in field techniques. CARE staff have now adopted many of these tools for work in other cities, which they carry out themselves.

One danger is that commissioned research will be disembodied, especially when demand originates in headquarters and not in the country office. Country-level staff may not see how the research fits and supports their work and view it as an additional burden. To reduce the burden and promote ownership, IFPRI took advantage of the project cycle to tie research more closely with project activities and build incrementally on previously planned research and evaluation. For example, the CARE urban livelihoods programme in Bangladesh needed to conduct a baseline survey; researchers modified modules in this survey to include data useful for a number of other studies, including the dynamics of urban livelihoods and the social status of women.

Dissemination

For a research organization, dissemination of knowledge is a primary mission. With the proliferation of information technologies even in developing countries, postings to the websites of headquarters, country offices or projects can disseminate information to multiple audiences (although fairly passively) at relatively low cost. More actively, research from the collaboration, produced in-house in a number of formats, reaches a variety of audiences through IFPRI's extensive mailing list.

Though these general guidelines are fairly concrete, the 'softer' aspects of institutional and interpersonal relations are often the fundamental determinants of success or failure. In the end, researchers have to think hard about soft things, like personal relations, organizational missions and management. These are not skills that come easily to those used to working independently on research issues they have chosen. Personalities and cultures that mesh or conflict can make or break the relationship. Flexibility and awareness of the need for continuous contact and mutual education over time as players and institutional perspectives change are essential.

Roper (2002) suggests that the organizations need to 'learn how to learn together'. By listening with respect and communicating openly and honestly, an organization can understand how and why the other does certain things in a certain way. Each can grow to appreciate the focus of and constraints upon the other. In most cases, this means working within pre-established structures, standard operating procedures and conceptual frameworks. The organizations can then work within those parameters to shape useful processes and outputs.

Bumpy bridges

The discussion so far makes collaboration seem almost easy. Yet, despite best efforts, attempts to construct bridges between the two types of organization are often quite bumpy experiences. From a researcher's perspective, chief causes include:

- short time horizon of the operational organization;
- demand for technical assistance;
- variation in schedule and focus of a project;
- differences over acceptable precision;
- limited capacity for appreciating and using research findings;
- concern for meeting reporting requirements.

Short time horizon

Operational organizations frequently feel that they do not have the luxury of commissioning research that takes place over months or years. NGO staff often do not fully recognize that if the information does not exist, failing to do the research will not provide the information they need any faster. It simply means that decisions will be based on less information.

Part of the frustration arises from staff who feel research generates the same data as their own management information systems. They find it hard to believe a researcher's claim that generating 'the same information' will take longer. This partly reflects a genuine need for less precision and partly a lack of appreciation of the research process. Researchers may also be wed to certain methods and approaches, and may need to be innovative in order to shorten the amount of time needed to obtain research outputs.

Operational organizations generally work with a shorter time horizon than research organizations. Particularly in the start-up phase of a project, they need information and assistance within a particular timeframe, one that was not always planned far ahead. The researcher may be able to respond to NGO demands in the shorter term by identifying discrete issues that take less time to investigate and by disseminating information as the research goes along.

The organizations may also find it useful to establish a medium-term workplan with specific tasks and outputs from the start, rather than working only under more general guidelines of, say, 'carry out operations research' or 'undertake an impact evaluation'. Such a workplan demonstrates value to an operational organization more clearly and fits more comfortably with its usual frame of operation of dealing with consultants with specific, time-bound tasks. This exercise can also alert the researcher to problems in issue identification, expectations, or capacity to use and disseminate the research.

Demand for technical assistance

Given the focus on project management, NGOs frequently look to researchers for day-to-day assistance. Although researchers may want to respond to these queries, getting involved in daily operations can pull them away from longer-term research – and often contractual – commitments. Both organizations must be clear about responsibilities and divisions of labour from the beginning. To maintain a focus on in-depth research, a research firm may turn over requests for technical assistance or routine reports, like baselines, to another organization, such as a consulting firm.

Variation in schedule and focus

Projects in the field hardly ever follow a perfectly linear trajectory. Problems with funding or partnerships can delay start-up. Parts of the project continue while others experience bottlenecks. Even the same project components may move differently because they are implemented at different times in different places. This can complicate research, which often presumes a stable progression of the project. Surveys must plan for starts and stops and adjust to variations in implementation, including changes in leadership and strategic direction. IFPRI has now found that in the start-up phase it is easier to undertake research that produces thematic information not specifically dependent on the project's progress. Until a project is functionally stable, useful research is more likely to focus on design issues, and not a rigorous determination of impact.

Differences over acceptable precision

NGOs seldom need information of academic quality, in part because they work in a world where the academic assumptions of 'all other things being constant' do not hold. Consequently, they are less appreciative and less willing to support academic-level rigour in terms of money or time. Findings from a few quickly formed focus groups or from more careful ethnographic research both produce words. Data from a poorly drawn sample or a carefully drawn one both produce numbers. To many NGO staff the difference in results (or quality) produced by these contrasting methods is not clear, provided 'expert consultants' have generated them both.

Explaining the concept of quality in data and the importance of methodological rigour is difficult but necessary. The researcher must be able to show how more and less rigorous processes affect the confidence the organization can place in the results of the study, and therefore the confidence it can place in its actions. At the same time, the researcher must be careful to weigh precision against need. The additional rigour may not, in fact, be necessary. An NGO may be satisfied with being confident that 90 per cent of the time the true value is within 10 percentage points, while academic standards would require 95 per cent confidence. In qualitative work, a reasonable, if not academically rigorous, selection of groups to interview may give sufficient insight into community relations to know what the primary problems are, or whether or not an approach will work. Appreciation of the needs of the other can allow for compromises that meet the needs of both researchers and NGO staff.

Capacity to own, direct and use research

The researcher will almost always need to develop the capacity of the NGO to own, direct, and use the research – and may have to do this repeatedly as staff change. In Bangladesh, CARE's research-oriented assistant country director, who initiated the original collaboration and guided it through the funding process, left. The collaboration was reconfigured to carry out thematic studies on project-related topics, but later project coordinators could not envision how to use the more general knowledge generated by these studies to improve their own project. Because of problems with start-up, usable outputs were delayed and lower-level staff and upper management saw few outputs of value to them from the project. Without genuine ownership of the collaboration by CARE, support dwindled and the collaboration was halted before the research was completed or findings disseminated.

Changes in the vision or strategy of other stakeholders, such as funders, can also impact the effectiveness of research collaboration. Urban issues had always had difficulty obtaining a place in USAID's Title II-funded programmes, but in Bangladesh a new and particularly unenthusiastic country director arrived just at the time of the initial funding submission. He questioned any investment in urban issues, particularly research, although this was only a small part of the overall proposal. After CARE staff took him to see the deprivation found in urban slums, he changed his mind and supported the work.

One major lesson from these experiences is that the researcher must constantly work with the project supervisors, staff, organizational management and donors to ensure broad support for the research, to create the capacity among stakeholders to see the benefits of such research, and ultimately use the data and findings. This is often not an easy task.

NGO staff seldom have training in how to apply conceptual models or general knowledge to their specific situation, or in the use of analytic skills and tools. Instead, they see the money spent on research as funds that could be used for direct programme support and data as simply fulfilling reporting requirements. In fact, research represents an investment in improving the project and data are the stock of information needed to do that.

Building the analytical, conceptual and data management capacities of staff (without transforming the NGO into a research organization) is essential to increase the NGO's sense of ownership and usefulness of research. On the analytical and conceptual side, effective collaboration requires that the NGO identify a project contact who 'buys into' the research, who champions it and who can identify useful outputs. This person should be able to think 'beyond the project'– that is, understand the value of sharing experiences with others beyond project staff and of generating information on issues beyond day-to-day operations (such as studies on governance systems or validation of indicators). This person is usually the project manager but could be another trusted staff person or intermediary.

On the data management side, staff should learn to access and analyse the data to answer specific questions about project design and management, thereby continuing to increase project effectiveness even after the final report has been delivered. In all cases, the research organization must be sure to provide information in usable, understandable formats (such as briefs, presentations and newsletters).

Whereas the management may previously have balked at paying 'high' costs for a one-off information-gathering exercise, with increased capacity the organization begins to see the advantage of commissioning high-quality data-gathering exercises. The costs of producing high-quality information become more reasonable with continued use of the data. Understanding, rather than criticizing, the organization's lack of research orientation leads to a sharpening of the contributions that both an operational and a research organization can make.

Concern for meeting reporting requirements

Finally, internal and donor requirements often drive the actions of operational NGOs. Monitoring and evaluation proceed along a pre-established path with pre-established indicators. The research may need to bend to that timetable and those indicators. In Bangladesh, for example, IFPRI made CARE's donor and internal reports part of the research plan. The more rigorous 'academic' reports or simpler summaries could serve most reporting purposes.

Conclusion

In conclusion, there are reasons and ways for a research organization to work with an operational organization. But researchers must understand NGOs' needs and perspectives, and likewise explain to them the focus and constraints of a research organization. The key is to identify the 'space' within NGOs where a research organization can contribute. Researchers can then use their comparative advantage to bridge the gap and answer questions important to the NGO in ways that fit with its institutional world.

Reference

Roper, L. (2002) 'Achieving successful academic–practitioner research collaborations', *Development in Practice*, 12(3&4): pp338–345

24

NGOs and Communication: Divorce over the Toothpaste

Alfonso Gumucio-Dagron

Introduction

Exactly the same happens with NGOs and communication as with multilateral organizations (UN) or bilateral agencies: they don't get it. Both imagine communication as institutional visibility or, in the best scenario, as information dissemination. None understands the role of communication as facilitating dialogue, enhancing participation in the decision-making process and ensuring sustainability of social and economic change.

This is particularly worrying in the world of development NGOs, since they are supposed to be closer to communities, working for the well-being of people at the grassroots, the 'poorest of the poor'. Communication should be their daily currency to relate to development issues and social change, but instead is generally ignored or misunderstood. There should be a perfect marriage between communication and non-governmental organizations to avoid red tape in their work, but instead, it is like a couple who don't get along because of the toothpaste or the toilet seat.

No matter how important 'communication' sounds in the discourse of all international development organizations, including the smallest national NGOs and the World Bank, the fact is that none, or very few, has a sincere, consequent and clear understanding of communication as a privileged approach to development and civic-driven social change.

This assertion is easily sustained when putting NGOs under the light of three main criteria:

1 Have they developed their own communication policy?
2 Have they allocated sufficient funds to communication?
3 Have they hired staff who are specialized in communication for development and social change?

The answer to these three questions might be 'no' three times in a row, particularly because the three criteria are interdependent. We cannot imagine better allocating funds or hiring high-level professional communication staff if there are no policies in place that commit the organization to an approach to communication that diverges from the business-as-usual information dissemination and propaganda.

Policies and strategies

Every organization involved in development has a defined policy and strategy that guides its operations and its mere existence. The policy is based on a philosophy of social change, a conceptual framework where the general objectives are set and justification is provided on 'why' the organization gets involved in a particular field of work.

Without analysis and internal discussion of the principles and without a vision and mission, an organization would have a hard time setting up a policy that guides its work; and without a policy there cannot be a strategy that lays out the concrete plan to accomplish. Organizations normally have a mission, a vision and a policy paper that covers the mains issues they are dealing with (health, human rights, education, etc.) but very seldom have they reflected on 'how' they communicate in a concrete reality in a geographical space or defined human universe.

Communication is essential to 'how' an intervention is implemented; at least that is what most organizations would declare. However very few have taken steps in the direction that is needed: discussion of what kind of communication is appropriate in order to define a philosophy or conceptual framework, as well as an institutional policy from which strategies will flow.

Allocation of funds

Most organizations allocate funds for 'communication', but their understanding of communication is so confused that the funds are usually utilized for information dissemination through mass media and/or for institutional propaganda through commercial advertising agencies. People with whom they work are absent since communication is conceived as a bunch of messages to deliver, and not as a process of establishing channels of dialogue with people.

Funding related to information and communication should be clearly separated, because the usual tendency is that information dissemination and institutional image building will take the lion's share and very little will be left for real communication activities that entail participation in the process of change.

Funding specifically marked for communication activities is the guarantee of civic-driven change where people have their say. It is very important that NGOs (and any other development organizations) transcend the vertical ways of operating, where decisions are made at the top by those who attract the funding or those that get it in the name of the communities in need.

The World Congress on Communication for Development (WCCD) held in Rome in 2006 clearly recommended that funds should be specifically assigned to communication for development. During the discussions at the WCCD, it was agreed that at least 6 per cent of the funding of each programme or project should be marked for communication for development.

Qualified staff

In the hypothetical scenario that an NGO has developed its conceptual framework, a policy paper and a strategy for communication for development and social change, and has also allocated a percentage of funding to the specific activities, the NGO still needs qualified and experienced professionals to lead the conceptual platform and to implement the strategy.

The word 'qualified' is not negligible because we have seen too much improvization both in NGOs and in other international development organizations, who are used to assigning communication responsibilities to anyone, even someone not related to communication, or outsourcing to advertising agencies.

The worst case I have seen is assigning communication responsibilities to staff who are otherwise 'doing nothing' (in other words, who have plenty of time for it). The second worst case I have seen too often is assigning communication responsibilities to medical staff (nurses, doctors) on health programmes or to engineers on safe water projects with the ridiculous argument that 'everyone has to be a communicator'. It is like saying that anyone should be able to compile statistics or draw up public health plans just because it is much needed.

This approach taken by development bureaucrats, never by communication specialists, leads to varnishing staff from any sector with a coat of short-term workshops where they learn generalities. In my work in UNICEF, in Africa and Latin America, I have seen staff permanently away from work because of this workshop culture that has blossomed.

Hiring journalists to do the work of communicators is also a bad idea and it doesn't work at all. It works for information dissemination, producing messages, posters or press conferences, but it doesn't work in support of a communication process that is inclusive and democratic, horizontal and dialogic.

At the World Congress on Communication for Development (WCCD) participants specifically argued that the academic field of communication for development needs to be strengthened to meet the needs of high-level posts for communication professionals in NGOs and other international development and aid organizations.

The Rome Consensus

The WCCD was a milestone for development communication, not only because of its discussions and final recommendations, which are the daily bread of development communicators in the world over decades, but particularly because of the level and influence of the three organizations that organized the congress: the Food and Agricultural Organization (FAO), the World Bank and the Communication Initiative.

The final document, the 'Rome Consensus', should be a key reference document for all organizations getting involved in another communication for another development. These were the recommendations:

1   Overall national development policies should include specific communication for development components
2   Development organizations should include communication for development as a central element at the inception of programmes
3   Communication for development capacity should be strengthened within countries and organizations at all levels. This includes people in their communities,

communication for development specialists and other staff, including through the further development of training courses and academic programmes

4 The level of financial investment should be expanded to ensure adequate, coordinated, financing of the core elements of communication for development as outlined under Strategic Requirements above. This includes budget line[s] for development communication

5 Policies and legislation that provide an enabling environment for communication for development should be adopted and implemented – including free and pluralistic media, the right to information and to communication

6 Development communication programmes should be required to identify and include appropriate monitoring and evaluation indicators and methodologies throughout the process

7 Partnerships and networks should be strengthened at international, national and local levels to advance communication for development and improve development outcomes

8 There should be a move towards a rights-based approach to communication for development.

And the entire document ended: 'As Nelson Mandela highlighted it is people that make the difference. Communication is about people. Communication for development is essential to make the difference happen.'[1]

The Role of Universities

Universities and research centres can play an important role in development when they break out of the ivory tower and apply to reality the theoretical construction they have been working on. In terms of communication, NGOs should outsource to universities that have communication departments with emphasis in communication and social change, rather than using advertising agencies to promote important development issues as if they were a soft drink or a travel destination.

True, very few universities are currently equipped to offer the profile of communication professionals that are needed. Most even equate 'communication' departments or faculties to the old journalism schools.[2] Someone, four decades ago, had the bright idea of changing the name of journalism studies to 'social communication', a brand that is now current in thousands of universities that, in fact, basically train journalists for the media (print, television, radio, film), for public relations (pretty faces) and to be advertising designers. All of these are technical careers that have little to do with the mission of higher education which is to develop science and knowledge. Thousands of these students graduate every year all over the world and too many are desperately looking for jobs in television, newspapers or advertising agencies. Often they end up writing corporate newsletters, press releases or organizing press conferences.

Ironically, on the other hand, many communication professionals are needed in development to support participatory processes for civic-driven change. When a development programme is looking for this profile of communicator, usually hundreds of journalists apply. Which is why things are as they are: just look at the zillions spent in ineffective campaigns for HIV-AIDS in Africa. In contrast, communication as a participatory process implemented by many NGOs in Brazil since the 1980s has contributed to halt HIV-AIDS. South Africa and Brazil had similar statistics in the early 1980s in relation to AIDS; today there is a world of difference.

Several thousand universities in the world offer studies in journalism (so called 'social communication') and hundreds offer postgraduate studies (diplomas, masters or other specialization) focusing on mass media, corporate 'communication' and the like. Fewer than 25 universities worldwide offer specialization in communication for development and social change.

Asia was the first region to acknowledge the importance of this field. More than 30 years ago the university of The Philippines at Los Baños started a development communication programme in support of rural community development. Today, it is the only university that offers Communication for Development studies at three levels: graduate, masters and PhD. In India, three universities hold the banner: the Centre of Communication for Development at the University of Gujarat and two masters degrees at University of Pantnagar and Jamia Millia Islamia in Delhi. Pakistan has the Centre for Rural Development Communication (CRDC) at the University of Sindh near Jamshoro.

Latin America has also traditionally been fertile ground for the development of communication studies, partly because it is in this region where dependency theories came to life and the first criticism of 'diffusion of innovation' – the US academic cornerstone for development communication – was formulated. The Universidad de La Plata in Argentina offers the prestigious masters degree on planning and management of communication programmes (PLANGESCO), while more recent and less established initiatives exist in Peru, Uruguay, Bolivia, Colombia, Guatemala and Cuba. Ironically two large countries with deep social inequalities, such as Brazil and Mexico, do not have universities offering specialized studies in communication for development and social change.

There are very few courses in Africa, where most are focused on journalism and democracy, which is understandable: the first and most urgent priority in countries that have lived or are still under strong authoritarian rules is to gain space for free press and freedom of expression. Communication for development should be the concern of NGOs or the United Nations concern, if at all, but not of universities, with one or two exceptions, such as the diploma and MA. Theatre and Media Communication in Development is offered by the University of Malawi.

Two universities in Spain (Universidad Internacional de Andalucia and Universidad de Salamanca) offer recently created masters degrees on communication for development. In Sweden, University of Malmo in conjunction with Roskilde University in Denmark, has promoted this emphasis in their communication studies. The United Kingdom offers an MSc in Media, Communication and Development at the London School of Economics (LSE), and though the word communication is not mentioned in the MA on Participation, Power and Social Change at the Institute for Development Studies (IDS) in Sussex, much of their work is conceptually similar to communication for development. A similar example is the Institute of Social Studies (ISS) in The Hague. Other European countries with large bilateral cooperation agencies and many development NGOs seem oblivious of the importance of communication in development and civic-driven change.

In the US and Canada we can only mention two examples. Ohio University has a prestigious and multicultural MA in International Affairs: Communication and Development Studies (MAIA), whereas The School of Environmental Design and Rural Development at The University of Guelph in Canada offers an online certificate in Communication Process: Bridging Theory and Practice.

It is worth noting that most of the specialized studies in communication for development have not grown out of the classic 'social communication' (journalism) schools, but from other areas related to research and praxis in rural development, health or human rights.

NGOs should develop better links with the universities mentioned above, in their respective regions, for at least two main reasons: a) to help to define the profile of studies needed for a facilitator of civic-driven change with development communication skills, and b) to hire from among university graduates the communicators they really need for their development programmes, instead of journalists or public relations managers.

Rights-based Approach

Most NGOs now claim that their work is conceptually guided by a 'rights-based approach'. This has become another buzzword not only for NGOs, but also for United Nations agencies and funds such as UNICEF.

Rights are entitlements and norms that establish constraints and obligations in the interactions between people and/or institutions, based on the principle that every human being is entitled to minimum conditions of freedom and dignity, regardless of nationality, origin, gender, skin colour, religion, language or any other status. Human rights protect people from political, legal, social and other abuses.

With respect to human rights, international laws include: procedural rights (to acquire information and access justice) and substantive rights (to life, health, education, culture, communication and freedom from discrimination, political rights). Rights are universal (apply to anyone and everywhere in the world), indivisible (they all have equal status for human dignity), interrelated and interdependent.

Because all human beings have equal rights without discrimination of any kind, participation and inclusion are a key element: all people are entitled to free and active participation in governance systems in which human rights and fundamental freedoms can be realized, and states are accountable for it.

The Rights-Based Approach (RBA) integrates human rights principles, norms and standards into policies, planning, implementation and evaluation, ensuring that development programmes and projects respect the human rights framework. Key elements of the RBA embrace identifying all relevant rights claims and obligations, including collective rights; using rights principles to guide policy; assessing and monitoring processes against rights-based criteria; addressing the underlying causes of rights violations, often due to inequitable power relations; strengthening the capacity of rights holders and duty bearers to claim their rights and meet their responsibilities; taking measures to respect rights, particularly for the most vulnerable (Campese et al, 2009).

The right to communicate is a human right, however it is often circumvented and reduced to 'freedom of expression' which is the right of those that already have the means to express themselves. Shouldn't the right to communicate also be part of the rights-based approach, particularly when this is the right that will allow people and communities to have a voice of their own and to participate in the decision-making process? Isn't it quite contradictory to put human rights at the centre of development while conveniently leaving aside the right to communicate? How often do we see the right to communicate in the platforms of those organizations declaring that they are very progressive because they subscribe to or use a rights-based approach?

Voices in Development

Development is a word with future. Although tainted by multiple meanings through history, and recently criticized because it often relates to more harm than good, it still synthesizes for people a horizon of better life through social change. The word echoes desires, dreams and expectations. Because of its multiple meanings, it has been complemented with adjectives, for precision sake, such as 'human development', or 'sustainable development' or 'endogenous development'.

Throughout history, two main concepts of development – and of communication – have clashed. After World War II and the Marshall Plan, development was strongly associated with economic growth (and still is). The 'modernization' paradigm that reigned mainly from 1945 to 1965 assumed that the origin of poverty resided in traditional societies that were unable, because of their culture, to reach the level of well-being of 'advanced' societies. This concept of development is unidirectional and attempts to measure development quantitatively in comparison with modern societies. In terms of communication, it assumes that information dissemination is the key to knowledge creation, thus mass media plays an important role in the 'diffusion of innovations' that can end poverty through adopting new behaviours.

From the early 1960s, a different concept of development grew in Third World countries, particularly in Latin America, where the modernization approach was severely questioned. The 'dependency' theories offered a structural perspective of poverty, based on the unfair international trade relations, as well as on local inequalities and lack of social justice. In terms of communication, it analyses the unbalances in information flows, the hegemonic place of mass media from the north, particularly from the United States, and the need to develop local voices and local media to strengthen local participation in the decision-making process. The MacBride report is one of the seminal contributions to this perspective (MacBride, 1980). The failure of development policies from the 1970s and the clash between two approaches to communication resulted in numerous new horizontal experiences of participatory communication for social change, and the appearance of new theoretical contributions from Antonio Pasquali, Luis Ramiro Beltran and Juan Diaz Bordenave, among others.

From the 1980s on, other theoretical variants have joined the discussion, such as the 'multiplicity' approach (Servaes, 1989) which attaches more importance to cultural identities and the global impacts of the world crisis, in all its manifestations: economic, financial, social, etc. The study of multiple relations between the centre and the periphery, the global and the local, are key to this approach, which promotes a development concept aiming at produce structural changes, very much as the dependency theory had suggested.

Human development, adopted by the United Nations as the ruler for its progress reports, no longer focuses on quantitative aspects and economic growth alone, but attempts to provide data on other important indicators, such as equity in access to resources, sustainability of resources and institutions, knowledge creation and exchanges and participation. This fourth element is crucial to the communication approach.

The international community has the technical tools to address development challenges, however technical solutions alone are often insufficient, because human beings are not pure numbers and in the real world development and social change will not be sustainable without the participation and voice of citizens. There are many lessons to be learned from practitioners and researchers, and from the theories and practices of the field of communication and other social sciences.

In its white paper *Making Governance work for the Poor*, the UK Department for International Development (DFID) defines good governance as not being just about government. 'It is also about political parties, parliament, the judiciary, the media, and civil society. It is about how citizens, leaders and public institutions relate to each other in order to make change happen.' The document points out that good governance requires three things: state capability – the extent to which leaders and government are able to get things done; responsiveness – whether public policies and institutions respond to the needs of citizens and uphold their rights; and accountability – the ability of citizens, civil society and the private sector to scrutinize public institutions and governments and hold them to account (DFID, 2006).

Even the World Bank acknowledges the importance of participatory communication in governance reform, development and social change:

> Communication has something unique to offer governance reform by facilitating the development of democratic practices that are not limited to the ballot box. These are practices that comprise the public surveillance of government activities, public debates within civil society regarding interlocking and often contesting interests, and publicizing social services. Communication approaches and techniques can be used to successfully deal with and mitigate the above-mentioned challenges. Communication links the constitutive elements of the public sphere – engaged citizenries, vibrant civil societies, plural and independent media systems, and open government institutions – and thus forms the framework for national dialogue through which informed public opinion is shaped about key issues of public concern and public policy. (World Bank, 2008)

The demand side of governance should consist in strengthening public will through participatory and deliberative approaches. Democratic engagement, central to civic-driven change, can be enabled and encouraged by public deliberation. Communities at all levels need to have the means to speak up with a collective and independent voice.

Again, too often the discourse – written by independent consultants – is well ahead of the ways things are implemented by pension-prone managers sitting in their offices. Reality shows that 'voices' are not really heard, and no effort is really made to amplify them. The truth is that loud voices usually demand a saying in the decision-making process, and this is so political that most development organizations shy away, even NGOs.

On the Ground

NGOs have an enormous responsibility on the ground, because they are closer to people than large development organizations, unless they become so large that they also lose contact with reality. There are many ways to intervene in the public sphere, and NGOs need to reason why and how they want to affect the balances of power where all stakeholders meet.

> In classical theory, the public sphere is the space between government and society in which private individuals exercise formal and informal control over the state: formal control through the election of governments and informal control through the pressure of public opinion. The media are central to this process. They distribute information necessary to citizens to make an informed choice at election time, they facilitate the formation of public opinion by providing an independent forum of debate and they enable people to shape the conduct of government by articulating their views. The media are thus the principle institutions of the public sphere. (Dahlgren and Sparks, 1991)

Is media enough? And then, what media and what contents? If NGOs intervene in the public sphere through mass media alone, they risk just adding messages to the information banks, without making a qualitative difference. Does society need more information dissemination to fill the gaps in the public sphere or does it need strong voices with real life stories? And then, what does it take to guarantee that voices are empowered and heard?

NGOs need to reflect on methodological and theoretical knowledge that includes communication policies and their socio-cultural impact in development; they need to promote through the media the presence of local cultures and knowledges as well as participation and citizenship for democracy; they need to support social networks through a process of appropriation of alternative community media, which means not only the management of technologies but the appropriation of the decision-making process of communication for civic-driven change. Thus the importance of the 'third sector' of media in development.

It is ironic that NGOs often prefer commercial media to public media and community media. The latter has proven its contribution over decades in promoting civic-driven change through participatory approaches. It easily connects communication with social processes to enhance the quality of democracy and strengthen the dialogue within the public sphere. Information products or messages are less important here than processes that help to build community through communication. The process of communication, rather than the messages, overflows the limits of information technologies and extends over the ensemble of social practices.

It's not difficult to understand how vital communication is for development and social change for a more sustainable planet. The ways in which we communicate or fail to communicate with one another are an indication of wider global problems. Failure of international bodies to alleviate conflict between and within nations is a good example of what goes wrong when communication breaks down. Missed opportunities in development, which have become so common, are a clear outcome of the failure to understand that effective and sustainable development is, above all, the result of a horizontal dialogue that contributes to create community.

Notes

1   www.comminit.com/redirect.cgi?m=5d1a07c1af1705fbb8161bbdc0d47768
2   Old journalism schools changed their name 40 years ago to 'communication schools', but they are still focusing on media (press, radio, TV), not on the communication processes which are essential to develop horizontal and participatory communication. Journalism is about messages, communication is about processes. Journalists are not communicators.

References

Biekart, K. and A. Fowler (eds) (2008) *Civic Driven Change: Citizens' imagination in action.* The Hague: Institute of Social Studies (ISS)

Campese, J., T. Sunderland, T. Greiber and G. Oviedo (eds) (2009) *Rights-based approaches: exploring issues and opportunities for conservation.* Bogor (Indonesia): CIFOR & IUCN

Dahlgren, P. and C. Sparks (eds) (1991) *Communication and citizenship: journalism and the public sphere.* London & New York: Routledge

DFID (2006*) Eliminating World Poverty: Making Governance Work for the Poor,* Department for International Development, London

DFID (2010) Governance, Development and Democratic Politics DFID's work in building more effective states *Good Governance* available at www.DFID.gov.uk/Global-Issues/How-we-fight-Poverty/Government/Good-Governance (last accessed July 2010)

Fuglesang, A. (1982) *About Understanding: ideas and Observations on Cross-Cultural Communication. Uppsala:* The Dag Hammarskjold Foundation

Gumucio, A. D. (2001) *Making Waves: Stories of Participatory Communication for Social Change.* New York: The Rockefeller Foundation

Hemer, O. and T. Tufte (eds) (2005) *Media & Global Change. Rethinking Communication for Development.* Goteborg: Nordicom

MacBride, S. (ed) (1980) *Many Voices, One World. Communication and society today and tomorrow.* Paris: UNESCO

Odugbemi, S. and T. L. Jacobson (2008) *Governance Reform under Real-World Conditions: Citizens, Stakeholders, and Voice.* Washington: World Bank

Servaes, J. (1989) *One world, multiple cultures: a new paradigm on communication for development.* Leuven: Acco

World Bank (2008) 'Reforming Governance Systems Under Real World Conditions' Brief for Policy Makers, Washington, DC: World Bank http://siteresources.worldbank.org/EXTGO-VACC/Resources/CommGapGovernancePolicyBrief_e.pdf (Accessed August 2010)

Part VII

Managing for Performance

25

Development Effectivness: Towards New Understandings

Shannon Kindornay and Bill Morton

Development Effectiveness and International Aid Actors

Over the last decade, official aid policy debates have increasingly centred on improving aid effectiveness. The origins for this focus can be traced to the 1995 OECD Development Assistance Committee statement, 'Shaping the 21st century'. Momentum grew in the 2000s, with a series of high level forums on aid effectiveness, including the 2005 meeting that resulted in the Paris Declaration. Along with the Millennium Development Goals, the Paris Declaration and its 2008 companion (the Accra Agenda for Action) now represent the key international frameworks for donor and developing country efforts on aid effectiveness.

Aid actors have also been interested in *development* effectiveness for many years, but the concept has only recently gained momentum on the international policy agenda. A number of multilateral and bilateral development agencies have engaged with the concept, and this is articulated in various levels of elaboration across their policies and programmes, and in different understandings of what is meant by development effectiveness. Civil Society Organizations (CSOs) have shown particular interest, and are developing a common policy platform on the issue, as well as analysing their own development effectiveness.

Development effectiveness is likely to be an important agenda item at the 2011 4th High Level Forum on Aid Effectiveness in Busan, South Korea.

While there is considerable consensus on the meaning of aid effectiveness, a common understanding of *development* effectiveness – and its implications for development policy – remains elusive. Instead, the term is used differently by different actors in different contexts. This chapter aims to make a contribution to thinking on development effectiveness by suggesting four categories under which it can be understood, based on how different aid actors describe and use the term.[1] The four categories consider development effectiveness as: 1) organizational effectiveness; 2) coherence or coordination; 3) development outcomes from aid; and 4) overall development outcomes. This research is not exhaustive, but rather represents a starting point for further discussion, and is part of a broader NSI research agenda on development effectiveness. Future studies will benefit by including more aid actors and sources, and in particular by consulting with southern stakeholders.

Aid Effectiveness and Development Effectiveness

Aid effectiveness generally refers to how effective *aid* is in achieving expected outputs and stated objectives of aid interventions. The Paris Declaration serves as a technical representation of this understanding, but does not define aid effectiveness. A 2008 independent evaluation of the Paris Declaration, however, suggests that an understanding of aid effectiveness can be extracted from the Declaration. Aid effectiveness can thus be defined as the 'arrangement for the planning, management and deployment of aid that is efficient, reduces transaction costs and is targeted towards development outcomes including poverty reduction'.[2] Under this definition, aid effectiveness focuses on how aid is used, although the evaluation suggests that it is generally assumed aid has a development-oriented intent.

In contrast, there is considerable scope for interpretation of the term 'development effectiveness' and a lack of clarity regarding what it means in practice. This is most accurately illustrated by the tendency of some analysts and aid agencies to make little distinction between aid effectiveness and development effectiveness, and in some cases, to use the terms interchangeably. The author of an Asian Development Bank Working Paper suggests that the meaning of development effectiveness is self-explanatory: it 'simply refers to the effectiveness of aid in development'. The author also advises that in the paper, 'expressions such as "development effectiveness" and "aid effectiveness" are used to convey the same ideas' and that 'aid effectiveness and development effectiveness are used interchangeably'.[3] Other agencies employ aid effectiveness language and concepts when discussing development effectiveness. The World Bank has published Reviews of Development Effectiveness since the early 1990s, but much of their discourse is framed within aid effectiveness principles and language that are now found in the Paris Declaration. AusAID's Office of Development Effectiveness also appears to consider development effectiveness primarily within an aid effectiveness context. It states its role is to monitor the quality and evaluate the impact of Australia's aid programme and describes its 2007 Annual Review of Development Effectiveness as an 'annual health check of the Australian aid program' (AusAID, 2008). While the review systematically assesses the effectiveness of Australian aid, it does not consider how other non-aid policy areas may have affected development outcomes.

Understanding Development Effectiveness: Four Categories

While the above suggests that some organizations make little distinction between aid effectiveness and development effectiveness, there are many examples in which this is not the case. For a range of actors examined for this study, aid effectiveness is too narrow to describe the results of the overall development process. A reading of their policies and aid strategies suggests four possible categories that serve as a starting point for conceptualizing understandings of development effectiveness. These categories are neither mutually exclusive nor exhaustive and some organizations have understandings that overlap between categories.

Development effectiveness as organizational effectiveness

The concept of development effectiveness has frequently been used by aid agencies, especially multilateral organizations, as a means of assessing the effectiveness of their own policies and programmes. Development effectiveness is thus considered from the supply side, in terms of how well an organization is achieving its stated objectives and goals. There are a number of examples of how multilateral organizations have considered development effectiveness in this way. The World Bank's Annual Reviews of Development Effectiveness look at development effectiveness in terms of organizational performance and outputs. In the 2005 Review, for instance, development effectiveness was measured on multiple levels, through the Bank's global programmes, country programmes and individual projects. The 2008 report assesses outcomes of the Bank's projects and country programmes, as well as its work in fostering global public goods.

The United Nations Development Programme (UNDP) has also published a number of Development Effectiveness Reports. Early reports distinguished between development and organizational effectiveness – but still focused on the efficiency and effectiveness of UNDP's own programmes and projects. The 2001 report suggests that organizational effectiveness measures time-bound organizational objectives and is about results-based management, whereas development effectiveness measures the impact of assistance and progress towards development goals and represents 'the extent to which an institution or intervention has brought about targeted change …'.[4] Despite making this distinction between development and organizational effectiveness, the report's discussion of development effectiveness remains confined to the development impact of UNDP itself, and does not consider external factors such as the role of other development agencies or the impact of non-aid sectors.

In its 2007 Development Effectiveness Report, the International Fund for Agricultural Development (IFAD) provides a useful definition of development effectiveness, suggesting it depends on the collective and coordinated actions by a range of national and external actors, and that it is therefore a measure of these actors' aggregate impact, with accountability for results shared by many. IFAD claims its 2007 Report has a broader scope than those of other organizations' development effectiveness reports, on the basis that it goes beyond reporting on operational effectiveness, and that it is more comprehensive, draws on wider sources and reports on results at the corporate as well as country level. Nevertheless, the report remains focused on development effectiveness in terms of IFAD's own organizational performance (IFAD, 2007).

Each of these examples demonstrates how key multilateral organizations interpret and apply a particular understanding of development effectiveness. As we will see below, UNDP's 2003 report signalled a deliberate move to go beyond considering development effectiveness in terms of organizational performance, and to instead adopt a broader analysis that looks at the final results of the overall development process and at the contribution of a range of relevant players.

Development effectiveness as coherence or coordination

Some actors view development effectiveness in terms of coordinating actions and the consistency of development-related policies. One view, for example, argues that development effectiveness recognizes that non-aid policies affect development processes, thus creating the need for policy coherence across various government departments and policy areas, such as trade, security and immigration. Some bilateral donors follow this understanding of development effectiveness and underline the importance of policy coherence while recognizing that aid is not the only factor affecting development. They emphasize Paris Declaration principles in their approach while policies derived from this conception focus specifically on how donors can improve development effectiveness through internal actions. 'Whole of government' approaches best reflect this rationale, but are often limited by constraints such as the vertical organization of government, wherein departments operate as silos focused on certain policy areas, making horizontal coordination and consistency across policies difficult to achieve. Institutional rivalry and claims on other objectives also limit policy coherence across departments.

Like other studies, the 'Mutual Review of Development Effectiveness in Africa' (Economic Commission for Africa/OECD, 2009) does not attempt to unpack the meaning of development effectiveness. It focuses on the policies that will promote development effectiveness (rather than on desired outcomes). These include supporting sustainable economic growth, investing in education, health and gender equality, promoting good governance and enhancing development finance (including an emphasis on domestic public resources). The review also identifies additional future policy priorities that are implicitly linked to development effectiveness, including advancing African interests in international negotiations on multilateral trade and climate change issues. Overall, the review provides important insights into the range of policies that African governments believe will promote development effectiveness, which supports a policy coherence view of development effectiveness, and which goes well beyond aid.

This view of development effectiveness is also reflected in the Center for Global Development's Commitment to Development Index.[5] This index rates rich countries' performance in supporting development outcomes according to their performance across a range of related policy areas, including aid, trade, migration, investment, environment, security and technology. The conflation of performance in all these policy areas into a single score represents an ambitious undertaking, but it nevertheless reflects an important underlying rationale: that development effectiveness depends on a range of variables and policy areas, and that good performance in one or two areas means little if it is undermined by development-unfriendly policy in other areas.

Development effectiveness as the development outcomes from aid

In this view, aid is measured in terms of development outcomes. Development effectiveness looks specifically at outcomes (rather than at policy areas, or at the efficiency of how each aid dollar is spent). This does not, however, mean aid and development effectiveness are mutually exclusive; rather, they are seen as mutually reinforcing concepts and agendas.

This view is seen predominantly in current CSO conceptions of development effectiveness. These recognize that development effectiveness is a broad concept that goes beyond aid and development cooperation, and that also considers issues such as trade, migration and finance and investment. The current CSO agenda on development effectiveness, however, chooses to focus on development effectiveness in an aid effectiveness context.

This is the result of CSOs' close engagement with the international aid effectiveness agenda and with policy discussions surrounding the 2005 Paris and 2008 Accra High Level Forums (HLF). In the lead up to the Accra HLF, the Better Aid platform, a global CSO grouping, released a policy brief that set out a civil society position on aid effectiveness. The brief signalled CSO's movement towards a development effectiveness agenda, underlining that aid effectiveness should be understood in terms of whether it is meeting development objectives, rather than in terms of improving aid delivery and management issues.[6] The brief challenged donors to move beyond the current technical aid effectiveness agenda, and to more clearly consider the development outcomes resulting from aid.

Following the Accra HLF and in the lead up to the 2011 Busan HLF, development effectiveness has become a major focus for CSOs, including for three related groups: the Better Aid Platform, the CSO Open Forum and the Reality of Aid network. Together, their key policy position is that the international aid effectiveness agenda should be reassessed and reformulated around a development effectiveness agenda. The Reality of Aid network suggests that the 2011 HLF should result in a new 'Busan Declaration', based on a development effectiveness framework. The network has signalled that its 2010 Reality of Aid Report will address the theme 'development effectiveness as the framework in aid and development cooperation through human rights, social justice and democratic development'.[7] In preparation for the 2011 Busan HLF, the Better Aid platform is planning multi-stakeholder consultations that are designed to further develop understandings of development effectiveness and to identify key issues for CSOs to take up with donors and developing countries. The consultations are also designed to inform a revised Policy Brief (due for release in 2010) that will set out a CSO policy position and that will form the basis for engagement with key official aid bodies such as the DAC Working Party on Aid Effectiveness. An early draft of the policy brief emphasizes the need to shift the aid effectiveness agenda towards discussions of development effectiveness and reinforces the Reality of Aid's articulation of the concept. The draft policy brief looks beyond 2011, suggesting that future development cooperation processes should be rights-based and should take into account key elements of social justice, including human rights, gender equality and decent work.[8]

CSOs have also formed the Open Forum for CSO Development Effectiveness, through which they are examining their own development effectiveness and are developing a set of common principles to guide both their own work and preparations for the Busan meeting. Reflecting the Better Aid view, statements made by Open Forum participants indicate they understand development effectiveness in terms of placing human rights, gender equality, environmental sustainability, social justice and democratic ownership at the heart of development.

The United Nations Development Fund for Women (UNIFEM) and the OECD-DAC have also used development effectiveness in terms that reflect CSO understandings. While UNIFEM tends to use the terms development and aid effectiveness interchangeably, it sees gender equality as a determinant of development effectiveness, arguing that it must be considered in all stages of development interventions. The OECD-DAC indicates that a consideration for human rights, gender equality and sustainability is important to achieving Paris Declaration goals. The outcome document to its 2007 workshop, 'Development Effectiveness in Practice', states that 'attention to these issues enhances development effectiveness' and that by addressing these concerns, development goals can be achieved.[9]

Development effectiveness as overall development outcomes

This view overlaps with the other understandings of development effectiveness described here and is the most comprehensive approach of the four categories. Development effectiveness is seen as a measure of the overall development process and is not just restricted to outcomes from aid. It incorporates external and internal factors and has implications for non-aid sectors. Importantly, development outcomes cannot be attributed to any one actor.

An independent review of DFID refers to two forms of effectiveness: operational and development.[10] According to the review, operational effectiveness is based on performance measures of the direct and attributable result of projects, but says very little about overall development outcomes. Development effectiveness, on the other hand, refers to the overall development outcome which, while highly relevant in assessing any aid programme, cannot be directly attributed to any one actor's activities. Development outcomes result from national and international forces, including aid interventions by various actors, the availability of domestic resources, global commodity prices, regional stability and many other determinants. When there is an improvement in overall development, it may arise from any number of factors such as enhanced domestic resource mobilization, improved terms of trade or the culmination of years of aid interventions: discerning exactly which factor has had the greatest effect may be extremely difficult. This is why the DFID review suggests that it is virtually impossible to illustrate a direct link between DFID's activities and progress towards the MDGs, despite its various contributions. For similar reasons, UNDP's 2003 Development Effectiveness Report shows that UNDP interventions could not explain progress in development processes in any given country or sector (UNDP, 2003). Under this view, responsibility for progress lies with all development partners.

UNDP has shifted from looking at how to maximize the value of aid towards placing development at the centre of the aid agenda. Its 2003 report signals a deliberate move from considering development effectiveness in terms of organizational performance towards a broader analysis that looks at the final results of the development process, and at the contribution of relevant players to overall development progress. This means assessing what works and what does not, and then assessing how aid flows can complement these factors. In a more comprehensive understanding of development, the report argues that 'development effectiveness is (or should be) about the factors and conditions that help produce sustainable development results – to make a sustained difference in the lives of people'. Development effectiveness is measured in outcomes, such as meeting human development goals and generating growth (which includes the quality of growth, equity, participation, and sustainability), rather than in terms of how money is spent. UNDP also claims that trade and global policies must also become more development friendly in order to meet the MDGs. Measuring outcomes in this way is consistent with CSO perspectives on development effectiveness, while the inclusion of non-aid factors reflects donors' concern for policy coherence and whole-of-government approaches. The UNDP approach combines the above categories to create a coherent, integrated approach to development effectiveness.

Conclusion and Further Research

As interest grows, it is likely that development effectiveness will gain more attention internationally: there are already indications that it will feature in discussions at the Busan HLF. While CSO momentum is clearly strong, a successful international agenda on development effectiveness will also depend on the active engagement of developing country governments and official aid agencies, and on their willingness to reformulate the current aid effectiveness agenda.

Also required is an appropriate forum where stakeholders can debate the issues, and ultimately move to joint commitments. While the 2011 HLF provides the most obvious starting point, the other possibility is the UN Development Cooperation Forum (DCF). The DCF aims at multi-stakeholder participation, and at ensuring a voice for all countries. At its first meeting, it addressed many aspects of development effectiveness outlined in this chapter, including donor policy coherency across aid and non-aid sectors, and responses to internationally agreed upon development goals, including gender equality, the environment and human rights. A development effectiveness approach could be an appropriate lens for the DCF to adopt in addressing its key work areas (mutual accountability, south-south cooperation and aid policy coherence) in the lead up to its 2010 High Level Meeting.

The creation of a development effectiveness agenda also depends on at least some level of agreement on what is meant by the term. This chapter has suggested four categories of understandings of development effectiveness. More research is required to address this in more detail and to explore the views of official aid agencies and southern stakeholders. Further study is also warranted on whether the four categories are valid and can be improved on, in order to deepen the discussion of development effectiveness and further understand how the concept can be put into practice.

Notes

1   We reviewed official documents of OECD-DAC donor countries, multilateral agencies and CSOs. We also considered non-DAC donors, but public information on their aid and development effectiveness policies was limited. Developing country perspectives have not been analyzed in any depth, owing in part to the predominance of literature on development effectiveness emanating from developed countries. This represents a gap in the research and could be addressed through further study.

2   See Stern et al, 2008.

3   See Quibria, 2004.

4   See UNDP, 2001.

5   www.cgdev.org/section/initiatives/_active/cdi/ (last accessed July 2010).

6   See ISG, 2008.

7   See Reality of Aid, 2009.

8   See Better Aid, 2009.

9   See OECD, 2007.

10   See Flint et al, 2002.

References

AusAID (2008) 'Annual Review of Development Effectiveness 2007', Commonwealth of Australia, available at www.ode.ausaid.gov.au/ (last accessed July 2010)

Better Aid (2009) 'Better Aid Policy Paper: Consultation Draft 1.0', draft

Economic Commission for Africa/OECD (2009) 'The Mutual Review of Development Effectiveness in Africa: Promise and Performance', www.oecd.org (last accessed July 2010)

Flint, M., Cameron, C., Henderon, S., Jones, S. and D. Ticehurst (2002) 'How Effective is DFID? An Independent Review of DFID's Organisational and Development Effectiveness', DFID Evaluation Report EV 640, available at www.dfid.gov.uk/Documents/publications/evaluation/ev640.pdf (last accessed July 2010)

IFAD (2007) 'Report on IFAD's Development Effectiveness', available at www.ifad.org/deveffect/ride/index.htm (last accessed July 2010)

ISG (2008) 'Better Aid: A civil society position paper for the 2008 Accra High Level Forum on Aid Effectiveness', available at www.betteraid.org (last accessed July 2010)

Lockhart, C. (2005) 'From aid effectiveness to development effectiveness: strategy and policy coherence in fragile states', Overseas Development Institute

OECD (2007) 'Workshop on development effectiveness in practice: Applying the Paris Declaration', outcome document available at www.oecd.org/dataoecd/30/20/38933324.pdf (last accessed July 2010)

Quibria, M. (2004) 'Development Effectiveness: What Does the Recent Research Tell Us?', Asian Development Bank OED Working Paper, Number 1, available at www.adb.org/evaluation (last accessed July 2010)

Reality of Aid (2009) 'The Reality of Aid 2010 Report Theme Statement', draft

Stern, E., with Laura Altinger, Osvaldo Feinstein, Marta Maranon, Nils-Sjard Schulz and Nicolai Steen Nielsen (2008) 'Thematic Study on the Paris Declaration, Aid Effectiveness and Development Effectiveness', Ministry of Foreign Affairs of Denmark, available at www.oecd.org/dataoecd/59/28/41807824.pdf (last accessed July 2010)

Tomlinson, B. (2008) 'The Accra Third High Level Forum on Aid Effectiveness: a CCIC Participant Assessment of the Outcomes, available at http://www.ccic.ca/_files/en/what_we_do/002_aid_2008-09_third_hlf_ccic_assessment.pdf (last accessed August 2010)

Tujan, T. (2009) 'Development Effectiveness: Claiming Rights and Achieving Development', CCIC: *Au Courant*, Winter 2009, available at http://www.ccic.ca/aucourant/aucourant_winter_2009/aucourant_winter_2009_e.html (last accessed August 2010

UNDP (2001) 'Development Effectiveness: Review of Evaluative Evidence', Evaluation Office, UNDP, available at www.undp.org/eo/documents/der2001.pdf (last accessed July 2010)

UNDP (2003) 'Development Effectiveness Report 2003: Partnership for Results', Evaluation Office, New York: UNDP.

UNIFEM (2008) 'Gender Equality for Development Effectiveness: National Development Planning in the Commonwealth of Independent States', available at www.unifem.org (last accessed July 2010)

World Bank (2005) 'Improving the World Bank's Development Effectiveness: What Does Evaluation Show?', World Bank Operations Evaluation Department, Washington: The World Bank

World Bank Group (2008) 'Annual Review of Development Effectiveness 2008: Shared Global Challenges', Washington: The World Bank

26

Measurement in Developmental Practice: From the Mundane to the Transformational

James Taylor and Sue Soal

Introduction

This chapter was inspired by a three-day exploration into measurement and its impact on development practice. Fourteen development practitioners from different parts of the world, fulfilling different functions in the development sector, participated in the process. What brought us together is a commitment to building a development practice that has the best chance of countering the societal forces that exclude, marginalize and undermine people's ability to develop to their fullest potential.

This is not in any way an attempt to capture the collective conclusions of the group process. Through this paper we share only what lives in, and between, the two of us after engaging with the others. As with all interactive learning processes it is impossible to claim exclusive ownership of the ideas, or to impose responsibility for them on others.

> We have been dilettantes and amateurs
> With some of our greatest notions
> For human betterment.
> We have been like spoilt children:
> We have been like tyrannical children;
> Demanding proof when listening is required
>
> Ben Okri (From: *Mental Fight*)

The tension between product and process is at the very core of the development industry. It is a defining characteristic of the sector that shapes the practices within it.

The products of development are many and varied, but the delivery of these is not the purpose of development. The purpose of development is to apply the resources (the product) through processes that transform relationships in society. The ultimate purpose of developmental interventions is always to ensure that the excluded, those at the margins, gain greater access to and control over the decisions and resources that directly affect their lives.

The tension in development, then, is between delivery of 'product' to the needy, and the facilitation of process that shifts power relations in favour of the less powerful. Through the lens of this tension, this paper explores measurement as an essential and inescapable element of development practice. It shares some of the impact measurement practices have had on this tension, as experienced by practitioners. It then proposes some essential characteristics and practices required for the type of measurement that appreciates and supports the ultimate purpose of developmental interventions.

The aim of this chapter is to contribute towards building a body of developmental practice that is effective. To be effective our combined efforts have to be transformational – those relationships and structures in society that restrict human potential have to be transformed. In the process of promoting good practice we join with all those who are starting to reject measurement practices that are counter-developmental.

Measurement and Its Impact on Development Practice

Increasingly measurement is being promoted as a critical tool for improving the outputs, effect and impact of physical and human resources. It is encountered at all levels of individual and organizational activity. Our individual contributions are measured in performance appraisals and the time and resources we use to do things are measured; our implementation is measured against our plans through the promotion of results-based management systems; our individual and organizational impact is assessed, our organizations are evaluated and measured against their stated objectives in order to be held accountable and to access resources to sustain ourselves. As development practitioners we are not alone in this. We are but a small part of a world that is dominated by a deep-seated belief in what is essentially a scientific and instrumentalist way of relating in and on the world.

As development practitioners we are bound to shape the use of measurement towards meeting the needs of our purpose. We cannot allow the process of measurement to undermine it. The simple logic of measurement can best serve the interests of development practice by gauging the extent to which 'what' we bring and 'how' we bring it contributes towards our achievement of our developmental purpose. Because of the immense difficulty and complexity of what we are attempting to achieve, measurement itself must be measured in its ability to contribute towards our learning. Our purpose is too urgent and important to waste time on activities that are subversive of that.

The experience of many who have been measuring, and have been measured, gives us some idea of the extent to which measurement is achieving its developmental objective. Below are some of the conclusions reached by practitioners from all levels of the 'aid chain'.

Measurement is an inherent ability that we all use

We all can and do measure. Measurement is not first and foremost a sophisticated technical skill, it is an intuitive ability. Single cell organisms can detect and measure subtle changes in their environment. Black eagles can measure when the communities of rock-rabbits they prey on are being over exploited and are in danger of becoming unsustainable.

Human beings from a very early age have an incredibly sophisticated ability to measure. Without even being conscious of doing it, they can measure the amount of oxygen in their blood and innumerable other body functions. They can assess the mood of their parent and their ability to undertake a range of risky activities. Human beings can plan activities ranging from children's games, to large and complex village celebrations, to intricate manufacturing processes. Those who plan and implement activities always have the ability to measure the extent to which they have succeeded in achieving their own objectives.

People do not have to be taught to measure. Measurement is central to how they have learned. They need to be reassured that they can measure and helped to adapt and apply their ability to new situations. All individuals and organizations are in some way, planning and measuring and learning.

Measurement facilitates accountability

Measurement has played a significant role establishing a more planned and organized approach to development practice. It is an integral part of planning, monitoring and evaluation. Through measurement the focus shifts from what we are doing to what we have achieved through our actions. Development agencies have had to become increasingly 'business-like'. Funds can no longer be raised without clear and logical strategic plans with clear objectives and indicators for success. Accounting for the use of funds is no longer simply a bookkeeping exercise. Life without performance appraisals and impact evaluations is unimaginable.

Learning to plan and measure our activities has improved our ability to account for ourselves. It has contributed much to improving our efficiency as delivery systems. In many instances it has made us more competitive, to the point where we win tenders from government to implement large and complex projects.

However we are nervous that these gains in our ability to measure the delivery of product can undermine our ability to focus our efforts on our ultimate purpose.

Measurement tends always towards the mundane

Within the dominant scientific paradigm, measurement reduces and standardizes. In order to make sense of complex systems and processes, measurement first uses models and frameworks to reduce them to manageable segments. In the process the models and frameworks standardize what is measured. The models and frameworks are usually drawn from the reality of the measurer and not the measured.

As a result measurement is most effective and easily applied to the more material and mundane. Those things that are not easily counted are simplified and superficialized.

To the developmental practitioner measurement does not convey what is most important. It is not that effective in capturing value. It focuses on 'what' you deliver and not on 'how' you deliver it: on the product and not the process, on the material not the relational, on the things not on the relationships that define them and on the outer and not the inner.

Measurement is really efficient and effective in conveying that which is easy to count. It is the best way for holding ourselves accountable for what we have done against what we planned to do. But despite all the attempts it remains inherently unsuitable as a means of appreciating what is of greatest value to us. It is not capable of capturing impact. We end up feeding each other with information that is only indirectly related to what we consider to be really important in our work. At times it is so distantly related to anything connected to our work that it borders on deceit.

Excessive measurement is a symptom of a particular phase of development

It is clear that some people have more of a need to measure than others. To those interested in observing and learning about development processes it is clear that measurement becomes more important at a certain phase of development. In the jargon of organization development the phase is called the 'scientific' or 'differentiated' phase. During this phase the differentiation of activities needs high levels of management, coordination and control. These highly measured and regulated systems have the ability to manipulate their environment and be enormously productive. But this power eventually tends to start turning inwards on itself. As measurement becomes an end in itself, it starts to stifle creativity and the ability to adapt.

In the pioneer phase organizations intuition, flexibility and the ability to respond are essential to success. Excessive measurement to a pioneer organization is as dangerous as no measurement is to a scientific phase organization. Excessive measurement is increasingly being recognized as a threat to productivity, creativity and even to trust, in those parts of the world where it is rampant. This fundamental principle of development does not only apply to organizations, but to individuals and even to societies in different phases of development. The use of measurement is only one of many things that changes in different phases of development.

One of the complicating factors in development is that northern and southern organizations are often at very different phases of development. They also operate out of vastly differing societal contexts and cultures.

Measurement is used as a means of centralizing control

Measurement is a very important part of our ability to adjust our behaviour in order to achieve desired results. We measure those things we want to control. Those who are being measured by others feel this very strongly. There is a major difference in being measured by someone who has power over you and measuring yourself. In the development sector there is much evidence that measurement is used to effect control. This is commonly experienced through processes such as evaluation and performance appraisal. Control is exercised simply by setting standards and benchmarks and making the judgements required for measurement. This ability to influence is further expanded through making recommendations, and actively supporting some activities and discouraging others.

Another very common experience in the sector is that those more powerful than you (those closer to the resources) pass their problems on to you down the line. If your donor is being challenged by their back-donor to account differently for their impact, you can be sure you are going to have to start doing things very differently in the near future.

This phenomenon is particularly rife in situations of so-called partnership. Many international agencies have stopped implementing in other countries and now support the activities of 'partner'[1] organizations. It is clear that many international agencies still have the need to extend their sphere of control beyond their relationship with their 'partner' to the relationship with the ultimate recipient of the service. For this reason the donor is not that interested in measuring its own success and ability in building the capacity of its partner, but is more interested in the success of its partner in delivering their services to the end user.

Measurement can dominate and devastate relationships

In many so-called partnerships measurement is experienced by the 'lesser' partner as dominating the quality and quantity of communication between the two parties. It is generally accepted that those providing the resources need to be reassured of the value of the work being done. But measurement is but a small part of fully appreciating the value of developmental work. Much of the more nuanced value achieved cannot be appreciated thorough short-term long distance measurement processes. More time needs to be spent in the kind of quality communication and relationship that facilitates 'really getting to know each other'.

The other simple fact that cannot be escaped is that all too often evaluations are experienced as traumatic, threatening processes that leave those evaluated feeling deeply frustrated, powerless and insecure. It is very common for evaluation to be experienced as a continuation of past oppressive relationships. All too often the evaluator is experienced as slipping into the role of colonizer as the evaluated slips into the role of the colonized. In Central Asia evaluations are nothing new. Organizations prepare themselves much as they did when they were a part of the centrally controlled Soviet Union. The process of one person evaluating another only contributes to improved relations between the two when immense skill, sensitivity and trust prevails.

In a business where positive shifts in the 'nature, quality and power in relationships over time' are central to its purpose, measurement needs to be used with great care. Anything that leaves 'partners' feeling less powerful is counter-productive, anti-developmental.

Measurement can undermine learning and trust

When we have a picture in our mind of what we hope to achieve before we act there is a strong chance that the outcomes of our actions will not 'measure up' exactly to our original picture. It is out of the tension created by this discrepancy that learning occurs. It is this tension that leads us to asking the learning questions. 'Why did my efforts not turn out as I had intended?' Ideally this process of questioning and learning leads to improved future practice.

All too often, however, this simple logical process simply does not take place. Because of the threatening nature of the process and consequences of measuring it is difficult even to admit that things have not turned out as planned. When it is impossible to avoid, the discrepancy is rationalized and justified in ways that do not involve the painful process of introspection. In relationships where there is insufficient trust it is simply not safe to look for and reveal one's inner weaknesses. If one does not look inside for the reasons why you are not able to achieve what is expected, you will not be able to change and improve. If it is not safe to look inside there is much that encourages the externalization of problems. It is often easier to blame something external to yourself – a person, a system, an event – but the developmental cost is heavy. By turning yourself into the victim you fall prey to the most counter-developmental of all forces.

All too often the learning that flows from measurement and evaluation stays at the level of information and does not impact on changed behaviour. At worst it actually adds to disempowerment.

Measurement ignores developmental timeframes

When development is understood as an inherent natural process it is accepted that each system has built into it its own development clock. It develops at its own pace. Similar types of systems have similar development time frames, but each individual progresses differently through it. Through our interventions into developing systems we can at best contribute towards unblocking stuckness – we can never speed up development beyond its natural pace without doing damage.

When measurement takes place outside of the implementation project cycle it frustrates itself by becoming unrealistic. It is good at keeping track of inputs and outputs but at the levels of effect and impact it is often too impatient to be helpful to developmental practitioners.

Measurement is becoming an imposed, standardized, specialist activity

Measurement is at its most powerful when we use it as an integral part of our ongoing cycles of purposeful action. However, we constantly experience measurement as something imposed by others and carried out by specialists. Those doing the measurement tend to use a very limited array of standardized models and methods. For the moment the 'logical framework' with a few lesser 'SMARTs' and 'SWOTs' dominate the development landscape. The problem lies not in the quality of these little models, but in their slavish application in all situations. This undifferentiated use of tools and techniques is non-developmental.

Our own measurement in our own way never suffices. We are all forced to report endlessly but it is never enough. Enormous amounts of money are being spent on specialist evaluations that are occasionally good enough to state what we already knew.

If measurement is to become a part of our own learning we must own and control the process.

Towards Developmental Measurement

The way measurement is being applied at present is succeeding most in enabling organizations and individuals to hold others accountable. While it is experienced as a powerful and formative force in relationships, its impact is not shifting power relations in favour of the less powerful. In this section we start exploring what developmental measurement might look and feel like. First we look at what developmental measurement must achieve. We suggest a few criteria for developmental measurement that could be used for measuring measurement itself. Criteria that will help us assess whether measurement is serving our developmental purpose.

And finally we share some characteristic elements of developmental measurement practice. Here we look more how it should be done. Not the detail, not standardized tools and techniques as there are more of these available than practitioners have the skill to use appropriately. We will look more at some basic principles of practice that should guide the practitioner in building their practice and their 'toolbox'.

Basic Requirements

Measurement must first do what it is good at, quickly and simply

Measurement is best at the more mundane material level. It is best at measuring inputs and outputs. On occasion it is also helpful at the level of effect or outcomes. These basic levels are absolutely vital for development practice, and form its foundation. After all, development does occur through the delivery of products and services and development organizations must be able to deliver their services properly, and account for the fact that they have. If they cannot do this they should not get the resources to continue functioning. If they cannot master this basic activity there is little chance that will become effective in the more complex developmental aspect of their practice.

Equally if those providing the resources cannot articulate clearly and simply what the basic minimum 'non-negotiable' accountability requirements are they are not fit to be stewards of development resources. The more technical 'accounting' type measurement at this level should simply be done – and done as simply as possible. Appropriate methods should be sought to ensure that it is not difficult to do. All too often it is made difficult by over complicated standardized and bureaucratic systems and procedures.

Planning, monitoring and evaluation at this level has made a very important contribution to the sector, but it is only the beginning. Those making resources available to anyone at any level in the chain must make this a condition. The developmental aspect of this part of measurement is to help 'partners' understand how easy it is by assisting them to find ways that are appropriate to them. What often confuses and confounds is the more common practice of imposing systems that are more suited to the provider of the resources.

Developmental measurement is transformational

Developmental practitioners that are committed to going beyond the delivery of product must find ways of using measurement to inform and build their practice. After the relatively simple measurement of product it must focus on purpose and process. Its focus must always be on the higher purpose of development, and avoid being drawn always into the easier to measure countable levels. It must face the challenge of ensuring that good practice is being informed by keeping the ultimate objective (of really challenging and changing the world) in mind.

The 'counting' type of measurement really struggles at this level. There are many efforts to combine the 'quantitative' with the 'qualitative'. The problem when we move into the realm of measuring relationships is that attribution becomes virtually impossible. One simply cannot attribute impact to input because of the complexity resulting from the interconnectedness of all things. Measuring changes in relationships has as much to do with emotion as it does with rationality. It is more about ideas and actions than information and data.

The concept and convention of measuring is getting in the way rather than helping us appreciate the impact of our efforts at the more complex levels of social and relational impact. There have been many creative efforts to quantify quality, but they remain locked into focusing on the objects rather than what happens between them. Perhaps we need to let go of the word 'measurement' when attempting to capture shifts and movements between social entities. We should consider the word 'capture' rather than measure or 'appreciate' (as in appreciative enquiry). We need to find a word that supports creative process rather than counting.

Developmental measurement must contain within it the ability to apprehend and describe changes in the nature and quality of relationships over time. But in addition to this it must succeed in rising above the mundane in order to contribute towards transforming relationships. Successful developmental measurement focuses intentions in ways that spark creativity. It does not reduce the complexity of life in order to capture it in small boxes. It faces the challenge of working holistically.

Measurement must improve the efficacy of practice

Measurement starts with practice, and should end in improved practice. It must always begin with clarifying and understanding plans and intentions; it then looks at what was done and achieved and compares it to what was intended. The circle must then be completed. The learning that is the product of measurement must result in improved future practice.

Despite all the rhetoric claiming that the purpose of measurement is learning (as well as accountability) it is difficult to detect its impact. The gap between knowledge about development practice and the actual quality of what is done in the name of development is unacceptable. A cost-benefit analysis of evaluations in the sector and their impact on improved practice would make us reconsider the resources invested in this activity. We know that a lot of measurement activity produces information that we simply do not have the capacity or time to process and use meaningfully.

Developmental measurement must improve the quality of practice of those being measured.

Measurement must contribute towards shifting relationships through learning

The tendency of measurement to centralize control is directly contrary to the developmental purpose. Developmental measurement must promote consciousness, openness, honesty and depth – particularly in one's relationship to self. It must be experienced first as contributing to ongoing learning, and secondly as a means of holding oneself accountable. If it experienced as being first for someone else, the potential to learn from the process will be minimized.

Measurement must build confidence through facing failure, celebrating success and learning from both. It must contribute towards relationships that empower, always from dependency through independence towards interdependence. Above all it must always leave the measured party more in control, rather than less.

Developmental measurement must constantly create the tension that prompts learning that results in change that impacts positively on relationships. What makes transformational learning different, and much more challenging, is the fact that in order to take on new forms you first have to let go of the old.

Principles for Measurement in Developmental Practice

Developmental measurement is always 'from the inside out'

Measuring someone else with the expectation that they will draw learning from the experience is in its essence instrumentalist, controlling and counter-developmental. Developmental measurement is measurement undertaken by yourself on the understanding that you are going to be the primary beneficiary of the learning.

The power in relationships starts shifting when individual parties become more conscious of, and connected to, the power that they have. It is not a 'top down' or 'bottom up' process. Power is not given through empowerment from the top or taken from the bottom without first finding a source of power from within. The power that transforms starts as an 'inside out' process. When power is wrested from the top to the bottom it tends simply to re-form rather than transform the relationships.

When evaluating and measuring yourself you start with your relationship with yourself. You have to accept full responsibility for your successes and failures, and the ability to change and improve. You always start with questions about your own purpose and practice. But to make sense of your impact on the world you need to explore and assess your relationships with others.

Developmental measurement is very different from the 'top-down' measurement of the recipient by the provider – it is circular, not linear. The principle of 'inside-out' suggests that after starting within, you proceed to review your relationships with others in all directions. Both vertical and horizontal relationships need to be included. In shifting power all relationships are important: those who have power over you, those over whom you have power and those who share your position and interests.

At times, particularly with periodic evaluations, there might be value in engaging an outsider in order to bring a different perspective, specialist skills or facilitation skills.

When this is done it is vital that the organization being evaluated own and control the process. They must decide what questions need to be asked, what the learning needs and accountability needs are. If outsiders are engaged to do some of the work they must be hired, instructed, managed, monitored and paid (or not paid) by the organization being evaluated. This arrangement increases the chance of the external service provider taking seriously the needs of the organization being evaluated.

The information and conclusions gained through this process are then used to account for yourself (becoming account-able!), rather than being held accountable by others. This fulfils the basic requirement of shifting power to 'the measured'. The organization providing resources already has power over the recipient. If there is any doubt about the honesty or 'objectivity' of the report they have every right to audit the organization. But this approach is being promoted from experience of 'partnerships' where the quality of relationships is such that there is enough knowledge of each other that this 'policing' is not necessary. By spending time, energy and resources building relationship with, rather than evaluating, your 'partner' you will know whether to trust them or not. Encouraging 'partners' to evaluate themselves contributes enormously to building relationship and trust.

What is being suggested is not that you don't involve others in your evaluations but that when you are involved in commissioning an evaluation it is understood that you are the primary learner expected to benefit from the process. The less powerful 'partner' is usually more than willing to be the subject of the evaluation if they know that your success and practice is being measured and judged and not theirs. What is then being measured is the more powerful 'partner's' impact on those they serve – on the quality of their services.

If organizations supporting others are concerned about their 'partner's' ability to measure and evaluate themselves they must not under any circumstances take over the task. Their developmental responsibility is to convince the organization that they have the ability to do it themselves. They must facilitate processes that connect their 'partners' to their own innate knowledge of measurement. This must then be built upon until they can design a process that is appropriate to their own skills, phase of development and needs.

If we all evaluate ourselves honestly and share our findings with each other we will be contributing to building a development sector that is worthy of its name, and a real chance of achieving its purpose. We must have the courage to challenge those who are not honest and hold them accountable for their dishonesty when it is a threat to our purpose.

Developmental measurement is not an event but an orientation

If developmental measurement is from the inside out then it is not something that is occasionally forced on you by those who have influence over you. Measurement is but one part of a self-consciousness orientation. It is a part of an orientation based on a belief that by acting with intent and a commitment to ongoing learning you can shape your world, and not be a victim. It stems from taking pride in what you do and responsibility for the effect it has on others. It is based on a self-critical questioning approach to life.

Measurement should be built into all formal aspects of your work including planning, monitoring and evaluation. But also in the less formal pondering, wondering and questioning that turns a job into a challenging life task.

Developmental measurement builds from the parts to the whole

Scientific measurement reduces things to the point where they can be counted. The value of its contribution stems from the fact that it is reductionist. It simplifies and standardizes. The logical framework approach to planning and measurement is a good example of this. It is designed to reduce the enormously complex social process to the point where they can fit into a series of boxes, and measured using 'SMART' objectives and 'OVIs' (objectively verifiable indicators). The point has already been made that these tools are effective at the level of input/output but decreasingly so towards impact.

To really 'appreciate' or 'capture' the changes that are of most importance to developmental practitioners we cannot reduce things of quality to quantities and little boxes. We cannot end up considering only that part of what is important to us that is easily measured – we need to be working with the whole. This is a very practical dilemma that faces all those responsible for reporting on their progress and achievements. Those closest to the actual 'coalface' of development practice are overwhelmed by the quantity of qualitative information they have. It is impossible for them to convey it to others without reducing its volume. They don't have the time to collate it all, and even if they did, it would be useless to those who need it.

But to the developmental practitioner the issue of quantity is secondary. The real concern is with quality. The potential learning for improved practice that can be drawn from the charts, graphs and tables of reduced information is very limited. Our challenge is to appreciate the whole – and this requires a completely different orientation and approach to that of the reductionist, rational and scientific. Developmental practice needs to draw as much from the creative arts as it does from science, it needs to draw on the 'right side of the brain', the intuitive as much as the rational.

When working with highly complex social systems it is not possible to engage with and make sense of the whole. In order to start gathering information on which to base some understanding you have to use models that give you a 'way in' to the system. These models assist in gathering, capturing and interrogating information that is meaningful. It helps us take the system apart, and understand the parts, their function and even something about how they relate to each other. But it is limited in its ability to help us understand the real meaning of the whole.

Taking one human individual as an example of a social system we can clarify the point. There are many models that help us make sense of the human being. Medical models help us understand the organs, their functions and relationships to each other. There are psychological models that help us gain insight into the workings of the mind. There are models that further differentiate between the body, mind, spirit and soul. There are methods to assist us in looking at how people have been shaped through their social interactions and relationships. Even if we were to apply all of these, we would not yet have a means of conveying the essence of the person. This is the challenge of holism – to capture the essence of the whole. The underlying principle is that the whole is always more than the sum of its parts.

The ability to capture and communicate the essence, or essential character, of complex systems and the relationships between them must be a core competence of the truly developmental practitioner. This is a skill that can, and must, be learned and developed. The ability to characterize is central to all art forms and developmental practice is as much an art as it is a science. There are practitioners already using this skill to great effect. It is providing people and organizations with insights into themselves that have more depth and meaning than other forms of measurement are capable of. There are simple and practical ways of doing it involving creative activities like storytelling, drawing and painting, characterization exercises, role-plays and the use of metaphors.

Again it takes courage to start implementing these approaches in a world dominated by scientific cynicism. There is however much proof that there is a side of all people that is more moved by a good story than a graph. There is no doubt that a story or a picture can capture more of the nuance and complexity of the human condition and potential than a graph ever will. Equally numbers have the enormous power of the finite. To meet the challenges we face in development we need to bring together capability of numbers to ground and bring down to earth, and the creative ability we have to capture the meaning of the stars.

Measurement is but a part of developmental practice

However vital measurement might be it is but a small part of development practice. Measurement is becoming a major focus in the development sector but its contribution must be kept in perspective. Ongoing measurement can play a significant role in informing and improving practice that has the best chance of contributing to developmental change. But in and of itself it has as much chance of undermining what we are trying to achieve as contributing towards it. The difficult part is achieving the shifts in relationships, not measuring them. When they happen they are all too easy to observe and appreciate.

At best measurement is but one aspect of the reflective learning part of developmental practice. It focuses attention on practice in order to improve it. Measurement will come into its own in development practice when it addresses the dilemmas and challenges that are most central to our task, when we develop the skills to engage in measurement in ways that bring complex systems to life rather than reduce them in order to control them. In seeking to understand our impact more deeply through measurement we must generate better questions rather than superficial answers. We must measure our practice in ways that inspire, challenge and make us more conscious, always building on the mundane towards transformation.

Measurement must be undertaken with courage in search of truth

In practice, measurement is too often undertaken with expediency and efficiency foremost in mind. Developmental measurement must not fall into the trap of supporting the pretence that development is easy and that we have the answers and ability to achieve what we are attempting. We don't! If our relationships are based on this premise we start off with a lie, and all our communications thereafter have to perpetuate it. The most critical relationship of all is with ourselves. We have to have the courage to ask ourselves the difficult questions, to challenge ourselves, to live with the reality of how long it really takes for developmental transformations to come about. Then we have to have the courage to share this with others – particularly those who have power over us. We have to call the big development bluff.

A quantum universe is enacted only in an environment rich in relationships. Nothing happens in the quantum world without something countering something else. Nothing is independent of the relationships that occur. I am constantly creating the world – evoking it, not discovering it – as I participate in all its many interactions. This is a world of process, not a world of things (Wheatly, 1994).

Notes

1   We use the word partner in inverted commas because we feel it is used inaccurately to describe all forms of relationship we have with each other – many of which do not in any way resemble partnerships. If interested read 'The Poverty of Partnership' available at www.cdra. org.za (last accessed July 2010).

References

Okri, B. (1997) Mental Fight, Weidenfeld & Nicolson
Wheatley, M. J. (1994) *Leadership and the New Science*, Berrett Koehler: San Francisco

Part VIII

Managing for Learning and Knowledge

27

Accountability and Learning: Exploding the Myth of Incompatibility between Accountability and Learning

Irene Guijt

When accountability is understood as reporting on predefined deliverables, it is often considered to be irreconcilable with learning. This conventional wisdom inhibits an appreciation of their connection.

In this chapter, the author exposes the flaws and traps in reasoning that keep accountability and learning apart. She provides practitioners with principles and basic good ideas that open up prospects for accountability and learning to complement each other.

You cannot be accountable if you do not learn. And you need to know how well you live up to performance expectations in order to learn. The tug of war between learning and accountability is nonsensical. They need each other. Understanding effectiveness requires both.

However, that is the theory. The daily reality is that tensions between the two are alive and kicking. This results in major headaches for many organizations and individuals, straining relationships up and down the 'aid chain'. Official policies that profess the importance of learning are often contradicted by bureaucratic protocols and accounting systems which demand proof of results against preset targets. In the process, data are distorted (or obtained with much pain) and learning is aborted (or is too ad hoc to make a difference).

Monitoring and evaluation (M&E) is a common site of a tug-of-war between the need for 'accountability' and the desire to ensure 'learning'. Often neither term is defined very clearly. Yet, people *do* seem convinced the two are methodologically and practically irreconcilable. This chapter first sets out reasons behind the perceptions and stubborn dilemmas that many working in aided-development processes face in satisfying demands to be both accountable and to learn. The issues involved are not unique to aid. They also hamper performance and innovation in business and government (Perrin, 2002). However, this chapter focuses on experiences in development initiatives that receive external funding.

The next section reviews underlying reasons for assuming incompatibility between accountability and learning. This setting the scene is followed by a section identifying

Figure 27.1 *Reconciling incompatibility*

two traps that appear to perpetuate the tensions and then two ideas that offer scope for reconciliation. Section three moves us on by discussing what kinds of capacities may be needed for both functions. The chapter ends with principles, practices and simple good ideas that open up prospects for accountability and learning to complement each other.

Understanding the Tug-of-war

So where does the purported tension lie? Development initiatives that receive external funding – be it from government, business or aid agencies – must sooner or later present their intentions following a certain format. This format requires statements about prede-fined goals and a specification of the activities and interim results that will lead to their achievement. These formats are known by many names – logframe approach, goal oriented project planning (ZOPP), Results-based Management (RBM), the list goes on. Informally, donors see the need for a more open-ended approach – without compro-mising the spirit of accountability – yet staff charged with monitoring progress, refer rigidly to original plans (see Guijt, 2008a).[1]

Documents produced by planning processes are, of course, only theories about what people think might happen. But they often become reality – the 'map' becomes the 'world'. And in so doing, it often turns into a rigidly followed contract that requires proof of deliverables as the heart of development effectiveness. This perspective is moti-vated by a need for 'accountability' and driven by a logic that views development as 'projectable change' (Reeler, 2007). In this way planning processes lock down plans into watertight projections of change which dictate the spirit of development as a controllable process in mutually reinforcing cycles.

And yet, every day, the world surprises us with its unexpected twists of events, which arise out of multiple variables and strands of efforts. Conscious labours to make a difference are part of a maelstrom of societal change that is dynamic, unpredictable and non-linear. Twenty years of efforts may eventually culminate in one giant policy victory – or not. Hence, the need to keep an eye on the context and 'learn one's way towards a solution'. Viewing development as an adaptive management process is often agreed as important, at least informally, by those involved. And in some organizations and donor-grantee relationships, plans are allowed to evolve, indicators are allowed to (dis)appear, strategies allowed to shift.

Notwithstanding such examples, accountability is a recurrent winner. There is a fundamental disconnect between the rhetoric about the need for learning in development and the reality of procedures that funding agencies require. How can it be that such patent contradiction exists in the rhetoric and practice of aid policy and allocation? My own experiences suggest that the following factors may play a role.

Practical Limitations: The most heard refrain from organizations seeking to be learning-oriented is 'we don't have time'. Reflection requires time to gather evidence, meet, analyse, agree and bed in new practices and policies. A culture of doing and delivering is common in development, and so reflection and learning has to be highly functional (Guijt, 2008b). This is compounded by overly ambitious goal-setting by development organizations themselves.

Capacity Constraints: Clearly different skills are needed to do statistical analysis than to facilitate transformational conversations in organizations – but often staff are not hired from a clear understanding of the capacities needed for accountability *and* learning. This issue is dealt with in more detail below.

Economic and Political Trends: The development sector is increasingly competitive in a world in economic crisis; more organizations and less money to go around. Profiling organizational uniqueness is increasingly important. Showing success using 'hard data' – of millions fed or schooled or housed or organized better – has an impact. Telling a more nuanced story about social change, involving contextual difficulties, messy partnerships and intangible but essential outcomes gets one nowhere.

Context Constraints (and Incentives): Some contexts (organizational or societal) are too closed to allow even minimum debate. Rigid administrative and legal regulations can paralyse potential learning processes or flexibility with accountability requirements. Incentives focus on meeting preset performance agreements and rarely applaud fundamental question-asking that may argue for strategic changes. Rigid accountability systems hinder learning. Staff may be punished for not achieving original agreed objectives even though they have learned what *is* feasible and effective. The simple solution would be to allow plans that do not live up to initial expectations to be renegotiated. But many (many!) people have suffered from frankly stupid accountability systems. These systems reward those with timid goals and punish those with ambitious goals. They reward those who make precise specifications of what will happen, and therefore reward those whose guesses will inevitably be shown to be wrong as 'life happens'. In so doing, they reward those who do not learn and adapt what they are doing – and punish those who do.[2]

Organizational Culture: Resources and responsibilities need to be allocated to accountability *and* learning. They *both* need to be embedded in specifications for project design or they won't happen. The nature of the senior managers is critical for the entire culture: the more curious, risk taking, feedback-asking – the more likely this will spawn similar behaviour elsewhere. In other cases, accountability may dominate.

Philosophical Simplicity: According to Reeler, the frameworks that dictate accountability in funding relationships are part of that problem: 'Created to help control the flow of resources, these frameworks have, by default, come to help control almost every aspect of development practice across the globe. Social processes are subordinated to the logistics of resource control, infusing a default paradigm of practice closely aligned with conventional business thinking'. This one-size-fits-all approach means that many managers act based on the assumption that there is more predictability and order in the world than exists (Snowden and Boone, 2007). They look at accountability and learning from an oversimplified understanding of reality. I will return to this critical issue below.

There are undoubtedly other drivers. But even this short list suggests that the dualistic behaviour of aid is a systemic property – a phenomenon that arises from the wider aid system and not from any individual component. In particular, these drivers all point to power dynamics as a key to break the status quo that locks the system into non-learning forms of accountability. This helps in understanding the tenacity of the problem. And implies that resolving the tension requires a new ideas set, not just changes in organizational systems and practices – ideas that include reconciling the anomalies between funders that stipulate funding conditionalities that encourage (dependent) grantees to report on results that may not have happened or do not result from their efforts. And so the system kids itself at deep levels. Tensions will continue to exist as long as these power inequalities are not challenged.[3] While the issue of power is significant for much that this chapter deals with, it is not the point of concentration.

Notwithstanding the aid sector's ongoing contradiction regarding power, a word of caution is needed here. There is a danger of creating and perpetuating a stereotype that pits the 'poor learning underdog' against the evils of 'accountability-obsessed funders'. While some organizations have only recently taken on the discipline of programme logic and have yet to experience its limitations, others are questioning the merits of this perspective and practice. The United Nations Development Programme (UNDP) recently produced a scathing evaluation of its own use of results-based management, opening the way for improvement (UNDP, 2007). Similarly, the German technical cooperation agency, Deutsche Gesellschaft für Technische Zusammenarbeit (GTZ), has acknowledged that its assumption that 'quality at entry' – involving a detailed situation analysis and goal-oriented planning – automatically led to quality and success has been contradicted by project practice. And some donors do give room to manoeuvre to grantees to shift plans or have flexible, responsive funding options, such as the UK Department for International Development (DFID) multi-year outcome based Challenge grants.

Is there a way to more systematically approach the supposed tug-of-war that enables greater synergy between these two needs? A new ideas set is part of the way forward.

Ideas That Trap and Ideas That Liberate

The aid system is trapped by two ideas that keep accountability and learning apart. First, accountability is, somehow, *not* considered learning. Second, the world and its processes of change are viewed in overly idealized terms that set up unrealistic accountability expectations. An alternative idea is proposed for each trap.

Trap 1: Defining learning and accountability to see convergence

Is learning at odds with accountability? What *are* they about in essence? We begin with the nature of learning.

Understanding learning

Learning in development has countless interpretations. Keeping it simple here, I consider learning to be the process of continual reflection about visions, strategies, actions and contexts that enable continual readjustments. Below are two useful distinctions in relation to capacity for learning: purposes and levels.

Purposes (and loops) of learning. Learning is needed for several purposes: (1) practical improvements, (2) strategic adjustments and changes and (3) rethinking the core driving values. These differences give rise to what is commonly known as single, double and triple loop learning. Single loop questioning focuses on 'are we doing things well' without questioning assumptions. Double loop questioning wonders 'are we doing the right things' which forces exploration of assumptions. Triple loop questioning bumps it up to another level by asking 'How do we know what it is "right" to do?'[4]

Learning entails not just pragmatic problem-solving but also reflection on the process by which this happens and the underlying perspective on knowledge. Seen like this, learning requires capacities for critical reflection, identifying assumptions, seeking evidence about what is going well or not, analysing multiple lines of evidence, relating evidence to expectations and analysing and negotiating possible consequences. These processes all require connecting people and their perspectives. Therefore the capacity to deal with power dynamics becomes essential.

Levels of learning. Similar to multiple levels of capacity explored in Chapter 3 of *Capacity Development in Practice* (Ubels et al, 2010), learning processes differ greatly in form and focus depending on the type and level at which they are pitched: individual, group, partnership, sector, societal or hierarchical.

Enabling learning at the individual level, in adults as the core implementers, is often linked to experiential learning. This framework for understanding adult learning processes is also used to structure collective learning. But collective learning takes place at different levels, each requiring additional skills. In my work in Brazil, for example, collective learning at the simplest level involved small groups around thematic interests, such as farmers involved in agro-forestry or honey production. Another collective level is organizational learning which occurs within the farmer trade unions or NGOs that support farmers. A third level is that of the partnership, which involves the different organizations and groups, each with their constituencies, staff or members.

But two other levels of learning are relevant for the aid sector, in general: sector-wide learning and societal learning. Sector-wide learning requires convening a large diversity of actors to reflect on ways forward. Such forms of learning are rare to find. Examples that I know include smaller initiatives with a sectoral focus, such as the Sustainable Food Lab (www.sustainablefoodlab.org, accessed November 2009) or large events such as the biannual International Aids Conference. Finally, societal learning occurs when different groups, communities and multi-stakeholder constituencies in society engage actively in a communicative process of understanding problematic situations, conflicts and social dilemmas and paradoxes, creating strategies for improvement, and working through the implementation.

When considering learning in terms of levels, additional capacities needed include facilitation, convening relevant people, process design, creative thinking and conflict resolution. And finally, it requires the capacity to read the context in order to give direction to the desired learning process:

- *Who* is being expected to learn?
- What *purpose* is the learning supposed to serve?
- What *level* is the learning process aimed at?

Understanding accountability

If learning is understood in the way described above, the connection to and potential for synergy with *accountability* can become clearer. But this also calls for a rethinking of how accountability is currently portrayed. The common view is this. When promises are made or finances (in the form of taxes, voluntary donations or membership fees) are raised on behalf of a group of people or a cause, it is considered justified to expect some feedback on how the money was used and if promises were kept, i.e. 'answerability'. If such feedback is found lacking, then sanctions may ensue – 'enforcement'. Hence accountability is essentially relational – as in answerable to others within a relationship of power (Goetz and Jenkins, 2004). 'To define accountability principles means to define who has the power to call for an account and who is obligated to give an explanation for their actions' (Newell and Bellour, 2002, p2).

However, there are variations modifying this term. There is *managerial accountability* which requires sending information 'upward', towards a board or funding agency. You can talk about *representative accountability*, when referring to the obligations of representatives to constituents. There is the option of *social accountability* with civil society exacting accountability, *principal-agent accountability* (motivating agents to achieve the goals of superiors), *mutual accountability*, in which values, aspirations and social relations form the glue. Increasingly, as used by Newell and Balfour and others, '*political* accountability' is extending beyond holding government and the judiciary to account, to including institutions that affect the poor, such as the World Trade Organization and the corporate sector. In this case, accountability is downward – citizens demanding of institutions that they be accountable to them. In all these variations, much effort is focused on compliance-checking and financial accountability – hence performing an external controlling function.

Critically important – and one of the places where accountability and learning converge – is that accountability can also be taken to mean taking responsibility for

---

Box 27.1

Clarifying what is meant by accountability in your context (Goetz and Jenkins, 2005, p4)

Who is seeking accountability?

From whom (or what) is accountability sought?

Where (in which forums and over what extent of geographic coverage) is accountability being sought?

How (through which means) are the powerful being held to account?

For what (which actions, and against which norms) is accountability being sought?

---

oneself. Understanding what you've done, being able to respond to questions about the basis of strategic decisions, the underlying theory of change and, of course, how money was spent. Such *strategic accountability* seeks to answer the question 'Did I/others/organizations/institutions act as effectively as possible?' In this sense, accountability is intrinsically about identity – feeling committed to one's ideas and strategies (Fry, 1995). Ebrahim (2005) echoes this by saying that: 'Organizational learning is more likely if internal accountability to mission, rather than upward accountability to donors, guides NGO reporting'. Being held accountable thus means having 'respond-ability'.

When considering accountability, the capacities needed include an ability to formulate clear performance expectations (of others and of self), gather and analyse evidence to understand effectiveness, draw conclusions about consequences and engage in a dialogue with those holding to account. Importantly, it requires reading the context in order to understand which version of accountability is operating (see Box 27.1).

An initial glance at the capacities required for accountability show a certain degree of convergence because the core tasks are similar. I return to this feature in section three.

Idea 1: Clarifying learning purposes – Including accountability

> 'Would you tell me, please, which way I ought to go from here?' Alice speaks to the Cheshire Cat. 'That depends a good deal on where you want to get to,' said the Cat.
>
> Lewis Carrol, *Alice in Wonderland*

Perhaps the words from *Alice in Wonderland* are a bit tired and overused. But how valid they remain! 'Learning' is one a term much bandied around with little care as to its direction (see 'Trap 1' above).

During work on participatory monitoring in Brazil in the late 1990s with farmers, trade unions and NGOs, time and again, the question returned of 'who will use this data'. Each time we thought we had agreed on end users of the data, practice proved otherwise. A publicly stated intention by the NGO or the trade unions that they would use the data meant nothing. The penny dropped when we started asking 'but what purpose will this information serve?'

Table 27.1 *Purposes served by 'learning'*

Type of learning	Core purpose
1 Financial accountability	Maintain financial viability or security
2 Operational improvement	Adjust implementation to be more efficient, effective
3 Strategic readjustment	Examine/question strategy (e.g., by identifying and testing underlying assumptions)
4 Capacity strengthening	Improve individual performance or that of the organization
5 Contextual understanding	Keep up-to-date on the context of implementation
6 Deepening understanding (research)	Understand key uncertainties better and to formulate new questions on which to focus
7 Self-auditing	Maintain transparency and therefore trust in (collective) use of resources
8 Advocacy	Push for political change/in public policies/with decision-makers
9 Sensitization	Sensitize others to build and sustain support for concerted action

Source: Guijt, 2008

Akin to the fundamental question of 'capacity for what', clarifying purpose means focusing on what the learning is *for*, not only what one is learning *about*. And in this process, *accountability becomes one among various learning purposes* – seeking and sharing information to ensure financial management and stability. This is why this idea focuses on clarifying 'learning' – it automatically brings you to 'accountability'.

The Brazilian experience focused on learning for those engaged in concerted action for institutional transformation. Increasingly, partnerships or alliances are emerging as the mechanism for social change endeavours. Five of these pertain to management of the development intervention: financial accountability; operational improvement; strategic adjustment; contextual understanding and capacity strengthening. Four learning purposes are also part of the development interventions themselves: research; self-auditing; advocacy and sensitization (see Table 27.1).

Not all purposes will be equally important to each organization or partnership at any one time, and some might not be needed, for example 'self-auditing' or 'policy influencing'. My point here is that 'learning' requires direction. This helps make it operational in terms of timeframe, required evidence-based, engagement of stakeholders and, importantly, required capacities. Each purpose, including financial and strategic accountability, can thus bring forth a custom-built learning process with purpose-specific capacities.

Trap 2: Predicting and controlling an idealized world

Nasrudin found a weary falcon sitting one day on his window-sill. He had never seen a bird like this before. 'You poor thing', he said, 'how were you to allowed to get into this state?' He clipped the falcon's talons and cut its beak straight, and trimmed its feathers. 'Now you look more like a bird', said Nasrudin. (Shah, 1983, p223)

In many ways, this trap concerns a more pernicious and entrenched idea than the first trap. But it is also more straightforward. It concerns a relentless pursuit of change based on an idealized image of the world and of the change process itself. Yet, like Nasrudin, we want the world to be in a certain way, to be able to mould it, shape it, know it, and control it.

In responding to uncertainty, Kurtz and Snowden (2006) usefully make a distinction between *naturalized* and *idealized* thinking. Those with *idealistic* glasses on, seek to close the gap between an ideal future state and their perception of the present. Those with a *naturalistic* take on life strive to understand enough of the present in order to be able to stimulate its evolution. They compare the two perspectives in terms of where expertise lies and the knowing-acting cycle as the core of an important aspect of capacity:

> Idealistic approaches tend to privilege *expert* knowledge, analysis and interpretation. Naturalistic approaches emphasise the inherent un-knowability of current and future complexities, and thus they de-privilege expert interpretation in favour of enabling emergent meaning at the *ground level*.

Shifting towards a more naturalized take on development means being willing and able to invest in resilience, act adaptively and accept the need to roll with the punches. This requires the ability to continually scan the context and have the creativity required to deal with what is perceived. Critical is *figuring out what capacities make people and their efforts better able to cope with the certainty of change and the uncertainty this brings*. Here context analysis is essential.

Idea 2: Adapting expectations of accountability and learning to contextual characteristics

Being clear about the nature of the context in which one is operating can help one understand what is needed and what is feasible in connecting accountability and learning. Put another way, from a capacity development perspective the nature of the context can give pointers towards priorities in terms the type of capabilities and links required.

Figure 27.2 shows one framework that helps to clarify diversity of context. The 'Cynefin framework' provides a basic understanding how to act in situations with different degrees of complexity, that is where cause-effect linkages become more or less clear and reliable (Snowden and Boone, 2007). The power of the framework lies in forcing the question of what can realistically be expected of decision-making responses, knowledge management processes and general working procedures, given that one is dealing with situations that have inherently different characteristics.

Both the 'simple' and 'complicated' domains are ordered and are well suited to fact-based management and capacities that are repetitious or routine. In the *simple domain*, expectations are clear, cause and effect are directly related and the known can be predicted, repeated and perceived. Deviations and variance from what was anticipated signal problematic procedures and suggest concrete directions for remedial action. Accountability is relatively straightforward in being outcome-oriented. In this domain, learning and accountability can be better linked by addressing the five reasons for disconnection discussed above.

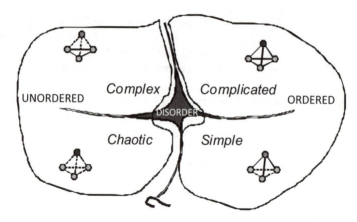

Figure 27.2 *Locating complexity*

The *complicated domain* relates to situations with more variables and elements that shape causes that, over time, exert their effects. Importantly, these effects can be known with expert input (anyone with relevant knowledge and experience). Analysis is needed to make sense of the interaction of different variables. Rather than categorization, 'sensing' what is happening is the entry point into analysis that enables a response or set of responses. Scenario planning and 'good practice' are at home in this domain. Accountability can remain outcome-oriented but, because more attention is paid to unpredictability and what can go awry, investing in learning becomes more critical. Expert consultation becomes a joint learning process and expected outcomes may shift as a result.

The domain that offers a 'liberating idea' is the *complex*. Here change follows an unpredictable trajectory. Cause and effect is only coherent retrospectively and cannot be repeated. It requires probing actionable options through safe-fail experimentation. It is the domain where accountability and learning depend on each other. Accountability is demonstrated by showing how learning has lead to adaptation or 'response-ability'. Capacity development is then about the increasing ability to gather the right information in order to make sense of what is going on in real time and to adjust accordingly.

This leaves us with the *chaotic domain* in which no clear cause-effect can be discerned and one is dealing with unknowables. Again, management best takes place through ongoing analysis of emerging patterns but requires action, then sensing what next step is needed and responding. Learning is embedded, while accountability becomes more akin to 'did we act as best as we could, given the little we knew under quickly changing circumstances'. Crisis task forces are at home within this domain.

Determining in what context one is operating – simple, complicated, complex, chaotic or disordered – allied to the purposes of learning and type of accountability enables appropriate capacity development choices. In other words; different capacities are needed to manage under distinct conditions.

Converging Capacities

In section two, capacities were identified that derived from the tasks that learning and accountability implied. If learning is to be a process of reflection that takes on the practical, the strategic and the transformational (and varied purposes), then diverse capacities are needed. The wide variety of different 'accountabilities' means that talking about capacity for accountability requires a choice. For accountability, I distinguish two core types – compliance-checking and strategic. Table 27.2 summarizes how these capacities relate to 'accountability' and 'learning', a list to which more could be added.

Two observations can be made about this table. First, there appears to be remarkable 'natural' convergence of capacities. This illustrates that there is greater overlap in terms of required capacities than perhaps seems obvious.

Second, there are important differences hidden within generic 'capacities'. For example, evidence gathering and analysis include a wide range of methodological options that will further dictate capacities. The capacity to undertake randomized control trials in order to 'prove impact' will require vastly different skills than undertaking a participatory impact assessment related to less intangible shifts in people's self-image. Hence it is critical to be precise about what, for example, process design capacities or reporting capacities are needed in order to ensure compliance versus those that are needed to ensure strategic accountability, or learning.

Table 27.2 *Capacities needed for accountability and learning under more complex conditions*

Capacities	Accountability		Learning
	Compliance	Strategic	
Process design (research and/or reflection)	X	X	X
Understand the context	X	X	X
Frame and revisit a theory of change	X	X	X
Formulate clear performance expectations	X	X	X
Identify assumptions	X	X	X
Make astute methodological choices	X	X	X
Gather evidence	X	X	X
Analyse multiple lines of evidence	X	X	X
Report findings and implications	X	X	X
Sense-making and critical reflection	X	X	X
Facilitation of reflection and dialogue		X	X
Creative thinking (consequences, alternatives)		X	X
Convene appropriate stakeholders		X	X
Negotiate differences and deal with power dynamics	X	X	X
Address cognitive biases and hazards	X	X	X

Arm-in-Arm: Principles, Practices and Basic Good Ideas to Resolve the Tension

Resolving the tension between accountability and learning is not about 'making it productive', a platitude that one often hears in relation to stubborn problems. It is about seeing them as part and parcel of the same need – a need for 'respond-ability' – akin to Chapter 5 in *Capacity Development in Practice*. These principles may offer some guidance for proceeding arm-in-arm.

1 Be clear that being accountable requires active learning activities and that engaging in learning includes processes to know whether one has delivered as promised. Therefore, there is *no inherent contradiction* between accountability and learning: 'The acid test of a good accountability system is that it encourages responsibility and promotes better performance' (Rogers, 2004). And this requires learning

2 Establish capacity development *preconditions by ensuring clarity*. Agree what one means by accountability (see Box 27.1) and what one can be held accountable for. And agree what one means by 'learning'. Such clarity will make more apparent if there is a big gap between expected processes, evidence, analysis, timing and capacities

3 Merge the *rhythms of accountability* with the learning rhythm of the organization or partnership. Identify when particular accountability needs must be met. Schedule learning processes to facilitate meeting of accountability requirements. For example, evidence gathering can be timed to feed into annual participatory reviews that generate conclusions and insights, which are subsequently shared with funding agencies and constituents

4 *Creatively merge needs*, for example, upward accountability requirements with strategic accountability and organizational learning needs. VECO Indonesia – a programme of Vredeseilanden Belgium – has opted to work with outcome mapping as it encourages more internal strategic reflection and accountability. At the same time, its main funder insists on a logframe format. VECO has constructed a format based on outcome mapping that dovetails with the logframe format, thus enabling donor financial accountability as a by-product

5 Understand the *nature* of one's intended change process and accommodate these methodologically and in terms of capacity. Start taking non-linearity and non-predictability more seriously *where this is appropriate*. Not everything is complex, nor is everything completely unpredictable

6 Processes of learning and accountability are essentially about bringing people and their perspective together to make sense of information and value performance in order to be able to respond. This means *engaging with the power dynamics* that exist between people, in hierarchies and in the aid sector in general. Having the skills to apply a power lens to these processes can help to strategize and create space for learning-oriented accountability – or accountability that feeds into learning.

Recommended Reading

The topics in this chapter have interesting connections to others in *Capacity Development in Practice*. Readers may wish to look at Chapter 12 which elaborates on public accountability which is tied to the area of monitoring and evaluation covered in Chapter 18, Chapters 19 and 20, providing a complement in terms of time frames for learning cycles and competencies and tools that support self-reflection.

The following is a short selection of useful resources as a starting point for further reading on this topic.

1   Argyris, C. and D. Schön (1978) *Organizational learning: A theory of action perspective*, Addison Wesley, Reading, Mass. (for an introduction to the core ideas, see www.infed.org/thinkers/argyris.htm, accessed November 2009)
     This classic text outlines key terms in organizational learning, both of which are central to surfacing and addressing assumptions and governing values. The first set of terms – theory-in-action and espoused theory – relates to the difference between the theories that are implicit in what we do (often tacit) and those that we use to explain to others or ourselves what we think we do. The second set of terms relates to whether learning occurs within the framework of given or chosen goals, plans, values, rules – so-called single loop learning. Another level of learning that requires questioning the assumed validity of these goals and plans is double loop learning, which can reframe the basic premises on which an organization operates. The book details how the two sets of ideas are related.

2   Ebrahim, A. (2005) *NGOs and Organizational Change. Discourse, Reporting and Learning*, Cambridge University Press
     This book explores change processes in NGOs, focusing on the relationships with international funders. This relationship impacts strongly on NGO change processes, leading to tensions in reporting requirements but also strategies used by NGOs to go their own way. It illustrates in sharp and insightful ways how the reporting requirements forces conceptualizations of work that in turn shape long-term development.

3   Land, T, V. Hauck and H. Baser (2009) 'Capacity Change and Performance. Capacity development: Between planned interventions and emergent processes. Implications for development cooperation', *Policy Management Brief,* 22, European Centre for Development Policy Management, Maastricht
     This provides a good introduction to how complexity thinking can help to reframe the expectations about capacity development as both process and product. It provides a useful comparison between planned interviews and emergent approaches by discussing key variables important in designing and implementing capacity development. It offers 12 implications for aid agencies who want to improve the capacity development they support.

4   Snowden, D. and M. Boone (2007) 'A Leader's Framework for Decision Making', *Harvard Business Review*, November 2007, pp69–76.
     An excellent overview of the Cynefin framework that focuses on the implications for leadership. It offers several ideas for managing under complex conditions and provides ample illustrates of how the simple, complicated, complex and chaotic demand different managerial responses.

Notes

1 See Schulpen and Ruben (2006) for a damning critique with respect to Netherlands official aid.
2 With thanks to Patricia Rogers for these ideas.
3 With thanks to Annelies Heijman.
4 Another version of triple loop learning considers 'are we learning as best as we can?' but this could be considered a special case of single and double loop learning.

References

Carroll, L. (1865) *Alice's Adventures in Wonderland*, Macmillan
Ebrahim, A. (2005) 'Accountability Myopia Can Impede NGO Learning and Mission', *Nonprofit and Voluntary Sector Quarterly*, Vol. 34, No. 1, pp56–87
Fry, R.E. (1995) 'Accountability in organizational life: Problem or opportunity for non-profits?', *Non-profit Management and Leadership*, Vol. 6, pp181–195
Goetz, A. and Jenkins, R. (2004) *Reinventing Accountability: Making Democracy Work for the Poor*, Palgrave, London
Guijt, I. (2008a) 'Seeking Surprise: Rethinking monitoring for collective learning in rural resource management', PhD thesis, Wageningen University, Wageningen
Guijt, I. (2008b) 'Assessing and Learning for Social Change', A Discussion Paper, Institute of Development Studies, Brighton
Kurtz, C. and Snowden, D. (2006) Bramble Bushes in a Thicket, available at www.cognitive-edge. com/ceresources/articles/52_Bramble_Bushes_in_a_Thicket.pdf (last accessed July 2010)
Newell, P. and Bellour, S. (2002) 'Mapping accountability: origins, contexts and implications for development', *IDS Working Paper 168*, Institute of Development Studies, Brighton
Perrin, B. (2002) 'Towards a New View of Accountability', paper presented to the European Evaluation Society annual conference, October 2002, Seville, Spain
Reeler, D. (2007) 'A Theory of Social Change and Implications for Practice, Planning, Monitoring and Evaluation', Community Development Resource Association, Cape Town
Rogers, P.J. (2004) 'Accountability' in Mathison, S. (ed) *Encyclopaedia of Evaluation*, Sage Publications, Newbury Park, CA
Shah, I. (1983) *The Exploits of the Incomparable Mulla Nasrudin*, Octagon Press
Schulpen, L. and Ruben, R. (2006) *Een gevoelige selectie. Analyse van de beoordelingssystematiek in het nieuwe Medefinancieringsstelsel* [A sensitive selection: Analysis of the assessment system in the ne co-financing framework], CIDIN, Nijmegen
Snowden, D. and Boone, M. (2007) 'A Leader's Framework for Decision Making', *Harvard Business Review*, November 2007, pp69–76
Ubels, J., Acquaye-Baddoo, N. and Fowler, A. (eds) (2010) *Capacity Development in Practice*, Earthscan, London.
UNDP (2007) 'Evaluation of Results-based Management in UNDP', UNDP, New York

28

Knowledge Management and Organizational Learning: An International Development Perspective

Ingeborg Hovland

Introduction

This chapter aims to review the current literature on knowledge management (KM) and organizational learning, particularly in relation to the international development field, in order to map out the rationale and objectives of KM and learning in this field, and to highlight gaps and emerging themes that will be of special interest to development actors and agencies. It is part of the Research and Policy in Development (RAPID) programme at the Overseas Development Institute (ODI).

Background

The purpose of ODI's RAPID programme is that better use be made of research in development policy and practice, in order to promote evidence-based and pro-poor policies. The programme focuses on four areas:

1   improved knowledge about research–policy links among development practitioners, policy-makers and researchers;
2   improved knowledge management and learning systems in southern and northern development agencies;
3   helping southern and northern researchers, practitioners and advocates to communicate research findings and influence policy more effectively;
4   improving awareness of the importance of research and how to access it among policy-makers and practitioners, especially in the UK.

This chapter is linked to the second focus area, namely improved knowledge management and learning systems in southern and northern development agencies. Since development policy and practice are largely formulated and implemented by various agencies – ranging from multilaterals, through bilaterals and governments, to NGOs – it is crucial to recognize the significant impact of organizational processes on the links between research, policy and practice.

This chapter reviews the current literature on KM and learning, paying particular attention to the literature on KM and learning in the international development field. Due to the substantial amount that has already been written on these issues, this paper does not present yet another guideline on 'how to do KM'. The common elements of a traditional KM organizational strategy are referred to briefly. These include: knowledge mapping; drawing up the value chain of an organization; gaining the support of top management; putting in place knowledge sharing systems and supportive information technology; updating intranet pages and staff contact information; strengthening Communities of Practice (teams or networks); using stories to communicate effectively; investing in new organizational processes; and encouraging cultural change within the organization. Those interested in the specific details and timing of these steps in a KM strategy will be able to find out more through the books, articles and reports summarized in the references. An accessible and easy-to-read introductory guide is 'Learning to Fly' (Collison and Parcell, 2001), and an introductory overview of the same issues applied to development agencies can be found in the report from Bellanet's 2000 KM Workshop (Bellanet International Secretariat, 2000) or on their KM4DEV wiki (http://wiki.km4dev.org/wiki, last accessed July 2010).

This chapter's primary aim is to review the current literature in order to map out the rationale and objectives of KM and learning within international development and to identify gaps and emerging themes. The chapter will be followed up by more operational work on these issues within ODI and practical recommendations on KM and learning will also be developed as part of the RAPID programme.

Previous work at ODI

ODI has already examined some of the issues related to KM and learning in international development through both published papers and projects. In 1998, *Development as Process* (Mosse et al, 1998) was published as part of the ODI Policy Studies Series. In particular, the book draws out the importance of social relationships, and the politics of information distribution and use in the context of development projects. It suggests that there is a need for new monitoring and evaluation criteria in the development sector, in order to be able to take into account intangible 'outputs' such as policy impact and institutional change. In 1999, an ODI Working Paper by Baumann, entitled 'Information and Power', reviewed the literature on information processes and the implications for process monitoring. The paper highlights the difficulties in assuming that people in an organization are willing to share their knowledge freely with other organizational staff. The paper suggests instead that it is more realistic to assume that actors will not be prepared to reveal the knowledge from which they derive their power. This has considerable implications for how to approach knowledge management and organizational learning.

The RAPID programme also builds on previous work at ODI concerning the dynamic of policy processes (Sutton, 1999), and an annotated bibliography and three-dimensional framework have been produced to more clearly map out the linkages between research and policy-making (De Vibe et al, 2002; Crewe and Young, 2002). In 2001, ODI established an Information and Communications Committee to advise on the design and implementation of a KM strategy in the institute. This objective has been strengthened with the appointment of a KM Research Officer in July 2003.

What is knowledge management and organizational learning?

What is knowledge management? As an introductory step it is useful to distinguish between raw information and knowledge (Edwards, 1994). Raw information may be widely available to a number of agencies, but only some organizations will be able to convert the information into relevant knowledge and to use this knowledge to achieve their aims. The processes by which they do this are known as KM strategies. In the section below on KM in the corporate sector, a further distinction will be made between first and second generation KM strategies. While the first generation focused on systematizing and controlling existing knowledge and knowledge sharing within an organization, the second generation KM strategies have shifted towards enhancing the conditions for innovation and knowledge creation (McElroy, 2000).

Challenges and advantages of KM are naturally related to challenges and advantages of organizational learning, and in the international development field these two sets of issues are often examined together. As with the two generations of KM strategies, an organization's ability to learn from past experiences can also be divided into first and second order strategies (Argyris, 1992). First order strategies concern 'single loop learning', aimed at correcting and modifying practices in order to fit in with an established policy. Second order strategies are those of 'double loop learning', which – in parallel with second generation KM strategies – aim to increase the organization's capacity to think creatively and act innovatively.

Review of the Literature

Knowledge management and learning in the development sector

The corporate sector has embraced KM and learning with the aim of improving organizational efficiency – measured in metrical figures of production and profit. In the development sector, organizational efficiency is also important, but it is far from the only aim. Many development agencies today work towards the Millennium Development Goals (MDGs) and measure their degree of success in terms of their impact on poverty reduction and policy change. In order to work towards these larger objectives, agencies not only need efficient internal coordination, but also increased ability to be responsive to the situation of the poor, and ability to influence debates and policy processes. The KM and learning needs of the development sector are therefore different in certain respects from those of the mainstream corporate sector, and recommendations from the corporate KM literature cannot be transferred indiscriminately. In recognition of this, development consultants and authors have started writing about KM and learning specifically in relation to different types of development organizations.

By far the most work has been carried out on KM and learning in northern or international development NGOs (INGOs). Some of this is linked to the literature on monitoring and evaluation (M&E). A lesser amount of work has also been carried out on KM in large donor agencies, such as the World Bank and some bilateral agencies (perhaps most prominently in Department for International Development, UK (DFID) and Sida). Very little work has focused on the particular KM and learning challenges faced by southern institutions, and even less on the specialized niche that ODI is especially interested in, namely KM and learning in research institutes and think-tanks, both northern and southern. Each of these types of organizations within the development sector are discussed in turn below.

Northern NGOs/INGOs

Changing role and context: The emergence of the information age in the 1990s coincided with the notable increase in numbers and relative influence of northern development NGOs. The rise of NGOs has prompted extensive reflection on the part they have to play in development, and in the current literature there is a widespread perception that the role of northern and international development NGOs is changing in significant ways. Northern NGOs are no longer regarded as unquestionably legitimate, but are expected to justify their own legitimacy by building credible relationships with southern communities and partners (Fowler, 1992). Northern NGOs are also no longer seen as neutral service delivery vehicles, but are taking on the roles of information broker and advocate in the interface between southern communities and national/international policy processes (Edwards, 1994).

Northern NGOs have another new role to play in building the capacity of southern civil society organizations to process knowledge and engage effectively in national/international development debates and decision-making processes (Keeble, 2002). All this requires NGOs to have high quality internal learning and information processing systems. In addition, calls for knowledge-based aid and the globalization of knowledge require NGOs to reflect on how their internal KM and learning systems interact with external information flows and policy trends (King, 2001).

Monitoring and evaluation: Although the KM and learning literature in the development field is by no means as copious as in the corporate sector, the changing context and role of northern NGOs has nonetheless generated a substantial amount of research, ranging from individual organizational guidelines (e.g. Powell, 2003, for Oxfam) and surveys of NGO learning (BOND, 2003), to academic attempts to develop a coherent theory of learning processes within NGOs (Davies, 1998). Much of the literature on learning processes situates itself within the field of monitoring and evaluation (M&E) (e.g. Marsden et al, 1994). Korten (1984) was one of the first authors to point out that organizations evaluate their errors in different ways. When organizations see errors as failures, staff will tend to hide their errors away and little learning will occur at an organizational level. On the other hand, if an organization sees errors as sources of information, staff will be encouraged to discuss past experiences and to carry forward new knowledge. Korten calls this the 'learning process approach'.

Recently, development agencies have also become interested in means of assessing not only their own learning, but also the intangible impact of their work – e.g. their policy influence. Corporate sector models of performance measurement, as discussed above, have largely avoided this area of intangible impact (focusing instead on how to measure their internal intangible assets and how to display these as metrical figures). In the development sector, a few complementary models have been suggested. In relation to M&E in development agencies and projects, the edited volume *Development as Process* (Mosse et al, 1998) proposes a new look at the role of monitoring information and organizational relationships. The book suggests that new M&E criteria should be developed in order to take into account intangible development outcomes such as policy impact and institutional change. In addition, such criteria should be monitored through a continuous process, rather than only at the end of a project, so that the information feedback can be used to guide practice on an ongoing basis. Even more recently, Lloyd-Laney (2003) has developed advocacy impact assessment guidelines, mapping out questions and issues that need to be taken into account when designing measurement indicators in this field. Indicators are suggested for the following dimensions: policy formulation and implementation, private sector change, civil society strengthening, democratization and improvements in the material situation of individuals.

Particular characteristics: It is worth noting, as King (2001) does, that on the whole the question of KM and learning in relation to development NGOs has led to a focus on internal organizational needs within northern NGOs, rather than a focus on the dramatic southern knowledge deficits. The current literature highlights several particular internal organizational characteristics of northern/international NGOs. These include the following:

- geographical distance between headquarters and field offices, which frequently leads to certain information gaps and learning tensions (Suzuki, 1998);
- the geographical range of NGOs can also be an advantage in that it gives them a comparative advantage in brokering information from the local, national and international level at the same time (Edwards, 1994);
- the NGO's ultimate 'customers' or 'beneficiaries' are not the same people as the NGO's donors, leading to different knowledge demands in relation to different groups (Roche, 1998);
- there is usually a high need for success stories to legitimate the NGO's existence, which may hinder learning (Roche, 1998);
- while NGOs continually try to bring about change in their environment, they are themselves often characterized by internal 'change fatigue', stemming from information overload and continuous demands for adaptation and response (Madon, 2000; O'Malley and O'Donoghue, 2001).

Emerging challenges: There are a few issues related to KM and learning that are especially challenging for northern/international NGOs:

- *Who benefits most: North or south?* In a sector that wishes to work towards the overarching goal of poverty reduction, it is important to consider whether the new KM trend contributes to this goal, or whether it is yet another process that benefits the north more than the south. As previously noted, questions of KM and learning in the development sector have predominantly centred on the internal knowledge needs and processes of northern agencies, rather than on the knowledge gaps and development in southern institutions. King (2001) suggests that northern KM projects should aim to escape from their present narrow focus and instead examine southern knowledge bases and knowledge systems, and find ways of supporting these

- *Invest in one-way or two-way information flows?* It is not enough for northern NGOs to improve the efficiency of their information flows without also considering the direction of these flows. Frequently there is far stronger pressure on NGOs to develop a one-way flow of information from the field and 'up' to headquarters and donors, rather than investing in a two-way flow (Edwards, 1994). This is related to the lack of analysis about the knowledge needs of southern communities. The new focus on partnerships between northern and southern institutions may be one way of dealing with this challenge, provided that the partnerships aim explicitly for mutual sharing of information and relevant learning (Drew, 2002)

- *Prioritize field-based or policy-related learning?* Northern NGOs today are expected to perform in far more areas than before. They must not only be engaged in field delivery, but also in research and reflection, debates and decision-making, advocacy and policy influence. This may sometimes lead to difficult choices between investment in field-based learning or policy-related learning (Madon, 2000). It may also generate tension between different types of information within an organization, as field-based information does not necessarily lead to the same strategic conclusions as policy-related information (Suzuki, 1998).

These emerging challenges for northern/international NGOs will be discussed further in Section 3.

Southern institutions

Organizations in different contexts: Organizations function in different ways within different cultural, political and economic contexts. This obviously has implications within the international development field. To put it crudely, the best KM, learning and evaluation strategies in the UK are not necessarily the best KM, learning and evaluation strategies in Uganda. Different groups and organizations (whether they are different due to political circumstances, economic resources, culture, social background or religion etc.) may have different associations to concepts such as 'leadership', 'cooperation', 'information', 'sharing' and 'monitoring'. One example of such differences is given by an anthropologist, Bailey, who examined the notion of 'leadership' in a peasant community in India. He found that traditional leaders function by commanding respect and giving orders; they never ask for 'cooperation'. Therefore, when outsiders such as higher-level politicians or development workers come to ask the villagers to cooperate so that everyone can learn together, 'to the villagers this seems either a joke or something to be very worried about, as a football player would be if he heard himself being urged on and urged to cooperate by the captain of the opposing team' (Bailey, 1971, p308).

The question of capacity building: The context and particular challenges facing southern institutions is an important topic because it has direct implications for how to approach local institutional capacity building, strengthen local democracy, and support southern engagement in development debates and decision-making. An illustrative example of this is a civil society organization in India – the Workers' and Farmers' Power Organization – which has found ways of using information in new ways to great effect (Jenkins and Goetz, 1999). They have waged a campaign to secure the right of ordinary people to gain access to information held by government officials, and through this have managed to contribute to greater local accountability. How are such southern civil society institutions strengthened, and what, if anything, do (northern) development agencies have to contribute to this process? Nicholson (1994) and Nuijten (1992) draw on experiences from Papua New Guinea and Mexico respectively to show that western-type institutional models do not automatically translate into a new context without significant adaptations and modifications. They suggest that capacity building projects in the south are overly based on ingrained notions of western organizational concepts and processes, and argue that the best contribution development agencies can make is to build on local understanding. To a certain degree, this is the same point made by Stiglitz (1999): capacity building or conditionality that is imposed from the outside will not produce lasting change, but only undermine people's incentives to develop their own capacities.

The public sector. Compared to the vast amount of literature on western institutions, relatively little research has been carried out so far on particular circumstances and challenges facing institutions in the south. The same is true of the literature on monitoring and evaluation (M&E), which is overly based on western experiences. However, a few studies on specific southern contexts have been carried out. Rondinelli (1993) examined public sector development programmes undertaken by southern governments, and found that they were generally excessively control oriented and top-down, thus cutting off the possibility of learning. He argues that this is in part due to expectations of external donors and aid agencies who place a lot of emphasis on coherent national development plans. Frequently, however, plans on paper can be far removed from the reality they are trying to influence.

World Bank research shifts the focus away from the potential tension between external donors and national governments, and instead highlights the tension between external institutional models and indigenous organizational forms (Dia, 1996). In line with new institutional economics theory, the institutional crisis affecting economic management in Africa is due to the structural disconnect between these different institutional forms. An institutional 'reconciliation paradigm' is proposed (Dia, 1996). However, another study of African organizations and management suggests that the success of such organizational reconciliation will depend in part on the size of the organization (Carlsson, 1998). Small businesses seem to be able to draw on different resources to adapt continually to new circumstances, many times out of pure necessity. However, larger organizations and public sector institutions are more constrained due to lack of economic resources, lack of trained personnel, a frequently unstable and therefore risk-averse environment and centralized state decision-making structures. This results in reduced capacity to manage change, and Carlsson concludes that public sector institutional processes in Africa tend to change as a result of changes in the environment in which they operate, rather than as a result of their own strategic aims.

The non-governmental sector. Hailey and James (2002) build on case studies of nine 'successful' South Asian NGOs in order to comment on how NGOs learn. They conclude that the single most important factor affecting organizational learning is a learning leader. The most important characteristic of the learning leaders in South Asia was not the particular internal organizational strategies that they put in place, but instead their ability to understand and work within a changing and complex environment. On the other hand, Uphoff's (1992) study from Sri Lanka suggests that the critical factor in non-governmental organizational capacity is not necessarily organized leadership. Uphoff examines the success of a large-scale irrigation system and argues that it worked well because it was not planned according to a predictable and fixed model, but rather evolved organically as farmers gradually engaged in flexible systems of cooperation.

Flexibility, however, is a difficult issue in many development contexts, due to different expectations of donors, policy-makers, practitioners and other participants. Non-governmental institutions are often required to provide proof of impact and effectiveness. The realities of M&E in southern organizations have been presented in a special issue of *Knowledge, Technology and Policy* where one of the common themes highlighted was 'donor fatigue'. Impact evidence was seen as 'something which is most frequently requested by funding agencies, most frequently promised by evaluators and least frequently delivered in evaluation reports' (Horton and Mackay, 1999). Another theme was the concern that methods used in the field are perceived to lag behind professional development in general.

Technology in southern institutions: Information and communication technologies (ICTs) are often promoted as the solution to many of the information and communication problems faced by organizations. However, ICT projects in southern institutions frequently fail or remain functional for only a brief period of time (Heeks, 2002). Heeks attributes this to a gap between the design of northern IT systems and the reality of southern institutions, which on the whole do not have the same level of technological infrastructure, local skills base or contextual stability as northern institutions. In addition, as Volkow (1998) points out, it is not enough to introduce IT systems if organizational management structures or other processes hinder the systems from functioning. Another challenge is the fact that ICT innovation and application in the north is mostly aimed at private companies, while in the south the main client is the public sector (Moussa and Schware, 1992). Public sector organizations have different requirements for handling information in relation to policy-making, consultation and reporting processes, and cannot necessarily adopt the same IT systems as the private sector. Policy recommendations on this issue vary from calls for intensive planning (Moussa and Schware, 1992), to suggestions about mixed teams of technical experts and organizational managers (Heeks, 2002), or knowledge partnerships and the need to engage the private sector (Chapman and Slaymaker, 2002).

Gaps in the Literature and Future Issues

There are a few gaps in the literature on KM and learning that are of particular importance to agencies working in the international development field. In this section they are presented under the four headings of responsiveness, impact on policy, impact of policy and southern engagement. These are issues that are relevant to development agencies in the current international development context, and which could usefully be linked to agencies' KM and learning strategies.

Knowledge management/learning and responsiveness

Viable civil society organizations (CSOs) provide a base from which the voice of the poor can be heard in decision and policy-making processes that affect their lives. However, this is only true if CSOs are able to assess and represent the situation of the poor accurately and to formulate appropriate responses. One of the factors determining the capacity of CSOs to do this is their ability to process information and use it in the most effective manner. Can improved KM and learning systems enable them to do this better, i.e. to respond to the situation of their 'beneficiaries' more accurately and effectively? Or is KM in this context an example of the self-absorbed practices that can sometimes make northern development agencies or elite-based southern CSOs revolve around themselves? Edwards (1994) answers this question by pointing to NGOs' democratic value base and their emphasis on openness and non-hierarchical communication channels. He argues that these inherent values will enable NGOs to use their information systems and processes to the benefit of the grassroots communities with which they work. King (2001) provides a less idealistic analysis of the situation, emphasizing that KM and learning processes do not automatically or necessarily make NGOs more responsive to southern needs. He voices concerns about the fact that northern NGOs have so far implemented KM to alleviate their own information blockages – based on the same rationale of efficiency and profit as corporate businesses – rather than using KM to address key questions of how they can contribute to knowledge development in the south.

How can a development organization's ability to be responsive be strengthened? A useful distinction can be made here between 'step thinking' and 'web thinking' (O'Malley and O'Donoghue, 2001). Step thinking can be illustrated, for example, by evaluation tied to the project cycle such as the 'before-during-after' approach (BOND, 2003). 'Learning before' starts by looking at lessons from past projects; 'learning during' a project consists of continuously reviewing project objectives; and 'learning after' a project is carried out by drawing together general reflections and lessons for the future. Web thinking, on the other hand, can be illustrated by partnership learning. The mutual organizational learning that goes on (or ideally should go on) in a partnership is an example of web thinking where different elements are brought into the picture at different points, where ideas are bounced off each other, and where the aim is to try and see the broader picture, without having a step by step answer (Drew, 2002). Any development agency will usually engage in both step thinking and web thinking as means of processing information and learning; the difference between agencies lies in the relative emphasis they give to one or the other of these approaches.

Further work is needed to examine the questions:

- Can KM/learning increase the responsiveness of southern and northern institutional processes to the situation of the 'beneficiaries'?
- Can KM/learning help to connect the voice of the poor with the institutional knowledge of development/civil society organizations?

Knowledge management/learning and impact on policy

Northern development NGOs are increasingly called on to carry out advocacy work based on evidence from the south, and to add value to policy debates both nationally and internationally. Yet experience indicates that NGO programme managers and policy officers are under perennial time and funds pressures to move quickly from concept to implementation, with less space than they would wish for undertaking comprehensive research to strengthen their evidence or undertaking analysis on how to influence policy effectively. Can improved KM and learning systems in development agencies enable them to influence policy processes more effectively? This is a key question that will need to be examined in future work on KM and learning in the international development field.

A related question concerns what type of knowledge and KM strategy will provide strategic advantage for a development organization wishing to strengthen its ability to influence. In theory one might distinguish between knowledge of the field (bottom-up learning) and knowledge of higher-level negotiation processes (top-down learning or centre-out learning). For development organizations it is important to have knowledge of the field in order to boost their legitimacy and influencing power (Fowler, 1992). This means they need to have good information systems in place in order to process information from the field quickly and effectively – from the right people, to the right people, at the right time (Madon, 2000). An emphasis on field knowledge also means that the higher levels of the organization have to be willing to learn from staff in field offices and 'on the ground'. However, in order to have an impact on policy, agencies also need knowledge of higher-level negotiation processes, i.e. knowledge of the channels through which to influence and how to go about influencing (Keeble, 2002). This is often a job for senior staff in a development NGO, or staff based at headquarters. They will communicate to field office staff the type of information they need and which channels the information should go through. In these situations learning takes place from the centre-out, i.e. field staff have to learn from the headquarters, based on the past experiences of headquarters staff.

Development agencies most frequently have to display knowledge of the field as well as knowledge of negotiation and policy processes. They need to make use of both bottom-up learning and centre-out learning in their organization. This situation brings with it much potential tension (Suzuki, 1998). Some of the same tension is shared by large corporations who have offices in different countries. However, agencies in the development sector have an added tension in that they are accountable to at least two different groups of people (Edwards, 1994). Business market analysts have a certain advantage over the NGO sector in that their clients are also their target group and financial supporters (for example, advertisements) (Roche, 1998). This usually means that if they have accurate knowledge of the consumers and their needs/demands, they have a good chance of making a profit. For development organizations, on the other hand, the 'clients' are separate from the funders and the two groups require different 'advertising' strategies. They also constitute two different target groups that organizations need to influence in different ways. This creates a need for strategic knowledge in development organizations that is somewhat further split between knowledge of the field and knowledge of negotiation processes than would be the case in a corporate firm.

This is worth bearing in mind when applying ideas from much of the KM literature to international development organizations. For example, Senge (1990), based on analysis of businesses in the corporate sector, speaks of 'the learning organization' as if the whole organization was one harmonious entity where all sections and staff are willing to learn together. This conclusion must be modified in line with the particular tensions experienced by development organizations. Against this background, further work is needed to examine the questions:

- Can KM/learning help to connect different types of institutional knowledge within the same organization?
- Can KM/learning help to connect institutional knowledge and policy-making processes?
- Can KM/learning increase southern and northern development organizations' impact on policy?

Knowledge management/learning and impact of policy

It is usual to speak of capacity for 'research uptake' into a policy process. However, it is of little use to influence a policy process unless the policy actually has some impact. This suggests that one should also speak of the capacity for 'policy uptake': how much of a policy is taken up into practice, and how quickly does it happen? How are policies bypassed, reinterpreted, modified and sometimes drastically changed as they are implemented? Why do some policies simply evaporate? There are several factors that influence whether or not, and to what extent, policy ideas and formulations are picked up and acted on by the agents who are the official implementers of policy. The central issue in relation to KM/learning is whether improved KM and learning systems can enable development agencies to translate policy into practice more effectively.

There is increasing interest in examining these issues in the UK. In 1999 the Economic and Social Research Council established the Evidence Based Policy and Practice Initiative, a collaborative network of seven research units aiming to bring social science research closer to the decision- making process (see www.evidencenetwork.org, last accessed July 2010). One of the research units involved has produced a framework for understanding the 'evidence into practice' process, emphasising, among other things, the shift from 'researcher as disseminator' to 'practitioner as learner' (Nutley et al, 2002).

However, there are very few case studies documenting what actually happens to development policies in practice. The examples that do exist, mainly within the sociological and anthropological field, only serve to highlight the need for more research on this issue. Lipsky (1980) examines what happens at the point where public policy is translated into practice in human service bureaucracies such as schools, courts and welfare agencies. He argues that in the end policy comes down to the people who actually implement it (the teachers, lawyers, social workers, etc.). They are the 'street-level bureaucrats' and are able to change the planned impact of policy to a large degree. In many instances this is not an intentional action by the street-level bureaucrats, but rather a natural reaction to various pressures such as limited resources, continuous negotiation with headquarters and relations with clients.

Another illustrative example is provided by Mosse (2002). At a recent workshop framed by concerns about how DFID could become a learning organization, he presented a case study of policy–practice linkages in a rural development DFID project in India. He argued that in this case the policy of participatory development did not primarily serve the function of guiding action. Rather, it served the function of legitimizing the action that was taken. Thus, the policy process in this project was not a process where policy was followed through in practice, but instead a matter of practice needing to be followed up by the correct policy model, in order to interpret and justify the actions that had been taken. The representations used concerning 'participatory development' served as successful marketing devices that convinced superiors, secured funds from donors and garnered higher political support.

As these two cases show, the link between policy and practice can be tenuous and frequently the policy–practice dynamic is played out in a different way from that which the policy-makers and donors had intended. There is therefore a need to learn more about the relationship between policies and practice in international development, focusing on the question of how and under what conditions practitioners take policies into account in their everyday work and in their dealings with donors. Further work is needed to develop an understanding of the following issues:

- Can KM/learning help to connect development policy with implementation of development programmes and projects?
- Can KM/learning increase the ability of institutions to translate policy into institutional practice?
- Can KM/learning increase the ability of institutions to take practice into account in their policy models?

Knowledge management/learning and southern engagement

Northern NGOs are called upon to develop new roles. They now have a role to play in a relationship of mutual exchange with southern NGOs, which involves both information sharing and joint contributions to policy processes. In some situations, northern NGOs will be called on to support and strengthen the capacity of southern CSOs to engage with national and international debates and decision-making (Keeble, 2002). As southern-based agencies improve their own capacity to produce and disseminate research, and as they gain increased access to research from northern agencies and international networks, they gain power to engage more effectively in national and international debates and policy-making processes. As DFID's latest Research Policy Paper argues:

> The evidence suggests that the capacity of developing countries to generate, acquire, assimilate and utilize knowledge will form a crucial part of their strategies to reduce poverty. (Surr et al, 2002, pv)

Can improved KM and learning systems in development agencies enable them to bridge the gap between northern and southern development institutions more effectively, facilitating not only northern contributions to southern concerns, but also southern involvement in international development debates? Or will KM prove to be a luxury that only northern and international agencies can afford, thus widening the gap between north and south?

One way of avoiding a situation where KM primarily works to the benefit of northern agencies, while passing southern agencies by, is to combine KM and learning concerns with an explicit focus on southern knowledge needs and challenges. In some southern contexts, the most obvious challenges relate to information infrastructure – including the need for increased and improved technical, financial, institutional and human resources (KFPE, 2001). In the edited volume by KFPE, several means of addressing this situation – aimed at northern agencies – are outlined. For example, northern institutions can cultivate partnerships with southern institutions – of which a central component can be information exchange: they can offer visiting fellowship positions in their institutions to southern colleagues or offer to co-host conferences and workshops that bring northern and southern agency staff together; they can engage in more demand-driven research, in association with southern partners; and they can specialize in institutional strengthening in specific geographic regions and/or related to specific international development themes.

Finally, then, further work is needed to examine the questions:

- Can KM/learning help to connect southern institutions and northern institutions/processes?
- Can KM/learning (in both southern and northern agencies) contribute to increased southern engagement in international development debates?

References

Argyris, Chris (1992) *Overcoming Organizational Defences: Facilitating Organizational Learning*, Boston: Allyn and Bacon

Bailey, F.G. (1971) 'The Peasant View of the Bad Life', in Teodor Shamin (ed) *Peasants and Peasant Societies*, Harmondsworth, UK: Penguin

Bellanet International Secretariat (2000) 'Knowledge Management for Development Organisations' Report of the Knowledge Management Brighton Workshop, 26–28 June 2000, at the University of Sussex (available at http://idl-bnc.idrc.ca/dspace/bitstream/10625/18243/1/116291.pdf, last accessed July 2010)

BOND (2003) 'Learning from Work: An opportunity missed or taken?', BOND survey, London: British Overseas NGOs for Development (available at http://portals.wi.wur.nl/files/docs/ppme/learningfromwork.pdf, last accessed July 2010)

Carlsson, Jerker (1998) 'Organization and leadership in Africa', in Lennart Wohlgemuth, Jerker Carlsson and Henock Kifle (eds) *Institution Building and Leadership in Africa*, Uppsala: Nordic Africa Institute

Chapman, Robert and Tom Slaymaker (2002) 'ICTs and Rural Development: Review of the Literature, Current Interventions and Opportunities for Action', ODI Working Paper 192. London: Overseas Development Institute (available at www.odi.org.uk/publications, last accessed July 2010)

Collison, Chris and Geoff Parcell (2001) *Learning to Fly: Practical Lessons from one of the World's Leading Knowledge Companies*, Oxford: Capstone

Crewe, Emma and John Young (2002) 'Bridging Research and Policy: Context, Evidence and Links', ODI Working Paper 173. London: Overseas Development Institute (available at www.odi.org.uk/publications, last accessed July 2010)

Davies, Rick (1998) Order and Diversity: Representing and Assisting Organisational Learning in Non-Government Aid Organisations, PhD thesis, Swansea: Centre for Development Studies, University of Wales (available at www.mande.co.uk/docs/thesis.htm, last accessed July 2010)

De Vibe, Maja, Ingeborg Hovland and John Young (2002) 'Bridging Research and Policy: An Annotated Bibliography', ODI Working Paper 174. London: Overseas Development Institute (available at www.odi.org.uk/publications, last accessed July 2010)

DFID (2000) Doing the Knowledge: How DFID Compares with Best Practice in Knowledge Management, London: Department for International Development (available at www.dfid.gov.uk, last accessed July 2010)

Dia, Mamadou (1996) Africa's management in the 1990s and beyond: Reconciling indigenous and transplanted institutions. Washington DC: World Bank

Drew, Roger (2002) 'Learning in Partnership: What constitutes learning in the context of south-north partnerships?', BOND Discussion Paper. London: British Overseas NGOs for Development

Edwards, Michael (1994) 'NGOs in the age of information' IDS Bulletin 25(2): 117–24.

Fowler, Alan (1992) 'Prioritizing Institutional Development: A New Role for NGO Centres for Study and Development', IIED Gatekeeper Series No. 35. London: International Institute for Environment and Development

Hailey, John and Rick James (2002) 'Learning Leaders: The Key to Learning Organisations', *Development in Practice*, 12(3/4): 398–408

Heeks, Richard (2002) 'Failure, success and improvisation of information systems projects in developing countries' Development Informatics Working Paper 11. Manchester: Institute for Development Policy and Management, University of Manchester (available at http://unpan1.un.org/intradoc/groups/public/documents/nispacee/unpan015601.pdf, last accessed July 2010)

Horton, Douglas and Ronald Mackay (eds) (1999) 'Evaluation in Developing Countries: Experiences with Agricultural Research and Development', *Knowledge, Technology and Policy*, Special Issue 11(4)

Jenkins, Rob and Anne Marie Goetz (1999) 'Accounts and Accountability: Theoretical Implications of the Right-to-Information Movement in India', *Third World Quarterly*, 20(3): 603–22

Keeble, Sally (2002) 'The Role of Northern Civil Society in International Development', Speech by the Parliamentary Under-Secretary of State for International Development at the BOND Annual General Meeting, 11 July (available at www.dfid.gov.uk, last accessed July 2010)

KFPE (2001) Enhancing Research Capacity in Developing and Transition Countries. Berne: Swiss Commission for Research Partnerships with Developing Countries (KFPE)

King, Kenneth (2001) '"Knowledge Agencies": Making the Globalisation of Development Knowledge Work for the World's Poor?', Learning to Make Policy Working Paper 9. Edinburgh: Centre of African Studies, University of Edinburgh (available at http://www.mekonginfo.org/HDP/Lib.nsf, last accessed July 2010)

Korten, David (1984) 'Rural Development Programming: The Learning Process Approach' in David Korten and Rudi Klauss (eds) *People-Centered Development: Contributions toward Theory and Planning Frameworks*, West Hartford, CT, USA: Kumarian Press

Lipsky, Michael (1980) *Street-level Bureaucracy: Dilemmas of the Individual in Public Services*, New York: Russell Sage Foundation

Lloyd-Laney, Megan (2003) Advocacy Impact Assessment Guidelines. Wallingford, Oxon: Communications and Information Management Resource Centre (CIMRC) (available at http://www.research4development.info/SearchResearchDatabase.asp?OutPutId=65302, last accessed July 2010)

Madon, Shirin (2000) 'International NGOs: Networking, information flows and learning' Development Informatics Working Paper Series 8. Manchester: Institute of Development Policy and Management, University of Manchester (available at http://unpan1.un.org/intradoc/groups/public/documents/NISPAcee/UNPAN015542.pdf, last accessed July 2010)

March, James G. (1991) 'Exploration and exploitation in organizational learning', *Organization Science*, 2(1): 71–87

Marsden, David, Peter Oakley and Brian Pratt (1994) 'Measuring the Process: Guidelines for Evaluating Social Development', NGO Management and Policy Series 3. Oxford: International NGO Training and Research Centre

McElroy, Mark (2000) 'Second-Generation KM: A White Paper' Knowledge Management 4(3)

Mosse, David (2002) 'The Western India Rainfed Farming Project: Seminar and Discussion', PARC Document 8, presented at a DFID learning organization seminar, 5 July 2002. Birmingham: Performance Assessment Resource Centre, International Organisation Development Ltd (available at www.livelihoods.org/post/Docs/WIRFP.doc, last accessed July 2010)

Mosse, David, John Farrington and Alan Rew (eds) (1998) *Development as Process: Concepts and Methods for Working with Complexity*, London: Overseas Development Institute and Routledge

Moussa, Antoun and Robert Schware (1992) 'Informatics in Africa: Lessons from World Bank Experience', *World Development*, 20(12): 1737–52

Nicholson, Trish (1994) 'Institution building: Examining the fit between bureaucracies and indigenous systems' in Susan Wright (ed) *Anthropology of Organizations*, London: Routledge

Nuijten, Monique (1992) 'Local organization as organizing practices: Rethinking rural institutions' in Norman Long and Ann Long (eds) *Battlefields of Knowledge*, London: Routledge

Nutley, Sandra, Isabel Walter and Huw Davies (2002) 'From Knowing to Doing: A framework for understanding the evidence-into-practice agenda', Discussion Paper 1. St Andrews, UK: Research Unit for Research Utilisation, University of St Andrews

O'Malley, Dolores and Geoff O'Donoghue (2001) *NGOs and the Learning Organisation*, London: British Overseas NGOs for Development

Powell, Mike (2003) *Information management for development organisations*, 2nd edition. Oxford: Oxfam Development Guidelines Series. Oxford: Oxfam

Roche, Chris (1998) 'Organizational assessment and institutional footprints' in Alan Thomas, Joanna Chataway and Marc Wuyts (eds) *Finding out Fast: Investigative Skills for Policy and Development*, London: Sage and the Open University

Rondinelli, Dennis (1993) *Development Projects as Policy Experiments: An Adaptive Approach to Development Administration*, London: Routledge

Schein, Edgar (1992) 'The Learning Leader as Culture Manager' in *Organizational Culture and Leadership*, San Francisco: Jossey-Bass Publishers

Senge, Peter (1990) *The Fifth Discipline: The Art and Practice of the Learning Organisation*, New York: Doubleday/Currency

Song, Steve (1999) Guidelines on the use of electronic networking to facilitate regional or global research networks. Ottawa: International Development Research Centre (available at http://www.idrc.ca/en/ev-33951-201-1-DO_TOPIC.html, last accessed July 2010)

Stacey, Ralph (1995) 'The Role of Chaos and Self-Organization in the Development of Creative Organizations', in Alain Albert (ed) *Chaos and Society*, Amsterdam: IOS Press

Stiglitz, Joseph (1999) 'Public Policy for a Knowledge Economy', Remarks at the Department for Trade and Industry and Centre for Economic Policy Research, London, 27 January 1999 (available at www.worldbank.org/html/extdr/extme/jssp012799a.html, last accessed July 2010)

Surr, Martin, Andrew Barnett, Alex Duncan, Melanie Speight, David Bradley, Alan Rew and John Toye (2002) Research for Poverty Reduction: DFID Research Policy Paper. London: Department for International Development, UK (DFID) (available at www.dfid.gov.uk, last accessed July 2010)

Sutton, Rebecca (1999) The Policy Process: An Overview. ODI Working Paper 118. London: Overseas Development Institute (ODI) (available at www.odi.org.uk/publications, last accessed July 2010)

Suzuki, Naoki (1998) *Inside NGOs: Learning to Manage Conflicts between Headquarters and Field Offices*, London: Intermediate Technology Development Group Publishing

Uphoff, Norman (1992) *Learning from Gal Oya: Possibilities for Participatory Development and Post-Newtonian Social Science*, Ithaca, NY: Cornell University Press

Volkow, Natalia (1998) 'Strategic Use of Information Technology Requires Knowing How to Use Information', in Chrisanthi Avgerou (ed) Implementation and Evaluation of Information Systems in Developing Countries, Proceedings of the Fifth International Working Conference of the International Federation for Information Processing, Working Group 9.4, 18–20 February 1998, Bangkok

Part IX

Managing Resources

29

Options, Strategies and Trade-offs in Resource Mobilization

Alan Fowler

... many CSOs can benefit by stepping back from their day-to-day demands ... to take a strategic view of resource enhancement possibilities. (Schearer et al, 1997)

Resources steer organizations. How you raise the resources you need, and from which source, has a strong influence on what an organization is and what it can be.[1] This chapter examines how resources impact on NGDOs. It provides a framework of 14 resource options and characteristics against which different options can be assessed for their likely effects.

The chapter starts with a cautionary note about equating money with sustainability. Finance is a necessary, but not sufficient, condition. The subsequent section takes a broad view of what is going on in terms of resource supply and demand that is likely to affect NGDO strategies. Then, using insights from theories of resource dependency, the chapter identifies the strategic choices available, together with the major trade-offs they imply. The options are then used for the analysis and discussion to be found in the rest of the chapters that make up Part II of *The Virtuous Spiral* (Fowler, 2000).

Fixing the Financial Fixation

There is an old American school of thought arguing that the final measure of non-profit performance is continuity in raising money.[2] If the organization is not doing something right for someone, it will eventually wither away and die.[3] As the saying goes, you can fool some people all of the time and all of the people some of the time, but you can't fool all of the people all of the time. This holds particularly true for NGDOs that, in many countries, are the object of government mistrust and public suspicion. They face a tough test in ensuring resource continuity.

The underlying point is that success at resource mobilization is the standard by which NGDOs should be judged. This is the ultimate 'bottom line'. No resources means no organization. Consequently, a perceived threat to resource supply leads to a natural tendency to concentrate on finding new sources as if this is what solely matters. As described below, such a threatening perception exists, leading to a concerted effort to look for alternatives.

A concern to secure an NGDO's resource base – away from international aid – started in the late 1980s. The book *Towards Greater Financial Autonomy*, was probably a seminal start to what has followed.[4] The approach adopted by the writers was for NGDOs to become completely self-financing. This goal is no longer seen to be realistic or necessarily desirable. It has been displaced by a number of trends. For a start, this book was written before the 'discovery' of civil society in relation to development. This new concept provided both a framework for and impetus to investment in studies, training courses and specialist organizations, such as the International Fund Raising Group and the World Alliance for Citizen Participation (CIVICUS).[5] Another change has been the adoption of partnership by all and sundry in the official aid industry. Collaboration and cross-financing between sectors of government, business and civil society is now a common part of a financing agenda. Further, there is a growing assert-iveness and increase in claim-making by NGDOs on government for subsidies to help provide public goods and services. If governments are prepared to provide tax and other concessions to attract businesses – a forgone income – why shouldn't NGDOs have a right to support for the added value of social provisions?

But the last point leads to one reason why resource mobilization is not the sole answer to organizational sustainability. As Part I *The Virtuous Spiral* argues, the case to be made rests on demonstrated NGDO performance. In its turn, maintaining performance requires an organization that can learn and adapt to environmental changes and to stay its civic self in the process – the topic of this chapter and of Part III of *The Virtuous Spiral*. In short, organizational sustainability is more than just a question of dollars and cents.[6] Sustaina-bility pivots in the interplay between resources, impact and organizational regeneration. With this fact in mind, we turn to the issue of resource mobilization.

NGDOs and Resource Supply and Demand

All organizations are both shaped by and shape their environments. The degree to which both occur varies enormously. For example, transnational corporations resulting from recent mergers in the banking, oil, transport and communications industries can and do wield enormous economic clout, as well as producing far-reaching social effects in terms, for example, of employment.[7] Nevertheless, they have to continue to raise and retain capital by generating value for shareholders. And, as the Monsanto case illustrates, they also have to maintain a positive reputation with present and future consumers. Apparent arrogance about the merits of genetic engineering and the bene-fits of 'terminator genes' tarnished the Monsanto brand name, causing loss of consumer trust, market valuation and share price.

The damage to public image was so severe that the name Monsanto was dropped in a merger with another corporation.

Despite a perception that northern governments are all-powerful, their behaviour is increasingly bounded by the demands of globalization, particularly the free movement of capital and elimination of trade barriers. Unless they make conditions for domestic and inward investment attractive, capital will go elsewhere. In addition, in an increasingly democratic world, the regimes elected to control the bureaucratic machines and public resources must satisfy enough citizens if they wish to remain in power. Hence, governments must behave in ways that recognize international competition for resource and produce policies and outputs that ensure public acceptance of domestic taxation.

The contribution of non-profit organizations to a country's economy may be more than people realize.[8] Nevertheless, they remain modest economic actors overall. However, through public pressure and interest groups, size is not necessarily the determinant of impact. Non-profits can have significant effects in terms of politics and policy if their agendas resonate with, and are sufficiently sustained by, civil society. The impact of civic institutions depends on public trust and support, even if this is expressed through public finance.

These generalizations indicate that no matter the type – or how big or how small – organizations are continually challenged to adjust and optimize their exchanges with the world outside their boundaries. The current flurry of studies, proposals and initiatives aimed at improving the sustainability of NGDO resources, especially money, can be seen as an accelerated adjustment to both perceived and real changes to their environment. The major contextual changes influencing NGDOs can be looked at in terms of alterations in supply and demand.

Supply-side Dynamics

On the supply side, the rapid growth of southern and eastern NGDOs has been fed by and resulted in a heavy dependence on foreign aid.[9] Aid resources reach them both directly from official donors and northern NGDOs and indirectly via loans and grants to their governments.[10] There is an overall trend of official aid to finance southern NGDOs directly in-country and to bring them into projects and programmes to be implemented by governments. Southern NGDO experience of these modalities is mixed, summed up in the question: are we partners or contractors?[11] This question reflects a strategic issue for NGDOs that reappears in subsequent chapters of *The Virtuous Spiral*. The fact that it matters so much relates to the substantial degree that NGDOs rely on official aid.

The past decade has seen a decline by 21 per cent in the real levels of finance allocated to overseas development assistance. After steady reduction in real terms, a recent increase in official aid, the first since 1994, added US$3.2 billion to the 1997 level of $48.3 billion. This amounts to a growth of 8.9 per cent. At 0.23 per cent of donor GNP, this level still falls far short of the agreed target of 0.7 per cent.[12]

However, even these improving figures should be read with caution. Detailed study suggests that official figures suffer from conscious, elevating distortions.

> Recently, aid flows have tended increasingly to benefit activities that do not fit the Organisation for Economic Cooperation's (OECD) strict definition of aid. Changes in OECD conditionality and in donor ideology after the Cold War also appear to weight the scale against recipient countries.

Official data from the OECD support the view that there was no resource shift to the East and that official aid was additional. Closer examination, however, suggests that changes in reporting and recording have artificially boosted ODA figures, thus hiding both indications of a geographical shift and a decline in ODA in the strict sense of a proportion of Gross National Domestic Product. Further findings of the study suggest that:

- Changes in the OECD's interpretation of ODA have increased officially declared aid in the 1990s
- The inclusion of expenditures directed at 'solving global common problems' – not development aid according to OECD definitions – has boosted
- A new ideology of donors and new forms of conditionality could be used to justify giving less aid
- New conditionalities have shifted the balance against recipient countries. State-led development appears at times to have been substituted by state-subsidized private sector activity, often favouring investors from donor countries.[13]

In sum, aid as originally understood is probably still decreasing, while policy conditions are changing the parameters by which it can be accessed and by whom.

For NGDOs, the effect of this supply-side trend has been very mixed. On the one hand, donor policies that develop civil society and concentrate on poverty are opening NGDO access to official funds, some previously assigned to government.[14]

Consequently, the total finance available to NGDOs has increased from about US$6 billion at the beginning of the decade to about $13 billion today. Private funding has remained more or less static while other, previously very limited sources – such as for-profit activity or business support – are increasing minimally. Consequently, the proportion of official, tax-derived, funds in the NGDO total has increased from about 20 to about 50 per cent.[15] In other words, NGDOs have become more tied to official aid and hence more exposed to changes in its policies and priorities.

However, a growth in official aid to and through NGDOs is very unevenly distributed geographically and between NGDO types.[16] Latin American NGDOs continue to experience a rapid drop in the foreign aid available to them. A similar reduction is being felt in the East Asian 'tiger economies'.[17] At the same time, poverty focus and political considerations are starting to concentrate official assistance. A poverty focus is moving foreign aid towards countries in South Asia and sub-Saharan Africa with a high number or high proportion of people who are poor. Politics directs aid to countries, either emerging from civil war, as for example in Cambodia, or a communist history, such as Vietnam and Laos, that would benefit from private enterprise, voluntary association, civic growth and finance for social compensation programmes during a period of transition.[18]

The bureaucratic threshold for gaining access to official aid is high. It requires 'spare' resources for pre-investments in participatory investigation and writing proposals. It also requires a high degree of 'development literacy' and professional competence. For many southern NGDOs both of these commodities are in short supply, and this therefore benefits their northern counterparts. In addition, there is still a tendency for foreign donors to prefer, or in the case of Canada require, a domestic NGDO in funding to southern NGDOs. Therefore, again, the south is relatively disadvantaged in terms of access.[19]

An additional feature feeding the supply of resources to NGDOs is the global instability caused by climatic and man-made disasters. What this means for the demand side is explained below. On the supply side it means a growing proportion of aid allocated to humanitarian action – currently amounting to some 7 per cent of the total in 1997, up from 2.6 per cent in 1990.[20] Again, northern NGDOs tend to have more capacity to respond and deliver than their southern counterparts, which is one reason why the United Nations High Commission for Refugees (UNHCR) is intent on local capacity building in the south.[21]

NGDO access to domestic funds is dependent on the political economy of a country, its historical and cultural circumstances and legal conditions. Together, they create an environment that determines the extent to which NGDO resources can be mobilized locally and with what types of strategies and degrees of difficulty. Where there is a tradition of NGDO-type intermediary organizations, government support, civic awareness and propensity to give are likely to be already established. However, at risk of gross generalization, the purpose of such support is likely to be the provision of institutional welfare rather than development as currently understood.[22]

Conversely, there are countries where informal relations and reciprocal networks – the 'economy of affection' common to sub-Saharan Africa[23] – are the foundation for social support. The notion of funding an intermediary runs counter to the needs of sustaining social capital and a system of mutual obligation. An emerging and enlightened middle class may be prepared to finance NGDOs, but mass support is less probable. And even middle class support is more likely to be premised on social welfare rather than activism.

Where NGDOs have been active in establishing a new, democratic political order, as in much of Latin America and in South Africa, relations with the new regimes could be expected to result in policies that open government funding to NGDOs. The question arising is: on what terms does this occur? Can and will such support be accessible in ways that respect the autonomy that was an essential feature of the NGDO contribution to political reform? Alternatively, will the new regime expect NGDOs to continue as 'brothers and sisters in arms', by playing an uncritical supportive role?[24]

For countries now adopting a market economy while retaining single party, communist-inspired political systems, as in China, the whole notion of autonomy is questioned. In China, despite an unclear legal status and ambiguous regulations, that are not uncommon elsewhere,[25] both domestic and foreign NGDOs are required to have a 'partnering' governmental or party institution.[26] Government resources – salary maintenance and subsidies, for example – are consequently a common foundation of domestic NGDO operations and sustainability, albeit with some modest progress in fund-raising from Chinese citizens.[27]

Finally, recent developments in China reflect a common problem faced by many NGDOs when trying to gain access to domestic resources; this is the problem of political and social legitimacy.[28] Where NGDOs are perceived to be a product of external interventions, colonial history or extensions and instruments of foreign aid and its masters, the foundation for domestic support is inevitably weak. In countries newly independent from the Soviet Union and in Russia itself, a new breed of non-profit organization is already perceived as a cover for organized crime, or simply to provide employment generation for those establishing them.[29] The basic ethics of voluntarism and trust in philanthropic intentions are insufficiently present or, if present, are more likely to be expressed through long standing, informal and intimate relationships – not through support to intermediary NGDOs.

From these broad generalizations, it is apparent that the present supply-side picture is both positive and negative for NGDOs. Crudely put, an NGDO's ability to capitalize on supply-side shifts depends on where it is on the globe and if it is northern or southern with already good capacity for development and/or emergency work.

The Demand Side

The demand side for NGDO development work is dominated by policy shifts associated with aid conditions and particular aspects of globalization. On the policy front there is consistent pressure for governments to do less, and do better at what they should do well. Typical tasks are sound economic management; creation and maintenance of an enabling environment for business and citizen initiatives; a fair and just application of the law; protection of human rights; provision of social safety nets as a last resort; and ensuring physical security for the population. Correspondingly, people should carry a bigger responsibility for their own welfare and costs of social service. They must learn to expect less from government services and hopefully, in much of sub-Saharan Africa, less state predation as well. In parallel, public ownership of productive enterprises should be reduced, if not eliminated, as should barriers to trade and capital flows under rules and agreements of the WTO.

Within this global policy framework, it is assumed that the social costs of adapting to the economic demands of globalization – such as unemployment or impoverishment – will only be short-term. The eventual acceleration in national economic growth because of more efficient market operation and investment, together with lowering prices – as international comparative advantages of factor inputs 'kick in' – will produce benefits for everyone in the end. In sum, there are transition costs of globalizing adjustment that temporarily overlay and add to the social impact of structural reform in state–society relations. Aside from the realism of the assumptions underlying the growth model being employed,[30] the demand-side question for NGDOs is: who wins and who loses from the additive effects of adjusting and structural changes? A crude answer is those – the poor and marginalized – already least able to cope before and while these two transitions were underway. The nature and breadth of this category are situationally dependent. But the general scenario is one of growing disparities between an emerging group of a few super-rich, a growing but insecure middle class and a perpetual category of the poor, relying for survival on subsistence, mutual support and public subsidy.

Identifying who is most likely to lose has been discussed in previous chapters of *The Virtuous Spiral*. But whoever they may be, the structural nature of the anticipated shift in state functions will inevitably create a public service demand on southern NGDOs. The demand is akin to that already manifested in the majority of their domestic counterparts in the north. Domestic non-profit organizations, predominantly in the north, fulfil a 'Third Way' welfare substitution and social service role based on a social compact or contract financed by a mix of government subsidy, contracts and user fees for service[31] – the developmental dimension of NGDOs will be under pressure unless their response offers an adequate counterweight. This is an important dimension of the strategic choices that NGDOs face in selecting how they want to mobilize domestic resources.

Combined, the forces sketched above are poverty inducing, and not just in the short term, for the capitalist free-market economic model has no intrinsic redistribution method or intention. Equity remains in the realm of politics and public choice. Consequently, the demand for policy advocacy should remain high on an NGDO agenda. However, as previously alluded to, will this be possible if there is greater dependency on public funds? Compromise in policy assertiveness is therefore another strategic issue and choice to be made in selecting a resource mobilization path.[32]

Southern governments have mixed views about the real agenda of aid conditions and its lessening of their role – not to mention a reduction in the potential for patronage on which much of their politics is based.[33] Nothing as clear-cut as a state-NGDO compact yet exists in most southern countries where overt or covert mistrust on both sides is attended by increasing exploratory engagement.[34]

Nevertheless, for heavily aid-dependent countries it is reasonable to anticipate that aid conditions reflecting donor domestic policies will push their way down the aid chain into the state-society arena, creating expectations of, and funds for, an NGDO service role. Spill-over of funders' domestic policies have usually had this effect in the past. For example, the Thatcher-Reagan era of supposed state retrenchment corresponded with the introduction of the cruder forms of structural adjustment conditions on recipients of aid. Subsequent refinements to adjustment and the drive for partnership with everyone for development corresponds to the Clinton-Major era, now reinforced by 'Third Way' harmony of the Clinton-Blair-Schröder and guarded Jospin quartet in their ode to 'social-liberalism'.[35]

However, governments are also under pressure to be more efficient so that taxes can be kept low, competitive and attractive for international business and knowledgeable manpower. This requirement can increase an interest in learning from NGDOs about how more can be done with less. Hence innovation and experimentation may be an NGDO niche role that is better appreciated and called upon, but probably in domains selected by government and not by NGDOs themselves, unless they make it happen. Southern NGDOs and their governments can also be allies, for example in setting out positions in terms of the rules and practices of WTO. Through their international contacts, NGDOs are sometimes better placed to gather information and help develop government capacity for negotiation, as happened prior to and during the WTO Seattle debacle. However, to expand this type of demand would require a change of the typical government perception that NGDOs are 'the opposition' and insufficiently professional or internationally connected enough to have anything valuable to offer.[36]

Another potential source of demand on NGDOs will not come from government, but will be directed against it. Greater and less inhibited flows of information across borders and a more educated public are forces for greater assertiveness towards state policies and actions. In other words, NGDOs can be at the forefront of increased popular activism for pro-poor structural reforms and trading conditions. One example is the month-long tour, in June 1999, of a caravan of southern peoples' organizations through G8 industrialized countries as a symbolic protest highlighting the negative impact of the global trading system on their lives and livelihoods.

Alongside structural and transition demands on NGDOs are the natural and man-made disasters that help them gain public profile and substantial resources that, on occasion, can cross-subsidize development work or at least secure a better cash flow. Hurricane Mitch devastated parts of Central America in 1999; a cyclone hit and killed 8000 people in Orissa in India in November, 1999; Turkey and Taiwan sustained major damage and loss of life through earthquakes in 1999. Conflicts in Kosovo, Africa's Great Lakes region, Sierra Leone, southern Sudan and atrocities in other locations, like East Timor, all conspire to maintain local and global instability and human tragedy. These instabilities and the humanitarian demands they cause – in 1997 some 14 million refugees and asylum seekers and 19 million internally displaced people – create opportunities for NGDO humanitarian action. Much of this support is provided by official sources and channelled through northern NGDOs.[37] The question currently being asked is whether or not this work can move beyond UN-NGDO subcontracting to a more equitable arrangement of pre-agreed 'task-sharing'.[38]

Overall, there is every reason to expect a continuation in the escalation of demand for certain types of NGDO activity. The biggest source is state unburdening through substitution for government welfare and social services – health, education, water and sanitation, for example. It would be burying one's head in the sand to suggest that, faced with government cutbacks, this role is not what poor people would want NGDOs to play. Non-service roles, such as advocacy for reform, innovation and government reinforcement, are also possibilities, but are unlikely to be of a comparable size or as prevalent. For the foreseeable future, humanitarian demands will continue to arise.

Setting supply possibilities against the profile of demand in a given context – and making the right choices – is an important part of creating a resource mobilization strategy. Another element is examining and dealing with trade-offs in terms of the implications for the organization itself associated with different courses of action. The concept of resource dependency can, and without them knowing it, does, help NGDOs in making trade-offs.

Moving from Dependency: Criteria for Resource Mobilization

Within changes in supply and demand, NGDOs have to make decisions about where to invest their energies in terms of mobilizing local resources. From a sustainability perspective, one task is to reduce resource vulnerability. But an NGDO is vulnerable in another way as well. Strategic choices in terms of resources have a ramification beyond their reliability. Why? Because the choices made can also affect what the organization stands for, which equates to a second task of protecting its mission and identity. In more technical terms, the profile of resources employed co-determines organizational identity. Using ideas generated by theories of contingency and resource dependency, this section explores various aspects of this dual vulnerability as a foundation for understanding the trade-offs NGDOs employ when choosing which resources to mobilize and how.[39]

Resource dependency

A contingent view pays central attention to the transactions and exchanges between an organization and its environment. On the input side, an organization is dependent on what the environment has to offer in terms of resources. On the output side, organizations can act to alter the environment in ways that increase, secure or stabilize the resources it requires. Typically, this is through providing goods and services that society wants and values, as well as pursuing interests in the political arena. NGDOs do both. For example, they draft proposals for funding and submit them to donors, while simultaneously seeking to change the conditions donors use to allocate their resources in order to make them more accessible. Their ability to do the latter depends on being seen to produce something of social value. In terms of organizational types, 'pure' non-profit organizations are particularly susceptible to change in the characteristics of their resources. This is because they do not control their generation as profits, like business; nor do they control their extraction as taxes from citizens, the resource base of government. Consequently, those providing resources to NGDOs can, and do, exert a significant element of control or power. Even if not their intention, it is a common, almost inevitable effect, paralleling the problem of CBO dependency described in Chapter 2 of *The Virtuous Spiral*. The consequences of resource instability, therefore, fall more heavily on NGDOs than on those funding them. The relations between NGDOs and typical resource providers, donors and governments, are heavily unbalanced: funders typically exercise more control over NGDOs than NGDOs do over their funders.

As a result, NGDOs are particularly sensitive to the stability of resources they rely on. In unstable periods, as sketched above, they have to adjust their external relationship to try to restore continuity and stability. A vital issue is how to do this in ways that are not at the cost of mission and identity. The phenomenon of an NGDO's client group or activities altering because of changes in resource conditions has been called 'mission creep' or 'goal displacement'. One result is an inconsistency between mission and action on the ground. Another result is internal confusion as the gap between rhetoric and reality increases – not an uncommon feature of NGDO behaviour.

Sensitivity also depends on how critical the resource is for organizational functioning and outputs. Typically, because the project-mode of development funding is averse to paying general overheads, resources that cover an NGDO's core costs are usually the most critical. As we will see, this translates into a compelling desire to set up endowments that generate untied funds.

In appraising alternative resources, NGDOs face the issue of maintaining autonomy in their own decision-making. Being able to negotiate fair terms without compromising on freedom of internal decision-making is important, as is the ability to say 'no' when it is necessary. Such ability can be eroded to different degrees by different sources of resources. This raises the issue of proportionality. Excessive reliance on a single source of funding not controlled by the organization is a normal sign of high vulnerability, high sensitivity, high criticality and low autonomy. It is not necessarily indicative of low consistency if the mission of both parties is sufficiently similar, but this problem comes readily into play if the provider shifts policy or perspective.

Finally, an NGDO must assess the organizational implications of taking on a new type of financial resource. How much internal adjustment will need to be made? What management and human resource demands will arise? How compatible will new resources be with existing processes, values and culture? Low compatibility brings significant organizational demands; high compatibility brings few if any.

The concepts used above help in understanding the factors involved in NGDOs' strategic choices for resource mobilization.

- *Vulnerability:* an NGDO's ability to suffer costs imposed by external events. Highly vulnerable NGOs are unable to cope, invulnerable NGDOs are unaffected
- *Sensitivity:* the degree and speed at which changes in a resource impact on the NGDO. Low sensitivity means that external changes do not cause immediate severe disruption, high sensitivity means that they do
- *Criticality:* the probability that an existing resource can be replaced by another for the same function. Highly critical resources – such as core support – cannot be easily replaced; resources with low criticality can
- *Consistency:* an ability to alter a resource profile without compromising mission and identity. High consistency resources mean that an NGDO is less forced to compromise than if it is to gain access to low consistency resources. Typically, swapping donors creates a consistency challenge as each has its own conditions and preferences[40]
- *Autonomy:* the degree to which the resource affects the ability to say 'no' when it is needed. Turning away or not pursuing available resources – when the demand side is essentially infinite – is not easy but it should always be possible. If it is not possible, NGDO decision-making is effectively enslaved to the dictates of others. It is not autonomous. Hence autonomy is reflected in an NGDO's freedom in decision-making about resources it wishes to access and the outputs and social value it will provide
- *Compatibility:* the degree of similarity between new and existing resources that call for minor to major modification to the organization's processes, structure and functioning; for example, creating a new department or recruiting staff with different professional cultures, values and aspirations.

An NGDO with a resource profile characterized by low vulnerability, low sensitivity, low criticality, high consistency, substantial autonomy and high compatibility is likely to be more agile and adaptive than an NGDO with the opposite profile. Common sense would suggest that an NGDO that achieves the preferred profile is not only more insightful but also has its strategic house in order – it is capacitated. As we will see in Part III of *The Virtuous Spiral*, achieving this condition has a lot to do with reputation, learning, leadership, a secure identity and self-awareness.

All the foregoing feeds into two features that dominate thinking behind the many efforts currently being put into NGDO resource mobilization. They can be summed up in two words: 'dependency' and 'diversification'. Given the high degree of NGDO reliance on foreign funds and the perceived unreliability of this source, the basic goal of resource mobilization is to reduce dependency on foreign aid by diversifying the resource base.[41] For example, studies in the US confirm that '... diversified revenue sources are more likely to be associated with a strong financial position than concentrated revenue sources.'[42] The question arising is how do NGDOs go about this task in relation to the six aspects of resource dependency summarized above? This is the topic of the next section that sets the guiding structure for the rest of Part II of *The Virtuous Spiral*.

Strategic options, trade-offs and dilemmas

What strategic options do NGDOs have as they seek to reduce vulnerability and dependency? What trade-offs and dilemmas do they face in making the best choices? This concluding section sets out the way in which the next four chapters of *The Virtuous Spiral* answer these questions..

Strategic options

The major options available to NGDOs in terms of diversifying and localizing their resource base are summarized in Figure 29.1.

The first major strategic choice is between human and material resources and finance. Given that NGDO dependency is essentially monetary, the latter tends to dominate over the former. But the former option is most likely to avoid the dilemma of mission creep and introducing inconsistency. Mobilizing volunteer and community resources is also a strategy that keeps an NGDO closest to the real commitment of CBOs and, hence, to sustained impact.

Within the financial option, NGDOs face two immediate decision paths. One is to generate financial resources itself, the topic of Chapter 6 of *The Virtuous Spiral*. This keeps the NGDO in greater control. The threat to autonomy is likely to be minimal. Own control also means that vulnerability to outsiders is not necessarily increased, that

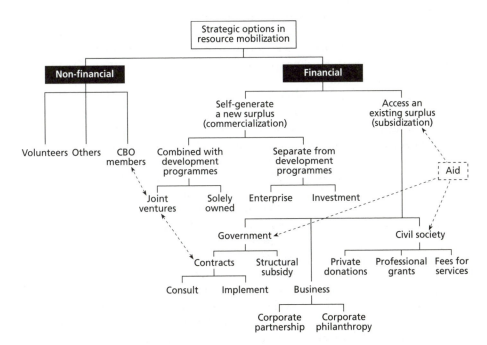

Figure 29.1 *NGDO options in resource mobilization*

Box 29.1 *The Social Capital Fiduciary Fund of Argentina (FONCAP)*

In July 1997, the executive branch of the Argentine government signed the decree creating FONCAP. The initiative was generated in the Argentine Secretariat of Social Development and its main purpose is to get community organizations to become the leading players in the creation of a structure to provide financial services to the huge quantity of small economic units. It is hoped that this would make it possible to build a consolidated and independent social sector. From this perspective, it is the intent of FONCAP that access to credit should improve the economic conditions of the most needy families and help to generate bonds of trust and links between social and public sector organizations and the national private sector and international cooperation sector. The fund is designed to last 30 years and has been started with US$40 million in capital from the national budget.

Source: Personal communication Mariano Valderrama, director of CEPES

---

sensitivity can be decreased and that critical resources can be replaced because the NGDO decides where to put the surplus it produces.

An alternative option is to access a surplus created by others, the focus of Chapter 7 in *The Virtuous Spiral*. This choice brings with it issues of reduced autonomy, heightened sensitivity and vulnerability, a threat to consistency, but the possibility of reducing high dependency on foreign aid. The probability of such negative aspects actually occurring depends, in turn, on the source generating the financial surplus: government, business or civil society.

For NGDOs, potential drawbacks of opting to gain access to a surplus produced by others must be set against the benefits of diversification. This is where proportionality comes into play. Simply shifting from a heavy dependency on foreign aid to a heavy dependency on domestic government revenues may make things worse, rather than better. The effect will depend on state-society relations and the willingness of government to negotiate rather than impose conditions. There is no straightforward answer. It is a question of judgement.

Figure 29.1 is a simplified version of a much more complex reality. All sorts of linkages and combinations are not shown. For example, it is quite possible that joint ventures with CBOs are made possible by the CBOs' own access to government funds as well as from their own resources. In turn, government finance to CBOs may be from its own resources, such as from the Social Capital Fiduciary Fund of Argentina (FONCAP) described in Box 29.1 or from aid grants or loans. World Bank social funds are a typical example of the latter.[43] In fact, in the period 1993–1997 some 40 per cent of World Bank funded projects made some provision for NGDO/CBO involvement. Within these projects, about 80 per cent of funds were designated for supporting CBOs.[44] In addition, NGDOs may raise capital to start up self-generating enterprises from voluntary and in-kind contributions (Chapters 5 and 6 of *The Virtuous Spiral*). Nevertheless, the framework corresponds reasonably well with the division of options that NGDOs face in practice.

Moreover, these options are not a question of either/or. Sensible NGDOs look to all three major strategic possibilities as they seek to diversify and reduce aid dependency. For example, in its 25-year history, BRAC (Bangladesh Rural Advancement Committee) has used all of them (Chapter 8 of *The Virtuous Spiral*) the latest additions being the establishment of a bank (transforming the credit-based rural development programme) and a

Table 29.1 *Probable effects of different resource options*

Resource factor/ likely impact	Non-financial option	Finance option: Self-generating a surplus	Finance option: Gaining access to an existing surplus
Vulnerability	Reduced	Reduced	Increased
Sensitivity	Reduced	Reduced	Increased
Criticality	Unchanged	Reduced	Unchanged
Consistency	Reinforced	Retained	Reduced
Autonomy	Unchanged	Reinforced	Reduced
Compatibility	High	Moderate	Source dependent

fee-paying university. Few NGDOs become as complex as BRAC in terms of its strategic mix. But NGDOs should be able to explore all possibilities, while bearing in mind that the organizational and management difficulties they pose multiply as the mix expands.

In terms of overall strategic choice, Table 29.1 summarizes likely effects on the six factors described in the previous section for each of the three major resource options discussed so far. It can be seen that the non-financial and self-financing options are more likely to beneficially alter an NGDO's resource profile as it moves away from aid dependency than the third alternative – gaining access to a financial surplus generated by someone else. Shifting from aid dependency to dependency on local sources other than your own generated internally is the less advantageous choice. The rest of the chapters in Part II of *The Virtuous Spiral* explain why in more detail.

Entries in the third column are the least certain: the outcome of tapping a surplus generated by others is so highly dependent on the specific source. However, like donor agencies, whoever it is will have an agenda and interests that will need to be satisfied if agreement is to be reached. Some compromise will be inevitable. Hence, dependency on the stability and reliability of resources generated by others will at least remain, but is more likely to increase, particularly where the source is not 'developmental' in its nature, for example businesses.[45]

Resource trade-offs and NGDO positioning

Finally, we need to pay attention to two major organizational concerns. This is the effect that resource diversification can have on:

1 an NGDO's contribution to society;
2 its ability to act in its own terms.

In short, what role does an NGDO play and produce that is of social value? In addition, how autonomous is the organization from governments that also have social responsibilities and agendas or corporations that want to be more citizen-like in their behaviour? These two factors critically affect an NGDO's position and identity in society and are shown as the axes of strategic choice in Figure 29.2.

The nature of the resource base constructed by NGDOs determines both what they do and their distance from the state. In terms of contribution to society, their impact lies

Maintaining Activities – Strategies for Sustaining Resources

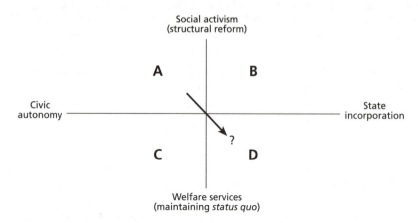

Figure 29.2 *Important trade-offs in NGDO strategic positioning*

along a vertical axis with, at its base, welfare provision that responds to state and market failure without attempting to change the structure of each: their work essentially maintains the status quo. The other extreme is where NGDOs are solely concerned about reforming how state, market and society work in favour of the poor and marginalized. Their agenda is activism and structural change.

The horizontal axis signals NGDO distance from state or corporate influence or control over their internal affairs, particularly decision-making about what role to play in society.[46] In the case of China, domestic NGDOs are closely allied with state and party. At the other extreme are NGDOs not affiliated to the state in any way at all. Within whatever the law allows, they enjoy complete freedom of decision-making that may or may not correspond to government agendas and priorities. Foundations deriving income from market investments may enjoy this degree of autonomy. This horizontal axis is therefore a very rough guide to an NGDO's 'civicness'.

The combination of role and autonomy locates NGDOs somewhere in this graphic framework. If recent data on non-profit organizations in industrialized countries are anything to go by, most organizations appear to inhabit quadrants 'C' and 'D'. In terms of services, the ratio between welfare and recreation and advocacy is about 70:30. While in terms of revenues, the split between government finance, fees for service and private giving is in the order of 40:50:10.[47]

Not surprisingly, quadrant 'B' is relatively uninhabited. Public finance for 'autonomous' non-profits to pursue reform agendas 'against' those providing the finance is almost a contradiction in terms. The bulk of resources in this quadrant come from private giving, especially from philanthropic foundations.

Many NGDOs would consider themselves – or would like to be – somewhere in quadrant 'A'.[48] However, the summary of forces shaping supply and demand, suggests a pressure from NGDOs to move towards quadrant 'C'. In political terms, such a move would imply that NGDO legitimacy is altering from civic to public with direct accountability to citizens being replaced by accountability to and through public bodies.[49] The trade-offs NGDOs make in terms of changing their resource base will influence whether or not this happens.

The issue of staying true to 'civic' position and role underlies much of NGDO self-questioning and soul-searching as they consider what to do in a 'future beyond aid'. Three chapters of *The Virtuous Spiral* therefore examine what occurs when NGDOs address these and other dilemmas. The starting point is a critical look at the current fashion to recast NGDOs as 'social entrepreneurs'. This concept should, it is believed, help NGDOs retain their position in quadrant 'A'. The question is, will it?

Chapter Summary

Using a resource dependency perspective, this chapter covers strategic options, choices and trade-offs associated with resource mobilization towards sustainability. Generally speaking, the goal in changing the resource profile is to reduce dependency on foreign aid by diversifying towards domestic sources.

There are major shifts in resource supply and demand that shape the NGDO operating environment. The overall picture is of an uneven change in availability of aid resources for NGDOs that is often not being made good by domestic sources, especially from government. Hence, there is the fear that some NGDOs will not survive.

Environmental changes are to the disadvantage of some types of NGDOs and to the gain of others that are already better resourced and more capable. There is a squeeze on weaker, middle-sized NGDOs and those that do not have a clear 'niche', to the benefit of larger, often northern, organizations. Increasing humanitarian demands are reinforcing this differential impact of changes in resource levels and conditions for NGDO access.

Six concepts assist in understanding the factors NGDOs take into account when assessing options. They are:

- vulnerability: an NGDO's ability to suffer costs imposed by external events affecting the resource;
- sensitivity: the degree and speed at which changes in a resource will impact on the NGDO;
- criticality: the probability that an existing resource can be replaced by another for the same function;
- consistency: an ability to alter a resource profile without compromising mission and identity;
- autonomy: the degree to which the resource affects free decision-making and ability to negotiate terms and say 'no' when necessary;
- compatibility: the degree of similarity in organizational demands between new and existing resources.

NGDOs face a primary division in the types of resources they can mobilize. They can choose between non-financial and financial sources and, within the latter, between generating funds themselves or tapping into finance generated by others. A comparative table suggests that the first two options are most likely to bring positive change in the above six factors. The latter option is more prone to creating contrary effects and to introduce organizational stress. However, the extent to which this occurs depends on which sub-source is accessed.

An important trade-off for NGDOs is one which links the profile of resources to its position in society in terms of its role and 'civicness', or distance from government. The external environment is tending to push NGDOs to more welfare roles and closer proximity to government and business. Countering or accommodating this trend is an important feature of strategic decision-making.

Notes

1 For example, see Smillie and Helmich, 1993, 1999.
2 This does not necessarily hold true for self-financing foundations whose endowments generate revenue irrespective of whether or not they bring any benefit to society.
3 Kanter, 1979.
4 Vincent and Campbell, 1989.
5 Following on from Vincent and Campbell are a number of important studies that are required reading for anyone interested in the resource dimension of sustainability. See Bennett and Gibbs, 1996; Norton, 1996; Fox and Schearer, 1997; Cannon, 1999; and Holloway, 1999a, 1999b.
6 Brown, 1998.
7 For a critical analysis of corporate power, see Korten, 1995.
8 Salamon and Anheier, 1999.
9 Informed observers suggest that international aid accounts for some 95 per cent of the funds employed by southern NGDOs.
10 For a detailed analysis of paths for aid flows, see Fowler, 1997:135–148.
11 This question is also being posed by northern NGDOs. See Smillie et al, 1996; INTRAC, 1998.
12 *Development Information Update*, no 1, Development Initiatives, Evercreech, July 1999.
13 Raffer, 1999, abstracted in <http://www.ids.ac.uk/id21/static/9ckr1.html> 23 October.
14 For official aid and civil society, see van Rooy, 1998. For examples of poverty focus see DFID, 1997, a White Paper produced by the UK Department for International Development, London.
15 Firm figures on NGDO funding levels and distribution of sources are notoriously difficult to find. For attempts, see Fowler, 1992, 1999; OECD, 1999.
16 For details of trends in aid allocations, see *Geographical Distribution of Financial Flows to Aid Recipients*, OECD, 1999 <http:www.oecd.org>.
17 Valderrama, 1999, Aldaba, 1999.
18 For the situation of non-profit-making organizations in Vietnam, see Sidel, 1997. The Netherlands has just gone through a review designed to reduce aid concentration countries from about 60 to 20.
19 INTRAC, 1998.
20 Data supplied by Development Initiatives derived from DAC data sheets. With thanks to Judith Randell.
21 UNHCR, 1994.
22 Public support to religious institutions and orders is typical, as are contributions to funds established by a royal family, as in Thailand. Development per se is seldom the intention.
23 Hyden, 1980, 1983.

24 This debate has been a significant feature of NGO-ANC relations pre- and post-apartheid.
25 Ge Yunsong, 1999. The issue of legislative frameworks is receiving significant attention. See for example, ICNPL, 1996; CIVICUS, 1997.
26 Zhu Youhong, 1999; Young and Woo, 1999.
27 One example is the Chinese Youth Development Foundation (CYDF) – with roots in the Communist Youth League – that has successfully mobilized nongovernmental resources from affluent Chinese in Hong Kong, to improve access to primary schools.
28 Gao Bingzhong, 1999.
29 To counter this public image, the Charities Aid Foundation (CAF) will be training journalists on the work of NGOs so that '… they may overcome their instinctive distrust of charities as covers for organised crime'. *CAF Bulletin*, September 1999.
30 Bretton Woods Project, 1999.
31 Fowler, 1994; Kendall, 1999; Salamon et al, 1999.
32 Such a compromise has been characterized as 'creeping self-censorship': Edwards, 1993.
33 Kapur, 1997.
34 In some countries, the situation is said to be deteriorating, exemplified by more stringent and disempowering laws for non-profit-making organizations: van Tuijl, 1999.
35 Bourdeau, 1999.
36 There is also the tactical issue of overcoming government 'ego' and a historically conditioned view in many developing countries that government always knows best about everything all the time.
37 IFRCRCS (International Federation of Red Cross and Red Crescent Societies), 1998.
38 Weiss, 1998.
39 See Pfeffer and Salancik, 1978. For an application to NGDOs, see Hudock, 1995.
40 For a case study, see Holloway, 1997; Sobhan, 1997.
41 There are ways of establishing a diversification index to assess present conditions and compare future options; Chang and Tuckman, 1994.
42 Ibid, p273.
43 Schmidt and Marc, 1994.
44 Gibbs et al, 1999, pxii.
45 This does not mean that businesses do not have a developmental impact. They do and it is quite profound. The point is that the perspective of their support is not social development or equity as such.
46 A common proxy for autonomy is the proportion of tax money in an NGDO's budget. However, this is too simplistic because the degree of influence a state exerts through its funds depends on the nature of the political system. Unlike two-party majority rule, proportional representation seems to exert a tempering influence on the propensity of states to interfere with the non-profit-making organizations they fund. The development foundations in Germany and the Netherlands enjoy substantial autonomy despite significant government funding that can amount to 95 per cent of their total. Transitions in political regime do not, unlike in Britain and America, lead to significant directionality being exerted by the incoming party. For example, in the case of Britain, the Labour government treats NGDOs as a particular type of development contractor, rather than civic entities with autonomous agendas. Reform to donor funding 'windows' for NGDOs – the Civil Society Challenge Fund and Participatory Partnership Agreements – are premised on applicants having a sufficiently similar agenda to DIFD itself.
47 Salamon, et al, 1999.
48 This self-perception is not as applicable as many would imagine. In terms of money volume, NGDOs are providers of social services, increasingly drawing on a subsidy provided by international aid.
49 Fowler, 1999:5.

References

Aldaba, F. (1999) 'The Future of Philippine NGOs: No Escape from the Market in a World with Declining Aid', paper presented at a conference on NGOs in a Global Future, 8–11 January, Birmingham

Bennett, J. and Gibbs, S. (1996) *NGO Funding Strategies: An Introduction for Southern and Eastern NGOs*, International NGO Training and Research Centre, Oxford

Bretton Woods Project (1999) *Questioning the IMF, World Bank Growth Model*, The Bretton Woods Project, London

Brown, D. R. (1998) 'Evaluating Institutional Sustainability in Development Programmes: Beyond the Dollars and Cents', *Journal of International Development*, 10(1): pp55–70

Cannon, L. (1999) *Life Beyond Aid: Twenty Strategies to Help Make NGOs Sustainable*, Interfund, Johannesburg

Chang, C. and Tuckman, H. (1994) 'Revenue diversification among non-profits', *Voluntas*, 5(3):pp273–290

CIVICUS (1997) *Legal Principles for Citizen Participation: Towards a Legal Framework for Civil Society Organisations*, CIVICUS, Washington, DC

DFID (1997) *Eliminating World Poverty: A Challenge for the 21st Century*, White Paper on International Development, Department for International Development, London

Edwards, M. (1993) 'Does the doormat influence the boot?: critical thoughts on UK NGOs and international advocacy', *Development In Practice*, 3(3): pp163–175, Oxfam, Oxford

Fowler, A. (1992) 'Distant Obligations: Speculations on NGO Funding and the Global Market', *Review of African Political Economy*, 55: pp9–29, Sheffield, November

Fowler, A. (1994) 'Capacity Building and NGOs: A Case of Strengthening Ladles for the Global Soup Kitchen?', *Institutional Development*, 1(1): pp18–24, PRIA, Delhi

Fowler, A. (1997) *Striking a Balance: A Guide to Enhancing the Effectiveness of Non-Governmental Organisations in International Development*, Earthscan, London

Fowler, A. (1999) 'NGDOs as a Moment in History: Beyond Aid to Civic Entrepreneurship?' paper presented at a conference on NGOs in a Global Future, 8–11 January, Birmingham

Fowler, A. (2000) *The Virtuous Spiral*, Earthscan, London

Fox, L. and Schearer, B. (eds) (1997) *Sustaining Civil Society: Strategies for Resource Mobilization*, CIVICUS, Washington, DC

Gao Bingzhong (1999) 'The Rise of Associations and their Legitimation Problems', paper presented at an International Conference of the Development of Non-profit Organisations and the China Project Hope, Beijing, November

Ge Yunsong (1999) 'On the Establishment of Social Organisations under Chinese Law', paper presented at an International Conference of the Development of Nonprofit Organisations and the China Project Hope, Beijing, November

Gibbs, C., Fumo, C. and Kuby, T. (1999) *Nongovernmental Organizations in Bank-Supported Projects: A Review*, Evaluation Department, World Bank, Washington, DC

Holloway, R. (1999a) *Towards Financial Self-Reliance: A Handbook of Approaches to Resource Mobilisation for Citizens' Organisations in the South – Trainer's Manual*, Beta Edition, Aga Khan Foundation, Geneva

Holloway, R. (1999b) *Towards Financial Self-Reliance: A Handbook of Approaches to Resource Mobilisation for Citizens' Organisations in the South*, Beta Edition, Aga Khan Foundation, Geneva

Holloway, R. (1997) *Exit Strategies: Transitioning from International to Local NGO Leadership*, PACT, New York

Hudock, A. (1995) 'Sustaining Southern NGOs in Resource-Dependent Environments', *Journal of International Development*, 7(4): pp653–668

Hyden, G. (1980) *Beyond Ujamaa in Tanzania: Underdevelopment and an Uncaptured Peasantry*, Heinemann, London

Hyden, G. (1983) *No Short Cuts to Progress: African Development Management in Perspective*, University of California Press, Berkeley

ICNPL (1996) *Global Standards and Best Practices for Laws Governing Non-Governmental Organizations*, study commissioned by the World Bank, International Centre for Non-Profit Law, Washington

IFRCRCS (1998) *World Disasters Report 1997*, International Federation of Red Cross and Red Crescent Societies, Geneva, Oxford University Press, Oxford

INTRAC (1998) *Direct Funding from a Southern Perspective – Strengthening Civil Society?* International NGO Training and Research Centre, Oxford

Kanter, R. (1979) 'The Measurement of Organizational Effectiveness, Productivity, Performance and Success: Issues and Dilemmas in Service and Non-Profit Organizations', *PONPO Working Paper*, 8, Yale University, Institution for Social and Policy Studies, Institute of Development Research, Boston

Kapur, D. (1997) 'New Conditionalities of the International Financial Institutions' in *International Monetary and Financial Issues for the 1990s*, pp127–138, Research Papers for the Group of 24, III, United Nations, New York and Geneva

Korten, D. (1995) *When Corporations Rule the World*, Earthscan, London

Norton, M. (1996) *The Worldwide Fundraiser's Handbook: A Guide to Fundraising for Southern NGOs and Voluntary Organisations*, Directory of Social Change, London

OECD (1999) *The Facts about European NGOs Active in International Development*, Organisation for Economic Cooperation and Development, Paris

Pfeffer, J. and Salancik, G. (1978) *The External Control of Organizations: A Resource Dependence Perspective*, Harper and Row, New York

Raffer, K. (1999) 'More Conditions and Less Money: Shifts in aid policies during the 1990s', paper presented at the Development Studies Association Conference, University of Bath, 11 September

Salamon, L. and Anheier, H. (1999) *The Emerging Sector Revisited: A Summary*, Center for Civil Society Studies, Johns Hopkins University, Baltimore

Salamon, L. et al (1999) *Global Civil Society: Dimensions of the Nonprofit Sector*, Institute for Policy Studies, Center for Civil Society Studies, Johns Hopkins University, Baltimore

Schearer, B., de Oliveira, M. and Tandon, R. (1997) 'A Strategic Guide to Resource Enhancement', in Fox, L. and Schearer, B. (eds) Sustaining Civil Society: Strategies for Resource Mobilisation, CIVICUS, Washington, DC

Schmidt, M. and Marc, A. (1994) 'Participation in Social Funds', *Environment Department Papers*, No 004, The World Bank, Washington, DC

Sidel, M. (1997) 'The emergence of the voluntary sector and philanthropy in Vietnam: functions, legal regulation and prospects for the future', *Voluntas*, 8(3): pp283–302

Smillie, I. and Helmich, H. (eds) (1993) *Non-Governmental Organisations and Governments: Stakeholders for Development*, OECD, Paris

Smillie, I. and Helmich, H. (eds) (1999) *Stakeholders: Government–NGO Partnerships for Development*, Earthscan, London

Smillie, I., Douxchamps, F., Sholes, R. and Covey, J. (1996) 'Partners or Contractors? Official Donor Agencies and Direct Funding Mechanisms: Three Northern *The Virtuous Spiral* Case Studies – CIDA, EU and USAID', *Occasional Paper Series*, 11, International NGO Training and Research Centre, Oxford

Sobhan, B. (1997) 'Partners or Contractors? The Relationship Between Official Aid Agencies and NGOs in Bangladesh', *Occasional Paper Series*, 14, International NGO Training and Research Centre, Oxford

UNHCR (1994) *Partnership in Action (PARINAC): Oslo Declaration and Plan of Action*, UNHCR, Geneva

Valderrama, M. (1999) 'Latin American NGOs in an Age of Scarcity: When Quality Matters', paper presented at a conference on NGOs in a Global Future, 8–11 January, Birmingham

van Rooy, A. (ed) (1998) *Civil Society and the Aid Industry*, Earthscan, London

van Tuijl, P. (1999) 'NGOs and Human Rights: Sources of Justice and Democracy', *Journal of International Affairs*, 52(2): pp493–512

Vincent, F. and Campbell, P. (1989) *Towards Greater Financial Autonomy*, A Manual on Financing Strategies and Techniques for Development NGOs and Community Organisations, IRED, Geneva

Weiss, T. (ed) (1998) *Beyond UN Subcontracting: Task-Sharing with Regional Security Arrangements and Service-Providing NGOs*, Macmillan, Basingstoke

Young, N. and Woo, A. (1999) *An Introduction to the Non-Profit Sector in China*, Charities Aid Foundation, London, draft

Zhu Youhong (1999) 'Social Innovation of China's Third Sector: views on the birth and development of non-profit organisations',paper presented at an International Conference of the Development of Nonprofit Organisations and the China Project Hope, Beijing, November

30

Social Entrepreneurship: of NGOs and the Market

Georgina M. Gomez and A.H.J. (Bert) Helmsing

Introduction

There is a growing consensus that, to be sustainable under conditions of uncertainty, economies need three types of actors: government, private businesses and non-government organizations (Stiglitz, 2009). Links between government and business, and government and non-government organizations, have been extensively explored but connections between business and civil society organizations, in general, have received considerably less attention.

Social and collective enterprises, defined as private (non-governmental) and autonomous organizations that provide goods and services with an explicit aim of benefiting the community, were the typical actor at the crossroads of civil society and the market economy. In more recent years they have been joined by a number of non-government organizations (NGOs) that are also venturing into economic activities, with or without commercial motivation. While in the past non-government organizations (NGOs) focused on advocacy, subsidized service delivery and/or alternative development models, some of them are gradually increasing their participation in entrepreneurial activities in the regular market economy. They started competing for funding and open tenders, taking risks in innovative economic sectors, pursuing profits (at least to ensure their financial sustainability), adopting managerial tools such as personnel incentives, managing links to other economic actors like suppliers and clients, accumulating capital, investing in assets and trying to develop new solutions in the private sector for the economic problems of their target populations. The venturing of NGOs in the regular economy, at times starting up or partnering with semi-independent social enterprises and other times forming new divisions within the organization, has resulted in a process of hybridization of their structures, mission and vision. In turn, it has exposed them to a new series of challenges and trade-offs. NGOs now need to balance their broad social goals with playing a for-profit game in which they encounter rivals that are well established in a profit-maximizing mentality.

This chapter discusses the hybridization process by which NGOs adopt an economic role in the market economy that includes direct participation as social enterprises, cooperation partnerships with governments, for-profits and other non-profits, regulation

...ctors by influencing the decisions of other economic agents and the contesta-
...conomic actions of businesses. It seeks to explain the motivations of actors at
...ads between NGOs and the market economy and categorize the areas of action.

Actors between Civil Society and Market Economy

Economic entities with social goals have existed for a long time (Monzón Campos, 1997). Charities and non-profit organizations have been formed in Europe since the Middle Ages to provide health and other social services and reduce risks through mutual insurance. In the 19th century agricultural cooperatives, credit unions and savings banks spread across Europe. In the same period workers' cooperatives appeared as a response to the harsh working conditions of industrialization. They promoted the interests of their members and an improvement of the quality of life of disadvantaged groups. However, in the second half of the 20th century social and health services were assimilated by the state. Public welfare systems expanded to support the weakest segments of the population and, through taxation, redistribute the fruits of economic growth. As a result, the participation in the economy of non-profit organizations lost ground, but this was only temporary.

By the 1970s the trend changed. Welfare states had retreated and non-profits were growing again. A new generation of 'social enterprises' emerged at the end of the 1970s (Defourny and Nyssens, 2008). Economic growth rates declined and unemployment rose. In that context, the traditional welfare state model was unable to distribute welfare sufficiently. Social exclusion and inequalities increased. Equal access to social services was curtailed, particularly for those with non-standard needs. Against that background, groups of citizens have embraced a number of remedial actions within civil society. They have created a number of new social enterprises as a reaction to the insufficiency of social and community services and not enough jobs being available to ensure full employment.

Social enterprises are conceived with both economic and social goals in sight. They are owned or managed by groups of citizens whose material interests are subject to the limits imposed by their specific social intentions. The public-benefit goals of social enterprises include the promotion of social cohesion and participation at the local level; making informal activities acceptable or bringing them closer to formal legality; favouring the integration of minorities and disadvantaged groups; contributing to economic and community development; and facilitating equal access to basic services to deprived and marginalized communities. At the same time, they pursue economic goals like the creation of employment opportunities, the generation or diversification of income for poverty alleviation and poverty reduction and the supply of merit goods like education, health and drinkable water. They combine these roles using resources that would not otherwise be allocated to meet welfare and development needs (Borzaga et al, 2008).

Examples of social enterprises include: a) voluntary organizations, linked to religious groups or not, that supply services; b) mutual and self-help associations that integrate the work of marginalized groups such as undocumented migrants, landless farmers, informal street vendors; c) public social entities within local improvement strategies that promote innovation and start-ups in high-risk economic sectors of social interest, like incubators and business development in renewable energy and technology; d) cooperative organizations of particular stakeholders within a locality; e) voluntary organizations, charities, foundations and other non-profits engaged in public service provision particularly oriented to those that cannot access those services otherwise; f) associations and foundations that establish subsidiary commercial entities to raise revenues for public benefit (Borzaga et al, 2008).

Social enterprises have recently been joined at the crossroads between civil society and markets by a number of traditional NGOs now venturing into entrepreneurial activities. These are organizations that were committed to advocacy, interest representation and alternative development models. They are now incurring into the regular economy in a broad number of areas while mostly maintaining advocacy and subsidized service delivery activities. In that sense, they are relative newcomers in dealing with the market economy and pose a new way of engaging it. While social enterprises are oriented to satisfying the needs of particular types of stakeholders that invest or work in it, NGOs participating in the market economy aim to serve a broader community. Besides, although the distribution of the profits of social enterprises is banned or at least limited by statutes and binding laws, they operate in parallel or as a complement to businesses, while the NGOs that ventured in the market economy pursue a qualitative transformation of the ways they operate. The incursion of NGOs in the market economy thus strengthens the role of civil society in regulating the institutions of the market economy, a kind of action which challenges some mainstream assumptions of what NGOs are supposed to do and how markets are supposed to work.

What Guides the Activities between Market Economy and Civil Society?

There are two main theoretical views to explain the position of civil society organizations at the crossroads between civil society and the market economy (Evers and Laville, 2004). The first one is founded in the American tradition, which focuses on the direct participation of civil society groups in the economy. It follows the point of view of the ownership of an organization and categorizes them in three types: for-profit, non-profit and state-owned. Non-profits are studied mainly within a public economics perspective. The seminal thinking on the American-based views on non-profits was set by the Yale University's Institution for Social and Policy Studies in the mid-1980s. Susan Rose-Ackerman introduced the main volume of the series stating that it 'may change the way economists think about both markets and government' because it 'concentrates on a fuller consideration of alternative institutional forms and types of markets' (Rose-Ackerman, 1986, p 3). The 'private non-profits' were seen as an organizational option different from both for-profit firms and public agencies and their managers were termed 'ideological entrepreneurs' (Rose-Ackerman, 1996). This theoretical tradition draws on three sets of theories to explain the participation of non-profits in the economy: the presence of market failure and/or government failure (Weisbrod, 1986; Kingma, 1997), the ideological motivations of the stakeholders and leaders (Rose-Ackerman, 1996) and the entrepreneurship theories that emphasize opportunities and resources (Badelt, 1997; Steinberg, 1997).

The second view is prevalent in Europe and analyses civil society organizations that participate in the economy in the light of political and sociological theories. It empha-sizes their 'non-governmental' nature as political actors and groups them under the name of 'Third sector' or 'social economy'. NGOs are seen as a special type of non-profit organization, in the sense that their non-government aspect takes precedence over their non-profit nature (Evers and Laville, 2004). Some authors refer to them as the 'political non-profits' (Becchetti and Huybrechts, 2007, p744) because they have an interest-representation role to play, particularly in voicing the needs of fragmented and excluded communities, that combines and takes precedence over an economic or productive role alone (Cafferata, 1997).

In this tradition, there are four main theoretical views to explain how NGOs combine the representation of interests with a role in the economy (Kramer, 2000). The first one is the *political economy theory*. This emphasizes the political struggle between groups pursuing different goals. NGOs represent the interests of stakeholders and participate in the economy engaging the government and the private sector actors as an expression of the goals of those groups. For example, an NGO attempting to block the privatization or the introduction of user fees in a public service may organize to provide the service itself. It would be representing the interests of its members while at the same time adopt an economic function. The second theory is the *market ecology theory*, which considers that NGOs are a reaction to what happens in the environment or context in which they are embedded. For instance, emergency relief organizations are formed in response to a natural disaster and some afterwards adopt a reconstruction or development role, building infrastructure and housing. The third is the *institutional perspective*, which mostly includes the previous two, but adds a historical dimension. NGOs evolve and develop distinctive activities in reaction to external forces but also out of their own evolu-tion. As they gain experience and become stable participants in the economy, they may go from running a micro-credit programme themselves to offering capital and capacity building to young micro-credit institutions or advising mainstream banks to create a micro-credit department. Finally, the *open systems perspective* sees NGOs as actors of mixed rationalities that juggle between representing the interests of households and holding busi-ness and government in check. They engage in various activities and encompass interests and priorities. They participate in the delivery of public services for their members, even in competition with government and for-profit enterprises and establish partnerships with the private sector in areas where interests are aligned. For example, they may run a micro-credit programme, offer funding to young institutions, advocate for the regula-tion of the activity and associate in a venture fund with private for-profit banks.

To the extent that a synthesis is at all possible, the intersection between civil society and the market economy is thus populated by politically-driven collective actors. These can take a series of actions in the economy to channel the representation of interests bred in the realm of civil society. The choice of what they do in the economy is defined by: a) the internal interests of members, staff and stakeholders; b) the changes in constraints and opportunities in the context, and c) what other actors and organizations do, including businesses and government.

To be more specific, what has motivated the recent incursion of civil society organizations into the market economy? Part of it is evolutionary. In the 1970s and 1980s NGOs grew in number and legitimacy, multiplying the variety of collective interests represented and sometimes pursuing alternative development models. By the 1990s they were no longer constrained to address governments alone but had learnt to advocate with business too.

In addition, their evolutionary learning process has also led them to accumulate skills and advantages in relation to government and business (Valentinov, 2008). One advantage is that they are better positioned to reduce the cost of searching for, processing, and communicating information because they are nearer the opportunities and constraints of their members and users. A second advantage is that they are capable of aligning partners by peer pressure. Together, these allow them to deal with multiple relations and tailor their interventions to diverse groups. They can promote economic and social innovation and mobilize persons with specialized skills to provide a customized output. They have autonomy and chose their role freely, though constrained to the requirements of public funding. They can also base their actions on more than one entry point, in contrast to business and government that have only one entry point: economic need and political representation, respectively.

The shift is also related to a change in constraints and opportunities experienced by organizations that operate in the realm of civil society, as posed by Anheier and Themudo (2002). Opportunities have multiplied and NGOs are dynamic in diversification and innovation. Among development NGOs Helmsing and Knorringa (2009) recently noted a rising awareness that programmes of income generation for the poor face different constraints and have to be sustainable in a market context in order to achieve structural poverty reduction. NGOs have begun to realize that the market economy provides opportunities, and that they can support the poor when specific measures are taken. The combination of these changing opportunities and constraints has led them to turn to entrepreneurship dynamics with social goals and have thus started a wide range of programmes in the regular economy that would not have been acceptable for civil society organizations in the past. For example, income generation programmes have traditionally had a supply-side focus on production and this has changed drastically to an enterprise development focus, first in market niches and gradually mainstreaming small and medium enterprise products.

Finally, Dees (1998) suggests that the shift of some NGOs to entrepreneurial activities is linked to the need to access extra funding to stay afloat, subsidize other activities or reduce their dependence on donors and constituents (and the constraints they pose). While this is certainly attractive to NGOs, the move to venture into the market economy is related to changes at the strategic level. It is the consequence of a different frame of mind blending goals and motivations entailed in the hybridization process.

There have also been changes in the private sector that made it possible and sometimes desirable for them to accommodate civil society organizations venturing in the market economy. Businesses began to see – sometimes by social pressure rather than own will – that their search for profits irrespective of damage to local communities and planet would no longer be tolerated and would produce heavy losses in the long run. Some sources place the disaster of the Brent Spar as a turning point in this process of precarious convergence.

After the debacle over Greenpeace's successful campaign against the sinking of the Brent Spar in the Atlantic, Shell's Chief Executive, C.A.J. Herkstroter added weight to the argument that there is a new paradigm in state, market and civil society relationships: Sustainable development requires collaborative thinking and partnerships with other non-business organizations ... These partnerships only make sense in the global scheme: to address poverty in the Third World, as much as to deal with pollution control ... business can't tackle all the issues nor can it do it alone. (Heap, 1998, p5)

Areas of Action in the Intersection between Civil Society and Market Economy

Social enterprises rely on the contributions of their members – in money, work and kind – in order to provide goods and services in the economy. In addition, NGOs participating in the economy also regulate and organize others, provide services by partnering with (independent) social enterprises, advocate for sustainable development or responsible production, do emergency relief after a war or disaster and coordinate networks integrated by businesses, government and other NGOs. This section will explore and categorize the actions performed by social enterprises at the crossroads between civil society and the market economy.

Resolving systemic market failure

The first area is to resolve systemic market failure. In contrast with the neoclassical definition, systemic market failure refers to the incapacity of market relations to establish themselves due to the lack of capacities of the agents and/or lack of necessary institutions to regulate the exchange relationship (Helmsing, 2006). What NGOs do in this area is related to facilitating the work of local governments, other NGOs, CBOs and community organizations that are better positioned to resolve market and/or government failures but do not have enough capacities or resources to act effectively on their own. In other words, this area of action is focused on capacity development, facilitating information flows, redistributing donations' funding and generally linking potential partners with each other.

For example, international NGOs support households, small producers and their associations to acquire the capacities and organizational skills to gain or improve access to local or international markets. Development NGOs serve as institution-builders, act as brokers between large and small businesses across north and south, facilitate connections between businesses, support the capacity building of co-operatives and producers' associations to improve their access to (inter)national value chains or fair trade standards, centralize knowledge and learning, disseminate information and generally strengthen the capacities and competences of poor and small producers in the south. They promote inclusion and access to those groups affected by systemic market failure, working also on their empowerment by strengthening their bargaining position. They are 'political' in the sense that they seek to rectify a situation which is not neutral in terms of power distribution; i.e. market failure is detrimental to some and beneficial to others.

An important role within this area of action that has been gaining prominence in the last few years is that of NGOs as brokers of connections and networks. In such cases the NGO is neither the main decision-maker nor the strongest partner in the network, nor the largest owner of funds or expertise. In the broker role, NGOs are usually smaller in scale than some of the private actors that participate in the network, have fewer funds available, less expertise and less decision-making power. However, it still occupies the central position in the network because all the other actors are connected to each other only through the NGO, at least initially. The relationship with them is not based on commonalities and collaboration but on negotiation and being at the centre of information that flows between actors whose interests may still need to go through a process to become compatible. NGOs can perform such a 'broker' role for two reasons. Firstly, they have often existing links with informal groups which other actors (state or for-profit enterprises) may be unable or unwilling to forge. Secondly because of the NGO's reputation and the social values it has shown to represent, other actors accept the NGO as a bridging actor.

The challenges in the broker role are centred on how to acquire expertise in order to best balance asymmetries of power between the other actors in the network, how to learn faster, how to anticipate problems in the field and manage the divergent interests and expectations of other members of the network. In addition, it may confront the NGO with dilemmas of how far to stick to its social goals or relax its own values to be able to keep the network together. In the case of development NGOs, they place themselves in the broker role by facilitating links between private sector actors in the south and in the north. They then experience a set of new challenges when it comes to protecting the interests of their beneficiaries in the south: corporate buyers in the north are clearly more powerful than small producers in the south. The broker role, therefore, triggers a new set of discussions and decision-making within NGOs and often requires specific skills as moderators and negotiators. In addition, a new service that NGOs can offer suitable businesses in the north is to facilitate access to small producers in the south, as dialogue partners respected by both parties.

Expanding participation in imperfect markets

The second area of action is direct participation in imperfect markets, defined in the neoclassical way of markets that do not clear or perform exchanges. When market and/ or government failure cannot be resolved by supporting communities or households' organizations that need to gain or improve access, NGOs may choose to become participants in the economy themselves. This may require forming an ad hoc social enterprise to deliver particular services on a non-profit or limited profit basis, *even if* charging partially or fully user fees. In the long run, these activities can sometimes be left to independent social enterprises or for-profits to do on a commercial basis, as it happened in the case of micro-credit once it was mainstreamed. NGOs then move to less profitable groups, those not covered by the private sector actors, or try further innovations to develop new ways of delivering services, which entails higher risks of failure. Examples of these activities are Business Development Services to small and medium enterprises, microfinance, marketing in fair trade channels, investment funds for start-ups in the south with favourable conditions for the debtor, improving the logistics or some link in a value chain (e.g. warehousing, quality certification, logistics, processing).

There is a wide spectrum of possibilities between providing services which are entirely for free or recovering costs to the point of making profits. Affordability for the clients may mean that they recover costs at best, and if they manage to generate a profit, it is often used to subsidize other activities. Dees (1998) poses that some cost recovery is desirable for signalling reasons, even if the funds are available, and increase the NGO's independence and flexibility. In general, most of these activities can be run commercially in the medium term.

Reducing government failure

The third area of action is addressing government failure coupled with market failure. In those conditions, communities of stakeholders organize themselves to secure the access to basic services by forming social enterprises. In the past development NGOs provided basic services to the poor and excluded, but already some time ago they shifted to supporting governments and civil society organizations in the south to run their own service delivery. Typical examples are services like health, education, housing, solid waste collection, drinking water and special emergency relief. Many different categories exist, including individual initiatives, new activities launched by non-profit organizations, public-private partnerships with a social aim. It is the traditional channel for direct poverty alleviation, but it has two additional dimensions: to integrate the work of the unemployed and to link with local governments. All forms of partnerships are increasingly important as a way to enhance social responsibility at the local level and contribute to channelling human, monetary and non-monetary resources towards the pursuit of goals valued by the community.

Regulatory reform

The fourth area of action is the regulation of market institutions. NGOs push for changes in the rules of the market economy in favour of a myriad of social goals: the disadvantaged segments of society, environmentally sustainable practices, consumers' protection and so on. This is a relatively new development of the traditional advocacy work of NGOs, by which they represent the values of some segments of society and press governments and businesses to abandon socially undesirable practices. It tends to be a confrontational type of relationship with the private sector, including various ways to exert pressure on business to establish codes of conduct and sector-wide agreements (e.g. Fairwear in the garment industry), campaigning with consumers (e.g. Fair Trade and biological products for a responsible consumption), lobbying for state regulation or explicit appeals to more sustainable business practices. NGOs address businesses in an appeal to their ethical grounds, threatening with 'blame and shame' campaigns and raising awareness of their responsibility with society and environment. They do this individually or collectively, in coalitions with other actors and NGOs.

A relatively new concept which NGOs are tapping into to press companies for a change in their production and commercial practices is Corporate Social Responsibility (CSR). Business managers, and a small army of consultants, are busy developing and implementing a multitude of standards and codes of conduct to convince consumers and NGOs of their companies' responsible behaviour. This responsibility translates into respecting and enhancing labour and environmental standards in the production processes of their suppliers in developing countries. Some authors ascribe to NGOs the potential to act as catalysts of change in introducing new norms in consumption behaviour, to punch beyond their weight, and to push for norms to become mainstreamed (Knorringa, 2007).

NGOs can play an important role for frontrunner companies in CSR by helping to create a 'level playing field' focussing their actions to reduce 'unfair competition' from less responsible firms and by lobbying other stakeholders and the state for policies that provide incentives for greater social and environmental responsibility of all firms.

The proliferation of standards which in a dynamic context can be seen to play a role in raising the level of the playing field, at the same time may complicate the implementation for businesses and constitute an entry barrier for small producers willing to enter markets in the north. NGOs therefore have to find a balance between differentiation and harmonization of standards.

Channelling growth in philanthropy

The fifth area of action is channelling private philanthropy. NGOs interact with companies and private donors to appeal for charity donations or for new modalities of private philanthropy. In recent times, these are the private persons that do not just donate funds but want to be able to make a difference for sustainable development, contribute their skills or influence the agenda of development NGOs. Unable or unwilling to do it themselves, they often prefer to contact established NGOs to run business-like projects in the developing world. However, their donations tend to come with a number of new constraints to which the NGO needs to adapt: a clearer business language and mentality and the perception that being a donor entitles the grantor to interfere in the execution of the project. These tensions need to be analyzed by the recipient NGOs before the funds are accepted.

Concluding Remarks: Managing Hybridization

In order to foster economic and social innovation, there is a need for collaboration and complementation of roles among organizations of different types because there is more than one solution to attain welfare objectives. Consequently, it should be possible to select intervention instruments in relation to a set of strategic and organizational alternatives, avoiding the exclusive adoption of only one of these, as was the case, for instance, with the almost unlimited state activity in public enterprises in the past. 'The right question for social policy is … not the choice between one sector or the other, but how to combine them most effectively in economic and social terms.' (Svetlik, 1991, p11)

This process of sharing or competing for spaces represents an inter-penetration of actors and sectors that may generate positive results. Social enterprises have existed in that arena for a long time, but in recent years traditional NGOs are also venturing into entrepreneurial activities that engage private sector actors and the market economy. The intersection between civil society and the market economy has hosted a series of shifts in terms of hybridization: various actors partnering with a common goal, blended values among actors and the accommodation of diverse interests of stakeholders.

The hybridization process brings new challenges to NGOs moving into the market economy that need to be addressed and managed. Moving away from the non-profit into the commercial arena often undermines the essence of NGOs, which are defined by a distinct moral stance centred on a common social purpose. In the long-run, some suffer from mission drift and only keep their names as such but little of the social motivation that has originated them. Given the upside to participating in the market economy, it should be possible to perform an economic goal in the market without endangering that morality. After all, a multiplicity of goals is consistent with the multi-stakeholder context in which civil society organizations thrive.

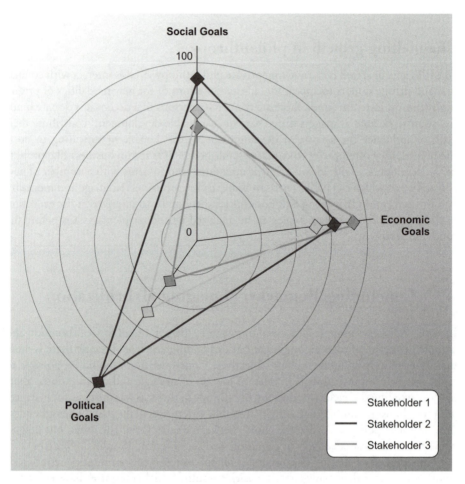

Figure 30.1 *Possible solutions for blending goals within NGOs*

The success or failure in blending values depends on the governance structures set in place within the NGOs, which will set limits to the trade-offs between interests (economic, social and political). The various stakeholders have minimum and maximum thresholds of what they consider acceptable in terms of how far they are willing to compromise one goal to achieve another. If these constraints are specified, there would be a number of solutions which are acceptable to all stakeholders, although probably none of them is the optimum for each one of them independently. The first basic element to manage hybridization is to ensure forums of participation and negotiation within the NGOs where divergent interests can be blended and the limits of possible solutions can be identified. The second structure of governance to manage hybridization is to create incentives within such structures that would set clear limits of what is acceptable, for example, including poor clients in management boards of social enterprises that implement cost recovery fees, or small producers in the board of trading companies that sell their produce, or venture capitalists in the management boards of micro-finance organizations. The decision-making body – the board of management – would then operate as an arena for blending values and not simply for conflict resolution.

In graphic terms, the possible solutions for blending goals could be depicted as in Figure 30.1, in which different stakeholders express their targets with respect to the various goals the NGO pursues, using the governance structures already in place. The minimums and maximums in each type of goal represent the solutions which the various stakeholders would find acceptable together.

References

Anheier, H. and A. Ben-Ner (1997) 'Economic theories of non-profit organisations. A Voluntas Symposium' *Voluntas* 8: pp93–96

Anheier, H. and N. Themudo (2002) 'Organisational forms of global civil society: implications of going global', in M. Glasius, M. Kaldor and H. Anheier (eds) *Global Civil Society*. Oxford: Oxford University Press, pp191–216

Badelt, C. (1997) 'Entrepreneurship theories of the non-profit sector', *Voluntas* 8: pp162–178

Becchetti, L. and B. Huybrechts (2007) 'The Dynamics of Fair Trade as a Mixed-form Market', *Journal of Business Ethics* 81:pp 733–750

Ben-Ner, A. (2002) 'The shifting boundaries of the mixed economy and the future of the nonprofit sector', *Annals of Public and Cooperative Economics* 73(1): pp5–40

Borzaga, C., G. Galera and R. Nogales (2008) Social Enterprise: A new model for poverty reduction and employment generation. An examination of the concept and practice in Europe and the Commonwealth of Independent States. UNDP and EMES European Research Network, available at http://emes.net/fileadmin/emes/PDF_files/News/2008/11.08_EMES_UNDP_publication.pdf (last accssed July 2010)

Cafferata, R. (1997) 'Nonprofit organisations, privatization and the mixed economy. A managerial economics perspective', *Annals of Public and Cooperative Economics* 68(4): pp665–688

Dees, G. (1998) 'Enterprising non-profits', *Harvard Business Review*, January–February: pp55–67

Defourny, J. and M. Nyssens (2008) 'Social enterprise in Europe: recent trends and developments', *Social Enterprise Journal* 5(3):pp 202–228

Dorward, A., J. Kydd, J. Morrison and C. Poulton (2005) 'Institutions, Markets and Economic Co-ordination: Linking Development Policy to Theory and Praxis', *Development and Change* 36(1): pp1–25

Emerson, J. (2003) 'The Blended Value Proposition: Integrating social and financial returns', *California Management Review* 45(4): pp35–51

Evers, A. and J.L. Laville (eds) (2004) *The Third Sector in Europe.* Cheltenham, UK: Edward Elgar

Heap, S. (1998) NGOs and the private sector: Potential for partnerships? INTRAC

Helmsing, A.H.J. (2006) Local economic development: enterprise and livelihood in Africa, in M. and P. Van Lindert (eds) *Development matters. Geographical studies on development processes and policies.* Utrecht: Utrecht University, pp199–214

Helmsing, A.H.J. and P. Knorringa (2009) 'Enterprise Development Interventions by Dutch Development NGOs: Is there increased involvement of private sector actors and does that make a difference?' in P. Hoebink (ed), *The Netherlands Yearbook on International Coopera-tion 2008.* Assen: Van Gorcum, pp105–128

Kingma, B. (1997) 'Public good theories of the non-profit sector: Weisbrod revisited' *Voluntas* 8: pp135–148

Knorringa, P. (2007) Asian drivers and the future of responsible production and consumption. Exploring a Research Question and Hypotheses for Future Research. Institute of Social Studies

Kramer, R. (2000) 'A Third Sector in the Third Millennium?' *Voluntas* 11(1): pp1–23

Monzón Campos, J.L. (1997) 'Contributions of Social Economy to the General Interest', *Annals of Public and Cooperative Economics* 68(3): pp397–408

Rose-Ackerman, S. (ed) (1986) *The economics of nonprofit institutions. Studies in structure and policy.* New York and Oxford: Oxford University Press

Rose-Ackerman, S. (1996) 'Altruism, nonprofits, and economic theory', *Journal of Economic Literature*

Steinberg, R. (1997) 'Overall evaluation of economic theories', *Voluntas* 8: pp179–204

Stiglitz, J. (2009) 'Moving beyond market fundamentalism to a more balanced economy', *Annals of Public and Cooperative Economics* 80(3): pp345–360

Svetlik, I. (1991) 'The future of welfare pluralism in post-communist countries', in A. Evers and I. Svetlik (eds) *New welfare mixes in care for the elderly.* Vienna: European Center for Social Welfare Policy and Research, pp13–24

Valentinov, V. (2008) 'Non-Market Institutions in Economic Development: The Role of the Third Sector', *Development and Change* 39(3): pp477–485

Weisbrod, B. (1986) 'Toward a theory of the voluntary nonprofit sector in a three-sector economy', in S. Rose-Ackerman (ed) *The economics of nonprofit institutions. Studies in struc-ture and policy.* New York and Oxford: Oxford University Press, pp21–24

Part X

Leadership

31

'Trees Die From the Top': International Perspectives on NGO Leadership Development

John Hailey and Rick James

Introduction

Capacity building is a concept beset by conflict and confusion. It is open to a variety of different interpretations. For some it is concerned with building the organizational capacities of individual non-governmental organizations (NGOs) to survive and fulfil their mission; while for others it is broader, involving building the capacity of civil society as a whole and strengthening the capacity of key stakeholders (including communities, families and individuals) to participate in the political and social arena (Eade, 1997). Clearly there is no one universally accepted definition of capacity building as the diversity of literature in this area demonstrates (Eade, 1997; James, 1998; 2002; Lewis, 2001; Sahley, 1995; Smillie and Hailey, 2001). Furthermore, capacity building, as a term is not easily translated into different languages and perhaps not surprisingly, is rarely used outside the development community or the non-profit sector.

Despite this confusion both donors and NGOs have increasingly prioritized capacity building. Recent research by INTRAC's (International NGO Training and Research Centre) new Praxis Programme into organizational capacity building has highlighted the growing interest in the dynamics and effectiveness of different types of capacity building interventions – including leadership development (Praxis, 2004).

NGO Leadership

Leadership development is but one element of the wider capacity building work, but it is increasingly viewed as a critical element. The increasing role and significance of non-profit and civil society organizations in the international arena means that the leadership of such organizations face increasingly complex managerial problems (Eade, 2000; Edwards, 1999; Fowler, 1997; Hailey, 2000; Lewis, 2001; Smillie, 1995). This is particularly apparent in the NGO community, which faces particular management challenges distinct from those faced by governments or the for-profit sector. NGOs have a social change mission and specifically work with vulnerable people and marginalized groups who have often been ignored or overlooked by government services and the mainstream social services. NGOs are intermediary organizations bridging donors and beneficiaries and therefore have to constantly respond to multiple constituencies or clients. The leadership of such development NGOs face extraordinary challenges as they work with very limited resources in uncertain and volatile political and economic circumstances to help the most marginalized and disadvantaged members of their communities.

There is increasing recognition of the crucial role of leadership in meeting these challenges. There is also a new awareness of the important role of leadership in the development of the NGO community and the powerful influence of individual leaders in shaping the destiny of local NGOs (Fowler, 1997; Hailey and James, 2002; Kelleher and McLaren, 1996; Smillie and Hailey, 2001). Despite this awareness, there is only a small body of research into the role of NGO leaders and dynamics of leadership in international NGOs. This lack of research is an issue of particular concern because leadership development is now a priority capacity building need for many NGOs in the developing world. Studies by the International Forum on Capacity Building – an international coalition of NGOs concerned with developing their organizational and managerial capacity – have consistently prioritized the need to develop a new generation of NGO leaders (1998, 2001). CIVICUS has referred to the growing deficit in leadership abilities. In particular they pointed to rapid turnover of NGO staff in leadership positions into business and government and the difficulty NGOs have in replacing them (CIVICUS, 2002). All too often this failure of leadership results in programmatic dysfunctionality and even organizational collapse – and the apocryphal warning that 'trees die from the top' rings all too true.

As a consequence, there is a new awareness of the need to better understand the influences on, and the characteristics of, NGO leaders. There is also an appreciation of the need to learn from innovative approaches to leadership development. Unfortunately the lack of research into NGO leadership means that there is little understanding of the different roles and responsibilities of such NGO leaders, or analysis of the skills and competencies needed. One can easily identify the large body of literature on broader macro-development issues (the socio-economic context of development, the political and policy context, civil society, human rights, sustainability, the role of aid, etc.). There is also another body of research focused on specific micro issues (project activities, fieldwork, community participative processes, specialist sectoral interests, etc.). But there is surprisingly little research into the 'meso' issues of how the people and organizations that implement much development activity are managed, motivated or led.

NGO Leadership: The Research Issues

To date leadership research has focused predominantly on the role and character of leaders in the for-profit sector and not the non-profit or public sector (Adair, 2002; Bennis and Nanus, 2004; Kotter, 1996). Most of it is based on studies in the developed industrialized countries of the north, with a particular focus on the individualistic, low power distance cultures of North American or Europe. Furthermore, while there is a small, but growing body of research into leadership in the non-profit sector, most of it is based on the experience of US non-profits and is concerned with the work of Boards rather than individual leaders. Allison (2002) reviewed the number of books concerned with non-profit management carried by www.Amazon.com, and estimated that only about 10 per cent were concerned with non-profit leadership – virtually all of which were based on the US experience and were concerned with board and governance issues. As a result much of the current leadership research is not relevant to the different political and cultural contexts in which NGO leaders work (Fowler et al, 2002; Smillie and Hailey, 2001).

The dearth of research into leadership in NGOs is a matter of concern considering the highly personalized nature of leadership in the sector. The sector is full of anecdotal stories about the detrimental impact of paternalistic founder leaders, 'charismatic autocrats,' or 'the guru syndrome' (Hailey, 1999). It has been suggested that the paternalistic nature of leadership in the NGO sector is a natural consequence of the high levels of commitment and shared sense of ownership common to many NGOs (Fowler, 1997). On the one hand such leaders demonstrate a drive and commitment, and a remarkable ability to mobilize people and resources. While on the other hand they are criticized for dominating organizations, being unaccountable and failing to adapt to changing circumstances. Chambers (1997, p76) points out that such NGO leaders can achieve many things through their 'guts, vision and commitment', but the way they use power is a 'disability' that jeopardizes organizational effectiveness. He argues such charismatic leaders are 'vulnerable to acquiescence, deference, flattery and placation' (Chambers, 1997, p76). They are not easily contradicted or corrected. As a result they actively suffocate promising initiatives that may threaten their power base, relationships or position of patronage.

This lack of a developed body of research in this area may be partly explained by an unwillingness to accept that the management and leadership styles commonly found in NGOs are so highly personalized. Another explanation for the lack of research may arise from the perception that the concept of leadership is antithetical to the participatory culture espoused by many NGOs. In a sector that believes itself to be more value driven, participatory and less managerialist than the for-profit business sector, there is an unwillingness to concede the important influence of any one individual leader. It has also been hypothesized that because non-profits give greater credence to ideas of equality and participatory democracy they only encourage research that focuses on these values, and actively discourage research that emphasizes the role of specific individuals (Allison, 2002).

NGO Leaders: Attributes and Characteristics

Despite these concerns there are now a small number of studies that are beginning to analyse the role and performance of NGO leaders, and develop a better understanding of the dimensions of NGO leadership and the skills and competencies needed. This research highlights a number of different dimensions of NGO leadership.

As with the mainstream leadership research, most studies still emphasize the personal characteristics and attributes of individual leaders. For example, Uphoff's studies (Uphoff and Esman,1998) into the dimensions of effective rural development programmes highlight the role of key individuals, who have often come from outside the rural community studied, and who play a catalytic role in inspiring, initiating and guiding innovative rural development processes. He identifies this group of unusually able and motivated individuals as development entrepreneurs or social innovators.

In a similar vein the study by Smillie and Hailey (2001) into the management of some of the larger local NGOs in Bangladesh, India and Pakistan highlighted the crucial role of individual leaders in the development and growth of these organizations. The NGOs studied had become sizeable organizations in their own right with well-established reputations in their local communities and with international donors. They face the challenge of working with some of the most vulnerable and disadvantaged people in the world today (South Asia represents 40 per cent of the world's absolute poor). The leaders studied had a highly personalized and distinctive leadership style. They appear pragmatic, rational and aspirational. However, on more detailed analysis it is clear from the case studies collected as part of this research that the leaders of the NGOs studied demonstrated a striking ability to balance competing demands on their time and energy with their own values and ambitions. They appeared both managerial and value driven. They had clear and ambitious development aspirations and an ability to understand and work with what resources they had and the volatile environment in which they found themselves. These 'development leaders' had developed a distinct character and leadership style that can be characterized as being value-driven, knowledge-based and responsive.

In practice this meant that they have a clear vision, a firm value-set and a strong sense of commitment to helping the rural poor which they were able to share with, and use to inspire, others. Second, they had a willingness to learn and experiment, to apply new technologies or organizational forms and draw on science or other sources of applied or professional knowledge. Third, a curiosity and ability to analyse the external environment, follow trends and respond to changing circumstances. Fourth, communication and interpersonal skills that enabled them to motivate staff and engage with a cross-section of society. Fifth, the ability to balance diverse demands and play different roles.

Such 'development leaders' seem to have a chameleon-like ability to adapt to different roles, styles or organizational needs (Hailey, 2002). They have the ability to combine ideals and values with analysis, technical expertise and professionalism while still being able to communicate a vision and motivate a range of staff, stakeholders and beneficiaries. They demonstrate the ability to balance a diversity of demands and roles according to the circumstances and the individuals involved. They also demonstrate the ability to balance personal commitment to a vision with the urgent needs of local communities, the demands of donors and the vested interests of politicians and local pressure groups. This ability to balance competing demands and develop strategies is able to help them cope with the exigencies of complex and difficult external environments and appears to be one of the hallmarks of successful NGO leaders.

NGO Leadership in Context

While much research focuses on the traits and attributes of individual leaders, one cannot overlook the influence that culture and wider contextual issues play in determining the strategies that different NGO leaders adopt. Social identity theory argues that leadership behaviour is bound up with leaders' definitions of themselves in relation to the group – their social identity (Haslam, 2001). As such leadership is not a person so much as a relationship. It is a dynamic process of mutual influence between leaders and followers. As Mayo pointed out 50 years ago, 'The desire to stand well with one's fellows, the so-called human instinct of association, easily outweighs the merely individual interest and logical reasoning upon which so many spurious principles of management are based' (quoted in Haslam, 2001, p17). Yet despite this it seems that still, 'most studies of leadership are divorced from the broader social context within which these roles and qualities emerge' (Haslam, 2001, p58).

A small number of NGO studies do also explore leadership in the wider context. For example, Fowler et al (2002) in their analysis of the determinants of civic leadership in Kenya emphasized the importance of the wider institutional framework in determining the performance of NGO leaders. This is an area that needs considerable further investigation, and new research being commissioned by INTRAC's Praxis Programme has prioritized this theme as part of its broader review of new and innovative approaches to capacity building. However, in any analysis of the dynamics and dimensions of NGO leadership, it is clear that NGO leaders work in an environment that is largely out of their control and changing very rapidly.

This is most apparent in communities and societies being devastated by HIV/AIDS, where local NGOs and their leadership have to develop a range of new strategies and skills to enable them to function. As discussed below, an increasingly HIV-infected world provides a salutary illustration of the impact of the wider context on leadership behaviour and change.

NGO Leadership in an HIV-infected World

The stark statistics for HIV/AIDS are terrifying. Three million people are dying each year – 500 times the loss of life on 11 September 2001. Countries like Malawi are losing more teachers each year than are being trained, 70 per cent of major hospital capacity is taken up by HIV+ patients, and orphans now amount to 8 per cent of the population. Such statistics become even more frightening when we dare to think through the implications over the next 10 years, when irrespective of changes in infection rates the situation will deteriorate as those already infected get sick and die.

The impact of HIV on leaders *infected* by the virus is increasingly obvious and distressing, and yet the impact on leaders *affected* by the virus is more widespread and subversive. Leaders, in countries like Malawi, are not just leaders in their organizations (and having to bear the weight of HIV in their workplace), but are also leaders in their extended and rapidly extending families (James, 2004a). There is a close relationship between personal identities, the community and a wider network of relationships and responsibilities (Jackson, 2004). Such local leaders, therefore, cannot divorce themselves from their societal and family perceptions and expectations of them.

The pressures they have to deal with include the impact on their family life and emotional well-being, physical exhaustion, as well as the financial costs and the drain on their time. NGO leaders in Malawi spend a significant proportion of their time and income in visiting sick relatives and friends. Many are expected to give up more than 10 per cent of their working time to family funerals. It is not infrequent for NGO leaders to go into significant debt in order to pay for these funerals. They are also the ones expected to take into their households the orphaned children of their siblings as well as to educate them. Not surprisingly such expenses, on top of normal 'living' expenses can create very serious financial worries.

This has a considerable impact on their capacity to lead and manage. Many NGO leaders in sub-Saharan Africa are close to burnout. It is impossible to fully appreciate the impact of the personal trauma and depth of grief in countries where so many family members are sick and dying. This emotional, physical and financial exhaustion is affecting their performance as leaders. They have less time and patience to consult, manage and motivate their staff. As a result they may take hasty and often autocratic decisions out of frustration, rather than considered thought. Grief can give way to despair leaving the leader unable to inspire the staff.

Faced with these pressures and the impact on personal health and well-being local leaders are beginning to devise strategies to cope with the demands they face. These include managing family expectations of what they can contribute, risking social ostracism by being more selective in what funerals to attend and insisting that the cultural funeral and mourning processes be shortened. None of these changes is easy, but leaders see them as the only way they can balance the competing demands of their professional lives with their personal lives.

Balanced leadership

This highlights that one of the crucial attributes of NGO leadership is the ability to balance such competing pressures, yet maintain a personal integrity based on personal values and deep-rooted contacts with the community within which they work. Because of their work with the poor and most vulnerable they are at the frontline of development work and as such subject to a range of contextual pressures ranging from the widespread impact of HIV/AIDS as explored above, or just the product of local political machinations.

NGOs, as part of an active civil society, are inherently part of a wider political process. As a result their work is susceptible to politically inspired restrictions, and NGO leaders are commonly perceived as a political threat that needs to be subverted or removed. This can be exemplified by what happened to two of the NGO leaders interviewed as part of the review of South Asian NGOs (Smillie and Hailey, 2001). One of these, the late Omar Ashgar Khan, who had founded and led the radical Pakistani advocacy and development NGO, Sungi, was persuaded to join the cabinet in General Musharaf's new military government to give it greater credibility and depth. Another of those interviewed, Qazi Faruque Ahmed leader of the Bangladeshi NGO, Proshika, was imprisoned in 2004 for his opposition of the present government.

Apart from the impact of such tangible contextual issues, there is the unquantifiable and intangible influence of caste, class, religion and culture. There is an ongoing debate as to the influence of culture on management strategies and leadership styles (Jackson, 2004). Contradictory evidence suggests that on the one hand, the more participative and collective leadership style that many NGOs espouse are shaped by the collectivist nature of society found in much of the developing world. On the other hand, the more autocratic approach adopted by individual NGO leaders is the product of the high power distance dimensions common to these cultures.

Running through much of the findings of this research is the fact that few of these NGO leaders would have survived unless they were able to balance the competing pressures they face, and adopt coping strategies that are operationally effective and incorporate their own values and aspirations. They demonstrate a remarkable ability to adopt different management styles yet still being true to their values and aspirations. They balance a range of pressures and the demands of different stakeholders without losing their identity. They can innovate without jeopardizing the viability of their organizations, and know how to use knowledge and promote learning without losing sight of practical needs. In conclusion, they demonstrate a range of attributes and traits that are hard to emulate, or develop through traditional training approaches.

The Challenge of Leadership Development

Capacity building is as much about self-development as it is about institutional or associational development. The development and empowerment of a new generation of NGO leaders should be seen as one of the crucial elements of any investment in building the NGO community in all its forms. The challenge for those involved in capacity building work is how to design interventions that can develop NGO leaders who can thrive, not just cope with, the complex environment in which most NGOs operate. Leadership development programmes need to explore the context into which leaders work and the expectations of those they work with if they are to be relevant and effective. It is clearly not about reducing leadership to a checklist of characteristics or competencies to be worked on and ticked off. Leadership is a tacit process. It is complex, dynamic and highly personal. It is clear that effective leadership is contingent on the environment, culture and context in which it is rooted. Leadership styles develop and evolve to suit the context and culture in which they operate. They cannot be simplistically transferred.

But as well as being contextually rooted, they cannot ignore the importance of the individual dimension. Recent evidence from the Leadership and Management Dynamics programme run by South African-based Vision Quest has emphasized the value of helping leaders think through their values and vision and so have a clearer sense of their own identity (James, 2004b). Key to this programme is its focus on confidence-building and greater self-awareness. It is based on the belief that the more leaders or the senior staff become aware of their strengths and weaknesses and can develop strategies to work with these, then the more effective they will be. As with many of the more respected leadership programmes they take a holistic approach to the individual, and so look at different elements of the personal state – the socio-emotional, the physical, the spiritual and the mental. But fundamental to the success of this programme is that it both provides hope and helps individual leaders to identify the core purpose of their life – their quest. This clearer sense of their own identity then enables them to balance the competing stakeholder demands in the environment without compromising core values.

Conclusion

The evidence from the research reviewed in this paper has emphasized the importance of individual attributes as well as the complexities in the environment in determining leadership behaviour. The competing challenges and the limited resources that most NGO leaders have to work with suggest that such development leaders need a set of attributes and competencies above and beyond those found in most managers or senior executives. In particular they need the personal integrity, political acumen and managerial ability to balance the competing pressures they face from the environment in which they work, the communities with whom they work, the donors who fund their work and the staff or volunteers with whom they work.

It is clear that management in this sector is different from management in other sectors. They are vulnerable to the exigencies of donors, the political sensitivities of governments and the needs and imperatives of the local community. Development NGOs are susceptible to the unpredictable demands of an uncertain development environment, or the consequences of such catastrophes as the global spread of HIV/AIDS or endemic poverty. The challenge for the future is how will such organizations find or develop a new generation of managers or leaders who can meet these challenges. We need to develop a better understanding of the role they should perform in light of the trends facing the NGO community and civil society in general, over the next 20 years. Based on this analysis it will then be possible to identify the attributes and competencies that NGO leaders need to have to handle future demands placed on them. It will then be possible to identify the systems and processes that NGOs need to establish to ensure that the necessary leaders are in place and equipped with the necessary attributes or competencies. This has implications for wider human resource strategies, and the way that NGOs both recruit and retain key staff, as well as the processes they use to develop the skills and competencies needed by the next generation of leaders.

If this new generation of development leaders is not identified, encouraged and developed then the apocryphal warning that 'trees die from the top' may have more than a ring of truth in it. The fear is that unless NGOs invest more in developing leadership capacity, and introduce the appropriate systems and processes to support leadership development and implement leadership succession policies, then they will suffer from endemic strategic drift or be pulled apart by the competing forces they face on a daily basis.

References

Adair, J. (2002) *Effective Strategic Leadership*, Macmillan, London
Allison, M. (2002) 'Into the fire: Boards and executive transitions', *Nonprofit Management & Leadership*, 12(4), pp341–351
Bennis, W. and Nanus, B. (2004) *Leaders*, HarperCollins, New York
Chambers, R. (1997) *Whose Reality Counts: Putting the First Last*, IT Publications, London
CIVICUS (2002) Connecting civil society worldwide Newsletter No. 175, August, Johannesburg, South Africa

Eade, D. (1997) *Capacity Building: An Approach to People-Centred Development*, Oxfam, Oxford

Eade, D. (2000) *Development & Management*, Oxfam, Oxford

Edwards, M. (1999) 'NGO performance – What breeds success? New evidence from South Asia', *World Development*, 27(2), pp361–374

Fowler, A. (1997) *Striking a Balance: A Guide to Enhancing the Effectiveness of NGOs in International Development*, Earthscan, London

Fowler, A., Ng'ethe and Owiti, J. (2002) *Determinants of Civic Leadership in Kenya*, IDS Working Paper, University of Nairobi, Nairobi, Kenya

Hailey, J. (1999) *Charismatic Autocrats or Development Leaders*, Paper presented to the Development Studies Association Conference, Bath, UK

Hailey, J. (2000) 'Learning NGOs', in D. Lewis and T. Wallace (eds) *New Roles and Relevance: Development NGOs and the Challenge of Change*, Kumarian, West Hartford, CT, pp63–72

Hailey, J. (2002) *Development Leaders: Issues in NGO leadership*, Paper presented to EIASM Conference on Leadership Research, Oxford, UK

Hailey, J. and James, R. (2002) 'Learning leaders: The key to learning organisations', *Development in Practice*, 12(3), pp398–408

Haslam, A. (2001) *Psychology in Organisations: The Social Identity Approach*, Sage, London

International Forum for Capacity Building (1998, 2001) *Southern NGO Capacity Building: Issues and Priorities*, PRIA, New Delhi, India

Jackson, T. (2004) *Cross-Cultural Management and NGO Capacity Building*, Praxis notes, Praxis website, INTRAC: www.intrac.org/cgi-bin/search.cgi?x=0&y=0&q=praxis

James, R. (1998) *Demystifying Organisation Development: Practical Capacity Building Experiences from African NGOs*, INTRAC, Oxford

James, R. (2002) *People and Change: Exploring Capacity Building in African NGOs*, INTRAC, Oxford

James, R. (2004a) *Dodging the Fists: The Crushing Blows of HIV/AIDS on Leaders in Malawi*, Praxis notes, Praxis website, INTRAC: www.intrac.org/cgi-bin/search.cgi?x=0&y=0&q=praxis

James, R. (2004b) *What Can We Learn From the Vision Quest Approach to Leadership Development?* Praxis notes, Praxis website, INTRAC: www.intrac.org/cgi-bin/search.cgi?x=0&y=0&q=praxis

Kelleher, D. and McLaren, K. (1996) *Grabbing the Tiger by the Tail: NGO Learning for Organisational Change*, Canadian Council for International Cooperation, Ottawa, Canada

Kotter, J. (1996) *Leading Change*, Harvard Business School Press, Cambridge, MA

Lewis, D. (2001) *Management of Non-Governmental Development Organisations: An Introduction*, Routledge, London

Praxis (2004) *Introduction to Capacity Building Research*, Praxis website, INTRAC, available at www.intrac.org/cgi-bin/search.cgi?x=0&y=0&q=praxis

Sahley, C. (1995) *Strengthening the Capacity of NGOs: Cases of Small Enterprise Development Agencies in Africa*, INTRAC, Oxford

Smillie, I. (1995) *The Alms Bazaar*, IT Publications, London

Smillie, I. and Hailey, J. (2001) *Managing for Change: Leadership, Strategy and Management in Asian NGOs*, Earthscan, London

Uphoff, N. and Esman, M. (1998) *Reasons for Success: Learning from Instructive Experiences in Rural Development*, Kumarian, West Hartford, CT

32

Developing Leaders? Developing Countries?

Henry Mintzberg

Introduction

A visit to Ghana, with the hosts interested in developing leaders and the guest interested in developing countries, led to a questioning of both. Three approaches to development are discussed. The top-down government planning approach, discredited with the fall of communism, has been replaced by an outside-in 'globalization' approach, which is now promoted as the way to develop an economy. But has any nation ever developed by throwing itself open to foreign companies, capital, experts and beliefs? The notable success stories, including the USA, point to a third approach, inside-up indigenous development, which has worked in concert with state intervention. Globalization thus denies developing countries the very basis by which other countries developed. This argument is woven together with a corresponding one about the development of leaders, which must also happen indigenously, from the life experiences of individuals, not programmes that purport to create leaders. We have had enough of hubris in the name of heroic leadership, much as we have had enough of foreign experts pretending to develop the 'developing' countries.

Questions for Development

We develop leaders. And we develop countries. So we believe. We also believe that we develop countries by developing leaders. Perhaps we need to develop our thinking.

I visited Ghana recently. I had spent little time in Africa, and came with the usual question: how can such a 'developing' country be developed? But something troubled me about this formulation. Did it have to do with the word 'developing', so often a euphemism for the absence of economic development? Do countries stop developing because outsiders are so intent on developing them?

I was the guest of the Kweku Hutchful Foundation of Ghana, which had invited me with a different question: how can Ghanaian leaders be developed? Something troubled me about this formulation too. That word again? Do we really 'develop' leaders? On my second day, three Ghanaian colleagues and I were walking through the botanical gardens near Accra when one of them asked me what I thought of multinational enterprises. 'Not much, at least in places like this', I answered, knowing where that question was coming from. That led the Ghanaians into a discussion of why there had to be so much control of domestic operations by foreign headquarters. Do they really understand the local needs? Just because some 'best practice' works in New York, does that mean it will work in Accra? They felt that even many of the international NGOs and 'development' agencies, not only the IMF, act in much the same way.

We mused about how US managers might react to consultants arriving from Ghana with their 'best practice': 'It worked in Accra so it is bound to work in New York!' Then we realized there is a prominent example of just that.

Leadership as heroic or engaging?

That example came up again the next day when I visited Dr Kwame Bediako at what was described to me as his centre for developing leaders. So I expected to get a good dose of empowerment, team building and all the rest of that leadership jargon. But Dr Bediako turned out to be a theologian, astute and well published, and concerned with moral leadership. He was especially interested in the African and Ghanaian approach to leadership. 'So how do you teach leadership here?' I asked, and he shot back 'We just show it'.

The telling example that Dr Bediako brought up is that of a fellow Ghanaian named Kofi Annan, who has 'shown it' rather profoundly in New York, indeed in perhaps the most difficult organization in that city, the United Nations (UN). Here is a truly global organization that has improved remarkably under his stewardship, although hardly in the fashionable style of 'turning around' beloved of so many of New York's ostensibly global corporations. Annan may have spent most of his career outside Ghana, and had some of his higher education in the USA, but to Dr Bediako, who was at school with him, his approach to leadership is decidedly African and Ghanaian. As one of Annan's advisers told a journalist, he 'runs the UN like an old-fashioned African village, with long discussions among the elders, periods of reflection and eventually a decision' (BBC News, 28 February 1998).

Dr Bediako talked about a tradition of service, of honesty and of modesty to describe Annan's style – hardly labels one would use for those corporate chief executives pulling down their huge bonuses in New York. Of course, he can hardly control his organization the way they control theirs, doing the great deals and imposing the grand strategies on everyone else. But perhaps he knows better. He has, after all, spent his career in the organization he runs; he was not parachuted in from above and beyond: Kofi Annan is the first career employee to head up the UN, so he knew what was wrong and appreciated that it had to be fixed carefully and patiently, by engaging the staff rather than intimidating them. Kofi Annan listens, Dr Bediako said, and brings people together, no simple matter in the tangle of relationships that surrounds and infuses the UN. Words prominently used for his tenure include moral and courageous.

Accordingly, Kofi Annan's re-election to a second term came with the support of nations all over the world, rich and poor, as well as of the UN staff itself. Imagine the leader of an organization chosen with reference to the led! But as Dr Bediako pointed out, that recognition is what makes someone a leader.

Table 32.1 *Two ways to manage*

Heroic leadership	Engaging management
1 Managers are important people, quite apart from others, who develop products and deliver services.	1 Managers are important to the extent that they help other people to be important.
2 The higher 'up' these managers go, the more important they become. At the 'top', the chief executive is the corporation.	2 An organization is an interacting network, not a vertical hierarchy. Effective leaders work throughout; they do not sit on top.
3 Down the hierarchy comes the strategy – clear, deliberate and bold – emanating from the chief who takes the dramatic acts. Everyone else 'implements'.	3 Out of the network emerge strategies, as engaged people solve little problems that grow into big initiatives.
4 Implementation is the problem because while the chief embraces change, most others resist it. That is why outsiders must be favoured over insiders.	4 Implementation is the problem because it cannot be separated from formulation. That is why committed insiders are necessary to resist ill-considered charges imposed from above and without.
5 To manage is to make decisions and allocate resources – including those human resources. Managing thus means analysing, often calculating, based on facts, from reports.	5 To manage is to bring out the energy that exists naturally within human beings. Managing thus means engaging, based on judgement, rooted in context.
6 Rewards for increasing performance go to the leadership. What matters is what's measured, shareholder value in particular.	6 Rewards for making the organization a better place go to everyone. Human values matter, though few of these can be measured.
7 Leadership is thrust upon those who thrust their will on others.	7 Leadership is a sacred trust earned from the respect of others.

The leadership style so prevalent in the USA today might be termed 'heroic': the great one imposed on the wayward organization to turn it around, dramatically – all too often by firing much of its staff. How much honesty, let alone moral courage, does that take? (It is worth noting that to turn around is to end up facing the same way.)

I think of true leaders as 'engaging': they engage others with their thoughtfulness and humility because they engage themselves in what they are doing – and not for personal gain. Such leaders bring out the energy that exists naturally within people. If there is a heroic dimension to their behaviour, it is not by acting heroically so much as by enabling other people to act heroically. (See Table 32.1 that contrasts heroic with engaging styles of leadership.) Is this kind of leadership developed? Was Kofi Annan 'developed'? Do these 'developing' countries – or 'developed ones' for that matter – need to develop heroic leaders?

Time for indigenous development?

After I had spent some time in the countryside and met various people, the Hutchful Foundation organized a workshop over a day and a half to discuss the issues of leadership and development. This brought together about 20 Ghanaians from all sectors: the Ministry of Health, the National Union of Students, the Employers Association, a variety of NGOs, Ghanaian and international, as well as entrepreneurs, academics and consultants.

By this time, my concerns about both forms of development were becoming clearer and I discussed them with the group. Perhaps we don't develop leaders so much as foster the conditions that bring leadership out, in context. And key among these conditions has to be the self-respect that derives from working things out for ourselves, individually and collectively. And that, in turn, is fostered by organizations that can likewise stand on their own feet and find their own ways of doing things, building on the best of their own cultural traditions.

The passive importation of techniques, controls and beliefs, via outside agencies and experts that run around solving everyone else's problems, may be the very problem of development.

'Globalization' certainly develops the 'global' corporations of the wealthy world. But does it develop the poor countries of the developing one? Or is this just another form of outside exploitation, of which Africa has had more than its share? Is it, therefore, time for indigenous development, of countries and leaders alike?

From Enterprise to Enterprises

One thing seemed clear. Ghana does not lack enterprise. Go into its streets, and you are struck by the pervasiveness of markets and personal initiative, more than enough to put the USA to shame. At a red light in New York, you might be approached by a squeegee kid or two; in Accra, your car is surrounded by a virtual supermarket of people trying to sell you everything imaginable. What Ghana lacks is enterprises. With the success of the Grameen Bank in Bangladesh, so-called microfinance – loans of small sums to self-employed craftspeople and the like – has become the prominent example of indigenous development. But development at that level may not be the problem, any more than imposed development at the corporate level. The need seems to exist at some level between the two: indigenous enterprises incorporated beyond the efforts of a few individuals – what has been called the 'missing middle'.

I happened to have stopped in northern Italy on my way to Ghana, and Carlo Alberto Carnevale of the Bocconi School of Management took me to Bergamo. He told me it is the richest city in this, one of the wealthiest parts of Europe, and most of the wealth was built by small, indigenous enterprises, often with just a dozen or so people. 'We Italians don't like organization', he said, and agreed when I replied that 'You like community'. Stock-option incentives probably figure less prominently here than elsewhere in the developed west, he explained. What really drives the people is the opportunity to go out on their own, to be entrepreneurs. And the existing enterprises often help their people do that, by turning employees into partners. (Benetton nearby has become famous for generating so many enterprises around it.) So here, deep inside the EU, is evidence of another approach to economic development, quite aside from globalization (although companies such as Benetton certainly benefit from it).

The Dogma of Development

Sometimes a conceptual framework can help us to see the obvious, especially when it is obscured by dogma. So at the workshop, these ideas were elaborated more formally, as the three models shown in the accompanying figure, to help get us beyond 'developing countries' and 'globalization'.

Two models of national development have become popular in turn. The first, labelled planned development in Figure 32.1, is shown as 'top-down' because it is driven by the state, whether the central planning and control of communist governments or the extensive intervention of more moderate ones, to create infrastructure. With the fall of the communist regimes, accompanied by the discrediting of state intervention, a second model, of international, or global, development – globalization so-called – replaced it as the answer to all economic needs. From a belief that the state must drive development came the attitude that the state must stay out of it, other than to ensure contract law and accounting procedures, etc. The rest would be taken care of by corporations, foreign as well as domestic, on that so-called 'level playing field'. (Note that I am using the term globalization here beyond the taking down of trade barriers, to include the full opening up of economies to foreign direct investment, outside enterprises and experts of all kinds.)

This has certainly sounded good to the multinationals, not to mention their home-country governments, as well as to free-market economists. But many other people, without the convenient self-interest of the former or the ideological conviction of the latter, have been less sure. And they have hardly been encouraged by the aggressiveness with which the wealthy countries have forced this globalization on the poorer ones, at least to sell their own manufactured goods, while closing their own markets to many of the very products these countries can sell – in agriculture and textiles, for example. It is really quite startling how anyone could have tolerated this hypocrisy at all, let alone most of the world for so many years. The issue is not whether honest economists decry such behaviour – of course they do. It is how these economists could have pursued the free-trade agenda so doggedly in the presence of such distortions. Of course, there is one obvious explanation as to why people on the receiving end have tolerated this situation: conceptually they have had nowhere else to turn. After the fall of communism, as noted above, globalism became the only model in town, so to speak; the answer to all the world's problems, development included. With what other theory was any developing country to stand up to the likes of the IMF or the WTO, let alone The Economist, issue after issue? How else to develop a modern economy?

The Failure of Forced Development

This form of development is labelled 'outside-in' in Figure 32.1, not only because the foreign corporations descend on the host economy with their money and their experts, but also because even the domestic firms are supposed to subscribe to this imported set of beliefs. There is nothing in globalization that responds to host-country conditions, save cosmetic modifications to the products and the ideology for local consumption.

Approaches to Development

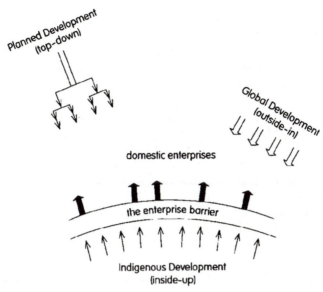

Figure 32.1 *Approaches to development*

Indeed, the ideology treats local communities, often even democratically elected national governments, as threats to globalization, and so as forces to be marginalized.

For more reasons than this, however, the globalization ideology is seriously flawed. It has simply not been working in many of the places in greatest need of development (see, for instance, Stiglitz, 2002). Perhaps this can be explained by the comments above: globalization does not build on a country's unique strengths, does not respect its social traditions, does not allow the autonomy necessary to grow indigenous leaders and enterprises. All too often, it is forced development, imposed against the natural inclinations and even the will of the people. Is that any way to foster a developmental mindset, let alone a democratic society?

Pride, dignity and corresponding confidence do not figure prominently in mainline economic theory: they cannot be measured. But they figure prominently in just about every story of success, whether of countries or of leaders. How people feel about themselves, personally and collectively, influences the energy with which they develop themselves. Think about Great Britain during its empire, Japan of the 1970s and 1980s, the USA throughout its history. Of course, the first and last of these examples suggest how the pride of one country can undermine the pride of others.

The trouble with the 'outside-in' model is that it is based on imitation, and imitations are often second rate, because copying is a mindless activity. People don't learn. This is not to argue that learning cannot be stimulated by the experience of others. Quite the contrary, some of the best learning is informed by that experience. Japan was famous for copying after World War II, but its economy 'took off' when it grew beyond that, from the mindlessness of imitating to the thoughtfulness of adapting, by tailoring the innovations of other countries to its own culture. We learn from others when we do it for ourselves.

One last point about globalization: is it now working, even for those countries so intent on promoting it? Put differently, are developed economies being further developed by their large multinational enterprises functioning according to this model?

This is a complex question that I can hardly answer here. But a good deal of recent evidence certainly gives cause for concern. We know about the key role of small and medium enterprises in job creation, especially when they work in cooperative local networks, as in northern Italy. We also know about the driving force of new technologies, which comes largely from the developing enterprises of the so-called 'new economy' more than from the developed ones of the old. Indeed, it is from the developed ones that we have been getting the litany of recent scandals, whether as outright corruption or simple strategic failure.

A good deal of the blame for both can be placed on a key component of globalization, namely its obsession with 'shareholder value', which is just a fancy label for pushing up the price of the stock. 'Shareholder value' hardly promotes broader human values, which are so necessary in all forms of development. Consider, in the USA, the casual dismissal of people at the drop of the share price, the sham of executive compensation that has destroyed the leadership of so many corporations, the corruption of politics through corporate donations. If the USA has succumbed to this ideology turned dogma, how is a country like Ghana supposed to cope?

The triumph of balance

We are certainly dependent on economic forces, just as we are dependent on social and political ones. But we have allowed the former to dominate the latter because of our mistaken belief that capitalism triumphed over communism, in other words, that the markets of economics proved their superiority over the controls of governments.

The fact is that capitalism never triumphed at all. Balance triumphed. Under the communism of Eastern Europe, the political power of the state dominated. The wealthy countries of the west, in contrast, combined strong markets with influential governments and vibrant social sectors in between (of so-called NGOs, cooperatives, etc.). But in their mistaken belief about the supremacy of one of these sectors, the Western countries are now going out of balance on the other side, in favour of markets, the private sector and economic forces in general. The result is a mindless corruptive greed increasingly reminiscent of communism itself. (For a fuller discussion of these consequences, see Mintzberg et al, 2002.)

So the key to healthy development, whether in a rich country or a poor one, is a certain balance of the economic, the social and the political. And that requires the recognition of a third model, labelled indigenous development in Figure 32.1. It is shown as 'inside-up,' because here domestic enterprises grow out of personal enterprise. This model is not meant to replace the other two – we have no need for another dogma – but to take a prominent place alongside them. For it is in the combined applications of the three models that the real success stories can be found.

Consider the greatest economic success story of them all. The USA did not depend on an imposed ideology or outside experts for its development. Quite the contrary, it developed significantly through the efforts of its own people, in their own way. But not alone. The state was there too, and it intervened significantly: in land grants to farmers, railroads and mining companies; with industrial policies and direct government funding for fledging industries; through military spending that stimulated the economy (and still does); and, of course, by the use of tariff barriers. There was also some direct foreign investment, for example by the British in the US railroads.

Likewise, indigenous development played the key role in Japan and Germany after World War II, in South Korea more recently and in Great Britain long before. And this was likewise reinforced by the strong intervention of the state, most notably in Japan, which also allowed a certain amount of 'outside-in' – but on its own terms.

Let me express this critical point in the form of the following question: has any country ever developed primarily through the 'outside-in' model, the equivalent of globalization today, based on the wholesale importation of beliefs, expertise and capital? Clear examples are difficult to find. If not, then why are the developed countries forcing on others a model that never worked for themselves?[1]

The Sham of Globalization in the Name of Development

The answer to the question, how else to develop a modern economy, thus seems to be as always, namely in the very way modern economies themselves became modern: through a great deal of indigenous development, supported by the concerted intervention of the state, reinforced by the appropriate use of outside help.

Alice Amsden, professor of political economy at MIT, asked in a New York Times commentary on 31 January 2002: 'what enabled those companies in developing countries that have been dramatically successful to grow and flourish'. Her answer:

> … in their countries, business and government worked closely together to strengthen domestic industry. Foreign enterprises were discouraged, by deliberate red tape, from entering certain industries, so that national companies could get a head start. State-owned banks lent money at subsidized rates to help local firms acquire the technologies and capital equipment they needed.

Yet now, Amsden says, nations must 'disallow government intervention in the economy beyond establishing minimal norms' and, according to new WTO proposals, must 'void [the right] to regulate multinationals and promote domestic businesses'. In other words, they must forfeit the 'freedom [that] has been critical to most economic modernizations that have had any lasting success'.

A nice little game this is: deny others the very basis for your own success. Level the playing field so that the New York Giants can take on some high-school team from Accra. And in so doing, promote the further success of your own economy, even if that has to be on the backs of some of the world's poorest people. (Bear in mind that the Roman Coliseum had a level playing field. And the lions always won.)

To dump this globalization dogma on these countries, therefore, is just plain unconscionable. Shame on all of us for allowing our economists and corporations to perpetrate this self-serving sham in the name of development. For years, we used communism as our excuse for economic colonialism. Now it is 'free trade'.

This is not to dismiss the 'outside-in' model any more than the other two. Foreign corporations can bring in fresh ideas, modern techniques and new processes; they can provide certain financing; and they can allow for the scale necessary in some contemporary forms of manufacturing. But this has to be done on the host country's own terms, for only the host country can ever look after its own interests. In other words, the 'outside-in' model has to be discredited only as the answer to development, not as a component of it. Of course, the same must be true for the other two models, namely 'top-down' state intervention and 'inside-up' indigenous development bearing in mind, however, that the latter is the especially weak link in so many poor countries today.

From Micro to Middle Enterprises

Accordingly, the issue on which we focused our workshop in Accra was breaking through what is shown in the figure as 'the enterprise barrier,' going from micro to middle enterprises. As Dr Bediako had put it, 'We suffer from a lack of institution building'.

We began by searching for examples of indigenous development, namely companies that had broken through this barrier in a decisive way, and could therefore serve as role models. Initially, there was silence in the room; no-one could think of any! Then an interesting thing happened. As one example came up, more followed, and soon there was an outpouring of stories. The problem, apparently, is not the absence of indigenous development so much as its obscurity: we get blinded by the multinational stars. (Right before our eyes, in fact. The most evident example never even came up. I was struck by the beauty of the hotel we were in – this was no ordinary fancy global hotel. I learned later that it was built by two Ghanaians who had worked as taxi drivers in the USA before coming home and establishing some smaller hotels, eventually to put together the financing for this one.)

As the examples came out, we ordered them into various approaches to indigenous enterprise development, to suggest the richness of the possibilities.

The most obvious is the family enterprise. This is usually thought of as small and marginal, indeed vulnerable at times of succession. Yet much of the development of Taiwan, Hong Kong and Singapore has involved family enterprises grown to enormous scale. And it is the same with some of the most prominent corporations of India, and earlier of the USA, for that matter, including DuPont and (still) Johnson's Wax.

A second approach we called spin-off, because one enterprise spins off entrepreneurs who create others, as in the story of northern Italy. Other examples raised at the workshop included the Korean immigrants in the USA and the Ibo of Nigeria, who help each other start enterprises, and also certain multinationals in Ghana that have encouraged this. Spin-off development creates a kind of crystalline growth of the economy.

Another is the cooperative approach, where people band together in some sort of community to pool their economic efforts. The label 'cooperative' has a negative connotation in many developing countries, where it became an excuse for state intervention.

But here we had in mind true cooperatives, controlled by members each of whom has an equal share that cannot be sold to others.

Similar to this is what we called the network approach, because the cooperation extends beyond formal ownership. People connect to do their business, much as they do around the world in that network called the World Wide Web. Ghana, for example, has its 'market queens', who draw sellers of particular commodities into informal affiliations, which sometimes raise money for their common goals.

We also discussed the fostering of indigenous development through the building of capabilities. There is certainly a key role for government here, by helping to make financing available, establishing a legal framework conducive to the creation of domestic enterprises, disseminating key information and encouraging all kinds of networks to carry this on. Examples were also provided of how social-sector organizations – NGOs and various trade associations, etc. – can help, especially in encouraging networking and the dissemination of information. Hope was expressed that more foreign corporations could be encouraged to act in similar ways, by promoting indigenous enterprises that could serve them as solid partners. There are good examples of this; there need to be many more.

There also need to be more examples of cooperation among different sectors within countries. The support of 'community' is especially important in economic development. For example, my colleague at McGill, Paola Pérez-Alemán has shown how the footwear industry and agro-industry in Chile have achieved considerable success through 'the relations between firms; the reorientation of trade associations; and the state's role as facilitator of collective learning processes' (Pérez-Alemán, 2000, p41). Key to this, in her view, are non-profit associations in the social sector that draw the players together. In fact, another colleague, Margaret Graham (1998), has shown something similar in the relationship between US government and industry in the successful introduction of aluminium to aircraft in the 1920s.

Earlier I referred to the 'missing middle', of which there has been some discussion. For example, economist Paul Vandenberg of the International Labour Office has noted that 'Manufacturing in much of Africa is structured around a number of large integrated firms, using foreign technology, at one end, and many smaller indigenous firms, at the other. In between there is a relative vacuum or missing middle which has been identified but not adequately explained.' He wrote this in 1997; it apparently remains inadequately explained today, although there is no shortage of proposed reasons, ranging from an underdeveloped middle class and the domination of the multinationals to domestic government corruption (see, for example, Kadenge, 2001). But one thing is clear: we shall find no answers by looking in the wrong place. Forced development is the wrong place. Imagine if some of the enormous amount of energy and intellect now devoted to the promotion of globalization went into finding ways to develop these missing middles.

Fostering Leadership

Where does this leave us with developing leaders? About where it has left us with developing countries. Outside programmes no more develop leaders than outside institutions develop countries. Indeed, the more we try to develop leaders, the more we seem to get hubris. Perhaps that is because singling people out to be developed as leaders encourages that heroic view of leadership, out of context instead of rooted in it. We have had quite enough of self-indulgence in the name of leadership lately.

Jay Conger published an interesting book, entitled *Learning to Lead* (1992), about short leadership development courses. He took four of them himself, in each of the main approaches, which he labelled personal growth, conceptual understanding, feedback and skill building. He found that all had significant flaws, but concluded that together they may be effective. Perhaps he should have concluded that the very notion of developing leaders is flawed. If leaders cannot be developed, then what can be done? Three things, I believe.

First, leadership can be fostered, much like economic development. In other words, we can foster the conditions that give rise to indigenous leadership, particularly those of thoughtful self-reliance. A key reason why globalization is dysfunctional for developing countries is that it encourages a kind of dependency antithetical to the emergence of indigenous leadership. Fostering leadership depends significantly on context: it is the person in the situation that gives rise to leadership. As Richard Holbrooke, former US Ambassador to the UN, put it, 'Kofi Annan is the right man at the right time from the right place' (Associated Press, 30 June 2001). Of course, right places can be encouraged. Morgan McCall of the University of Southern California, who has written extensively on how leaders learn in their jobs, stresses that people should be offered challenges in a variety of difficult jobs, which leaves them 'little chance but to learn and develop new abilities' (McCall, 1998, p5).

Second, people can be developed. Not as leaders, but as human beings, in their beliefs and behaviours, their thoughtfulness and self-respect. But that probably happens mostly in the early years, at home and in school. We do, after all, raise children, not just have them. And this requires a culture that prizes basic human values and educates children to think for themselves, to do what seems fundamentally right rather than to accept some pat dogma. Dr Bediako would no doubt say that Kofi Annan is the product of a society that takes its Christian beliefs seriously.

Third, we can develop managerial practice, not separate from leadership but intrinsic to it. That separation also encourages the heroic view of leadership, up on a pedestal, disconnected from the daily functioning of the organization. True leaders are in touch, on the ground: they have to manage, just as managers have to lead. We can promote management development in a classroom that brings managers together with their colleagues to reflect thoughtfully on their own experience. They can, in other words, just show it to each other! (For our own efforts in this regard, see www.impm.org (last accessed July 2010) and also www.imhl.ca in healthcare).

Developing the developed

The people I met in Ghana, from all walks of life, were mostly warm, considerate and thoughtful. There was a relaxed sense of equality in the places I visited. At the workshop, everyone spoke up with no sense of a pecking order; a person I invited to meet me there, who had written to me as a student years earlier, walked in and took a spare seat next to the minister. No-one seemed to notice (except me). Ghana certainly needs to develop economically; perhaps the 'wealthy' west could stand to develop socially.

At the workshop we discussed economic and social development. Which is the driver? Economic forces certainly drive social ones: material wealth helps to sustain democracy, improve healthcare and provide education. But social forces drive economic ones too: a deeply rooted sense of democracy seems necessary for sustained economic development. The two must work in tandem, like two feet walking, just as indigenous development must work with engaging management.

Social development has certainly benefited from economic development in the developed west – the economically developed west. But are we sustaining that relationship? Do shareholder value and heroic leadership, etc. now promote, or do they undermine, social development? Globalization focuses on the economic and assumes that the social will follow obediently behind. There is growing evidence, however, that the opposite is now occurring: globalization is weakening our social structures and undermining our democratic institutions; in the United States it may now be contributing to a growing poverty. It is certainly throwing our societies out of balance. Will it, therefore, eventually weaken our economies too?

'Unhappy is the land that has no heroes', comments a character in Bertolt Brecht's *Life of Galileo*. 'No', replies another, 'unhappy is the land that needs heroes'. If we can get past our need for heroic leadership, and past the narrow metrics of our economists, then perhaps we will be able to take a good look at ourselves, instead of having to run around developing others, both countries and leaders. Then, perhaps, we can start back on the tricky road to developing balance.

Note

1   Ireland may seem to be the closest, but it was already rather developed and a member of the EU before its surge in recent years. In fact, Ireland may now be paying the price for a lack of attention to indigenous development.

References

Brecht, Bertolt (1995, trans. John Willett) *Life of Galileo*, Arcade Publishing

Conger, Jay (1992) *Learning to Lead: The Art of Transforming Managers into Leaders*, San Francisco, CA: Jossey-Bass

Graham, Margaret B.W. (1988) 'R&D and competition in England and the United States: the case of the aluminum dirigible', *Business History Review*, 62(2):261–285

Kadenge, Judy (2001) 'Barriers to Growth: A Case of the "Missing Middle" in Kenya', Working Paper, Nottingham, UK Nottingham Business School

McCall Jr, Morgan M.W. (1988) 'Developing executives through work experience', *Human Resource Planning*, 11(1):1–12

Mintzberg, Henry, Robert Simons and Kunal Basu (2002) 'Beyond selfishness', *Sloan Management Review*, Fall:67–74

Pérez-Alemán, Paola (2000) 'Learning, adjustment and economic development: transforming firms, the state and associations in Chile', *World Development*, 28(1):41–55

Stiglitz, Joseph E. (2002) 'Globalism's discontents', *The American Prospect*, 13(1):1–14 January
Vandenberg, Paul (1997) 'Technology, institutions and the structure of production in Africa: explaining the missing middle', *SOAS Economic Digest*, 1(2), available at www.soas.ac.uk/ SED/Issue1-2/paul2.html (retrieved 10 November 2004)

Index